Fodor's

SAN FRANCISCO

W9-AHX-576

Welcome to San Francisco

With its myriad hills and spectacular bay, San Francisco beguiles with natural beauty, vibrant neighborhoods, and contagious energy. From the hipster Mission District to the sassy Castro, from bustling Union Square to enduring Chinatown, this dynamic town thrives on variety. The city makes it wonderfully easy to tap into the good life, too: between San Francisco's hot arts scene, tempting boutiques, parks perfect for jogging or biking, and all those stellar locavore restaurants and cocktail bars, it's the ultimate destination for relaxed self-indulgence.

TOP REASONS TO GO

★ **Foodie heaven:** Top restaurants, hip ethnic favorites, farmers' markets, food trucks.

★ **Distinctive neighborhoods:** Buzzing, walkable streets invite discovery.

★ **Golden Gate Bridge:** Electric orange and towering, this glorious span inspires awe.

★ **Waterfront activities:** Whether you hike, bike, or stroll it, the bay is magnetic.

★ **Accessible art:** From famous street murals to top-notch museums, art is everywhere.

Contents

Fodor's Features

MAPS

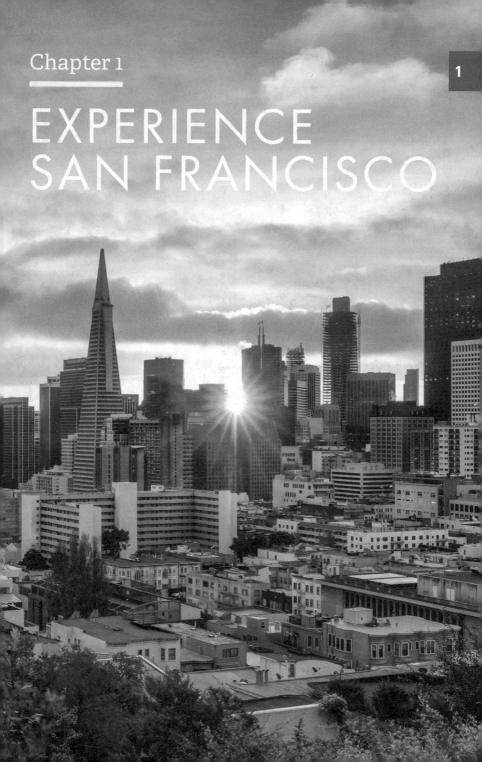

Chapter 1

EXPERIENCE SAN FRANCISCO

25 ULTIMATE EXPERIENCES

San Francisco offers terrific experiences that should be on every traveler's list. Here are Fodor's top picks for a memorable trip.

1 Ride a Cable Car

Clatter and jiggle up mansion-topped Nob Hill, then hold on for the hair-raising descent toward Fisherman's Wharf, with sun glittering off the bay and Alcatraz in the distance. *(Ch. 3, 5, 6, 7, 13)*

2 Wander Through Chinatown

Have delicious dim sum, watch the nimble hands at Golden Gate Fortune Cookie Factory, then take in the hundreds of red lanterns at Tin How Temple. *(Ch. 3)*

3 Frolic in Golden Gate Park

San Francisco's green beating heart, a 3-mile-long park, stretches from the Haight to the Pacific Ocean, and offers museums, gardens, and two windmills. *(Ch. 10)*

4 See a Classic Film at the Castro Theatre

One of America's last great independent theaters, this grand 1922 playhouse is a hodgepodge of art deco, Spanish, and Asian influences and features a pipe organ that entertains preshow. *(Ch. 11)*

5 Picnic in the Presidio

Almost 50% larger than Golden Gate Park, the Presidio is home to public art, an extensive network of hiking trails, a historic fort, two cemeteries, and Sunday picnic events. *(Ch. 8)*

6 Browse City Lights Bookstore

A San Francisco landmark, this independent shop and publisher was a Beat-era hangout for writers and remains a vital part of the city's literary scene. Browse three levels of books. *(Ch. 6)*

7 Visit Mission Dolores and Dolores Park

Mission Dolores's 18th-century chapel, with its painted wooden ceiling, is the oldest standing building in the city. Just down the road, Dolores Park is a favorite with the locals. *(Ch. 12)*

8 Gaze Upon the Palace of Fine Arts

Perched on a lagoon near the Marina's yacht harbor, this beautiful terra-cotta domed structure was built in 1915 for an expo and has been a popular photo op ever since. *(Ch. 8)*

9 Take In the Views at Coit Tower

The tower itself is just okay; it's all about the city and bay views here. Also, it sits at the top of Telegraph Hill's Filbert Steps, a steep stairway through glorious gardens. *(Ch. 6)*

10 Find a Ghost at Alcatraz

Walk the cellblock of America's most infamous federal pen as you hear about desperate escape attempts and notorious crooks like Al "Scarface" Capone and George "Machine Gun Kelly." *(Ch. 7)*

11 Eat at the Ferry Building

Discover cafés, restaurants, a farmers' market, and merchants peddling everything from wine and olive oil to oysters and mushrooms. Plaza tables offer great people-watching. *(Ch. 7)*

12 See Your Favorite Band at the Fillmore

This is *the* club that all the big names want to play. Catch a show and view the amazing collection of rock posters upstairs, then get free apples and posters on the way out. *(Ch. 13)*

13 Feel the Wind on Twin Peaks

Windswept and desolate, Twin Peaks yields sweeping vistas of San Francisco and neighboring counties. You can get a real feel for the city's layout here. *(Ch. 11)*

14 Dive Into Urban Ruins at the Sutro Baths

Explore the ruins and staircases of what was once the largest indoor saltwater swimming pool in the world, to a soundtrack of pounding Pacific waves. *(Ch. 9)*

15 Tipple at the Tonga Room & Hurricane Bar

Since the 1940s this kitschy tiki bar has served up signature mai tais with a backdrop of fake palm trees, a lagoon (bands play pop standards on a floating barge), and faux monsoons. *(Ch. 5)*

16 Walk Across a Rainbow in the Castro

Take your selfies at the rainbow crosswalks at 18th and Castro, check out the Rainbow Honor Walk honoring brave pioneers, and visit the GLBT Historical Society Museum. *(Ch. 11)*

17 Seek Out the Mission's Murals

Street art is at its most concentrated in the Mission, where small alleys and other spots have become magnets for artists creating murals, many with themes of social justice and Latino heritage. *(Ch. 12)*

18 Explore SFMOMA

With about 170,000 square feet of galleries, SFMOMA is one of the largest museums in America devoted to modern and contemporary art. It's easy to spend a day here. *(Ch. 4)*

19 Amble Across the Golden Gate Bridge

Walking the 1.7 miles to Marin County—steel shaking beneath your feet, and the water 200 feet below—is much more than a superlative photo op (though it's that, too). *(Ch. 8)*

20 Explore Historic North Beach

Signs of the area's Italian heritage linger on in establishments like century-old foccacia purveyors Liguria Bakery and trattorias along Columbus Avenue. *(Ch. 6)*

21 Slide on Seward Street

Designed by a 14-year-old in the 1970s, the side-by-side steep, concrete slides for grown-up kids in the Seward Mini Park remain a random pocket of joy in a rapidly changing city. *(Ch. 11)*

22 Play Vintage Games at the Musée Mécanique

This quirky "museum" has more than 300 antique arcade games from the early days of mechanization, including coin-operated fortune-tellers, moving dioramas, and an arm-wrestling machine. *(Ch. 7)*

23 Admire the Redwoods of Muir Woods

Walking among some of the last old-growth redwoods on the planet, trees hundreds of feet tall and a millennium or more old, is a magical experience. *(Ch. 14)*

24 Stand in Line at Tartine

Experience loaves of tangy country bread and morning buns dusted with brown sugar, cinnamon, and orange zest at this cult Mission District bakery. *(Ch. 12)*

25 Climb the Vallejo Steps

Though very steep, the walk up to Ina Coolbrith Park and beyond is possibly the most pleasurable thing to do on Russian Hill, thanks to glorious city views. *(Ch. 5)*

WHAT'S WHERE

1 Union Square and Chinatown. Hotels and upscale stores are plentiful around bustling Union Square. Nearby Chinatown is entirely different and not to be missed, with live fish flopping around on ice, the scent of incense and vanilla, and bargains announced in myriad Chinese dialects.

2 SoMa and Civic Center. Anchored by SFMOMA and Yerba Buena Gardens, SoMa is a once-industrial neighborhood in transition, with luxury condos, stylish restaurants, and cool dance clubs, but some parts are still gritty. Monumental city government buildings and performing arts venues dominate Civic Center, but it's also a chronic magnet for unhoused people. Locals love Hayes Valley, the chic little neighborhood west of City Hall.

3 Nob Hill and Russian Hill. Topped by staid, elegant mansions and luxury hotels that ooze reserve and breeding, Nob Hill is old-money San Francisco. Russian Hill's steep streets hold a vibrant, classy neighborhood that's very au courant. Locals flock to

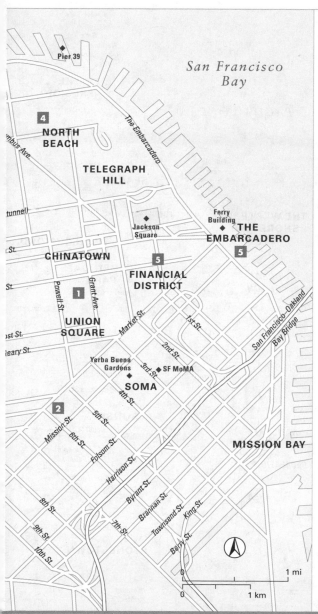

Polk and Hyde Streets, the main commercial avenues, for excellent neighborhood eateries and fantastic window-shopping.

4 North Beach. The city's small, historically Italian neighborhood makes even locals feel as if they're on holiday. In the morning, fresh focaccia beckons, and there are few better ways to laze away an afternoon than in one of North Beach's cafés or at City Lights Bookstore.

5 On the Waterfront. This area includes Fisherman's Wharf, the Embarcadero, and the Financial District and offers access to boats to Alcatraz. If you wander the touristy shops and attractions of Fisherman's Wharf, Pier 39, and Ghirardelli Square, the only locals you'll meet will be the ones with visitors in tow. The city's northeastern waterfront Embarcadero area is anchored at the foot of Market Street by the Ferry Building and its marketplace, filled with culinary delights. The promenade that starts in back has great views of the bay. In the Financial District, Jackson Square is a pleasant diversion for history buffs.

WHAT'S WHERE

6 The Marina and the Presidio. With fancy wine shops, trendy boutiques, fashionable cafés and restaurants, and pricey waterfront houses, the Marina is home to many young urban professionals. The exquisite 1915 Palace of Fine Arts is here, too. Locals go to the Presidio, the huge, wooded shoreline park west of the Marina, for an amble on the sand in the shadow of the Golden Gate Bridge.

7 The Western Shoreline. A natural gem underappreciated by locals and visitors alike, the city's windswept Pacific shore stretches for miles.

8 Golden Gate Park. Covering more than 1,000 acres of greenery, with sports fields, two windmills, museums, gardens, a playground, and small lakes, Golden Gate Park is San Francisco's backyard.

9 The Haight, the Castro, and Noe Valley. If you're looking for '60s souvenirs, the Haight has them, along with some of the city's loveliest Victorian houses (and most aggressive panhandling). Hip locals come for the secondhand shops, cheap brunch,

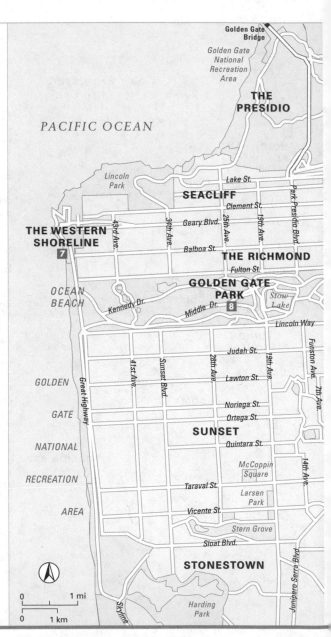

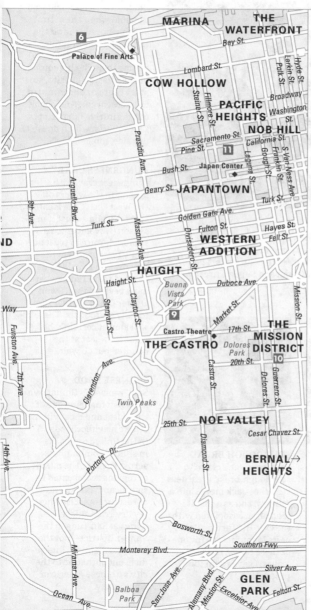

and low-key bars and cafés. The Castro is proudly rainbow-flag-waving, in-your-face fab, and it's a friendly neighborhood that welcomes visitors of all stripes. Catch a film at the vintage Castro Theatre. South of the Castro, Noe Valley is a cute, pricey neighborhood favored by young families. The main strip, 24th Street, is lined with coffee shops, eateries, and boutiques.

10 The Mission District. When the sun sets, people descend on the Mission from all over the Bay Area for destination restaurants, excellent value-price global eateries, and a hip bar scene. Colorful murals are a major draw during the day. Neighborhoods to explore near the Mission include Dogpatch, Bernal Heights, and Potrero Hill.

11 Pacific Heights and Japantown. The Pacific Heights neighborhood boasts some of San Francisco's most opulent real estate and grand Victorians—but in most cases you'll have to be content with an exterior view. A tight-knit Japanese American population supports Japantown, of interest to visitors mostly for the shopping and dining opportunities.

What to Eat and Drink in San Francisco

MICHELIN-STARRED CUISINE
Northern California's culinary intensity and creativity have earned six restaurants three Michelin stars. The Bay Area's three-star Atelier Crenn and Single Thread are especially hot now.

LOCAL WINE
San Francisco sits smack dab in wine paradise, and you should drink deep. To the north are Napa and Sonoma, including the Russian River Valley. To the northeast lie the Sierra Foothills; to the south, the Central Coast. Chardonnay is a major varietal of the area.

SOURDOUGH BREAD
San Francisco's claim to sourdough-bread greatness stretches back more than a century, and as a result it's a food often associated with the city. Hit Tartine Bakery or its Manufactory for one of these tangy, fermented loaves. Leave room for pastries!

MISSION BURRITO
Named for San Francisco's Mission District, this burrito has three identifiers: the size (gigantic), the variety of ingredients (including rice, considered unusual when these first became popular), and the tightly packed weight. Taqueria La Cumbre claims to be the inventor of the Mission burrito, so start there or do your own field research. (And check out definitive burrito spot La Taqueria, which doesn't use rice, too.)

DUNGENESS CRAB
Dungeness crab, with a habitat in the waters off the West Coast, is a local specialty and a must if in season (November to early summer). You can try it at many restaurants in the Bay Area, but you'd be hard pressed to find somewhere more revered than Swan Oyster Depot, a great spot for any seafood fix. There will almost certainly be a line for a seat at the counter, but do wait.

CHINESE FOOD
San Francisco's Chinatown is known for being one of the oldest and most vibrant ethnic neighborhoods in the United States. As in similar communities across the U.S., the number of regions represented is significant, as is the number of restaurants. Elsewhere, try dry-fried chicken wings at San Tung in the Sunset District—not the most "authentic" Chinese dish, but authentic to the city's Chinese American community.

Dungeness crab

CIOPPINO
San Francisco's diverse history and incredible confluence of cultures makes for unique dishes like cioppino, which is essentially the Bay Area's own version of bouilla-baisse. The dish is credited to Italian immigrants who began fishing California's generous waters. With a broth made from tomatoes and red wine, this seafood-filled soup is worth seeking out.

BRUT IPA
On the more experimental end of the San Francisco beer spectrum is Brut IPA, a brand-new style of beer whose creation is credited to Kim Sturdavant, who was the brewmaster at now-closed Social Kitchen & Brewery. It's unusual to see a truly new style of beer emerge, but Brut IPA—designed to mimic aspects of champagne—is pale, hoppy, bone-dry, and a true San Francisco original.

OAKLAND'S SOUL FOOD
Thanks to authors like Toni Tipton-Martin and Michael Twitty, America has begun to more fully recognize the cultural debt that is owed to African American cooks. While 3,000 miles from the American South, Oakland, which is home to a long-standing and historic African American commu-nity, offers some of the best soul food on the West Coast. Head to Brown Sugar Kitchen for some classic fried chicken and waffles or fried shrimp and catfish.

LOCAL COFFEE
Local chains like Blue Bottle Coffee (now more global), Four Barrel, and Réveille have cult followings. Be sure to support independently owned coffee shops as you wander: there's no shortage of talent or expertly roasted beans.

Best Photo Ops in San Francisco

THE PAINTED LADIES

Familiar to fans of the 1990s' TV show *Full House*, the so-called Painted Ladies or Seven Sisters are a row of seven colorful and beautifully maintained Queen Anne–style houses just off Alamo Square Park. Take photos at midday for clear city views.

TWIN PEAKS

These two adjacent peaks near Noe Valley are at the near geographic center of San Francisco, with an elevation of 925 feet. Especially pretty (and popular, but chilly) at sunrise and sunset, the peaks provide sweeping 180-degree views of the Bay Area, with a great perspective on downtown San Francisco, the Bay Bridge, and the tips of the Golden Gate Bridge.

THE PALACE OF FINE ARTS

This stirringly lovely terra-cotta–color domed structure on a lagoon near the Marina's yacht harbor has an otherworldly quality about it. Built in 1915 for an exposition, the palace is a San Francisco architect's version of a Roman ruin, and it's been eliciting gasps ever since. It's a popular wedding spot, which is good if you like happy couples in your photos.

LANDS END COASTAL TRAIL

This 4-mile trail winds and twists along the rugged cliffs of San Francisco Bay, offering stunning views of the Golden Gate Bridge and surprisingly woodsy forest. At the 1.3-mile mark, turn left at the wooden staircase to explore Mile Rock Beach and the Lands End Labyrinth. On a clear day, you can see the Golden Gate Bridge in the distance.

THE PRESIDIO

As the gateway to the Golden Gate Bridge, San Francisco's 1,500-acre Presidio is part of the National Park System and offers incredible views of the bridge and the sprawling landscape that surrounds it. The Presidio also abuts Baker Beach, a stretch of sand with an alternative perspective.

TREASURE ISLAND

Tiny, man-made Treasure Island is generally off the tourist track, so your photos won't be crowded with selfie-takers. Sitting right in the middle of San Francisco Bay, it offers gorgeous views of the San Francisco skyline, especially at night when everything is lit up.

MUIR WOODS NATIONAL MONUMENT

Naturalist John Muir wrote, "Most people are on the world, not in it—have no conscious sympathy or relationship to anything about them ..." It's hard not to feel connected as you walk the shaded paths of Muir Woods amid the towering majesty of the redwood groves.

HAWK HILL

At a high point on the south-facing Marin Headlands, Hawk Hill lies opposite the city with vistas of the Pacific and of the Golden Gate Bridge as it enters San Francisco. True to its name, it's also a great spot for nature watching. Hawk Hill is the site of the autumnal raptor migration and also serves as a habitat for the Mission Blue Butterfly.

BERNAL HEIGHTS

This somewhat stumpy-looking mound rises unenthusiastically above the houses of the surrounding neighborhood. But, pictures taken *from* Bernal Heights Hill offer 360-degree panoramic views. Take a sunset stroll here for stunning San Fran shots.

UNION SQUARE

This lively and central location is a great spot to capture cable cars as they rumble by. Also, the towering Dewey Monument pillar, topped triumphantly by Nike, the Greek goddess of victory, is a legitimately beautiful sculpture. Relax on the steps and soak in or photograph the city.

Under the Radar

KABUKI SPRINGS & SPA
Enter the peaceful lobby and prepare to be transported at the Japanese-style communal baths at this Japantown spa popular with locals of all ages. The extensive spa menu includes facials, salt scrubs, and mud and seaweed wraps. Enjoy banging the gong if fellow bathers are ruining your zen with chitchat.

PIER 24
Just beneath the Bay Bridge along the Embarcadero, Pier 24 provides a fantastic space for displaying photography of all sizes and styles and is home to world-class photography exhibitions.

16TH AVENUE STEPS
At the base of this glorious stairway mosaic in the Inner Sunset, you can take in the beautiful artwork, from an underwater theme to dragonflies and butterflies and even a starry night skyscape. At the top, you get beautiful city views.

EL TECHO
In a city where rooftop bars are a rarity, this Mission spot near Lolinda restaurant draws crowds with a retractable roof and heat lamps, along with cocktails, street-style food, and a city panorama.

FLEA MARKETS
The Alemany Flea Market held every Sunday year-round sells secondhand merch, collectibles of all kinds, and artisan goods. Other options are the smaller Inner Sunset Flea Market and the eclectic Berkeley Flea Market, with treasures including art, body oils, and tools from around the world.

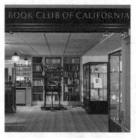

BOOK CLUB OF CALIFORNIA
A secret haven for book lovers, this club holds a collection of more than 10,000 volumes and ephemera, with many books about the history of California and the evolution of printing in the state. You don't have to be a member to attend frequent exhibitions.

THE WARMING HUT
Walking over the Golden Gate Bridge can be a blustery experience at any time, but head down to sea level and you'll find a port in a storm. The Warming Hut offers warm drinks and gifts, and it's the perfect spot to stock up on picnic supplies to enjoy while exploring the waterfront.

16th Avenue Steps

CHURCH OF 8 WHEELS
You haven't lived until you've roller-skated in church, specifically at the former Sacred Heart Church in the Western Addition, now a bonafide roller disco for holy and not-so-holy rollers. Friday and Saturday nights are for adults only, with plenty of old-school funk to get your groove on.

POLLY ANN AND MITCHELL'S
San Francisco is filled with hip ice cream shops, but two of the older shops (both in business for over 50 years) stand out for their unusual offerings. Polly Ann Ice Cream has ice cream flavors like Thai tea, lychee, and black sesame. Mitchell's offers tropical flavors, including *langka* (jackfruit) and *ube* (purple yam).

MT. DAVIDSON
In the shadow of Twin Peaks, but actually taller, this "mountain" the next hill over is topped with a eucalyptus-filled park. Finding the road up is tricky (entrance at Dalewood and Myra Ways), but once there you'll have amazing views—while tourists look for parking on Twin Peaks.

What to Watch and Read

THE MALTESE FALCON
There was a time when the city's most notorious antiheroes weren't billionaires in T-shirts but rather chain-smoking, hard-boiled detectives. In The Maltese Falcon, detective Sam Spade crisscrosses an atmospheric 1930s San Francisco to locate a jeweled statue. The novel, written by Dashiell Hammett, is a legendary piece of noir fiction, and the 1941 film, which starred an in-his-prime Humphrey Bogart and was nominated for three Oscars, is a must-watch.

THE JOY LUCK CLUB
San Francisco's Chinatown is one of the largest and most famous immigrant enclaves in the United States. Amy Tan's 1989 novel and the 1993 film based on it provide a glimpse into the lives of four women who emigrated from China and their relationships with their American-born daughters. The film's grounding anchor is San Francisco, the city that ultimately becomes the home of the four matriarchs, who tell their stories while playing mah-jongg.

THE ROCK
Set on Alcatraz, San Francisco's infamous island prison, The Rock (1996) sets Nicholas Cage and Sean Connery against a rogue unit of special-forces Marines who threaten to launch rockets filled with nerve gas into the city unless they're paid a ransom of $100 million.

THE MAYOR OF CASTRO STREET
Randy Shilts's 1982 biography of gay civil rights icon Harvey Milk is perhaps the most well-regarded and authoritative reckoning of his life to date. Milk was a bombastic, emblematic figure whose advocacy and brutal murder permanently shaped the political landscape of San Francisco and the entire United States.

INFINITE CITY: A SAN FRANCISCO ATLAS
In this 2010 book, Rebecca Solnit offers her own narrative of the city as well as those of collaborating artists, writers, and mapmakers. The end result is a fascinating visual representation of San Francisco's many diverse geographical and cultural layers.

MRS. DOUBTFIRE
Robin Williams had a stunning, iconic career, but for people of a certain generation Mrs. Doubtfire (1993) is perhaps his most recognizable film role. Williams plays a freshly divorced dad in San Francisco who dresses up as an older British nanny to care for his children. The beautiful, Victorian-style "Mrs. Doubtfire House," at 2640 Steiner Street in the Pacific Heights neighborhood, is a popular attraction even though it can be viewed only from the street.

TALES OF THE CITY
Few books offer such a longitudinal view of a place, but Armistead Maupin's stories started running in serial format in the San Francisco Chronicle in 1978, as well as the San Francisco Observer in later years, before they were compiled into novels. As a result the books (there are now nine) are grounded in the events of the day, so the AIDS epidemic is represented and gay characters play an important and influential role. The latest novel was published in 2014.

GUN, WITH OCCASIONAL MUSIC
Set in San Francisco and Oakland, Jonathan Lethem's 1994 novel, a compelling, not-quite-dystopian vision of the near-yet-distant future, highlights what San Francisco might become with just a little (okay, a lot of) rampant genetic experimentation.

VERTIGO

One of Alfred Hitchcock's career-defining films, *Vertigo* (1958) follows the relationship between a detective-turned-investigator and the woman he was hired to follow. Filmed on location in San Francisco and the surrounding Bay Area, the movie offers a smorgasbord of quintessential sights, bringing both presence and authenticity to a captivating story of love, mystery, and murder.

MR. PENUMBRA'S 24-HOUR BOOKSTORE

Robin Sloan's 2012 novel about a curiously quirky used-book store in San Francisco does double duty. Not only is it a story of mystery, love, code-breaking, secret societies, and adopted and inherited culture, it's also a narrative about the potential dangers of rapid technological advancement (and of rejecting technology), tribalism, and other issues currently impacting San Francisco.

THE ROOM

Set in San Francisco, *The Room* (2003) is widely considered to be one of the worst films ever produced, and for good reason. It's a disjointed mess with atrocious acting, a nonsensical plot, and a script that almost defies belief. However, thanks to its sheer ridiculousness (and raucous midnight screenings at arthouse theaters), both *The Room* and its creator, director, and principal actor Tommy Wiseau have become cult film legends. It's also impossible to mention *The Room* without noting *The Disaster Artist,* the 2017 dramatic mockumentary detailing its inception and production, which is also incredibly fun to watch.

SILICON CITY: SAN FRANCISCO IN THE LONG SHADOW OF THE VALLEY

Written by a documentary filmmaker, *Silicon City* (2018) interviews a broad swath of San Franciscans, including both older bohemians who are concerned about the changes to their longtime home and technocratic millennials pushing a future tied to rapid growth. Cary McClelland's book delves into San Francisco's cultural shifts through the eyes of both new and longtime residents and examines how people of differing backgrounds, and philosophies, live side-by-side.

THE CHEZ PANISSE CAFÉ COOKBOOK

Located in Berkeley, Chez Panisse taught lessons to cooks, chefs, and diners that now seem so obvious—cook with fresh ingredients, eat local meat and produce, and treat your guests like friends. While the ethos of Chez Panisse is deliberately unstuffy, the Chez Panisse Café—which sits upstairs from the main dining room—is even looser and a little more bohemian. The *Chez Panisse Café Cookbook* (1999) by Alice Waters captures this and is as much about relationships and culinary philosophy as it is about recipes. If you can't make it to the restaurant itself, this book will help get you there in flavor and in spirit.

ZODIAC

When people think of the San Francisco Bay Area, serial killers don't typically come to mind. This wasn't the case during the late '60s though, when the city and its surrounding areas were terrorized by a person known only as the "Zodiac Killer." Seven people were killed, and the assailant—who to this day remains unknown—sent taunts, cryptic codes, and ciphers to local newspapers, causing both curiosity and panic. Robert Graysmith's book (1986) and the David Fincher film adaptation (2007) each chronicle the efforts to catch the Zodiac Killer and are well-received thrillers.

San Francisco with Kids

ON THE MOVE

Adventure Cat sailing. Them: playing on the trampoline at the bow of this 55-foot catamaran. You: enjoying a drink and the bay sunset on the stern deck.

Cable cars. This one's a no-brainer. But don't miss the **Cable Car Terminus** at Powell and Market Streets, where conductors push the iconic cars on giant turntables, and the **Cable Car Museum,** where you can see how cable cars work.

F-line trolleys. Thomas the Tank Engine fan in tow? Hop on one of the F-line's neat historic streetcars. ■**TIP→ Bonus: this line connects other kid-friendly sights, like Fisherman's Wharf, Pier 39, and the San Francisco Railway Museum.**

SNEAK IN SOME CULTURE

Mission District murals. Kids can appreciate the colorful murals in the Mission's alleys and on buildings, especially if you follow it up with a meal at one of the area's excellent eateries.

Walt Disney Family Museum. Older children may appreciate the videos and displays about the life and times of the man behind Mickey Mouse, including a detailed model of Disneyland.

Stern Grove Festival. Enjoying a delicious picnic in a eucalyptus grove, your kids might not even complain that they're listening to—gasp—classical music (or Latin jazz or opera).

THE GREAT OUTDOORS

Aquatic Park beach. Does your brood include a wannabe Michael Phelps? Then head to this popular beach, one of the few places around the city where it's safe to swim. ■**TIP→ Many other Bay Area beaches have powerful currents that make swimming dangerous.**

Golden Gate Promenade. If your kids can handle a 3.3-mile walk, this one's a beauty—winding from Aquatic Park Beach, through the Presidio, to Fort Point Pier near the base of the Golden Gate Bridge.

Muir Woods National Monument. If these redwood trees look tall to you, imagine seeing them from 2 or 4 feet lower.

Stow Lake. When feeding bread to the ducks gets old, rent a rowboat or pedal boat at this Golden Gate Park favorite.

JUST PLAIN FUN

Dim sum. A rolling buffet from which kids point and pick—likely an instant hit during a break on a Chinatown stroll.

Fisherman's Wharf, Hyde Street Pier, Ghirardelli Square, and Pier 39. The phrase "tourist trap" may come to mind, but in this area you can clamber around old ships, snack on chocolate, and laugh at the sea lions.

Musée Mécanique. How did people entertain themselves before PlayStation (or TV)? Come here to find out.

Oracle Park. Emerald grass, a hot dog in your hand, baseball … and suddenly, you're 10 again, too.

San Francisco Zoo. Between Grizzly Gulch, Lemur Forest, and Koala Crossing, you can make a day of it.

Yerba Buena Gardens. Head here for ice-skating, bowling, a carousel, a playground, and the Children's Creativity Museum, a hands-on arts-and-technology center.

LEARN A THING OR TWO

California Academy of Sciences. Penguins, free-flying tropical butterflies, giant snakes … what's not to like?

Exploratorium. Hands-on children's creativity museum.

Top Walking Tours

All About Chinatown On a delightful two-hour, behind-the-scenes look at the neighborhood, owner Linda Lee and her guides explore historic buildings and new murals, stroll through a food market, and stop at a Buddhist temple. At herbal markets, you'll learn the therapeutic benefits of ginseng, geckos and more. A dim sum lunch is an added option. ✉ *San Francisco* ☎ *415/982–8839* ⊕ *allaboutchinatown. com* ⬛ *From $55, $85 with lunch.*

Chinatown Alleyway Tours To learn about the modern Chinatown community, join up with one of the young guides at this youth-led nonprofit. Tour leaders, who all grew up here, discuss Chinatown's history and current social issues. ✉ *San Francisco* ☎ *415/984–1478* ⊕ *www.chinatownalleywaytours.org* ⬛ *From $23.*

Don Herron's Dashiell Hammett Tour Brush up on your noir slang and join trench-coated guide Herron for a walk by the mystery writer's haunts and the locations from some of Hammett's novels. At four hours for $20, it's one of the best deals going. See the website for tours or arrange one of your own. ✉ *Civic Center* ⊕ *www.donherron.com* ⬛ *$20.*

Foot! Fun Walking Tours You'll likely find yourself breathless with laughter, not just gasping after a steep hill. The tour leaders are all entertainers and history buffs; they've got offerings like the Nob Hill tour "Hobnobbing with Gobs of Snobs." ☎ *415/793–5378* ⊕ *www.foottours.com* ⬛ *From $30.*

Local Tastes of the City Tours If you want to snack your way through a neighborhood as you walk it, consider hanging with cookbook author Tom Medin or one of his local guides. You'll learn why certain things just taste better in San Francisco—like coffee and anything baked with sourdough. You'll also gorge yourself into oblivion: the North Beach tour, for instance, might include multiple stops for coffee and baked goods. ✉ *San Francisco* ☎ *415/665–0480*, ⊕ *www.sffoodtour.com* ⬛ *From $69.*

Precita Eyes Mural Walks For an insider's look at the Mission District's vibrant murals, contact this place for the latest information on tours. The nonprofit organization has nurtured this local art form since 1977. Walks are on weekends, but you can arrange private tours at other times. Muralists lead the tours. ✉ *San Francisco* ☎ *415/285–2287* ⊕ *www. precitaeyes.org* ⬛ *From $20.*

San Francisco City Guides An outstanding free service supported by the San Francisco Public Library since 1978, these walking tours have themes that range from individual neighborhoods to local history (the gold rush, the 1906 quake, ghost walks) to architecture. Although the tours are free and the knowledgeable guides are volunteers, it's appropriate to make a donation for these nonprofit programs. ✉ *San Francisco* ☎ *415/557–4266* ⊕ *www.sfcityguides.org* ⬛ *Free; $15 donation suggested.*

Wok Wiz Chinatown Tour The late cookbook author and Chinatown booster Shirley Fong-Torres founded Wok Wiz, and her team continues to lead these walks. Conversation topics include folklore and, of course, food. The tour called "I Can't Believe I Ate My Way Through Chinatown!" includes breakfast and lunch. ☎ *415/795–8303* ⊕ *www.wokwiz. com* ⬛ *From $35.*

Free and Almost Free

Despite—or perhaps because of—the astronomical cost of living here, San Francisco offers loads of free diversions. Here are our picks for the best free things to do in the city, in alphabetical order by category. Also check out ⊕ *sf. funcheap.com* for a calendar of random, offbeat, and often free one-offs.

FREE MUSEUMS AND GALLERIES
■ Fort Point National Historic Site

■ Octagon House

■ San Francisco Cable Car Museum

■ San Francisco Railway Museum

■ Wells Fargo Museum

FREE MUSEUM TIMES
The first week of every month brings a bonanza of free museum options. Just be aware that free times can draw crowds.

■ Asian Art Museum, first Sunday of every month

■ de Young Museum, first Tuesday of every month

■ GLBT Historical Society Museum, first Saturday of every month

■ Legion of Honor, first Tuesday of every month

■ Yerba Buena Center for the Arts (galleries), first Tuesday of every month

FREE CONCERTS
■ The Golden Gate Park Band plays free public concerts on Sunday afternoon, April through October, on the Music Concourse in the namesake park.

■ The San Francisco Conservatory of Music offers frequent free recitals year-round at its Civic Center home.

■ Stern Grove Festival concerts are held in the Sunset on Sunday afternoon from June through August, ranging from opera to jazz to pop music.

■ Yerba Buena Gardens Festival hosts many concerts and performances from May through October, including Latin jazz, global music, dance, and even puppet shows.

FREE TOURS
■ The free San Francisco City Guides walking tours (note: a $15 donation is suggested) are easily one of the best deals going. Knowledgeable, enthusiastic guides lead walks that focus on a particular neighborhood, theme, or historical period.

■ City Hall offers free tours of its grandiose HQ on weekdays.

MORE GREAT EXPERIENCES FOR $7 OR LESS
■ Do your own walking tour of the Mission District's fantastic outdoor murals, then grab a bite at a taqueria.

■ Walk across the Golden Gate Bridge— an obvious but breathtaking choice.

■ Choose a perfect treat at the Ferry Building's fabulous marketplace and stroll the waterfront promenade.

■ Tour the grounds around the Palace of Fine Arts, circling its lagoon. Next, walk through the Presidio to the Letterman Digital Arts Center campus to see the Yoda fountain and life-size figure of Darth Vader inside the building beyond.

■ Take the kids to Koret Children's Quarter in Golden Gate Park and go for a ride ($2) on a vintage carousel.

■ Hike up to the top of Telegraph Hill for sweeping city and bay views.

SAN FRANCISCO'S CABLE CARS

The moment it dawns on you that you severely underestimated the steepness of the San Francisco hills will likely be the same moment you look down and realize those tracks aren't just for show—or just for tourists.

Van Ness Ave.. California
59
& Market Streets

Sure, locals rarely use the cable cars for commuting these days. (That's partially due to the $8 fare—hear that, Muni?) So you'll likely be packed in with plenty of fellow sightseers. You may even be approaching cable-car fatigue after seeing its image on so many souvenirs. But if you fear the magic is gone, simply climb on board, and those jaded thoughts will dissolve. Grab the pole and gawk at the view as the car clanks down an insanely steep grade toward the bay. Listen to the humming cable, the clang of the bell, and the occasional quip from the gripman. It's an experience you shouldn't pass up, whether on your first trip or your fiftieth.

HOW CABLE CARS WORK

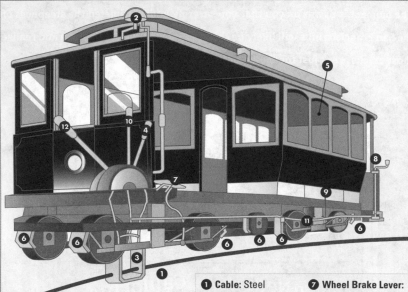

The mechanics are pretty simple: cable cars grab a moving subterranean cable with a "grip" to go. To stop, they release the grip and apply one or more types of brakes. Four cables, totaling 9 miles, power the city's three lines. If the gripman doesn't adjust the grip just right when going up a steep hill, the cable will start to slip and the car will have to back down the hill and try again. This is an extremely rare occurrence—imagine the ribbing the gripman gets back at the cable car barn!

Gripman: Stands in front and operates the grip, brakes, and bell. Favorite joke, especially at the peak of a steep hill: "This is my first day on the job, folks . . ."

Conductor: Moves around the car, deals with tickets, alerts the grip about what's coming up, and operates the rear wheel brakes.

❶ Cable: Steel wrapped around flexible sisal core; 2 inches thick; runs at a constant 9½ mph.

❷ Bells: Used for crew communication; alerts other drivers and pedestrians.

❸ Grip: Vice-like lever extends through the center slot in the track to grab or release the cable.

❹ Grip Lever: Left-hand lever; operates grip.

❺ Car: Entire car weighs 8 tons.

❻ Wheel Brake: Steel brake pads on each wheel.

❼ Wheel Brake Lever: Foot pedal; operates wheel brakes.

❽ Rear Wheel Brake Lever: Applied for extra traction on hills.

❾ Track Brake: 2-foot-long sections of Monterey pine push down against the track to help stop the car.

❿ Track Brake Lever: Middle lever; operates track brakes.

⓫ Emergency Brake: 18-inch steel wedge, jams into street slot to bring car to an immediate stop.

⓬ Emergency Brake Lever: Right-hand lever, red; operates emergency brake.

ROUTES

Cars run at least every 15 minutes, from around 6 am to about 1 am.

Powell–Hyde line: Most scenic, with classic Bay views. Begins at Powell and Market streets, then crosses Nob Hill and Russian Hill before a white-knuckle descent down Hyde Street, ending near the Hyde Street Pier.

Powell–Mason line: Also begins at Powell and Market streets, but winds through North Beach to Bay and Taylor streets, a few blocks from Fisherman's Wharf.

California line: Runs from the foot of Market Street, at Drumm Street, up Nob Hill and back. Great views (and aromas and sounds) of Chinatown on the way up. Sit in back to catch glimpses of the bay. ■TIP➔ Take the California line if it's just the cable-car experience you're after—the lines are shorter, and the grips and conductors say it's friendlier and has a slower pace.

RULES OF THE RIDE

Tickets. There are ticket booths at all three turnarounds. You must purchase your ticket in advance.

■TIP➔ If you're planning to use public transit a few times, or if you'd like to ride back and forth on the cable car without worrying about the price, consider a one-day (or multiday) Muni Visitor Passport. You can get passports online, at the Powell Street turnaround, at the TIX booth on Union Square, or the Fisherman's Wharf cable-car ticket booth at Beach and Hyde streets. Also consider Muni Mobile or a Clipper Card; see sfmta.com. Cash purchases require exact change.

All Aboard. You can board on either side of the cable car. It's legal to stand on the running boards and hang on to the pole, but keep your ears open for the gripman's warnings. ■TIP➔ Grab a seat on the outside bench for the best views.

Most people wait (and wait) in line at one of the cable car turnarounds, but you can also hop on along the route. Board wherever you see a white sign showing a figure climbing aboard a brown cable car; wave to the approaching driver, and wait until the car stops.

Riding on the running boards can be part of the thrill.

CABLE CAR HISTORY

HALLIDIE FREES THE HORSES

In the 1850s and '60s, San Francisco's streetcars were drawn by horses. Legend has it that the horrible sight of a car dragging a team of horses downhill to their deaths roused Andrew Smith Hallidie to action. The English immigrant had invented the "Hallidie Ropeway," essentially a cable car for mined ore, and he was convinced that his invention could also move people. In 1873, Hallidie and his intrepid crew prepared to test the first cable car high on Russian Hill. The anxious engineer peered down into the foggy darkness, failed to see the bottom of the hill, and promptly turned the controls over to Hallidie. Needless to say, the thing worked . . . but rides were free for the first two days because people were afraid to get on.

SEE IT FOR YOURSELF

The Cable Car Museum (✉ 1201 Mason St, ⊕ cablecarmusem.org) is one of the city's best free offerings and an absolute must for kids. (You can even ride a cable car there, since all three lines stop between Russian Hill and Nob Hill.) The museum, which is inside the city's last cable-car barn, takes the top off the system to let you see how it all works. Eternally humming and squealing, the massive powerhouse cable wheels steal the show. You can also climb aboard a vintage car and take the grip, let the kids ring a cable-car bell (briefly, please!), and check out vintage gear dating from 1873.

■ TIP→ The gift shop sells cable car paraphernalia, including an authentic gripman's bell (it'll sound like Powell Street in your house every day). For significantly less, you can pick up a key chain made from a piece of worn-out cable. Books, T-shirts, hats, and models are also on sale.

CHAMPION OF THE CABLE CAR BELL

Each fall (though the month can vary widely : check ⊕ sfmta.com for update) the city's best and brightest come together to crown a bell-ringing champion at Union Square. The crowd cheers gripmen and conductors as they stomp, shake, and riff with the rope. But it's not a popularity contest; the ringers are judged by former bell-ringing champions and others who take each ping and gong very seriously.

Chapter 2

TRAVEL SMART

Updated by
Ava Liang Zhao

★ **STATE CAPITAL**
Sacramento

👫 **POPULATION**
881,549 (San Francisco city)

💬 **LANGUAGE**
English

$ **CURRENCY**
U.S. Dollar

📠 **AREA CODE**
415

⚠ **EMERGENCIES**
911

🚗 **DRIVING**
On the right

⚡ **ELECTRICITY**
120–220 v/60 cycles;
plugs have two or three
rectangular prongs

🕙 **TIME**
Pacific Time; 3 hours behind
New York

🌐 **WEB RESOURCES**
www.sftravel.com
www.visitcalifornia.com
www.sfgate.com
www.sfexaminer.com

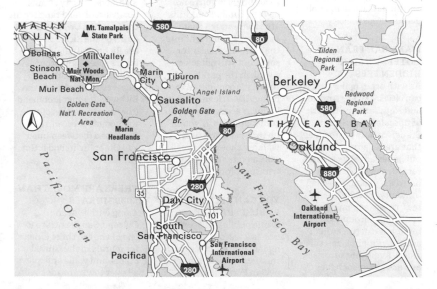

Know Before You Go

PACK FOR SAN FRANCISCO, NOT CALIFORNIA

California has drawn in many a traveler with endless sunny days, but the average high in the Bay Area is only 63.8°F and nights tend to drop into the low 50s. So, while the city is beautiful, it doesn't exactly have beach weather. Even summer is marked by foggy, windy conditions.

SAN FRAN HAS A HIGH RATE OF STREET HOMELESSNESS

San Francisco is famous for a great many things, but for a multitude of reasons, including the city's acute lack of affordable housing, this unfortunately includes homelessness. The circumstances that lead to people being unhoused are varied and often tragic, and the reality of the problem can be jarring and upsetting: expect to see tent cities and panhandling, as well as used drug paraphernalia and human waste in public places across the city.

MANY SAN FRAN HOTELS CHARGE HIDDEN FEES

As with other major American cities, like Los Angeles and New York, the majority of upscale hotels in San Francisco now charge fees that are separate from the published advertised room rate for the hotel. Often listed as "Urban," "Resort," "Amenity," and/or "Facility" fees, these tack-on rates are usually around $25 per night but can run as high as $85 per night (sometimes more). Avoid any surprises and ask about such fees before you book or when you are checking in (and feel free to contest them in person and on social media).

THE HILLS ARE PRETTY, JUST NOT SO MUCH ON THE WAY UP

The city's hills offer spectacular views, but they can also be physically challenging, particularly for those with limited stamina or mobility. Exploring on foot is both possible and rewarding, but it's important to plan accordingly if you're not up for a climb. Some hills are steep enough that they have steps built right into the sidewalk (easier for some, but still not exactly a walk in the park!), and the city is committed to being ADA-friendly, which includes accessible public transportation. If you're up to it, pack practical walking shoes; if not, take advantage of public transportation.

YOU CAN RELY ON PUBLIC TRANSIT

While public transportation is a feature of every major city, few places have the sheer variety offered by San Francisco. The Bay Area Rapid Transit (BART) system is a mix of both heavy rail and subway and serves San Francisco, Oakland, and a variety of suburban areas. At the same time, San Francisco has hybrid Muni buses, Muni Metro Light Rail, cable cars, historic streetcars, electric trolleys, and a range of privately run options, such as taxis, app-based rideshares, electric bicycles, and motorized scooters. Many parts of the public transportation network are quite well run, though buses fall prey to traffic and sometimes run behind schedule. Between the public and the private options, you should have a fairly easy time getting to where you need to go.

KNOW WHICH RICHMOND YOU'RE RENTING IN

The Richmond District, also known as "the Richmond," is a neighborhood in the northwest corner of San Francisco; Richmond is a city 20 miles northeast of San Francisco in the East Bay. Drilling further down on the Richmonds, the Richmond neighborhood's sub-neighborhoods include Outer Richmond (the western portion of the Richmond), Inner Richmond (the eastern portion of the Richmond), and Central Richmond (between Inner and Outer Richmonds). Got all that?

THERE ARE MORE THAN 1,000 MURALS

Along with L.A. and Chicago, San Francisco is one of the top three cities for murals in the United States, and walls and alleys all over town are adorned with vivid colors and poignant messages. The Mission alone boasts almost 500. Some highlights are the Chris Ware mural at 826 Valencia, the multitude of murals in Balmy Alley and Clarion Alley, and the Hidden Garden Steps.

THE PIERS ARE TOURIST TRAPS, BUT THAT'S OKAY

San Francisco's public piers are absolutely, 100% a set of loud and crowded tourist traps. There's a reason the piers are such a famous tourist magnet—they're kind of awesome! The straight, weatherworn expanse of Fisherman's Wharf is iconic, and Pier 39's basking sea lions and multitude of vendors make it a lively and popular destination. Even if you don't think of yourself as the kind of person that these sights would appeal to, give them a shot. Wander along the Embarcadero, stop for some crab legs and oysters along the way, and enjoy one of the most leisurely parts of the city.

SIDE TRIPS ARE A MUST

San Francisco is a vibrant and engaging place, but you'll be doing yourself a disservice if you only stick to the major tourist neighborhoods. The city of Oakland has been transformed in recent years, with pockets of Piedmont Avenue and other streets lined with hip restaurants, bars, and shops. Berkeley is home not just to a famous university but also to a variety of museums, cafés, and legendary restaurants. And don't forget all that incredible wine to be had in nearby Sonoma and Napa.

PRIVATE PARKS ARE PUBLIC

It's a little-known fact that cities often require privately owned buildings to provide public spaces. In San Francisco those are known as POPOS (Privately Owned Public Open Space), and they're all over the city just waiting for you to come sit, feel like a local, and use the bathroom. These spaces are legally required to be labeled with visible signage indicating both how they can be accessed and what their hours of operation are. In the off chance those signs are hard to find (or simply aren't there), the San Francisco Planning Department provides a searchable, interactive map (⊕ *sfplanninggis.org/POPOS/*) that lets you see which sites have amenities, such as bathrooms, food, tables, and seating.

IT'S NOT CHEAP

San Francisco is not only one of the most expensive cities in the entire world in which to live, it's also an expensive one to visit. Between the high prices of flights, hotels, and meals, if you're budget-conscious you'll need to plan a bit to maximize your resources. CityPASS (⊕ *www.citypass. com*) bundles together public transit passes and museum tickets for both ease and savings, and the customizable Go City pass (⊕ *gocity.com/en-us*) lets you build your own itinerary from scratch while still economizing. The city's public transportation network also sells unlimited-ride day passes.

YOUR DOG IS VERY WELCOME

If you're a dog lover or like to travel with your dog, San Francisco is a good option for you. There are hundreds of acres in and around the city where your pup can romp off-leash, and every neighborhood has one or two parks with sizable dog-run areas. People are just out and about everywhere with their dogs, socializing with other people with dogs. There are dog-friendly bars; dog-friendly beaches, like Baker Beach, Ocean Beach, and Lands End Beach; dog-friendly cabs; dog-friendly gyms, pet-friendly apartment rentals and hotels; dog-friendly wineries in Napa; and lots of dog-friendly walking tours. In April, the annual DogFest is a huge celebration of all things canine in Duboce Park.

CHECK OPENING INFORMATION

The ongoing impact of COVID-19 means that it's best to check opening times and days before visiting sights, restaurants, and other places. At this writing, for example, cable-car service is expected to resume later in fall 2021, but not all lines (check sfmta.com for updates). For more information about COVID-related closures and reopenings, see the San Francisco city government's website (⊕ *sf.gov/topics/ reopening*).

Getting Here and Around

Air

The least expensive airfares to San Francisco are priced for round-trip travel and should be purchased in advance. Airlines generally allow you to change your return date for a fee; most low-fare tickets, however, are nonrefundable. (But if you cancel, you can usually apply the fare to a future trip, within one year, to any destination the airline flies.)

Nonstop flights from New York to San Francisco take about 5½ hours, and with the 3-hour time change, it's possible to leave JFK by 8 am and be in San Francisco by 10:30 am. Some flights may require a midway stop, making the total excursion between 8 and 9½ hours. Nonstop times are approximately 1½ hours from Los Angeles, 3 hours from Dallas, 4½ hours from Chicago, 5½ hours from Atlanta, 11 hours from London, 12 hours from Auckland, and 13½ hours from Sydney.

AIRPORTS

The major gateway to San Francisco is **San Francisco International Airport (SFO)**, 15 miles south of the city. It's off U.S. 101 near Millbrae and San Bruno.

Oakland International Airport (OAK) is across the bay, not much farther away from downtown San Francisco (via I–80 East and I–880 South), but rush-hour traffic on the Bay Bridge may lengthen travel times considerably.

San Jose International Airport (SJC) is about 40 miles south of San Francisco; travel time depends largely on traffic flow, but plan on 1½ hours with moderate traffic.

Depending on the price difference, you might consider flying into Oakland or San Jose. Oakland's an easy-to-use alternative because there's public transportation between the airport and downtown San Francisco. Getting to San Francisco from San Jose, though, can be time-consuming and costly via public transportation. Heavy fog is infamous for causing chronic delays into and out of San Francisco.

GROUND TRANSPORTATION FROM SAN FRANCISCO INTERNATIONAL AIRPORT

Transportation signage at the airport is color-coded by type and is quite clear. A taxi ride to downtown costs around $60; rideshare companies like Lyft and Uber are a popular option and start around $25 for a shared ride into the city. Airport shuttles are inexpensive and generally efficient. Lorrie's Airport Shuttle and SuperShuttle both stop at the lower level near baggage claim and take you anywhere within the city limits of San Francisco. They charge around $17 each way, depending on where you're going. Both sell tickets online; you can print them out before leaving home.

Shuttles to the East Bay, such as Bay-Porter Express, depart from a lot near the lower level; expect to pay between $38 and $47. Inquire about the number of stops a shuttle makes en route to or from the airport; some companies, such as East Bay Shuttle, have nonstop service, but they cost a bit more. Marin Door to Door operates van service to Marin County starting at $78 for the first passenger, and a few bucks more for each additional person. Marin Airporter buses cost $23 (cash only, unless reserved ahead online) and require no reservations but stop only at designated stations in Marin; buses leave every 30 minutes, on the half hour and hour, from 5 am to midnight.

You can take BART directly to downtown San Francisco; the trip takes about 30 minutes and costs $9.65. There are both booths with attendants and vending machines for ticket purchases. Trains leave from the international terminal every 15 or 20 minutes, depending on the day or time.

Another inexpensive way to get to San Francisco (though not as convenient as BART) is via two SamTrans buses: No. 292 (50 minutes) and the KX (35 minutes). Fares are $2.25 from SFO, $4.50 to SFO. Board the SamTrans buses on the lower level.

To drive to downtown San Francisco from the airport, take U.S. 101 North to the Civic Center/9th Street, 7th Street, or 4th Street/Downtown exits. If you're headed to the Embarcadero or Fisherman's Wharf, take Interstate 280 North (the exit is to the right, just north of the airport, off U.S. 101) and get off at the 4th Street/King Street exit. King Street becomes the Embarcadero a few blocks east of the exit. The Embarcadero winds around the waterfront to Fisherman's Wharf.

FROM OAKLAND INTERNATIONAL AIRPORT

A taxi to downtown San Francisco costs around $80; rideshare companies like Lyft and Uber offer rides for around $50. BayPorter Express and other shuttles serve major hotels and provide door-to-door service to the East Bay and San Francisco. SuperShuttle operates vans to San Francisco and Oakland. Marin Door to Door serves Marin County for $78 for the first passenger, and a few bucks more for each additional person.

The best way to get to San Francisco via public transit is to take BART, which is free upon boarding but requires ticket purchase at the Coliseum/Oakland International Airport BART station (BART fares vary depending on where you're going; the ride to downtown San Francisco from here costs $10.20).

If you're driving from Oakland International Airport, take Airport Drive east to Interstate 880 North to Interstate 80 West over the Bay Bridge. This will likely take at least an hour.

FROM SAN JOSE INTERNATIONAL AIRPORT

A taxi to downtown San Jose costs about $20 to $25; a trip to San Francisco runs about $150 to $165. Rideshare companies like Lyft and Uber offer rides to downtown San Jose starting around $12; a trip to San Francisco starts around $55.

To drive to downtown San Jose from the airport, take Airport Boulevard east to Route 87 South. To get to San Francisco from the airport, take Route 87 South to Interstate 280 North. The trip will take roughly two hours.

At $10.50 for a one-way ticket, Caltrain provides the most affordable option for traveling between San Francisco and San Jose's airport. However, the Caltrain station in San Francisco at 4th and Townsend Streets isn't in a conveniently central location. It's on the eastern side of the South of Market (SoMa) neighborhood and not easily accessible by other public transit. You'll need to take a taxi or walk from the nearest bus line. From San Francisco, it takes 90 minutes to reach the Santa Clara Caltrain station, from which a free shuttle runs every 15 minutes (every 30 minutes on nights and weekends), whisking you to and from the San Jose International Airport in 15 minutes.

⊙ Boat

Several ferry lines run out of San Francisco. Blue & Gold Fleet operates a number of routes, including service to Sausalito ($13 one-way) and Tiburon ($13 one-way). Tickets are sold at Pier 39; boats depart from Pier 41 nearby. Alcatraz Cruises, owned by Hornblower Cruises and Events, operates the ferries to Alcatraz Island ($42, including audio tour and National Park Service ranger-led

Getting Here and Around

programs) from Pier 33, about a half-mile east of Fisherman's Wharf. Boats leave 14 times a day (more in summer), and the journey itself takes 30 minutes. Allow at least 2½ hours for a round-trip jaunt. Golden Gate Ferry runs daily to and from Sausalito and Larkspur ($13.50 and $13 one-way), leaving from Pier 1, behind the San Francisco Ferry Building. The Alameda/Oakland Ferry operates daily between Alameda's Main Street Terminal, Oakland's Jack London Square, and San Francisco's Pier 41 and the Ferry Building ($7.20 one-way); some ferries go only to Pier 41 or the Ferry Building, so ask when you board. Purchase tickets on board.

Bus

Greyhound serves San Francisco with buses from many major U.S. cities; within California, service is limited to hub towns and cities only. The Greyhound depot is located at the Salesforce Transit Center, in the SoMa district. Tickets can be purchased online; seating is on a first-come, first-served basis. Cash, checks, and credit cards are accepted.

Cable-Car

Don't miss the sensation of moving up and down some of San Francisco's steepest hills in a clattering cable car. Jump aboard as it pauses at a designated stop, and wedge yourself into any available space. Then just hold on. At this writing, cable-car service is set to resume later in fall 2021, but not all lines; check sfmta.com for updates.

The fare (for one direction) is $8. Buy tickets in advance at the kiosks at the cable-car turnarounds at Hyde and Beach Streets and at Powell and Market

Tracking Cheap Gas

Determined to avoid the worst prices at the pump? Check the GasBuddy website (⊕ *www.sanfran-gasprices.com*), which tracks the lowest (and highest) gasoline costs in the Bay Area. It also has a handy price-mapping feature and a master list of local gas stations.

Streets. Or consider MuniMobile or a Clipper Card; see ⊕ *sfmta.com*. Cash purchases require exact change.

The heavily traveled Powell–Mason and Powell–Hyde lines begin at Powell and Market Streets near Union Square and terminate at Fisherman's Wharf; lines for these routes can be long, especially in summer. The California Street line runs east and west from Market and California Streets to Van Ness Avenue; there's often no wait to board this route.

Car

Driving in San Francisco can be a challenge because of the one-way streets, snarly traffic, and steep hills. The first two elements can be frustrating enough, but those hills are tough for unfamiliar drivers.

Be sure to leave plenty of room between your car and other vehicles when on a steep slope. This is especially important when you've braked at a stop sign on a steep incline. Whether with a stick shift or an automatic transmission, every car rolls backward for a moment once the brake is released. So don't pull too close to the car ahead of you. When it's time to pull forward, keep your foot on the brake while tapping lightly on the accelerator. Once the gears are engaged, let up on the brake and head uphill.

■TIP→ Remember to curb your wheels when parking on hills—turn wheels away from the curb when facing uphill, toward the curb when facing downhill. You can get a ticket if you don't do this.

Market Street runs southwest from the Ferry Building, then becomes Portola Drive as it rounds Twin Peaks (which lie just south of the giant radio-antennae structure Sutro Tower). It can be difficult to drive across Market. The major east–west streets north of Market are Geary Boulevard (it's called Geary Street east of Van Ness Avenue), which runs to the Pacific Ocean; Fulton Street, which begins at the back of the Opera House and continues along the north side of Golden Gate Park to Ocean Beach; Oak Street, which runs east from Golden Gate Park toward downtown, then flows into northbound Franklin Street; and Fell Street, the left two lanes of which cut through Golden Gate Park and empty into Lincoln Way, which continues to the ocean.

Among the major north–south streets are Divisadero, which heading south becomes Castro Street at Waller Street and continues just past César Chávez Street; Van Ness Avenue, which heading south becomes South Van Ness Avenue after it crosses Market Street; and Park Presidio Boulevard, which heading south from the Richmond District becomes Crossover Drive within Golden Gate Park and empties into 19th Avenue.

GASOLINE
Gas stations are hard to find in San Francisco; look for the national franchises on major thoroughfares, such as Market Street, Geary Boulevard, Mission Street, or California Street.

Take the 511

Several transportation organizations—the Metropolitan Transportation Commission, the California Highway Patrol, the California Department of Transportation, and more—pool their data into a free, one-stop telephone (☎ 511) and Web (⊕ www.511.org) resource for all nine Bay Area counties. The service provides the latest info on traffic conditions, routes, and fares for all public transit and also has info about bicycle and other transportation. The phone line operates 24/7 toll-free.

PARKING
San Francisco is a terrible city for parking. In the Financial District and Civic Center neighborhoods, parking is forbidden on most streets between 3 or 4 pm and 6 or 7 pm. Check street signs carefully to confirm because illegally parked cars are towed immediately. Downtown parking lots are often full, and most are expensive. The city-owned Sutter-Stockton, Ellis-O'Farrell, and 5th-and-Mission garages have the most reasonable rates in the downtown area. Large hotels often have parking available, but it doesn't come cheap; many charge in excess of $40 a day for the privilege.

ROAD CONDITIONS
Although rush "hours" are 6–10 am and 3–7 pm, you can hit gridlock on any day at any time, especially over the Bay Bridge and leaving and/or entering the city from the south. Sunday-afternoon traffic can be heavy as well, in particular over the bridges.

Getting Here and Around

The most comprehensive and immediate traffic updates are available through the city's 511 service, which can be accessed online (⊕ *www.511.org*), where real-time data shows you the traffic on your selected route, or by calling 511. On the radio, tune in to an all-news radio station, such as KQED 88.5 FM or KCBS 740 AM/106.9 FM.

Be especially wary of nonindicated lane changes.

San Francisco is the only major American city uncut by freeways. To get from the Bay Bridge to the Golden Gate Bridge, you'll have to take surface streets, specifically Van Ness Avenue, which doubles as U.S. 101 through the city.

RULES OF THE ROAD

The speed limit on city streets is 25 mph unless otherwise posted. A right turn on a red light after stopping is legal unless posted otherwise, as is a left on red at the intersection of two one-way streets.

Ⓜ Metro/Public Transport

BART

BART (Bay Area Rapid Transit) trains, which run until midnight, travel under the bay via tunnel to connect San Francisco with Oakland, Berkeley, and other cities and towns beyond. Within San Francisco, stations are limited to downtown, the Mission, and a couple of outlying neighborhoods.

Trains travel frequently from early morning until evening on weekdays. After 8 pm weekdays and on weekends, there's often a 20-minute wait between trains on the same line. Trains also travel south from San Francisco as far as Millbrae. BART trains connect downtown San

Francisco to San Francisco International Airport; the ride costs $9.65.

Intracity San Francisco fares are $2.10; intercity fares are $3.70 to $11.45. BART bases its ticket prices on miles traveled and doesn't offer price breaks by zone. The easy-to-read maps posted in BART stations list fares based on destination, radiating out from your starting point of the current station.

During morning and evening rush hour, trains within the city are crowded—even standing room can be hard to come by. Cars at the far front and back of the train are less likely to be filled to capacity. Smoking, eating, and drinking are prohibited on trains and in stations.

BUS OPERATORS

Outside the city, AC Transit serves the East Bay, and Golden Gate Transit serves Marin County and a few cities in southern Sonoma County.

MUNI

The San Francisco Municipal Railway, or Muni, operates light-rail vehicles, the historic F-line streetcars along Fisherman's Wharf and Market Street, buses, and the world-famous cable cars. Light-rail travels along Market Street to the Mission District and Noe Valley (J line), Ingleside (K line), and the Sunset District (L, M, and N lines) while also passing through the West Portal, Glen Park, and Castro neighborhoods. The N line continues around the Embarcadero to the Caltrain station at 4th and King Streets; the T-line light-rail runs from the Castro, down Market Street, around the Embarcadero, and south past Mission Bay and Hunters Point to Sunnydale Avenue and Bayshore Boulevard. Muni provides 24-hour service on select lines to all areas of the city.

On buses and streetcars, the fare is $2.50. Exact change is required, and dollar bills are accepted in the fare boxes. For all Muni vehicles other than cable cars, 90-minute transfers are issued free upon request at the time the fare is paid. These are valid for unlimited transfers in any direction until they expire (time is indicated on the ticket). Cable cars cost $8 and include no transfers *(see Cable-Car Travel)*.

One-day ($13), three-day ($31), and seven-day ($41) Visitor Passports valid on the entire Muni system can be purchased at several outlets, including the cable-car ticket booth at Powell and Market Streets and the visitor information center downstairs in Hallidie Plaza. A monthly ticket is available for $81, which can be used on all Muni lines (including cable cars) and on BART within city limits. The San Francisco CityPass ($76), a discount ticket booklet to several major city attractions, also covers all Muni travel for seven consecutive days.

■TIP➔ **Save money by purchasing your Passports on MuniMobile, the mobile ticketing app of the San Francisco Metropolitan Transportation Authority (SFMTA).**

Taxi

Taxi service is notoriously bad in San Francisco, and finding a cab can be frustratingly difficult. Popular nightlife locales, such as the Mission, SoMa, North Beach, and the Castro, are the easiest places to hail a cab off the street; hotel taxi stands are also an option. If you're going to the airport, make a reservation or book a shuttle instead. Taxis in San Francisco charge $3.50 for the first 0.5 mile (one of the highest base rates in the United

States), 55¢ for each additional 0.2 mile, and 55¢ per minute in stalled traffic; a $4 surcharge is added for trips from the airport. There's no charge for additional passengers; there's no surcharge for luggage. For trips farther than 15 miles outside city limits, multiply the metered rate by 1.5; tolls and tip are extra.

That said, San Francisco's poor taxi service was a direct factor in the creation of ridesharing services, such as Uber and Lyft, which are easy to use and prominent throughout the city and its surrounding areas. San Franciscans generally regard taxis as a thing of the past and use ridesharing on a day-to-day basis. If you're willing to share a car with strangers, a trip within the city can run as low as $4; rates go up for private rides and during peak-demand times. These services are especially economical when going to or from the airport, where a shared ride starts at about $25—half the cost of a cab.

Train

Amtrak trains travel to the Bay Area from some cities in California as well as the greater United States. The Coast Starlight travels north from Los Angeles to Seattle, passing the Bay Area along the way, but contrary to its name, the train runs inland through the Central Valley for much of its route through Northern California; the most scenic stretch is in Southern California, between San Luis Obispo and Los Angeles. Amtrak also has several routes between San Jose, Oakland, and Sacramento. The California Zephyr travels from Chicago to the Bay Area, with spectacular alpine vistas as it crosses the Sierra Nevada range. San Francisco doesn't have an Amtrak train

Getting Here and Around

station but does have an Amtrak bus stop at the Ferry Building, from which shuttle buses transport passengers to trains in Emeryville, just over the Bay Bridge. Shuttle buses also connect the Emeryville train station with BART and other points in downtown San Francisco. You can buy a California Rail Pass, which gives you 7 days of travel in a 21-day period, for $159.

Caltrain connects San Francisco to Palo Alto, San Jose, Santa Clara, and many smaller cities en route. In San Francisco, trains leave from the main depot, at 4th and Townsend Streets, and a rail-side stop at 22nd and Pennsylvania Streets. One-way fares are $3.75 to $15, depending on the number of zones through which you travel; tickets are valid for four hours after purchase time. A ticket is $8.25 from San Francisco to Palo Alto, at least $10.50 to San Jose. You can also buy a day pass ($7.50–$30) for unlimited travel in a 24-hour period. It's worth waiting for an express train for trips that last from 1 to 1¾ hours. On weekdays, trains depart three or four times per hour during the morning and evening, but only once or twice per hour during daytime non-commute hours and late night. Weekend trains run once per hour, though there are two bullet trains per day, one in late morning and one in early evening The system shuts down after midnight. There are no onboard ticket sales. You must buy tickets before boarding the train or risk paying up to $230 for fare evasion.

Essentials

Activities

Bikers and hikers traverse the majestic Golden Gate Bridge, bound for the Marin Headlands or the winding trails of the Presidio. Runners, strollers, and cyclists head for Golden Gate Park's wooded paths, and water lovers satisfy their addictions by kayaking, sailing, kite-surfing, and even swimming in the bay and along the rugged Pacific coast.

Prefer to watch from the sidelines? The Giants (baseball) play in San Francisco, as do the Golden State Warriors (basketball; at the Chase Center in Mission Bay); the A's (baseball) play in Oakland; and the 49ers (football) are based in Santa Clara. But the city has plenty of other periodic sporting events to spectate, including that roving costume party, the Bay to Breakers race in May. For events listings and local perspectives on Bay Area sports, pick up a copy of the *San Francisco Chronicle* (⊕ *www.sfchronicle. com*), *SFGate* (⊕ *www.sfgate.com*), or the *San Francisco Examiner* (⊕ *www. sfexaminer.com*).

BASEBALL
Oakland Athletics
BASEBALL/SOFTBALL | FAMILY | Baseball's Oakland Athletics, also called the Oakland A's, has a loyal following among locals in Oakland and enjoys a fierce rivalry with the San Francisco Giants just across the bay. The team hopes to move from its RingCentral Coliseum stadium to a proposed new waterfront ballpark at Jack London Square, perhaps in 2023, but Major League Baseball is also allowing the team to consider relocating to another city; stay tuned. ⊠ *RingCentral Coliseum, 7000 Coliseum Way, Oakland* ☎ *877/493–2255 box office* ⊕ *mlb.com/ athletics.*

★ **San Francisco Giants**
BASEBALL/SOFTBALL | FAMILY | Three World Series titles (2010, 2012, and 2014) and the retro-modern design of Oracle Park lead to sellouts for nearly every home game the National League team plays, so make plans in advance. ⊠ *Oracle Park, 24 Willie Mays Plaza, between 2nd and 3rd Sts., SoMa* ☎ *415/972–2000* ⊕ *www. mlb.com/giants.*

BIKING
San Francisco is known for its treacherously steep hills, so it may be surprising to see so many cyclists. This is actually a great city for biking—there are ample bike lanes, it's not hard to find level ground with great scenery (especially along the water), and if you're willing to tackle a challenging uphill climb, you're often rewarded with a fabulous view—and a quick trip back down.

FOOTBALL
San Francisco 49ers
FOOTBALL | State-of-the-art Levi's Stadium, 45 miles south of San Francisco, has more than 13,000 square feet of HD video boards. Home games usually sell out far in advance. Ticketmaster (*www.ticketmaster.com*) and StubHub (*www.stubhub.com*) are sources for single-game tickets. ⊠ *Levi's Stadium, 4900 Marie P. DeBartolo Way, from San Francisco, take U.S. 101 S to Lawrence Expressway and follow signs, Santa Clara* ☎ *800/745–3000 Ticketmaster, 866/788– 2482 StubHub, 415/464–9377 Santa Clara stadium* ⊕ *www.49ers.com.*

RUNNING
San Francisco is spectacular for running. There are more than 7 miles of paved trails in and around **Golden Gate Park**; circling **Stow Lake** and then crossing the bridge and running up the path to the top of Strawberry Hill is a total of 2½ miles. An enormously popular route is the 2-mile raised bike path that runs

Essentials

from Lincoln Way along the ocean, at the southern border of Golden Gate Park, to Sloat Boulevard, which is the northern border of the San Francisco Zoo. (Stick to the park's interior when it's windy, as ocean gusts can kick up sand.) From Sloat Boulevard, you can pick up the **Lake Merced** bike path, which loops around the lake and the golf course, to extend your run another 5 miles.

The paved path along the **Marina** provides a 1½-mile (round-trip) run along a flat, well-maintained surface and has glorious bay views. Start where Laguna Street meets Marina Boulevard, then run west along the Marina Green toward the Golden Gate and St. Francis Yacht Clubs, near the docks at the northern end of Marina Boulevard. On weekends beware: you'll have to wind through the crowds—but those views are worth it. You can extend your Marina run by jogging the paths through the restored wetlands of Crissy Field, just past the yacht harbor, then up the hill to the Golden Gate Bridge.

The *San Francisco Bike Map & Walking Guide*, available at booksellers or through the San Francisco Bicycle Coalition (⊕ *sfbike.org/resources/maps-routes)*, which indicates hill grades on city streets by color, is a great resource. Online, check the **San Francisco Road Runners Club** site (⊕ *www.sfrrc.org)* for some recommended routes and links to several local races.

🍴 Dining

San Francisco is one of America's top food cities. Some of the biggest landmarks are restaurants, and, for some visitors, chefs are just as big a draw as Alcatraz. In fact, on a Saturday, the Ferry Building—a temple to local eating—may attract more visitors than the Golden Gate Bridge.

Chefs are drawn to the superb ingredients plucked from the soil and the sea. Chances are that the Meyer lemons, fava beans, or strawberries on your plate that are preserved, pureed, or pickled were harvested within the last 48 hours, if not this morning. The briny abalone, crab, oysters, squid, and tuna that are poached, seared, smoked, or carpaccio'ed are caught just offshore. You will also get to taste unusual varieties, like lollipop kale, *agretti* greens, and yuzu citrus.

Today the most interesting kitchens are using these ingredients in regional cuisines, like Korean, Japanese, Italian, or South American. So get ready to dig into kung pao pastrami, porcini doughnuts with raclette béchamel, and yucca gnocchi. That fig-on-a-plate reputation? That's so last decade.

But the playground isn't just in haute cuisine kitchens. Culinary hot spots are just as likely to be a burger, pizza, or barbecue joint—with a few classically trained chefs dedicating their lives to making a better margherita pizza. And you can just as easily find superb *banh mi,* ramen noodles, and juicy *al pastor* tacos in the kitchens of Little Saigon, Japantown, or the Mission District.

The impact of the COVID-19 pandemic on the restaurant scene in the Bay Area, as in many other parts of the globe, has been widespread and severe. Many restaurants and bars have responded with adjusted hours, changed menus, and limited indoor or only outdoor seating. Call the restaurant or check their website for the latest information. One upside is that temporary parklets and pedestrian-friendly slow streets may become permanent fixtures, lending an air of alfresco European leisure to the streets of San Francisco.

RESERVATIONS

Snagging reservations at restaurants with a lot of buzz has gotten notoriously difficult, with 5:30 or 9:30 often the pick. These choices aren't terrible, if you plan on it. For a reservation at peak dining hours, though, our best advice is to call as far in advance as possible—try eating there earlier in the week if the Friday and Saturday tables are full. You can also try calling a restaurant in the early afternoon the day of, when they're making their reservation confirmation calls and may have a last-minute opening. If you're calling a few days ahead of time, ask if you can be put on a waiting list. Also, ask whether there's a bar or counter you can dine at—these are usually offered first-come, first-served. Some places set aside tables for walk-in business (and not for advance reservations), in which case you can just show up and make the most of the wait. As a last resort, many popular San Francisco restaurants are also open for lunch.

HOURS

Unless otherwise noted, the restaurants listed are open daily for lunch and dinner. Prime time for dinner is around 7:30 or 8 pm, and although there are places for night owls to fuel up, most restaurants stop serving around 10 pm. Restaurants, along with bars and clubs, may serve alcohol between the hours of 6 am and 2 am.

WHAT TO WEAR

In general, San Franciscans are neat but casual dressers; only at the top-notch dining rooms do you see a more formal style. But the way you dress may influence how you're treated—and where you're seated. Generally speaking, jeans will suffice at most table-service restaurants in the $ to $$$ range. A few pricier restaurants require jackets, and some insist on ties. In reviews, we mention

dress only when men are required to wear a jacket or a jacket and tie. Note that shorts, sweatpants, and sports jerseys are rarely appropriate. When in doubt, call the restaurant and ask.

CHILDREN

As in many other cities, small kids generally aren't seen in the fanciest restaurants. For families with young children, we recommend many family-friendly places with great food. Restaurants that are particularly good for families are marked as such.

PARKING

Most high-end restaurants offer valet parking—worth considering in crowded neighborhoods, such as North Beach, Russian Hill, Union Square, and the Mission. There's often a nominal charge and a time restriction on validated parking.

PRICES

If you're watching your budget, be sure to ask the price of daily specials. The charge for these dishes can sometimes be out of line with the menu. If you eat early or late, you may be able to take advantage of a prix-fixe deal not offered at peak hours. Many upscale restaurants offer lunch deals with special menus at bargain prices. Credit cards are widely accepted, but some restaurants (particularly smaller ones) accept only cash. Also, keep in mind that a restaurant listed as $$$ may actually have a good deal or two, such as an early prix-fixe dinner or a great bar scene and good, reasonably priced bar food to go with it.

Prices in the reviews are the average cost of a main course at dinner or, if dinner is not served, at lunch.

Essentials

What It Costs

$	$$	$$$	$$$$
AT DINNER			
under $17	$17–$26	$27–$36	over $36

TIPPING AND TAXES

In most restaurants, tip the waiter 18%–20%. (To figure out a 20% tip quickly, just move the decimal spot one place to the left of your pretax bill and double that.) Bills for parties of six or more sometimes include the tip (you can always add more). A few restaurants in the Bay Area are experimenting with a gratuity-included policy for all parties. There are only a handful of such places, and the movement is led by some of the best chefs. Tip at least $1 per drink at the bar; $2 if it's a labor-intensive cocktail. Also be aware that some restaurants, now required to fund the city's new universal-health-care ordinance, are passing these costs along to their customers indirectly instead of raising menu prices—usually in the form of a 3%–4% surcharge or a $1–$3.50-per-head charge. (San Francisco sales tax is currently at 8.5%.)

Immunizations

There are no immunization requirements for visitors traveling to the United States for tourism.

Internet

The city of San Francisco offers free Wi-Fi service in selected parks and areas in and around the city. All public libraries also provide Internet access, and most hotels have a computer stationed in the lobby with free (if shared) high-speed access for guests. Some hotels can charge a small fee to provide a high-speed connection in the room; others offer it free of charge. In addition, many cafés throughout San Francisco, Marin County, and the East Bay offer complimentary Wi-Fi, but a few continue to charge a fee. For a list of free hotspots, check the OpenWiFiSpots site (⊕ www.openwifispots.com).

Lodging

San Francisco accommodations are diverse, ranging from cozy bed-and-breakfasts and kitschy motels to chic boutique hotels, grande dames, and sleek high-rises. Though the tech boom has skyrocketed the prices of even some of the most dependable low-cost options, some Fodor's faves still offer fine accommodations without prices that rival the city's steep hills. In fact, the number of reasonably priced accommodations is impressive.

When contemplating a stay in San Francisco, consider timing. Many business-oriented hotels offer weekend deals (such properties are busiest from Monday through Thursday), with the opposite often true at lodgings geared more to leisure travelers. When there's a big convention in town, even the humblest accommodations can double in price or more.

For travelers looking for a more intimate experience with local hosts, vacation rental properties booked through Airbnb or VRBO may be the way to go. Prices are often cheaper, especially if shared among a group of guests who plan to do some of the cooking themselves.

Once you settle into your perfect room, remember this advice: when in doubt, ask the concierge. This holds true for almost any request, whether you have special needs or burning desires—if anyone can get you tickets to that sold-out show or a table at the hottest restaurant, it's the concierge.

RESERVATIONS

Reservations are always advised, especially during the peak seasons—from August through November, during the Oracle Convention week and Salesforce Dreamforce Convention in fall, and weekends in December. Celebrations like Chinese New Year (late January or early February), Mother's Day and Bay to Breakers (mid-May), and Gay Pride (June) also require reservations.

FACILITIES

When pricing accommodations, always ask what facilities are included and what entails an additional charge. One big unexpected extra might be parking fees, which are off the charts in San Francisco; another is the per-night "resort" or "amenity" fee that may be added to rates at more expensive hotels. A seemingly expensive hotel that provides free parking and a hearty breakfast, for instance, can end up costing you less than one that charges for parking and breakfast. All the hotels listed have private baths, central heating, and private phones unless otherwise noted. Many places don't have air-conditioning, but you probably won't need it. Even in September and October, when the city sees its warmest days, the temperature rarely climbs above 70°F.

Nearly all hotels have Wi-Fi available, and though many offer the service for free, some charge for quicker connections, multiple devices, or both. Larger hotels often have high-speed checkout capability. Pools are a rarity, but most large properties have gyms or health clubs, and sometimes full-scale spas; hotels without facilities usually have arrangements for guests at nearby gyms, sometimes for a fee. At the end of each review, we state whether any meals (and in San Francisco, this means breakfast) are included in the

room rate. Mirroring a trend elsewhere in the country, some hotels no longer provide room service, so if that's an amenity you require, be sure to inquire.

PARKING

Several properties on Lombard Street and in the Civic Center area have free parking (but not always in a covered garage), and occasionally hotel package deals include parking. Hotels in the Union Square and Nob Hill areas charge $30 to $70 per day for garage parking; many hotels charge extra fees for SUVs. Some bed-and-breakfasts have limited free parking available, but many don't, requiring you to park on the street. Depending on the neighborhood, this can be easy or quite difficult, so ask for realistic parking information when you call. Some hotels offer a choice of valet parking with unlimited in-out privileges or self-parking. The cost is generally less for the latter in part because no tip is involved. Given the expense of parking, and the ease of getting around San Francisco on public transportation, you may well want to leave the car at home or wait to rent one until you're ready to leave town.

PRICES

San Francisco hotel prices rank among the highest in the country. Weekend rates for double rooms in high season (typically summer for leisure travelers) average about $250 a night citywide except during large conventions, such as those hosted by Oracle and Salesforce, when even the humblest downtown lodgings command $500 or more. At other times, even in high season, decent lower-cost accommodations are relatively plentiful, especially in comparison to New York, Washington, and other big cities. Most hotels price rooms dynamically with rates for dates a few days forward or months down the line fluctuating from hour to hour depending on availability.

Where Should I Stay?

	NEIGHBORHOOD VIBE	PROS	CONS
Union Square	Union Square is a hub for visitors; you'll find a wide range of choices—and prices—for lodging.	Excellent shopping. Home to the theater district. Great transit access to other neighborhoods.	Often crowded and noisy. Many panhandlers. Close to the Tenderloin, a still-seedy part of town. Take cabs at night.
SoMa	SoMa is square one for the business set, with luxury high-rises, old classics, and a few bargains.	Near the museums and Yerba Buena Gardens. Steps from the convention center. Many fine eateries.	Construction in the area may mean traffic snarls. As with many changing neighborhoods, street life takes many forms. Be cautious walking around at night.
Financial District	A mini Midtown Manhattan, where properties cater to business travelers.	Excellent city and bay views, which are spectacular by night. Easy access to restaurants and nightclubs.	Some streets are iffy at night. Hotels are on the pricey side. Many businesses close at night and on weekends.
Nob Hill	Synonymous with San Francisco's high society, this area contains some of the city's best-known luxury hotels.	Many hotels boast gorgeous views and notable restaurants. Easy access to Union Square and Chinatown.	Hotels here will test your wallet, while the area's steep hills may try your endurance.
Civic Center	A wide mix of lodgings scattered throughout this area.	Many cultural offerings and government offices surround this central hub. Not too far from Union Square.	Away from touristy areas. A large homeless population lives in the area.
Fisherman's Wharf/ North Beach	Mostly chain hotels by the wharf; lodgings get funkier and smaller in North Beach.	Near attractions like Ghirardelli Square and Pier 39. Cable-car lines and bay-cruise piers are nearby.	City ordinances limit wharf hotels to four stories, so good views are out. The wharf is very touristy.
Pacific Heights/Cow Hollow/The Marina	A few tony accommodations in quietly residential Pacific Heights. In Cow Hollow, mostly motels along Lombard Street, a busy traffic corridor.	These three areas are away from the more tourist-oriented areas; visitors have a chance to explore where locals eat and shop. Lots of free parking.	Getting downtown from these neighborhoods can be challenging via public transportation. Some complain of the fraternity-like bar scene in the Marina.

you have your heart set on a particular property and its prices are high for your desired dates, it's wise to check back often either online or by phone.

You'll sometimes, but not always, find a hotel's best rates on its website. If looking for a same-day room, check out apps, such as HotelTonight, or access the last-minute pages of Expedia and other travel sites for the best deals. Whenever you're making a reservation, inquire about special rates and packages.

Prices are the lowest cost of a standard double room in high season.

What It Costs			
$	$$	$$$	$$$$
HOTELS			
under $200	$200– $300	$301– $400	over $400

Nightlife

After hours, the city's business folk and workers give way to costume-clad party-goers, hippies and hipsters, downtown divas, frat boys, and those who prefer something a little more clothing-optional. Downtown and the Financial District remain pretty serious even after dark, and Nob Hill is staid, though you can't beat views from penthouse lounges, the most famous being the Top of the Mark (in the InterContinental Mark Hopkins). Nearby North Beach is an even better starting point for an evening out.

Always lively, North Beach's options include family-friendly dining spots, historic bars from the city's bohemian past (among them Jack Kerouac's old haunts), and even comedy clubs where stars like Robin Williams and Jay Leno cut their teeth. In SoMa there are plenty of places

to catch a drink before a Giants game and brewpubs to celebrate in afterward. SoMa also hosts some of the hottest dance clubs, along with some saucy gay bars. While Union Square can be a bit trendy, even the swanky establishments have loosened things up in recent years.

Heading west to Hayes Valley, a more sophisticated crowd dabbles in the burgeoning "culinary cocktail movement." Up-and-coming singles gravitate north of here to Cow Hollow and the Marina. Polk Gulch was the city's gay mecca before the Castro and still hosts some wild bars, but things get downright outlandish in the Castro District. Indie hipsters of all persuasions populate the Mission and Haight Districts by night. Keep in mind, though, that some of the best times San Francisco has to offer are off the beaten path. And a good party can still be found in even the sleepiest of neighborhoods, such as Bernal Heights and Dogpatch.

Sports bars and hotel bars tend to be open on Sunday, but others may be closed. A few establishments—especially wine bars and bars attached to restaurants—also close on Monday.

🧳 Packing

Walking shoes. A pair of comfortable walking shoes is your must-pack item. This is a walking town, with notoriously steep and uneven streets, and if you fail to pack for it, your feet will pay. If you are planning an outdoorsy day or side trip from the city, you will need a pair of hiking boots or shoes with good treads.

A good raincoat. San Francisco is in California, but it doesn't adhere to your idea of California weather. It does stay mild year-round, but this is a peninsula surrounded by water on three sides, so you will want to plan for foggy mornin

Essentials

Sweaters. San Francisco weather can be a bit unpredictable. One minute you could be comfortable, and the next, shivering with the cold. Having a sweatshirt or sweater with you at all times will alleviate this.

Scarf. Lightweight and easy layers offset those sudden chills. In spring or from September to November, you can bring a lightweight one, but you will want warmer options for the rest of the year.

Backpack. A lightweight daypack is handy for toting those layers, along with sunscreen, a hat (the sun *does* often come out), and a change of shoes if you are planning a variety of activities, say, hiking, sightseeing, and then drinks.

Wine-bottle protectors. If your visit to San Francisco allows time to visit Napa and Sonoma's amazing vineyards, you may well want to bring a few bottles of wine home with you. Protect those precious liquid souvenirs (and everything in your suitcase) with bubble-wrap wine-bottle protectors.

Passport

All visitors to the United States require a passport that is valid for six months beyond your expected period of stay.

Performing Arts

The heart of the mainstream theater district lies on or near Geary Street, mostly west of Union Square, though touring Broadway shows land a little farther afield at big houses like the Orpheum and the Golden Gate. But theater can be found all over town. For a bit of culture shock, slip out to eclectic districts, maybe the Mission or the Haight, where smaller theater companies reside and short-run and one-night-only performances happen on a regular basis.

The city's opera house and symphony hall present the musical classics, and venues like the Fillmore and the Warfield host major rock and jazz talents, but the city's extensive festival circuit broadens the possibilities considerably. Stern Grove presents a popular, free summer music festival; Noise Pop is the premier alt-rock showcase; and Hardly Strictly Bluegrass is a beloved celebration of bluegrass, country, and roots music, attracting hundreds of thousands of attendees from all over every year.

Safety

San Francisco is generally a safe place for travelers who observe all normal urban precautions. Use common sense and, unless you know exactly where you're going, steer clear of certain neighborhoods late at night, especially if you're walking alone. Be alert in the following areas, or avoid them:

The Tenderloin. Thought to be named for a cut of steak, this neighborhood west of Union Square and above Civic Center can be a seedy part of town, with drug dealers, homeless people, hustlers, and X-rated joints. It's roughly bordered by Taylor, Polk, Geary, and Market Streets. Avoid coming here after dark, especially if you're walking.

Western Addition. Past incidents of gang activity have made this neighborhood somewhat sketchy. Don't stray too far off Fillmore Street.

Civic Center. After a show here, walk west to Gough Street; avoid Market Street between 6th and 10th.

Some areas in Golden Gate Park. These include the area near the Haight Street entrance, where street kids often smoke and deal drugs, and around the pedestrian tunnels on the far west end of the park.

Like many large cities, San Francisco has many homeless people. Although most are no threat, some are more aggressive and can persist in their pleas for cash until it feels like harassment. If you feel uncomfortable, don't reach for your wallet.

COVID-19

COVID-19 brought travel to a virtual standstill for most of 2020 and into 2021, but vaccinations have made travel possible and safe again. However, each destination (and each business within that destination) may have its own requirements and regulations. Travelers may expect to continue to wear a mask in public and obey any other rules. Given how abruptly travel was curtailed at the onset of the pandemic, it is wise to consider protecting yourself by purchasing a travel insurance policy that will reimburse you for cancellation costs related to COVID-19. Not all travel insurance policies protect against pandemic-related cancellations, so always read the fine print.

🛍 Shopping

Each neighborhood has its own distinctive finds, whether it's 1960s housewares, cheeky stationery, or vintage Levi's. If shopping in San Francisco has a downside, it's that real bargains can be few and far between. Sure, neighborhoods like the Lower Haight and the Mission have thrift shops and other inexpensive stores, but you won't find many discount outlets in the city, where rents are sky-high and space is at a premium.

Serious shoppers head straight to Union Square, San Francisco's main shopping area and the site of most of its department stores, including Macy's, Neiman Marcus, and Saks Fifth Avenue. Nearby are such platinum-card international

boutiques as Yves Saint Laurent, Cartier, Emporio Armani, Gucci, Hermès, and Louis Vuitton.

Seasonal sales, usually in late January and late July into August, are good opportunities for finding deep discounts on clothing. The *San Francisco Chronicle* and *San Francisco Examiner* advertise sales. For smaller shops, check the free *SF Weekly*, which can be found on street corners every Wednesday. Sample sales are usually held by individual manufacturers, so check your favorite company's website before visiting.

💲 Tipping

Tipping Guidelines for San Francisco	
Bartender	About 15%, starting at $1 a drink at casual places
Bellhop	$1–$5 per bag, depending on the level of the hotel
Hotel concierge	$5 or more, if he or she performs a service for you
Hotel doorman, room service, or valet	$3–$4
Hotel maid	$5 a day (either daily or at the end of your stay, in cash)
Taxi driver	15%–20%, but round up the fare to the next dollar amount
Tour guide	10% of the cost of the tour
Waiter	18%–20%, with 20% being the norm at high-end restaurants

Essentials

Visa

Except for citizens of Canada and Bermuda, most visitors to the United States must have a visa. If you are from one of the 38 designated members of the Visa Waiver Program, then you only require an ESTA (Electronic System for Travel Authorization) as long as you are staying for 90 days or less. However, some changes were made in the Visa Waiver Program in 2015, and nationals of Visa-Waiver nations who have traveled to Iran, Iraq, Libya, Somalia, Sudan, Syria, or Yemen no longer qualify for ESTA. Also, if you have been denied a visa to visit the United States, your application for the ESTA program most likely will be denied.

 When to Go

You can visit San Francisco comfortably any time of year, though summer is high season for leisure travelers, including families with children. Thanks to its proximity to the Pacific Ocean, the city has fairly consistent weather throughout the year. Possibly the best months are September and October, when the summerlike weather (warmer than August) at that time brings outdoor concerts and festivals. The climate here always feels Mediterranean and moderate—with a foggy, sometimes chilly bite. The temperature rarely drops below 40°F, and anything warmer than 80°F is considered a heat wave. Be prepared for rain in winter, especially December and January. Winds off the ocean can add to the chill factor. That old joke about summer in San Francisco feeling like winter is true at heart, but once you move inland, it gets warmer. (And some locals swear that the thermostat has inched up in recent years.)

Contacts

✈ Air

CONTACTS Oakland International Airport. (*OAK*). ✉ *1 Airport Dr., Oakland* ☎ *510/563-3300* ⊕ *www.oaklandairport.com.* **San Francisco International Airport.** (*SFO*). ✉ *McDonnell and Links Rds.* ☎ *800/435-9736, 650/821-8211* ⊕ *www.flysfo.com.* **San Jose International Airport.** (*SJC*). ✉ *1701 Airport Blvd., San Jose* ☎ *408/392-3600* ⊕ *www.flysanjose.com.*

⛴ Boat

CONTACTS Alameda/ Oakland Ferry. ☎ *877/643-3779* ⊕ *sanfrancisco-bayferry.com.* **Alcatraz Cruises.** ☎ *415/981-7625* ⊕ *www.alcatrazcruises.com.* **Blue & Gold Fleet.** ☎ *415/705-8200* ⊕ *www.blueandgoldfleet.com.* **Ferry Building Marketplace.** ✉ *1 Ferry Bldg., at foot of Market St. on Embarcadero* ⊕ *www.ferrybuildingmarketplace.com.* **Golden Gate Ferry.** ☎ *415/923-2000* ⊕ *www.goldengateferry.org.*

🚌 Bus

CONTACTS Greyhound. ✉ *Salesforce Transit Center, 425 Mission St., SoMa* ☎ *415/495-1569* ⊕ *www.greyhound.com.*

🚊 Public Transport

BART Bay Area Rapid Transit. (*BART*). ☎ *510/465-2278* ⊕ *www.bart.gov.*

MUNI San Francisco Municipal Transportation Agency. (*Muni*). ☎ *311, 415/701-3000* ⊕ *www.sfmta.com.*

🚕 Taxi

CONTACTS Flywheel Taxi. ☎ *415/970-1300* ⊕ *flywheeltaxi.com.* **Luxor Cab.** ☎ *415/282-4141* ⊕ *www.luxorcab.com.* **National Veterans Cab.** ☎ *415/648-4444.* **Yellow Cab.** ☎ *415/333-3333* ⊕ *yellowcabsf.com.*

🚆 Train

CONTACTS Amtrak. ☎ *800/872-7245* ⊕ *www.amtrak.com.* **Caltrain.** ☎ *800/660-4287* ⊕ *www.caltrain.com.* **San Francisco Caltrain station.** ✉ *700 4th St., near Townsend St., SoMa* ☎ *800/660-4287* ⊕ *www.caltrain.com/ stations.*

📍 Visitor Information

SAN FRANCISCO San Francisco Visitor Information Center. ✉ *Moscone Center, 749 Howard St. , between 3rd and 4th Sts., SoMa* ☎ *415/391-2000* ⊕ *www.sftravel.com.*

METRO AREA Marin Convention & Visitors Bureau. ✉ *1 Mitchell Blvd., Suite B, at Redwood Hwy., San Rafael* ☎ *415/925-2060, 866/925-2060* ⊕ *www.visitmarin.org.* **Visit Berkeley Information Center.** ✉ *2030 Addison St., Suite 102, Berkeley* ✛ *1 block north of Downtown Berkeley BART station* ☎ *800/847-4823, 510/549-7040* ⊕ *www.visitberkeley.com.*

STATE Visit California. ✉ *555 Capitol Mall, Suite 1100, Sacramento* ☎ *877/225-4367, 916/444-4429* ⊕ *www.visitcalifornia.com.* **California Welcome Center.** ✉ *Pier 39 , Beach St. and the Embarcadero , Bldg. B, 2nd level* ☎ *415/716-5897* ⊕ *www.visitcwc.com.*

A Waterfront Walk: The Ferry Building to Fisherman's Wharf

One of the great pleasures of San Francisco is a stroll along the bay, with its briny scent, the cry of the gulls, and boats bobbing on the waves. The flat, 2-mile walk along the Embarcadero from the Ferry Building offers a chance to take in some of the city's block-buster sights, along with spectacular bay vistas.

THE FERRY BUILDING: FOODIE MECCA

Standing sentry at the foot of Market Street, the **Ferry Building** offers organic, seasonal delights from such local treasures as Mariposa Baking Company and Humphry Slocombe Ice Cream. Take your picnic to a bench out back and take in the bay and the Bay Bridge.

EMBARCADERO: NEW LIFE FOR OLD PIERS

Heading north on the Embarcadero (the piers go up in number), watch for a mélange of historical info on black-and-white pillars, engraved in the sidewalk, and on plaques. These line **Pier 1,**, where the giant paddle wheeler *San Francisco Belle* docks. **Pier 7** juts out far into the bay; an evening stroll here is lovely (if chilly) under the street lamps.

Just two blocks beyond at Pier 15 is the city's excellent hands-on science museum, the **Exploratorium.**

NORTH BEACH DETOUR: LEVI'S AND COIT TOWER

Near Pier 17, a left on Union and a right on Battery leads to **Levi Strauss headquarters,** where visitors can shop for jeans at a ground-level retail store. Back across Battery, **Levi's Plaza** is one of the most manicured parks in town.

A Waterfront Walk: The Ferry Building to Fisherman's Wharf

WHERE TO START:
In front of the Ferry Building.

TIME/LENGTH:
30–60 minutes at a moderate pace, without stops. With a picnic and park breaks, this walk could be a three-hour affair. The total distance is 2 miles.

WHERE TO STOP:
At the cable-car turnaround or resting your feet at the Buena Vista.

BEST TIME TO GO:
Sunny days are best for strolling the waterfront. Start off at the Ferry Building in the morning, ideally on a Saturday, when farmers' market stalls fill the plaza. The street-theater scene from Pier 39 to Fisherman's Wharf is liveliest on weekends, too.

WORST TIME TO GO:
Rain puts a huge damper on this walk, which is all about being outside. Weekends are bustling, but they can mean large crowds at the big-ticket attractions—Alcatraz and Fisherman's Wharf.

GETTING AROUND:
If you're driving, park at the north end—it's much cheaper—and do the walk backward from north to south. Pedicabs will offer rides along the way, and the light-rail F-line is always available for the weary.

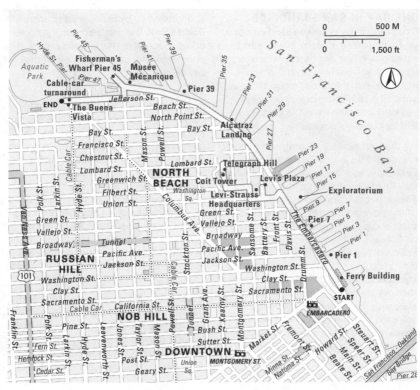

Consider heading west on Filbert or Greenwich and ascending one of the steep staircases clinging to **Telegraph Hill** for spectacular views and a peek into the lush stairway gardens along the way up to **Coit Tower.** Then return down the stairs to continue along the Embarcadero.

EMBARCADERO NORTH END: TOURIST SAN FRANCISCO

Continuing north up the Embarcadero, **Alcatraz Landing** (Pier 33) is a good spot to pick up souvenirs even if you're not taking the highly recommended tour. **Pier 39** is just around the corner, with its cornucopia of souvenir vendors; thankfully, sea lion–watching is still free.

A few blocks farther north is **Fisherman's Wharf** , at Pier 45. Bypass the wax museum and make a beeline for the fabulous vintage arcade **Musée Mécanique** (at the foot of Taylor Street). For crab- and bunny-shape sourdough loaves, stop by Boudin Bakery, just down Taylor on Jefferson.

LAST STOP: HISTORIC VESSELS AT THE HYDE STREET PIER

Follow the towering masts to the foot of Hyde Street and the collection of exquisitely restored ships there. Afterward, head up Hyde to the **cable-car turnaround,** where you can grab an Irish coffee at the **Buena Vista,** which opened in 1916.

Great Itineraries

ONE DAY IN SAN FRANCISCO

If you have a day or less in San Francisco, your sightseeing strategy is very simple: either pick one major museum or one attraction you really want to see and work the rest of your day around that, or avoid all major attractions altogether, and just walk and take the cable car to get a feel for the city's diverse neighborhoods.

For the former, we'd recommend the San Francisco Museum of Modern Art (or SFMOMA, as it's known) and the **Golden Gate Bridge.** For the latter, start in **Union Square,** but don't be too early: the focus of this neighborhood is shopping, and most doors don't open until 10 am (11 am on Sunday). At the cable-car turnaround at Powell and Market Streets, hop aboard either line and ride over Nob Hill and into **Chinatown.** Browse the produce stalls and markets, peruse herb shops, and explore alleyways. Have your camera ready as you pass from Chinatown into **North Beach,** the old Italian quarter: Broadway looking down Columbus and Grant is one of the most interesting cultural intersections of the city. Walk Columbus Avenue—stopping for espresso, of course—then head toward Coit Tower up Filbert Street, which becomes the Filbert Steps, one of the city's many stairways. Keep your eyes—and ears—open for the famous wild parrots of **Telegraph Hill.** Take in the views at the top and Coit Tower's WPA-era murals of California's history, then head back into North Beach for dinner or cocktails.

THREE DAYS IN SAN FRANCISCO
DAY 1

With more time, you have a chance to see the sights, eat all the amazing food, and really get to know the city. The **Mission** neighborhood is the first stop, for breakfast and coffee, perhaps a cappuccino at Four Barrel Coffee and croissants Tartine. With some pastries in hand

and fortified by caffeine, head to nearby **Dolores Park.** The park's southwest corner offers your first of many steep climbs. It also presents a panoramic view of the city skyline.

It's a short walk to Castro Street, the heart of the city's gay population and culture. Allow time to browse the shops and snap some photos of the ornate marquee and giant rainbow flag at the classic movie palace **Castro Theatre** at Castro and Market. From here, it's a steep climb, but short mileage-wise trek, to the city's "it" corridor, Divisadero and its chic cafés and vintage shops. At Hayes Street, hang a right and ahead is **Alamo Square Park,** with the backdrop of the beautifully painted Painted Ladies Victorian homes, made famous by the TV show *Full House.* This is *the* view of San Francisco.

It's all downhill from here … at least until the late afternoon. Stroll down the hill along Hayes Street and check out the sleek boutiques of Hayes Valley. Lunch just a few blocks away at Zuni Café, a fine-dining staple that defines California Cuisine.

Back on your feet, continue down Market Street, San Francisco's "Champs-Élysée," which sadly is also one of its more struggling corridors, as is evident in the street life. There are many important sights to see here, including the Twitter headquarters and its must-photograph "@Twitter" sign at Market and 10th Street. Walk one block off Market Street to admire magnificent **City Hall** and its grand rotunda. Catch a ride here to the beautiful Chinatown Gate entrance to **Chinatown** at Grant and Bush Street. Continue along Grant Street to Columbus Avenue and explore North America's oldest Chinatown. Hang a left at Columbus; after it crosses Broadway, Chinatown evolves into the city's Italian neighborhood, North Beach. The Italian influence continues to dwindle but can be found in cozy espresso cafés, like Mario's Bohemian Cigar Store Cafe overlooking Washington Square Park. After a much-needed espresso jolt, get ready for another steep climb up **Telegraph Hill,** home of a community of parrots and Coit Tower, with its mesmerizing views at the top.

Back down the hill, immediately head to Columbus Avenue and have a coffee or a drink. Wrap up the day with dinner at Mister Jiu's, the city's game-changing contemporary Chinese restaurant by chef Brandon Jew. Everything is stellar and has an intriguing spin, but be sure to start with the prawn toast and sea urchin *cheong fun.*

DAY 2

Start in Union Square and admire the grand outdoor plaza that could fit in any European capital. It's surrounded by the city's luxury department stores, and the 97-foot Victory Monument column commemorating Commodore George Dewey's defeat of the Spanish fleet at Manila in 1898 resides in the center. Give your legs a rest this morning and take the Powell-Hyde cable car that weaves up and down Nob Hill and Russian Hill from its loading spot by Union Square. After the requisite selfies as you dangle from the outdoor poles, get off the cable car at Lombard Street. This flower-adorned, curvy street is best viewed in the morning before there are more tourists than blossoms. When you're ready, walk a block or two away and request a car to head to Pier 33, where the **Alcatraz** boats depart. Generally, 2½ to 3 hours is a good amount of time for the boat ride and tour of "The Rock," a federal prison until the '60s. ■TIP➜ **Avoid disappointment and secure Alcatraz tickets in advance online.**

Back on the mainland, walk along the **Embarcadero,** a former elevated freeway turned palm tree–lined thoroughfare along the bay that is the de facto official venue for San Francisco joggers and stroller walking. For lunch, head to the **Ferry Building,** which is indeed the public transit ferry terminal, in addition to being a spectacular food hall filled with all sorts of vendors and artisans showcasing why the Bay Area is one of the greatest places to eat in the world. Save room for desserts such a chocolates by Recchiuti. As a bonus, if it's Tuesday, Thursday, or Saturday, the city's most extensive farmers' market gathers outside the building.

Spend the late afternoon in the sprawling **San Francisco Museum of Modern Art (SFMOMA),** a magnificent museum of modern art that is a 460,000-square-foot behemoth, with more than 1,000 works from its large collection on display. You won't make it through all the galleries, so start with highlights, like the third-floor sculpture garden with a living wall and signature works by the likes of Wayne Thiebaud and Andy Warhol, plus Alexander Calder's mobiles. If you want to linger a little longer here, dine at SFMOMA's in-house restaurant, In Situ.

Finally, take a short car ride up steep Nob Hill to two grande dame hotels of the city, the Fairmont and the Huntington. Their two bars are San Francisco classics for wildly different reasons. The Big 4 in the Huntington is all about piano music, dim lighting, an old-school vibe, and stiff classic cocktails. The Fairmont's Tonga Room is as kitsch as it gets with its lagoon and ultra-tiki atmosphere. The mai tais aren't so bad, either. Choose one for a nightcap. Or both.

Great Itineraries

DAY 3

After you've explored the city's urban and residential sides, this final day is all about nature. If it's a weekend, get a head start on the brunch crowds by racing out toward the Pacific. Then, enjoy San Francisco's "unofficial official meal" at Outerlands, a surfer-cool, reclaimed wood–paneled restaurant that is often cited as the city's best brunch. If it's a weekday, Outerlands still has a terrific breakfast and lunch menu that isn't too different from weekend brunch. Walk a few blocks to Ocean Beach and enjoy the sea salt–kissed air.

If there were more time today to do it, the walk all the way to the **Golden Gate Bridge** is one of the most stunning in the country, but it would take several hours. Take a car to Baker Beach, just to the western edge of the bridge. The views from here of the bridge are magnificent, even dreamy. Afterward, climb up the steep Battery to Bluffs Trail, hang a left on Lincoln Boulevard, follow the trail along the road for another gorgeous Golden Gate overlook, and follow the trail to the Golden Gate Bridge's parking lot. The views from the bridge are beautiful, but the experience can take a lot of time … and is frightening if you are even vaguely afraid of heights. Today, bypass the popular walk across the bridge and follow the steps down to Fort Point at its base. The walk from here to Crissy Field, an expansive grassy area that used to be a military airfield, is one of the more spectacular in the whole Bay Area. There are two bridges in view, the skyline, and lots of fresh air. Yes, welcome to California. End your walk at the Palace of Fine Arts, an elegant, colossal monument built in 1915 for the Panama–Pacific International Exposition world's fair.

For one final neighborhood, dinner, and drink, use the "Mrs. Doubtfire home" as the starting address, at 2640 Steiner Street. This is the heart of Pacific Heights, the city's deep-pockets district, with splendid mansions and views on each block. Walk down nearby Fillmore Street and admire the price tags and high-end boutiques. Then, for your final dinner, head to the wildly inventive State Bird Provisions, to enjoy a feast of globe-spanning contemporary creations served dim sum–style. ■**TIP**➔ **Make reservations at State Bird Provisions at least a month in advance.**

IF YOU HAVE MORE TIME

With more time, you can begin to explore the Bay Area. Cross the bay to **Oakland** or **Berkeley** and check out Oakland's restaurants and coffee spots or spend an afternoon scouting the university in Berkeley. Alternatively, you can head north from the city to majestic **Muir Woods National Monument**; if you've never seen the redwoods—the tallest living things on earth—this is a must. World-famous Napa Valley or lower-key Sonoma County each merit an overnight stay.

Chapter 3

UNION SQUARE AND CHINATOWN

Updated by
Trevor Felch

● Sights	⑪ Restaurants	🛏 Hotels	● Shopping	🍸 Nightlife
★★★☆☆	★★★☆☆	★★★★★	★★★★★	★☆☆☆☆

NEIGHBORHOOD SNAPSHOT

TOP EXPERIENCES

■ **Ross Alley:** Breathe in the scented air as you watch the nimble hands of workers at Chinatown's Golden Gate Fortune Cookie Factory on this narrow one-block, shop-lined alley first built in 1849 in the days of the gold rush.

■ **Chinatown walk and dine:** Stroll down Grant Avenue and Stockton Street, Chinatown's main thoroughfares, and enjoy steamed pork buns and red-bean sesame balls from the decades-old shops along the way.

■ **Shopping in and around Union Square:** Prime your credit cards and dive right in, from department stores like Bloomingdale's to the boutiques of Maiden Lane.

■ **Tin How Temple:** Climb the narrow stairway to this space in Chinatown with hundreds of red lanterns, then step onto the tiny balcony and take in the alley scene below.

■ **Union Square:** Grab a seat and soak up the grandeur—and the sun—in the heart of the city's signature plaza.

GETTING HERE

In these two neighborhoods, cars equal hassle. Traffic is slow and parking is pricey. Take advantage of the confluence of public transit at Powell and Market Streets: buses, Muni light-rail vehicles and BART (Powell Street Station for both), cable cars, and F-line streetcars run here.

It's an easy walk to Chinatown from Union Square, and both Powell lines of the cable-car system pass through.

PLANNING YOUR TIME

■ Set aside at least an hour to scope out the stores and sights around Union Square—or most of the day if you're a shopper—but don't bother arriving before 10 am, when the first shops open.

■ Allow at least two hours to tour compact Chinatown. Come on a weekday (it's less crowded) and before lunchtime (busiest with locals). You won't need more than 15 or 20 minutes at any of the sights, but exploring the shops and alleys and having a few bites along the way is, indeed, the whole point.

QUICK BITES

■ **Eastern Bakery.** Claiming to be Chinatown's oldest bakery, this packed space is a must-stop, with the goods to back up its rep. Try the moon cakes and egg custard tarts. ✉ *720 Grant St., Chinatown* ⊕ *www.easternbakery.com.*

■ **Good Mong Kok Bakery.** At this line-around-the-corner, no-English-spoken bakery, the delicious dim sum is strictly to-go, so picnic at Woh Hei Yuen Park on Powell Street. ✉ *1039 Stockton St., Chinatown* ⊕ *www.goodmongkok.com.*

The Union Square area bristles with big-city bravado, while just a stone's throw away is a place that feels like a city unto itself, Chinatown.

The two areas share a strong commercial streak, although manifested very differently. In Union Square—a plaza but also the neighborhood around it—the crowds zigzag among international brands, trailing glossy shopping bags. A few blocks north, people dash between small neighborhood stores, their arms draped with plastic totes filled with groceries or souvenirs.

Union Square

The city's finest department stores put on their best faces in Union Square, along with such exclusive emporiums as Tiffany & Co. and Bulgari, and such big-name retailers as Nike, Apple, H&M, and Disney. Visitors lay their heads at several dozen hotels within a three-block walk of the square, and the downtown theater district is nearby. Union Square is shopping-centric; nonshoppers will find fewer enticements here.

 Sights

Lotta's Fountain
FOUNTAIN | Saucy gold rush–era actress, singer, and dancer Lotta Crabtree so excited the city's miners that they were known to shower her with gold nuggets and silver dollars after her performances. The peculiar, rather clunky gold-colored fountain adorned with regal lions was her way of saying thanks to her fans. Given to the city in 1875, the fountain became a meeting place for survivors after the 1906 earthquake. Each April 18,

the anniversary of the quake, San Franciscans gather at this quirky monument. An image of redheaded Lotta herself, in a very pink, rather risqué dress, appears in one of the Anton Refregier murals in Rincon Center. ⊠ *Traffic triangle at intersection of 3rd, Market, Kearny, and Geary Sts., Union Sq.*

Maiden Lane
NEIGHBORHOOD | Known as Morton Street in the raffish Barbary Coast era, this former red-light district reported at least one murder a week during the late 19th century, though things cooled down after the 1906 fire: these days Maiden Lane is a chic, designer-boutique-lined pedestrian mall stretching two blocks, between Stockton and Kearny Streets. Wrought-iron gates close the street to traffic most days between 11 and 5, when the lane becomes an alfresco hot spot dotted with umbrella-shaded tables. It's also popular with photographers and Instagrammers for its quaint-chic aesthetic. At **140 Maiden Lane** is the only Frank Lloyd Wright building in San Francisco, fronted by a large brick archway. The curving ramp and skylights of the interior, which houses exclusive Italian menswear boutique Isaia, are said to have been his model for the Guggenheim Museum in New York. ⊠ *Between Stockton and Kearny Sts., Union Sq.*

Union Square
PLAZA | The marquee destination for big-name shopping in the city and within walking distance of many hotels, Union Square is home base for many visitors. The Westin St. Francis hotel and Macy's

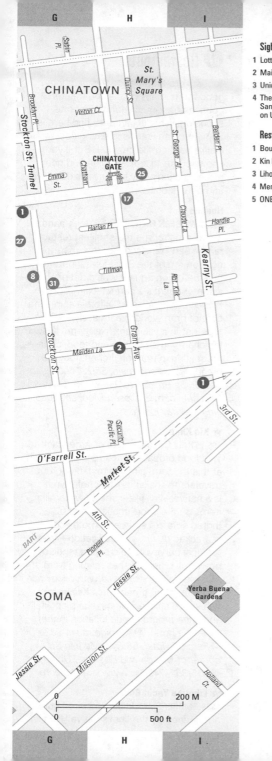

Sights ▼

1 Lotta's Fountain **I5**
2 Maiden Lane **H5**
3 Union Square............. **F5**
4 The Westin St. Francis San Francisco on Union Square......... **F5**

Restaurants ▼

1 Bouche................... **G3**
2 Kin Khao **E7**
3 Liholiho Yacht Club **A4**
4 Mensho Tokyo SF....... **A6**
5 ONE65..................... **F6**

Hotels ▼

1 Axiom Hotel San Francisco............ **F8**
2 Beresford Arms......... **B5**
3 The Cartwright Hotel Union Square **E4**
4 The Clift Royal Sonesta Hotel **C6**
5 Club Donatello **D5**
6 Cornell Hotel de France **E3**
7 Golden Gate Hotel **D3**
8 Grand Hyatt San Francisco Union Square............ **G4**
9 Hilton San Francisco Union Square............ **D7**
10 Hotel Abri................. **E7**
11 Hotel Adagio, Autograph Collection... **B6**
12 Hotel Beresford........... **D4**
13 Hotel Bijou................ **E8**
14 Hotel Emblem San Francisco............ **E4**
15 Hotel G San Francisco .. **E5**
16 Hotel Nikko San Francisco............ **E7**
17 Hotel Triton **H3**
18 Hotel Zeppelin........... **D5**
19 The Inn at Union Square......... **E4**
20 JW Marriott San Francisco Union Square............ **D4**
21 Kensington Park Hotel...................... **E4**
22 Kimpton Sir Francis Drake Hotel.............. **F4**
23 King George Hotel **E6**
24 The Marker San Francisco........... **C6**
25 Orchard Garden Hotel...................... **H2**
26 Orchard Hotel **F3**
27 Palihotel San Francisco............ **G3**
28 Parc 55 San Francisco, a Hilton Hotel............. **E8**
29 San Francisco Marriott Union Square............. **F4**
30 Staypineapple San Francisco........... **B6**
31 Taj Campton Place San Francisco........... **G4**
32 Villa Florence............. **F6**
33 Warwick San Francisco............ **C5**
34 The Westin St. Francis San Francisco on Union Square......... **F5**

line two of the square's sides, and Saks, Neiman Marcus, and Tiffany & Co. edge the other two. Four globular contemporary lamp sculptures by the artist R. M. Fischer preside over the landscaped, 2½-acre park anchored by the monument to Admiral George Dewey. The area also has a café with outdoor seating, an open-air stage, and the city's favorite holiday season ice-skating rink—along with a kaleidoscope of characters: office workers sunning and brown-bagging, street musicians, shoppers taking a rest, kids chasing pigeons, and a fair number of homeless people. The constant clang of cable cars traveling up and down Powell Street helps maintain a festive mood. ✉ *Bordered by Powell, Stockton, Post, and Geary Sts., Union Sq.*

The Westin St. Francis San Francisco on Union Square

HOTEL—SIGHT | Built in 1904 and barely established as the most sumptuous hotel in town before it was ravaged by fire following the 1906 earthquake, this grande-dame hotel designed by Walter Danforth Bliss and William Baker Faville reopened in 1907 with the addition of a luxurious Italian Renaissance–style residence designed to attract loyal clients from among the world's rich and powerful. The hotel's checkered past includes the ill-fated 1921 bash in the suite of the silent-film superstar Fatty Arbuckle, at which a woman became ill, leading to her death. Arbuckle endured three sensational trials for rape and murder before being acquitted, by which time his career was kaput. In 1975, Sara Jane Moore, standing among a crowd outside the hotel, attempted to shoot then-President Gerald Ford. Of course, the grand lobby contains no plaques commemorating these events. **■ TIP→ Some visitors make the St. Francis a stop whenever they're in town, soaking up the lobby ambience or enjoying a cocktail at the Clock Bar or lunch at the Oak Room Restaurant.** ✉ *335 Powell St., at Geary St., Union Sq.* ☎ *415/397–7000* 🌐 *westinstfrancis.com.*

🍴 Restaurants

Tourists are attracted to this neighborhood for its many hotels and theater houses but primarily for its first-rate shopping. What is harder to find here is authentic San Francisco eating (locals dislike battling the crowds). But if you know where to look, you can find good places tucked away in narrow side alleys and hotel lobbies.

Bouche

$$$$ | **MODERN FRENCH** | They don't hand out awards for the the smallest restaurant in San Francisco, but this charmer right on top of the Stockton Tunnel outside Union Square would definitely be a contender. It's a perfect example of a French bistro given a California spin—the best of both worlds seamlessly cooked together in a value prix-fixe menu. **Known for:** charming ambience and food; counter seating in front of kitchen; fougasse bread. [$] *Average main: $55* ✉ *603 Bush St., Union Sq.* ☎ *415/956–0396* 🌐 *www.bouchesf.com* 🕒 *Closed Mon. and Tues. No weekday lunch.*

★ Kin Khao

$$$ | **THAI** | Casual eaters of Americanized Thai food probably won't recognize much at this modern, dimly lit restaurant, but travelers to Thailand—the chef-owner is a native—will likely see a few familiar items on the short, focused menu. Ingredients are sourced—more accurately, tracked down with dedication—from regional purveyors to create a range of powerful, unique dishes ranging from a mushroom curry mousse with crispy rice cakes to rabbit green curry. **Known for:** fish sauce chicken wings; sharp cocktails and wine program; odd location in the back of a hotel. [$] *Average main: $32* ✉ *Parc 55 Hotel, 55 Cyril Magnin St., corner of Mason and Ellis Sts., Union Sq.* ☎ *415/362–7456* 🌐 *www.kinkhao.com.*

★ Liholiho Yacht Club

$$$$ | **MODERN AMERICAN** | Inspired but not defined by the chef's native Hawaii,

A monument to Admiral George Dewey stands tall in Union Square, a spacious plaza surrounded by hotels and big-name shops.

Ravi Kapur's lively restaurant is known for big-hearted, high-spirited cooking, including contemporary riffs on poke and Spam but also squid served with crispy tripe and manila clams in coconut curry. The dining room and front bar area are perpetually packed, and are dominated by an enormous photo of a beaming woman who happens to be none other than the chef's mother. **Known for:** beef tongue on poppy-seed steamed buns "bao"; giant mains that serve two to four people; beautifully composed cocktails. [$] *Average main: $42 ✉ 871 Sutter St., Union Sq. ☎ 415/440–5446 🌐 lycsf.com ⏲ Closed Sun. No lunch.*

Mensho Tokyo SF

$$ | JAPANESE | Look for the lines on busy Geary Street where Union Square blurs into the edges of the Tenderloin, and that's where eager ramen fans will find what is generally considered the city's leading bowl of ramen. This was the first U.S. outpost of a prominent Tokyo-based ramen shop, and the quality and consistency of its noodles and broths continue to be spectacular in this tiny space. **Known for:** "tori paitan" chicken ramen; excellent vegan ramen; open late. [$] *Average main: $20 ✉ 672 Geary St., Union Sq. ☎ 415/800–8345 🌐 mensho.tokyo ⏲ Closed Mon. and Tues. No lunch.*

ONE65

$$$ | FRENCH | It's hard to describe this ode to France's many culinary specialties without a map diagram, as this is a full six-story, four-concept venue just a block from Union Square. The shimmering gem of the house is upstairs, the exquisite fine-dining tasting menu space O' by Claude Le Tohic; the other floors are taken up by a modern cocktail bar (Elements), a more casual bistro and grill, and a ground-floor bakery and patisserie. **Known for:** bistro is one of the area's few noteworthy sit-down lunch spots; patisserie's macarons; stellar house-baked breads. [$] *Average main: $34 ✉ 165 O'Farrell St., Union Sq. ☎ 415/814–8888 🌐 www.one65sf.com.*

Union Square Backstory

The heart of San Francisco's downtown since 1850, Union Square takes its name from the violent pro-Union demonstrations staged here before the Civil War. At center stage, Robert Ingersoll Aitken's *Victory Monument* commemorates Commodore George Dewey's victory over the Spanish fleet at Manila in 1898. The 97-foot Corinthian column, topped by a bronze figure symbolizing naval conquest, was dedicated by Theodore Roosevelt in 1903; it withstood the 1906 earthquake. After the earthquake, the square was dubbed "Little St. Francis" because of the temporary shelter erected for residents of the St. Francis hotel. Actor John Barrymore (grandfather of actress Drew Barrymore and a notorious carouser) was among the guests pressed into volunteering to stack bricks in the square. His uncle, thespian John Drew, remarked, "It took an act of God to get John out of bed and the United States Army to get him to work."

Hotels

Scores of hotels—populated by first-time visitors, corporate travelers, and savvy globetrotters—surround Union Square, which is a central shopping district. (It's also where you'll find a large number of San Francisco's homeless people.) Easy access to public transportation, attractions, the Financial District, and Moscone Center convention activity has influenced major hotel chains to set up shop here, but you'll also find boutique hotels, several inns, and, a few blocks off Union Square, some value options.

★ Axiom Hotel San Francisco

$$ | **HOTEL** | Green, pet-friendly, and equipped with high-speed fiber-optic Wi-Fi, the tech-oriented Axiom—a splashy refresh of a 1908 hotel—nimbly provides a boutique experience business and leisure travelers applaud. **Pros:** fun, hip vibe; nicely designed rooms and bathrooms; on-site café open morning to night. **Cons:** the smallest rooms are notably tiny; somewhat congested area; some guests find panhandlers intimidating. [$] *Rooms from: $229* ✉ *28 Cyril Magnin St., at 5th and Market Sts., Union Sq.* ☎ *415/392–9466* 🌐 *www.axiomhotel.com* 🛏 *152 rooms* 🍴 *No meals.*

Beresford Arms

$ | **HOTEL** | **FAMILY** | Fancy moldings and 10-foot-tall windows grace the red-carpeted lobby of this brick Victorian listed on the National Register of Historic Places that has rooms of varying size and setup. **Pros:** good value for the neighborhood; suites with kitchenettes and Murphy beds are a plus for families; excellent bathrooms. **Cons:** no a/c; older architecture and design aren't for everyone; can be noisy at night. [$] *Rooms from: $169* ✉ *701 Post St., Union Sq.* ☎ *415/673–2600* 🌐 *www.beresford.com* 🛏 *95 rooms* 🍴 *Free Breakfast.*

The Cartwright Hotel Union Square

$$ | **HOTEL** | A relatively inexpensive Union Square–area option (look for online specials), this 1913 Edwardian is part of the Best Western chain's Premier Collection, and it retains a period feel, especially in the tile-floor lobby with a fireplace and adjoining wood-paneled bar. **Pros:** comfortable pillow-top beds; free Wi-Fi; staff that cares. **Cons:** few amenities; small bathrooms; uninspired decor. [$] *Rooms from: $255* ✉ *524 Sutter St., Union Sq.*

☎ 415/421–2865, 800/780–7234 🌐 *www.bestwestern.com* 🛏 *114 rooms* 🍴 *No meals.*

The Clift Royal Sonesta Hotel
$$ | **HOTEL** | Built for the 1915 Panama-Pacific International Exposition world's fair, this longtime favorite at the edge of Union Square and Nob Hill nicely bridges the gap between hip modern and timeless classic style with a swanky lobby and nicely polished rooms that have some decorative touches inspired by that major early-20th-century global event when the hotel was born. **Pros:** discreet and helpful staff; one of the city's top hotel bars, the Redwood Room; close to public transportation, shopping, and theaters. **Cons:** street noise (book on upper floors to avoid); nearby neighborhood can be rough; room designs seems a little simple compared to peers at price point. [$] *Rooms from: $239* ✉ *495 Geary St., Union Sq.* ☎ *415/775–4700* 🌐 *www.sonesta.com/sanfrancisco* 🛏 *372 rooms* 🍴 *No meals.*

Club Donatello
$$ | **HOTEL** | A Tuscan-themed owners' club and boutique hotel may hardly be a traditional San Francisco accommodations arrangement, but it's the setup for one of the prime Union Square places to stay for luxury without grande-dame prices or pomp and circumstance. **Pros:** giant-size rooms by SF standards; on-site Zingari Ristorante; feels more like a home than a hotel. **Cons:** located away from the main areas of Nob Hill and Union Square; some may find it strange to share space and facilities with residents; not particularly stylish. [$] *Rooms from: $206* ✉ *501 Post St., Union Sq.* ☎ *415/441–7100* 🌐 *www.clubdonatello.org* 🛏 *45 rooms* 🍴 *No meals.*

★ Cornell Hotel de France
$ | **HOTEL** | In their six-story, 1910 structure, hosts Claude and Micheline Lambert have created a bit of Paris a few blocks from Union Square, with rooms individually decorated with pastel colors, a stenciled ceiling, and prints of works by Picasso, Chagall, Klimt, and other European artists. **Pros:** excellent room quality and design for the price; updated bathrooms; special packages and discounts. **Cons:** several blocks from the center of things; surrounding area mildly dodgy after dark; small lobby. [$] *Rooms from: $144* ✉ *715 Bush St., Union Sq.* ☎ *415/421–3154* 🌐 *www.cornellhotel.com* 🛏 *50 rooms* 🍴 *Free breakfast.*

Monument to San Francisco

In front of the Grand Hyatt hotel at 345 Stockton Street gurgles an intricate bronze fountain depicting whimsical bas-relief scenes of San Francisco. It's one of many local public works by San Francisco sculptor Ruth Asawa. Look closely at this one and you can find an amorous couple behind one of the Victorian bay windows.

★ Golden Gate Hotel
$$ | **B&B/INN** | **FAMILY** | Travelers looking for charming accommodations around Union Square will enjoy this four-story Edwardian building with bay windows, an original birdcage elevator, hallways lined with historical photographs, and rooms decorated with antiques, wicker pieces, and Laura Ashley bedding and curtains. **Pros:** friendly staff; spotless rooms; good location if you're a walker. **Cons:** some rooms share a bath; resident cat and dog, so not good for guests with allergies; some rooms on the small side. [$] *Rooms from: $234* ✉ *775 Bush St., Union Sq.* ☎ *415/392–3702, 800/835–1118* 🌐 *www.goldengatehotel.com* 🛏 *23 rooms* 🍴 *Free Breakfast.*

Grand Hyatt San Francisco Union Square
$ | **HOTEL** | **FAMILY** | Location is the main draw at this hotel, where rooms done

in warm autumnal tones, with textured custom furniture, original artwork, and teak beds, are showing their age but still offer high-tech features: windows can be blacked out from your bed, and you can stream from your mobile or other device to a swiveling flat-screen. **Pros:** stellar views from upper floors; spacious rooms with floor-to-ceiling windows; weekend deals. **Cons:** small bathrooms; corporate feel; self-parking is in one of the city's busiest garages. [$] *Rooms from: $194* ✉ *345 Stockton St., Union Sq.* ☎ *415/398–1234* 🌐 *www.hyatt.com* 🛏 *668 rooms* 🍴 *No meals.*

Hilton San Francisco Union Square

$$ | HOTEL | This is the largest hotel in California—sometimes the lobby feels like downtown at rush hour—and many rooms in the silvery tower enjoy views that rank among San Francisco's finest. **Pros:** great views from Cityscape Lounge; outdoor pool—a rarity in this area; nice setups for working from the room. **Cons:** area is dodgy day and night; Wi-Fi is only free if you're a Hilton member; some rooms show wear. [$] *Rooms from: $201* ✉ *333 O'Farrell St., Union Sq.* ☎ *415/771–1400* 🌐 *www.hiltonsanfranciscohotel.com* 🛏 *1,919 rooms* 🍴 *No meals.*

Hotel Abri

$ | HOTEL | Near Union Square shops, theaters, and restaurants, this appealing hotel has small but tastefully appointed rooms with smart TVs, device docking stations, comfortable bedding, and fancy bath products. **Pros:** lots of online specials offer great values; excellent work-from-room setup; great location for walking and public transit. **Cons:** no on-site gym or restaurant; area can be dicey at times; on-street parking very difficult. [$] *Rooms from: $169* ✉ *127 Ellis St., Union Sq.* ☎ *866/823–4669, 415/392–8800* 🌐 *hotelabrisf.com* 🛏 *91 rooms* 🍴 *No meals.*

Hotel Adagio, Autograph Collection

$ | HOTEL | The Spanish-colonial facade of this 16-story theater-row hotel complements its chic interior, with good-size rooms that have beautiful sea-blue carpets and plenty of tech amenities for working or relaxing after sightseeing. **Pros:** Marriott-run property with boutique-hotel charm; central location for lots of sightseeing; good drinks and scene at lobby bar, the Mortimer. **Cons:** street noise; area can be dicey at night; adjacent to a popular outdoor bar. [$] *Rooms from: $159* ✉ *550 Geary St., Union Sq.* ☎ *415/775–5000* 🌐 *www.hoteladagiosf.com* 🛏 *171 rooms* 🍴 *No meals.*

Hotel Beresford

$ | HOTEL | For many budget travelers the Beresford's pluses—reasonable prices, central location, and sightseeing assistance—outweigh minuses that include the small rooms, outdated decor, and no air-conditioning. **Pros:** hotel's White Horse Tavern is a delightful pub; pleasant sitting areas within rooms; free Wi-Fi. **Cons:** no a/c; small rooms; old-fashioned look and vibe can seem scruffy. [$] *Rooms from: $165* ✉ *635 Sutter St., Union Sq.* ☎ *415/673–9900, 800/533–6533* 🌐 *www.beresford.com* 🛏 *114 rooms* 🍴 *Breakfast.*

Hotel Bijou

$ | HOTEL | This beautifully designed boutique hotel bordering the Tenderloin impresses with gorgeous art-deco styling in touches such as floor-to-ceiling gold-painted steel peacock screens and starburst tile in the lobby. **Pros:** nicely laid-out rooms; luxurious pillow-top beds; beautiful on-site bar/restaurant, Gibson. **Cons:** borders a dicey neighborhood; small rooms; per-night "destination fee" means free Wi-Fi isn't free. [$] *Rooms from: $189* ✉ *111 Mason St., at Eddy St., Union Sq.* ☎ *415/771–1200, 800/771–1022* 🌐 *www.hotelbijou.com* 🛏 *65 rooms* 🍴 *No meals.*

Hotel Emblem San Francisco

$ | **HOTEL** | Inspiration is everywhere at this intimate hotel, with a prominent literary theme that celebrates San Francisco's Beat poets, from its lobby wall of books and poetry-laced carpet to in-room libraries and typewriters. **Pros:** fun, creative vibe; excellent eating and drinking options; amenities available by request include diffusers, a humidifier, and bath bombs. **Cons:** some guests might feel the hotel is trying too hard to be hip; no on-site fitness option; some rooms on the small side. [$] *Rooms from: $159* ✉ *562 Sutter St., Union Sq.* ☎ *415/433–4434* 🌐 *www.viceroyhotelsandresorts.com/en/emblem* 🛏 *96 rooms* 🍴 *No meals.*

Hotel G San Francisco

$ | **HOTEL** | Both homey and innovative, the Hotel G has tiled lobby floors, large windows, and high ceilings (giving even the smallish standard rooms an airy feel) that pay homage to the building's century-plus history, while smart TVs, Bluetooth radios, Nespresso machines, and Wi-Fi keep it firmly in the present. **Pros:** fun design; one of the city's top bars on property; great central location. **Cons:** street noise; wooden or concrete flooring can be loud; some guests complain about small bathrooms and small windows. [$] *Rooms from: $159* ✉ *386 Geary St., Union Sq.* ☎ *415/986–2000* 🌐 *www.hotelgsanfrancisco.com* 🛏 *149 rooms* 🍴 *No meals.*

★ Hotel Nikko San Francisco

$$ | **HOTEL** | **FAMILY** | Known for impeccable service and satin-smooth style, this youngish grande dame takes its visual cues from traditional kimonos and Japanese calligraphy, with rooms that soothe upscale business and leisure travelers with muted colors offset by judicious splashes of stronger hues. **Pros:** polished multilingual staff; very dog-friendly, including a pet terrace; large indoor rooftop pool. **Cons:** slightly formal vibe doesn't work for some travelers; obligatory $34 fee for fitness center and pool use makes some travelers feel nickel-and-dimed; so-so surrounding neighborhood. [$] *Rooms from: $200* ✉ *222 Mason St., Union Sq.* ☎ *415/394–1111, 800/248–3308* 🌐 *www.hotelnikkosf.com* 🛏 *532 rooms* 🍴 *No meals.*

Hotel Triton

$ | **HOTEL** | With a strong location at the convergence of Chinatown, the Financial District, and Union Square, this boutique anchor attracts a design-conscious crowd and is highlighted by its intricately decorated lobby featuring marble floors, a wood-beam ceiling, and art from around the world. **Pros:** arty environs; Carrara marble bathrooms and showers; beautiful Café de la Presse next door offers discount for guests. **Cons:** rooms and baths are on the small side; hallways feel cramped; room decor feels a bit dated to some guests. [$] *Rooms from: $160* ✉ *342 Grant Ave., Union Sq.* ☎ *415/394–0500* 🌐 *www.hoteltriton.com* 🛏 *140 rooms* 🍴 *No meals.*

★ Hotel Zeppelin

$ | **HOTEL** | A frothy homage to 1950s Beat writers, 1960s hippies and rockers, and other local agents of change, the hip Hotel Zeppelin appeals to a youngish crowd with high-tech amenities and an inviting, sometimes boisterous, game room with a full-size Bingo board, quick-shot basketball wall, and other entertainments. **Pros:** plucky design; fun-loving vibe; responsive concierge reachable by text for advice or requests. **Cons:** smallish rooms; some guests find pace too frenetic; service can seem too informal. [$] *Rooms from: $166* ✉ *545 Post St., Union Sq.* ☎ *415/563–0303, 888/539–7510* 🌐 *www.hotelzeppelin.com* 🛏 *196 rooms* 🍴 *No meals.*

The Inn at Union Square

$$$ | **B&B/INN** | Built in 1922 and smartly updated, this six-story inn is strictly 21st century, with amenities that include high-quality bath products, soft robes, free high-speed Wi-Fi (included in the

daily $16 amenity fee), and in-room service tablets. **Pros:** nicely laid-out rooms; evening wine and cheese; dreamy Beautyrest Victoria Park Plush beds. **Cons:** some rooms can be noisy; interiors feel stuffy; cramped hallways. ⓢ *Rooms from: $309* ✉ *440 Post St., Union Sq.* ☎ *415/397-3510* ⊕ *www.unionsquare. com* ➘ *30 rooms* ⦿ *Free Breakfast.*

JW Marriott San Francisco Union Square

$$ | HOTEL | Bullet elevators whisk guests skyward from the grand, third-floor marble lobby with a Matisse-inspired bronze sculpture to contemporary guest rooms that are outfitted with business-oriented clientele in mind and situated around a dramatic, 19-story atrium. **Pros:** large rooms; luxurious bathrooms; spectacular public spaces. **Cons:** lacks character; service is polite but not particularly warm; expensive parking. ⓢ *Rooms from: $209* ✉ *515 Mason St., Union Sq.* ☎ *415/771-8600* ⊕ *www.jwmarriottunionsquare.com* ➘ *344 rooms* ⦿ *No meals.*

Kensington Park Hotel

$$ | HOTEL | Built in the 1920s in a Moorish and Gothic style, this former Elks Club retains its period feel and features, with rich marble and dark-wood accents, crystal chandeliers, vaulted ceilings, and antique furnishings in the lobby and vintage touches in the comfortable guest rooms. **Pros:** friendly personal service; no amenity fees; period feel. **Cons:** some rooms have street noise; rooms average 220 square feet; bathrooms are small. ⓢ *Rooms from: $224* ✉ *450 Post St., Union Sq.* ☎ *415/788-6400, 800/553-1900* ⊕ *www.kensingtonparkhotel.com* ➘ *93 rooms* ⦿ *No meals.*

Kimpton Sir Francis Drake Hotel

$$ | HOTEL | Beefeater-costumed doormen welcome guests into the ornate, high-ceilinged lobby of this 1928 landmark whose rooms are equipped with 21st-century tech amenities but evoke the hotel's heyday with regal headboards and plush white comforters. **Pros:** plenty of character; Lizzie's Starlight bar with panoramic views and popular drag brunch; fun perks like wine hour and yoga mats in each room. **Cons:** small rooms and baths; room decor may feel dated to some; hectic entrance. ⓢ *Rooms from: $299* ✉ *450 Powell St., Union Sq.* ☎ *415/392-7755, 800/795-7129* ⊕ *www. sirfrancisdrake.com* ➘ *416 rooms* ⦿ *No meals.*

King George Hotel

$$ | HOTEL | With its compact yet thoughtfully designed rooms and its Mason Social Club, a lively, Union Jack–theme bar/living room/game room, the King George has upped its game to match its service and hospitality, points of pride since the hotel's 1914 opening. **Pros:** colorful rooms are hardly sterile; rooms often at a very good rate; marble bathrooms. **Cons:** low ceilings in hallways; location on the edge of the Tenderloin unnerves some guests; baths and some closets are minuscule. ⓢ *Rooms from: $249* ✉ *334 Mason St., Union Sq.* ☎ *415/781-5050* ⊕ *www.kinggeorge. com* ➘ *153 rooms* ⦿ *No meals.*

The Marker San Francisco

$ | HOTEL | Behind a cheery 1910 Beaux-Arts facade and with smartly designed public spaces, the Marker delivers a comfortable experience amid the theater district hubbub, plus one of the area's better restaurant-and-bars with the Italian-themed Tratto. **Pros:** desk and lots of outlets for working from the room; colorful, nicely appointed rooms; Beekind bath products are luxurious and sustainable. **Cons:** close to sketchy Tenderloin neighborhood; some discount-rate rooms are very small; windowless fitness center is very basic. ⓢ *Rooms from: $199* ✉ *501 Geary St., Union Sq.* ☎ *415/292-0100, 800/237-2508* ⊕ *www.themarkersf.com* ➘ *208 rooms* ⦿ *No meals.*

★ Orchard Garden Hotel

$$ | HOTEL | Feel virtuous and eco-friendly while enjoying a junior terrace room with private outdoor space and views of downtown at this service-oriented

and environmentally friendly boutique hotel close to the Financial District and Chinatown that was the city's first LEED-certified hotel. **Pros:** free Wi-Fi and no resort fees; rooftop deck with sweeping city views; noise-reducing walls and windows. **Cons:** no on-site fitness center; lacks character of older establishments; minimalist aesthetic won't appeal to all travelers. [$] *Rooms from: $239* ✉ *466 Bush St., Union Sq.* ☎ *877/525–7749* 🌐 *www.theorchardgardenhotel.com* 🛏 *86 rooms* 🍴 *No meals.*

Orchard Hotel

$$ | **HOTEL** | Unlike many of the area's other boutique hotels, which occupy century-old buildings, the Orchard was built in 2000—though the marble lobby, with dramatic architectural embellishments like arched openings, vaulted ceilings, and stone floors, evokes another era. **Pros:** cutting-edge technology; sizable rooms; green pedigree. **Cons:** can be pricey (but look for deals on hotel website); uphill from Union Square; area outside hotel is safe but a tad grungy. [$] *Rooms from: $269* ✉ *665 Bush St., Union Sq.* ☎ *877/525–7750* 🌐 *www.theorchardhotel.com* 🛏 *104 rooms* 🍴 *No meals.*

Palihotel San Francisco

$ | **HOTEL** | Situated at the foot of the Stockton Tunnel, this beautiful property has seen a revolving door of owners in recent years and is now under the careful, hip eye of the Palisociety boutique hotel group, but its strong suits continue to be food and drink, a prime location, and a modern-meets-vintage aesthetic in rooms and public areas. **Pros:** superb cocktail bar; historic property; artsy decor. **Cons:** smallish rooms (but large suites have soaking tubs); city noise; can have sketchy characters in the block by tunnel entrance. [$] *Rooms from: $175* ✉ *417 Stockton St., Union Sq.* ☎ *415/400–0500* 🌐 *www.palisociety.com/hotels/san-francisco* 🛏 *82 rooms* 🍴 *Free Breakfast.*

Parc 55 San Francisco, a Hilton Hotel

$$ | **HOTEL** | One of the largest hotels in town, the Parc 55 brims with activity, but its size is by no means overwhelming, thanks to features like the acclaimed Kin Khao restaurant and spacious standard rooms with flat-screen TVs, Wi-Fi (free for Hilton members), handsome desks, and ergonomic chairs. **Pros:** close to public transportation, shops, and restaurants; some rooms have stellar views from bay windows; good-size rooms compared to other hotels in the neighborhood. **Cons:** the immediate area can be seedy at night; mediocre fitness center; rooms can feel a bit dated. [$] *Rooms from: $236* ✉ *55 Cyril Magnin St., near 5th and Market Sts., Union Sq.* ☎ *415/392–8000* 🌐 *www.parc55hotel.com* 🛏 *1,024 rooms* 🍴 *No meals.*

San Francisco Marriott Union Square

$ | **HOTEL** | **FAMILY** | Business travelers appreciate the 30-floor Marriott's attention to their needs with easily accessible plugs, movable desks, ergonomic chairs, and laptop connectors to flat-screen TVs—and its prime location near shopping, restaurants, nightspots, and public transportation. **Pros:** convenient location; in-room pull-out sofas and roll-away bed options a plus for families with children; generally solid service. **Cons:** noisy street; lacking in atmosphere; bland fitness center. [$] *Rooms from: $169* ✉ *480 Sutter St., Union Sq.* ☎ *415/398–8900, 866/912–0973* 🌐 *www.marriott.com* 🛏 *400 rooms* 🍴 *No meals.*

★ Staypineapple San Francisco

$$ | **HOTEL** | Three blocks west of Union Square and loaded with high- and low-tech amenities, this Pineapple Hospitality boutique property delivers value in a stylish package, starting with the lobby's paintings and sculptures and the giant black-and-white art above the adjacent bar. **Pros:** cheery and stylish decor; loaded with amenities and extras like loaner bikes and afternoon pineapple cupcakes; fun vibe. **Cons:** many rooms are

small; $30 per day amenity fee to cover Wi-Fi and those "extras"; some visitors find hotel's neighborhood intimidating after dark. $ Rooms from: $215 ✉ 580 Geary St., Union Sq. ☎ 415/441–2700, 866/866–7977 ⊕ www.staypineapple. com ⇨ 93 rooms ⦿ No meals.

Taj Campton Place San Francisco

$$ | HOTEL | Beauty and highly attentive service remain the hallmarks of this top-tier hotel, whose rooms are elegantly decorated in a contemporary Italian style, with sandy earth tones and handsome pearwood paneling and cabinetry. **Pros:** discreet, attentive service; Michelin-starred French-influenced Cal-Indian restaurant; rooftop fitness center. **Cons:** some questionable characters and busy sidewalk right outside hotel; smallest rooms 250 square feet; $30 obligatory resort fee a surprising annoyance to many guests. $ Rooms from: $265 ✉ 340 Stockton St., Union Sq. ☎ 415/781–5555 ⊕ www.tajcamptonplace.com ⇨ 110 rooms ⦿ No meals.

Villa Florence

$ | HOTEL | A stylish refuge amid the Powell Street whirlwind, this boutique hotel welcomes guests to rooms that feel comfortable, upbeat, and expansive—gray and white predominate, with magenta accents and gold-veined mirrors. **Pros:** easy access to shopping, theater, and public transportation; business meeting room named for Machiavelli (imagine the possibilities); stylish, somewhat upscale rooms. **Cons:** small lobby; noise from cable cars; free breakfast is just coffee and one pastry. $ Rooms from: $149 ✉ 225 Powell St., Union Sq. ☎ 415/397–7700, 844/838–8701 reservations ⊕ www.villaflorence.com ⇨ 189 rooms ⦿ Free Breakfast.

Warwick San Francisco

$$ | HOTEL | The handsome, if small, rooms at this 1913 theater district hotel evoke an aristocratic feel with geometric wallpaper, black-and-white framed historic photos curated by the San Francisco Public Library, and ornate wooden furnishings. **Pros:** artsy rooms with timeless feel; gorgeously appointed on-site cocktail bar and paella restaurant well above par for a hotel; good online rates. **Cons:** older property with thin walls; small rooms; some guests complain of street noise. $ Rooms from: $225 ✉ 490 Geary St., Union Sq. ☎ 415/928–7900 ⊕ www. warwickhotels.com/san-francisco ⇨ 74 rooms ⦿ No meals.

The Westin St. Francis San Francisco on Union Square

$$ | HOTEL | The survivor of two major earthquakes, some headline-grabbing scandals, and even an attempted presidential assassination, this richly appointed and superbly located grande dame dating to 1904 is comprised of the landmark building, renovated in 2018, and a modern 32-story tower whose glass elevators reveal Union Square views from the upper floors. **Pros:** prime Union Square location; correctly named Heavenly Bed; Chateau Montelena wine-tasting room and the excellent Clock Bar. **Cons:** rooms in original building can be small; public spaces lack the panache of days gone by; no dinner at on-site Oak Room Restaurant. $ Rooms from: $209 ✉ 335 Powell St., Union Sq. ☎ 415/397–7000, 888/627–8546 ⊕ www.marriott. com ⇨ 1,195 rooms ⦿ No meals.

🍸 Nightlife

Known mostly for high-end shopping and the surrounding theater district, the square has its own share of nightlife. You'll find places pouring interesting cocktails, a good mix of locals and tourists, and nods to nightspots and eras past.

BARS

Benjamin Cooper

BARS/PUBS | There's no sign outside, and don't come hungry because oysters are the only food served—but once you climb the stairs and find a seat at the bar, you're in for a treat. Discreetly located in the rear of the Hotel G, this craft cocktail destination is one of the city's most innovative, quirky cocktail bars. ⊠ *398 Geary St., Union Sq.* ☎ *415/986–2000* ⊕ *benjamincopersf.com.*

Le Colonial

BARS/PUBS | Down an easy-to-miss alley off Taylor Street is what appears to be a two-story plantation house in the center of the city. Without being kitschy, the top-floor bar successfully evokes French-colonial Vietnam, thanks to creaky wooden floors, Victorian sofas, a patio with potted palms, and tasty French-Vietnamese food and tropical cocktails. You'll find local jazz bands playing early in the week, but come the weekend this is a full-on DJ-driven dance party. ⊠ *20 Cosmo Pl., off Taylor St., between Post and Sutter Sts., Union Sq.* ☎ *415/931–3600* ⊕ *www.lecolonialsf.com.*

Lizzie's Starlight

BARS/PUBS | Forget low-key drinks—the only way to experience what is arguably SF's definitive upscale sky-high bar and lounge with a view is to dress up, bring the credit card, and enjoy the swanky, refined modern decor of this San Francisco legend (for decades it was the consummate local party host Harry Denton's Starlight Room) on the Sir Francis Drake Hotel's 21st floor. Sunday brunch brings a popular drag show, and the small dance floor is packed on Friday and Saturday nights (when cover charges start at 9 pm). Jackets are preferred for men. ⊠ *Kimpton Sir Francis Drake Hotel, 450 Powell St., between Post and Sutter Sts., Union Sq.* ☎ *415/395–8595* ⊕ *lizziesstarlightsf.com.*

Mikkeller Bar San Francisco

BARS/PUBS | Beer nerds rejoice every time they step through the door from the dicey sidewalk of Mason Street and are greeted by 40 shiny taps serving the celebration creations of the namesake Danish brewer plus some of the world's most in-demand small production beers. This is hardly a proper pub or beer dive—the exposed-brick interior and zigzag-shape bar are as chic as any fashionable drinking spot in town. Don't miss the house-made sausages. ⊠ *34 Mason St., Union Sq.* ☎ *415/984–0279* ⊕ *mikkeller.com.*

Redwood Room

BARS/PUBS | Opened in 1933 and updated many times, including in 2019, this lounge at the Clift Hotel is a San Francisco icon. The art-deco bar itself and the wood-paneled room are constructed from a single old redwood tree, giving a distinct only-in-California sense of place. Cocktails are a mix of high-quality classics and slightly creative newcomers. ⊠ *The Clift Royal Sonesta Hotel, 495 Geary St., at Taylor St., Union Sq.* ☎ *415/929–2372 for table reservations* ⊕ *redwoodroomsf.com.*

Performing Arts

THEATER

American Conservatory Theater

THEATER | One of the nation's leading regional theater companies presents about eight plays a year, from classics to contemporary works, often in repertory. The season runs from early fall to late spring. In December ACT stages a beloved version of Charles Dickens's *A Christmas Carol.* ⊠ *415 Geary St., Union Sq.* ☎ *415/749–2228* ⊕ *www.act-sf.org.*

Curran Theater

THEATER | Some of the biggest touring shows come to this local gem, which has hosted classical music, dance, and stage performances since its 1925 opening. Productions are of the long-running Broadway musical variety, such as *Stomp, Harry Potter and the Cursed Child,* and *The Book of Mormon.* ⊠ *445 Geary St., at Mason St., Union Sq.* ☎ *415/358–1220* ⊕ *sfcurran.com.*

EXIT Theatre

THEATER | *The* place for absurdist and experimental theater, this three-stage black-box venue also presents the annual **Fringe Festival** in September. ⊠ *156 Eddy St., between Mason and Taylor Sts., Tenderloin* ⊕ *www.theexit.org.*

📷 Shopping

Serious shoppers head straight to Union Square, San Francisco's main shopping area and the site of most of its department stores, including Macy's, Neiman Marcus, and Saks Fifth Avenue. Nearby are such platinum-card international boutiques as Yves Saint Laurent, Cartier, Emporio Armani, Gucci, Hermès, and Louis Vuitton.

The **Westfield San Francisco Centre,** anchored by Bloomingdale's and Nordstrom, is notable for its gorgeous atriums and top-notch dining options.

■ TIP→ **Most retailers in the square don't open until 10 am or later, so there isn't much advantage to getting an early start unless you're grabbing breakfast nearby. If you're on the prowl for art, be aware that many galleries are closed on Sunday and Monday.**

ART GALLERIES

Hang Art

ART GALLERIES | A spirit of fun imbues this inviting space that showcases local, emerging artists. Prices range from a few hundred dollars to several thousand, making it an ideal place for novice collectors to get their feet wet. ⊠ *567 Sutter St., 2nd fl., near Mason St., Union Sq.* ☎ *415/434–4264* ⊕ *hangart.com.*

CLOTHING

Cable Car Clothiers

CLOTHING | This classic British menswear store, open since 1939, is so fully stocked that a whole room is dedicated to hats, pants are cataloged like papers in file cabinets, and entire displays showcase badger-bristle shaving brushes.
■ TIP→ **The cable-car logo gear, from silk**

ties to pewter banks, makes for dashing souvenirs. ⊠ *110 Sutter St., Suite 108, Union Sq.* ☎ *415/397–4740* ⊕ *cablecarclothiers.com.*

Levi's

CLOTHING | A San Francisco icon, founded in 1853, Levi's offers every style, size, color, and cut of 501s for men and women at its massive flagship store. You can even get a custom fitting if you book ahead of time. ⊠ *815 Market St., at 4th St., Union Sq.* ☎ *415/501–0100* ⊕ *www.levi.com.*

ELECTRONICS

Apple Store Union Square

CAMERAS/ELECTRONICS | Apple's flagship San Francisco store is a two-level, open-air tech temple to Macs, iPads, iPhones, Apple Watches, and the people who use them. Inside, it's more about getting your iPhone fixed at the Genius Grove, but outside everyone is using those phones to take pictures of the modern structure. ⊠ *300 Post St., at Stockton St., Union Sq.* ☎ *415/486–4800* ⊕ *www.apple.com.*

FURNITURE, HOUSEWARES, AND GIFTS

Samuel Scheuer

HOUSEHOLD ITEMS/FURNITURE | A San Francisco staple since the 1930s, this decadent shop draws designers and other fans for its luxurious bed and bath items and linens. The pretty tablecloths, runners, napkins, fragrant candles, and luxurious bath accessories are popular gifts. ⊠ *340 Sutter St., between Grant Ave. and Stockton St., Union Sq.* ☎ *415/392–2813* ⊕ *www.scheuerlinens.com.*

Williams Sonoma

HOUSEHOLD ITEMS/FURNITURE | Behind striped awnings and a historical facade lies the massive mother ship of the Sonoma-founded kitchen-store empire. La Cornue custom stoves beckon you inward, and two grand staircases draw you upward to the world of dinnerware, linens, and chefs' tools. Antique tart tins, eggbeaters, and pastry cutters from the personal collection of founder Chuck Williams line the walls. ⊠ *340 Post St., between Powell and Stockton Sts., Union Sq.* ☎ *415/362–9450* ⊕ *www. williams-sonoma.com.*

JEWELRY

Shreve & Co.

JEWELRY/ACCESSORIES | Along with gems in dazzling settings, San Francisco's oldest retail store—it's been in business since 1852—carries luxury watches by Jaeger-LeCoultre and others. On Saturdays well-heeled couples scope out hefty diamond engagement rings. ⊠ *150 Post St., at Robert Kirk La., Union Sq.* ☎ *415/421–2600* ⊕ *shreve.com.*

TEXTILES

★ Britex Fabrics

TEXTILES/SEWING | Walls of Italian wool in deep, rich colors, yards of faille-striped silk, and neat stacks of fresh cotton prints await your creative touch. A San Francisco institution for more than 60 years, the two-story Britex also sells an endless variety of buttons as well as thread and trim. If sewing is your thing, this will be a visit to paradise. It's closed on weekends. ⊠ *117 Post St., between Grant Ave. and Kearny St., Union Sq.* ☎ *415/392–2910* ⊕ *www.britexfabrics. com.*

Chinatown

A few blocks uphill from Union Square is the abrupt beginning of dense and insular Chinatown—the oldest such community in the country. When the street signs have Chinese characters, produce stalls take up most of the sidewalk, and whole roast ducks hang in deli windows, you'll know you've arrived. (The neighborhood fills the 17 blocks and 41 alleys bordered roughly by Bush, Kearny, and Powell Streets and Broadway.) A number of neighborhood businesses closed or struggled during the COVID-19 pandemic, and, as in other parts of San Francisco and in cities around America, the community is seeing an unfortunate rise in anti–Asian American incidents. The city is trying hard to support this landmark neighborhood and keep its largely elderly population safe.

Chinatown is very much both a residential *and* a tourist neighborhood, with some overly tourist-focused souvenir shops. Yet it is still an incredibly unique, welcoming place that residents love to share. Each day sees a joyful mix of curious visitors eating pork buns and gazing at the architecture, while longtime locals walk by after to shop for the night's dinner. Join the flow along Grant Avenue and its side streets: good-luck banners of crimson and gold hang beside dragon-entwined lampposts and pagoda roofs, and honking cars chime in with shoppers bargaining in Cantonese or Mandarin.

◉ Sights

Chinatown Gate

BUILDING | At the official entrance to Chinatown, stone lions flank the base of the pagoda-topped gate; the lions, dragons, and fish up top symbolize wealth, prosperity, and other good things. The four Chinese characters immediately beneath the pagoda represent the philosophy of Sun Yat-sen, the leader who unified China in the early 20th century. Sun Yat-sen, who lived in exile in San Francisco for a few years, promoted the notion of friendship and peace among all nations based on equality, justice, and goodwill. The vertical characters under the left pagoda read "peace" and "trust," the ones under the right pagoda "respect" and "love." The whole shebang telegraphs the internationally understood message of "photo op." Immediately beyond the gate, dive into souvenir shopping on Grant Avenue, Chinatown's tourist strip. ⊠ *Grant Ave. at Bush St., Chinatown.*

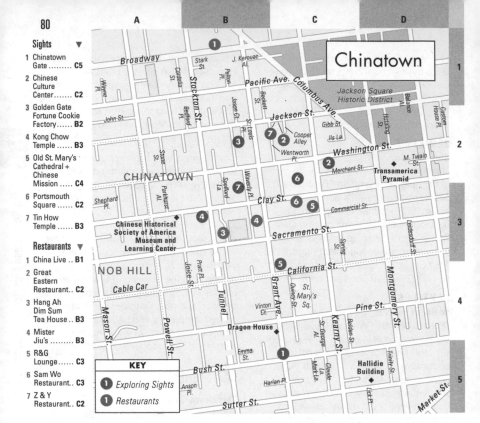

Chinese Culture Center

COLLEGE | Chiefly a place for the community to gather for calligraphy and tai chi workshops, the center operates a gallery with interesting temporary exhibits by Chinese and Chinese American artists. Excellent political, historical, and food-focused walking tours of Chinatown depart from the gallery; call the center or visit its website for details. ⊠ *Hilton San Francisco Financial District, 750 Kearny St., 3rd fl., Chinatown* ☎ *415/986–1822* ⊕ *www.cccsf.us* ⊠ *Center and gallery free (donations suggested), tour $40* ⊙ *Closed Sun.*

Golden Gate Fortune Cookie Factory

FACTORY | **FAMILY** | Follow your nose down Ross Alley to this tiny but fragrant cookie factory. Two workers sit at circular motorized griddles and wait for dollops of batter to drop onto a tiny metal plate, which rotates into an oven. A few moments later, out comes a cookie that's pliable and ready for folding. It's easy to peek in for a moment, and hard to leave without getting a few free samples and then buying a bagful of fortune cookies for snacks and wisdom later. ⊠ *56 Ross Alley, between Washington and Jackson Sts., west of Grant Ave., Chinatown* ☎ *415/781–3956* ⊕ *www.goldengatefortunecookies.com* ⊠ *Free.*

Kong Chow Temple

RELIGIOUS SITE | The god to whom its members pray represents honesty and trust, and this ornate temple sets a somber, spiritual tone right away with a sign warning visitors not to touch *anything*. Chinese stores and restaurants often display his image because he's thought to bring good luck in business. Chinese immigrants established the

Chinatown Gate is an inviting entrance to the second-largest Chinatown outside of Asia.

temple in 1851; its congregation moved to this building in 1977. Take the elevator up to the fourth floor, where incense fills the air. You can show respect by placing a dollar or two in the donation box and by leaving your phone stowed. Amid the statuary, flowers, and richly colored altars (red wards off evil spirits and signifies virility, green symbolizes longevity, and gold connotes majesty), a couple of plaques announce that "Mrs. Harry S. Truman came to this temple in June 1948 for a prediction on the outcome of the election ... this fortune came true." The area around the temple has major ongoing construction that should end by early 2022. ■TIP→ **The temple's balcony has a good view of Chinatown.** ⊠ *855 Stockton St., 4th fl., Chinatown* ☎ *415/788–1339* 🖾 *Free.*

Old St. Mary's Cathedral + Chinese Mission
RELIGIOUS SITE | Dedicated in 1854, this church served as the city's Catholic cathedral until 1891. The verse below the massive clock face beseeched naughty Barbary Coast boys: "Son, observe the time and fly from evil." Across the street from the church in **St. Mary's Square,** a statue of Sun Yat-sen towers over the site of the Chinese leader's favorite reading spot during his years in San Francisco. On Tuesdays at 12:30 pm, the church hosts free chamber music concerts (⊕ *noontimeconcerts.org*). ■TIP→ **A surprisingly peaceful spot, St. Mary's Square also has a couple of small, well-kept playgrounds, perfect for a break from the hustle and bustle of Chinatown.** ⊠ *660 California St., at Grant Ave., Chinatown* ⊕ *www. oldsaintmarys.org.*

Portsmouth Square
PLAZA | Chinatown's living room buzzes with activity: the square, with its pagoda-shape structures, is a favorite spot for morning tai chi, and by noon dozens of men huddle around Chinese chess tables, engaged in competition. Kids scamper about the square's two grungy playgrounds. Back in the late 19th century this land was near the waterfront. The square is named for the USS *Portsmouth*, the ship helmed by Captain John Montgomery, who in 1846 raised

the American flag here and claimed the then-Mexican land for the United States. A couple of years later, Sam Brannan kicked off the gold rush at the square when he waved his loot and proclaimed, "Gold from the American River!" Robert Louis Stevenson, the author of *Treasure Island,* often dropped by, chatting up the sailors who hung out here. Some of the information he gleaned about life at sea found its way into his fiction. A bronze galleon sculpture, a tribute to Stevenson, anchors the square's northwest corner. A plaque marks the site of California's first public school, built in 1847. ✉ *Bordered by Walter Lum Pl. and Kearny, Washington, and Clay Sts., Chinatown* 🌐 *sfrecpark.org.*

★ Tin How Temple

RELIGIOUS SITE | In 1852, Day Ju, one of the first three Chinese to arrive in San Francisco, dedicated this temple to the Queen of the Heavens and the Goddess of the Seven Seas, and the temple looks largely the same today as it did more than a century ago. Duck into the inconspicuous doorway, climb three flights of stairs, and be surrounded by the aroma of incense in this tiny, altar-filled room. In the entryway, elderly ladies can often be seen preparing "money" to be burned as offerings to various Buddhist gods or as funds for ancestors to use in the afterlife. Hundreds of red-and-gold lanterns cover the ceiling; the larger the lamp, the larger its donor's contribution to the temple. Gifts of oranges, dim sum, and money left by the faithful, who kneel while reciting prayers, rest on altars to different gods. Tin How presides over the middle back of the temple, flanked by one red and one green lesser god. Taking photographs is not allowed. ✉ *125 Waverly Pl., between Clay and Washington Sts., Chinatown* 🎟 *Free, donations accepted.*

🍴 Restaurants

Once you step beneath the gateway on Grant Avenue and meander the alleyways, into the restaurants and bakeries along Jackson, Clay, and Washington Streets, you might be surprised at what you'll find. A food market, along Stockton, is a riot of unusual fruits, vegetables, and other delicacies. Restaurants feature the cuisine of (mostly) China's Guangdong Province, that is, the Cantonese style, but you'll also find restaurants focused on Sichuan cuisine, the cuisine of Hunan, and dishes from Shanghai. The area has several bakeries and takeout dim sum specialists.

China Live

$$ | **CHINESE** | It's been compared to a Chinatown version of Eataly or the Ferry Building, but in reality George Chen's ultra-ambitious market, restaurant, bar, and fine-dining-experience project on Broadway is its own incredibly unique place. The main ground-floor Market Restaurant excels at a wide variety of specialties from dumplings to duck, served in a refined, industrial-style dining room surrounded by different cooking areas; upstairs, the intimate Eight Tables is one of San Francisco's most elaborate special-occasion tasting-menu experiences. **Known for:** sheng jian bao pork dumplings; opening "nine essential flavors of Chinese cuisine" small-bites dish at Eight Tables; outstanding tea selection. [$] *Average main: $24* ✉ *644 Broadway, Chinatown* ☎ *415/788–8188* 🌐 *chinalivesf.com.*

Great Eastern Restaurant

$$ | **CHINESE** | **FAMILY** | Dine here for fresh, simply prepared Cantonese-style cuisine, especially the seafood—it hails from tanks that occupy a corner of the street-level main dining room—as well as kid favorites, such as stir-fried noodles, cashew chicken, and fried rice. The dim sum starts at 10 am, but there aren't

Continued on page 87

CHINATOWN

Chinatown's streets flood the senses. Incense and cigarette smoke mingle with the scents of briny fish and sweet vanilla. Rooflines flare outward, pagoda-style. Loud Cantonese bargaining and honking car horns rise above the sharp clack of mah-jongg tiles and the eternally humming cables beneath the street.

Most Chinatown visitors march down Grant Avenue, buy a few trinkets, take a few photos of paper lanterns and dragon-draped lamp posts, and call it a day. Do yourself a favor and dig deeper. This is one of the largest Chinese communities outside Asia, and there is far more to it than buying a back-scratcher near Chinatown Gate. To get a real feel for the neighborhood, wander off the main drag. Step into a temple or an herb shop and wander down a flag-draped alley.

Whatever you do, don't leave without eating something. Noodle houses, bakeries, tea houses, and dim sum shops seem to occupy every other storefront. There's a feast for your eyes as well: in the market windows on Stockton and Grant, you'll see hanging whole roast ducks, fish, and shellfish swimming in tanks, and strips of shiny, pink-glazed Chinese-style barbecued pork.

CHINATOWN'S EARLY HISTORY

The Street of Gamblers (Ross Alley), 1898 (top). The first Chinese telephone operator in Chinatown (bottom).

Sam Brannan's 1848 cry of "Gold!" didn't take long to reach across the world to China. Struggling with famine, drought, and political upheaval at home, thousands of Chinese jumped at the chance to try their luck in California. Most came from the Pearl River Delta region, in the Guangdong province, and spoke Cantonese dialects. From the start, Chinese businesses circled around Portsmouth Square, which was conveniently central. Bachelor rooming houses sprang up, since the vast majority of new arrivals were men. By 1853, the area was called Chinatown.

COLD WELCOME

The Chinese faced discrimination from the get-go. Harrassment became outright hostility as first the gold rush, then the work on the Transcontinental Railroad petered out. Special taxes were imposed to shoulder aside competing "coolie labor." Laws forbidding the Chinese from moving outside Chinatown kept the residents packed in like sardines, with nowhere to go but up and down—thus the many basement establishments in the neighborhood. State and federal laws passed in the 1870s deterred Chinese women from immigrating, deeming them prostitutes. In the late 1870s, looting and arson attacks on Chinatown businesses soared.

The coup de grace, though, was the Chinese Exclusion Act, passed by the U.S. Congress in 1882, which slammed the doors to America for "Asiatics." This was

Chinatown's Grant Avenue.

Women and children flooded into the neighborhood after the Great Quake.

the country's first significant restriction on immigration. The law also prevented the existing Chinese residents, including American-born children, from becoming naturalized citizens. With a society of mostly men (forbidden, of course, from marrying white women), many San Franciscans hoped that a Chinatown neighborhood would not have a strong presence in the city.

OUT OF THE ASHES

When the devastating 1906 earthquake and fire hit, city fathers thought they'd seize the opportunity to kick the Chinese out of Chinatown and get their hands on that desirable piece of downtown real estate. Then Chinatown businessman Look Tin Eli had a brainstorm of Disneyesque proportions.

He proposed that Chinatown be rebuilt, but in a tourist-friendly, stylized, "Oriental" way. Anglo-American architects would design new buildings with pagoda roofs and dragon-covered columns. Chinatown would attract more tourists—the curious had been visiting on the sly for decades—and add more tax money to the city's coffers. Ka-ching: the sales pitch worked.

PAPER SONS

For the Chinese, the 1906 earthquake turned the virtual "no entry" sign into a flashing neon "welcome!" All the city's immigration records went up in smoke, and the Chinese quickly began to apply for passports as U.S. citizens, claiming their old ones were lost in the fire. Not only did thousands of Chinese become legal overnight, but so did their sons in China, or "sons," if they weren't really related. Whole families in Chinatown had passports in names that weren't their own; these "paper sons" were not only a windfall but also an uncomfortable neighborhood conspiracy. The city caught on eventually and set up an immigration center on Angel Island in 1910. Immigrants spent weeks or months being inspected and interrogated while their papers were checked. Roughly 250,000 people made it through. With this influx, including women and children, Chinatown finally became a more complete community.

A GREAT WALK THROUGH CHINATOWN

■ Start at the Chinatown Gate and walk ahead on Grant Avenue, entering the souvenir gauntlet. (You'll also pass Old St. Mary's Cathedral.)

■ Make a right on Clay Street for a great view of the Transamerica Pyramid ahead. The *Ross Alley 1889* mural to your right depicts a Chinatown alley (a stop on this walk) after the Chinese Exclusion Act. Next, turn left and walk to spacious Portsmouth Square.

■ Head up Washington Street to the Old Chinese Telephone Exchange building, now the East West Bank. Across Grant, look left for Waverly Place. Here Free Republic of China (Taiwanese) flags flap over some of the neighborhood's most striking buildings, including Tin How Temple.

■ At the Sacramento Street end of Waverly Place stands the First Chinese Baptist Church of 1908. Across the way, Mister Jiu's restaurant bridges the gap between the neighborhood's history and modern seasonal California dining. Make a U-turn at Sacramento Street and visit the Tin How Temple (No. 125) on your return toward Washington Street.

■ Head back to Washington Street and check out the many herb shops.

■ Follow the scent of vanilla down Ross Alley to the Golden Gate Fortune Cookie Factory, where many fortunes and crunchy, crescent-shape cookies have been produced since 1962.

■ Turn left on Jackson Street; ahead is the real Chinatown's main artery, Stockton Street, where most residents do their grocery shopping. Both sides of Stockton Street in this stretch north to Broadway alternate between herbal stores, bustling markets, butcher and fish shops, and on-the-go dim sum stops like Good Mong Kok Bakery and Wing Sing Dim Sum. Look toward the back of stores for Buddhist altars with offerings of oranges and grapefruit. From here you can loop one block east back to Grant.

any carts—you order off a paper sheet, and the dumplings come out of the kitchen piping hot. **Known for:** shrimp dumplings; ornate pagoda-roof exterior; then-President Barack Obama ate takeout from here. [$] *Average main: $22* ✉ *649 Jackson St., Chinatown* ☎ *415/986–2500* 🌐 *www.greateasternsf.com* 🕒 *Closed Tues.*

Hang Ah Dim Sum Tea House

$ | CHINESE | Enjoying the barbecue pork buns and curry chicken at this Chinatown icon dating to 1920 is a bite into both culinary history and San Francisco's past. Located on an alley, it's one of the smaller, more homey, and less frenetic sit-down dim sum choices in the city, with a small dining room simply decorated with pieces of Chinese art and a few Bruce Lee movie posters. **Known for:** being the country's first dim sum house; soup dumplings; red-bean bun desserts decorated like cute animals. [$] *Average main: $12* ✉ *1 Pagoda Pl., between Sacramento and Clay Sts., Chinatown* ☎ *415/982–5686* 🌐 *hangahdimsumsf.com.*

Mister Jiu's

$$$ | CHINESE | Brandon Jew's ambitious, graceful restaurant offers the chef's delicious contemporary, farm-to-table interpretation of Chinese cuisine that sometimes tweaks classic dishes with a California spin (hot-and-sour soup with nasturtiums) or enhances fresh produce with unique Chinese flavors (local asparagus with smoked tofu). The elegant dining room—accented with plants and a chrysanthemum chandelier—provides beautiful views of Chinatown, while the menu breathes new life into it. **Known for:** sea urchin cheong fun (rice noodle rolls); standout cocktails; large-format roast duck with pancakes. [$] *Average main: $29* ✉ *28 Waverly Pl., Chinatown* ☎ *415/857–9688* 🌐 *misterjius.com* 🕒 *Closed Sun. and Mon. No lunch.*

Look Up!

When wandering around Chinatown, don't forget to look up! Above the chintziest souvenir shop might loom an ornate balcony or a curly pagoda roof. The best examples are on the 900 block of Grant Avenue (at Washington Street) and at Waverly Place.

R&G Lounge

$$ | CHINESE | FAMILY | Salt-and-pepper Dungeness crab is a delicious draw at this bright, three-level Cantonese eatery that always has a packed crowd for its crustacean specialties—crab portions are easily splittable by three—and dim sum. A menu with photographs will help you sort through other Hong Kong culinary specialties, including Peking duck and shrimp-stuffed bean curd. **Known for:** three treasures with shrimp and black bean sauce; stir-fry "special beef" for land lovers; high-energy crowd of all ages. [$] *Average main: $20* ✉ *631 Kearny St., Chinatown* ☎ *415/982–7877* 🌐 *www.rnglounge.com.*

Sam Wo Restaurant

$ | CHINESE | Few restaurants in San Francisco—or the country—can match the history of this city treasure that has been around since 1908 (with a brief closure in 2012) and now resides in a narrow, two-story space across the street from Portsmouth Square. You'll want to try as much as possible from the menu, which is a unique mix of Cantonese dishes, a few items from other regions of China, a couple Southeast Asia–inspired noodles, and more familar Chinese American fare. **Known for:** iconic sign; jook (rice porridge); BBQ pork noodle roll, a great appetizer to share. [$] *Average main: $11* ✉ *713 Clay St., Chinatown* ☎ *415/989–8898* 🌐 *samworestaurant.com* 🕒 *Closed Tues.*

Signs along Chinatown's busy streets tempt strollers and shoppers.

Z & Y Restaurant

$$ | **SICHUAN** | San Francisco's signature Sichuan restaurant is a wonderful place to sample the often spicy, mouth-numbing (that's the "mala" heat, then the cooling effect of the peppers and chilies) cuisine of that northern China region. It's a long menu, so ask for advice from the servers or do some research before sitting down at one of the red tablecloth–covered tables in the bustling room. **Known for:** house spicy fresh fish; "couple's delight" beef-three-ways appetizer; energetic dining room full of regulars, so book ahead. [$] *Average main: $23* ✉ *655 Jackson St., Chinatown* ☎ *415/981–8988* 🌐 *zandyrestaurant.com* 🕒 *Closed Tues.*

🍸 Nightlife

Away from the bustle of Chinatown's streets, you'll find sake bars, beer pubs, and a few high-quality craft cocktail bars filled with both locals and tourists.

BARS

Cold Drinks Bar

BARS/PUBS | China Live's stylish upstairs, vintage Shanghai–inspired bar focuses on scotch and intricate cocktails with no shortage of creativity. The renowned AvroKO firm's sharp-as-a-tuxedo design, with dramatic lighting and a black-and-gold motif, is as glamorous a setting for drinking as any in this city. ✉ *644 Broadway, 2nd fl., Chinatown/North Beach* ☎ *415/788–8188* 🌐 *chinalivesf.com.*

Moongate Lounge

BARS/PUBS | The upstairs, slightly more casual and hip bar/lounge companion to Mister Jiu's is a destination in its own right. Lunar themes are everywhere, from the drinks' names and colors to the mystical lighting and design accents in a suave space that previously was a banquet room. Smaller bites have the same seasonal and technique-driven Chinese-Californian bent as the more upscale food downstairs. ✉ *28 Waverly Pl., Chinatown* ☎ *415/857–9688* 🌐 *misterjius.com.*

◉ Performing Arts

Noontime Concerts at Old St. Mary's Cathedral

MUSIC | The Gothic Revival church, completed in 1872 and rebuilt after the 1906 earthquake, hosts a notable—and free—chamber-music series on Tuesday at 12:30. ✉ 660 California St., Chinatown ☎ 415/777–3211 ⊕ www.noontimeconcerts.org.

◉ Shopping

The intersection of Grant Avenue and Bush Street marks the gateway to Chinatown. The area's 24 blocks of shops, restaurants, and markets are a nonstop tide of activity. Dominating this cityscape are the sights and smells of food: crates of bok choy, tanks of live crabs, cages of live partridges, and hanging whole chickens. Racks of Chinese silks, colorful pottery, baskets, and carved figurines are displayed chockablock on the sidewalks, alongside fragrant herb shops where your bill might be tallied on an abacus. And if you need to knock off souvenir shopping for the kids and coworkers in your life, the dense and multiple selections of toys, T-shirts, mugs, magnets, decorative boxes, and countless other trinkets make it a quick, easy, and inexpensive proposition.

ART GALLERY

Jessica Silverman Gallery

ART GALLERIES | One of the city's leading galleries devoted to emerging contemporary artists resides along Chinatown's main thoroughfare after spending the 2010s in the Tenderloin. Jessica Silverman has been instrumental in launching the careers of several artists and constantly puts together interesting exhibitions that, based on her prolific career, might one day end up at a major art festival or museum. ✉ 621 Grant Ave., Chinatown ☎ 415/255–9508 ⊕ jessicasilvermangallery.com.

Old Chinese Telephone Exchange ◉

In a time when we rely on our smartphones to remember numbers for us, it's impressive that the workers at the Old Chinese Telephone Exchange (743 Washington Street) were required to memorize each subscriber's name. Per the San Francisco Chamber of Commerce in 1914: "These girls respond to calls that are given (in English or one of five Chinese dialects) by the name of the subscriber instead of by his number—a mental feat that would be impossible for most high-schooled American misses."

CLOTHING

Kim + Ono

GIFTS/SOUVENIRS | Hand-painted robes, kimonos, formal dresses, and jackets are sold at this longtime family-owned spot now run by the second generation. Chic Asia-inspired gifts and smaller items make great souvenirs. The store is closed Monday through Thursday. ✉ 729 Grant Ave., Chinatown ☎ 415/989–8588 ⊕ kimandono.com.

FOOD AND DRINK

Hing Lung Co.

FOOD/CANDY | It's impossible to miss this Stockton Street Cantonese BBQ butchery icon—just look for the air-drying ducks and pigs hanging from above. Roast duck, crispy roast pork, and succulent honey BBQ pork are the marquee items on the concise menu, and must-try signature tastes of Chinatown history. This isn't a café or an eatery—order a half pound of a few meats and enjoy it as a snack on the go or to bring back to the hotel/condo for dinner. ✉ 1261 Stockton St., Chinatown ☎ 415/397–5521.

★ **Vital Tea Leaf**

FOOD/CANDY | Tea enthusiasts will feel at peace in this bright, spacious, hardwood-floor haven for sipping. You'll find more than 400 different varieties of tea here, and the staff is extremely knowledgeable on the health benefits of each and every one. ✉ *1044 Grant Ave., between Jackson St. and Pacific Ave., Chinatown* ☎ *415/981–2388* ⊕ *vitaltealeaf.net.*

FURNITURE, HOUSEWARES, AND GIFTS
The Wok Shop

HOUSEHOLD ITEMS/FURNITURE | The store carries woks, of course, but also anything else you could need for Chinese cooking and eating—bamboo steamers, ginger graters, wicked-looking cleavers—plus artistic chopstick holders and accessories for Japanese cooking, including sushi paraphernalia and tempura racks. ✉ *718 Grant Ave., at Sacramento St., Chinatown* ☎ *415/989–3797* ⊕ *www.wokshop. com.*

TOYS AND GADGETS
Chinatown Kite Shop

TOYS | The family-run shop has been selling bright, fun-shaped kites—dragons, butterflies, sharks—since the 1960s. There's a lot more than kites, too, with feng shui items, art tiles, and even iPhone cases that can go home as local souvenirs ✉ *717 Grant Ave., near Sacramento St., Chinatown* ☎ *415/989–5182* ⊕ *www.chinatownkite.com.*

Chapter 4

SOMA AND CIVIC CENTER

WITH THE TENDERLOIN AND HAYES VALLEY

Updated by
Trevor Felch

4

 Sights
★★★☆☆

Restaurants
★★★☆☆

 Hotels
★★★★☆

 Shopping
★★★☆☆

Nightlife
★★★★☆

NEIGHBORHOOD SNAPSHOT

TOP EXPERIENCES

■ **San Francisco Museum of Modern Art (SFMOMA):** Explore the vast trove of modern masterpieces at this sprawling museum, one of the largest in the country dedicated to modern art.

■ **Asian Art Museum:** Stand face-to-face with a massive gold Buddha at one of the world's most expansive collections of Asian art.

■ **Club-hopping in SoMa:** Shake it with the cool, friendly crowd that fills SoMa's dance clubs until the wee hours, and all weekend long at the EndUp.

■ **Yerba Buena Gardens:** Gather picnic provisions and choose a spot on the grass in downtown's oasis.

■ **SFJAZZ Center:** Experience the amazing acoustics at Hayes Valley's intimate temple to jazz.

■ **SF Opera, Ballet, and Symphony:** Enjoy San Francisco's world-class performing arts companies in the shadow of spectacular City Hall.

GETTING HERE

For most SoMa visitors who stick close to the area around Yerba Buena Gardens and the Moscone Center, getting here is a matter of walking roughly 10 minutes from Union Square, less from Market Street transit.

It's best to reach Civic Center by Muni light-rail, bus, or F-line. Hoofing it from Union Square takes you through the often seedy Tenderloin neighborhood and is a bit of a trek.

After dark, a cab or rideshare may be prudent for both of these neighborhoods.

PLANNING YOUR TIME

■ You could spend all day museum-hopping in SoMa. Allow at least two hours for gigantic SFMOMA. An hour each should do it for the Museum of the African Diaspora, the Contemporary Jewish Museum, and the Yerba Buena Center for the Arts, a little less than that for the smaller museums.

■ SoMa after dark is another adventure entirely. More interested in merlot or megaclubs than Matisse? Start here around 8 pm for dinner, then move on to a bar or dance spot. *See Restaurants and Nightlife for our top recommendations.*

■ Plan on spending at least two hours at the Asian Art Museum and no more than a half hour at City Hall. Except for these two mainstays, you'll have little reason to visit the Civic Center area unless you have tickets to the opera, symphony, or other cultural event. Hayes Valley and its restaurants and boutiques merit a leisurely one-hour look-see.

To a newcomer, the SoMa (short for "south of Market") and Civic Center Districts may look like cheek-by-jowl neighbors—they're divided by Market Street. To locals, though, these areas are separate entities, especially since Market Street itself is considered such a strong demarcation line. Both communities have a core of cultural sights, as well as their share of sketchy blocks. North of Civic Center lies the western section of the Tenderloin neighborhood, while to the east is hip Hayes Valley.

SoMa

SoMa is less a neighborhood than a sprawling area of wide, traffic-heavy boulevards lined with office skyscrapers and ultrachic condo high-rises. The COVID-19 pandemic hit this area particularly hard, as many of the neighborhood's office workers and residents departed with the increase in working from home for tech companies. Still, it's a noteworthy area for locals and tourists who are drawn to the cultural offerings and concentration of eateries and bars, including a number of destination restaurants. In terms of sightseeing, gigantic and impressive SFMOMA tops the list, followed by the specialty museums of the Yerba Buena arts district.

SoMa was once known as "South of the Slot" (read: the Wrong Side of the Tracks) in reference to the cable-car slot that ran up Market Street. Ever since gold-rush miners set up their tents here in 1848, SoMa has played a major role in housing immigrants to the city.

The 2010s influx of techies (and their money) changed the neighborhood once again: the skid row of 6th Street, between Market and Mission Streets, now coexists with trendy bars and cafés that cater to Twitter's headquarters. Once a scary section of SoMa, the neighborhood is trying hard to rebrand itself as the hip Mid-Market area.

Map labels: Jackson St., Jackson Square Historic District, Washington St., Maritime Plaza, Portsmouth Square, M. Twain Pl., Clay St., Embarcadero Center, Commercial St., Sacramento St., DOWNTOWN, California St., St. Mary's Sq., Pine St., Montgomery St., Sansome St., Kearny St., Grant Ave., Sutter St., Stockton St., Powell St., Union Square, Tunnel, MONTGOMERY ST., California Historical Society, New Montgomery St., Minna St., Natoma St., Ecker St., 1st St., Fremont St., 2nd St., Hawthorne St., Market St., Yerba Buena, Mission St., 4th St., Metreon, Moscone Convention Center, Folsom St., 3rd St., Howard St., Natoma St., Tehama St., Clementina St., Folsom St., 5th St., SOMA, 4th St., Perry St., 80, 80, Bryant St., Harrison St., Hall of Justice and Co. Jail, 6th St., Harriet St., Boardman Pl., Gilbert St., Brannan St., Bluxome St., Townsend St., 8th St., S.F. Tennis Club, Sutter St.

SoMa, Civic Center, Tenderloin, and Hayes Valley

Sights ▼
1 Asian Art Museum...... D6
2 @Twitter sign C7
3 City Hall C6
4 Contemporary Jewish Museum (CJM) H4
5 GLIDE Church E4
6 Louise M. Davies Symphony Hall.......... B7
7 Museum of the African Diaspora (MoAD)....... H4
8 San Francisco LGBT Center............. A9
9 San Francisco Museum of Modern Art H4
10 San Francisco Public Library D6
11 War Memorial Opera House B7
12 Yerba Buena Gardens.. H4

Restaurants ▼
1 Benu...................... I4
2 Birdsong F6
3 Brenda's French Soul Food C5
4 Californios E9
5 The Cavalier............. G5
6 54 Mint F5
7 The Fly Trap.............. I5
8 Hayes Street Grill....... B7
9 In Situ H4
10 Lers Ros.................. B7
11 Marlowe I7
12 Mourad I4
13 Nightbird................. B7
14 Nojo Ramen Tavern B7
15 Petit Crenn.............. A7
16 Pläj B7
17 Rich Table B8
18 Robin B6
19 ROOH...................... I5
20 Saison.................... B8
21 Souvla.................... A7
22 Suppenküche A7
23 Town Hall I2
24 25 Lusk I6
25 Zero Zero H6
26 Zuni Café................. B8

Quick Bites ▼
1 Blue Bottle Coffee....... F5
2 Johnny Doughnuts B6

Hotels ▼
1 Four Seasons Hotel San Francisco........... G4
2 Hotel Zelos San Francisco........... G4
3 Hotel Zetta San Francisco........... G5
4 Inn at the Opera........ B7
5 InterContinental San Francisco........... G5
6 The Mosser Hotel....... G4
7 Palace Hotel, San Francisco........... H3
8 Park Central Hotel San Francisco........... H4
9 The Parsonage.......... A8
10 Phoenix Hotel C5
11 The St. Regis San Francisco........... H4
12 San Francisco Marriott Marquis G4
13 San Francisco Proper Hotel.............. E6
14 W San Francisco H4

Sights

@Twitter sign

BUILDING | Those who want to take a picture of the @Twitter sign at Twitter's headquarters or, yes, tweet from Twitter can see the sign prominently displayed outside the gorgeous art-deco building that houses the company's main offices at Market and 10th Streets. You can tweet inside while shopping in the building's ground-floor market or picking up lunch from the vendors around the market's small café/bar area. To truly appreciate this micro-neighborhood, enjoy a local beer across Market Street at The Beer Hall or catch some music with craft cocktails at Mr. Tipple's—both are prime happy-hour spots for the Mid-Market crowd. ⊠ *1355 Market St., at 10th St., SoMa* ☎ *415/767-5130* ⊕ *visitthemarket.com.*

Contemporary Jewish Museum (CJM)

MUSEUM | Noted architect Daniel Libeskind designed the postmodern CJM, whose impossible-to-ignore diagonal blue cube juts out of a painstakingly restored power substation. A physical manifestation of the Hebrew toast *l'chaim* (to life), the cube may have obscure philosophical origins, but Libeskind created a unique, light-filled space that merits a stroll through the lobby even if the current exhibits (the museum is non-collecting and does not have permanent holdings, so they change regularly) don't entice you into the galleries. Exhibits, usually two or three at a time, vary, from a look at the history of Levi Strauss to an immersive series about the 19th-century Jewish immigrant and photographer Shimmel Zohar. ■**TIP→ San Francisco's best Jewish deli, Wise Sons, operates a counter in the museum. Try the company's popular smoked salmon bagel sandwich or a slice of chocolate babka.** ⊠ *736 Mission St., between 3rd and 4th Sts., SoMa* ☎ *415/655-7800* ⊕ *www.thecjm.org* 🎫 *$16* ⊗ *Closed Mon.–Wed.*

Museum of the African Diaspora (MoAD)

MUSEUM | Dedicated to the influence that people of African descent have had in places all over the world, MoAD focuses on temporary exhibits in its four galleries over three floors. With floor-to-ceiling windows onto Mission Street, the museum fits perfectly into the cultural scene of Yerba Buena and is well worth a 30-minute foray. Most striking is its front-window centerpiece: a three-story mosaic, made from thousands of photographs, that forms the image of a young girl's face. ■**TIP→ Walk up the stairs inside the museum to view the mosaic photographs up close—Malcolm X is there, Muhammad Ali, too, along with everyday folks—but the best view is from across the street.** ⊠ *685 Mission St., SoMa* ☎ *415/358–7200* ⊕ *www.moadsf.org* 🎫 *$10* ⊗ *Closed Mon. and Tues.*

★ San Francisco Museum of Modern Art (SFMOMA)

MUSEUM | Opened in 1935, the San Francisco Museum of Modern Art was the first museum on the West Coast dedicated to modern and contemporary art, and after a three-year expansion designed by Snøhetta, it emerged in 2016 as one of the largest modern art museums in the country and the revitalized anchor of the Yerba Buena arts district. With gallery space over seven floors, the museum displays only a portion of its more than 33,000-work collection and has numerous temporary exhibits. You could spend a day here, but allow at least two hours; three is better. The museum's holdings include art from the Doris and Donald Fisher Collection, one of the world's greatest private collections of modern and contemporary art. Highlights here include deep collections of works by German abstract expressionist Gerhard Richter and American painter Ellsworth Kelly and an Agnes Martin gallery. The third floor is dedicated to photography. Also look for seminal works by Diego Rivera, Alexander Calder, Matisse, and Picasso. Don't miss the third-floor sculpture terrace. The first floor is free to the public and contains four large works as well as the museum's shop and expensive restaurant. Ticketing, information, and one gallery are on the second floor; save time and reserve timed tickets online. ✉ *151 3rd St., SoMa* ☎ *415/357–4000* 🌐 *www.sfmoma.org* 🎟 *$25.*

Yerba Buena Gardens

CITY PARK | FAMILY | Not much south of Market Street encourages lingering outdoors, with this notable exception: these two blocks encompass the Yerba Buena Center for the Arts, the Metreon, and Moscone Convention Center, but the gardens themselves are the everyday draw. Office workers and convention-goers escape to the green swath of the East Garden, the focal point of which is the memorial to Martin Luther King Jr. Powerful streams of water surge over large, jagged stone columns, mirroring the enduring force of King's words, which are carved on the stone walls and on glass blocks behind the waterfall. Moscone North is behind the memorial, and an overhead walkway leads to Moscone South and its rooftop attractions. ■ **TIP→ The gardens are liveliest during the week and especially during the Yerba Buena Gardens Festival, from May through October (www.ybgfestival.org), with free performances.**

Atop the Moscone Center perch a few lures for kids. The historic Looff carousel (*$5 for two rides; $3 with museum admission*) twirls daily 10–5. The carousel is attached to the Children's Creativity Museum (☎ *415/820–3320,* 🌐 *creativity.org*), a high-tech, interactive arts-and-technology center (*$13*) geared to children ages 3–12. Just outside, kids adore the slides, including a 25-foot tube slide, at the play circle. Also part of the rooftop complex are gardens, an ice-skating rink, and a bowling alley. ✉ *Bordered by 3rd, 4th, Mission, and Folsom Sts., SoMa* 🌐 *yerbabuenagardens.com* 🎟 *Free.*

🍴 Restaurants

Hip SoMa covers a large area that swings from chic residential lofts and 19th-century warehouses turned trendy eateries to slightly dingy sidewalk scenes, particularly near the police station and in the higher numbers (7th through 10th nearer to Market). It has the rowdy ballpark and the genteel South Park within its fold. The restaurants near here fuel the mostly young and single local crowd who work in tech (Pinterest, Yelp, Twitter, and Adobe are nearby, and so is the train to Silicon Valley). Also, interesting chef-owned restaurants are finding their footing here, such as Benu and Saison.

★ Benu

$$$$ | MODERN AMERICAN | Chef Corey Lee's three-Michelin-star fine dining mecca is a must-stop for those who hop from city to city collecting memorable meals. At this tasting menu–only restaurant, each course is impossibly meticulous, a marvel of textures and flavors. **Known for:** high-end dining; phenomenal wine pairings and list of bottles; stellar service. [$] *Average main: $325* ✉ *22 Hawthorne St., SoMa* ☎ *415/685–4860* 🌐 *www.benusf.com* 🕒 *Closed Sun. and Mon. No lunch.*

★ Birdsong

$$$$ | MODERN AMERICAN | Despite its gritty location a block from Market Street's roughest section, this sweeping, elaborate tasting-menu restaurant is a destination for discerning fine-dining lovers from all over the country. Chef and co-owner Christopher Bleidorn is now spreading his wings after working in the kitchen at some of San Francisco's top kitchens (Atelier Crenn, Saison, Benu), and each of the 11 or so dishes he creates for each diner is a masterpiece in presentation and taste. **Known for:** dishes involving wood-fired and luxurious elements; beautiful open-kitchen setting; abstract versions of comfort dishes like clam chowder. [$] *Average main: $225*

✉ *1085 Mission St., SoMa* ☎ *415/369–9161* 🌐 *www.birdsongsf.com* ⏲ *Closed Sun. and Mon. No lunch.*

★ Californios

$$$$ | MODERN MEXICAN | Most restaurant discussion in San Francisco during the COVID-19 pandemic sadly revolved around the closings, except for a few exciting openings like this Californian-Mexican tasting-menu concept by chef Val M. Cantu that relocated in 2021 from its Mission District digs to a larger, ultrachic home in SoMa's former Bar Agricole space. **Known for:** house-made tortillas used in brilliant ways; wonderful patio; hard to get reservations. [$] *Average main: $223* ✉ *355 11th St., SoMa* ☎ *415/757–0994* 🌐 *www.californiossf.com* ⏲ *Closed Sun. and Mon. No lunch.*

The Cavalier

$$$ | MODERN BRITISH | British pub grub gets a Nor Cal makeover at this Anna Weinberg–Jennifer Puccio production: like the pair's other collaborations (Marlowe, Park Tavern, Leo's Oyster Bar), it's chic and loud, yet deliciously comforting thanks to refined but homey dishes like the city's best fish-and-chips. The darkly painted space, with high ceilings and large arched windows, is decorated with stuffed animal heads and paintings imparting a British vibe that attracts the clubby tech crowd. **Known for:** Brussels sprouts chips; cocktails with gin; lively atmosphere. [$] *Average main: $30* ✉ *Hotel Zetta, 360 Jessie St., SoMa* ☎ *415/321–6000* 🌐 *www.thecavaliersf.com* ⏲ *Closed Sun. and Mon.*

54 Mint

$$$ | ITALIAN | Overlooking the always interesting Mint Plaza, a busy European-style plaza that surrounds the former U.S. Mint, this brick-walled, cozy-modern restaurant is one of San Francisco's best examples of a Roman trattoria, with both rustic traditional cooking and gentle spins on classic recipes. **Known for:** bottarga, sea urchin, and burrata bruschetta; any homemade pasta; creative Negroni variations. [$] *Average main: $31* ✉ *16 Mint Plaza, SoMa* ✥ *Plaza can be accessed from 5th St. or Mission St.* ☎ *415/543–5100* 🌐 *54mint.com.*

The Fly Trap

$$ | MODERN AMERICAN | Though the restaurant has been around in various iterations since the 19th century, it's really the pistachio meatballs that put this place on the San Francisco culinary map. It continues to attract SoMa crowds to the relaxed, tablecloth-free bar and dining room with Cal-Med fare like smoked trout with cucumber "linguine" and lamb chops with lentils, kale, and pear. **Known for:** signature cheeseburger; well-made, creative cocktails; fun classic-meets-modern vibe. [$] *Average main: $25* ✉ *606 Folsom St., SoMa* ☎ *415/243–0580* 🌐 *www.flytrapsf.com* ⏲ *No lunch weekdays; no dinner Sun.*

★ In Situ

$$$ | CONTEMPORARY | Benu chef Corey Lee's restaurant at SFMOMA is an exhibition of its own, with a rotating menu comprised of dishes from 80 famous chefs around the world. You might taste David Chang's sausage and rice cakes, René Redzepi's wood sorrel granita, or Wylie Dufresne's shrimp grits. **Known for:** global culinary influences; sleek space that fits the modern art vibe; most refined daytime option in an area without many sit-down lunch choices. [$] *Average main: $30* ✉ *151 3rd St., SoMa* ☎ *415/941–6050* 🌐 *insitu.sfmoma.org* ⏲ *Closed Tues. and Wed. No dinner Mon.*

Marlowe

$$$ | AMERICAN | Hearty American bistro fare and hip design draw crowds to this Anna Weinberg–Jennifer Puccio enterprise. The menu boasts one of the city's best burgers, and the dining room gleams with white penny-tile floors and marble countertops. **Known for:** refined takes on comfort food like roast chicken and deviled eggs; strong drinks; festive atmosphere. [$] *Average main: $29* ✉ *500 Brannan St., SoMa* ☎ *415/777–1413* 🌐 *marlowesf.com.*

Mourad

$$$$ | MOROCCAN | With Mourad's stunning, grand design, it's easy to get distracted from the intricate cocktails and excellent cooking served here on the ground level of the magnificent 1920s art-deco PacBell building (later known as the headquarters for Yelp). However, chef-owner Mourad Lahlou is the great voice for his native Morocco's cuisine in the Bay Area, and this restaurant is his showcase, where dish after dish is as splendid as the bathrooms' tile work and the chandeliers above the dining room. **Known for:** glass-enclosed wine cellar "bridge" above the bar and dining room; family-style chicken and short rib dinners; za'atar flatbread and spreads. [$] *Average main: $42* ✉ *140 New Montgomery St., #1, SoMa* ☎ *415/660–2500* 🌐 *www.mouradsf.com* 🕓 *No lunch weekends.*

ROOH

$$$ | MODERN INDIAN | Traditional Indian dishes get a captivating, innovative spin at this SoMa hot spot that is tucked away far from the neighborhood's main restaurant areas. Look for tandoori octopus, masala jackfruit tacos, and other exciting dishes, all complemented by equally inventive cocktails and a splashy, colorful space. **Known for:** SF's best butter chicken; the naan and chutneys; best dining choice before a Giants game. [$] *Average main: $30* ✉ *333 Brannan St., SoMa* ☎ *415/525–4174* 🌐 *www.roohsf.com* 🕓 *Closed Mon. No lunch.*

★ Saison

$$$$ | MODERN AMERICAN | This Michelin-starred restaurant consistently answers the question of what you get for $298 per person with a culinary adventure of many courses, prepared by a crew overseen by chef Joshua Skenes. The team teases the deepest flavors from premium ingredients in dishes that may highlight fire-grilled antelope, followed by a broth of its grilled bones, or the signature, showstopping sea urchin on grilled bread. **Known for:** destination dining in a 19th-century building; world-class wine list; polished start-to-finish experience. [$] *Average main: $298* ✉ *178 Townsend St., SoMa* ☎ *415/828–7990* 🌐 *www.saisonsf.com* 🕓 *Closed Sun. and Mon.*

Town Hall

$$$ | MODERN AMERICAN | American fare with Southern flair is the headline at this power broker's pit stop where barbecue gulf shrimp, juicy fried chicken, and butterscotch-chocolate *pot de crème* highlight a menu with enough variety to satisfy nearly everyone and portions to satisfy almost every appetite. The converted-warehouse space, with dark-wood floors, exposed brick walls, and contemporary art, comfortably blends old with new. **Known for:** must-order cornbread and veal meatballs; lunchtime scene; mix of classic New Orleans and creative cocktails. [$] *Average main: $30* ✉ *342 Howard St., SoMa* ☎ *415/908–3700* 🌐 *townhallsf.com* 🕓 *No lunch weekends.*

25 Lusk

$$$ | MODERN AMERICAN | Tucked off an alley, this sleek two-story (plus rooftop) bastion of American cuisine serves a hefty helping of glamour with its food. The lights are low, the wines are well chosen, and the menu offers dishes that range from green-tea crab noodle salad to caviar and buckwheat blinis. **Known for:** sexy ambience; seafood dishes; more casual, equally fun rooftop restaurant sibling. [$] *Average main: $33* ✉ *25 Lusk St., SoMa* ☎ *415/495–5875* 🌐 *www.25lusk.com.*

Zero Zero

$$ | ITALIAN | Convention-goers and locals alike love the Cal-Ital pizzas and house-made pasta for dinner, with a Negroni, at this longtime favorite near the Moscone Center. Ingredients are fresh and seasonal, and portions are affordable and easy to share. **Known for:** stoner garlic bread; good soft-serve ice cream; strong wine and cocktails program. [$] *Average main: $24* ✉ *826 Folsom St., SoMa* ☎ *415/348–8800* 🌐 *www.zerozerosf.com* 🕓 *No lunch. Closed Sun. and Mon.*

Coffee and Quick Bites

Blue Bottle Coffee

$ | **CAFÉ** | Oakland-born Blue Bottle Coffee can now be found all over the Bay Area, on the East Coast, and even in Japan. However, this Mint Plaza coffee shop inside a 1912 building (fun fact: it appeared in *The Maltese Falcon*) remains its spiritual flagship for coffee geeks eager to gawk at the glitzy brewing equipment for sale, then enjoy perfect espresso pulls, powerful Oji cold brew, and meticulously made drip coffee from the three-light Japanese siphon bar. **Known for:** excellent cappuccinos; small selection of delicious cookies, pastries, and sandwiches; prime people-watching. [$] *Average main: $5* ✉ *66 Mint St., SoMa* ☎ *510/653–3394* 🌐 *bluebottlecoffee.com/cafes/mint-plaza* 🕑 *No dinner.*

Hotels

SoMa's burgeoning lodging scene, spawned by the Moscone Convention Center, Oracle Park, and the conglomeration of museums and high-end eateries, includes some of the city's greenest chain operations, and boutique hotels are opening that cater to techie conventioneers. In SoMa, you won't want to take leisurely evening strolls, as the streets can occasionally get sketchy after dark.

Four Seasons Hotel San Francisco

$$$$ | **HOTEL** | Occupying floors 5 through 17 of a skyscraper, the Four Seasons delivers subdued elegance in rooms with contemporary artwork, fine linens, floor-to-ceiling windows that overlook Yerba Buena Gardens or downtown, and bathrooms with soaking tubs and glass-enclosed showers. **Pros:** near museums, galleries, restaurants, shopping, and clubs; terrific fitness facilities; luxurious rooms and amenities. **Cons:** in-house restaurant/bar has delicious eats and drinks but lacks personality; rooms can feel sterile; Market Street entrance can have aggressive street life outside. [$] *Rooms from: $490* ✉ *757 Market St., SoMa* ☎ *415/633–3000* 🌐 *www.fourseasons.com/sanfrancisco* 🛏 *277 rooms* 🍴 *No meals.*

Hotel Zelos San Francisco

$ | **HOTEL** | A high-style haven on the top five floors of the green-tiled Pacific Building (built in 1907), the Zelos offers a luxurious oasis above the busiest part of town, with spacious rooms decked out in muted alligator-pattern carpeting, earth-toned drapes, and sleek furniture echoing a 1930s sensibility. **Pros:** snappy design; convenient to public transit including cable cars; home to one of the city's premier cocktail bars. **Cons:** rates soar during large conventions; too much of a scene for some guests; some rooms have no street views. [$] *Rooms from: $180* ✉ *12 4th St., SoMa* ☎ *415/348–1111, 888/459–3303* 🌐 *hotelzelos.com* 🛏 *202 rooms* 🍴 *No meals.*

★ **Hotel Zetta San Francisco**

$ | **HOTEL** | With a playful lobby lounge, London-style brasserie The Cavalier, and slick-yet-homey tech-friendly rooms, this trendy redo behind a stately 1913 neoclassical facade is a leader on the SoMa hotel scene. **Pros:** tech amenities and arty design; in-room spa services; noteworthy fitness center. **Cons:** lots of hubbub and traffic; no bathtubs; aesthetic too frenetic for some guests. [$] *Rooms from: $198* ✉ *55 5th St., SoMa* ☎ *415/543–8555* 🌐 *hotelzetta.com* 🛏 *116 rooms* 🍴 *No meals.*

InterContinental San Francisco

$$ | **HOTEL** | The arctic-blue glass exterior and subdued, Zen-like lobby may mimic an airport concourse, but it's merely a prelude to expansive, spectacularly thought-out guest rooms supplied with all the ultramodern conveniences sophisticated travelers expect. **Pros:** excellent restaurant and above-average hotel bar; tends to be less pricey than its peers; state-of-the-art air filtration system. **Cons:** decor may seem short on character; borders a rough area; a few blocks

off the major tourist path. $ *Rooms from: $220* ☒ *888 Howard St., SoMa* ☎ *415/616–6500, 877/666–3243* ⊕ *www.intercontinentalsanfrancisco.com* ⟿ *550 rooms* ❙◎❙ *No meals.*

The Mosser Hotel

$ | HOTEL | A compatible pairing of contemporary decor with original 1913 architectural elements entices a budget-minded clientele to this family-owned eight-floor hotel just south of Market Street. **Pros:** doesn't feel like a chain; lowest-priced rooms a bargain for downtown; nice freebies like Wi-Fi and morning coffee and muffins. **Cons:** some rooms share a bath; breakfast is just a muffin; need to leave hotel for fitness center. $ *Rooms from: $115* ☒ *54 4th St., SoMa* ☎ *415/986–4400, 800/227–3804* ⊕ *www.themosser.com* ⟿ *166 rooms* ❙◎❙ *Free Breakfast.*

Palace Hotel, San Francisco

$$ | HOTEL | Open since 1875 and rebuilt after the 1906 earthquake, this legendary hotel continues to be one of the city's elite places to stay, with a prominent location at the border of SoMa and downtown plus a delightful mix of modern amenities (an indoor lap pool beneath a glass-domed ceiling) and deluxe architectural details of a bygone era. **Pros:** oozes history and Gilded Age grandeur; well-trained staff; excellent fitness center. **Cons:** smallish rooms with even smaller baths; west-facing rooms can be warm and stuffy; street noise (ask for an upper-floor room). $ *Rooms from: $254* ☒ *2 New Montgomery St., SoMa* ☎ *415/512–1111* ⊕ *www.sfpalace.com* ⟿ *556 rooms* ❙◎❙ *No meals.*

Park Central Hotel San Francisco

$$ | HOTEL | Rising 36 stories over the bustling downtown and SoMa areas, this Hyatt-affiliated hotel revels in views from light, contemporary, but not overly artsy rooms with floor-to-ceiling windows. **Pros:** good location by sights and public transit hubs; very comfortable beds; even the smallest rooms are spacious. **Cons:** some

street noise; local neighborhood lacks evening excitement post-pandemic; daily "destination" fee. $ *Rooms from: $206* ☒ *50 3rd St., SoMa* ☎ *415/974–6400* ⊕ *www.parkcentralsf.com* ⟿ *681 rooms* ❙◎❙ *No meals.*

San Francisco Marriott Marquis

$$ | HOTEL | The distinctive design of the 40-story Marriott has been compared to a parking meter and a jukebox, but the guest rooms, decorated in tasteful neutrals, satisfy the business set with ergonomic chairs, wide desks, and a host of technological amenities. **Pros:** spectacular views from upper-floor rooms; in the cultural district; staffed, full-service business center. **Cons:** pricey parking; frenetic lobby and street entrance; rooms fill quickly during conferences. $ *Rooms from: $204* ☒ *780 Mission St., SoMa* ☎ *415/896–1600, 888/575–8934* ⊕ *www.marriott.com* ⟿ *1,500 rooms* ❙◎❙ *No meals.*

★ The St. Regis San Francisco

$$$$ | HOTEL | Across from Yerba Buena Gardens and SFMOMA, the luxurious and modern St. Regis is favored by celebrities, such as Lady Gaga and Al Gore, and others drawn to guest rooms and suites decorated with subdued cream colors, leather-textured walls, and window seats offering city views. **Pros:** excellent views; stunning lap pool and luxe spa; art by local artists on display. **Cons:** expensive rates; restaurant isn't on par with the rest of the hotel; cramped space for passenger unloading. $ *Rooms from: $489* ☒ *125 3rd St., SoMa* ☎ *415/284–4000* ⊕ *st-regis.marriott.com* ⟿ *260 rooms* ❙◎❙ *No meals.*

W San Francisco

$$ | HOTEL | FAMILY | Chic, urban, and compact, the W's colorful and newly renovated guest rooms come with an abstract "gold rush" theme (both the 1800s one and the current tech wave) and include such homey comforts as upholstered window seats, pillow-top mattresses, and sleek baths with MOMO amenities

by Davines. **Pros:** sophisticated digs; in the heart of the cultural district; locally sourced snacks and exciting cocktails at TRACE restaurant and Living Room bar. **Cons:** on-the-go vibe not for everyone; at a busy intersection; area's street people may unsettle some guests. [$] *Rooms from: $259* ✉ *181 3rd St., SoMa* ☎ *415/777–5300* 🌐 *marriott.com* 🛏 *404 rooms* 🍴 *No meals.*

Nightlife

In modern, industrial SoMa you'll find everyone from loyal Giants fans celebrating with beers at one of the neighborhood's breweries to the gay biker crowd that explodes onto the patio of the Lone Star Saloon in fog or sunshine. Everyone else is apt to wind up at one of the handful of hip nightclubs open into the wee hours. The area is also home to some of the city's leading cocktail bars and to concerts at DNA Lounge.

BARS

★ City Beer Store

BARS/PUBS | Called CBS by locals, this friendly tasting room meets liquor mart has a wine bar's sensibility. Perfect for both connoisseurs and the merely beer curious, CBS stocks hundreds of different bottled beers, and more than a dozen are on tap to enjoy on the patio or the bar seats in front of a whimsical mural depicting aquatic animals flying around the Bay Bridge. ✉ *1148 Mission St., between 7th and 8th Sts., SoMa* ☎ *702/941–0349* 🌐 *www.citybeerstore.com.*

The Hotel Utah Saloon

BARS/PUBS | This funky spot—off the beaten path of the area's nightlife—is in a building dating back to 1908 and presents a mix of local bands and young national touring acts performing rock, indie pop, alt-country, and everything in between. The low-ceiling performance space is small, with a few tables. Grab the signature hummus or a Utah burger and one of 12 beers on tap from the bar. The bar area is just as popular as the music. Monday is open-mic night. ✉ *500 4th St., at Bryant St., SoMa* ☎ *415/546–6300* 🌐 *www.hotelutah.com.*

MoMo's

BARS/PUBS | This stylish restaurant and trendy bar has an outdoor patio perfect for sunny days; it's a popular spot before and after games. The pizzas, salads, and sandwiches are fine, but the bar is really all about its proximity to Oracle Park or being a prime setting for relaxed weekend day-drinking. ✉ *760 2nd St., at King St., SoMa* ☎ *415/227–8660* 🌐 *www.sfmomos.com.*

★ The Pied Piper

BARS/PUBS | The Palace Hotel's clubby, wood-paneled watering hole takes its name from the 1909 Maxfield Parrish mural *The Pied Piper of Hamelin,* which covered most of the wall behind the bar for a century. In 2013, the hotel management put it up for auction, but locals howled in protest. The painting then went to a restorer before returning to the bar, which draws an upscale clientele for two-olive martinis, Manhattans, and other trad libations. ✉ *The Palace Hotel, 2 New Montgomery St., off Market St., SoMa* ☎ *415/512–1111* 🌐 *www.piedpipersf.com.*

Terroir

WINE BARS—NIGHTLIFE | The focus at this quaint wine bar is on natural (and mostly old-world) vintages, though it's not impossible to find local offerings, too. The space may be small, but the selection is not: hundreds of different wines, stacked along the walls, compete for your attention. Not sure about Jura wines or the difference between Poulsard and Trousseau? The staff is always eager to help. The bar also serves a small selection of artisanal cheeses and charcuterie to pair with the wines. **■ TIP→ Go on a weekday and head to the candlelit loft above the bar. It's the best seat in the house.** ✉ *1116 Folsom St., at 7th St., SoMa* ☎ *415/558–9946* 🌐 *terroirsf.com.*

The View Lounge

BARS/PUBS | Art-deco-influenced floor-to-ceiling windows frame superb views on the 39th floor of the San Francisco Marriott Marquis. You won't feel out of place here just getting a drink or two rather than dinner, but the small bites are usually delicious. It can get crowded at happy hour on weekdays and all night on weekends. ✉ *San Francisco Marriott Marquis, 780 Mission St., between Mission and Market Sts., SoMa* ☎ *415/896–1600* ⊕ *marriott.com.*

BREWPUBS AND BEER GARDENS

ThirstyBear Organic Brewery

BREWPUBS/BEER GARDENS | This eco-friendly brewpub is the perfect pit stop for those on a budget who don't want to compromise. ThirstyBear is the only certified organic brewery within city limits, and the beers here are handcrafted variations on traditional styles. The bar's tapas menu features seasonal produce (mostly local), paella, and sustainably harvested seafood. The upstairs pool hall is ideal for large groups. ✉ *661 Howard St., at Hawthorne St., SoMa* ☎ *415/974–0905* ⊕ *thirstybear.com.*

21st Amendment Brewery

BREWPUBS/BEER GARDENS | Known for its range of beer types, this popular brewery has multiple taps going at all times. In the summer, the Hell or High Watermelon—a wheat beer—gets rave reviews. ■**TIP**➜ **Serious beer drinkers should try the Back in Black, a black IPA-style beer this brewpub helped pioneer.** The space has an upmarket warehouse feel, though exposed wooden ceiling beams, framed photos, whitewashed brick walls, and hardwood floors help keep it cozy. It's a good spot to warm up before a Giants game and an even better place to party after they win. ✉ *563 2nd St., between Bryant and Brannan Sts., SoMa* ☎ *415/369–0900* ⊕ *www.21st-amendment.com.*

CABARET

AsiaSF

CABARET | Saucy, sexy, and fun, this is one of the best places in town for a drag-show virgin. The entertainment, as well as the gracious food service, is provided by some of the city's most gorgeous transgender women, who strut in impossibly high heels on top of the catwalk bar, vamping to tunes like "Cabaret" and "Big Spender." The creative Asian-influenced cuisine is surprisingly good. ■**TIP**➜ **Go on a weekday to avoid the bachelorette parties.** Make reservations, or risk being turned away. ✉ *201 9th St., at Howard St., SoMa* ☎ *415/255–2742* ⊕ *asiasf.com.*

DANCE CLUBS

DNA Lounge

DANCE CLUBS | The music changes nightly at the venerable DNA Lounge, and one of the highlights is **Bootie.** Every Saturday night, this popular mash-up unites hard-core and indie rockers, hip-hop devotees, and emo fans. Three bars and dance floors on two levels mean that DNA is rarely uncomfortably crowded. ■**TIP**➜ **The action spills into the pizza joint next door, so you don't have to stop dancing if you suddenly get hungry.** ✉ *375 11th St., between Harrison and Folsom Sts., SoMa* ☎ *415/626–1409* ⊕ *www.dnalounge.com.*

The EndUp

DANCE CLUBS | Sometimes 2 am is way too early: with an all-night (and most of the morning) dance party starting at 10 pm on Saturday, the EndUp is by far SF's most popular after-hours place, with possibly the best sound system in the city. ■**TIP**➜ **Said system is cranked. Even the cool kids wear earplugs.** It's usually open from 10 pm Saturday until 4 am Monday, and 10 pm–4 am weekdays, but times can vary based on each event. It can be a bit of a meat market, but this San Francisco institution doesn't adhere to any particular scene. ✉ *401 6th St., at Harrison St., SoMa* ☎ *415/896-5530* ⊕ *theendupsf.com.*

4

SoMa and Civic Center SOMA

111 Minna Gallery

CAFES—NIGHTLIFE | It doesn't get more trendy, modern-day San Francisco than this gallery and coffee shop by day, bar and dance club by night in a warehouse space on a small side street just south of Mission Street. It draws a mix of techies networking and the trendy art crowd hobnobbing. Dance events typically take place on Friday and Saturday from 9 pm until 2 am, though the bar opens around 5. ⊠ *111 Minna St., between 2nd and New Montgomery Sts., SoMa* ☎ *415/974–1719* ⊕ *111minnagallery.com* ⊙ *Gallery closed weekends.*

GAY NIGHTLIFE
Lone Star Saloon

BARS/PUBS | Open since 1989, this watering hole is popular with bikers, bears, and the men who love them. The inside bar has an old-style-tavern feel, with a pool table and a long wooden bar you half expect the bartender to sling a beer down. Weekend "Beer Busts" unfold on the great outdoor patio bar. Expect a big crowd on a sunny day. The scene here isn't particularly female-friendly, and the action can get steamy during events like Gay Pride or the Folsom Street Fair. ⊠ *1354 Harrison St., near 9th St., SoMa* ☎ *415/863–9999* ⊕ *www.lonestarsf.com.*

SF Eagle

BARS/PUBS | This spacious indoor-outdoor leather bar is a holdover from the days before AIDS and SoMa's gentrification. The Sunday afternoon "Beer Busts" (3–6) remain a high point of the leather set's week, and Thursday nights are given over to live music. This remains a welcoming place for people from all walks of life. ⊠ *398 12th St., at Harrison St., SoMa* ⊕ *thesfeagle.com.*

 # Performing Arts

DANCE
Alonzo King LINES Ballet

DANCE | Since 1982 this company has been staging the fluid and gorgeous ballets of choreographer and founder Alonzo King, sometimes in collaboration with top-notch global musicians. Ballets incorporate both classical and modern techniques, with experimental set design, costumes, and music. The San Francisco seasons are in spring and fall. ⊠ *26 7th St., SoMa* ☎ *415/863–3040, ext. 221* ⊕ *linesballet.org.*

Robert Moses' Kin

DANCE | Founded in 1995 by choreographer Robert Moses and known for its provocative themes, the Kin dance company makes a study of race, class, culture, and gender with the use of eclectic movements, such as jazz, hip-hop, and ballet. Performances take place at studios and theaters around the SoMa neighborhood. ⊠ *301 8th St., Suite 200, SoMa* ☎ *415/252–8384* ⊕ *www.robert-moseskin.org.*

MOVIE THEATERS
San Francisco Cinematheque

FILM | In the spotlight are experimental film and digital media. Cinematheque hosts screenings throughout the city, but most are at the Yerba Buena Center for the Arts at 701 Mission Street. It also produces the annual Crossroads Film Festival each year at SFMOMA. ⊠ *SoMa* ☎ *415/552–1990* ⊕ *www.sfcinematheque.org.*

PERFORMING ARTS CENTERS
Yerba Buena Center for the Arts

ARTS CENTERS | Across the street from SFMOMA and abutting a lovely urban garden, this performing arts complex schedules interdisciplinary art exhibitions, touring and local dance troupes, music, film programs, and contemporary theater events. You can depend on the quality

Oracle Park: Where Giants Tread

The size of Oracle Park hits you immediately—the field, McCovey Cove, and the Lefty O'Doul drawbridge all look like miniature models. At just under 13 acres, the San Francisco Giants' ballpark is one of the country's smallest. After Boston's Fenway Park, Oracle Park has the shortest distance to the wall; from home plate it's just 309 feet to the tall right-field wall. But there's something endearing about its petite stature—not to mention its location, with yacht masts poking up over the outfield and the blue bay sparkling beyond. From 1960 to 2000 the Giants played at Candlestick Park, which was in one of the coldest, windiest parts of the city. (Giants' pitcher Stu Miller was famously "blown off the mound" here during the 1961 All-Star Game.)

In 2000 the Giants played their first game at Oracle Park (then called Pacific Bell Park and later SBC Park and AT&T Park). All told, $357 million was spent on the privately funded facility, and it shows in the retro redbrick exterior, the quaint clock tower, handsome bronze statues, and above-average food. There isn't a bad seat in the house, and the park has an unusual level of intimacy and access. Concourses circle the field on one level, and in some ticketed areas you can stand inches from players as they exit the locker rooms. At street level, non-ticket-holders can get up close

outside a gate in right field. The giant Coke bottle and mitt you see beyond the outfield are part of the Coca-Cola Fan Lot playground. Don't miss the edible garden, the model cable car, and the ballpark specialty Crazy Crab crab sandwich, all located in the centerfield area. Diehards may miss the grittiness of Candlestick, but it's hard not to love this park. It still feels new but has an old-time aura and has become a San Francisco institution. Park tours are led daily at 10:30 and 12:30 and cost $22.

The Famous "Splash Hit"

Locals show up in motorboats and inflatable rafts, ready to scoop up home-run balls that clear the right-field wall and land in McCovey Cove. Hitting one into the water isn't easy: the ball has to clear a 25-foot wall, the elevated walkway, and the promenade outside. Barry Bonds had the first "splash hit" on May 1, 2000.

Getting There

Parking is very limited and pricey ($35 and up). Take public transportation. Muni lines N and T (to CalTrain/Mission Bay and Sunnydale, respectively) stop in front of the park, and Muni bus lines 10, 30, 45, and 47 stop within a few blocks. Or arrive in style—take the ferry from Jack London Square in Oakland (⊕ www.sanfranciscobayferry.com).

of the productions at Yerba Buena. Film buffs often come here for screenings by the San Francisco Cinematheque (⊕ www.sfcinematheque.org), which showcases experimental film and digital media. And dance enthusiasts can attend concerts by a roster of city companies that perform here, including Smuin

Ballet (⊕ www.smuinballet.org), ODC/Dance (⊕ www.odcdance.org), and Alonzo King's LINES Ballet (⊕ www.linesballet.org). Lamplighters (⊕ www.lamplighters.org), an alternative opera that specializes in Gilbert & Sullivan, also performs here. ⊠ 701 Mission St., SoMa ☎ 415/978–2787 ⊕ ybca.org.

🛍 Shopping

The South of Market district, once the bastion of light industry, is still framed by warehouses, but today it's best known for its trendy pockets of quaint restaurants, edgy clubs, and airy art spaces, as well as for being home to the offices of major tech companies like Dropbox, Twitter, and Airbnb. A smattering of antiques shops and other dealers occupy some of the former warehouse spaces, and there are a few clothing outlets. At the other end of the spectrum is the Metreon, a massive shopping center. At the corner of 4th and Mission Streets, it has a few stores of note, among them Chronicle Books, along with a 16-screen cinema and a slew of eateries.

ART GALLERIES

ArtHaus
ART GALLERIES | This one-story gallery south of Market provides an intimate space for both local and New York artists to display their contemporary work. Gallery owners Annette Schutz and James Bacchi are very approachable and include a diverse range of mediums as well as rotating shows beneath their roof. ✉ *228 Townsend St., between 3rd and 4th Sts., SoMa* ☎ *415/977–0223* ⊕ *www.arthaus-sf.com.*

The Bond Latin Gallery
ART GALLERIES | Some of the vibrant works on show in this cozy yet light Latin American art gallery come from such artists as Diego Rivera, Laura Hernandez, and Francisco Toledo. The charming owners will make you want to return. ✉ *631 Howard St., Suite 120, SoMa* ☎ *415/362–1480* ⊕ *www.bondlatin.com.*

Crown Point Press
ART GALLERIES | What started as a print workshop in 1962 now includes studios as well as a large, airy gallery where etchings, intaglios, engravings, and aquatints by local and internationally renowned artists are displayed. ✉ *20 Hawthorne St., between 2nd and 3rd*

On the Horizon

The **Mexican Museum**, which presents Latino art and culture, will add a new destination to the Yerba Buena cultural zone, occupying the bottom four floors of a new luxury condo tower. Accredited as a Smithsonian affiliate, the museum has a collection of 17,000 works. Construction is well under way at the site on Mission and 3rd Streets, and it is scheduled to open in summer 2022.

See ⊕ *www.mexicanmuseum.org* for updates.

Sts., SoMa ☎ *415/974–6273* ⊕ *crownpoint.com* ☽ *Closed Sun.*

Hackett Mill
ART GALLERIES | This gallery prides itself on its friendly staffers, who will educate you about the art or leave you alone, whichever you prefer. Some of the artists here include Conrad Marca-Relli, Esteban Vincente, Kenzo Okada, and Robert De Niro Sr. Specialties are American modern, postwar abstract expressionist, and Bay Area figurative art. ✉ *145 Natoma St., Suite 400, SoMa* ☎ *415/362–3377* ⊕ *www.hackettmill.com.*

Varnish Fine Art
ART GALLERIES | Jen Rogers and Kerri Stephens's gallery specializes in thought-provoking works such as those by San Francisco–based artist Brian Goggin, known for his public art piece *Defenestration*. Ransom & Mitchell, two other noteworthy locals the gallery represents, blend photography and set design to create a truly surreal visual experience. This gallery is open by appointment only. ✉ *16 Jessie St., Suite C120, near 1st St., SoMa* ☎ *415/433–4400* ⊕ *www.varnishfineart.com.*

BOOKS

Alexander Book Company

BOOKS/STATIONERY | The three floors here are stocked with literature, poetry, and children's books, with a focus on hard-to-find works by men and women of color. ✉ *50 2nd St., between Jessie and Stevenson Sts., SoMa* ☎ *415/495–2992* ⊕ *www.alexanderbook.com.*

★ Chronicle Books

BOOKS/STATIONERY | A local beacon of publishing produces inventively designed fiction, cookbooks, art books, and other titles, as well as diaries, planners, and address books—all of which you can purchase at its home near Oracle Park in an old maritime machine shop and warehouse. ✉ *680 2nd St., SoMa* ☎ *415/537–4200* ⊕ *www.chroniclebooks.com.*

FOOD AND DRINK

DECANTsf

WINE/SPIRITS | Wine geeks love the retail choices to bring home and the exciting offerings being poured at this hybrid wine store–bar slightly below street level. This is the place to ask questions about quieter regions and rarely seen grapes— the co-owners are gifted sommeliers and love to share their wine passion with guests. ✉ *1168 Folsom St., SoMa* ☎ *415/913–7256* ⊕ *decantsf.com.*

K&L Wine Merchants

WINE/SPIRITS | More than any other wine store in the city, this one has an ardent cult following around town. The friendly staffers promise not to sell what they don't taste themselves, and weekly events—on Friday from 5 pm to 6:30 pm and Saturday from noon to 3 pm—open the tastings to customers. The best-seller list for varietals and regions for both the under- and over-$30 categories appeals to the wine lover in everyone. ✉ *855 Harrison St., near 4th St., SoMa* ☎ *415/896–1734* ⊕ *www.klwines.com.*

JEWELRY AND COLLECTIBLES

★ SFMOMA Museum Store

JEWELRY/ACCESSORIES | The museum's shop is an excellent stop for unique souvenirs, including its large selection of watches and jewelry, as well as artists' monographs and artful housewares. Posters, calendars, children's art sets and books, and art books for adults round out the merchandise. ✉ *151 3rd St., between Mission and Howard Sts., SoMa* ☎ *415/357–4035* ⊕ *museumstore. sfmoma.org.*

Activities

BASEBALL

★ San Francisco Giants

BASEBALL/SOFTBALL | **FAMILY** | Three World Series titles (2010, 2012, and 2014) and the retro-modern design of Oracle Park lead to sellouts for nearly every home game the National League team plays, so make plans in advance. ✉ *Oracle Park, 24 Willie Mays Plaza, between 2nd and 3rd Sts., SoMa* ☎ *415/972–2000* ⊕ *www. mlb.com/giants.*

Civic Center

San Francisco's eye-catching, gold-domed City Hall presides over this patchy neighborhood bordered roughly by Franklin, McAllister, Hyde, and Grove Streets. The optimistic "City Beautiful" movement of the early 20th century produced the Beaux Arts–style complex for which the district is named, including City Hall, the War Memorial Opera House, and the old public library, now the home of the Asian Art Museum. The wonderful Main Library on Larkin Street between Fulton and Grove Streets is a modern variation on Civic Center's architectural theme.

The Civic Center area may have been set up on City Beautiful principles, but illusion soon gives way to reality. The buildings are grand, but many of the city's most destitute residents eke out an existence on the neighborhood's streets and plazas. Tickets to shows, concerts, operas, or ballet at one of the grand performance halls are the main reason many venture here, and major city events like the Pride parade and Giants' victory celebrations draw big crowds.

Sights

★ Asian Art Museum

MUSEUM | You don't have to be a connoisseur of Asian art to appreciate a visit to this museum whose monumental exterior conceals a light, open, and welcoming space. The fraction of the museum's collection on display (about 2,500 pieces out of 18,000-plus total) is laid out thematically and by region, making it easy to follow historical developments.

Begin on the third floor, where highlights of Buddhist art in Southeast Asia and early China include a large, jewel-encrusted, exquisitely painted 19th-century Burmese Buddha and clothed rod puppets from Java. On the second floor you can find later Chinese works, as well as exquisite pieces from Korea and Japan. The ground floor is devoted to temporary exhibits and the museum's wonderful gift shop. During spring and summer, visit on Thursday evenings for extended programs and sip drinks while a DJ spins tunes. ⊠ *200 Larkin St., between McAllister and Fulton Sts., Civic Center* 🖀 *415/581–3500* ⊕ *asianart.org* ⊠ *$15, free 1st Sun. of month; $8 Thurs. 5–8* ⊙ *Closed Tues. and Wed.*

★ City Hall

GOVERNMENT BUILDING | This imposing 1915 structure with its massive gold-leaf dome—higher than the U.S. Capitol's—is about as close to a palace as you're going to get in San Francisco: the classic granite-and-marble behemoth was modeled after St. Peter's Basilica in Rome. Architect Arthur Brown Jr., who was also behind Coit Tower and the War Memorial Opera House, designed an interior with grand columns and a sweeping central

staircase. The 1899 structure it replaced had taken 27 years to erect, but it collapsed in about 27 seconds during the 1906 earthquake.

City Hall was seismically retrofitted in the late 1990s, but the sense of history remains palpable, and you can learn about it on a tour. Some noteworthy events that have taken place here include the hosing of civil-rights and freedom-of-speech protesters (1960); the assassinations of Mayor George Moscone and openly gay supervisor Harvey Milk (1978); the torching of the lobby by angry members of the gay community in response to the light sentence given to the former supervisor who killed both men (1979); and the first domestic partnership registrations of gay couples (1991). In 2004, Mayor Gavin Newsom took a stand against then-current state and federal law by issuing marriage licenses to same-sex partners.

Across Polk Street from City Hall is **Civic Center Plaza,** with lawns, walkways, seasonal flower beds, a playground, and an underground parking garage. This sprawling space is generally clean but somewhat grim, as many homeless people hang out here. ⊠ *1 Dr. Carlton B. Goodlett Pl. , bordered by Van Ness Ave. and Polk, Grove, and McAllister Sts., Civic Center* 🖀 *415/554–4000, 415/554–6139 tour reservations* ⊕ *sfgov.org/cityhall/city-hall-tours* ⊠ *Free* ⊙ *Closed weekends.*

★ Louise M. Davies Symphony Hall

ARTS VENUE | Fascinating and futuristic-looking, this 2,739-seat hall is the home of the San Francisco Symphony. The glass wraparound lobby and pop-out balcony high on the southeast corner are visible from outside, as is the Henry Moore bronze sculpture on the sidewalk at Van Ness Avenue and Grove Street. The hall's 59 adjustable Plexiglas acoustical disks cascade from the ceiling like hanging windshields. Concerts range from typical symphonic fare to more unusual performers and combinations, such as singer Al Green and film screenings with a live orchestra performing the score. Scheduled tours (about 75 minutes) on Monday take in Davies and the nearby War Memorial Opera House. ⊠ *201 Van Ness Ave., Civic Center* ☎ *415/552–8338* ⊕ *www.sfsymphony.org* ☑ *Tours $7.*

San Francisco Public Library

LIBRARY | Topped with a swirl like an art-deco nautilus, the library's seven-level glass atrium fills the building with light. Local researchers take advantage of centers dedicated to gay and lesbian, African American, Chinese, and Filipino history. ■TIP→ **The sixth-floor San Francisco History Center has fun exhibits of city ephemera, including—a treat for fans of noir fiction—novelist Dashiell Hammett's typewriter.** ⊠ *100 Larkin St., at Grove St., Civic Center* ☎ *415/557–4400* ⊕ *sfpl.org.*

War Memorial Opera House

ARTS VENUE | After San Francisco's original opera houses were destroyed in the 1906 quake, architect Arthur Brown Jr. was commissioned to design this stunning Renaissance-style building. Taking its name as a tribute to the city's soldiers lost in World War I, the War Memorial Opera House was inaugurated in 1932 with a performance of *Tosca.* It has since played host to two major historic events: the drafting of the United Nations charter in 1945 and the ceremony six years later in which the United States restored sovereignty to Japan. Modeled after its European counterparts, the building has a vaulted and coffered ceiling, marble foyer, two balconies, and a huge silver art-deco chandelier that resembles a sunburst. The San Francisco Opera performs here from September into December and in summer; the opera house hosts the San Francisco Ballet from February through May, with December *Nutcracker* performances. Tours are available in conjunction with Davies Symphony Hall; check online. ⊠ *301 Van Ness Ave., Civic Center* ☎ *415/621–6600* ⊕ *sfwarmemorial.org.*

Nightlife

Lawyers, politicians, and others in the government biz populate this neighborhood by day, and at night the scene tends to remain buttoned-up.

MUSIC CLUBS
Warfield

MUSIC CLUBS | A former movie palace is now one of the city's largest rock-and-roll venues, with folding chairs or standing space (depending on the event) downstairs and theater seating upstairs. The historic venue has booked everyone from Prince and the Grateful Dead to the Pretenders and the Killers. ⊠ *982 Market St., at Taylor St., Civic Center* ☎ *415/345–0900* ⊕ *www.thewarfieldtheatre.com.*

Performing Arts

DANCE
★ **San Francisco Ballet**

DANCE | For ballet lovers, the nation's oldest professional company is reason alone to visit the Bay Area, as SFB's performances under the direction of Helgi Tomasson have won critical raves. The primary season runs from February through May. The repertoire includes full-length ballets such as *Don Quixote* and *Sleeping Beauty*; the December presentation of *The Nutcracker* is truly spectacular. The company also performs bold new dances from star choreographers such as William Forsythe and Mark Morris, alongside modern classics by George Balanchine and Jerome Robbins. Tickets are available at the **War Memorial Opera House.** ⊠ *War Memorial Opera House, 301 Van Ness Ave., at Grove St., Civic Center* ☎ *415/865–2000* ⊕ *www.sfballet.org.*

MUSIC

★ San Francisco Opera

OPERA | Founded in 1923, this internationally recognized organization has occupied the War Memorial Opera House since the building's completion in 1932. From September through December and June through July, the company presents a wide range of operas, from *Carmen* to an operatic version of *It's a Wonderful Life* . The opera often takes on ambitious world premieres and sometimes presents unconventional, edgy projects designed to attract younger audiences. Translations are projected above the stage during most non-English productions. ⊠ *War Memorial Opera House, 301 Van Ness Ave., at Grove St., Civic Center* 🖀 *415/864–3330 tickets* ⊕ *sfopera.com.*

★ San Francisco Symphony

MUSIC | One of America's top orchestras performs from September through May, with additional summer performances of light classical music and show tunes. The symphony is known for its daring programming of 20th-century American works, often performed with soloists of the caliber of André Watts, Gil Shaham, and Renée Fleming. Legendary maestro Michael Tilson Thomas retired in 2020, and music lovers are eager to listen to the opening post-pandemic concerts of the new music director, Esa-Pekka Salonen. ⊠ *Louise M. Davies Symphony Hall, 201 Van Ness Ave., at Grove St., Civic Center* 🖀 *415/864–6000* ⊕ *www.sfsymphony.org.*

SPOKEN WORD AND READINGS

★ City Arts & Lectures

READINGS/LECTURES | Each year this program includes more than 20 fascinating conversations with writers, composers, actors, politicians, scientists, and others. The Sydney Goldstein (formerly the Nourse) Theater, in the Performing Arts Center, is usually the venue. Past speakers have included Diane Keaton, Ken Burns, and Linda Ronstadt. ⊠ *Sydney Goldstein Theater, 275 Hayes St., Civic Center* 🖀 *415/392–4400* ⊕ *www.cityarts.net.*

THEATRE

New Conservatory Theatre Center

THEATER | This three-stage complex focuses on contemporary gay- and lesbian-themed works and newer small-production musicals, as well as other events, including educational plays and classes for young people. ⊠ *25 Van Ness Ave., between Fell and Oak Sts., Civic Center* 🖀 *415/861–8972* ⊕ *www.nctcsf.org.*

Shopping

Civic Center is often abuzz with protests, performances, and political rallies. Come here to get a glimpse of the mayor or pick up some fresh produce at the twice-weekly farmers' market.

FARMERS' MARKETS

Heart of the City Farmers' Market

OUTDOOR/FLEA/GREEN MARKETS | Twice a week (Wednesday and Sunday), vendors at the city's only farmer-operated farmers' market sell heaps of fresh produce, along with baked goods, jams, potted herbs, and plenty of delicious snacks and on-the-go lunches from local artisans. The market can get busy; come early (it opens at 7 am) for the largest selection. ⊠ *United Nations Plaza, along Market St., Civic Center* 🖀 *415/558–9455* ⊕ *hotcfarmersmarket.org.*

Tenderloin

Stretching west of Union Square and north of Civic Center, the Tenderloin could be the city's poster child for urban challenges: low-income families huddle in tiny apartments; single-room-occupancy hotels offer shelter a step up from living on the street; drug dealing and prostitution are common; and very few green spaces break up the monotony of high-rises. So why would anyone go out of their way to come here? Well, exceptional Vietnamese food, for one thing, but these days more than just the great pho is luring people to the Tenderloin. Trendy watering holes and coffee shops are springing up, with a handful of intrepid hipsters moving into the hood after them. The Tenderloin may be on its way to becoming the next Mission, but for now it remains a gritty slice of San Francisco.

■ TIP→ Some parts of the Tenderloin are more dangerous than others, and a single street can change from block to block. Little Saigon's Larkin Street corridor is relatively safe during the day, as are most streets north of Ellis (an area that realtors insist on calling the TenderNob for its proximity to Nob Hill). Avoid walking the last two blocks of Turk Street and Golden Gate Avenue before they meet Market Street, along with Hyde Street and Leavenworth Street between Ellis Street and Turk Street. Locals would advise visitors not to walk alone or look at their phone when walking here.

👁 Sights

GLIDE Church

RELIGIOUS SITE | For a rockin' gospel concert and an inclusive, feel-good vibe, head to Glide, where Reverend Emeritus Cecil Williams, a bear of a man and a local celeb do-gooder, and other engaging pastors lead a hand-clapping, shout-it-out, get-on-your-feet Sunday "celebration." The diverse crowd—gay and straight, all colors of the rainbow, religious and not—is large and enthusiastic. You might recognize the church from the Will Smith film *The Pursuit of Happyness.* ✉ *330 Ellis St., at Taylor St., Tenderloin* ☎ *415/674–6000* 🌐 *www.glide.org.*

🍴 Restaurants

A land of dive bars, package-liquor stores, panhandlers, and … some of the best pho and bánh mì in the city, this seedy district of low rents encompasses Little Saigon. Locals know to come here for great cheap eats, including not just Vietnamese but naans and masalas. This is one of San Francisco's rougher neighborhoods—one of the last holdouts.

Little Saigon 🍴

The best Vietnamese food in the city can be found along Larkin Street between Turk and O'Farrell Streets, where Vietnamese Americans own most of the businesses. Marketing types call this corridor Little Saigon; locals associate it with the Tenderloin. You can find cheap, often fantastic food here, particularly pho (beef- or chicken-broth noodle soup). Check out Turtle Tower (*645 Larkin St.*) for pho, Hai Ky Mi Gia (*707 Ellis St.*) for braised duck-leg noodles, and Sing Sing (*309 Hyde St.*) or Saigon Sandwich (*560 Larkin St.*) for banh mi (Vietnamese sandwiches).

Brenda's French Soul Food

$$ | **CREOLE** | The good times are rolling—and the crowds coming—to this longtime Polk Street destination that is the city's definitive choice for New Orleans cooking. Brunch is always the locals' preferred meal here, but it's just as good to come for a weekday lunch of gumbo or a fried chicken dinner when the scene is a little more subdued than the real NOLA French Quarter. **Known for:** delicious beignets; broiled oysters; lots of charm and fun. [$] *Average main: $19* ✉ *652 Polk St., at Eddy St., Tenderloin* ☎ *415/345–8100* 🌐 *frenchsoulfood.com* 🕒 *Closed Tues. and Wed.*

Lers Ros

$ | **THAI** | Skip the "same old" pad thai and try something new at this authentic Thai standby. Thai herb sausage and papaya salad with salted egg are good appetizers to share, while the pork belly with crispy rind and basil leaves and duck *larb* (meat salad) come packed with flavor and heat. **Known for:** exciting, rarely seen dishes; extensive menu; post-drinking hangout. [$] *Average main: $16* ✉ *730 Larkin St., Tenderloin* ☎ *415/931–6917* 🌐 *lersros.com.*

Hotels

Between Union Square, Nob Hill, and Civic Center, the Tenderloin contains some hip boutique hotels and happening bars (plus some of the best Vietnamese and Thai food in the region). Be advised that many transients live here; the streets can feel seedy even during the day.

Phoenix Hotel

$ | **HOTEL** | A magnet for the boho crowd, the Phoenix is retro and low-key, with colorful furniture, white bedspreads, and original pieces by local artists, as well as modern amenities like free Wi-Fi. **Pros:** mellow staffers set the cool tone; heated outdoor pool but no resort fee; free parking. **Cons:** somewhat seedy location; no elevators; frequent party vibe isn't for everyone. [$] *Rooms from: $189* ✉ *601 Eddy St., Tenderloin* ☎ *415/776–1380* 🌐 *www.phoenixsf.com* 🛏 *44 rooms* 🍴 *No meals.*

★ San Francisco Proper Hotel

$$ | **HOTEL** | Inside the magnificent, flatiron-shape Beaux-Arts building—given a modern refresh in the mid-2010s—is one of the city's most spectacular places to stay, a sharp, upscale, ultra-hip boutique hotel; in contrast, outside is one of the roughest intersections for streetlife in San Francisco. **Pros:** gorgeous lobby; excellent restaurant and cocktails; tech elements like wireless speakers and smart TV. **Cons:** price may seem high for difficult location; too cool for many tastes; $30 daily fee for amenities. [$] *Rooms from: $220* ✉ *1100 Market St., Tenderloin* ✥ *Entrance at 45 McAllister St.* ☎ *415/737–7777, 888/730–4299 reservations* 🌐 *properhotel.com/san-francisco* 🛏 *131 rooms* 🍴 *No meals.*

Nightlife

This neighborhood is best known for its grit and realism, but despite this the Loin is centrally located and, depending on your reservation time at Bourbon & Branch, the perfect place to start (or end) your night on the town.

BARS

★ Bourbon & Branch

BARS/PUBS | Although this spot reeks of Prohibition-era speakeasy cool, it's not exclusive: everyone is granted a password, though it's *highly* recommended to book a reservation. The place has sex appeal, with tin ceilings, bordello-red silk wallpaper, intimate booths, and low lighting; loud conversations and cell phones are not allowed. The menu of expertly mixed cocktails and quality bourbon and whiskey is substantial, with cocktails leaning more in the spirit-forward direction. A speakeasy within the speakeasy called Wilson & Wilson is more exclusive, but just as funky. ✉ *501 Jones St., at O'Farrell St., Tenderloin* ☎ *415/346–1735* 🌐 *www.bourbonandbranch.com.*

Edinburgh Castle Pub

BARS/PUBS | Work off your fish-and-chips and Scottish brew with a turn at the dartboard or pool table at this divey pub. It's popular with locals and Brits, who congregate at the long bar or in the scattered seating areas, downing single-malt Scotch or pints of Fuller's. The pub holds weekly trivia nights and occasional Scottish cultural events (January's Robert Burns celebration is a favorite). Be aware that the surrounding neighborhood is gritty. ✉ *950 Geary St., between Larkin and Polk Sts., Tenderloin* ☎ *415/885–4074.*

MUSIC CLUBS

Great American Music Hall

MUSIC CLUBS | You can find top-drawer entertainment at this eclectic concert venue. Acts range from the best in blues, folk, and jazz to up-and-coming college-radio and American-roots artists to indie rockers. The colorful marble-pillared club, built in 1907 as a bordello, also accommodates dancing at some shows. Pub grub is available most nights. ✉ *859 O'Farrell St., between Polk and Larkin Sts., Tenderloin* ☎ *415/885–0750* 🌐 *slimspresents.com/great-american-music-hall.*

Performing Arts

THEATER

Golden Gate Theatre

THEATER | Stylishly refurbished, this movie theater is now primarily a musical house. Touring productions of popular Broadway shows and revivals are its mainstays. ✉ *1 Taylor St., at Golden Gate Ave., Tenderloin* ☎ *888/746–1799* 🌐 *www.shnsf.com.*

★ Orpheum Theatre

THEATER | The biggest touring shows, such as *Hamilton* and *The Lion King*, are performed at this gorgeously restored 2,200-seat venue. The theater itself, opened in 1926, is as much an attraction as the shows. It was modeled after a 12th-century French cathedral and is considered one of the most beautiful theaters in the world; the interior walls have ornate stonework, and the gilded plaster ceiling is perforated with tiny lights. ✉ *1192 Market St., at Hyde and 8th Sts., Tenderloin* ☎ *888/746–1799* 🌐 *broadwaysf.com.*

Activities

SPAS

Onsen Bath & Restaurant

SPA | An excellent dining experience *and* Japanese bathhouse together is an unlikely combination for the gritty Tenderloin, but once you get past the front door, this is one of the city's great treasures for massages and a sauna session. Accompany a treatment with delightful seasonal cooking and grilled skewers at the connected restaurant. ✉ *466 Eddy St., Tenderloin* ☎ *415/441–4987* 🌐 *www.onsensf.com* 🎟 *$40 for the baths, massages from $140.*

Hayes Valley

A chic neighborhood due west of Civic Center, Hayes Valley has terrific eateries, cool watering holes, and great browsing in its funky clothing, home-decor, and design boutiques. Locals love this quarter, but without any big-name draws it remains off the radar for many visitors.

Sights

San Francisco LGBT Center

LOCAL INTEREST | Night and day, the center hosts many social activities, from mixers and youth game nights to holiday parties and slam poetry performances. ✉ *1800 Market St., at Octavia St., Hayes Valley* ☎ *415/865–5555* 🌐 *www.sfcenter.org.*

Restaurants

Hayes Valley is home to several hip and haute dining destinations, centered around Hayes Street, perfect for pretheater dining. The low-key vibe in the wine bars and cafés makes it easy to feel like a local.

Hayes Street Grill

$$$ | **SEAFOOD** | You'll snag a table if you arrive at this longtime (since 1979) standby just as music lovers are folding their napkins and heading off for a show at the nearby Opera House or SFJAZZ Center. Fresh, sustainable, often local seafood lures the faithful here, as well as peak seasonal produce from the nearby region. **Known for:** simple yet excellent fish preparations; choice of sauces; white-tablecloth dining in timeless atmosphere. [$] *Average main: $31* ✉ *320 Hayes St., Hayes Valley* ☎ *415/863–5545* 🌐 *www.hayesstreetgrill.com* 🕒 *Closed most Mon. No lunch weekends.*

★ Nightbird

$$$$ | **MODERN AMERICAN** | Chef-owner Kim Alter's solo debut is this small, charming, seasonally focused tasting-menu destination that is an oasis of calm away from the frantic traffic of Gough Street. The five-course and five-bite menus (think of it like a 10-course tasting menu) are always beautifully orchestrated, served by a staff that seems to always anticipate the next question or request, making this one of the more relaxed and (relatively) affordable splurges of San Francisco's gastronomic elite restaurants. **Known for:** quail egg amuse-bouche; tiny art-deco adjacent bar, Linden Room; three-course theater menu before weeknight shows. [$] *Average main: $145* ✉ *330 Gough St., Hayes Valley* ☎ *415/829–7565* 🌐 *www.nightbirdrestaurant.com* 🕓 *Closed Sun. and Mon. No lunch.*

Nojo Ramen Tavern

$$ | JAPANESE | For a little bonhomie before the symphony, it's hard to go wrong with this buzzy (and typically crowded) ramen spot. Noodles are the star of the menu, and deservedly so, but you'll also find *izakaya*-style small plates, including pot stickers and chicken fritters. **Known for:** focused on ramen with chicken-based (paitan) broth; comfort food like chicken teriyaki; long lines. [$] *Average main: $19* ✉ *231 Franklin St., Hayes Valley* ☎ *415/896–4587* 🌐 *www.nojosframen.com* 🕓 *Closed Mon. No lunch weekdays.*

Petit Crenn

$$$$ | FRENCH | Chef Dominique Crenn's sequel to her Michelin-starred Atelier Crenn is more casual but no less accomplished. Here, the French chef keeps her focus on seafood and vegetables, inspired by her family home in the French coastal region of Brittany and presented as a seven-course prix-fixe menu. **Known for:** any dish with oysters; meat-free (but fish included) prix-fixe menu; homey yet modern atmosphere. [$] *Average main: $105* ✉ *609 Hayes St., Hayes Valley* ☎ *415/864–1744* 🌐 *www.petitcrenn.com* 🕓 *Closed Mon.*

Pläj

$$$$ | SWEDISH | The only Swedish restaurant in San Francisco is tucked behind the lobby of the Inn at the Opera and serves refreshing cuisine—fish pickled, smoked, or cured. Chef Roberth Sundell is from Stockholm, and although the aquatic fare might be the highlight, the Swedish meatballs with lingonberries is a treasured family recipe and truly a must-order. **Known for:** beet-cured gravlax; homemade aquavits (Scandinavian spirits); special vegan menu. [$] *Average main: $38* ✉ *333 Fulton St., Hayes Valley* ☎ *415/294–8925* 🌐 *www.plajrestaurant.com* 🕓 *No lunch.*

★ Rich Table

$$$ | MODERN AMERICAN | Sardine chips and porcini doughnuts are popular bites at co-chefs (and husband and wife) Evan and Sarah Rich's lively, creative restaurant; mains are also clever stunners, including pastas like the sea urchin *cacio e pepe*. The room's weathered-wood wallboards repurposed from a Northern California sawmill give it a homey vibe. **Known for:** tough-to-get reservations; freshly baked bread; seasonal ingredients. [$] *Average main: $34* ✉ *199 Gough St., Hayes Valley* ☎ *415/355–9085* 🌐 *www.richtablesf.com* 🕓 *No lunch.*

Robin

$$$$ | SUSHI | The classic Japanese *omakase* experience (the chefs select the sushi and other small bites for guests) gets translated with a distinct seasonal Californian influence at Adam Tortosa's hip, modern restaurant made up of counter seats and a handful of tables. It's been packed since it opened in 2017 and for good reason—the raw fish preparations are magnificent, and it's a relative deal where diners can name the price between $89 and $189, depending on their desire to splurge. **Known for:** exquisite nigiri with creative garnishes; caviar–potato chip bite; equally strong sake and wine lists. [$] *Average main: $120* ✉ *620 Gough St., Hayes Valley* ☎ *415/548–2429 text only*

🌐 *robinsanfrancisco.com* ⏲ *Closed Mon. and Tues. No lunch.*

Souvla
$ | **GREEK** | Join the lines, get ready to Instagram, and enjoy the superb Cali-Greek pita sandwiches and salads at the flagship of this small, slowly growing San Francisco fast-casual (or self-described "fast-fine") concept. The menu keeps it simple with four proteins (roasted white sweet potato or a trio of spit-roasted meats), but the secret to the magic is how each protein is prepartnered with captivating sauces and fresh garnishes (same for salads and sandwiches), turning a simple-sounding white sweet potato sandwich into a stellar meal. **Known for:** lamb leg with harissa-spiked yogurt; Greek frozen yogurt with baklava crumbles; prime location for picking up a picnic for Patricia's Green or Alamo Square Park. [$] *Average main: $15* ✉ *517 Hayes St., Hayes Valley* ☎ *415/400–5458* 🌐 *www.souvla.com.*

Suppenküche
$$ | **GERMAN** | Nobody goes hungry—and no beer drinker goes thirsty—at this lively, hip outpost of simple German cooking in Hayes Valley. The hearty food—bratwurst and sauerkraut, potato pancakes with house-made applesauce, meat loaf, braised beef, pork loin, schnitzel, spaetzle—is tasty and kind to your wallet, and the imported brews are first-rate. **Known for:** seating at common tables; any of the sausages; quick service. [$] *Average main: $26* ✉ *525 Laguna St., Hayes Valley* ☎ *415/252–9289* 🌐 *www.suppenkuche.com* ⏲ *Closed Mon. No lunch weekdays.*

★ Zuni Café
$$$ | **MODERN AMERICAN** | After one bite of Zuni's succulent brick-oven-roasted whole chicken with warm bread salad, you'll understand why the two-floor café is a perennial star. Its long copper bar is a hub for a disparate mix of patrons who commune over oysters on the half shell and cocktails and wine. **Known for:** seasonal Californian cooking at its best; under-the-radar lunch and late-night burger; beloved margarita. [$] *Average main: $35* ✉ *1658 Market St., Hayes Valley* ☎ *415/552–2522* 🌐 *zunicafe.com* ⏲ *Closed Mon. and Tues.*

Coffee and Quick Bites

Johnny Doughnuts
$ | **BAKERY** | **FAMILY** | San Francisco diners used to drive to Marin County or track down a traveling truck to enjoy the namesake specialty of this outstanding shop before it settled down in a sunlight-drenched space with a few tables. The dreamy, fluffy doughnuts made with organic wheat flour (milled at cool temperatures for freshness) and local ingredients might be the city's best, whether it's a strawberry-peach-jam-filled Bismarck or a chocolate-glazed vegan doughnut (which uses roasted sweet potato). **Known for:** creative flavors; coffee drinks using beans from Equator roastery in Marin; crodough (a croissant-doughnut). [$] *Average main: $5* ✉ *392 Fulton St., Hayes Valley* ☎ *415/400–5078* 🌐 *www.johnnydoughnuts.com.*

Hotels

Hayes Valley should be called Hip Valley. Head-turning urbanites stroll past the boutiques, cafés, and high-end eateries day and night. But this wasn't always the case, and there still is a dodgy element to the streets off the main drag. Travelers can find a couple modest inns atop gourmet eateries.

Inn at the Opera
$$ | **B&B/INN** | Within walking distance of Davies Symphony Hall and the War Memorial Opera House, this inn with small rooms with dark wood furnishings caters to season-ticket holders for the opera, ballet, and symphony; it's also been the choice for stars of the music, dance, and opera worlds, from Luciano Pavarotti to Mikhail Baryshnikov. **Pros:** staff goes the extra mile; good on-site

dining; prime location but a quiet block. **Cons:** no air-conditioning; sold out far in advance during opera season; difficult parking. [$] *Rooms from: $215* ✉ *333 Fulton St., Hayes Valley* ☎ *415/863–8400,* 🌐 *www.shellhospitality.com/inn-at-the-opera* 🛏 *48 rooms* 🍴 *Free Breakfast.*

★ The Parsonage

$$ | B&B/INN | The two owners of this 1883 Victorian house, a historic landmark, have created a one-of-a-kind bed-and-breakfast steps from the lower Haight and Hayes Valley, with many of the original mantelpieces, fireplaces, and mirrors, as well as the ornate ceiling molding, still intact. **Pros:** handmade McRoskey mattresses; relaxed, welcoming atmosphere; superior breakfasts. **Cons:** street parking only; bygone-era feel not for everyone; two-night minimum. [$] *Rooms from: $260* ✉ *198 Haight St., Hayes Valley* ☎ *415/863–3699* 🌐 *www.theparsonage.com* 🛏 *5 rooms* 🍴 *Free Breakfast.*

🍸 Nightlife

Chic Hayes Valley is known for its wine and cocktail lounges with dark lighting and plenty of atmosphere, making it easy to spend a pleasant evening moving from bar to bar and having small bites.

BARS

Absinthe Brasserie & Bar

BARS/PUBS | The popular restaurant's nearly two dozen specialty cocktails—or even a plain old Manhattan—make a trip just to the bar worthwhile. The classic but modern French cuisine, California and French wines, and beautiful vintage bistro decor are terrific, too, so it's best to pair a cocktail with a few bites before or after a show. ✉ *398 Hayes St., at Gough St., Hayes Valley* ☎ *415/551–1590* 🌐 *absinthe.com.*

Anina

BARS/PUBS | This floral-and-tropics-themed bar boasts one of the prime patios in San Francisco (come early or it's in the shadows), plus excellent, non-fussy craft cocktails. Next door, its sibling bar, Brass Tacks, has equally noteworthy cocktails but a completely different, dimly lit, intimate atmosphere. ✉ *482 Hayes St., Hayes Valley* 🌐 *www.aninasf.com.*

Birba

WINE BARS—NIGHTLIFE | With a charming rear garden and an excellent selection of lesser-known European vintages, this wine bar is a local favorite for a leisurely happy hour or date night. It's a little removed from the main Hayes Valley action, so the crowd tends to be regulars, who come in frequently to try a new Greek rosé or a Touriga from Portugal. Bites are limited to mostly cheese, charcuterie, and smoked or tinned fish, but everything is beautifully composed. ✉ *458 Grove St., Hayes Valley* 🌐 *www.birbawine.com.*

Fig & Thistle

WINE BARS—NIGHTLIFE | The Golden State's wines are the specialty at this rustic-feeling bar with a relaxed vibe; the tall windows overlook busy Gough Street. Natural and biodynamic wines from the greater West Coast and around the world are also poured, pairing nicely with cheese selections. ✉ *429 Gough St., Hayes Valley* ☎ *415/651–9905* 🌐 *www.figandthistlesf.com.*

Hôtel Biron Wine Bar and Art Gallery

WINE BARS—NIGHTLIFE | Sharing an alley-like block with the backs of Market Street restaurants, this tiny, cavelike (in a good way) spot displays the work of local artists on its brick walls. The well-behaved twenty- to thirtysomething clientele enjoys the off-the-beaten-path quarters, the wines from around the world, the soft lighting, and the hip music. ✉ *45 Rose St., off Market St. near Gough St., Hayes Valley* ☎ *415/703–0403.*

The Mint Karaoke Lounge

BARS/PUBS | A mixed gay-straight crowd that's drop-dead serious about its karaoke—to the point where you'd think an *American Idol* casting agent was in attendance—comes here seven nights a week. Regulars sing everything from Simon and Garfunkel songs to disco classics in front of an attentive audience. Do *not* walk onstage unprepared! Check out the songbook online to perfect your debut before you attempt to take the mic. Hit the ATM beforehand, as everything here is cash-only. ⊠ *1942 Market St., between Duboce Ave. and Laguna St., Hayes Valley* ☏ *415/626–4726* ⊕ *themint.net.*

★ **Smuggler's Cove**

BARS/PUBS | With the decor of a pirate ship and a slew of rum-based cocktails, you half expect Captain Jack Sparrow to sidle up next to you at this offbeat, Disney-esque hangout. But the folks at Smuggler's Cove take rum so seriously they've even had it made for them from distillers around the world, which you can sample along with more than 550 other offerings. A punch card is provided so you can try the entire menu (featuring 80-plus cocktails). The small space fills up quickly, so arrive early. The same owner also has a gin-centric cocktail bar, Whitechapel, a few blocks away on Polk Street, where the cocktails are equally special and the outrageous decor echoes a vintage London Underground station. ⊠ *650 Gough St., at McAllister St., Hayes Valley* ☏ *415/869–1900* ⊕ *www.smugglerscovesf.com.*

🎭 Performing Arts

DANCE
RAWdance CONCEPT Series

DANCE | This modern-day salon is made for both dance aficionados and those just ballet-curious. The choreography is colorful and "outside the lines" of your usual dance troupe. In true bohemian spirit, admission is pay-what-you-can (suggested donation is $10–$25), and sometimes food is served as well. ⊠ *1446 Market St., Hayes Valley* ☏ *415/729–3959* ⊕ *rawdance.org.*

MUSIC
★ **SFJAZZ Center**

MUSIC | Jazz legends Branford Marsalis and Herbie Hancock have performed at the snazzy center, as have Rosanne Cash, Dianne Reeves, and world-music favorite Esperanza Spalding. The sight lines and acoustics here are impressive, as are the second-floor tile murals. Shows often sell out quickly. ⊠ *201 Franklin St., Hayes Valley* ☏ *866/920–5299* ⊕ *www.sfjazz.org.*

🛍 Shopping

A community park called Hayes Green breaks up a crowd of cool shops just west of Civic Center. Art galleries and stores selling hip home decor, clothing, shoes, and handcrafted jewelry predominate. The density of unique shops and the absence of chains make Hayes Valley a favorite destination for local shoppers.

BOOKS
The Green Arcade

BOOKS/STATIONERY | For environmental, political, and sustainable books, look no further. With deep roots in the community, energetic artwork, and an atmosphere that encourages reading, this is a good place to hide away; the comfy chairs and warm vibe make it hard to leave. ⊠ *1680 Market St., at Gough St., Hayes Valley* ☏ *415/431–6800* ⊕ *thegreenarcade.com.*

Isotope Comic Book Lounge

BOOKS/STATIONERY | For full-frontal nerdity in a chic modern setting, pay a visit to SF's premier comic book hangout. You'll find a great selection of graphic novels and artwork by popular and local artists, as well as lively after-hours events. ⊠ *326 Fell St., at Gough St., Hayes Valley* ☏ *415/621–6543* ⊕ *www.isotopecomics.com.*

CLOTHING
Dish
CLOTHING | Many of the women's clothes displayed within this spare space are romantic, minus the frills. Look for the chic dresses of local designer Kathryn McCarron, as well as clothing and accessories by more widely known brands like MOTHER Denim and Apiece Apart. ⊠ *541 Hayes St., between Laguna and Octavia Sts., Hayes Valley* ☎ *415/252–5997* ⊕ *www.dishboutique.com.*

FOOD AND DRINK
Arlequin Wine Merchant
WINE/SPIRITS | If you like the wine list at Absinthe Brasserie & Bar, you can walk next door and pick up a few bottles from its highly regarded joint establishment. This small, unintimidating shop carries hard-to-find wines from small producers. Why wait to taste? Crack open a bottle on the patio of sibling restaurant Arbor out back. ⊠ *384 Hayes St., near Gough St., Hayes Valley* ☎ *415/863–1104* ⊕ *www.arlequinwinemerchant.com.*

Miette Patisserie & Confiserie
FOOD/CANDY | There is truly nothing sweeter than a cellophane bag tied with colorful ribbon and filled with malt balls or floral meringues from this Insta-friendly candy and pastry store. Grab a gingerbread cupcake or a tantalizing macaron or some shortbread. The pastel-color cake stands make even window-shopping a treat. It's open Thursday–Sunday. ⊠ *449 Octavia Blvd., between Hayes and Linden Sts., Hayes Valley* ☎ *415/626–6221* ⊕ *www.miette.com.*

True Sake
WINE/SPIRITS | Though it would be reasonable to expect a Japanese aesthetic at the first store in the United States dedicated entirely to sake, you might instead hear dance music thumping quietly in the background while you browse. Each of the many sakes is displayed with a label describing the drink's qualities, with food-pairing suggestions. ⊠ *560 Hayes St., between Laguna and Octavia Sts., Hayes Valley* ☎ *415/355–9555* ⊕ *www.truesake.com.*

HANDICRAFTS AND FOLK ART
F. Dorian
CRAFTS | In addition to scarves, jewelry, and other crafts from around the world, this decorative-arts store carries brightly colored glass and ceramic works by local and international artisans, plus beautiful votive candles. ⊠ *370 Hayes St., between Franklin and Gough Sts., Hayes Valley* ☎ *415/861–3191* ⊕ *www.fdorian.com.*

JEWELRY AND ACCESSORIES
Metier
JEWELRY/ACCESSORIES | For boutique shopping that's anything but hit or miss, browse through this unusual selection of jewelry by artists like Gabriella Kiss, Harwell Godfrey, and Gillian Conroy. The one-of-a-kind rings, charms, and pendants have won this boutique an obsessively loyal following. Shopping is by appointment only. ⊠ *546 Laguna St., between Linden and Hayes Sts., Hayes Valley* ☎ *415/590–2998* ⊕ *www.metiersf.com.*

SHOES
Paolo Shoes
SHOES/LUGGAGE/LEATHER GOODS | If you're looking for gorgeous handcrafted Italian leather shoes, this is *the* place in San Francisco to find them. From knee-high boots to contoured heel pumps, Paolo Iantorno's selection will make your heart miss a beat. The prices might as well; they hover around the $250 mark, but all shoes are made in quantities of 25 or fewer pairs. ⊠ *524 Hayes St., between Octavia and Laguna Sts., Hayes Valley* ☎ *415/552–4580* ⊕ *paoloshoes.com.*

Chapter 5

NOB HILL AND RUSSIAN HILL

WITH POLK GULCH

Updated by
Trevor Felch

 Sights
★★☆☆☆

 Restaurants
★★★☆☆

 Hotels
★★★★☆

 Shopping
★★☆☆☆

 Nightlife
★★☆☆☆

NEIGHBORHOOD SNAPSHOT

TOP EXPERIENCES

■ **Macondray Lane:** Duck into this secret, lush garden lane and walk its narrow, uneven cobblestones.

■ **Vallejo Steps area:** Make the steep climb up to lovely Ina Coolbrith Park, then continue up along the glorious garden path of the Vallejo Steps to a spectacular view at the top.

■ **San Francisco Art Institute:** Contemplate a Diego Rivera mural and stop at the café for cheap organic coffee and a priceless view of the city and the bay. It may be the best—and cheapest—way to spend an hour in the neighborhood.

■ **Cable Car Museum:** Ride a cable car all the way back to the barn, hanging on tight as it *clack-clack-clacks* its way up Nob Hill, and then go behind the scenes at the museum.

■ **Playing "Bullitt" on the steep streets:** For the ride of your life, take a drive up and down the city's steepest streets on Russian Hill. A trip over the precipice of Filbert or Jones will make you feel as if you're falling off the edge of the world.

GETTING HERE

The thing about Russian and Nob Hills is that they're both especially steep hills. If you're not up for the hike, a cable car is certainly the most exciting way to reach the top. Take the California line for Nob Hill and the Powell–Hyde line for Russian Hill. Buses serve the area as well, such as the 1–California bus for Nob Hill, but the routes run only east–west. The cable cars tackle the steeper north–south streets. Driving yourself is a hassle, since parking is a challenge on these crowded, precipitous streets.

PLANNING YOUR TIME

■ Since walking Nob Hill is (almost) all about gazing at exteriors, touring the neighborhood during daylight hours is a must. The sights here don't require a lot of visiting time—say a half hour each at the Cable Car Museum and Grace Cathedral—but allow time for the walk itself. An afternoon visit is ideal for Russian Hill, so you can browse the shops. You could cover both neighborhoods in three or four hours. Finish up with a sunset cocktail at a swanky hotel lounge or the retro-tiki Tonga Room.

QUICK BITES

■ **The Boy's Deli.** Tucked into the back of a tiny produce market is a counter serving up some of the biggest, juiciest, best sandwiches in town for lunch—strictly to go. Try the turkey-bacon-pesto Sanfranpsycho sandwich. ⊠ *Polk & Green Produce Market, 2222 Polk St., between Green and Vallejo Sts., Russian Hill* ⊕ theboysdeli.com.

■ **Swensen's Ice Cream.** The original Swensen's has been a neighborhood favorite for traditional ice cream since it opened in 1948. An antique sign still fronts the tiny, cash-only shop. ⊠ *1999 Hyde St., at Union St., Russian Hill* ⊕ www.swensensicecream.com.

In place of the quirky charm and cultural diversity that mark other San Francisco neighborhoods, Nob Hill exudes history and good breeding. Topped with some of the city's most elegant hotels, gloriously Gothic Grace Cathedral, and private blue-blood social clubs, it's the pinnacle of privilege. One hill over, across Pacific Avenue, is another old-family bastion, Russian Hill. It may not be quite as wealthy as Nob Hill, but it's no slouch—and it's got jaw-dropping views.

Nob Hill

Nob Hill was officially dubbed during the 1870s when the "Big Four"—Charles Crocker, Leland Stanford, Mark Hopkins, and Collis P. Huntington, who were involved in the construction of the transcontinental railroad—built their hilltop estates. The lingo is thick from this era: those on the hilltop were referred to as "nabobs" (originally meaning a provincial governor from India) and "swells," and the hill itself was called Snob Hill, a term that survives to this day. By 1882 so many estates had sprung up on Nob Hill that Robert Louis Stevenson called it "the hill of palaces." The 1906 earthquake and fire, though, destroyed all the palatial mansions except for portions of the James Flood brownstone. History buffs may choose to linger here, but for most visitors, a casual glimpse from a cable car will be enough.

⇨ *For more details on the Cable Car Museum, see the Cable Cars feature in Chapter 1, Experience San Francisco.*

 Sights

Cable Car Museum
MUSEUM | FAMILY | One of the city's best free offerings, this museum is an absolute must for kids. You can even ride a cable car here—all three lines stop between Russian Hill and Nob Hill. The facility, which is inside the city's last remaining cable-car barn, takes the top off the system to let you see how it all works. Eternally humming and squealing, the massive powerhouse cable wheels steal the show. You can also climb aboard a vintage car and take the grip, let the kids ring a cable-car bell (briefly), and check out vintage gear dating from 1873. ⊠ *1201 Mason St., at Washington St., Nob Hill* 🕾 *415/474–1887* ⊕ *www.cablecarmuseum.org* 🎫 *Free.*

Collis P. Huntington Park

CITY PARK | The elegant park west of the Pacific Union Club and east of Grace Cathedral occupies the site of a mansion owned by the "Big Four" railroad baron Collis P. Huntington. He died in 1900, the mansion was destroyed in the 1906 fire, and in 1915 his widow—by then married to Huntington's nephew—donated the land to the city for use as a park. The Huntingtons' neighbors, the Crockers, once owned the *Fountain of the Tortoises,* based on the original in Rome's Piazza Mattei. ■TIP➔ **The benches around the fountain offer a welcome break after climbing Nob Hill.** ✉ *Taylor and California Sts., Nob Hill* ⊕ *sfrecpark.org.*

Fairmont San Francisco

HOTEL—SIGHT | The hotel's dazzling opening was delayed a year by the 1906 quake, but since then, the marble palace has hosted presidents, royalty, movie stars, and local nabobs. Things have changed since its early days, however: on the eve of World War I, you could get a room for as low as $2 per night, meals included. Nowadays, prices go as high as $18,000, which buys a night in the eight-room, contemporary art–filled penthouse suite.

Swing through the opulent lobby on your way to tea (served on weekends from 1:30 to 3:30) at the Laurel Court restaurant; peek through the foyer's floor-to-ceiling windows for a glimpse of the hotel's garden and beehives, where the honey served with tea is produced. Don't miss an evening cocktail (a mai tai is in order) in the kitschy Tonga Room, complete with tiki huts and a floating bandstand. When exiting or entering the hotel's main entrance, snap a picture with the 8-foot-tall bronze Tony Bennett statue outside the lobby. This site was selected as the statue's home to commemorate the singer's 90th birthday because his first performance of "I Left My Heart in San Francisco" was in the hotel's Venetian Room. ✉ *950 Mason*

Close-Ups on the Brocklebank ⊙

The grand Brocklebank Apartments, on the northeast corner of Sacramento and Mason Streets across from the Fairmont San Francisco hotel, might look eerily familiar. In 1958 the complex was showcased in Alfred Hitchcock's *Vertigo* (Jimmy Stewart starts trailing Kim Novak here), and in the 1990s it popped up in the television miniseries based on Armistead Maupin's *Tales of the City.*

St., Nob Hill ☎ *415/772–5000* ⊕ *www. fairmont.com/san-francisco.*

★ Grace Cathedral

RELIGIOUS SITE | Not many churches can boast an altarpiece by Keith Haring and two labyrinths, but this one, the country's third-largest Episcopal cathedral, does. The soaring Gothic-style structure took 14 (often interrupted) years to build, beginning in 1927 and eventually wrapping up in 1964. The gilded bronze doors at the east entrance were taken from casts of Lorenzo Ghiberti's incredible *Gates of Paradise,* designed for the Baptistery in Florence, Italy. A sculpture of St. Francis by Beniamino Bufano greets you as you enter.

The 34-foot-wide limestone labyrinth is a replica of the 13th-century stone maze on the floor of Chartres Cathedral. All are encouraged to walk the 1/8-mile-long labyrinth, a ritual based on the tradition of meditative walking. There's also a granite outdoor labyrinth on the church's northeast side. The AIDS Interfaith Chapel, to the right as you enter Grace, contains a bronze triptych by the late artist Keith Haring and panels from the AIDS Memorial Quilt. ■TIP➔ **Especially dramatic times to view the cathedral are during**

Walking the Hills

Start a tour of Nob Hill and Russian Hill with a cable-car ride up to **California** and **Powell Streets** on Nob Hill (all lines go here). Walking two blocks west, you can pass all the Big Four mansions-cum-hotels on the hill. Peek at the Keith Haring triptych in impressive **Grace Cathedral** and stroll around beautiful **Huntington Park**. While on top of the hill, walk over to the southeast corner of Clay and Jones Streets, home to the art-deco Clay-Jones Apartments building (the highest point on Nob Hill). Next, enjoy the view of the Bay Bridge and the Transamerica Pyramid from the intersection, then head down to the **Cable Car Museum** to see the machinery in action. Next, make your way to Russian Hill—a cable car is a fine way to reach the peak—to visit some of the city's loveliest hidden lanes and stairways. At **Mason** and **Vallejo Streets**, head up the **Vallejo Steps**, passing contemplative, terraced **Ina Coolbrith Park** and private gardens. Take in the sweeping city and bay view from the top of the hill, then head right on **Jones Street** and duck under the trellis to shady **Macondray Lane**. For another alleyway photo-op, head a block west to Leavenworth and briefly backtrack south to see **Waldo Alley**, where clever locals dressed up its sign pole with red and white stripes as an ode to the namesake "Where's Waldo" puzzle-book character. From here it's a five-block hike to crooked **Lombard Street**. If you've still got some steam, go another block to see **Diego Rivera's mural** and the surprise panoramic view from the **San Francisco Art Institute**.

Tuesday-evening yoga (6 pm), Thursday-night evensong (5:15 pm), and special holiday programs. ✉ *1100 California St., at Taylor St., Nob Hill* ☎ *415/749–6300* ⊕ *www.gracecathedral.org* ☜ *Free; tours $25.*

InterContinental Mark Hopkins Hotel

HOTEL—SIGHT | Built on the ashes of railroad tycoon Mark Hopkins's grand estate (constructed at his wife's urging; Hopkins himself preferred to live frugally), this 19-story hotel built in 1926 displays a combination of French château and Spanish Renaissance architecture, with noteworthy terra-cotta detailing. Over the decades it has hosted statesmen, royalty, and Hollywood celebrities. The 11-room penthouse was turned into a glass-wall cocktail lounge in 1939: the Top of the Mark is remembered fondly by thousands of World War II veterans who jammed the lounge before leaving for overseas duty. Wives and sweethearts watching the ships depart gave the room's northwest nook its name—Weepers' Corner. ■**TIP**➜ With its 360-degree views, the lounge is a wonderful spot for a grand brunch or a nighttime drink. ✉ *999 California St., at Mason St., Nob Hill* ☎ *415/392–3434* ⊕ *www.sfmarkhopkins.com.*

Nob Hill Masonic Center

ARTS VENUE | Erected by Freemasons in 1957, the hall is familiar to locals mostly as a concert and lecture venue, where such notables as Van Morrison and Al Gore have appeared. But you don't need a ticket to check out the outdoor war memorial or artist Emile Norman's impressive lobby mosaic. Mainly in rich greens and yellows, it depicts the Masons' role in California history. ✉ *1111 California St., Nob Hill* ☎ *415/776–7457* ⊕ *sfmasonic.com.*

Pacific-Union Club

BUILDING | The former home of silver baron James Clair Flood cost a whopping $1.5 million in 1886, when even a stylish Victorian like the Haas-Lilienthal House in Pacific Heights cost less than $20,000. All that cash did buy some structural stability. The Flood residence (to be precise, its shell) was the only Nob Hill mansion to survive the 1906 earthquake and fire. The Pacific-Union Club, a bastion of the wealthy and powerful, purchased the house in 1907 and commissioned Willis Polk to redesign it; the architect added the semicircular wings and third floor. The ornate fence design dates from the mansion's construction. It is now a members-only private social club. ✉ *1000 California St., Nob Hill.*

🍴 Restaurants

Nob Hill, the most famous hill in a city of hills, is known for its iconic hotels—the Fairmont, the Mark, the Ritz-Carlton, the Huntington—and for its views. Unfortunately, the food isn't as unparalleled as the scenic outlooks. Real estate is expensive, so it's not the place for chefs to roll the dice on a new venture. But what you will find are hotel dining rooms and established institutions.

AltoVino

$$$ | **MODERN ITALIAN** | Hiking up Nob Hill can feel like trekking up a mountain, so the "alto" is indeed an apropos part of the name of this Italian neighborhood favorite run by husband-and-wife team Nick Kelly and Calli Martinez (he's the chef; she's the wine director). Kelly's menu effortlessly dances between haute and rustic Italian cooking, often with distinct California elements, and he's a master of pastas and in-house butchery. **Known for:** superior collection of Italian wines; secondi that are actually as special as the primi; beautifully upscale dining room that could be in a Nob Hill mansion. [$] *Average main: $32* ✉ *1358 Mason St., Nob Hill* ☎ *415/529–2435* 🌐 *www.altovinosf.com* 🕒 *Closed Mon. and Tues. No lunch weekdays.*

Del Popolo

$$ | **PIZZA** | **FAMILY** | The puffy, perfectly charred Neapolitan pizzas from this Lower Nob Hill neighborhood bistro-pizzeria are the stuff of legend. Del Popolo gained a cult following after beginning as a state-of-the-art pizza truck outfitted with a wood-fired oven, and the crowds continue to gather nightly for the stellar pies—though being a restaurant means that it also has a convivial, cozy dining room, friendly servers, and great wines. **Known for:** margherita pizza; stunning firewood-filled arch backdrop behind the wood-fired oven; delightful salads and antipasti. [$] *Average main: $20* ✉ *855 Bush St., Nob Hill* ☎ *415/589–7940* 🌐 *delpopolosf.com* 🕒 *Closed Sun. and Mon. No lunch.*

★ Sons & Daughters

$$$$ | **AMERICAN** | The constantly evolving tasting menu that chef-owner Teague Moriarty serves at his standout restaurant serves as a primer for how to do highly seasonal cuisine the right way. Though the preparations are intricate and often luxurious, there is a pretention-free, contemporary type of elegance on the plate and throughout the small, immaculate space that makes this one of the most relaxed (and fun) fine-dining experiences in the city. **Known for:** refined, cozy but chic dining room anchored by an ornate fireplace; excellent house-made bread; attentive service. [$] *Average main: $175* ✉ *708 Bush St., Nob Hill* ☎ *415/994–7933* 🌐 *www.sonsanddaughterssf.com* 🕒 *Closed Mon. and Tues. No lunch.*

☕ Coffee and Quick Bites

The Coffee Movement

$ | **CAFÉ** | Nob Hill's design and architecture tend to be resolutely old-school, except with this impossibly hip coffee shop located right by the Cable Car Museum. Coffee and espresso drinks are excellent here, plus there's a tasting flight of the day's offerings for the most avid coffee nerd. **Known for:** perfect cappucinos; popular with the Instagram set; friendly baristas. [$] *Average main: $5* ✉ *1030 Washington St., Nob Hill* ☎ *510/828–4933* 🌐 *thecoffeemovement.com* 🕐 *No dinner.*

Le Beau Market
$$ | DELI | FAMILY | One block from the highest point of Nob Hill, this is the epicenter of activity for neighborhood residents, who love the dauntless Le Beau, one of the few remaining family-run grocery stores in the city. It's fun to just browse around and soak up the charming atmosphere, and their sandwiches are a highlight. **Known for:** turkey butta sandwich; barbecue chicken sandwich; charming staff and vibe. [$] *Average main: $13* ✉ *1263 Leavenworth St., at Clay St., Nob Hill* ☎ *415/885–3030* 🌐 *www.lebeaumarket.com.*

Hotels

The steep Nob Hill is alive with hostelries proffering treatment fit for (and provided to) kings, queens, and politicians. Stay here, and at the end of a long day of sightseeing, a cable car can whisk you practically to your hotel's doorstep. The dining scene can be a schlep from your hotel, but the allure of sleeping atop San Francisco can erase that inconvenience. Note that many hotels charge "urban fees" or "amenity fees," so you may want to call in advance to confirm the true daily rate.

Fairmont San Francisco
$$$ | HOTEL | Dominating the top of Nob Hill like a European palace, the Fairmont indulges guests in luxury: rooms in the main building, adorned in sapphire blues with platinum and pewter accents, have high ceilings, decadent beds, and marble bathrooms; rooms in the newer Tower, many with fine views, have a neutral color palette with bright-silver notes. **Pros:** huge bathrooms; stunning lobby; great location. **Cons:** some older rooms are small; hills can be challenging for those on foot; $30 per night Urban Experience amenities fee. [$] *Rooms from: $301* ✉ *950 Mason St., Nob Hill* ☎ *415/772–5000, 866/550–4491* 🌐 *www.fairmont.com/san-francisco* 🛏 *606 rooms* 🍴 *No meals.*

Hotel Vertigo
$ | HOTEL | Scenes in Alfred Hitchcock's classic thriller *Vertigo* were shot in this ornate hotel (it was a speakeasy during Prohibition), and designer Thomas Schoos has infused the guest rooms with whimsical tributes—consider the tangerine highlights and the horse-head lamps, not to mention the classic *Vertigo* swirl logo along the walls. **Pros:** tons of personality; artsy decor; central location. **Cons:** borderline neighborhood; no a/c; $20 nightly Urban Fee for Wi-Fi and coffee and tea. [$] *Rooms from: $139* ✉ *940 Sutter St., between Leavenworth and Hyde Sts., Nob Hill* ☎ *415/885–6800, 855/532–2216* 🌐 *www.hotelvertigosf.com* 🛏 *102 rooms* 🍴 *No meals.*

★ The Huntington Hotel
$$ | HOTEL | Stars from Bogart and Bacall to Picasso and Pavarotti have stayed in this hotel famed for its spacious, high-ceilinged rooms and suites, most of which have great views of Grace Cathedral and Huntington Park or the bay and the fog rolling across the city skyline. **Pros:** good-size rooms; first-rate spa with city views; impressive service from greeting to farewell. **Cons:** up a steep hill from downtown; expensive restaurant; ultracontemporary aesthetic doesn't work for some guests. [$] *Rooms from: $266* ✉ *1075 California St., Nob Hill* ☎ *415/474–5400* 🌐 *www.huntingtonhotel.com* 🛏 *134 rooms* 🍴 *No meals.*

InterContinental Mark Hopkins
$$ | HOTEL | The circular redbrick drive of this towering 1926 architectural landmark leads to an opulent, mirrored, marble-floor lobby that's the gateway to luxurious rooms aglow with gold,

cream, and yellow tones. **Pros:** spectacular views from upper floors; steeped in history; last-minute deals often possible online. **Cons:** decor too old-style for some guests; small bathrooms in some rooms and suites; steep climb from Union Square. [$] *Rooms from: $209* ✉ *999 California St., Nob Hill* ☎ *415/392–3434* 🌐 *www.intercontinentalmarkhopkins.com* 🛏 *380 rooms* 🍴 *No meals.*

Petite Auberge

$ | **B&B/INN** | The French provincial room decor of Petite Auberge—bright flowered wallpaper and an armoire that compensates for little or no closet space—pleases Francophiles seeking Old World charm. **Pros:** a classic hotel with strong character that doesn't feel old; cute outdoor courtyard; personalized service. **Cons:** guests staying front of house complain of street noise; lowest price rooms can be too tight of a squeeze; limited amenities. [$] *Rooms from: $189* ✉ *863 Bush St., Nob Hill* ☎ *415/928–6000* 🌐 *www.petiteaubergesf.com* 🛏 *26 rooms* 🍴 *Free breakfast.*

★ The Ritz-Carlton, San Francisco

$$$ | **HOTEL** | A tribute to beauty and attentive, professional service, the Ritz-Carlton emphasizes luxury and elegance, which are evident in the Ionic columns that grace the neoclassical facade and the crystal chandeliers that illuminate marble floors and walls in the lobby. **Pros:** terrific service; beautiful furnishings throughout; lobby wine-tasting lounge. **Cons:** nothing is a bargain; hilly location; no pool. [$] *Rooms from: $364* ✉ *600 Stockton St., at Pine St., Nob Hill* ☎ *415/296–7465, 800/542–8680* 🌐 *www.ritzcarlton.com/sanfrancisco* 🛏 *336 rooms* 🍴 *No meals.*

Stanford Court San Francisco

$$ | **HOTEL** | Railroad baron Leland Stanford's mansion once stood at the top-tier central location where the Stanford Court is today, and the warm tones and handsome leather chairs are reminiscent of a grander time. **Pros:** attention to technological detail; classic yet modern style; off-season packages. **Cons:** $30 nightly Urban Bundle fee ; cheaper rooms are small and lack much design interest; exterior rooms get outside noise. [$] *Rooms from: $254* ✉ *905 California St., Nob Hill* ☎ *415/989–3500* 🌐 *www.stanfordcourt.com* 🛏 *393 rooms* 🍴 *No meals.*

White Swan Inn

$ | **B&B/INN** | A cozy library with a crackling fireplace and comfortable chairs and sofas is the heart of this inviting English-style bed-and-breakfast, a sister property to the French-style Petite Auberge next door. **Pros:** cozy antidote to nearby chain hotels; nice lounge and patio area; unique touches like board games and its own city treasure hunt. **Cons:** thin walls can make for noisy rooms; nearby streets can feel gritty at night; some rooms in need of an update. [$] *Rooms from: $169* ✉ *845 Bush St., Nob Hill* ☎ *415/775–1755* 🌐 *www.whiteswaninnsf.com* 🛏 *26 rooms* 🍴 *Free Breakfast.*

🍸 Nightlife

Whether you're wandering the streets or kicking back inside a bar, Nob Hill delivers fantastic city views, the very best of which can be experienced from the Top of the Mark.

BARS

★ Big 4 Bar

BARS/PUBS | Dark-wood paneling and green leather banquettes lend a masculine feel to the bar at the Huntington Hotel, where the over-30 crowd orders single-malt Scotch and stiff martinis. To accompany your whiskey, try the potpies or French onion soup. This place is a San Francisco history lesson and trip back in time, complete with nightly piano music. To get more out of the experience, read up on the Big Four railroad barons—Stanford, Hopkins, Crocker, and the hotel's namesake—before you go. ✉ *The Huntington Hotel, 1075 California St., at Taylor St., Nob Hill* ☎ *415/771–1140* 🌐 *www.huntingtonhotel.com.*

Stookey's Club Moderne

BARS/PUBS | With swing jazz on the soundtrack, bartenders in white jackets, and an immaculately detailed 1930s art-deco interior, it's always a trip back to the Bing Crosby–Ella Fitzgerald era at this charming Lower Nob Hill cocktail bar. The drinks on the menu are as classic and timeless as the Victrola in the back corner. ✉ *895 Bush St., Nob Hill* ☎ *415/771–9695* ⊕ *www.stookeysclub-moderne.com.*

Tonga Room and Hurricane Bar

BARS/PUBS | Since the 1940s, the Tonga Room has supplied the city with high Polynesian kitsch. Fake palm trees, grass huts, a lagoon (three-piece combos play pop standards on a floating barge), and faux monsoons—courtesy of sprinkler-system rain and simulated thunder and lightning—grow more surreal as you quaff the bar's signature mai tais and other fruit-flavored cocktails. Avoid peak times because both locals and tourists love this tropical getaway on weekend evenings. ✉ *Fairmont San Francisco, 950 Mason St., at California St., Nob Hill* ☎ *415/772–5144* ⊕ *www. tongaroom.com.*

Top of the Mark

BARS/PUBS | A famous magazine photograph immortalized the bar atop the Mark Hopkins as a hot spot for World War II servicemen on leave or about to ship out. The view remains sensational. Entertainment on many evenings ranges from solo jazz piano to six-piece jazz ensembles (sometimes with a cover charge). Drinks and small bites can vary in quality, but you're really here to drink in the view and history. ✉ *InterContinental Mark Hopkins, 999 California St., at Mason St., Nob Hill* ☎ *415/392–3434* ⊕ *www.topofthemark.com.*

Shopping

With superb vistas and European-st[yle] shops and eateries, this leafy neighbo[r]hood is a favorite destination for Saturday-morning and after-work shoppers.

CLOTHING

Cris

CLOTHING | This upscale designer consignment shop for women (the locals' best-kept secret) is full of nearly new items for a lot less than new prices. Chloé and Chanel are a couple of the many high-end labels to grace the racks. Not only is this shop brimming with one-of-a-kind tops, dresses, and coats, but it smells like a spring garden. To top it all off, they include a sprig of fresh flowers with every purchase. ✉ *1813 Polk St., Nob Hill* ✛ *between Washington and Jackson Sts.* ☎ *415/474–1191* ⊕ *shopcrisconsignment. com* ⊘ *Closed Mon. and Tues.*

Activities

SPAS

Nob Hill Spa

FITNESS/HEALTH CLUBS | Warning: after experiencing this serene and luxurious spa's treatments, you'll start to *expect* champagne after a massage. Unique features include the eucalyptus steam bath and a gorgeous infinity pool that overlooks the city through a glass wall. Following your appointment, you can hang here: relax in the Zen room or just read on the sundeck. Regulars love the 80-minute Nourishing Seaweed facial, the 50-minute Lavender Salt Scrub skin-exfoliation treatment, and the Table Thai massage, 80 minutes of pure indulgence. ✉ *The Huntington Hotel, 1075 California St., at Mason St., Nob Hill* ☎ *415/345–2888* ⊕ *www.hunting-tonhotel.com* ☞ *Massages and scrubs from $170.*

Sights ▼

Restaurants ▼

Quick Bites ▼

Hotels ▼

Russian Hill

Essentially a tony residential neighborhood of spiffy pieds-à-terre, Victorian flats, Edwardian cottages, and boxlike condos, Russian Hill has some of the city's loveliest stairway walks, sweetest hidden garden-ways, and steepest streets—not to mention wonderful bay views. Several stories explain the origin of Russian Hill's name. One legend has it that Russian farmers raised vegetables here for Farallon Islands seal hunters; another attributes the name to a Russian sailor of prodigious drinking habits who drowned when he fell into a well on the hill. A plaque at the top of the Vallejo Steps gives credence to the version that says sailors of the Russian-American Company were buried here in the 1840s. Be sure to visit the sign for yourself—its location offers perhaps the finest vantage point on the hill.

Sights

★ Ina Coolbrith Park

CITY PARK | If you make it all the way up here, you may have the place all to yourself, or at least feel like you do. The park's terraces are carved from a hill so steep that it's difficult to see if anyone else is there or not. Locals love this park because it feels like a secret no one else knows about—one of the city's magic hidden gardens, with a meditative setting and spectacular views of the bay peeking out from among the trees. A poet, Oakland librarian, and niece of Mormon prophet Joseph Smith, Ina Coolbrith introduced Jack London and Isadora Duncan to the world of books. For years she entertained literary greats in her Macondray Lane home near the park. In 1915 she was named poet laureate of California. ⊠ *Vallejo St. between Mason and Taylor Sts., Russian Hill* ⊕ *www. sfparksalliance.org.*

★ Lombard Street

NEIGHBORHOOD | The block-long "Crookedest Street in the World" makes eight switchbacks down the east face of Russian Hill between Hyde and Leavenworth Streets. Residents bemoan the traffic jam outside their front doors, but the throngs continue. Join the line of cars waiting to drive down the steep hill, or avoid the whole mess and walk down the steps on either side of Lombard. You take in super views of North Beach and Coit Tower whether you walk or drive—though if you're the one behind the wheel, you'd better keep your eye on the road lest you become yet another of the many folks who ram the garden barriers. ■TIP→ **Can't stand the traffic? Thrill seekers of a different stripe may want to head two blocks south of Lombard to Filbert Street. At a gradient of 31.5%, the hair-raising descent between Hyde and Leavenworth Streets is one of the city's steepest. Go slowly!** ⊠ *Lombard St. between Hyde and Leavenworth Sts., Russian Hill.*

★ Macondray Lane

NEIGHBORHOOD | San Francisco has no shortage of impressive, grand homes, but Macondray Lane is the quintessential hidden garden. Enter under a lovely wooden trellis and proceed down a quiet, cobbled pedestrian lane lined with Edwardian cottages and flowering plants and trees. A flight of steep wooden stairs at the end of the lane leads to Taylor Street—on the way down you can't miss the bay views. If you've read any of Armistead Maupin's *Tales of the City* books, you may find the lane vaguely familiar. It's the thinly disguised setting for parts of the series' action. ⊠ *Between Jones and Taylor Sts., and Union and Green Sts., Russian Hill.*

San Francisco Art Institute

COLLEGE | The number-one reason for a visit to this art college is Mexican master Diego Rivera's *The Making of a Fresco Showing the Building of a City* (1931), in the student gallery to your immediate left inside the entrance. Rivera himself is in the fresco—his broad behind is to the viewer—and he's surrounded by his assistants. They in turn are surrounded by a construction scene, laborers, and city notables, such as sculptor Ralph Stackpole and architect Timothy Pflueger. *Making* is one of three San Francisco murals painted by Rivera. The school itself has seen substantial changes on the academic side because of budget issues and the COVID-19 pandemic, but the mural still remains, as does the panoramic view from the courtyard café.

The **Walter & McBean Galleries** (*415/749–4563; closed Sun. and Mon.*) exhibit the often provocative works of established artists. ✉ *800 Chestnut St., Russian Hill* ☎ *415/771–7020* 🌐 *sfai.edu* 🎟 *Galleries free.*

★ Vallejo Steps

VIEWPOINT | Several Russian Hill buildings survived the 1906 earthquake and fire and remain standing. Patriotic firefighters saved what's become known as the **Flag House** (*1652–56 Taylor St.*) when they spotted the American flag on the property. The owner, a flag collector, fearing the house would burn, wanted it to go down with "all flags flying." At the southwest corner of Ina Coolbrith Park, it is one of a number of California shingle–style homes in this neighborhood, several of which the architect Willis Polk designed.

Polk drew up the plans for the nearby **Polk-Williams House** (*Taylor and Vallejo Sts.*) and lived in one of its finer sections, and he was responsible for **1034–1036 Vallejo,** across the street. He also laid out the Vallejo Steps themselves, which climb the steep ridge across Taylor Street from the Flag House. The precipitous walk up to Ina Coolbrith Park and beyond is possibly the most pleasurable thing to do while on Russian Hill, rewarding you with glorious views. **■ TIP→ If the walk up the steps will be too taxing, park at the top by heading east on Vallejo from Jones and enjoy the scene from there.** ✉ *Taylor and Vallejo Sts., steps lead up toward Jones St., Russian Hill.*

🍴 Restaurants

Despite its name, don't expect Russian food here. Instead, this area bordering Nob Hill caters to the post-college crowds, who want to live near buzzy Polk Street. They mix in with the upper-crust San Franciscans who live in the art-deco high-rises with views. Many romantic bistros are tucked away on tree-lined Hyde Street.

Elephant Sushi

$$ | **SUSHI** | Excellent, somewhat affordable sushi is the main event at this locals' favorite, so get ready to add your name to the waiting list; then watch the cable cars go by on Hyde Street. Luckily, post-wait, the creative sushi rolls and excellent, high-quality fish, as nigiri or sashimi, are always a delight. **Known for:** homey, casual spot; prime seats watching sushi chefs at back counter; no reservations, so substantial waits at peak times. [$] *Average main: $25* ✉ *1916 Hyde St., Russian Hill* ☎ *415/440–1905* ⏲ *Closed Mon. No lunch.*

Harris' Restaurant

$$$$ | **STEAKHOUSE** | Red-meat connoisseurs will appreciate this old-school restaurant, home to some of the best dry-aged steaks in town, including Kobe-style Wagyu rib eye, which guests can see aging in a window along the street. Take this opportunity to enjoy a generous martini or Manhattan, and you may feel transported back in time at one of the city's few lavish, wood-paneled classic steakhouses. **Known for:** classic atmosphere with horseshoe-shaped leather booths; extensive wine list; live jazz. [$] *Average main: $60* ✉ *2100 Van Ness Ave., Russian Hill* ☎ *415/673–1888* 🌐 *www.harrisrestaurant.com* ⏲ *Closed Mon. dinner. No lunch.*

Helmand Palace

$$ | **AFGHAN** | This handsomely outfitted spot will introduce you to the aromas and tastes of traditional Afghan cooking, including sauces and spices that recall India's cuisine as well as an emphasis on lamb that brings to mind Turkey and Greece. Highlights of the reasonably priced menu include *aushak* (leek-filled ravioli served with yogurt and ground beef) and *kaddo* (a sweet-savory dish of sugared pumpkin in a beef sauce). **Known for:** basmati rice pudding; neighborhood gem; generous portions. [$] *Average main: $19* ✉ *2424 Van Ness Ave., Russian Hill* ☎ *415/345–0072* 🌐 *www.helmandsf.com* 🕑 *No lunch.*

Seven Hills

$$$ | **MODERN ITALIAN** | Just before the COVID-19 pandemic, this longtime Nob Hill favorite moved a few blocks down the Hyde Street cable-car line into a new, far more spacious home in Russian Hill. The setting might be livelier and grander, but the consistently excellent contemporary-upscale Italian cuisine and superb wine list remain as great as ever. **Known for:** excellent pastas; well-curated wine list focused on Italy and California; any burrata or house-made charcuterie appetizer. [$] *Average main: $32* ✉ *1896 Hyde St., Russian Hill* ☎ *415/775–1550* 🌐 *www.sevenhillssf.com* 🕑 *No lunch.*

Coffee and Quick Bites

Hot Sauce and Panko

$ | **KOREAN FUSION** | After its home in the Inner Richmond was demolished, this quaint, family-run Korean fried chicken–focused establishment moved east to Russian Hill. As in their old digs, the cramped, takeout-centric restaurant still serves quite possibly the leading wings in the city. **Known for:** more than a dozen sauce options (they're for sale, too); waffles for DIY fried chicken sandwiches; closes at 7 pm. [$] *Average main: $12* ✉ *1468 Hyde St., Russian Hill* ☎ *415/359–1908* 🌐 *hotsauceandpanko.com* 🕑 *Closed Mon. and Tues.*

Nightlife

Union Larder

BARS/PUBS | Some call it a wine bar, some call it a restaurant—whatever this cheery, modern industrial–designed Hyde Street spot is, it's truly wonderful and refreshingly casual. A rarity for its length, the excellent list of wines by the glass is always impressive. Nicely composed small plates, cheese, and house-made charcuterie are worthy companions to all the Chardonnay and Zinfandel. ✉ *1945 Hyde St., Russian Hill* ☎ *415/323–4845* 🌐 *unionlarder.com* 🕑 *Closed Mon. No lunch Sun. and Tues.-Thurs.*

Polk Gulch

Polk Gulch, the microhood surrounding north–south Polk Street, hugs the western edges of Nob Hill and Russian Hill but is nothing like either. It's actually two microhoods: Upper Polk Gulch, fairly classy in its northern section, runs from about Union Street south to California Street; Lower Polk Gulch, the rougher southern part, continues down from California to Geary or so.

Polk Gulch was the Castro before the Castro. It was the city's gay neighborhood into the 1970s, hosting San Francisco's first pride parade in 1972 and several festive Halloween extravaganzas. The area became known for transgender bars and gay prostitution but has "straightened" out—lost its edge, some would say. Today the friendly saloon the Cinch, the last remnant of gay Polk, and a few holdovers from that earlier time share space with newer mid-range restaurants, a passel of bars and nightclubs, and some browsable, funky stores, not to mention two great doughnut shops.

Downhill and down-market from its hilltop neighbors, Polk Gulch has seen some gentrification on certain blocks (especially north of California Street) from the tech-boom years of the 2010s, but the Upper Gulch still has a fraternity-house party vibe. The Lower Gulch feels closer in spirit to the edgy Tenderloin, which it borders. Come to see a lively, scrappy, down-to-earth slice of the city that's forever in transition.

🍴 Restaurants

★ Acquerello

$$$$ | ITALIAN | At this true San Francisco dining gem, chef and co-owner Suzette Gresham has elicited plenty of swoons over the years with high-end but soulful Italian cooking that is worth every penny. Her cuttlefish "tagliatelle" is a star of the menu, which features both classic and cutting-edge dishes. **Known for:** sensational prix-fixe dining with a variety of options; city's premier Italian cheese selection; extensive Italian wine list. [$] *Average main: $115* ✉ *1722 Sacramento St., Polk Gulch* ☎ *415/567–5432* 🌐 *www.acquerellosf.com* 🕒 *Closed Sun., Mon. and Tues. No lunch.*

House of Prime Rib

$$$$ | STEAKHOUSE | Simply known as "HOPR" by regulars, Van Ness's temple to a British Sunday roast feast is one of San Francisco's most timeless—and unique—dinner experiences. Waiters continuously wheel the prime rib carving stations around a sprawling complex that feels like the vast dining hall of a Cotswolds manor, complete with fireplaces and chandeliers: it's all quite a production. **Known for:** worthy martinis to go with tender prime rib; ambience of a London high-society club; leaving you too full for dessert. [$] *Average main: $50* ✉ *1906 Van Ness Ave., Polk Gulch* ✣ *between Washington and Jackson Sts.* ☎ *415/885–4605, 415/885–4606* 🌐 *www.houseofprimerib.net* 🕒 *No lunch.*

★ Lord Stanley

$$$ | AMERICAN | Wife-and-husband team Carrie and Rupert Blease bring European training and a Californian sensibility to their sophisticated but approachable Michelin-starred cooking, pairing refined technique with earthy and inventive charm. You may find kimchi dip accompanying *brandade* (creamed cod) beignets, or roast duck served with sweet-and-sour cabbage heart. **Known for:** excellent wine list; new interpretations of California cooking; attentive service. [$] *Average main: $35* ✉ *2065 Polk St., Polk Gulch* ☎ *415/872–5512* 🌐 *www.lordstanleysf.com.*

★ Swan Oyster Depot

$$ | SEAFOOD | Half fish market and half diner, this small, slim, family-run seafood operation, open since 1912, has no tables, just a narrow marble counter with about 18 stools. Some locals come in to buy perfectly fresh salmon, halibut, crabs, and other seafood to take home; everyone else hops onto one of the rickety stools to enjoy a dozen oysters, other shellfish, or a bowl of clam chowder—the only hot food served. **Known for:** memorable Dungeness crab Louie salad; long lines; payment is cash only. [$] *Average main: $26* ✉ *1517 Polk St., Polk Gulch* ☎ *415/673–1101* 🌐 *swanoysterdepot.us* 💳 *No credit cards* 🕒 *Closed Sun. No dinner.*

☕ Coffee and Quick Bites

Bob's Donuts

$ | BAKERY | FAMILY | Polk Street's legendary 24-hour doughnut shop has been a neighborhood anchor since the 1960s. It's a Bay Area favorite for good reason—the homemade doughnuts, whether an apple fritter or classic raised maple, are always excellent, at 10 am or 10 pm. **Known for:** cake crumb doughnut; Bob's Challenge for the most devoted doughnut lovers; timeless, low-key atmosphere with a few tables. [$] *Average main: $3* ✉ *1621 Polk St., Polk Gulch* ☎ *415/776–3141* 🌐 *www.bobsdonutssf.com.*

Maison Danel

$ | CAFÉ | Paris's joie de vivre is everywhere at this *salon de thé*-patisserie-bakery that looks like it should be in Saint-Germain-des-Prés rather than on Polk Street. The sweets and baked goods are just as magnificent as the vintage Parisian atmosphere, making this a joyfully tough place for indecisive pastry lovers. **Known for:** afternoon tea and lunch/brunch; "Paris-San Francisco" version of the famous Paris Breast dessert pastry; macarons. [$] *Average main:* ✉ *1030 Polk St., Polk Gulch* ☎ *415/685–5900* 🌐 *www.maisondanel.com* 🕓 *Closed Tues. and Wed.*

🍸 Nightlife

Sassy, vibrant, and even a little crass, Lower Gulch, the southern half of this neighborhood—Polk Street from Geary Street to a little beyond California Street—was the heart of San Francisco's pre-Castro gay mecca. Things mostly settle down north of California in the Upper Gulch section, though even straight bars like Kozy Kar live up to this hood's feisty reputation.

BARS

Amelie

WINE BARS—NIGHTLIFE | A slice of modern French life, this cozy and romantic wine bar is an ideal spot for oenophiles, with a list strong in French selections. Vintage-theater seating is available up front—perfect for mingling with strangers. The prices are reasonable, the pours handsome. **■ TIP→ Sit at the red-lacquer bar to learn about wine and pick up a French phrase or two.** ✉ *1754 Polk St., at Washington St., Polk Gulch* ☎ *415/292–6916* 🌐 *www.ameliewinebar.com.*

Kozy Kar

BARS/PUBS | Outrageous and full of sexual energy, this tiny space with an even tinier dance floor may be the heterosexual equivalent of San Francisco's gay-bar scene. The drinks are stiff, but if they overwhelm you—or you just want to have fun—there's a waterbed for you to lounge on. Cartoons and '80s movies play on various televisions. Pay attention and you'll catch frames of porn mixed in for good measure, but if you miss them, don't worry: the bar and the floors are lined with vintage centerfolds. It may all be on the racy side, but it's never creepy or uncomfortable. ✉ *1548 Polk St., at Sacramento St., Polk Gulch* ☎ *415/346–5699* 🌐 *www.kozykar.com.*

Macondray

BARS/PUBS | Polk Street has no shortage of bars, but if you're looking for a refined craft cocktail, this relative newcomer named for the famous nearby alley is pretty much the only option. The cheery, plant-filled bar serves excellent, never precious drinks, balancing the line between serious and fun. Curiously, the food menu leans toward seafood like rock crab–stuffed eggs and a signature lobster roll (the owners are from New England). ✉ *2209 Polk St., Polk Gulch* ☎ *415/829–3464* 🌐 *www.macondraysf.com.*

GAY NIGHTLIFE

The Cinch Saloon

BARS/PUBS | This Wild West–motif neighborhood gay bar has pinball machines, pool tables, and a smoking patio. Several theme nights and drag shows are on the schedule. The Cinch is not the least bit trendy, which is part of the charm for regulars. ✉ *1723 Polk St., between Washington and Clay Sts., Polk Gulch* ☎ *415/776–4162.*

Chapter 6

NORTH BEACH

Updated by
Coral Sisk

Sights	Restaurants	Hotels	Shopping	Nightlife
★★☆☆☆	★★★☆☆	★☆☆☆☆	★★★☆☆	★★★★☆

NEIGHBORHOOD SNAPSHOT

TOP EXPERIENCES

■ **Espresso:** Or cappuccino, americano, mocha: however you take your caffeine, this is the neighborhood for it. Grabbing a coffee constitutes sightseeing here, so find a worthy spot and get to work.

■ **Colorful watering holes:** The high concentration of bars with character, like Specs' and Vesuvio, makes North Beach perfect for a pub crawl.

■ **Filbert Steps:** Walk down this dizzying stairway from Telegraph Hill's Coit Tower, past lush private gardens and stunning bay views—and listen for the hill's famous screeching parrots.

■ **Grant Avenue:** Check out independent boutiques, rambling antiques shops, and cavernous old-time bars, all chockablock on narrow Grant Avenue. The best stuff is crowded into the four blocks between Columbus Avenue and Filbert Street.

■ **Browsing books at City Lights:** Illuminate your mind at this Beat-era landmark. Its ample book selection, author events, and keen staff make it just as cool as ever.

QUICK BITES

Liguria Bakery. The Soracco family has been baking Liguria's focaccia *genovese* in North Beach for more than a century, and their fresh-baked Italian flatbreads (such as plain, rosemary, and tomato slathered with green onions) are the city's best. Their oven is the same traditional one they opened with. Bring cash and arrive before noon: when the focaccia is gone, the bakery closes. ⊠ *1700 Stockton St., at Filbert St., North Beach.*

Mario's Bohemian Cigar Store Cafe. This intimate, triangular spot with a beautiful antique oak bar serves great hot focaccia sandwiches, sourcing from Liguria Bakery. Try the toasted combo (ham, salami, cheese), the breaded eggplant, or the meatball drenched in marinara. On sunny days, take your order across the street to Washington Square for a San Francisco picnic. ⊠ *566 Columbus Ave., North Beach.*

GETTING HERE

■ The Powell–Mason cable-car line can drop you within a block of Washington Square Park, in the heart of North Beach. The 30–Stockton and 15–3rd Street buses run to the neighborhood from Market Street. Once you're here, North Beach is a snap to explore on foot. Most of it is relatively flat, but climbing Telegraph Hill to reach Coit Tower is another story entirely.

PLANNING YOUR TIME

■ There's no bad time of day to visit this quarter. The cafés buzz from morning to night, the shops along main drags Columbus Avenue and Broadway tend to stay open until at least 6 or 7 pm, and late-night revelers don't start checking their watches until about 2 am. Sunday is quieter, since some shops close (though the iconic City Lights bookstore is open daily, until midnight).

■ Plan to spend a few hours here. It's all about lingering, and the only major "sightseeing" spot is Coit Tower. The walk up to the tower is strenuous but rewarding; if you can tough it out, make time for it. If you're driving, keep in mind that parking is difficult, especially at night.

San Francisco novelist Herbert Gold called North Beach "the longest-running, most glorious, American bohemian operetta outside Greenwich Village." Indeed, to anyone who has spent some time in its eccentric old bars and cafés, North Beach evokes everything from the Barbary Coast days to the no-less-rowdy Beatnik era.

Italian delis appear frozen in time, rife with homages to writers Jack Kerouac and Allen Ginsberg, and the area is dotted with adult-entertainment meccas nodding to North Beach's bawdy history, the modern equivalent of its once-wild sin city legacy. Although the outdoor café tables seem like a contrived scene of European alfresco dining, the real heart and soul of this part of the city remains inside the iconic enclaves, away from the throngs of tourists.

The neighborhood truly was a beach at the time of the gold rush—the bay extended into the hollow between Telegraph and Russian Hills. Among the first immigrants to Yerba Buena during the early 1840s were young men from the northern provinces of Italy. The Genoese started the fishing industry in the newly renamed boomtown of San Francisco, as well as a much-needed produce business. Later, Sicilians emerged as leaders of the fishing fleets and eventually as proprietors of the seafood restaurants lining Fisherman's Wharf. Meanwhile, their Genoese cousins established banking and manufacturing empires.

North Beach was once an almost exclusively Italian American neighborhood, but today the area's premium rental market has driven away what was left of its Italian residents to other neighborhoods. The neighborhood lies alongside a still-robust Chinese community that is now being joined by transplanted yuppie populations. Still, walk down narrow Romolo Place (off Broadway east of Columbus) or Genoa Place (off Union west of Kearny) or Medau Place (off Filbert west of Grant) and you can catch a hint of the Italian roots of this neighborhood. Locals may think the city's finest Italian restaurants are elsewhere, but North Beach has some gems and is, after all, the place that puts folks in mind of Italian food, with addresses worth seeking out despite some kitschy traps. The street foods of choice are bags of focaccia or massive subs from Liguria Bakery, Molinari's, or Freddie's, eaten warm or cold. Random aromas fill the air: coffee beans, cured salami, Italian *dolce*, and—depending on the corner you've turned—pungent garlic.

A North Beach Walk

To hit the highlights of the neighborhood, start off with a browse at Beat landmark **City Lights Bookstore**. For cool boutique shopping, head north up **Grant Avenue**. Otherwise, it's time to get down to the serious business of people-watching. Make a left onto **Columbus Avenue** when you leave the bookstore and walk the strip until you find a respectable coffee café or pastry display howling your name.

Sugar-loaded, continue down Columbus to **Washington Square**, where you can walk or take the 39 bus up **Telegraph Hill** to Coit Tower's views. Be sure to take in the gorgeous gardens along the **Filbert Steps** on the way down. Finally, reward yourself by returning to **Columbus Avenue** for a drink at one of the atmosphere-steeped watering holes like **Vesuvio** or **Specs'**.

Sights

★ City Lights Bookstore

STORE/MALL | The exterior of this famous literary bookstore is iconic in itself, from the replica of a revolutionary mural destroyed in Chiapas, Mexico, by military forces to the art banners hanging above the windows. Designated a landmark by the city, the hangout of Beat-era writers and independent publishers remains a vital part of San Francisco's literary scene. Browse the three levels of poetry, philosophy, politics, fiction, history, and local zines, to the beat of creaking wood floors.

Back in the day, writers like Allen Ginsberg and Jack Kerouac would do their reading here (and even receive mail in the basement). The late poet Lawrence Ferlinghetti, who cofounded City Lights in 1953, cemented its place in history by publishing Ginsberg's *Howl and Other Poems* in 1956. The small volume was ignored in the mainstream … until Ferlinghetti and the bookstore manager were arrested for obscenity and corruption of youth. In the landmark First Amendment trial that followed, the judge exonerated both men. *Howl* went on to become a classic.

Stroll Kerouac Alley, branching off Columbus Avenue next to City Lights, to read the quotes from Ferlinghetti, Maya Angelou, Confucius, John Steinbeck, and the street's namesake embedded in the pavement. ✉ *261 Columbus Ave., North Beach* ☎ *415/362–8193* ⊕ *www.citylights.com.*

Coit Tower

VIEWPOINT | Among San Francisco's most distinctive skyline sights, this 210-foot tower is often considered a tribute to firefighters because of the donor's special attachment to the local fire company. As the story goes, a young gold rush–era girl, Lillie Hitchcock Coit (known as Miss Lil), was a fervent admirer of her local fire company—so much so that she once deserted a wedding party and chased down the street after her favorite engine, Knickerbocker No. 5, while clad in her bridesmaid finery. When Lillie died in 1929, she left the city $125,000 to "expend in an appropriate manner … to the beauty of San Francisco." You can ride the elevator to the top of the tower to enjoy the 360° view of the Bay Bridge and the Golden Gate Bridge; due north is Alcatraz Island. Most visitors saunter past the 27 fabulous Depression-era murals inside the tower that depict California's economic and political life, but take the time to appreciate the first New

City Lights bookstore is a literary icon with three floors of books and zines.

Deal art project, supported by taxpayer money. It's also possible to walk up and down (if you're in shape): a highlight is the descent toward the Embarcadero via the **Filbert Steps,** a series of stairways that are a shaded green oasis in the middle of the city. ✉ *Telegraph Hill Blvd. , at Greenwich St. or Lombard St., North Beach* ☎ *415/362–0808* ⊕ *sfrecpark.org* ✉ *Free; elevator to top $9.*

Grant Avenue
NEIGHBORHOOD | Originally called Calle de la Fundación, Grant Avenue is the oldest street in the city, but it's got plenty of young blood. Here, dusty bars such as the Saloon mix with independent boutiques and odd curio shops, as well as curated gourmet shops such as Italian Slow Food import store Sotto Casa and fancy wine and cheese shop Little Vine. While the street runs from Union Square through Chinatown, North Beach, and beyond, the fun stuff in this neighborhood is jammed into the four blocks from Columbus Avenue north to Filbert Street. ✉ *North Beach.*

Sentinel Building
BUILDING | A striking triangular shape and a gorgeous green patina make this 1907 flatiron building at the end of Columbus Avenue unmissable, and the Financial District's skyscrapers make a great backdrop for it. In the 1970s local filmmaker Francis Ford Coppola bought the building to use for his production company. The ground floor houses Coppola's swanky wine bar, **Café Zoetrope** . ✉ *916 Kearny St., at Columbus Ave., North Beach.*

★ Telegraph Hill and the Filbert Steps
NEIGHBORHOOD | Residents here have some of the city's best views, as well as the most difficult ascents to their aeries. The hill rises from the east end of Lombard Street to a height of 284 feet and is capped by Coit Tower. If you brave the slope, though, you can be rewarded with a "secret treasure" San Francisco moment. Filbert Street starts up the hill, then becomes the **Filbert Steps** when the going gets too steep. You can cut between the Filbert Steps and another flight, the **Greenwich Steps,** on

The Birds

While on Telegraph Hill, you might be startled by a chorus of piercing squawks and a rushing sound of wings. No, you're not about to have a Hitchcock bird-attack moment. These small, vivid green parrots with cherry-red heads number in the hundreds; they're descendants of former pets that escaped or were released by their owners. (The birds dislike cages, and they bite if bothered ... must've been some disillusioned owners along the way.)

The parrots like to roost high in the aging cypress trees on the hill, chattering and fluttering, sometimes taking wing en masse. They're not popular with some residents, but they did find a champion in local bohemian Mark Bittner, a former street musician. Bittner began chronicling their habits, publishing a book and battling the homeowners who wanted to cut down the cypresses. A 2003 documentary, *The Wild Parrots of Telegraph Hill*, made the issue a cause célèbre. In 2007, City Hall, which recognizes a golden goose when it sees one, stepped in and brokered a solution to keep the celebrity birds in town. The city would cover the homeowners' insurance worries and plant new trees for the next generation of wild parrots.

up to the hilltop. As you climb, you pass some of the city's oldest houses and are surrounded by beautiful, flowering private gardens. In some places the trees grow over the stairs, so it feels like you're walking through a green tunnel; elsewhere, you'll have wide-open views of the bay. The cypress trees that grow on the hill are a favorite roost of local avian celebrities, the wild parrots of Telegraph Hill; you'll hear the cries of the cherry-headed conures if they're nearby. And the telegraphic name? It comes from the hill's status as the first Morse code signal station back in 1853. ⊠ *Bordered by Lombard, Filbert, Kearny, and Sansome Sts., North Beach.*

Washington Square

PLAZA | Once the daytime social heart of San Francisco's Italian district, this grassy patch has changed character numerous times over the years. The Beats hung out here in the 1950s, hippies camped out in the 1960s and early '70s, and nowadays you're more likely to see picnickers and residents doing community dance, yoga, or tai chi. You might also see homeless people hanging out on the benches and young locals sunbathing or running their dogs. Lillie Hitchcock Coit, in yet another show of affection for San Francisco's firefighters, donated the statue of two firemen with a rescued child. Camera-toting visitors focus on the Romanesque splendor of **Saints Peter and Paul Church** (Filbert St. side of square), a 1924 building with Disneyesque stone-white towers that are local landmarks. Mass reflects the neighborhood; it's given in English, Italian, and Chinese. ⊠ *Bordered by Columbus Ave. and Stockton, Filbert, and Union Sts., North Beach* ⊕ *sfrecpark.org.*

🍴 Restaurants

One of the city's oldest neighborhoods, North Beach continues to speak Italian, albeit in fewer households than it did when Joe DiMaggio was hitting home runs at the local playground.

Columbus Avenue, North Beach's primary commercial artery, and nearby side streets boast dozens of moderately priced Italian restaurants and coffee bars that San Franciscans flock to for a dose of strong community feeling. But beware, there are a few tourist traps that are after the college crowd, who come here for cheap drinks and then want to fill up on cheap food.

Barbara Pinseria & Cocktail Bar
$$ | **ITALIAN** | Calabrian-born SF resident Francesco Covucci is determined to continue the Italian legacy of North Beach with trendy, casual, quality-driven regional Italian eateries (he also owns Il Casaro Pizzeria at 348 Columbus Ave.). Here you can slam Roman-style *pinsa* , which is a modern style of ciabatta-shape pizza made of a multigrain flour mix and gourmet toppings like burrata and pesto or pear, walnut, and Gorgonzola. **Known for:** Roman pasta specialties like cacio e pepe; casual industrial-chic decor with wooden tables and tiled bar; craft cocktails and wines from Italy and California. [$] *Average main: $20* ✉ *431 Columbus Ave., North Beach* ☎ *415/445–3009* 🌐 *www.sfbarbara.com.*

Da Flora
$$ | **ITALIAN** | The original ownership has changed to wife-and-husband duo chef Jen McMahon and Oakland native Darren Lacy (front of house), who strive to create the neighborhood's most thoughtful Italian dining experience. Handwritten menus and linen napkins set the tone for ingredient-driven, high-quality regional Italian–inspired cuisine. **Known for:** house-baked focaccia and fresh pastas; red walls and cozy, romantic decor; decadent Italian desserts. [$] *Average main: $25* ✉ *701 Columbus Ave., North Beach* ☎ *415/981–4664* 🌐 *daflora.com* 🕒 *Closed Sun.–Tues. No lunch.*

Il Casaro Pizzeria & Mozzarella Bar
$$ | **PIZZA** | During a period when North Beach was undergoing a sort of upheaval, Francesco Covucci stepped on the scene to bring his concept for a modern, casual Italian pizzeria with quality-driven imported Italian ingredients to the storied quarter. Although hailing from Calabria (an agriculturally marked region of Southern Italy neighboring Campania, Italy's pizza bastion), he succeeds in leaving an authentic footprint on a Neapolitan-style pizzeria and also offers appetizers involving imported buffalo milk mozzarella and burrata. **Known for:** 'nduja pizza (a spicy chili soft paste-like salami from Calabria where the owner is from); fresh mozarella; traditional snacks like polpette and cured meats (like wild boar and truffle salame). [$] *Average main: $18* ✉ *348 Columbus Ave., North Beach* ☎ *415/677–9455* 🌐 *www.ilcasaropizzeria.com.*

Il Pollaio
$ | **CAFÉ** | One of North Beach's last blue-collar eateries has immense character, as if a *rosticceria* (a type of casual roast meat eat-in or take-away) was plopped here from a small quarter of Rome. This is a simple spot to get classic, hearty meals like half a roasted chicken and sides. **Known for:** an icon for a chicken or rib-eye dinner since 1984; simple, cafeteria-style tables and chairs; BYOB option, though there's wine and beer. [$] *Average main: $15* ✉ *555 Columbus Ave., North Beach* ☎ *415/362–7727* 🌐 *www.ilpollaiosf.com* 🕒 *Closed Sun.*

The Italian Homemade Company
$ | **ITALIAN** | **FAMILY** | In Italy, the bastion of fresh pasta is Emilia-Romagna, and a trio of entrepreneurs hailing from the region give respect to its claim to carb fame in a mini-empire of fast-casual pasta eateries, with the one in North Beach as its flagship. Come for treats like slabs of lasagna that fool you into thinking you're calorie loading in Bologna, as well as stuffed ravioli and gnocchi. **Known for:** varieties of piadina (Italian flatbreads with meats, cheeses, and vegetables); mix-and-match pastas and sauces; great quality for the price. [$] *Average main: $13* ✉ *716 Columbus Ave., North Beach* ☎ *712–8874* 🌐 *italianhomemade.com.*

★ **Maykadeh**
$$ | **MIDDLE EASTERN** | Persian dining is mostly done in homes, with fine dining a modern concept, but Maykadeh hits the mark with authenticity in Persian cooking

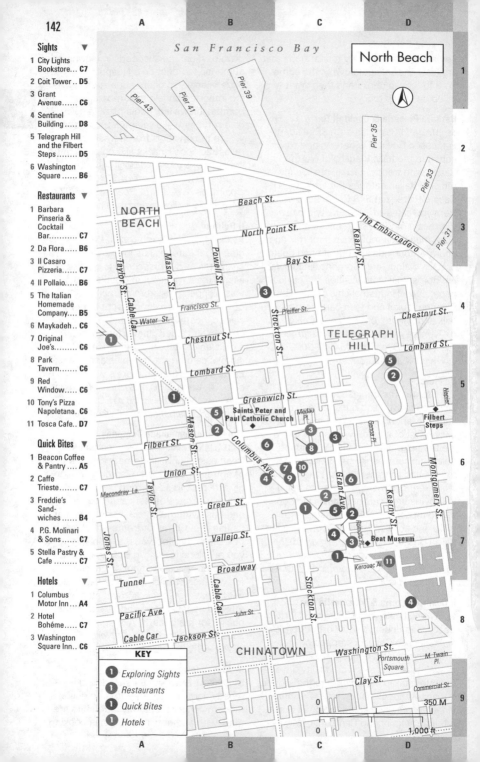

Sights ▼

1 City Lights Bookstore... **C7**
2 Coit Tower .. **D5**
3 Grant Avenue...... **C6**
4 Sentinel Building **D8**
5 Telegraph Hill and the Filbert Steps **D5**
6 Washington Square **B6**

Restaurants ▼

1 Barbara Pinseria & Cocktail Bar........... **C7**
2 Da Flora **B6**
3 Il Casaro Pizzeria...... **C7**
4 Il Pollaio..... **B6**
5 The Italian Homemade Company.... **B5**
6 Maykadeh .. **C6**
7 Original Joe's........ **C6**
8 Park Tavern....... **C6**
9 Red Window..... **C6**
10 Tony's Pizza Napoletana. **C6**
11 Tosca Cafe.. **D7**

Quick Bites ▼

1 Beacon Coffee & Pantry **A5**
2 Caffe Trieste....... **C7**
3 Freddie's Sandwiches **B4**
4 P.G. Molinari & Sons **C7**
5 Stella Pastry & Cafe **C7**

Hotels ▼

1 Columbus Motor Inn ... **A4**
2 Hotel Bohéme..... **C7**
3 Washington Square Inn .. **C6**

North Beach

San Francisco Bay

Pier 43
Pier 41
Pier 39
Pier 35
Pier 33
Pier 31

The Embarcadero

NORTH BEACH

Beach St.
North Point St.
Bay St.
Taylor St. Cable Car
Mason St.
Powell St.
Francisco St.
Water St.
Chestnut St.
Stockton St.
Pfeiffer St.
Chestnut St.
Lombard St.
Kearny St.

TELEGRAPH HILL

Lombard St.
Greenwich St.
Saints Peter and Paul Catholic Church
Medau Pl.
Genoa Pl.
Filbert Steps
Napier
Montgomery St.
Columbus Ave.
Filbert St.
Union St.
Macondray La.
Taylor St.
Green St.
Grant Ave.
Kearny St.
Mason St.
Jones St.
Vallejo St.
Romolo Pl.
Beat Museum
Broadway
Kerouac Al.
Tunnel
Pacific Ave.
Cable Car
John St.
Jackson St.
Cable Car
CHINATOWN
Washington St.
Portsmouth Square
M. Twain Pl.
Clay St.
Commercial St.

KEY

① Exploring Sights
① Restaurants
① Quick Bites
① Hotels

0 ———— 350 M
0 ———— 1,000 ft

as well as saucy, elevated, French-influenced twists. Those in the know come for succulent lamb specialties with saffron rice, served in a dining room with an old-school, white-shirt-and-tie vibe. **Known for:** loyal following of Iranians, Iranian Americans, and Persian food enthusiasts; eggplant dip appetizer; kebabs and marinated meats good for sharing. $ *Average main: $24 ⊠ 470 Green St., North Beach* ☎ 415/362–8286 ⊕ *maykadehrestaurant.com.*

Original Joe's

$$$ | ITALIAN | After a fire destroyed the old-school Italian American restaurant's Tenderloin building in 2007, it moved to North Beach; the "new" place has its charms, but it's quite a different restaurant, with far more sophisticated decor that includes some mid-century design elements. Original Joe's took over the former location of Fior D'Italia and carried on that space's legacy as a destination for fine dining, now marrying a higher-end experience with classic Italian American fare like eggplant parmigiana, saucy meatballs, and fettuccine dishes. **Known for:** classic Cal-Ital food; Joe's housemade ravioli; excellent bar. $ *Average main: $29 ⊠ 601 Union St., North Beach* ☎ 415/775–4877 ⊕ *originaljoessf.com.*

Park Tavern

$$$ | AMERICAN | Offering curated comfort food in a dining room with a vibe like a luxe cabin, this upscale American tavern on pretty Washington Square has been a hit from the day it opened in 2011. You can sit at the bar and snack on crispy frites and tartare starters or opt for a proper sit-down complete with a twice-baked potato and American Wagyu steak. **Known for:** meaty American food; excellent roast chicken; dishes using preserved lemons. $ *Average main: $30 ⊠ 1652 Stockton St., North Beach* ☎ 415/989–7300 ⊕ *parktavernsf.com* ☾ *No lunch weekdays.*

O Pioneers!

The corner of Broadway and Columbus Avenue witnessed an unusual historic breakthrough. Here stood the Condor Club, where in 1964 Carol Doda became the country's first dancer to break the topless barrier. A bronze plaque honors the milestone (only in SF).

Red Window

$$ | TAPAS | Pandemic opening and hardly Italian, this colorful small plates Spanish-style tapas/pinxos bar deserves a spot especially if you need a quick bite before heading off to dinner with an appetite stimulating vermouth-based aperitif. The food is delicious, with delightful ambiance and a not-to-miss for anyone who could use a night off from Italian. **Known for:** excellent low-ABV cocktails made tableside; patatas bravas piled into thin slices and then fried; fun, welcoming atmosphere. $ *Average main: $15 ⊠ North Beach* ☎ 415/757–0600 ⊕ *www.theredwindow.com* ☾ *Closed Mon. and Tues. No lunch Wed. and Thurs.*

Tony's Pizza Napoletana

$$ | PIZZA | FAMILY | Repeatedly crowned the World Champion Pizza Maker at the World Pizza Cup in Naples, Tony Gemignani is a carb-friendly legend in the city for his flavorful dough and myriad versions. The multiple gas, electric, and wood-burning ovens in his casual, modern pizzeria turn out many different styles of pies—the famed Neapolitan-style Margherita, but also Sicilian, Roman, and Detroit styles—with salads, antipasti, homemade pastas, and calzone rounding out the menu. **Known for:** Cal-Italia pie with aged balsamic drizzle; vibes like an NYC pizza parlor; slice stand next door if you can't wait. $ *Average main: $26 ⊠ 1570 Stockton St., North Beach* ☎ 415/835–9888 ⊕ *tonyspizzanapoletana.com.*

Tosca Cafe

$$$$ | ITALIAN | The leather booths and chairs are in high demand at this dark and clubby boho classic from 1919, where well-heeled locals and visitors delight in food that skews to the Cal-Italian genre, meaning local catches and seasonal produce as well as Italian flair in dishes such as halibut crudo and meatballs swimming in red sauce. The dinner menu is prix fixe, and there's a stylish Sunday brunch with choices like polenta pancakes and salt cod hash. **Known for:** Italian cocktails; raw bar and caviar menu; Tuscan fried chicken. [$] *Average main: $75* ✉ *242 Columbus Ave., North Beach* ☎ *415/986–9651* 🌐 *toscacafesf.com* 🕓 *No lunch.*

Coffee and Quick Bites

Beacon Coffee & Pantry

$ | CAFÉ | A glance at the menu board—with third-wave options like pour over—and at the bags of craft roasted coffee at the register will clue you in that Beacon takes its coffee seriously. A bit down from the heart of the Columbus strip, the white-tiled space with wood floors is a no-nonsense coffee enthusiast's pit stop for a hot shot or cold brew. **Known for:** kitchen items sold in pantry shop; gourmet pastries; house-made salads and sandwiches. [$] *Average main:* ✉ *805 Columbus Ave., North Beach* ☎ *415/814–2551* 🌐 *www.beacon-sf.com.*

Caffe Trieste

$ | CAFÉ | A visit to Caffe Trieste will give a glimmer of North Beach soul, along with generous slices of cake and possibly the best cappuccino in town that isn't trying to be part of a hipster latte-art competition. Open since 1956 and claiming to be the West Coast's first espresso coffeehouse, this fixture draws a diverse crowd, from young artists writing to the tune of their espresso buzz to old-timers reading the paper as they sip their drip cup. **Known for:** Saturday afternoon music; neighborhood vibe; retail annex next door. [$] *Average main:* ✉ *601 Vallejo St., at Grant Ave., North Beach* ☎ *415/392–6739* 🌐 *coffee.caffetrieste.com* 🕓 *No dinner.*

Freddie's Sandwiches

$ | ITALIAN | For a take-out sando shop for those in the North Beach know, Freddie's is where you need to go. The calling cards of this off-the-tourist-track time capsule, owned by Ed Sweileh, are the combo layered with mortadella, pressed ham, cheese, and salami galore, and the protein trio turkey, ham, and bacon club. **Known for:** corner store vibe of a place around since 1926; plenty of sandwich choices in a variety of sizes; excellent value for the price. [$] *Average main: $10* ✉ *300 Francisco St., North Beach* ☎ *415/433–2882* 🌐 *orderfreddiessandwiches.com* 🕓 *No dinner.*

★ Molinari Delicatessen

$ | DELI | The whip-quick, no-nonsense, food-smart staff behind the counter at this take-out delicatessen have been serving up the most delicious, and quite possibly the biggest, sandwiches in town since 1896 in this location alone. Grab a number, revel in the time warp that Sinatra in the background provides, marvel at the Italian-style cured meats, and let the artists build you an unforgettable combo; then head to Washington Square Park for a picnic. **Known for:** Italian combo sandwich; family business has old-time Italian vibe; traditional Italian products. [$] *Average main: $14* ✉ *373 Columbus Ave., at Vallejo St., North Beach* ☎ *415/421–2337* 🌐 *www.molinarisalame.com* 🕓 *Closed Sun. No dinner.*

Stella Pastry & Cafe

$ | BAKERY | For a quarter so rich in Italian history, North Beach sadly lacks authentic Italian *dolce* (sweet) offerings; indeed, this lone sweets bakery is it. Stella has been around since 1942 and has since changed hands from the original owners but still sticks to offering an array of Italian-American-style biscotti, tiramisu, and cannoli with creamy, cloyingly sweet predilections. **Known for:** Sacripantina cake, heavy with zabiglione; coffee and cappucino; American-style cannoli. [$] *Average main: $4* ✉ *446 Columbus Ave., North Beach* ☎ *415/986–2914*.

Hotels

The bright lights and frenetic energy of North Beach have long appealed to travelers. Value boutique hotels blend in well with the cafés, delis, clubs, and artsy shops near Washington Square Park. Most accommodations are best for couples or solo travelers, as rooms tend to be petite.

Columbus Motor Inn
$ | HOTEL | FAMILY | Close to Chinatown and Fisherman's Wharf, this affordable lodging with basic rooms decked out with oversize pillows, earth-toned bedding, and large flat-screen TVs is a great pick if you brought your family and have a car to park. **Pros:** free parking; affordable rooms deep-cleaned regularly; lively location. **Cons:** lacks amenities; decor is not stylish; street-facing accommodations can be noisy. [$] *Rooms from: $120* ✉ *1075 Columbus Ave., North Beach* ☎ *415/885–1492* 🌐 *www.columbusmotorinn.com* 🛏 *45 rooms* 🍴 *No meals.*

Hotel Bohème
$$ | HOTEL | Located in the heart of North Beach, this small hotel takes you back in time with cast-iron beds, large mirrored armoires, and memorabilia recalling the Beat generation—whose leading light, Allen Ginsberg, often stayed here (legend has it that in his later years he could be seen sitting in a window, typing away). **Pros:** convenient to North Beach shops and pastry spots; homey rooms; helpful staff. **Cons:** street parking is scarce; no a/c; small rooms. [$] *Rooms from: $225* ✉ *444 Columbus Ave., North Beach* ☎ *415/433–9111* 🌐 *hotelboheme.com* 🛏 *15 rooms* 🍴 *No meals.*

Washington Square Inn
$ | B&B/INN | Surrounded by fine shops and cafés, this inn overlooking North Beach's tree-lined Washington Square Park has individually decorated rooms with high-thread-count sheets on comfortable beds and up-to-date technological amenities like docking stations; many rooms have gas fireplaces. **Pros:** central location with many restaurants nearby; reasonable (off-site) parking fees; free Wi-Fi. **Cons:** no a/c; some rooms are small; old-style decor. [$] *Rooms from: $150* ✉ *1660 Stockton St., at Filbert St., North Beach* ☎ *415/981–4220, 800/388–0220* 🛏 *15 rooms* 🍴 *Breakfast.*

Nightlife

North Beach contains a suave mixture of watering holes, espresso cafés, late-night gelato ops, and strip clubs. Vesuvio is a must-visit for literary fans.

BARS

Bodega
WINE BARS—NIGHTLIFE | For a glass (or a bottle) of natural wine served with delicious, fresh small plates from burrata and radish salads to flavorful sweet potato tacos, head to this popular neighborhood wine bar a bit farther down Columbus. The owner, a young Iranian woman, runs the place seamlessly with a laser focus on a rotating selection of artisanal wines from small producers, mainly in France, Italy, and California. The eclectic, casual atmosphere and music selections pair well with the wine and snack options. Brunch is served weekends. ✉ *700 Columbus St., North Beach* ☎ *415/634–7002* 🌐 *www.bodegasf.com.*

15 Romolo
BARS/PUBS | Easy to miss on an alley and overshadowed by neighboring adult-entertainment venues that are parallel along the Columbus strip, this craft cocktail den with a Basque theme serves up tipples of sherry, a few thoughtful wine picks, and creative cocktails. Pair your

Topped by Coit Tower, Telegraph Hill has spectacular bay and city views.

drink with tasty, Spanish-driven bistro snacks, such as pressed tuna baguette sandos, house-made pickles, *pintxos* (Basque tapas with bread), and *croquetas* (a fried snack). With a non-Internet jukebox and a photo booth, this place oozes vintage hipster vibes but with old-world sensibilities. ✉ *15 Romolo Pl., off Broadway east of Columbus Ave., North Beach* ☎ *415/398–1359* ⊕ *www.15romolo.com.*

Specs' Twelve Adler Museum Cafe

BARS/PUBS | If you're into bohemian dive bars, you can groove on this hidden hangout for artists, poets, and heavy-drinking old-timers. Specs' Bar is a women-owned and -run institution and a beloved fixture not only in San Francisco but the country. It's one of the few remaining old-fashioned watering holes in North Beach that still smack of the Beat years and the 1960s. Though it's just off a busy street, Specs' is strangely immune to the hustle and bustle outside. ✉ *12 William Saroyan Pl., off Columbus Ave., between Pacific Ave. and Broadway, North Beach* ☎ *415/421–4112* ⊕ *www.specsbarsf.com.*

Tony Nik's

BARS/PUBS | For a dive bar with old San Francisco soul (considering there are few legends like this left), go no furtherfor a nightcap involving an old-fashioned, martini, or Negroni after a night of pizza crushing or any carb-fueled meal, really. If you can, hang out at the bar with and quickly become acquainted with the charming owner/bartender. Tony Nik's is an icon to local bar history, around since Prohibition and with a lot of the same details intact. ✉ *1534 Stockton St., North Beach* ☎ *415/693–0990.*

★ Vesuvio

BARS/PUBS | If you're hitting only one bar in North Beach, it should be this one. The low-ceilinged second floor of this raucous boho saloon hangout, little altered since its 1960s heyday (when Jack Kerouac frequented the place), is a fine vantage point for watching the colorful Broadway and Columbus Avenue intersection. Another part of Vesuvio's appeal is its diverse clientele, from older neighborhood regulars and young couples to bacchanalian posses. ✉ *255 Columbus Ave., at Broadway, North Beach* ☎ *415/362–3370* ⊕ *www.vesuvio.com.*

COMEDY
Cobb's Comedy Club
COMEDY CLUBS | Well-known stand-up comics have appeared at this club, though there's more emphasis on up-and-comers. You might also see local sketch comedy and comic singer-songwriters. No one under 18 is admitted, and there is a minimum drink purchase in addition to the entrance fee. Free Zoom shows (tip requested) are a good place to get a taste. ✉ *915 Columbus Ave., at Lombard St., North Beach* ☎ *415/928–4320* ⊕ *www.cobbscomedy.com.*

MUSIC CLUBS
Bimbo's 365 Club
MUSIC CLUBS | The plush main room and adjacent lounge of this club, here since 1951, retain a retro vibe perfect for the "Cocktail Nation" programming that keeps the crowds entertained. For a taste of the original San Francisco nightclub scene, you can't beat it. Indie low-fi and pop bands such as Mustache Harbor and Tainted Love have played here. ✉ *1025 Columbus Ave., at Chestnut St., North Beach* ☎ *415/474–0365* ⊕ *www. bimbos365club.com.*

The Saloon
MUSIC CLUBS | Hard-drinkin' in-the-know locals favor this raucous spot, renowned for great blues. Built in the 1860s, the onetime bordello is purported to be the oldest bar in the city. This is not the place to order anything mixed besides maybe a gin and tonic, and don't expect it to be quaffable. Get a bottle or can of beer, enjoy the scene, and chat with anyone next to you. Just keep quiet when the music is jamming. ✉ *1232 Grant Ave., near Columbus Ave., North Beach* ☎ *415/989–7666* ⊕ *sfblues.weebly.com.*

Shopping

Small eateries, cafés, and shops selling clothing, antiques, and vintage wares cluster tightly around Washington Square Park and Columbus Avenue. Be sure to check out the four blocks of Grant Avenue north from Columbus. Book lovers must stop at literary landmark City Lights Bookstore on Columbus.

CLOTHING
AB Fits
CLOTHING | The affable staff can help guys and gals sort through the jeans selection, one of the hippest in the city, from hyperlocal to international brands. On-staff experts pride themselves on being able to match the pants to the person. Occasional release parties are hosted: sign up for the mailing list to get a taste of local fashion and art life combined. ✉ *1519 Grant Ave., between Filbert and Union Sts., North Beach* ☎ *415/982–5726* ⊕ *www.abfits.com.*

Knitz and Leather
CLOTHING | Local artisans Julia Relinghaus and Katharina Ernst have been producing one-of-a-kind and custom products of extraordinary craftsmanship for over 30 years. Ernst's bold knitted sweaters and accessories will help you stand out from the crowd, and Relinghaus's exquisite, high-quality leather jackets for men and women are the kind of investment you make for fine leather. ✉ *1453 Grant Ave., North Beach* ☎ *415/391–3480.*

FOOD AND DRINK
Graffeo Coffee Roasting Company
FOOD/CANDY | Forget overly roasted (burnt) mystery coffees if you're snagging a bag from this emporium and working roastery, open since 1935 and one of the best-loved coffee stores in a city devoted to high-quality roasted java. The shop sells craft roast whole-bean bags only. It's worth the jaunt if only for the aromas. ✉ *735 Columbus Ave., at Filbert St., North Beach* ☎ *415/986–2420* ⊕ *www. graffeo.com.*

Sotto Casa

FOOD/CANDY | A specialty Italian grocer for lovers of Slow Food, this shop is owned by Abruzzo-born Lorenzo Scarpone, who founded SF's Slow Food chapter; he also moonlights as a wine importer. Stop by for dried pastas from ancient villages like Gragnano; imported Italian specialty cheeses; aged balsamic vinegar from Modena; holiday cookies and specialties; and canned goods, such as San Marzano tomatoes. Also on offer are Roman roasted coffee and bottles of extra-virgin olive oil from Scarpone's family's production in Abruzzo. ✉ *1351 Grant Ave., North Beach* ☎ *415/475–7774* ⊕ *www.sotto-casa.com.*

Victoria Pastry Company

FOOD/CANDY | In business since the early 1900s and a throwback to the North Beach of old, this bakery has display cases full of Italian pastries (although most hard-core Italian food experts would disapprove of them), traditional holiday cookies, and buttercream-based cakes. ✉ *700 Filbert St., between Columbus Ave. and Powell St., North Beach* ☎ *415/781–2015.*

★XOX Truffles

FOOD/CANDY | The decadent confection comes in countless bite-size flavors here, from the traditional (cocoa-powder-coated Amaretto) to the unusual (flavored with rum-coconut liqueur and coated with coconut flakes). There's something for everyone, even vegans (soy truffles). Bonus: all espresso drinks come with a complimentary truffle. ✉ *754 Columbus Ave., between Greenwich and Filbert Sts., North Beach* ☎ *415/421–4814* ⊕ *xoxtruffles.com.*

FURNITURE, HOUSEWARES, AND GIFTS

Biordi Art Imports

HOUSEHOLD ITEMS/FURNITURE | A North Beach landmark, this store sells ceramics of the quality found in the artisan clusters of Italy. The excellent selection of hand-painted Italian pottery, imported mainly from Tuscany, Umbria, and Sicily, has been shipped worldwide by this proud, family-run business since it was opened by Italian immigrants in 1946 (the current owners are an Italian-American couple). Their specialty is Umbrian Deruta ceramics and some Palio di Siena Contrade pieces, and they work directly with generational artisans. Ceramic sets can be ordered in any combination. ✉ *412 Columbus Ave., at Vallejo St., North Beach* ☎ *415/392–8096* ⊕ *biordi.com.*

MUSIC MEMORABILIA

San Francisco Rock Posters & Collectibles

ANTIQUES/COLLECTIBLES | The huge selection of rock-and-roll memorabilia, including posters, handbills, and original art, makes this spot a groovy cave for the nostalgic vintage '60s. Also available are posters from more recent shows, many at the legendary Fillmore Auditorium. ✉ *1851 Powell St., between Filbert and Greenwich Sts., North Beach* ☎ *415/956–6749* ⊕ *rockposters.com.*

PAPER AND STATIONERY

Lola of North Beach

BOOKS/STATIONERY | For an alternative to Hallmark with a SF vibe, try this intimate shop offering gadgets, knickknacks, and tongue-in-cheek novelties, plus cards, stationery, and postcards. Many products make great souvenirs, from Golden Gate Bridge onesies for babies to city-skyline socks for adults. Local artists are well represented. ✉ *454 Columbus Ave., North Beach* ☎ *415/678–5327* ⊕ *www.lolaofnorthbeach.com.*

Chapter 7

ON THE WATERFRONT

FISHERMAN'S WHARF, EMBARCADERO, AND THE FINANCIAL DISTRICT

Updated by
Trevor Felch

👁 **Sights**
★★★☆☆

🍴 **Restaurants**
★★★☆☆

🛏 **Hotels**
★★☆☆☆

🛍 **Shopping**
★★☆☆☆

🍸 **Nightlife**
★★☆☆☆

NEIGHBORHOOD SNAPSHOT

TOP EXPERIENCES

■ **Ferry Building:** Join locals eyeing produce and foods prepared by some of the city's best chefs at San Francisco's premier Saturday farmers' market.

■ **Hyde Street Pier:** Sing sea chanteys and raise the sails aboard the 19th-century square-rigged ship *Balclutha*, then hit the Buena Vista for an Irish coffee.

■ **Alcatraz:** Go from a scenic bay tour to "the hole" — solitary confinement in absolute darkness—while inmates and guards tell you stories about what life was really like on the Rock.

■ **F-line:** Grab a polished wooden seat aboard one of the city's vintage streetcars and clatter down the tracks toward the Ferry Building's spire.

■ **Exploratorium:** Play with the ultimate marble run or explore yourself in the Science of Sharing exhibit at this spectacular hands-on science museum.

GETTING HERE

The Powell–Hyde and Powell–Mason cable-car lines both end near Fisherman's Wharf. The walk from downtown through North Beach to the northern waterfront is lovely, and if you stick to Columbus Avenue, the incline is relatively gentle. F-line trolleys run all the way down Market to the Embarcadero, then north to the wharf.

QUICK BITES

Cafe de Casa. Start the morning on the outskirts of Fisherman's Wharf with an acai bowl and Brazilian coffee, or enjoy puffy chicken-and-cheese-filled *coxinha* pastries as an afternoon snack at this cheery stop by a quiet, grassy square. ⊠ *2701 Leavenworth St., Fisherman's Wharf* ⊕ *cafedecasa.com.*

Terminus Cafe and Bar. Café by day, with coffee, a stellar kale-and-chicken salad, and sandwiches, and then a post-work drinks-only bar in the evening: this tile-decorated spot at the end of the California Street cable-car line is a great stop between the Ferry Building and downtown. ⊠ *16 California St., Financial District* ⊕ *www.terminussf.com.*

PLANNING YOUR TIME

■ If you're planning to go to Alcatraz, be sure to buy your tickets in advance, as tours frequently sell out. Alcatraz ferries leave from Pier 33—so there isn't a single good reason to suffer Pier 39's tacky, overpriced attractions. If you're a sailor at heart, though, definitely spend an hour with the historic ships of the Hyde Street Pier.

FERRIES

■ The bay is a huge part of San Francisco's charm, and getting out on the water gives you an attractive and unique (though windy) perspective on the city. ■TIP→ **A ride on a commuter ferry is cheaper than a cruise, and just as lovely.**

■ The **Blue & Gold Fleet** (⊕ *www.blueandgoldfleet. com*) offers scenic bay cruises around Alcatraz and under the Golden Gate Bridge. They also operate the commuter ferries Golden Gate Ferry and San Francisco Bay Ferry.

■ The **Red and White Fleet** (⊕ *redandwhite.com*) offrs cruises to the Golden Gate Bridge and the Bay Bridge—and beautiful sunset trips—all of which deliver splendid views of San Francisco

San Francisco's waterfront neighborhoods have fabulous views and utterly different personalities. Kitschy, overpriced Fisherman's Wharf struggles to maintain the last shreds of its existence as a working wharf, while Pier 39 is a full-fledged consumer circus. The Ferry Building draws well-heeled locals with its culinary pleasures, firmly connecting the Embarcadero and downtown. Between the Ferry Building and Pier 39, a former maritime no-man's-land, are the Exploratorium, a $90 million cruise-ship terminal, Alcatraz Landing, fashionable waterfront restaurants, and restored, pedestrian-friendly piers.

Fisherman's Wharf

The crack of fresh Dungeness crab, the aroma of sourdough warm from the oven, the cry of the gulls—in some ways you can experience Fisherman's Wharf today as it has been for more than 100 years. Italians began fishing these waters in the 19th century as immigrants to booming Barbary Coast San Francisco. Family businesses established generations ago continue to this day—look for the Alioto-Lazio Fish Company, selling crab fresh off the boat here since the 1940s, and Alioto's Restaurant, a Sicilian seafood Wharf staple since 1925.

As the local fishing industry has contracted and environmental awareness has changed fishing regulations, Fisherman's Wharf has morphed. Fewer families make a living off the sea here, fewer fishing boats go out, and more of the wharf survives on tourist dollars. You'll see more schlock here than in any other neighborhood in town: overpriced food alongside discount electronics stores, bargain-luggage outlets, and cheap T-shirts and souvenirs.

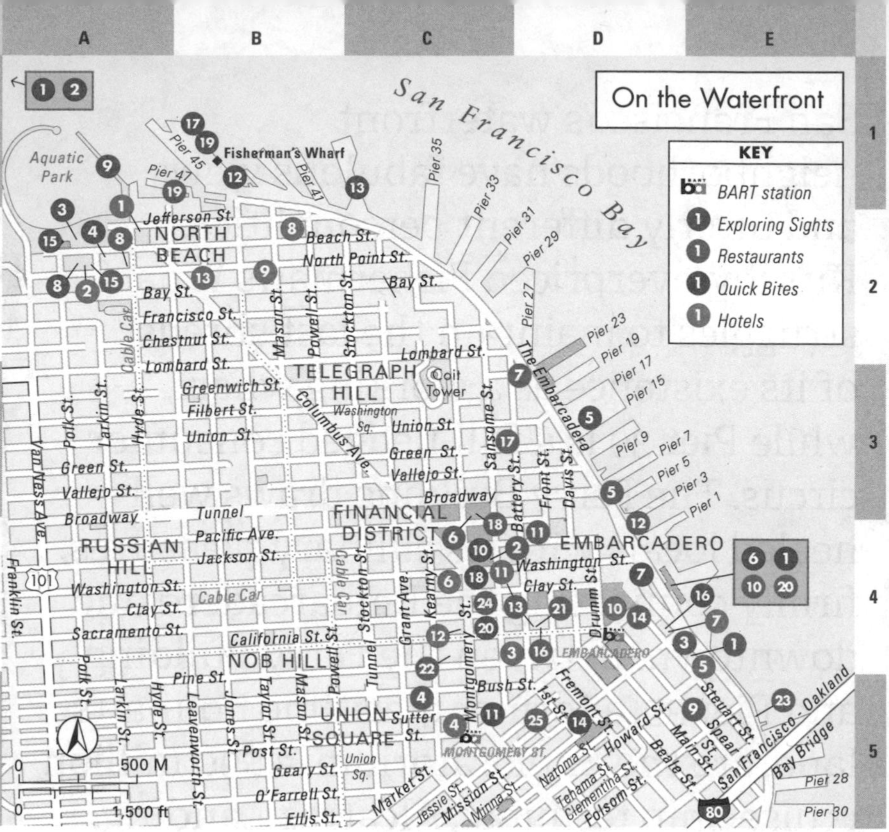

Sights

1 Alcatraz.................. A1
2 Angel Island State Park A1
3 Aquatic Park A2
4 Cartoon Art Museum... A2
5 Exploratorium D3
6 Ferry Building D4
7 F-line... .... D4
8 Ghirardelli Square A2
9 Hyde Street Pier A1
10 Jackson Square Historic District C4
11 Market Street buildings..................C5
12 Musée Mécanique B1
13 Pier 39....................C1
14 Salesforce Park......... D5
15 San Francisco National Maritime Museum A2
16 San Francisco Railway Museum D4
17 SS *Jeremiah O'Brien*.....B1
18 Transamerica Pyramid...................C4
19 USS *Pampanito*......... B1
20 Wells Fargo History Museum C4

Restaurants

1 Angler.....................E4
2 BIX.........................C4
3 Boulevard................ D4
4 Café Claude C5
5 Coqueta................... D3
6 Cotogna....................C3
7 Fog City D3
8 Gary Danko.............. A2
9 GOZU....................... E5
10 Hog Island Oyster Company D4
11 Kokkari Estiatorio....... D4
12 La Mar Cebicheria Peruana.................. D4
13 Michael Mina D4
14 One Market.............. D4
15 Palette Tea House A2
16 Perbacco D4
17 Piperade...................C3
18 Quince C3
19 Scoma's.................. B1
20 The Slanted Door....... D4
21 Tadich Grill............... D4
22 The Vault Garden........C4
23 Waterbar E5
24 Wayfare Tavern..........C4
25 Yank Sing D5

Quick Bites

1 Gott's Roadside D4

Hotels

1 Argonaut Hotel.......... A2
2 Fairmont Heritage Place, Ghirardelli Square A2
3 Four Seasons Hotel San Francisco at Embarcadero.............C4
4 Galleria Park Hotel C5
5 Harbor Court Hotel E4
6 Hilton San Francisco Financial District.........C4
7 Hotel Vitale D4
8 Hotel Zephyr............. B2
9 Hotel Zoe Fisherman's Wharf B2
10 Hyatt Regency San Francisco........... D4
11 Le Méridien San Francisco........... D4
12 Omni San Francisco Hotel......................C4
13 San Francisco Marriott Fisherman's Wharf B2

It's enough to send locals running for the hills, but there are things here worth experiencing. Explore maritime history aboard the fabulous ships of the Hyde Street Pier, amuse yourself early-20th-century style with the mechanical diversions at Musée Mécanique, and grab a bowl of chowder or some Dungeness crab from one of the stands along Jefferson Street to get a taste (and distinct shellfish aroma) of what made Fisherman's Wharf what it is in the first place. If you come early, you can avoid the crowds and get a sense of the Wharf's functional side: it's not entirely an amusement-park replica.

Sights

Angel Island State Park

NATIONAL/STATE PARK | For an outdoorsy adventure and some fascinating though sometimes disturbing history, consider a day at this island northwest of Alcatraz, the bay's largest natural island. Used by the Coast Miwok as a favored camp, explored by Spaniards in 1775, and declared a U.S. military reserve 75 years later, the island was used as a screening ground for Asian, mostly Chinese, immigrants—who were often held for months, even years, before being granted entry—from 1910 until 1940. You can visit the restored Immigration Station, from the dock where detainees landed to the barracks where you can see the poems in Chinese script they etched onto the walls.

In 1963 the government designated Angel Island a state park. Today people come for picnics, hikes such as one to the top of Mt. Livermore and a scenic 5-mile path that winds around the island's perimeter, and tram tours that explain the park's history. Blue & Gold Fleet is the only Angel Island ferry service with departures from San Francisco; boats leave from Pier 41. ⊠ *Pier 41, Fisherman's Wharf* ☎ *415/435–1915 park information and ferry schedules,*

415/705–8200 Blue and Gold Fleet ⊕ *www.parks.ca.gov* ✉ *$19.50 round-trip for ferry and admission.*

Aquatic Park

BEACH—SIGHT | This urban beach, surrounded by Fort Mason, Ghirardelli Square, and Fisherman's Wharf, is a quarter-mile-long strip of sand. The gentle waters near shore are shallow, safe for kids to swim or wade, and fairly clean. Locals come out for quick dips in the frigid water. Members of the **Dolphin Club** and the **South End Rowing Club** come every morning for a swim, and a large and raucous crowd braves the cold on New Year's Day. **Amenities:** food and drink; showers; toilets. **Best for:** sunset; swimming; walking. ⊠ *San Francisco Maritime National Historical Park, 499 Jefferson St., at Hyde St., Fisherman's Wharf* ⊕ *www.nps.gov/safr.*

Cartoon Art Museum

MUSEUM | Krazy Kat, Zippy the Pinhead, Batman, and other colorful cartoon icons greet you at the Cartoon Art Museum, established with an endowment from the late cartoonist-icon Charles M. Schulz. The museum's strength is its changing exhibits, which have highlighted subjects such as emerging artists, the evolution of animation, and the artwork in a book about actor/activist George Takei's childhood experiences in an internment camp for Japanese Americans during World War II. Serious fans of cartoons—especially those on the quirky underground side—will likely enjoy the exhibits; those with a casual interest may be bored. The store here carries cool titles to add to your collection. ⊠ *781 Beach St., Fisherman's Wharf* ☎ *415/227–8666* ⊕ *www. cartoonart.org* ✉ *$10.*

Ghirardelli Square

STORE/MALL | Most of the redbrick buildings in this complex were once part of the Ghirardelli factory, which the prominent chocolate company purchased in 1893. Tourists visit to pick up the famous chocolate and indulge in ice cream sundaes at this dessert paradise (Ghirardelli's factory is now in the East Bay), though you can purchase the chocolates all over town and save yourself a trip to what is essentially a mall. But it's still a must-visit destination for chocolate lovers. Placards throughout the square describe the factory's history, and the giant Ghirardelli sign above the square, erected in 1923, remains one of the city's visual icons. ⊠ *900 N. Point St., Fisherman's Wharf* ☎ *415/775–5500* ⊕ *www.ghirardellisq.com.*

★ **Hyde Street Pier**
MUSEUM | FAMILY | If you want to get to the heart of the Wharf, there's no better place to do it than at this pier. Don't pass up the centerpiece collection of historic vessels, part of the **San Francisco Maritime National Historical Park,** almost all of which can be boarded. The *Balclutha,* an 1886 full-rigged three-masted sailing vessel that's more than 250 feet long, sailed around Cape Horn 17 times. Kids especially love the *Eureka,* a side-wheel passenger and car ferry, for her onboard collection of vintage cars. The *Hercules* is a steam-powered tugboat, and the *C. A. Thayer* is a beautifully restored three-masted schooner.

Across the street from the pier and a museum in itself is the maritime park's **Visitor Center** (*499 Jefferson St., 415/447–5000*), whose fun, large-scale exhibits make it an engaging stop. See a huge First Order Fresnel lighthouse lens and a shipwrecked boat. Then stroll through time in the exhibit "The Waterfront," where you can touch the timber from a gold rush–era ship recovered from below the Financial District, peek into 19th-century storefronts, and see the sails of an Italian fishing vessel. ⊠ *Hyde and Jefferson Sts., Fisherman's Wharf* ☎ *415/561–7100* ⊕ *www.nps.gov/safr* ⊠ *Ships $15 (ticket good for 7 days).*

Musée Mécanique
MUSEUM | FAMILY | Once a staple at Playland at the Beach, San Francisco's early 20th-century amusement park, the antique mechanical contrivances at this time-warp arcade—including peep shows and nickelodeons—make it one of the most worthwhile attractions at the Wharf. Some favorites are the giant and rather creepy "Laffing Sal"; an arm-wrestling machine; the world's only steam-powered motorcycle; and mechanical fortune-telling figures that speak from their curtained boxes. Note the depictions of race that betray the prejudices of the time: stoned Chinese figures in the "Opium-Den" and clown-faced African Americans eating watermelon in the "Mechanical Farm." ■**TIP→ Admission is free, but you'll need quarters to bring the machines to life.** ⊠ *Pier 45, Shed A, Fisherman's Wharf* ☎ *415/346–2000* ⊕ *museemecaniquesf.com* ⊠ *Free.*

Pier 39
STORE/MALL | FAMILY | The city's most popular waterfront attraction draws millions of visitors each year, who come to browse through its shops and concessions hawking every conceivable form of souvenir. The pier can be quite crowded, and the numerous street performers may leave you feeling more harassed than entertained. Arriving early in the morning ensures you a front-row view of the sea lions that bask here, but if you're at Pier 39 to shop, be aware that most stores don't open until 9:30 or 10 (later in winter).

Follow the sound of barking to the northwest side of the pier to view the **sea lions** flopping about the floating docks. During the summer, orange-clad naturalists answer questions and offer fascinating facts about the playful pinnipeds—for example, that most of the animals here are males.

At the **Aquarium of the Bay** (☎ 415/623–5300 or 888/732–3483 ⊕ www.aquariumofthebay.org 🍴 $29.95), moving walkways transport you through a space surrounded on three sides by water filled with indigenous San Francisco Bay marine life, from fish and plankton to sharks. ⊠ Beach St., at Embarcadero, Fisherman's Wharf ⊕ www.pier39.com.

San Francisco National Maritime Museum
MUSEUM | FAMILY | You'll feel as if you're out to sea when you step aboard, er, inside this sturdy, ship-shape (literally), Streamline-Moderne structure, dubbed the Bathhouse Building and built in 1939 as part of the New Deal's Works Progress Administration. The first floor of the museum, part of the **San Francisco Maritime National Historical Park**, has stunningly restored undersea dreamscape murals and some of the museum's intricate ship models. The first-floor balcony overlooks the beach and has lovely WPA-era tile designs. ■TIP→ If you've got young kids in tow, the museum makes a great quick, free stop. Then pick up ice cream at Ghirardelli Square across the street and enjoy it on the beach or next door in Victorian Park, where you can watch the cable cars turn around. ⊠ Aquatic Park, foot of Polk St., Fisherman's Wharf ☎ 415/447–5000 ⊕ www.nps.gov/safr 🍴 Donation suggested.

SS *Jeremiah O'Brien*
LIGHTHOUSE | A participant in the D-Day landing in Normandy during World War II, this Liberty Ship freighter is one of two such vessels (out of more than 2,700 built) still in working order. On board you can peek at the crew's living quarters and the officers' mess hall. The large display of the Normandy invasion, one of many exhibits on board, was a gift from France. To keep the 1943 ship in sailing shape, the steam engine—which appears in the film *Titanic*—is operated dockside seven times a year on special "steaming weekends." Most recently, the ship escaped damage from a major 2020 fire at its home dock, Pier 45. Visitors can explore the ship at the dock or enjoy one of the bay cruises that happen on select days throughout the year. ⊠ Pier 45, Fisherman's Wharf ☎ 415/544–0100 ⊕ www.ssjeremiahobrien.org 🍴 $20.

USS *Pampanito*
LIGHTHOUSE | Get an intriguing, if mildly claustrophobic, glimpse into life on a submarine during World War II on this small, 80-person sub, which sank six Japanese warships and damaged four others. ■TIP→ There's not much in the way of interpretive signs, so opt for the audio tour (included with admission) to learn about what you're seeing. ⊠ Pier 45, Fisherman's Wharf ☎ 415/775–1943 ⊕ maritime.org/uss-pampanito 🍴 From $20.

🍴 Restaurants

To the north of the Ferry Building lies Fisherman's Wharf, a jumbled mix of seafood dining rooms, sidewalk vendors, and trinket shops that visitors religiously trudge through and San Franciscans invariably dismiss as a tourist trap. But even locals may come for a cracked crab.

Gary Danko
$$$$ | AMERICAN | This San Francisco classic for prix fixe dining has earned a legion of fans—and a Michelin star—for its namesake chef's refined and creative seasonal California cooking, displayed in dishes like glazed oysters with Ossetra caviar and juniper-crusted bison. The banquette-lined rooms, with stunning floral arrangements, are as memorable as the food and impeccable service. **Known for:** tableside cheese cart; soufflé for dessert; reservations are hard to get. 💲 Average main: $97 ⊠ 800 N. Point St., Fisherman's Wharf ☎ 415/749–2060 ⊕ garydanko.com ⏱ No lunch ⛧ Jacket required.

Palette Tea House
$$ | CHINESE | The biggest thing to happen to Ghirardelli Square since the chocolate factory left the neighborhood, this dim sum specialist from a popular local group (Koi Palace, Dragon Beaux) has been

Escape from Alcatraz

Federal-prison officials liked to claim that it was impossible to escape Alcatraz, and for the most part, that assertion was true. For seasoned swimmers, though, the trip has never posed a problem—in fact, it's been downright popular.

In the 1930s, in an attempt to dissuade the feds from converting Alcatraz into a prison, a handful of schoolgirls made the swim to the city. At age 60, fitness guru and native son Jack LaLanne did it (for the second time) while shackled and towing a 1,000-pound rowboat. Every year thousands take the chilly plunge during the annual Escape from Alcatraz Triathlon and Sharkfest Swim events. Heck, a dog made the crossing in 2005 and finished well ahead of most of the (human) pack. And since 2006, seven-year-old Braxton Bilbrey remains the youngest "escapee" on record. Incidentally, those reports of shark-infested waters are true, but the sharks are almost never dangerous species.

a hit for its modern take on the genre since opening in 2019. While the colorful dumplings and *bao* (steamed buns) are generally the headliners, the menu also includes several consistently strong rice dishes, noodles, and entrées, plus must-order salted egg lava bao to finish. **Known for:** xiao long bao (soup dumpling) platter; modern decor with brick walls and eye-catching yellow-and-red lamps overhead; refreshing find in a super-touristy destination. [$] *Average main: $24* ✉ *900 N. Point St., Suite B201A, Fisherman's Wharf* ☎ *415/347–8888* 🌐 *paletteteahouse.com.*

Scoma's

$$$$ | **SEAFOOD** | Ask locals where to eat at Fisherman's Wharf and you'll get a blank look, but the answer is this San Francisco classic that is undoubtedly the leader among its peers (or ... piers?). The Pier 47 spot was a coffee shop when brothers Al and Jay Scoma bought it in 1965 (the homey coffeehouse vibe still lingers around the retro-meets-contemporary bar), and the restaurant continues to be a great stop for excellent fresh fish and seafood preparations. **Known for:** excellent crab Louis; one of the city's best cioppinos; timeless atmosphere with all kinds of memorabilia. [$] *Average main: $43* ✉ *1965 Al Scoma Way, Pier 47, Fisherman's Wharf* ☎ *415/771–4383* 🌐 *scomas.com* 🕒 *Closed Tues. and Wed.*

Hotels

The hub of San Francisco's kitschy tourist trade, Fisherman's Wharf draws families to its chain hotels and smaller properties. Accommodations are generally playful, and many have swimming pools. The downside is that some lodgings lie far from other tourist attractions.

★ Argonaut Hotel

$$ | **HOTEL** | **FAMILY** | The nautically themed Argonaut's spacious guest rooms have exposed-brick walls, wood-beam ceilings, and best of all, windows that open to the sea air and the sounds of the waterfront; many rooms enjoy Alcatraz and Golden Gate Bridge views. **Pros:** hotel's seafood restaurant is above average for the neighborhood; near Hyde Street cable car; toys for the kids. **Cons:** nautical theme isn't for everyone; cramped public areas; far from crosstown attractions. [$] *Rooms from: $269* ✉ *495 Jefferson St., at Hyde St., Fisherman's Wharf* ☎ *415/563–0800,*

800/790–1415 reservations 🌐 *www.argonauthotel.com* 🛏 *252 rooms* 🍴 *No meals.*

Fairmont Heritage Place, Ghirardelli Square
$$$$ | RENTAL | FAMILY | Located in the former Ghirardelli chocolate factory, these one-to-three-bedroom "residences" deliver elevated comfort and style, with fully equipped gourmet kitchens, the factory's signature brick walls, plush bedding, in-room laundry facilities, fireplaces, and modern furniture in chocolate and lavender hues. **Pros:** bay and Alcatraz views from most rooms; outdoor terraces with firepits; pre-arrival grocery shopping can be provided. **Cons:** a trek from downtown; steep prices; limited food and beverage service. $ *Rooms from: $775* ✉ *900 N. Point St., Suite D100, Fisherman's Wharf* ☎ *415/268–9900* 🌐 *www.fairmont.com/ghirardelli* 🛏 *53 suites* 🍴 *No meals.*

Hotel Zephyr
$$ | HOTEL | FAMILY | Directly facing Alcatraz with unobstructed bay and island vistas, this Fisherman's Wharf hotel pays tribute to San Francisco's shipyard past and features an impressive outdoor adult playground with firepits, giant interactive games, and the Camper, a Shasta trailer converted into a grab-and-go food truck. **Pros:** creative decor; water views from many rooms; s'mores happy hour. **Cons:** very touristy immediate area; $25 per-night amenity fee and expensive parking; some housekeeping lapses. $ *Rooms from: $269* ✉ *250 Beach St., Fisherman's Wharf* ☎ *415/617–6555* 🌐 *www.hotelzephyrsf.com* 🛏 *361 rooms* 🍴 *No meals.*

Hotel Zoe Fisherman's Wharf
$$ | HOTEL | A little removed from the heart of the wharf area craziness, this smart-looking boutique hotel with guestroom interiors inspired by luxury Mediterranean yachts aims for subtle contemporary elegance in the form of lightly stained woods and soft-brown and cream fabrics and walls. **Pros:** cozy feeling; nice desks and sitting areas in rooms; open-air courtyard with firepits. **Cons:** rather congested touristy area; smaller rooms can feel too tight; resort fee catches some guests off guard. $ *Rooms from: $239* ✉ *425 N. Point St., at Mason St., Fisherman's Wharf* ☎ *415/561–1100, 800/648–4626* 🌐 *www.hotelzoesf.com* 🛏 *221 rooms* 🍴 *No meals.*

San Francisco Marriott Fisherman's Wharf
$ | HOTEL | FAMILY | Reliable and slightly refined, this chain property is a good choice for families and business travelers wanting to be on the fringes of Fisherman's Wharf, highlighted by a lobby that plays on the aquatic and wharf theme and smartly designed rooms with tech amenities. **Pros:** excellent work-from-room setup; comfortable bedding; relatively small and charming by Marriott standards. **Cons:** bland fitness center; on a busy street; nearby hotels have better views. $ *Rooms from: $169* ✉ *1250 Columbus Ave., Fisherman's Wharf* ☎ *415/775–7555* 🌐 *www.marriott.com* 🛏 *285 rooms* 🍴 *No meals.*

Nightlife

Come nightfall, the crowds that throng the northern waterfront during the day tend to thin out, and the nightlife scene here becomes almost quaint.

BARS

★ Buena Vista Cafe
BARS/PUBS | At the end of the Hyde Street cable-car line, the Buena Vista packs 'em in for its famous Irish coffee—which, according to owners, was the first served stateside (in 1952). The place oozes nostalgia with its white-jacketed bartenders and timeless atmosphere, drawing devoted locals as well as out-of-towners relaxing after a day of sightseeing. It's narrow and can get crowded, but this spot is a sip of history and provides a fine alternative to the overpriced tourist joints nearby. ✉ *2765 Hyde St., at Beach St., Fisherman's Wharf* ☎ *415/474–5044* 🌐 *www.thebuenavista.com.*

♿ Activities

BICYCLING

A completely flat, sea-level route, the Embarcadero hugs the eastern and northern bay and gives a clear view of open waters, the Bay Bridge, and sleek high-rises. The route from Pier 40 to Aquatic Park takes about 30 minutes to ride, and there are designated bike lanes the entire way. As you ride west, you'll pass the Bay Bridge, the Ferry Building, Coit Tower (look inland near Pier 19), and historic ships at the Hyde Street Pier. At Aquatic Park there's a nice view of the Golden Gate Bridge. If you're not tired yet, continue along the Marina and through the Presidio's Crissy Field. You may want to time your ride so you end up at the Ferry Building, where you can reward yourself with some great food. ■TIP➔ **Be alert—cars move quickly here, and streetcars and tourist traffic can cause congestion. Near Fisherman's Wharf you can bike on the promenade, but watch out for pedestrians.**

Bay City Bike

BICYCLING | With three locations in Fisherman's Wharf and one in the Haight, Bay City Bike isn't hard to find. The shop has an impressive fleet of rental bikes—many sizes and types—and friendly staff to help you map your biking adventure. ✉ *2661 Taylor St., at Beach St., Fisherman's Wharf* ☎ *415/346–2453* ⊕ *baycitybike.com* 💲 *From $32 per day.*

Blazing Saddles

BICYCLING | This outfitter with multiple locations around San Francisco also offers guided tours—most of which involve biking the Golden Gate Bridge—as well as self-guided options with their app. Go slowly on the bridge and watch for pedestrians. ✉ *2715 Hyde St., near Beach St., Fisherman's Wharf* ☎ *415/202–8888* ⊕ *www.blazingsaddles.com* 💲 *From $26 per day for rentals.*

No Uphill Battle

Don't want to get stuck slogging up 20-degree inclines? Then buy the foldout *San Francisco Bike Map & Walking Guide* ($4), which indicates street grades by color and delineates bike routes that avoid major hills and heavy traffic. Find it in bicycle shops and some bookstores or at the San Francisco Bicycle Coalition's website (⊕ *www.sfbike.org*).

BOATING AND SAILING

San Francisco Bay has year-round sailing, but tricky currents and strong winds make the bay hazardous for inexperienced navigators. However, on group sails you can enjoy the bay while leaving the work to the experts.

Adventure Cat Sailing Charters

BOATING | Near Fisherman's Wharf, Adventure Cat takes passengers aboard one of two 55-foot-long catamarans. The kids can sit and soak up the water spray on the trampoline-like net between the two hulls while adults sip drinks on the wind-protected sundeck. Bay cruises and sunset sails with drinks and light hors d'oeuvres are options. ✉ *Pier 39, Dock J, Fisherman's Wharf* ☎ *415/777–1630, 800/498–4228* ⊕ *www.adventurecat.com* 💲 *From $60 for a 90-minute bay cruise.*

WHALE-WATCHING

Between January and April, hundreds of gray whales migrate along the coast; the rest of the year humpback and blue whales feed offshore at the Farallon Islands. The best place to watch them from shore is Point Reyes in Point Reyes National Seashore, in Marin County *(see Chapter 14).*

For a better view, head out on a whale-watching trip. Seas around San Francisco can be rough, making motion-sickness tablets a must. Dress warmly, wear sunscreen, and pack rain gear and sunglasses; binoculars come in handy, too. Tour companies don't provide meals or snacks, so bring your own lunch and water. Make reservations at least a week ahead.

California Whale Adventures

WHALE-WATCHING | California Whale Adventures has year-round whale-watching trips, weekends only, and reservations are highly encouraged. In the fall you can take a great-white-shark tour (weekends only). All trips on *Wacky Jacky* , the company's 50-foot boat, leave from Fisherman's Wharf. ⊠ *Fisherman's Wharf* ☎ *650/579–7777* ⊕ *www.californiawhaleadventures.com* ✉ *From $100 per person, $200 per person for great white shark tour.*

Embarcadero

Stretching from below the Bay Bridge to Fisherman's Wharf, San Francisco's flat, accessible waterfront invites you to get up close and personal with the bay, the picturesque and constant backdrop to this stunning city. For decades the Embarcadero was obscured by a raised freeway and known best for the giant buildings on its piers that further cut off the city from the water. With the freeway gone and a few piers restored for public access, the Embarcadero has been given a new lease on life. Millions of visitors may come through the northern waterfront every year, lured by Fisherman's Wharf and Pier 39, but locals tend to stop short of these, opting instead for the gastronomic pleasures of the Ferry Building or using the palm-tree-lined sidewalks as a jogging route. Between the wharf and South Beach Park, though, you'll find tourists and San Franciscans alike soaking up the sun, walking out over the water on a long pier to see the sailboats, savoring the excellent restaurants and old-time watering holes,

and watching the street performers that crowd Embarcadero Plaza on a sunny day—these are the simple joys that make you happy you're in San Francisco, whether for a few days or a lifetime.

Sights

★ Alcatraz

JAIL | **FAMILY** | Thousands of visitors come every day to walk in the footsteps of Alcatraz's notorious criminals. The stories of life and death on "the Rock" may sometimes be exaggerated, but it's almost impossible to resist the chance to wander the cell block that tamed the country's toughest gangsters and saw daring escape attempts. Some infamous inmates included Al "Scarface" Capone, Robert "The Birdman" Stroud, and George "Machine Gun Kelly." The boat ride to the island is brief (15 minutes) but affords beautiful views, and the audio tour is highly recommended. Allow at least three hours for the visit and boat rides combined. Tour options include a regular daytime one, plus a Night Tour and an evening Behind the Scenes Tour. ■**TIP➔ Booking your tour ahead is absolutely essential to avoid disappointment.** ⊠ *Pier 33, Embarcadero* ☎ *415/981–7625* ⊕ *www.nps.gov/alca* ✉ *From $41.*

★ Exploratorium

MUSEUM | **FAMILY** | Walking into this fascinating "museum of science, art, and human perception" is like visiting a mad-scientist's laboratory, but one in which most of the exhibits are super-size and you can play with everything. Signature experiential exhibits include the Tinkering Studio and a glass Bay Observatory building, where the exhibits inside help visitors better understand what they see outside. Get an Alice-in-Wonderland feeling in the Distorted Room, where you seem to shrink and grow as you walk across the slanted, checkered floor. In the Shadow Box, a powerful flash freezes an image of your shadow on the wall; jumping is a favorite pose.

More than 650 other exhibits focus on sea and insect life, computers, electricity, patterns and light, language, the weather, and more. One surefire hit is the pitch-black, hands-on Tactile Dome ($15 extra; reservations required): crawl through ladders, slides, and tunnels, relying solely on your sense of touch. Don't miss a walk around the outside of the museum afterward for superb views and a lesson about the bay's sediment and water motion in the Bay Windows presentation. ⊠ *Piers 15–17, Embarcadero* ☎ *415/528–4444 general information, 415/528–4407 Tactile Dome reservations* ⊕ *www.exploratorium.edu* ⊠ *$30.*

★ **Ferry Building**
MARKET | The jewel of the Embarcadero, erected in 1896 and now home to an outstanding food marketplace, is topped by a 230-foot clock tower modeled after the campanile of the cathedral in Seville, Spain. On the morning of April 18, 1906, the tower's four clock faces stopped at 5:17—the moment the great earthquake struck—and stayed still for 12 months.

Today San Franciscans flock to the street-level marketplace, stocking up on supplies from local favorites, such as Acme Bread, Blue Bottle Coffee, El Porteño (empanadas), the gluten-free Mariposa Baking Company, and Humphry Slocombe (ice cream). The Slanted Door, the city's beloved high-end Vietnamese restaurant, is the fine dining favorite here, along with Hog Island Oyster Company and the seasonal Californian duo of Bouli Bar and Boulette's Larder. On the plaza side, the outdoor tables at Gott's Roadside offer great people-watching and famous burgers. On Saturday morning the plazas outside the building buzz with an upscale farmers' market. Extending south from the piers north of the building to the Bay Bridge, the waterfront promenade out front is a favorite among joggers and picnickers, with a view of sailboats plying the bay. True to its name, the Ferry Building still serves actual ferries: from its eastern flank they sail to Sausalito, Larkspur, Tiburon, and the East Bay. ⊠ *Embarcadero , 1 Ferry Building, at foot of Market St., Embarcadero* ☎ *415/983–8030* ⊕ *www. ferrybuildingmarketplace.com.*

F-line
TRANSPORTATION SITE (AIRPORT/BUS/FERRY/ TRAIN) | The city's system of vintage electric trolleys, the F-line, gives the cable cars a run for their money as a beloved mode of transportation. The beautifully restored streetcars—some dating from the 19th century—run from the Castro District down Market Street to the Embarcadero, then north to Fisherman's Wharf. Each car is unique, restored to the colors of its city of origin, from New Orleans and Philadelphia to Melbourne and Milan. ■ **TIP→ Pay with a Clipper card or purchase tickets on board; exact change is required.** ⊠ *San Francisco* ⊕ *www. streetcar.org* ⊠ *$2.75.*

San Francisco Railway Museum
MUSEUM | **FAMILY** | A labor of love brought to you by the same vintage-transit enthusiasts responsible for the F-line's revival, this one-room museum and store celebrates the city's streetcars and cable cars with photographs, models, and artifacts. The permanent exhibit includes the replicated end of a streetcar with a working cab—complete with controls and a bell—for kids to explore; the cool, antique Wiley birdcage traffic signal; and models and display cases to view. Right on the F-line track, just across from the Ferry Building, this is a great quick stop. ⊠ *77 Steuart St., Embarcadero* ☎ *415/974–1948* ⊕ *www.streetcar.org/ museum/* ⊠ *Free* ⊘ *Closed Mon.*

🍴 Restaurants

Locals and visitors alike flock here for gorgeous bay views, a world-class waterfront esplanade, and a Ferry Building that's much better known for its food than its boat rides. Some of the best

Did You Know?

San Francisco is only seven miles long by seven miles wide—which makes it really easy to see a lot in just one day.

bakers and cooks in the city have started here or have their satellites here.

Angler

$$$ | SEAFOOD | Immaculately fresh seafood and a wood-burning hearth are the centerpieces of this bustling yet luxurious Embarcadero sibling to Saison. The menu descriptions might be brief, but it's really all about the ingredients—whether it's "fresh from the live tank" geoduck (a large Pacific clam) or peak seasonal baby artichokes—fulfilling their full potential on the plate with a few smart embellishments. **Known for:** taxidermy-filled back room with Bay Bridge views; bigeye tuna tartare; Instagram-favorite radicchio salad. $ *Average main: $36* ⊠ *132 The Embarcadero, Embarcadero* ☎ *415/872–9442* ⊕ *anglerrestaurants.com/san-francisco* ☺ *Closed Sun. and Mon. No lunch.*

★ Boulevard

$$$$ | MODERN AMERICAN | Two local restaurant celebrities—chef Nancy Oakes and designer Pat Kuleto—are behind this high-profile, high-priced eatery in the historic 1889 Audiffred Building that's been attracting well-dressed locals and flush out-of-towners since 1993. A striking Belle Époque interior is the setting for sophisticated American food with a French accent, with a distinct local California produce twist in nearly every dish. **Known for:** any pork chop preparation; polished service; excellent desserts. $ *Average main: $41* ⊠ *1 Mission St., Embarcadero* ☎ *415/543–6084* ⊕ *www.boulevardrestaurant.com* ☺ *No lunch weekends.*

Coqueta

$$$ | SPANISH | With its Embarcadero perch, Bay Bridge views, and stellar Spanish tapas, celebrity chef Michael Chiarello's San Francisco restaurant is a big hit that's equal parts rustic and chic, a lively destination for both small bites and larger meals. Toothpicked *pintxos* (small snacks) like quail egg with Serrano ham are a tasty way to start, but the real draws are the inventive cocktails, luscious paella, and dazzling selection of cured meats. **Known for:** smoked salmon montadito (a small sandwich); sangria from a porrón (a pitcher that people also drink from); churros with chocolate. $ *Average main: $36* ⊠ *Pier 5, on the Embarcadero, near Broadway, Embarcadero* ☎ *415/704–8866* ⊕ *coquetasf.com.*

Fog City

$$ | AMERICAN | FAMILY | All but hidden on a far-flung stretch of the Embarcadero halfway between the Ferry Building and Pier 39, this 21st-century diner that's well worth the hike is best known for its updated classics. An inviting U-shape bar and tables-with-a-view attract a mix of FiDi (Financial District) locals and tourists who've wandered off the main sightseeing path into an excellent spot for great eats and to escape the crowds. **Known for:** wood-fired sourdough pizza; excellent cocktails; anything with fried chicken. $ *Average main: $25* ⊠ *1300 Battery St., Embarcadero* ☎ *415/982–2000* ⊕ *www. fogcitysf.com.*

GOZU

$$$$ | STEAKHOUSE | Chef-owner Marc Zimmerman introduced himself to the San Francisco dining scene running the kitchen for a local group of high-end steak houses, and his first personal restaurant project is the city's most compelling beef-centric dining experience. Elaborate preparations of prestigious Wagyu beef cooked on robata grills are the center of the $185 tasting menu and à la carte options at this minimalist chic Embarcadero restaurant. **Known for:** a steak restaurant that isn't a typical steak house; whiskeys list; counter seating overlooking the kitchen area. $ *Average main: $55* ⊠ *201 Spear St., Embarcadero* ☎ *415/523–9745* ⊕ *www.gozusf.com* ☺ *Closed Sun. and Mon. No lunch.*

Hog Island Oyster Company

$$ | SEAFOOD | A thriving oyster farm north of San Francisco in Tomales Bay serves up its harvest at this raw bar and restaurant in the Ferry Building, where devotees come for impeccably fresh oysters and clams on the half shell. Other mollusk-centered options include a first-rate seafood stew, grilled oysters, clam chowder, and "steamer" dishes, but the bar also turns out one of the city's best grilled cheese sandwiches, made with three artisanal cheeses on artisanal bread. **Known for:** crowds slurping dozens of oysters; local produce salads; superior Bloody Mary. [$] *Average main: $21* ✉ *1 Ferry Bldg., Embarcadero at Market St., Embarcadero* ☎ *415/391–7117* 🌐 *hogislandoysters.com.*

La Mar Cebicheria Peruana

$$$$ | **PERUVIAN** | Right on the water's edge, this casually chic outpost, global mega-chef Gastón Acurio's first outside Peru, imports the signature flavors of his home country's cuisine to San Francisco. Fresh seafood is a big draw here (though not the only one), including a long list of ceviches and the can't-miss *causas* (whipped potatoes topped with a choice of fish, shellfish, or vegetable salads). **Known for:** pisco cocktails; beautiful back patio; empanadas and tiradito (a dish with raw fish). [$] *Average main: $37* ✉ *Pier 1½, between Washington and Jackson Sts., Embarcadero* ☎ *415/397–8880* 🌐 *lamarsf.com.*

One Market

$$$$ | **MODERN AMERICAN** | A favorite for business lunches and special dinners, this white-tablecloth spot caters to suits brokering deals and well-dressed romantic dates, who carve their way through upscale dishes accented by local produce and often intricate sauces. Its menu skews seasonal and meaty, and its largish bar, which offers small bites and numerous cocktails, is popular for FiDi/precommute happy hour. **Known for:** tasty prime rib; Tonya Pitts's standout wine program; "Mark 'n Mike's" lunchtime NY deli restaurant-within-a-restaurant menu. [$] *Average main: $43* ✉ *1 Market St., Embarcadero* ☎ *415/777–5577* 🌐 *onemarket.com* 🕒 *Closed Sun. No lunch Sat.*

Piperade

$$$ | **BASQUE** | Longtime San Francisco chef Gerald Hirigoyen serves a rustic French-Basque menu that includes the namesake *piperade* (cooked peppers and tomatoes served with serrano ham and poached egg) and rack of lamb with cumin and date relish in a sexy, brick-walled dining room. Try a Basque wine for the full experience, and don't miss the orange-blossom beignets or the pastry cream–filled gâteau Basque with cherry preserves on the extensive dessert menu. **Known for:** the definitive Basque food destination in the city; garlic soup with rock shrimp, bacon, and egg; excellent service. [$] *Average main: $36* ✉ *1015 Battery St., Embarcadero* ☎ *415/391–2555* 🌐 *www.piperade.com* 🕒 *Closed Sun. and Mon. No lunch Sat.*

The Slanted Door

$$$$ | **VIETNAMESE** | Celebrated chef-owner Charles Phan has mastered the upmarket, contemporary Vietnamese menu, showcased in a large space with sleek wooden tables and chairs, a big bar, an enviable bay view, and dedicated clientele. There are too many signature dishes to count, including green-papaya salad, chicken clay pot, and shaking beef (tender beef cubes with garlic and onion); they don't come cheap, but they're always made with excellent ingredients. **Known for:** cellophane crab noodles; some of the city's best cocktails; bustling dining room with hard-to-get reservations. [$] *Average main: $38* ✉ *Ferry Bldg., 1 Ferry Bldg. #3, Embarcadero at Market St., Embarcadero* ☎ *415/861–8032* 🌐 *www.slanteddoor.com.*

Waterbar

$$$$ | **SEAFOOD** | You come for seafood with a view: sky-high aquariums dominate the dining room, and the bay is just beyond, but the biggest attraction is the food. Every fin and shell of the sea, from the oak-roasted Petrale sole to the roasted Sacramento sturgeon, is sustainably sourced. **Known for:** cured fish starters; ample oyster bar; delightful Pat Kuleto–designed interior. $ *Average main: $38* ✉ *399 The Embarcadero, between Folsom and Harrison Sts., Embarcadero* ☎ *415/284–9922* ⊕ *www.waterbarsf.com.*

☕ Coffee and Quick Bites

Gott's Roadside

$ | BURGER | FAMILY | A lunchtime favorite where gleaming metal countertops and hand-lettered boards recall the prime burger era, this Ferry Building stalwart boasts a view of Coit Tower and crowd-pleasing grub. This is a burger chain that cares about details: its dressings are house-made, its patties use freshly ground Niman Ranch beef, and its menu includes a wine list. **Known for:** ahi tuna "burger"; creative sandwich specials; wine list and good shakes. $ *Average main: $14* ✉ *1 Ferry Bldg., Suite 6, Embarcadero* ☎ *415/318–3423* ⊕ *www. gotts.com.*

Hotels

The boutique hotels along the Embarcadero are convenient, though at a cost. Rooms tend to be on the smallish side (this is the high-rent district), yet stylish. On the upside, views of the bay are dramatic, and easy access to the Ferry Building makes foodies rejoice.

Harbor Court Hotel

$ | HOTEL | Renovated in 2018, this Spanish Colonial Revival–style Embarcadero hotel has nice touches that enliven the guest quarters, including 42-inch high-definition TVs, quirky mathematical wall clocks, and lumbar pillows adorning beds with Frette linens, as well as a daily wine hour and the convenience of being attached to the Ozumo sushi restaurant. **Pros:** convenient and quiet location; friendly, professional staffers; Bay Bridge and Ferry Building views from some rooms. **Cons:** many rooms are noticeably small; some rooms lack views; $29 fee per night for amenities they don't require irks some guests. $ *Rooms from: $179* ✉ *165 Steuart St.,*

Embarcadero ☎ *415/882–1300, 888/538–8552* ⊕ *www.harborcourthotel.com* ⬩ *131 rooms* ⦿ *No meals.*

Hotel Vitale

$$$ | HOTEL | The emphasis on luxury and upscale relaxation at this eight-story property across the street from the bay is apparent: limestone-lined baths stocked with top-of-the-line products; the penthouse-level day spa with soaking tubs set in a rooftop bamboo forest; terraces on the fifth, seventh, and eighth floors with great waterfront views. **Pros:** excellent Americano Restaurant & Bar; spacious rooms; well-designed work-from-room setups with ergonomic chairs. **Cons:** not close to much nightlife; steep $40 per day amenities fee adds expense to an already pricey property; yet another charge for Wi-Fi beyond basic. $ *Rooms from: $319* ✉ *8 Mission St., Embarcadero* ☎ *415/278–3700* ⊕ *www.hotelvitale.com* ⬩ *200 rooms* ⦿ *No meals.*

Hyatt Regency San Francisco

$$ | HOTEL | This perfectly located property near the Ferry Building has a dramatic 17-story atrium lobby that starred in several 1970s flicks, most notably the disaster epic *The Towering Inferno* . All the guest rooms, furnished with comfortable "Hyatt Grand" beds, blackout curtains, and smart TVs, have floor-to-ceiling windows revealing city or bay views, and many have balconies. **Pros:** elegant design; near restaurants and shopping; even the smallest rooms a decent size. **Cons:** unremarkable dining choices; not all rooms have balconies; lacks intimacy. $ *Rooms from: $200* ✉ *5 Embarcadero Center, Embarcadero* ☎ *415/788–1234* ⊕ *hyatt.com* ⬩ *804 rooms* ⦿ *No meals.*

▼ Nightlife

The waterfront's eastern section stays busy at night, not a surprise given its expansive bay views and proximity to Union Square, Chinatown, the Financial District, and SoMa.

BARS
Hard Water
BARS/PUBS | The waterfront restaurant and bar with a stunning horseshoe-shape bar centerpiece pays homage to America's most iconic spirit—bourbon—with a wall of whiskeys and a lineup of specialty cocktails. The menu, crafted by Charles Phan of Slanted Door fame, is an ode to New Orleans cuisine and includes spicy pork-belly cracklings, BBQ oysters, must-try Nashville hot fried chicken, and other fun snacks. ⊠ *Pier 3, at The Embarcadero, Embarcadero* ☎ *415/392–3021* ⊕ *www.hardwaterbar.com.*

Pier 23 Cafe
BARS/PUBS | Beer arrives at your table in buckets at this waterfront bar, which has ample seating at plastic tables on a wooden deck. Although you'd expect to sit elbow to elbow with fishers, you're more likely to share the space with twenty- and thirtysomethings drawn by the cocktails and decent seafood dishes, and of course the prime vantage point for gazing across the bay. ⊠ *Pier 23, The Embarcadero, Embarcadero* ☎ *415/362–5125* ⊕ *www.pier23cafe.com.*

🎫 Performing Arts

SPOKEN WORD AND READINGS
Commonwealth Club of California
READINGS/LECTURES | The nation's oldest public-affairs forum hosts speakers as diverse as Jane Goodall and Bill Gates, covering topics from culture and politics to economics and foreign policy. Most events are open to nonmembers, and lectures are broadcast on local NPR affiliates. ⊠ *110 The Embarcadero, Embarcadero* ☎ *415/597–6705* ⊕ *www. commonwealthclub.org.*

🛍 Shopping

Four sprawling buildings of shops, restaurants, offices, and a popular independent movie theater—plus the Hyatt Regency hotel—make up the Embarcadero Center,

downtown at the end of Market Street. Most stores are branches of upscale national chains, such as Ann Taylor and Banana Republic. Also in this area is the Ferry Building, with a focus on local food and other vendors.

BOOKS
Book Passage
BOOKS/STATIONERY | Windows at this modest-size bookstore frame close-up views of the docks and San Francisco Bay. Commuters snap up magazines by the front door as they rush off to their ferries, and kids browse the Kids' Corner while Ferry Building visitors leisurely thumb through the thorough selection of cooking and travel titles. Author events take place several times a month. ⊠ *Ferry Building Marketplace, 1 Ferry Bldg. #42, at foot of Market St., Embarcadero* ☎ *415/835–1020* ⊕ *www.bookpassage.com.*

FARMERS' MARKETS
★ Ferry Plaza Farmers' Market
OUTDOOR/FLEA/GREEN MARKETS | The partylike Saturday edition of the city's most upscale and expensive farmers' market places baked goods, gourmet cheeses, smoked fish, and fancy pots of jam alongside organic basil, specialty mushrooms, heirloom tomatoes, and juicy-ripe locally grown fruit. Smaller markets also take place on Tuesday and Thursday year-round, rain or shine—and the many passionate San Francisco home cooks who frequent them will come even in a rainstorm. ⊠ *Ferry Plaza, at Market St., Embarcadero* ☎ *415/291–3276* ⊕ *www. ferrybuildingmarketplace.com.*

FOOD AND DRINK
Recchiuti Confections
FOOD/CANDY | Michael and Jacky Recchiuti began making otherworldly chocolates in San Francisco in 1997, using traditional European techniques. Now considered among the best confectioners in the world, they stock their store here with their full chocolate line, including several unique items like truffles inspired by red-wine pairings and a box of burnt

caramel truffles decorated with images of San Francisco's iconic places. ⊠ *Ferry Building Marketplace, 1 Ferry Bldg., Suite 30, Embarcadero at foot of Market St., Embarcadero* ☎ *415/834–9494* ⊕ *www. recchiuti.com.*

TOYS

Exploratorium

TOYS | FAMILY | The educational gadgets and gizmos sold here are so clever and engaging that kids won't know they're learning while playing. Space- and dinosaur-related games are popular, as are science videos and optical illusion gifts. ⊠ *Pier 15, at The Embarcadero and Green St., Embarcadero* ☎ *415/528–4390* ⊕ *www.exploratorium.edu.*

 Activities

BOATING AND SAILING

Rendezvous Charters

SAILING | This operator offers individually ticketed trips on large sailing yachts, including sunset sails and Sunday brunch cruises on a schooner. Ticketed trips tend to close from mid-October through March (although they continue to do private chartered sails throughout the year), so call in advance to confirm availability. ⊠ *Pier 40, Suite 4, South Beach Harbor, Embarcadero* ☎ *415/543–7333* ⊕ *www.rendezvouscharters.com* 🎫 *Sailings from $60.*

Financial District

During the latter half of the 19th century, when San Francisco was a brawling, extravagant gold-rush town, today's Financial District (FiDi, for short) was underwater. Yerba Buena Cove reached all the way up to Montgomery Street, and what's now Jackson Square was the heart of the Barbary Coast, bordering some of the roughest wharves in the world. These days, Jackson Square is a genteel and upscale neighborhood wedged between North Beach and the Financial District, but buried below

Montgomery Street lie remnants of those wild days: more than 100 ships abandoned by frantic crews and passengers caught up in gold fever rest under the foundations of buildings here.

The Financial District of the 21st century is a decidedly less exciting affair: it's all office towers with mazes of cubicles now. When the sun sets, this quarter empties out fast. The few sights here will appeal mainly to gold-rush history enthusiasts; others can spend time elsewhere.

◉ Sights

Jackson Square Historic District

NEIGHBORHOOD | This was the heart of the Barbary Coast of the Gay '90s—the 1890s, that is. Although most of the red-light district was destroyed in the fire that followed the 1906 earthquake, the remaining old redbrick buildings, many of them now occupied by advertising agencies, law offices, and antiques firms, retain hints of the romance and rowdiness of San Francisco's early days.

With its gentrified gold rush–era buildings, the 700 block of **Montgomery Street** just barely evokes the Barbary Coast days, but this was a colorful block in the 19th century and on into the 20th. Writers Mark Twain and Bret Harte were among the contributors to the spunky *The Golden Era* newspaper, which occupied No. 732 (now part of the building at No. 744).

Restored 19th-century brick buildings line Hotaling Place, which connects Washington and Jackson Streets, named for the **A. P. Hotaling Company whiskey distillery** (*451 Jackson St., at Hotaling Pl.*), the largest liquor repository on the West Coast in its day. The exceptional Gold Rush City walking tour offered by City Guides (☎ *415/557–4266,* ⊕ *www. sfcityguides.org*) covers this area and brings its history to life. ⊠ *Bordered by Columbus Ave., Broadway, and Washington and Sansome Sts., Financial District.*

Market Street buildings

BUILDING | The street, which bisects the city at an angle, has consistently challenged San Francisco's architects. One of the most intriguing responses to this challenge sits diagonally across Market Street from the Palace Hotel. The tower of the **Hobart Building** (No. 582) combines a flat facade and oval sides and is considered one of Willis Polk's best works in the city. East on Market Street is Charles Havens's triangular **Flatiron Building** (Nos. 540–548), another classic solution. At Bush Street, the **Mechanics Monument**, in recognition of the Donahue brothers who industrialized the city, holds its own against the skyscrapers that tower over the intersection. This homage to waterfront mechanics, which survived the 1906 earthquake (a famous photograph shows Market Street in ruins around the sculpture), was designed by Douglas Tilden, a noted California sculptor. The plaque in the sidewalk next to the monument marks the spot as the location of the San Francisco Bay shoreline in 1848. Telltale nautical details, such as anchors, ropes, and shells, adorn the gracefully detailed **Matson Building** (No. 215), built in the 1920s for the shipping line Matson Navigation. ⊠ *Between New Montgomery and Beale Sts., Financial District.*

Salesforce Park

CITY PARK | FAMILY | Ask a hundred San Franciscans about Salesforce Park and the city's tallest building, the 1,070-foot Salesforce Tower, and you'll get a hundred different opinions. The tower opened in 2018 and is now the second-tallest building west of the Mississippi. This splashy, impossible-to-miss glass, rocket-shape high-rise dominates the city's skyline and has become the symbol of the city's modern tech-money elite. It is photogenic, but some feel it might dominate photos of the city *too* often. Building visits are limited to employees and people coming for business purposes, so instead, enjoy a pastry from the street-level Boutique Crenn by

Whiskey Rhyme

The Italianate Hotaling building at 451 Jackson Street survived the disastrous 1906 quake and fire—a miracle considering the thousands of barrels of inflammable liquid inside. A plaque on the side of the structure repeats a famous query: "If, as they say, god spanked the town for being over frisky, why did he burn the churches down and save Hotaling's whiskey?"

Michelin-starred chef Dominique Crenn, and look up to try to see the top of the tower.

The true highlight of the Salesforce mini-neighborhood is Salesforce Park, a sprawling urban park with 13 ecosystems atop the four-block-long Salesforce Transit Center. It's a downtown green gem, a true civic accomplishment. This is a favorite destination for families, walkers, and workers trying to get fresh air on their lunch break. The park can be reached via elevators, escalators, or a thrilling gondola ride from the base of the Salesforce Tower at Fremont and Mission Streets. ⊠ *425 Mission St., Downtown* ✛ *Roughly between Beale and 2nd Sts., and Mission and Howard Sts.* ☎ *415/597-5000* ⊕ *salesforcetransitcenter.com.*

Transamerica Pyramid

BUILDING | It's neither owned by Transamerica nor is it a pyramid, but this 48-floor, 853-foot-tall obelisk *is* the most photographed of the city's high-rises. Excoriated in the design stages as "the world's largest architectural folly," the icon was quickly hailed as a masterpiece when it opened in 1972. Today it's probably the city's most recognized structure after the Golden Gate Bridge, and it's the second-tallest in the city after the Salesforce

Alcatraz as Native Land

In the 1960s, Native Americans attempted to reclaim Alcatraz, citing an 1868 treaty that granted Native Americans any surplus federal land. Their activism crested in 1969, when several dozen Native Americans began a 19-month occupation, supported by public opinion and friendly media.

The group offered to buy the island from the government for $24 worth of beads and other goods—exactly what Native Americans had been paid for Manhattan in 1626. In their "Proclamation: To the Great White Father and All His People," the group laid out the 10 reasons why Alcatraz was suitable for an Indian reservation "by the white man's own standards," among them: "There is no industry and so unemployment is very great," and "The soil is rocky and nonproductive, and the land does not support game." Federal agents removed the last holdouts in 1971, but each Thanksgiving Native Americans and others gather on the island to commemorate the takeover. In 2013 the park service restored the protesters' fading graffiti on the water tower, and today's visitors are still greeted with the huge message: "Indians Welcome. Indian Land."

Tower. You can't go up the pyramid, but the best views and photo-ops are of the building itself anyway. **■TIP→ A fragrant redwood grove along the east side of the building, with benches and a cheerful fountain of leaping frogs, is a placid downtown oasis in which to unwind.** ✉ *600 Montgomery St., Financial District* 🌐 *www.pyramidcenter.com.*

Wells Fargo History Museum

MUSEUM | At this fun two-story museum, you can get a taste of the early years of the gold rush when San Francisco had no formal banks and miners often entrusted their gold dust to saloon keepers. In 1852, Wells Fargo opened its first bank in the city on this spot, and the company soon established banking offices in mother-lode camps throughout California. One popular exhibit is a simulated ride in a replica of an early stagecoach. The museum also displays samples of nuggets and gold dust from mines, an old telegraph machine on which you can practice sending codes, and tools the '49ers used to coax gold from the ground. ✉ *420 Montgomery St., Financial District* ☎ *415/396–2619* 🌐 *www.wellsfargohistory.com* 🎫 *Free.*

🍴 Restaurants

The center of commerce, with some very good restaurants (housed in old Barbary Coast buildings), FiDi caters to the business elite with prices to match, but engineers and software developers looking for a fast lunch head to modest Indian and Chinese places, as well as superb sandwich shops.

BIX

$$$ | **AMERICAN** | With its Jazz Age vibe, live music, discreet alley location behind the Transamerica Pyramid, and spectacular bar and bi-level dining room, BIX would be worth a visit for the impressive setting alone. However, it's also one of the city's finest restaurants for special occasions that don't require a tasting menu; continental and upscale American fare get fresh modern takes, often with a few haute elements. **Known for:** all the classic cocktails; potato pillows with caviar; career servers who remember your name after one visit. [$] *Average main: $35* ✉ *56 Gold St., Financial District* ☎ *415/433–6300* 🌐 *bixrestaurant.com* 🕒 *Closed Sun. and Mon. No lunch.*

Continued on page 175

ALCATRAZ

"They made that place purely for punishment, where men would rot. It was designed to systematically destroy human beings . . . Cold, gray, and lonely, it had a weird way of haunting you—there were those dungeons that you heard about, but there was also the city . . . only a mile and a quarter away, so close you could almost touch it. Sometimes the wind would blow a certain way and you could smell the Italian cooking in North Beach and hear the laughter of people, of women and kids. That made it worse than hell."

—Jim Quillen, former Alcatraz inmate

Gripping the rail as the ferryboat pitches gently in the chilly breeze, you watch formidable Alcatraz rising ahead. Imagine making this trip shackled at the ankle and waist, the looming fortress on the craggy island ahead, waiting to swallow you whole. Thousands of visitors come every day to walk in the footsteps of Alcatraz's notorious criminals. The stories of life and death on "the Rock" may sometimes be exaggerated, but it's almost impossible to resist the chance to wander the cellblock that tamed the country's toughest gangsters and saw daring escape attempts of tremendous desperation.

LIFE ON THE ROCK

The federal penitentiary's first warden, James A. Johnston, was largely responsible for Alcatraz's (mostly false) hell-on-earth reputation. A tough but relatively humane disciplinarian, Johnston strictly limited the information flow to and from the prison when it opened in 1934. Prisoners' letters were censored, newspapers and radios were forbidden, and no visits were allowed during a convict's first three months in the slammer. Understandably, imaginations ran wild on the mainland.

A LIFE OF PRIVILEGE

Monotony was an understatement on Alcatraz; the same precise schedule was kept daily. The rulebook stated, "You are entitled to food, clothing, shelter, and medical attention. Anything else you get is a privilege." These privileges, from the right to work to the ability to receive mail, were earned by following the prison's rules. A relatively minor infraction meant losing privileges. A serious breach, like fighting, brought severe punishments like time in the Hole (a.k.a. the Strip Cell, since the prisoner had to strip) or the Oriental (an absolutely dark, silent cell with a hole in the ground for a toilet).

THE SPAGHETTI RIOT

Johnston knew that poor food was one of the major causes of prison riots, so he insisted that Alcatraz serve the best chow in the prison system. But the next warden at Alcatraz slacked off, and in 1950, one spaghetti meal too many sent the inmates over the edge. Guards deployed tear gas to subdue the rioters.

A PRISONER'S DAY

6:30 am: Wake-up call. Prisoners get up, get dressed, and clean cells.

6:50 am: Prisoners stand at cell doors to be counted.

7:00 am: Prisoners march single-file to mess hall for breakfast.

7:20 am: Prisoners head to work or industries detail; count.

9:30 am: 8-minute break; count.

11:30 am: Count; prisoners march to mess hall for lunch.

12:00 pm: Prisoners march to cells; count; break in cells.

12:20 pm: Prisoners leave cells, march single-file back to work; count.

2:30 pm: 8-minute break; count.

4:15 pm: Prisoners stop work, two counts.

4:25 pm: Prisoners march into mess hall and are counted; dinner.

4:45 pm: Prisoners return to cells and are locked in.

5:00 pm: Prisoners stand at their doors to be counted.

8:00 pm: Count.

9:30 pm: Count; lights out.

12:01 am–5 am: Three counts.

INFAMOUS INMATES

Fewer than 2,000 inmates ever did time on the Rock; though they weren't necessarily the worst criminals, they were definitely the worst prisoners. Most were escape artists, and others, like Al Capone, had corrupted the prison system from the inside with bribes.

Name Al "Scarface" Capone

On the Rock 1934–1939

In for Tax evasion

Claim to fame Notorious Chicago gangster and bootlegger who arranged the 1929 St. Valentine's Day Massacre.

Hard fact Capone was among the first transfers to the Rock and arrived smiling and joking. He soon realized the party was over. Capone endured a few stints in the Hole and Warden Johnston's early enforced-silence policy; he was also stabbed by a fellow inmate. The gangster eventually caved, saying "it looks like Alcatraz has got me licked," thus cementing the prison's reputation.

Name Robert "The Birdman" Stroud

On the Rock 1942–1959

In for Murder, including the fatal stabbing of a prison guard

Claim to fame Subject of the acclaimed but largely fictitious 1962 film *Birdman of Alcatraz*.

Hard fact Stroud was actually known as the "Bird Doctor of Leavenworth." While incarcerated in Leavenworth prison through the 1920s and '30s, he became an expert on birds, tending an aviary and writing two books. The stench and mess in his cell discouraged the guards from searching it—and finding Stroud's homemade still. His years on the Rock were birdless.

Name George "Machine Gun" Kelly

On the Rock 1934–1951

In for Kidnapping

Claim to fame Became an expert with a machine gun at the urging of his wife, Kathryn. Kathryn also encouraged his string of bank robberies and the kidnapping for ransom of oilman Charles Urschel. While stashed in Leavenworth on a life sentence, Kelly boasted that he would escape and then free Kathryn. That got him a one-way ticket to Alcatraz.

Hard fact Was an altar boy on Alcatraz and was generally considered a model prisoner.

NO ESCAPE

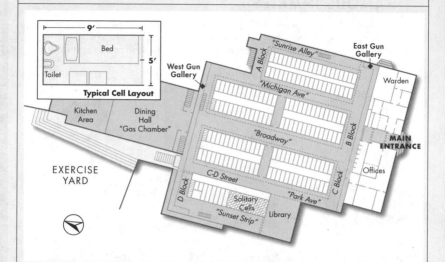

Typical Cell Layout — Bed, Toilet, 9', 5'

West Gun Gallery, East Gun Gallery, Warden, "Sunrise Alley", A Block, "Michigan Ave", Kitchen Area, Dining Hall "Gas Chamber", B Block, MAIN ENTRANCE, "Broadway", EXERCISE YARD, C-D Street, Offices, D Block, C Block, Solitary Cells, "Park Ave", "Sunset Strip", Library

Alcatraz was a maximum-security federal penitentiary with one guard for every three prisoners. The biggest deterrent to escape, though, was the 1.4 miles of icy bay waters separating the Rock from the city. Only a few prisoners made it off the island, and only one is known to have survived. And that story about the shark-infested waters? There are sharks in the bay, but they're not the man-eating kind.

Bloodiest Attempt: In 1946, six prisoners hatched a plan to surprise a guard, seize weapons, and escape through the recreation yard. They succeeded up to a point, arming themselves and locking several guards into cells, but things got ugly when the group couldn't find the key that opened the door to the prison yard. Desperate, they opened fire on the trapped guards. Warden Johnston called in the Marines, who shelled the cell house for two days in the so-called Battle of Alcatraz. Three ringleaders were killed in the fighting; two were executed for murder; and one, who was just 19 years old, got 99 years slapped on to his sentence.

Craftiest Attempt: Over six months, three convicts stole bits and pieces from the kitchen and machine shop to make drills and digging pieces. They used these basic tools to widen a vent into the utility corridor. They also gathered bits of cardboard, toilet paper, and hair from the prison's barbershop to make crude models of their own heads. Then, like teenagers sneaking out, they put the decoy heads in their cots and walked away—up the pipes in the utility corridor to the roof, then down a drainpipe to the ground. They set sail in a raft made from prison raincoats, and are officially presumed dead.

Most Anticlimactic: In 1962, one prisoner spent an entire year loosening the bars in a window. Then he slipped through and managed to swim all the way to Fort Point, near the Golden Gate Bridge. He promptly fell asleep there and was found an hour later by some teenagers.

6 TIPS FOR ESCAPING TO ALCATRAZ

"Broadway," once the cell blocks' busiest corridor.

1. Buy your ticket in advance. Visit the website for Alcatraz Cruises (☎ 415/981–7625 ⊕ cityexperiences.com) to scout out available departure times for the ferry. Prepay by credit card—the ticket price covers the boat ride and the audio tour—and print your ticket at home. Bring it to Pier 33 up to an hour before sailing and experience just a touch of schadenfreude as you overhear attendants tell scores of too-late passengers that your tour is sold out.

2. Dress smart. Bring that pullover you packed to ward off the chill from the boat ride and Alcatraz Island. Also: sneakers. Some Alcatraz guides are fanatical about making excellent time.

3. Go for the evening tour. You'll get even more out of the experience if you do it at night. The evening tour has programs not offered during the day, the bridge-to-bridge view of the city twinkles at night, and your "prison experience" will be amplified as darkness mournfully falls while you shuffle around the cell block.

4. Unplug and go against the flow. If you miss a cue on the excellent audio tour and find yourself out of synch, don't sweat it—use it as an opportunity to switch off the tape. No one will stop you if you walk back through a cell block on your own, taking the time to listen to the haunting sound of your own footsteps on the concrete floor.

5. Be mindful of scheduled and limited-capacity talks. Some programs only happen once a day; the schedule is posted in the cell house and at the dock on the island. Certain talks have limited capacity seating, so keep an eye out for a cell house staffer handing out passes shortly before the start time.

6. Talk to the staff. One of the island's greatest resources is its staff, who practically bubble over with information. Pick their brains, and draw them out about what they know.

PRACTICALITIES

Visitors at the Alcatraz dock waiting to depart "Uncle Sam's Devil's Island."

GETTING THERE

All cruises are operated by Alcatraz Cruises, the park's authorized concessionaire. Check ⊕ cityexperiences.com for all tour options and reservations. Please book in advance. Locals aren't kidding when they mention how often visitors are disappointed.

TIMING

The boat ride to Alcatraz is only about 15 minutes long, but you should allow about three hours for your entire visit. The delightful F-line vintage streetcars are the most direct public transit to the dock; on weekdays the 10-Townsend bus will get you within a few blocks of Pier 33.

FOOD

There is no food service on the boats or on the island. Food cannot be brought past the dock on the island, so don't even think about an Alcatraz picnic. Bottled water is okay, though. The café at Alcatraz Landing is closed. Plan your meals for before or after the trip.

STORM TROOPER ALERT!

When he was filming *Star Wars*, George Lucas recorded the sound of Alcatraz's cell doors slamming shut and used the sound bite in the movie whenever Darth Vader's star cruiser closed its doors.

KIDS ON THE ROCK

Parents should be aware that the audio tour, while engaging and worthwhile, includes some startlingly realistic sound effects. (Some children might not get a kick out of the gunshots from the Battle of Alcatraz—or the guards' screams, for that matter.) If you stay just one minute ahead in the program, you can always fast forward through the violent moments on your little one's audio tour.

Café Claude
$$ | **FRENCH** | Francophiles congregate here for that *je ne sais quoi,* right down to the delicious French onion soup, escargots, steak tartare, and coq au vin, especially Thursday through Sunday nights for live jazz. If you think this place looks straight out of Paris, it mostly is: the banquettes, zinc bar, light fixtures, and cinema posters were shipped from a defunct café in the City of Lights to this atmospheric downtown alley. **Known for:** steak frites; joie de vivre; cheese and charcuterie plates. [$] *Average main: $26* ✉ *7 Claude La., Financial District* ☎ *415/392–3505* 🌐 *cafeclaude.com* 🕒 *No lunch Sun.*

Cotogna
$$$ | **ITALIAN** | The draw at this urban trattoria—just as in demand as its fancier big sister, Quince, next door—is chef Michael Tusk's flavorful, rustic, seasonally driven Italian cooking, headlined by pastas, beautifully grilled or spit-roasted meats, and homemade gelato. The look is comfortably chic, with wood tables, quality stemware, and fantastic Italian and under-the-radar Californian wines by the bottle and glass. **Known for:** raviolo with brown butter and egg in center; very tough to get prime reservations; peak seasonal produce in antipasti. [$] *Average main: $29* ✉ *490 Pacific Ave., Financial District* ☎ *415/775–8508* 🌐 *www.cotognasf.com* 🕒 *Closed Mon. and Tues.*

Kokkari Estiatorio
$$$$ | **GREEK** | Satisfy your craving for outstanding Greek taverna food—albeit at luxe steak house prices—from a dizzying selection of mezes (small plates) such as stuffed grape leaves to main courses that showcase Athenian standards like moussaka, lemon-oregano chicken, and notable grilled lamb chops. There's a lively after-work scene in this chic farmhouse setting with wood-beamed ceilings, a roaring wood oven, and candlelight. **Known for:** grilled octopus; in-demand reservations; semolina custard wrapped in phylo. [$] *Average main: $37* ✉ *200 Jackson St., Financial District* ☎ *415/981–0983* 🌐 *kokkari.com* 🕒 *No lunch weekends.*

Michael Mina
$$$$ | **MIDDLE EASTERN** | The flagship outpost for this acclaimed chef remains a beacon of refined dining, with a Middle Eastern–inspired menu that loosely channels Mina's Egyptian family background with luxury elements and plenty of creativity in prix fixe menus. The restaurant's predecessor, Aqua, is where Mina first made a major name for himself in San Francisco before growing a worldwide restaurant empire, and you can still opt to include some of his early signature dishes, like lobster pot pie, here. **Known for:** romantic dates and power lunches; consummate service; superb wine program. [$] *Average main: $195* ✉ *252 California St., Financial District* ☎ *415/397–9222* 🌐 *www.michaelmina.net* 🕒 *No lunch weekends.*

Perbacco
$$ | **ITALIAN** | From the complimentary basket of skinny, brittle breadsticks to the pappardelle with short rib *ragù,* chef Staffan Terje's entire menu is a delectable paean to northern Italy. With a long marble bar and open kitchen, this brick-lined two-story space oozes big-city charm, attracting business types and Italian food aficionados alike to the FiDi well after evening rush hour ends. **Known for:** agnolotti del plin (a type of pasta filled with meat); house-made cured meats; vitello tonnato (cold veal with a tuna-flavored sauce) appetizer. [$] *Average main: $26* ✉ *230 California St., Financial District* ☎ *415/955–0663* 🌐 *www.perbaccosf.com* 🕒 *Closed Sun.-Tues. No lunch Sat.*

★ Quince
$$$$ | **MODERN AMERICAN** | To enjoy Michael Tusk's three-Michelin-starred contemporary California cuisine with a slight Italian influence, you'll have to splurge on an 8- to 10-course chef's tasting menu, but you'll be rewarded with seasonal items reaching the highest gastronomic

heights. The 1,400-bottle-strong wine list is top-notch, although it can get pricey (a steep corkage fee means you won't save much by bringing your own bottle), and the seamless service is both refined and welcoming. **Known for:** stellar pasta dishes in middle of menu; outstanding cocktails and amaro list; posh, dramatic dining room. [$] *Average main: $295* ✉ *470 Pacific Ave., Financial District* ☎ *415/775–8500* 🌐 *www.quincerestaurant.com* 🕓 *Closed Sun. No lunch.*

Tadich Grill

$$$ | **SEAFOOD** | Locations and owners have changed more than once since this old-timer started as a coffee stand on the waterfront in 1849, but the crowds keep coming. Try to snag one of the private booths (complete with a bell to summon the brusque, white-coated waiters) and sample seafood—always the name of the game here—such as the Dungeness crab cocktail or local sanddabs (a type of flounder). **Known for:** delicious cioppinos; one- (or three-) martini lunches; hangtown fry (a type of omelet from gold-rush days). [$] *Average main: $30* ✉ *240 California St., Financial District* ☎ *415/391–1849* 🌐 *tadichgrillsf.com* 🕓 *Closed Sun. No lunch Sat.*

The Vault Garden

$$$ | **MODERN AMERICAN** | The Financial District took a hit during the COVID-19 pandemic, but one silver lining was the opportunity for this restaurant inside the sky-touching 555 California Building to take over the sprawling, suddenly commuter-free plaza outside. "The Garden" is now a permanent fixture (and the swanky main indoor part is worth a dinner stop, too), featuring excellent seasonal California cuisine and a few elevated comfort classics that help lift this destination into the upper tier of SF dining options. **Known for:** Parker house rolls; photogenic food and atmosphere; excellent cocktails. [$] *Average main: $34* ✉ *555 California St., Financial District* ☎ *415/508–4675* 🌐 *thevault555.com* 🕓 *Closed Mon. No lunch Tues. and Wed.*

Wayfare Tavern

$$$ | **AMERICAN** | This energetic and upscale American tavern owned by TV chef and personality Tyler Florence is rich with upscale turn-of-the-20th-century Americana, including brick walls, comfortable booths, and a billiards room. It also tips its hat to tradition—and comfort — on the menu with deviled eggs, fresh seafood, and several signature dishes that are considered the best of their categories in the city (the burger with Marin brie, for one), plus noteworthy cocktails that complete the full experience. **Known for:** buttermilk-brined fried chicken with herbs; giant warm popovers start each meal; house-made doughnuts. [$] *Average main: $30* ✉ *558 Sacramento St., Financial District* ☎ *415/722–9060* 🌐 *www.wayfaretavern.com.*

Yank Sing

$$ | **CHINESE** | **FAMILY** | This bustling, lunch-only restaurant serves some of San Francisco's best dim sum to office workers on weekdays and boisterous families on weekends, and the take-out counter makes a meal on the run a satisfying compromise when office duties—or sightseeing—won't wait. The several dozen varieties prepared daily include the classic and the creative; steamed pork buns, shrimp dumplings, scallion-skewered prawns tied with bacon, and basil seafood dumplings are among the many delights. **Known for:** Peking duck; Shanghai soup dumplings; energetic vibe in dining room. [$] *Average main: $18* ✉ *49 Stevenson St., Financial District* ☎ *415/541–4949* 🌐 *yanksing.com* 🕓 *No dinner.*

Hotels

The large hotels here lure business travelers with some of the city's finest luxury accommodations—with hefty price tags to boot. With public transportation, Union Square, the Ferry Building, Chinatown, and North Beach a short walk away, leisure travelers find this area a good base as well.

Four Seasons Hotel San Francisco at Embarcadero

$$$$ | **HOTEL** | Previously a Mandarin Oriental hotel and then a Loews Regency, the city's second Four Seasons opened with little fanfare during the COVID-19 pandemic, but as in previous incarnations, each luxurious room has spectacular city and bay views; the hotel occupies the top 11 floors in one of San Francisco's tallest buildings. **Pros:** 40th-floor open-air sky deck; beautiful bathrooms with marble vanity; "Eye Spy from the Sky" game on 48th floor. **Cons:** in a business area that's quiet at night and on weekends; high price for pampering; not all rooms have soaking tubs. $ *Rooms from: $535* ✉ *222 Sansome St., Financial District* ☎ *415/276–9888* ⊕ *www.fourseasons.com/embarcadero* ⇩ *155 rooms* ⭤ *No meals.*

Galleria Park Hotel

$ | **HOTEL** | At the edge of the FiDi and Union Square areas, this boutique hotel manages to be both hip and welcoming, with modern touches on historical bones and smallish guest rooms with all the technological amenities modern travelers require. **Pros:** hotel's own park terrace with walking track; complimentary wine at daily Sipping Hour; in-house French brasserie Gaspar and Blue Bottle Coffee. **Cons:** relatively small bathrooms; city noise; $29 per night fee for extras like Wi-Fi, morning coffee, fitness room. $ *Rooms from: $189* ✉ *191 Sutter St., Financial District* ☎ *415/781–3060,* ⊕ *www.galleriapark.com* ⇩ *177 rooms* ⭤ *No meals.*

Hilton San Francisco Financial District

$$ | **HOTEL** | **FAMILY** | Business travelers patronize this hoppin' Hilton for its airy guest rooms and large work desks, but even in high season the weekend rates drop significantly, luring leisure travelers. **Pros:** has its own "technology lounge"; good-size rooms with bay or city views; great location at intersection of FiDi, Chinatown, and North Beach. **Cons:** congested downtown area; property

needs sprucing up; feels rather corporate. $ *Rooms from: $236* ✉ *750 Kearny St., Financial District* ☎ *415/433–6600* ⊕ *www.hilton.com* ⇩ *543 rooms* ⭤ *No meals.*

Le Méridien San Francisco

$ | **HOTEL** | The stylishly contemporary Le Méridien scores well on both form and function, with compelling artwork throughout the lobby and guest rooms outfitted with polished granite sinks, wall-size San Francisco maps, and floor-to-ceiling windows. **Pros:** spacious rooms; interesting artwork throughout; accommodating staff. **Cons:** this FiDi neighborhood grows sleepy after dark; restaurant and bar merely adequate; not a lot of amenities. $ *Rooms from: $169* ✉ *333 Battery St., Financial District* ☎ *415/296–2900* ⊕ *lemeridiensanfrancisco.com* ⇩ *360 rooms* ⭤ *No meals.*

Omni San Francisco Hotel

$$$ | **HOTEL** | In a 1926 Florentine Renaissance–style structure that once housed banks and other financial enterprises, the Omni draws travelers seeking historical flavor and a downtown location. **Pros:** comfortable rooms with historical flavor; great steak and martinis at on-site steak house; "get fit" kits for working out in-room, plus well-equipped fitness center. **Cons:** fee for in-room Wi-Fi if not an Omni member; traditional look not to everyone's taste; not much to do in immediate area at night and on weekends. $ *Rooms from: $319* ✉ *500 California St., Financial District* ☎ *415/677–9494* ⊕ *www.omnisanfrancisco.com* ⇩ *362 rooms* ⭤ *No meals.*

Nightlife

Not surprisingly, the nightlife scene here revolves around people recovering from extended workdays or still trying to seal the deal. Wiggle in among the shop talkers and enjoy a stiff martini.

BARS
Pagan Idol

BARS/PUBS | Giving the Tonga Room a run for its money as the most kitschy tiki bar in town, Pagan Idol features a secret back room complete with erupting volcano, giant tikis, and a starry night sky. The folks from Bourbon & Branch are behind this faux pirate ship, so even if the cocktails are served in goofy tiki glasses with paper umbrellas, rest assured they're top-shelf and on the money. ⊠ 375 Bush St., near Kearney St., Financial District ☎ 415/985–6375 ⊕ www.paganidol.com.

★ Rickhouse

BARS/PUBS | An after-work FiDi crowd fills this brick-walled and dimly lit, speakeasy-ish drinking spot, revered for its extensive whiskey menu and curated list of seasonal cocktails. It's a beautiful space with barrels aplenty, an evening oasis in a neighborhood that traditionally rolls up the sidewalks at sunset. ⊠ 246 Kearney St., near Bush St., Financial District ☎ 415/398–2827 ⊕ www.rickhousebar.com.

San Francisco Wine Society

WINE BARS—NIGHTLIFE | This cozy wine bar is in a little alley (just north of Market Street), and the location is part of the appeal, but the wines (with an emphasis on flights) and amuse-bouches make it truly worthwhile. A jumble of velvet chairs and love seats fills the space, and the bocce court outside is popular. ⊠ 408 Merchant St., at Battery St., Financial District ☎ 415/674–3567 ⊕ www.sanfranciscowinesociety.com.

The Treasury

BARS/PUBS | With a striking, almost elegant interior that has incredibly high ceilings compared with most bars (thanks to its Beaux-Arts space), this is a prime happy hour spot in the afternoon, then a citywide cocktail destination afterward. You can't go wrong with any of the cocktails, but the bar has a particular affinity for sherry, both in drinks and on its own in various styles. ⊠ 200 Bush St., Suite 101, Financial District ☎ 415/578–0530 ⊕ www.thetreasurysf.com.

COMEDY
Punch Line

COMEDY CLUBS | A launch pad for the likes of Robin Williams and Ellen DeGeneres, this place books some of the nation's top comedy talents. Headliners have included Dave Chappelle, Margaret Cho, and Amy Schumer. No one under 18 is admitted. ⊠ 444 Battery St., between Clay and Washington Sts., Financial District ☎ 415/397–7573 ⊕ www.punchlinecomedyclub.com.

🎭 Performing Arts

THEATER
42nd Street Moon

THEATER | This group produces delightful "semistaged" concert performances of rare chestnuts from Broadway's golden age of musical theater, such as Fiorello! and Follies in Concert. ⊠ Gateway Theatre, 215 Jackson St., Financial District ☎ 415/255–8207 ⊕ 42ndstmoon.org.

Theatre Rhinoceros

THEATER | A longtime queer theater stalwart for the city, Theatre Rhinoceros showcases gay and lesbian performers and playwrights at the Gateway Theatre. ⊠ Gateway Theatre, 215 Jackson St., Financial District ☎ 800/838–3006 tickets, 415/552–4100 offices ⊕ therhino.org.

Chapter 8

THE MARINA AND THE PRESIDIO

WITH COW HOLLOW

8

Updated by
Trevor Felch

👁 **Sights**
★★★★☆

🍴 **Restaurants**
★★★☆☆

🛏 **Hotels**
★★☆☆☆

🛍 **Shopping**
★★★★☆

🍸 **Nightlife**
★★☆☆☆

THE GOLDEN GATE BRIDGE

Two orange-red towers reach into the sky, floating above the mist like ghost ships on foggy days. If there's one image that instantly conjures San Francisco, it's the majestic Golden Gate Bridge, one of the most recognizable sights in the world.

Spanning the Golden Gate—the mouth of the San Francisco Bay, after which the bridge was named—between San Francisco and pastoral Marin County, the bridge has won both popular and critical acclaim, including being named one of the seven wonders of the modern world. With its simple but powerful art-deco design, the 1.7-mile suspension span and its 750-foot towers were built to withstand winds of more than 100 mph. It's also not a bad place to be in an earthquake: designed to sway almost 28 feet, the Golden Gate Bridge (unlike the Bay Bridge) was undamaged by the 1989 Loma Prieta quake. If you're on the bridge when it's windy, stand still and you can feel it swaying a bit.

✉ *Lincoln Blvd. near Doyle Dr. and Fort Point, Presidio,* ☎ *415/921–5858,* ⊕ *www.goldengate.org*

Pedestrians: Mar.–Oct., daily 5 am–9 pm; Nov.–Feb., daily 5 am–6:30 pm; hrs change with daylight saving time. Bicyclists: daily 24 hrs.

A DAY OVER THE BAY
Crossing the Golden Gate Bridge under your own power is a sensation that's hard to describe. Especially as you approach midspan, hovering more than 200 feet above the water makes you feel as though you're outside of time—exhilarating, a little scary (be careful taking selfies since the wind can steal phones!), definitely chilly. From the bridge's eastern-side walkway, the only

side pedestrians are allowed on, you can take in the San Francisco skyline and the bay islands; look west for the wild hills of the Marin Headlands, the curving coast south to Lands End, and the Pacific Ocean. On sunny days, sailboats dot the water, and brave wind-surfers test the often-treacherous tides beneath the bridge. A vista point on the Marin County side provides a spectacular city panorama. The views are fantastic however you cross—by foot, bicycle, or motorized vehicle—but driving or cycling will allow you to fully appreciate the bridge from multiple vantage points in and around the Presidio.

THE MAN WHO BUILT THE BRIDGE

In the early 1900s, San Francisco was behind the times. Sure, the city had the engineering marvel of the cable car and hundreds of streetcar lines, but as the largest U.S. city served mainly by ferries, this town needed a bridge. Enter Joseph Strauss, a structural engineer, dreamer, and poet who promised that not only could he build a bridge, but he could also do it on the cheap. At 5 feet, 3 inches tall, Strauss was a force of nature. He worked tirelessly over the next 20-odd years, first as a bridge booster and then overseeing its design and construction. Though the final structure bore little resemblance to his

If you want to ride across the bridge and avoid the crowds, bike early or on a weekday.

The iconic orange-red bridge is often enveloped by clouds of swirling fog known as "Karl."

original plan, Strauss guarded his legacy, refusing to recognize the seminal contributions of engineer Charles Ellis. In 2007, the Golden Gate Bridge District finally recognized Ellis's role, though Strauss, who died less than a year after the bridge's opening day in 1937, would be pleased with the inscription on his own statue, which stands sentry in the southern parking lot: "The Man Who Built the Bridge."

VISITING THE BRIDGE TODAY

Most visits start at Strauss Plaza, near the bridge's Welcome Center (⊕). At the outdoor exhibits, you can see the bridge rise before your eyes on hologram panels, learn about the features that make it art deco, and read about the personalities behind its design and construction. The surrounding Battery East Trail features several stunning viewpoints of the bridge and also connects the bridge with Crissy Field back down at sea level. City Guides (⊕ sfcity-guides.org) offers free walking tours of the bridge every Sunday at 11 am.

NEIGHBORHOOD SNAPSHOT

TOP EXPERIENCES

■ **Golden Gate Bridge:** Get a good look at the iconic span from the Presidio, then bundle up and walk over the water.

■ **Shopping in Cow Hollow and the Marina:** Browse hip boutiques and people-watch at stylish cafés on Union Street, Cow Hollow's main drag. Then head north to Chestnut Street.

■ **Palace of Fine Arts:** Bring a picnic to this beautiful faux-Roman remnant of the 1915 Panama-Pacific International Exposition and travel back in time to the city's post-earthquake-and-fire coming-out party.

■ **Crissy Field:** Join jogging, cycling, and kitesurfing locals along this restored strip of sand and marshland where the bay laps the shore, a stone's throw from the Golden Gate Bridge.

■ **Presidio wanderings:** Lace up your walking shoes and follow one of the wooded trails; the city will feel a hundred miles away.

GETTING HERE

For those without wheels, the free year-round shuttle PresidiGo, which runs two routes through the Presidio every half hour, is a dream. Pick up the shuttle at the transit center, usually at Lincoln Boulevard and Graham Street. (The Presidio has a temporary transit center in the Main Post parking area at Lincoln Boulevard and Anza Avenue through 2021.)

PLANNING YOUR TIME

Walking across the Golden Gate Bridge takes about an hour round-trip, but leave some time to take in the view on the other side. If you aren't in a hurry, plan to spend at least two to three hours in the Presidio, and be sure to allow 15 minutes to stroll around the stunning Palace of Fine Arts. In a pinch, make a 30- to 45-minute swing-through for the views. Shoppers can burn up an entire afternoon browsing the Marina's Chestnut Street and Cow Hollow's Union Street. Weekends are liveliest, while Mondays are quiet, since some shops close.

QUICK BITES

■ **Dynamo Donut & Coffee.** The tiny kiosk on the Marina's yacht harbor is the perfect spot to grab a pick-me-up before a stroll to the Palace of Fine Arts or along the beach. The doughnuts by a former Foreign Cinema pastry chef are universally terrific, from the vanilla bean standby to chocolate star anise, and there's locally roasted coffee for an extra prehike jolt. ⊠ *110 Yacht Rd., Marina* ⊕ *dynamodonut.com.*

■ **Gio Gelati.** This Union Street gelato maker is the place to go for authentic, airy gelato. The ingredients are top-notch—pistachios from Sicily, local fruits in season, a sour cherry variety from one part of Italy—and the results are delightful. ⊠ *1998 Union St., Cow Hollow* ⊕ *giogelati. com.*

■ **Wrecking Ball Coffee Roasters.** The Instagram set knows this Wi-Fi-free, almost seating-free Union Street roaster and café as the place with the pineapple wallpaper. Everyone enjoys some of the finest lattes and espresso shots around, usually to-go, but sometimes sipped on the low bench in front of that famous backdrop. ⊠ *2271 Union St., Cow Hollow* ⊕ *www.wrecking-ballcoffee.com.*

Yachts bob at their moorings, satisfied-looking folks jog along the Marina Green, and multimillion-dollar homes overlook the bay in the picturesque, if somewhat sterile, Marina neighborhood. Does it all seem a bit too perfect? Well, it got this way after the hard knock of Loma Prieta—the current pretty face was put on after hundreds of homes collapsed in the 1989 earthquake. Just west of this waterfront area is a more natural beauty: the Presidio. Once a military base, this beautiful, sprawling park is mostly green space, with hills, woods, and the marshlands of Crissy Field.

The Marina

Well-funded postcollegiates and the nouveaux riches flooded the Marina after the 1989 Loma Prieta earthquake had sent many residents running for more-solid ground, changing the tenor of this formerly low-key neighborhood. The number of fancy coffee emporiums skyrocketed, a bank became a Williams Sonoma store, and the local grocer gave way to a Pottery Barn. On weekends a young, fairly homogeneous, well-to-do crowd floods the cafés and bars. (Some things don't change—even before the quake, the Marina Safeway was a famed pickup place for straight singles, hence the nickname "Dateway.") South of Lombard Street is the Marina's affluent neighbor, Cow Hollow, whose main drag, Union Street, has some of the city's best boutique shopping and a good selection of restaurants and cafés. Joggers and kite-flyers head to the Marina Green, the strip of lawn between the yacht club and the mansions of Marina Boulevard.

 Sights

Fort Mason Center
ARTS VENUE | Originally a depot for the shipment of supplies to the Pacific during World War II, the fort was converted into a cultural center in 1977 and is now home to the vegetarian restaurant Greens and shops, galleries, and performance spaces.

The **Museo Italo Americano** (✉ *Bldg. C,* ☎ *415/673–2200,* ⊕ *museoitaloamericano.org,*☉ *closed Mon.*) is a small gallery that hosts one exhibit at a time, worth a glance if you're already at Fort Mason.

The temporary exhibits downstairs at the **SFMOMA Artists Gallery** (✉ *Bldg. A,* ☎ *415/441–4777,* ⊕ *www.sfmoma.org/artists-gallery ,*☉ *closed Sun. and Mon.*) can be great, but head upstairs and check out the paintings, sculptures, prints, and photographs for sale or rent. You won't find a Picasso or a Rembrandt, but where else can you get a $50,000 work of art to hang on your wall for $400 (a month)?

From March through September, Friday evening at Fort Mason means **Off the Grid** (⊕ *offthegridsf.com*); the city's food-truck gathering happens at locations around town, and this is one of the oldest and most popular. Check online for updates. ✉ *2 Marina Blvd., Marina* ☎ *415/345–7500 event information* ⊕ *fortmason.org.*

★ Palace of Fine Arts

BUILDING | At first glance this stunning, rosy rococo palace on a lagoon seems to be from another world, and indeed, it's the sole survivor of the many tinted-plaster structures (a temporary neoclassical city of sorts) built for the 1915 Panama-Pacific International Exposition, the world's fair that celebrated San Francisco's recovery from the 1906 earthquake and fire. The expo buildings originally extended about a mile along the shore. Bernard Maybeck designed this faux-Roman classic beauty, which was reconstructed in concrete and reopened in 1967. A victim of the elements, the Palace required a piece-by-piece renovation that was completed in 2008.

The pseudo-Latin language adorning the Palace's exterior urns continues to stump scholars. The massive columns (each topped with four "weeping maidens"),

great rotunda, and swan-filled lagoon have been used in countless fashion layouts, films, and wedding photo shoots. Other than its use for major events and exhibitions inside the building, it's really an outdoor architecture attraction that's perfect for an hour of strolling and relaxing. After admiring the lagoon, look across the street to the house at 3460 Baker Street. If the statues out front look familiar, they should—they're original casts of the "garland ladies" you can see in the Palace's colonnade. ✉ *3301 Lyon St., at Beach St., Marina* ☎ *415/886–1296* ⊕ *palaceoffinearts.com* 🎫 *Free.*

Wave Organ

PUBLIC ART | FAMILY | Conceived by environmental artist Peter Richards and fashioned by master stonecutter George Gonzales, this unusual wave-activated acoustic sculpture at the entrance of a harbor gives off subtle harmonic sounds produced by seawater as it passes through 25 tubes. The sound is loudest at high tide. The granite and marble used for walkways, benches, and alcoves that are part of the piece were salvaged from a gold rush–era cemetery. ✉ *83 Marina Green Dr., Marina* ✛ *North of Marina Green at end of jetty by Yacht Rd.; park in lot north of Marina Blvd. at Lyon St.* ⊕ *www.exploratorium.edu/visit/wave-organ.*

🍴 Restaurants

On a sunny day, the Marina is perhaps one of the most cheerful places in the city, with sweeping views of Marin and the Golden Gate Bridge and plenty of joggers and bicyclists. Residents tend to be a mix of the just-graduated, who are still very much into the nightclub scene, and the affluent inhabitants of the spectacular waterfront properties, who hit Chestnut Street after dark for good food.

A16

$$$ | **ITALIAN** | Named after a highway that runs through southern Italy, this trattoria specializes in the food from that region, done very, very well. The menu is stocked with pizza and rustic pastas like *maccaronara* with *ragù Napoletano* (a meat sauce) and house-made salted ricotta, as well as entrées like roasted chicken with caper salsa *verde*. **Known for:** spicy arrabbiata pizza; one of the city's best Italian wine programs; dark chocolate budino tart. [$] *Average main: $36* ✉ *2355 Chestnut St., Marina* ☎ *415/771–2216* 🌐 *www.a16pizza.com* 🕒 *Closed Mon.*

Causwells

$$ | **AMERICAN** | There are two personalities to Chestnut Street's sleek grown-up diner—the double-stack burger that draws burger hounds from dozens of miles away, and the rest of the honest, spruced-up comfort-food menu. It's a local institution that feels partially like a bistro and partially like a modern tavern, and a place where the buzz from signature mezcal paloma cocktails and delicious eats never disappears. **Known for:** house-made ricotta; excellent wine list full of bottles from lesser-known regions; feels like a party even on weeknights. [$] *Average main: $24* ✉ *2346 Chestnut St., Marina* ☎ *415/447–6081* 🌐 *www.causwells.com* 🕒 *Closed Mon. No lunch Tues.–Thurs.*

Greens

$$$ | **VEGETARIAN** | Owned and operated by the San Francisco Zen Center, this legendary vegetarian restaurant gets some of its fresh produce from the center's organic Green Gulch Farm. Despite the lack of meat, the hearty and often creative dishes—such as root vegetable *biryani* (mixed rice) with tamarind chutney—really satisfy, and floor-to-ceiling windows give diners a sweeping view of the Marina and the Golden Gate Bridge. **Known for:** magnificent wood-heavy decor headlined by a large redwood sculpture; mesquite-grilled tofu entrée; seasonal produce–driven pizzas. [$] *Average main: $27* ✉ *Bldg. A, Fort Mason, 2 Marina Blvd., Marina* ☎ *415/771–6222* 🌐 *greens-restaurant.com* 🕒 *Closed Mon.*

Tacolicious

$ | **MEXICAN** | Tacos and tequila draw a young and energetic crowd to this perennial hot spot. Tables with big groups or couples out on casual date nights are topped with chips and guacamole and laden with platters of tortillas bursting with *carnitas* (shredded pork) or shot-and-a-beer braised chicken. **Known for:** Baja-style Pacific cod tacos on homemade tortillas; chupitos (easy-drinking tequila mixed with fruit shots); no reservations. [$] *Average main: $16* ✉ *2250 Chestnut St., Marina* ☎ 🌐 *www.tacolicious.com.*

Coffee and Quick Bites

Le Marais Bakery

$ | **BISTRO** | **FAMILY** | With prime people-watching, perfect pastries, and lovely espresso drinks, this bakery-café is a quintessential slice of Paris on one of San Francisco's busiest streets. All the ingredients are top-notch (butter from Normandy, fruit from local orchards), and the results show that, whether you're just picking up a few treats for the road or having a leisurely shopping-break lunch at a sidewalk table. **Known for:** croissants or any croissant-related pastry; chocolate chip cookies; French café design, from bistro wicker chairs to the floor tiles at the entrance. [$] *Average main: $16* ✉ *2066 Chestnut St., at Steiner St., Marina* ☎ *415/359–9801* 🌐 *lemaraisbakery.com* 🕒 *No dinner weekends.*

Hotels

Marina is where the beautiful (and rich) go to see and be seen. However, that luxury is limited to homes because it's a heavily residential area; hotel options are mainly just reasonably priced, usually nondescript motor inns on Lombard

Street, with enticements that might include kitchenettes or free parking. The proximity to boutiques, eateries, and happening bars, as well as Crissy Field and the Presidio, make this area a popular choice.

Cow Hollow Motor Inn

$ | **HOTEL** | The rooms and suites at this modern motel are more spacious than average, featuring high-end Serta iComfort beds; some have views of the Golden Gate Bridge, and others overlook the shops, coffeehouses, and neighborhood businesses of Chestnut Street. **Pros:** free covered parking in building for one vehicle; nice desk/work area; easy walking distance to restaurants and bars. **Cons:** not much personality; standard rooms face a loud street; few amenities and unhelpful website. [$] *Rooms from: $185* ✉ *2190 Lombard St., Marina* ☎ *415/921–5800* 🌐 *www.cowhollowmotorinn.com* 🛏 *130 rooms* 🍴 *No meals.*

Marina Motel

$$ | **HOTEL** | **FAMILY** | Bougainvillea, fuchsia, and other foliage real and trompe l'oeil add color and verve to this 1939 motor court operated by the granddaughters of the original owners, creating a magical mood when everything's in bloom and hummingbirds flit through the quiet courtyard. **Pros:** wide variety of room sizes; full kitchens in several units; free parking is gold in this neighborhood. **Cons:** loud rooms facing Lombard Street; no a/c (usually not a problem in the Marina); rooms look a bit dated. [$] *Rooms from: $251* ✉ *2576 Lombard St., Marina* ☎ *415/921–3430* 🌐 *www.marinamotel.com* 🛏 *39 rooms* 🍴 *No meals.*

Nightlife

BARS

California Wine Merchant

WINE BARS—NIGHTLIFE | Part cluttered shop, part cozy bar, Chestnut Street's marquee wine destination is a longtime favorite for grabbing a glass or three. Wines featured always come from some of the state's most highly regarded vintners of all sizes and celebrity standings. The neighborhood has many wine bars, but this is where the locals go when the focus is on the wine itself. ✉ *2113 Chestnut St., Marina* ☎ *415/567–0646* 🌐 *www.californiawinemerchant.com.*

The Interval

BARS/PUBS | Even many locals don't realize that the Fort Mason Center is home to one of the city's most impressive and scene-free cocktail bars. As part of the Long Now Foundation, a nonprofit devoted to long-term thinking, the bar serves cocktails that reflect the group's approach, finding innovative ways to serve tried-and-true libations. The Navy Gimlet with clarified lime juice is a modern-day San Francisco classic. ✉ *Fort Mason Center, 2 Marina Blvd., Bldg. A, Marina* ☎ *415/496–9187* 🌐 *www.theinterval.org.*

COMEDY

BATS Improv

COMEDY CLUBS | In addition to teaching workshops on improvisation, this group based in a renovated warehouse stages performances such as "Improvised Shakespeare" and "Spontaneous Broadway." As is always the case for improv, the quality varies, but it's reliably fun. Tickets are reasonably priced, usually $15–$20. ✉ *Bayfront Theater, Fort Mason Center, Bldg. B, 3rd fl. , at Marina Blvd. and Buchanan St., Marina* ☎ *415/474–6776* 🌐 *www.improv.org.*

Performing Arts

THEATER

Magic Theatre

THEATER | Once the late Sam Shepard's favorite showcase, pint-size Magic presents works by rising and established playwrights who create thought-provoking plays that explore the world's diversity. It has produced a number of world premieres. ✉ *Fort Mason, Bldg. D, Laguna St.*

at Marina Blvd., Marina ☎ 415/441–8822 ⊕ www.magictheatre.org.

🛍 Shopping

CLOTHING

Marine Layer

CLOTHING | It doesn't take much time in San Francisco to learn about the city's frequent fog and chilly wind, both of which are the cozy inspiration for this local label's distinctive soft-textured, stylish clothing for men and women of all ages. If you're at any restaurant or event in the city, there's a good chance that several residents are wearing a Marine Layer design. ☒ 2106 Chestnut St., Marina ☎ 415/400–4136 ⊕ www.marinelayer.com.

Cow Hollow

Between old-money Pacific Heights and the well-heeled, postcollegiate Marina lies comfortably upscale Cow Hollow. The neighborhood's name harks back to the 19th-century dairy farms whose owners eked out a living here despite the fact that there was more sand than grass. A patch of grass remains a scarce commodity in this mostly residential area, but Cow Hollow does have a lively commercial strip, centered around Union Street. To get a feel for this accessible bastion of affluence, stroll down Union. Browse the cosmetics and jewelry stores, snazzy clothing boutiques, and shops selling home decor for every taste (if not budget), then rest your feet at one of the many good restaurants or sidewalk cafés.

👁 Sights

Octagon House

HOUSE | This eight-sided home sits across the street from its original site on Gough Street; it's one of two remaining octagonal houses in the city (the other is on Russian Hill), and the only one open to the public. White quoins accent each

of the eight corners of the pretty blue-gray exterior, and a colonial-style garden completes the picture. The house is full of antique American furniture, decorative arts (paintings, silver, rugs), and documents from the 18th and 19th centuries. Note that the home is only open on the second Sunday and second and fourth Thursday of each month (closed all January). ☒ 2645 Gough St., near Union St., Cow Hollow ☎ 415/441–7512 ⊕ nscda-ca. org/octagon-house/ 🌐 Free, donations encouraged ⊘ Closed Jan.; also closed Mon.–Wed., Fri., and Sat.

Vedanta Society Old Temple

RELIGIOUS SITE | A light-green pastiche of colonial, Queen Anne, Moorish, and Hindu opulence, with turrets battling red-top onion domes and Victorian detailing everywhere, this 1905 structure is considered the first Hindu temple in the West. Vedanta, an underlying philosophy of Hinduism, maintains that all religions are paths to one goal. It's an interesting building to study from the street. ☒ 2963 Webster St., Cow Hollow ☎ 415/922–2323 ⊕ www.sfvedanta.org.

🍴 Restaurants

Just up the hill from the Marina—and slightly quieter, with more young families—is Cow Hollow. Union Street is the main strip, dense with restaurants, cafés, and boutiques that mostly cater to the trendy A-list crowd. Wander even farther up the hills and you'll be in the thick of the manses of Pacific Heights.

★ Atelier Crenn

$$$$ | MODERN FRENCH | Dinner at the spectacularly inventive flagship of San Francisco's most celebrated chef of the moment, Dominique Crenn, starts with the presentation of a poem. Each course, many of which include produce from Crenn's own Bleu Belle Farm, and some of which have a slight French influence, is described by a line in the poem: the "Hidden beneath the bluffs" might be

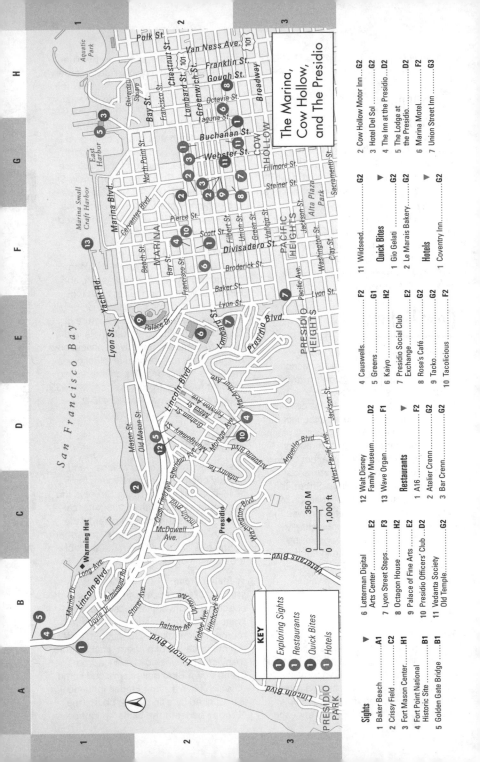

The Marina, Cow Hollow, and The Presidio

Sights ▶

1 Baker Beach A1
2 Crissy Field C2
3 Fort Mason Center H1
4 Fort Point National
   Historic Site B1
5 Golden Gate Bridge B1

6 Letterman Digital
   Arts Center E2
7 Lyon Street Steps F3
8 Octagon House H2
9 Palace of Fine Arts E2
10 Presidio Officers' Club D2
11 Vedanta Society
   Old Temple G2

12 Walt Disney
   Family Museum D2
13 Wave Organ F1

Restaurants ▶

1 A16 .... F2
2 Atelier Crenn G2
3 Bar Crenn G2

4 Causwells F2
5 Greens G1
6 Kaiyo H2
7 Presidio Social Club
   Exchange E2
8 Rose's Café G2
9 Tacko G2
10 Tacolicious F2

11 Wildseed G2

Quick Bites ▶

1 Gio Gelati G2
2 Le Marais Bakery G2

Hotels ▶

1 Coventry Inn F2

2 Cow Hollow Motor Inn G2
3 Hotel Del Sol G2
4 The Inn at the Presidio D2
5 The Lodge at
   the Presidio D2
6 Marina Motel F2
7 Union Street Inn G3

KEY

1 Exploring Sights
1 Restaurants
1 Quick Bites
1 Hotels

San Francisco Bay

0   350 M
0   1,000 ft

whole grilled Monterey abalone with a purée of its own liver and a grilled mussel sauce. **Known for:** extraordinary, whimsical tasting menu with fish and seafood but no meat; stellar desserts; hip-elegant atmosphere. $ *Average main: $365* ✉ *3127 Fillmore St., Cow Hollow* ☎ *415/440–0460* ⊕ *www.ateliercrenn. com* ⊗ *Closed Sun. and Mon. No lunch.*

Bar Crenn

$$$ | **FRENCH** | Dominique Crenn's sumptuous salon decked out with fur-draped bar stools, chandeliers, and lush velvet drapes is really a bar only in name. Yes, there's a bar pouring outstanding wines and it's possible to graze on warm *gougères* (savory cheese puffs) and oysters. **Known for:** Versailles-style furnishings; canelés de Bordeaux (a type of small pastry); fine Champagne. $ *Average main: $36* ✉ *3131 Fillmore St., Cow Hollow* ☎ *415/440–0460* ⊕ *www. barcrenn.com* ⊗ *Closed Sun. and Mon. No lunch.*

Kaiyo

$$ | **PERUVIAN** | San Francisco has a handful of Peruvian restaurants, but this uber-hip Union Street spot is the first "Nikkei" (Japanese-Peruvian) cuisine restaurant for diners to explore. Skip the pedestrian *pollo a la brasa* (rotisserie chicken) and have fun sampling around the *tiraditos* (dishes with raw fish) and sushi rolls. **Known for:** creative pisco cocktails; shrimp tempura and yellowtail Lima roll; no reservations, so lines can be long. $ *Average main: $18* ✉ *1838 Union St., Cow Hollow* ☎ *415/525–4804* ⊕ *kaiyosf. com* ⊗ *Closed Mon.*

Rose's Café

$$ | **AMERICAN** | **FAMILY** | Although it's open morning until night, this cozy café is most synonymous with brunch. Sleepy-headed locals turn up for delights like the smoked ham, fried egg, and Gruyère breakfast sandwich, and evening favorites lean toward roast chicken, pastas, and seasonal-rustic fare. **Known for:** pizzas for the morning and night;

house-baked goods; wonderful sidewalk patio. $ *Average main: $25* ✉ *2298 Union St., Cow Hollow* ☎ *415/775–2200* ⊕ *rosescafesf.com.*

Tacko

$ | **MEXICAN** | **FAMILY** | Tacos and lobster rolls aren't a standard duo, but they're the staples of the menu at this fast-casual favorite a block downhill from Union Street. The connection is Nantucket (ACK is Nantucket's airport code), as the owner grew up in New England and honors the Massachusetts summer destination in this eatery with an East Coast yacht club vibe and a mural featuring a map of the island. **Known for:** fish tacos "Nick's Way" with Jack cheese and both a crispy corn and a soft flour tortilla; California-style burrito with fries inside; Allagash White and Sam Adams on draft. $ *Average main: $11* ✉ *3115 Fillmore St., Cow Hollow* ☎ *415/796–3534* ⊕ *tackosf.com.*

Wildseed

$$ | **VEGETARIAN** | Vegan dining doesn't have to be boring, and this hip, bustling Union Street destination proves that plant-based cuisine can be exciting and delicious, along with being virtuous for the body (well, at least most dishes are) and better for the environment. The

8

The Marina and the Presidio COW HOLLOW

Park Yourself in a Parklet

Since 2010, San Francisco has been reclaiming parking spaces and turning them into parklets, tiny parks open to the public. These dot the city—more than five dozen and counting—from mobile, red-metal containers with built-in benches and plantings to Powell Street's eight-section high-design aluminum parklet. The Mission has the highest concentration, mostly along Valencia Street, but one of the most creative—an old Citroën van turned into seating and planters—is in front of the Rapha bike shop on Filbert near Fillmore in Cow Hollow.

And even if everyone in that parklet in front of a café is clutching a to-go cup, remember these are public spaces; look for the "Public Parklet" sign and grab a seat. For a parklet map, visit 🌐 *pavementtoparks.org.*

With the outdoor dining rules in place during the COVID-19 pandemic, the number of restaurant and bar parklets across the city has soared, with unique alfresco dining set-ups created out of necessity in every neighborhood. They have been such a hit that many of these pandemic parklets will stay permanently.

highly eclectic menu includes dishes from Mexican corn cakes with dairy-free queso to a spicy yellow Thai curry. **Known for:** mushroom-and-spinach patty Wildseed burger; terrific cocktails; beautiful green plants and wood-heavy interior design. [$] *Average main: $18* ✉ *2000 Union St., Cow Hollow* ☎ *415/872–7350* 🌐 *www.wildseedsf.com.*

Coffee and Quick Bites

Gio Gelati

$ | ITALIAN | FAMILY | San Francisco is filled with wonderful ice cream shops, but for the real-deal smooth, airy gelato, this Union Street gelato maker is the address to know. It's all about the ingredients here—pistachios from Sicily, local fruits in season, a sour cherry variety from a particular part of Italy—and the results are delightful whether it's a hot, sunny day or the fog feels as cool as the gelato. **Known for:** tiramisu flavor; Piemonte hazelnut flavor; espresso (in gelato or a proper espresso shot on its own). [$] *Average main: $7* ✉ *1998 Union St., Cow Hollow* ☎ *415/867–1306* 🌐 *giogelati.com.*

Hotels

Upscale urbanites toting iPhones and gazillion-dollar strollers call Cow Hollow home. Visitors will appreciate the boutiques lining Union Street, the excellent eateries, and the winning B&Bs and motor inns (some value-minded, others hip and refurbished) catering to in-the-know travelers.

Coventry Inn

$ | HOTEL | FAMILY | Among the many motels on busy Lombard Street, this is one of the cleanest and quietest, and the unusually spacious rooms have well-lighted dining and work areas that make this a favorite for those looking for comfort without a hefty price tag. **Pros:** some rooms have nice Golden Gate Bridge and bay views; free parking in building; good-quality beds. **Cons:** busy street; not much personality or charm; far from downtown sights. [$] *Rooms from: $158* ✉ *1901 Lombard St., Cow Hollow* ☎ *415/567–1200* 🌐 *coventrymotorinn.com* 🛏 *69 rooms* 🍴 *No meals.*

Hotel Del Sol

$ | **HOTEL** | **FAMILY** | This rejuvenated, beach-theme 1950s motor lodge with nicely appointed rooms and a fun, heated outdoor pool is all alone in a higher, hipper class of Cow Hollow/Marina boutique hotels. **Pros:** charming courtyard; great selection of suites; cheery design. **Cons:** fitness center is off-site; smallest rooms are truly tiny; parking fee high for this area, where there's often no charge. [$] *Rooms from: $175* ✉ *3100 Webster St., Cow Hollow* ☎ *415/921–5520, 877/433–5765* 🌐 *hoteldelsol.com* 🛏 *57 rooms* 🍴 *Breakfast.*

★ **Union Street Inn**

$$ | **B&B/INN** | Antiques, unique artwork, fine linens, and windows opening to a lovely courtyard or Union Street view make this charming Edwardian inn popular with honeymooners and those looking for a romantic getaway with an English countryside ambience. **Pros:** personal service; afternoon wine and cheese; beautiful secret garden. **Cons:** parking garage is two blocks away; old-fashioned decor not for all tastes; no elevator. [$] *Rooms from: $270* ✉ *2229 Union St., Cow Hollow* ☎ *415/346–0424* 🌐 *unionstreetinn.com* 🛏 *6 rooms* 🍴 *Breakfast.*

Nightlife

In between the Marina and Pacific Heights, this small yet affluent neighborhood has a similar scene to the bordering Marina district, but without the hefty price tags.

BARS

Balboa Cafe

BARS/PUBS | Here you'll spy young (thirty-something) and upwardly mobile former frat boys and sorority girls munching on tasty burgers served sandwich-style on a baguette—considered by some to be the best in town. Martinis are proper and stiff, bartenders always have something witty to say, and the wine list is one of the neighborhood's best. ✉ *3199 Fillmore St., at Greenwich St., Cow Hollow* ☎ *415/921–3944* 🌐 *www.balboacafe.com.*

The Black Horse London Pub

BARS/PUBS | Barely seven stools fit in San Francisco's smallest bar. Plus, there are just as many bottled beers (no taps) as seats, and be sure to bring some cash since credit cards aren't accepted. It's as bare-bones as it gets, but there's sports on TV, a fun dice game, and most important, a neighborhood camaraderie that is increasingly hard to find. ✉ *1514 Union St., Cow Hollow* ☎ *415/678–5697* 🌐 *www.blackhorselondon.com.*

Perry's

BARS/PUBS | One of San Francisco's oldest singles bars still packs 'em in, but it's also a favorite restaurant for all ages. You can dine on great hamburgers (and a stellar Reuben) as well as more substantial fare to pair with local beers and simple cocktails, while gabbing about the '49ers with the well-scrubbed, khaki-clad, baseball-cap-wearing patrons. It's just as known for the plaid tablecloths as it is for the fun, lively crowd. ✉ *1944 Union St., at Laguna St., Cow Hollow* ☎ *415/922–9022* 🌐 *www.perryssf.com.*

West Coast Wine & Cheese

WINE BARS—NIGHTLIFE | Whether you're in the mood for a Mendocino County rosé or an Oregon Pinot Noir, as the name suggests, you'll find it at this narrow, sleek locals' favorite. The kitchen isn't much more than a stovetop but does some pretty impressive work beyond cheese and charcuterie. Take advantage of the ability to order half pours and sample more wines. ✉ *2165 Union St., Cow Hollow* ☎ *415/376–9720* 🌐 *www.westcoastsf.com.*

🛍 Shopping

The former dairy pastures of yesteryear are a quaint yet sophisticated fashion and home-decor hot spot today. If you're tired of browsing the clothing and shoe stores, you can explore two of San Francisco's favorite longtime florist shops, The Bud Stop (✉ *2200 Union St.*) and Le Bouquet (✉ *2205 Union St.*). They're across the street from each other, creating the city's most flowery intersection.

CLOTHING

Current Clothing

CLOTHING | This Union Street shop's name perfectly sums up how in vogue its selection of women's clothing is. The local brand keeps thing edgy and comfortable but never veers too far in either direction for stylish tops, pants, skirts, dresses, and even tweed jackets. It is without question a San Francisco favorite for contemporary, fun, but functional designs. ✉ *1738 Union St., Cow Hollow* ☎ *415/400–5517* ⊕ *currentclothingsf.com.*

FOOD AND DRINK

The Caviar Company

FOOD/CANDY | "The Caviar Sisters" Petra and Saskia Bergstein created this sustainability-minded brand that has developed a cult following among caviar connoisseurs and chefs in the Bay Area. Their chic above-street-level boutique on Union Street allows the public to pick out some of the finest caviar products in town—and feel good about it. ✉ *1954 Union St., Cow Hollow* ☎ *415/580–7986* ⊕ *thecaviarco.com.*

The Epicurean Trader

FOOD/CANDY | Located around the city, this small group of markets presents a terrific selection of gourmet foods and high-quality artisanal food and drink products. It's best known for the extensive selections of craft spirits and cocktail ingredients, making this the shopping headquarters for San Francisco's home bartenders. ✉ *1909 Union St., Cow Hollow* ☎ *888/504–8118* ⊕ *theepicureantrader.com.*

PlumpJack Wines

WINE/SPIRITS | Cow Hollow's go-to wine boutique is much more than "the wine shop" co-founded by Governor Gavin Newsom in the early 1990s (when he was 26 years old). A nice selection of imported wines complements the well-priced, well-stocked collection of hard-to-find California wines here, creating one of the city's strongest wine rosters. Noe Valley has a sibling store. ✉ *3201 Fillmore St., at Greenwich St., Cow Hollow* ☎ *415/346–9870* ⊕ *plumpjackwines.com.*

FURNITURE, HOUSEWARES, AND GIFTS

ATYS

HOUSEHOLD ITEMS/FURNITURE | Gadgets and home accessories with a sleek modern design are imported from all over Europe and Japan and sold at this charming store in a courtyard off Union Street. Among the eye-catching items are levitating lights and French knives made of actual Golden Gate Bridge steel. ✉ *2149B Union St., between Fillmore and Webster Sts., Cow Hollow* ☎ *415/441–9220* ⊕ *atysdesign.com.*

Topdrawer

GIFTS/SOUVENIRS | This Japanese store sells everything from high-quality bento boxes to fine Tokyo-made pens and lots more, including colorful stationery, journals, eyeware, and travel bags. ✉ *1840 Union St., between Octavia and Laguna Sts., Cow Hollow* ☎ *415/771–1108* ⊕ *topdrawershop.com.*

SHOES, HANDBAGS, AND LEATHER GOODS

Birdie's

SHOES/LUGGAGE/LEATHER GOODS | Comfortable, chic flats are the beloved signature item at the flagship store of this shoe designer, with varieties ranging from the most comfortable slippers ever to sandals that could walk down a runway. These flexible shoes can work for the office or a casual night out. The Union Street boutique shows that multidimensional approach as well, with its plush design that invites lingering long after shoes have been purchased. ⊠ *1934 Union St., Cow Hollow* ☎ *415/263–9668* ⊕ *birdies.com.*

Shaw Shoes⁻

SHOES/LUGGAGE/LEATHER GOODS | Not much in Cow Hollow's retail scene has been around since the 1970s except this venerable luxury shoe store, a Union Street standby. Fine Italian leather shoes for men and women are the specialty, from sleek pumps to sharp flats, along with trendy, upscale sneakers and sandals. Designer sunglasses and handbags are also sold, so shoppers can look suave from head to toe. ⊠ *2001 Union St., Cow Hollow* ☎ *415/922–5676* ⊕ *shawshoes.net.*

 ## Activities

SPAS

Redmint

SPA | With an emphasis on traditional Chinese practices like acupuncture, sound therapy, and *chi nei tsang* (an abdominal treatment with massage and breathwork), plus unique herbal and antioxidant ingredients, this Union Street spa is a perfect stop for a mind and body wellness break or to pick up some unique hand creams or facial mists. The serene, immaculate complex seamlessly blends the indoors and outdoors and includes an herbal bar (think coffee shop, but for herbal drinks), a beautiful courtyard, and six private treatment areas. ⊠ *1958 Union St., Cow Hollow* ☎ *415/932–6987* ⊕ *www.redmint.com* 🗒 *acupuncture from $65, body treatments from $139.*

Spa Radiance

SPA | Elegant but casual Spa Radiance specializes in facials and draws the occasional celebrity. Try the "Super Duper Plus Facial," which adds LED light therapy to the treatment, or one of the relaxing massages or body treatments. ⊠ *3011 Fillmore St., between Union and Filbert Sts., Cow Hollow* ☎ *415/346–6281* ⊕ *www.sparadiance.com* 🗒 *massages from $140, facials from $180.*

Presidio

At the foot of the Golden Gate Bridge, one of city residents' favorite in-town getaways is the 1,400-plus-acre Presidio, which combines accessible nature-in-the-raw with a window on the past. For more than 200 years and under the flags of three nations—Spain, Mexico, and the United States—the Presidio served as an army post, but in 1995 the U.S. Army officially handed over the keys to the National Park Service. The keys came without sufficient federal funding, though, and it seemed the Presidio would be sold piecemeal to developers.

An innovative plan combining public and private monies and overseen by the Presidio Trust, the federal agency created to run the park, was hatched to help the Presidio become self-sufficient, which it did in 2013. The trust has found paying tenants, such as George Lucas's Industrial Light and Magic, the Walt Disney Family Museum, and a few thousand lucky San Franciscans who live in restored army housing. Now this spectacular corner of San Francisco—surrounded by sandy beaches and rocky shores, and with windswept hills of cypress dotted with historical buildings—is a thriving park for the far reaches of the city and technically a national park (it's part of the Golden Gate National Recreation Area, ⊕ *nps.gov/goga*). It's also a small community on its own with a gym, a few restaurants, and a beautifully renovated 600-seat theater where Bob Hope once performed. The Presidio has superb views (be sure to visit Inspiration Point and the cemetery for the most striking ones) and some of the best hiking and biking areas in San Francisco (Lovers' Lane Trail is a favorite for hikers); even a drive through this lush area is a treat. Start your visit at the Presidio Visitor Center (210 Lincoln Blvd., 415/561–4323, ⊕ *presidio.gov*; check for hours), then enjoy a day of exploring.

⊙ Sights

★ Baker Beach

BEACH—SIGHT | FAMILY | West of the Golden Gate Bridge is a mile-long stretch of soft sand beneath steep cliffs, beloved for its spectacular views and laid-back vibe (read: good chance you'll see naked people here on the northernmost end). Its isolated location makes it rarely crowded, but many San Franciscans know that there is no better place to take in the sunset than this beach. Kids love climbing around the old Battery Chamberlin. This is truly one of those places that inspires local pride. **Amenities:** parking (free); toilets. **Best for:** nudists, solitude; sunsets. ⊠ *Baker Beach, Presidio* ✛ *Accessed from Bowley St. off Lincoln Blvd.* ⊕ *www.parksconservancy. org* ⌷ *Free.*

Crissy Field

NATIONAL/STATE PARK | FAMILY | One of the most popular places for San Franciscans to get fresh air is this stretch of restored marshland along the sand of the bay, part of the Golden Gate National Recreation Area. Kids on bikes, folks walking dogs, and joggers share the paved path along the shore, often winding up at the Warming Hut, a combination café and fun gift store at its end, for a hot chocolate in the shadow of the Golden Gate Bridge. Midway along the Golden Gate Promenade that winds along the shore is the Greater Farallones National Marine Sanctuary Visitor Center, where kids can get a close-up view of small sea creatures and learn about the rich ecosystem offshore. Alongside the main green of Crissy Field, several renovated airplane hangars and warehouses are now home to the likes of rock-climbing gyms, an air trampoline park, and a craft brewery (the latter is not open to the public). The Quartermaster Reach Marsh by Crissy Field was reclaimed as wetland ecosystem in 2020 after being asphalt. It nicely connects the Presidio with Crissy Field for pedestrians. ⊠ *1199 E. Beach, Presidio* ✛ *Area north*

Coming Soon: Presidio Tunnel Tops ⊙

The 14-acre Presidio Tunnel Tops parkland (⊕ *presidiotunneltops.gov*) will debut by mid-2022 with beautiful green space connecting the Presidio Main Post to Crissy Field, all developed on top of the Presidio Parkway Tunnels. Residents and visitors will be able to take in stunning Golden Gate Bridge views during a picnic by the new meadow or stretch their legs on the walking paths. The park's Outpost area will be a spectacular playground for kids.

of Mason St. between Baker St. and Marine Dr. ⊕ *www.presidio.gov/places/crissy-field.*

Fort Point National Historic Site

MUSEUM | FAMILY | Dwarfed today by the Golden Gate Bridge, this brick fortress constructed between 1853 and 1861 was designed to protect San Francisco from a Civil War sea attack that never materialized. It was also used as a coastal-defense fortification post during World War II, when soldiers stood watch here. This National Historic Site is now a sprawling museum of military memorabilia. The building, which surrounds a lonely, windswept courtyard, has a gloomy air and is suitably atmospheric. It's usually chilly, too, so bring a jacket. The top floor affords a unique angle on the bay. ■ TIP→ **Take care when walking along the front side of the building, as it's slippery and the waves can have a dizzying effect.**

On the days when Fort Point is staffed (Friday and weekends), guided group tours and cannon drills take place. The popular, guided candlelight tours, available only in winter, book up in advance, so plan ahead. Living-history days take place throughout

The Presidio with Kids

If you're in town with children (and you have a car), the sprawling, bayside Presidio offers enough kid-friendly diversions for one very full day. Start off at **Presidio Wall Playground**, on the Presidio's southern edge, which has a disproportionate number of structures that spin. Swing by George Lucas's **Letterman Digital Arts Center** to check out the Yoda fountain; then head to the **Immigrant Point Overlook** on Washington Boulevard, with views of the bay and the ocean. Children love the pet cemetery, with its sweet, leaning headstones; it's near the stables, where you might glimpse some of the park police's equestrian members. Older kids might enjoy a

stop at the **Walt Disney Family Museum** (✉ *104 Montgomery St.* ☎ *415/345–6800*) to see the model of Disneyland and a replica of the ambulance jeep Walt Disney drove during World War I. The last stop is **Crissy Field**, where kids can ride bikes, skate, or run along the beach and clamber over the rocks; the view of the Golden Gate Bridge from below is captivating. Two nature centers here have fun, hands-on exhibits for kids. Finally, stop by the **Warming Hut**, at the western end of Crissy Field, for sandwiches and hot chocolate. You can also do a version of this day using the PresidiGo Shuttle, but you'll need to adapt your route according to the shuttle stops.

the year, when Union soldiers perform drills, a drum-and-fife band plays, and a Civil War–era doctor shows his instruments and describes his surgical techniques (gulp). ✉ *201 Marine Dr. , off Lincoln Blvd., Presidio* ☎ *415/561–4959* ⊕ *www.nps.gov/fopo* 🎫 *Free* ⊙ *Closed Mon.–Thurs.*

★ Golden Gate Bridge
BRIDGE/TUNNEL | Instantly recognizable as an icon of San Francisco, the two reddish-orange towers of the majestic Golden Gate Bridge rise 750 feet over the Golden Gate at the mouth of San Francisco Bay, linking the city and Marin County. Designed in simple but powerful art-deco style and opened in 1937, the 1.7-mile suspension span and the towers were built to handle winds of more than 100 mph. Crossing the bridge under your own power, by foot or bicycle, is exhilarating, a bit scary—and definitely chilly. From the bridge's eastern-side walkway, the panoramic views of the city skyline, Marin Headlands, and Pacific Ocean are magnificent. ✉ *Lincoln Blvd. , near Doyle Dr. and Fort Point, Presidio* ☎ *415/921–5858* ⊕ *www.goldengate.org* 🎫 *Free.*

Letterman Digital Arts Center
LOCAL INTEREST | **FAMILY** | Bay Area filmmaker George Lucas's 23-acre **Letterman Digital Arts Center,** a digital studio "campus" along the eastern edge of the land, is exquisitely landscaped and largely open to the public. If you have kids in tow or are a *Star Wars* fan yourself, make the pilgrimage to the **Yoda Fountain** (*Letterman Dr. at Dewitt Rd.*), between two of the arts-center buildings, then take your picture with the life-size Darth Vader statue in the lobby, open to the public on weekdays. The center's public restaurant, **Sessions,** is a good stop for a craft beer and some satisfying eats that often include produce or beef from Lucas's Skywalker Ranch. ✉ *1 Letterman Dr., Presidio* ⊕ *www.presidio. gov/places/letterman-digital-arts-center* ⊙ *Lobby closed weekends.*

Lyon Street Steps
VIEWPOINT | Get ready for a workout—and a spectacularly rewarding view at the top—when tackling the 332 steps at the eastern edge of the Presidio. There will likely be no shortage of exercise seekers bounding up the steps, but feel free to

conquer the climb slowly. The trimmed hedge landscaping is worthy of its own visit, but the views of the Presidio forests and the bay are the reason these steps are a top attraction. Equally stunning, though, are the opulent mansions surrounding them. ✉ *2545 Lyon St., Presidio Heights* ✥ *Between Green St. and Broadway* 🌐 *www.nps.gov/places/000/lyon-street-steps.htm.*

Presidio Officers' Club

MUSEUM | An excellent place to begin a historical tour of the Presidio, the Officers' Club offers a walk through time from the Presidio's earliest days as the first nonnative outpost in present-day San Francisco to more than a century as a U.S. Army post. Start with the excellent short film about life here from the time of the Ohlone people to the present, then peruse the displays of artifacts, including uniforms and weaponry. In the Mesa Room, you can literally see layers of history: parts of the original adobe wall from the 1790s, the brick fireplace in the 1880s commander's office, and the Mission revival–style fireplace in the 1930s billiard room. Excavation of the Presidio continues: outside, a canopy covers the Presidio Archaeology Field Station, where you can sometimes see archaeologists at work. Guided tours of the Archaeology Lab take place the first Saturday of each month. ✉ *50 Moraga Ave., Presidio* ☎ *415/561–5300* 🌐 *www.presidio.gov/officers-club* 🎟 *Free* 🕒 *Closed Mon.*

Walt Disney Family Museum

MUSEUM | **FAMILY** | This beautifully refurbished brick barracks is a tribute to the man behind Mickey Mouse, the Disney Studios, and Disneyland. The smartly organized displays include hundreds of family photos, and well-chosen videos play throughout. Disney's legendary attention to detail becomes evident in the cels and footage of Fantasia, Sleeping Beauty, and other animation classics. "The Toughest Period in My Whole Life" exhibit sheds light on lesser-known bits of history: the animators' strike at Disney Studios, the films Walt Disney made for the U.S. military during World War II, and his testimony before the U.S. House Un-American Activities Committee during its investigation of Communist influence in Hollywood. The liveliest exhibit, and the largest gallery, documents the creation of Disneyland with a fun, detailed model of what Disney imagined the park would be. Teacups spin, the Matterhorn looms, and that world-famous castle leads the way to Fantasyland. You won't be the first to leave humming "It's a Small World." In the final gallery, titled simply "December 15, 1966," a series of cartoons chronicles the world's reaction to Disney's sudden death. Worth checking for are periodic special exhibitions that take a deep dive into film themes or historical periods surrounding Disney's life. ✉ *Main Post, 104 Montgomery St., off Lincoln Blvd., Presidio* ☎ *415/345–6800* 🌐 *www.waltdisney.org* 🎟 *$25* 🕒 *Closed Mon.–Wed.*

🍴 Restaurants

Presidio Social Club Exchange

$$ | **AMERICAN** | **FAMILY** | American comfort classics meet seasonal California cooking in this restaurant in an old barracks building at the eastern edge of the Presidio. Like the military base/national park itself, the restaurant has a blend of the nostalgic past and the trendy present (spice-fried Cornish game hen; a Thursday prime rib special; shrimp cocktail), as well as a substantial "exchange" shop/takeout café and ample patio seating that allows diners to soak up the Presidio outdoor beauty. **Known for:** East–West chicken soup; French onion burger; barrel-aged cocktails. [$] *Average main: $26* ✉ *563 Ruger St., Presidio* ☎ *415/885–1888* 🌐 *www.presidiosocialclub.com* 🕒 *Closed Mon.-Wed. No brunch Thurs.-Fri. No dinner Sun.*

Art in the Presidio

Fans of Andy Goldsworthy, the British artist famed for his work with natural elements, will have a field day in the Presidio: the park contains four of his creations, all using materials reclaimed from the Presidio. *Spire*, created in 2008, is a 100-foot-high sculpture made of 37 Monterey cypress trees that reaches toward the sky in a grove near the Arguello Gate. Sadly, the sculpture was damaged by a fire in 2020 and is behind chain-link fences; its future remains uncertain. Near the intersection of Presidio Boulevard and West Pacific Avenue, Goldsworthy created *Wood Line* in 2011. Felled eucalyptus trees weave lines through a cypress grove in a work that the artist says "draws the place." In 2013, Goldsworthy moved inside for the installation *Tree Fall*, in the Presidio's Powder Magazine. He covered a tree trunk and the ceiling above it, a dome suspended above the historic structure's walls, with clay from the Presidio, which cracked into lovely patterns. The work is open for viewing weekends from 10 am to 4 pm. In 2014, Goldsworthy created *Earth Wall* in a wall around the patio at the Presidio Officers' Club. He collected curved eucalyptus branches from the site, affixed them in a sphere on the side of the concrete wall, then added a rammed-earth layer to the entire wall, burying the wood while thickening the wall. When it had dried, he used a chisel to reveal the ball, essentially excavating it in a nod to the layers of history at the Presidio. The Presidio Trust's website (🌐 *presidio.gov/places-internal*; click on one of the Goldsworthy sites) includes a 3-mile-loop walk that connects all four works.

Hotels

Long heralded as the place where upscale San Franciscans come to play, the Presidio has a few worthy lodgings, among them a fancy inn occupying former officers' quarters and a sleek lodge in a renovated barracks building. Though the area has just a couple restaurants and nightlife options are nonexistent, the Presidio's historic cachet, wealth of hiking trails, and gorgeous bay-view beaches entice tourists and locals alike, the latter escaping downtown for a restful staycation.

The Inn at the Presidio

$$$ | **B&B/INN** | Built in 1903, this two-story, Georgian revival–style structure once served as officers' quarters but these days is a standout boutique hotel where the rooms and suites have a nice sense of modern refinement and historical touches varying by the room, such as wrought-iron beds, vintage black-and-white photos, and Pendleton blankets. **Pros:** beautifully designed rooms, some with gas fireplaces; peaceful place away from the city's frenetic vibe; evening wine-and-cheese reception by firepits. **Cons:** lack of noise blocking because of old building; 2-night minimum on weekends; challenging to get a taxi/ride-share. [$] *Rooms from: $320* ✉ *42 Moraga Ave., Presidio* ☎ *415/800–7356* 🌐 *www.presidiolodging.com* 🛏 *26 rooms* 🍴 *Free breakfast.*

★ The Lodge at the Presidio

$$$ | B&B/INN | The three-story Lodge occupies former Army barracks, built in the 1890s, and is at the Main Post green's northwestern edge, allowing some rooms to have Golden Gate Bridge views; all rooms are far more upscale and chic than military accommodations, with large flat-screen TVs, well-appointed bathrooms, work stations, and dreamy, custom-made pillow-top mattresses. **Pros:** gorgeous, spacious rooms; charming staff; feels like a vacation from the city but within the city. **Cons:** traffic noise is fairly loud in rooms facing the Golden Gate Bridge; isolated from restaurants and nightlife; similar prices to downtown's more lavish luxury hotels. [$] *Rooms from: $320* ✉ *105 Montgomery St., Presidio* ☎ *415/561–1234* 🌐 *www.presidiolodging.com* 🛏 *42 rooms* 🍴 *Free breakfast.*

Activities

HIKING

Golden Gate Promenade

HIKING/WALKING | During this great walk you pass through Crissy Field, taking in marshlands, kite-flyers, beachfront, and windsurfers, with the Golden Gate Bridge as a backdrop. The 4.3-mile roundtrip trek (or bike ride) is flat and easy—it should take less than two hours round-trip. If you begin at Aquatic Park, you'll end up practically underneath the bridge at Fort Point Pier. ■ **TIP→ If you're driving, park at Fort Point and do the walk from west to east.** It can get blustery, even when it's sunny, so be sure to layer. ✉ *Presidio* 🌐 *www.presidio.gov.*

Presidio hiking trails

HIKING/WALKING | Hiking and biking trails wind through nearly 1,500 acres of woods and hills in the Presidio, past old redbrick military buildings and jaw-dropping scenic overlooks with bay and ocean views. The Bay Trail along Crissy Field to Fort Point, the steep Batteries to Bluffs Trail, and the winding forest stroll of the Ecology Trail are some of the standout hiking routes. Visit 🌐 *www.presidio.gov/trails* for hiking and biking maps. ✉ *Visitor Center, 210 Lincoln Blvd., near Montgomery St., Presidio* ☎ *415/561–4323* 🌐 *www.nps.gov/prsf.*

Chapter 9

THE WESTERN SHORELINE

Updated by
Ava Liang Zhao

⊙ Sights
★★★☆☆

🍴 Restaurants
★★★☆☆

🛏 Hotels
☆☆☆☆☆

🛍 Shopping
☆☆☆☆☆

🍸 Nightlife
☆☆☆☆☆

NEIGHBORHOOD SNAPSHOT

TOP EXPERIENCES

■ **Lands End:** Head down the gorgeous Coastal Trail near the (currently closed) Cliff House; you'll quickly find yourself in a forest with unparalleled views of the Golden Gate Bridge.

■ **Sunset at the Beach Chalet:** Top off a day of exploring with a cocktail overlooking Ocean Beach.

■ **Legion of Honor Museum:** Tear yourself away from the spectacular setting and eye-popping view, and travel back to 18th-century Europe through the paintings, drawings, and porcelain on display here.

■ **Ocean Beach:** Wrap up warmly and stroll along the strand on a brisk, cloudy day; you'll feel like a gritty local. Then thaw out over a bowl of steaming pho in the Richmond.

■ **Old-time San Francisco:** Wandering among the ruins of the Sutro Baths, close your eyes and imagine vintage San Francisco.

PLANNING YOUR TIME

The premier sights of the Western Shoreline are outdoors—gorgeous hiking trails and sandy stretches of coastline. The area is prone to low-lying fog and often biting chill, so bundle up before you start off on the Coastal Trail, which passes by the Legion of Honor museum. Continue west to catch the sunset from the Beach Chalet. If you don't want to do the entire 3-mile hike, you can spend an hour touring the museum, catch the stunning views just below it, and head to the beach.

GETTING HERE

To reach the Western Shoreline from downtown by Muni light-rail, take the N–Judah to Ocean Beach or the L–Taraval to the zoo. From downtown by bus, take the 38–Geary, which runs all the way to 48th and Point Lobos Avenues, just east of the Cliff House. Along the Western Shoreline, the 18–46th Avenue runs between the Legion of Honor and the zoo (and beyond).

QUICK BITES

■ **Arizmendi Bakery.** A Bay Area worker-owned cooperative, the bakery lures passersby with liberal slogans and baked goodies displayed in its large storefront window. The menu changes daily, offering different types of bread, sweet treats like scones, and pizza. Plop down $24 for a whole thin-crust pizza and enjoy it in the sidewalk parklet for a perfect beginning (or end) to a Golden Gate Park excursion. ⊠ *1331 9th Ave., Sunset* ⊕ *www. arizmendibakery.com.*

■ **Arsicault Bakery.** The search for the best, flakiest croissant in San Francisco ends at this tiny French bakery off Clement Street. Other popular items include an assortment of scones, cookies, and *kouign-amann* (a Breton pastry); coffee and tea complete your treat. Lines may be long but move fast and are well worth the wait. ⊠ *397 Arguello Blvd., Richmond* ⊕ *arsicault-bakery.com.*

Few American cities provide a more intimate and dramatic view of the power and fury of the surf attacking the shore than San Francisco does along its wild Western Shoreline.

From Lincoln Park in the north, along Ocean Beach from the Richmond south to the Sunset, a different breed of San Franciscan chooses to live in this area: surfers who brave the heaviest fog to ride the waves; writers who seek solace and inspiration in this city outpost; and dog lovers committed to giving their pets a good workout each day.

The Richmond

In the mid-19th century, the western section of town just north of Golden Gate Park was known as the Outer Lands, and it was covered in sand dunes and seen fit for cemeteries and little else. Today it's the Richmond, comprised of two distinct neighborhoods: the Inner Richmond, from Arguello Boulevard to about 20th Avenue, and the Outer Richmond, from 20th to the ocean. (More formally, this area of San Francisco is called the Richmond District. Just don't confuse the Richmond with Richmond, a city 20 miles away in the East Bay.) Clement Street, packed with solid dining options, from French to Burmese, and with numerous Chinese groceries, is the Inner Richmond's favorite commercial strip. The street makes for great strolling and even better eating. The Outer Richmond has its share of restaurants—most along Geary Boulevard, some along Clement—including the city's highest concentration of Russian eateries and bakeries. But this mostly residential neighborhood is about

the foggy hinterlands that stretch west to the coast: dramatic Lincoln Park with Golden Gate views, the (currently closed) Cliff House, and often-chilly, uncrowded Ocean Beach.

From Lands End in Lincoln Park, you have some of the best views of the Golden Gate—the name was given to the opening of San Francisco Bay long before the bridge was built—and the Marin Headlands. From the historic Cliff House south to the sprawling San Francisco Zoo, the Great Highway and Ocean Beach run along the western edge of the city (south of Golden Gate Park, you're in the Sunset). If you're here in winter or spring, keep your eyes peeled for migrating gray whales. The wind is often strong along the shoreline, summer fog can blanket the ocean beaches, and the water is cold and too dangerous for swimming. Don't forget your jacket!

##

Cliff House
LOCAL INTEREST | Three buildings have occupied this site—today owned by the National Park Service—since 1863, and the current building, a city landmark, dates from 1909. Spectacular ocean views have been bringing diners to the Cliff House's several restaurants for more than a century—you can see 30 miles or more on a clear day. Sitting on the Cliff House's observation deck is the **Giant Camera,** a camera obscura with its lens pointing skyward housed in a cute

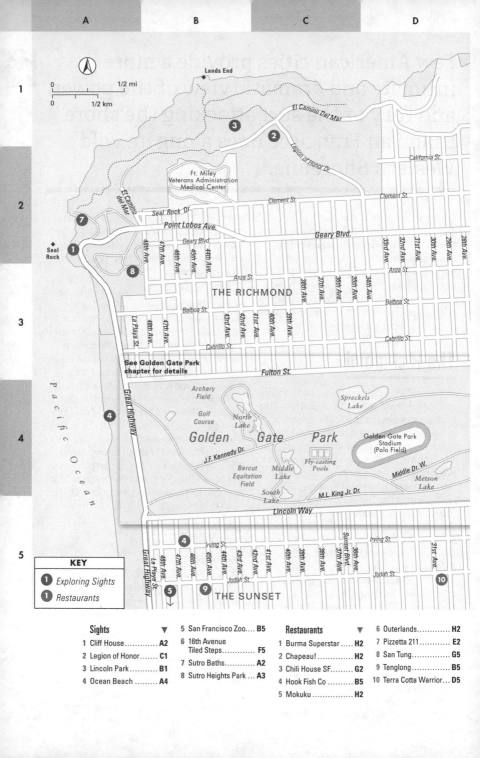

KEY

● Exploring Sights
● Restaurants

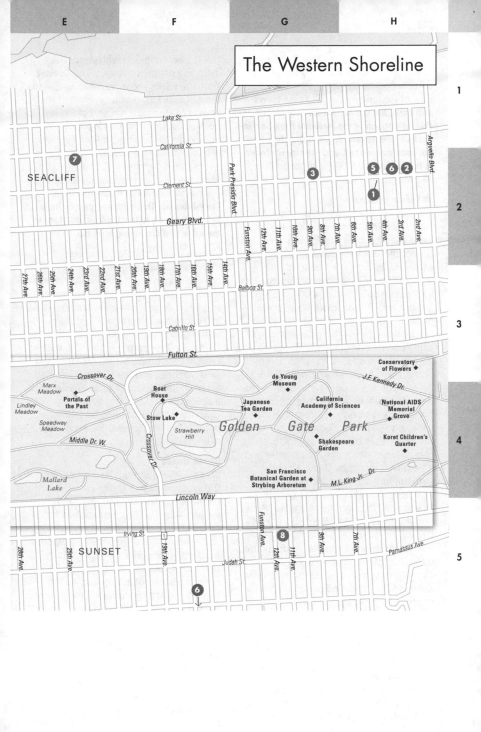

The Western Shoreline

yellow-painted wooden shack. Built in the 1940s and threatened many times with demolition, it's now on the National Register of Historic Places. ⚠ **Those views still exist, but the restaurants are closed at this writing while the National Park Service seeks a new tenant. A reopening date has not been announced, and the site is closed to the public.** ✉ *1090 Point Lobos Ave., Richmond* 🕾 ⊕ *www.nps.gov/goga.*

★ **Legion of Honor**

MUSEUM | Built to commemorate soldiers from California who died in World War I and set atop cliffs overlooking the ocean, the Golden Gate Bridge, and the Marin Headlands, this beautiful Beaux Arts building in Lincoln Park displays an impressive collection of 4,000 years of ancient and European art. A pyramidal glass skylight in the entrance court illuminates the lower-level galleries, which exhibit prints and drawings, European porcelain, and ancient Assyrian, Greek, Roman, and Egyptian art. The 20-plus galleries on the upper level display European art (paintings, sculpture, decorative arts, and tapestries) from the 14th century to the present day. The noteworthy Auguste Rodin collection includes two galleries devoted to the master and a third with works by Rodin and other 19th-century sculptors. An original cast of Rodin's *The Thinker* welcomes you as you walk through the courtyard. Also impressive is the 4,526-pipe Spreckels Organ; live concerts take advantage of the natural sound chamber produced by the building's massive rotunda. As fine as the museum is, the setting and view outshine the collection and also make a trip here worthwhile. ✉ *100 34th Ave. , at Clement St., Richmond* 🕾 *415/750–3600* ⊕ *legionofhonor.famsf.org* 🎟 *$15, free 1st Tues. of month; free Sat. for Bay Area residents* ⊘ *Closed Mon.*

★ **Lincoln Park**

CITY PARK | Although many of the city's green spaces are gentle and welcoming, Lincoln Park is a wild, 275-acre park in the Outer Richmond with windswept cliffs and panoramic views. The **Coastal Trail,** the park's most dramatic one, leads out to **Lands End**; pick it up west of the Legion of Honor (at the end of El Camino del Mar) or from the parking lot at Point Lobos and El Camino del Mar. Time your hike to hit Mile Rock at low tide, and you might catch a glimpse of two wrecked ships peeking up from their watery graves. ⚠ **Be careful if you hike here; landslides are frequent, and people have fallen into the sea by standing too close to the edge of a crumbling bluff top.**

Lincoln Park's 18-hole golf course (⊕ *www.lincolnparkgolfcourse.com)* is on land that in the 19th century was the Golden Gate Cemetery. (When digging has to be done in the park, human bones still occasionally surface.) Next door to the golf course on 33rd Avenue and California Street are the dazzling, mosaic Lincoln Park Steps, which rival the 16th Avenue Steps and the Hidden Garden Steps in the Sunset District. They provide a delightful backdrop for contemplation or an Instagram photo-op. ✉ *Entrance at 34th Ave. at Clement St., Richmond* ⊕ *sfrecpark.org.*

Ocean Beach

BEACH—SIGHT | Stretching 3 miles along the western side of the city from the Richmond to the Sunset, this sandy swath of the Pacific coast is good for flying kites, jogging, or walking the dog—but not for swimming. The water is so cold that surfers wear wet suits year-round, and riptides are strong—drownings are not infrequent. As for sunbathing, it's rarely warm enough here; think meditative walking instead of sun worshipping.

Paths on both sides of the Great Highway lead from Lincoln Way to Sloat Boulevard (near the zoo); the beachside path winds through landscaped sand dunes, and the paved path across the highway is good for biking and in-line skating (though you have to rent bikes elsewhere). The **Beach**

Lincoln Park is known for its golf course as well as cliffs and sweeping ocean views.

Chalet restaurant and brewpub is across the Great Highway from Ocean Beach, about five blocks south of the Cliff House. **Amenities:** parking (no fee); showers; toilets. **Best for:** solitude; sunset; walking. ⊠ *San Francisco ✛ Along Great Hwy. from Cliff House to Sloat Blvd. and beyond* ⊕ *www.parksconservancy.org.*

Sutro Baths

LOCAL INTEREST | Along the oceanfront, to the north of the Cliff House, lie the ruins of the once-grand glass-roof Sutro Baths. Today visitors can explore this evocative historical site and listen to the pounding surf. Adolph Sutro, eccentric onetime San Francisco mayor and Cliff House owner, built the bath complex in 1896 so that everyday folks could enjoy the benefits of swimming. Six enormous baths—freshwater and seawater—and more than 500 dressing rooms plus several restaurants covered 3 acres and accommodated 25,000 bathers. Likened to Roman baths in a European glass palace, the baths were for decades a favorite destination of San Franciscans. The complex fell into disuse after World War II, was closed in 1952, and burned down (under questionable circumstances) during demolition in 1966. To get here, park in the main Lands End parking lot and walk down toward the ruins by the ocean. ⊠ *1004 Point Lobos Ave., Richmond* ☎ *415/426–5240* ⊕ *www.nps.gov/goga.*

Sutro Heights Park

CITY PARK | Crows and other large birds battle the heady breezes at this cliff-top park on what were once the grounds of the home of Adolph Sutro, an eccentric mining engineer and former San Francisco mayor. An extremely wealthy man, Sutro may have owned about 10% of San Francisco at one point, but he couldn't buy good taste: a few remnants of his gaudy, faux-classical statue collection still stand (including the lions at what was the main gate). Monterey cypresses and Canary Island palms dot the park, and photos on placards depict what things looked like before the house burned down in 1896.

All that remains of the main house is its foundation. Climb up for a sweeping view of the Pacific Ocean and the Cliff House below (which Sutro once owned), and try to imagine what the perspective might have been like from one of the upper floors. San Francisco City Guides (*415/557–4266, www.sfcityguides.org*) runs a free Saturday tour of the park that starts at 2; you must reserve ahead. ✉ *Point Lobos and 48th Aves., Richmond* 🌐 *www.nps.gov/goga.*

🍴 Restaurants

The Richmond encompasses the land on the north side of Golden Gate Park, running to the ocean's edge. As for architecture eye-candy, there isn't much, but this is the land of authentic Asian food, particularly in the Inner Richmond, known as the new Chinatown, covering Clement Street from about 2nd to 13th Avenues. On the main thoroughfares of Clement, Balboa, and Geary Streets, you'll find bargain dim sum, Burmese salads, Korean barbecue, and noodle soups of all persuasions.

Burma Superstar

$ | **ASIAN** | Locals make the trek to the "Avenues" for this perennially crowded spot's flavorful, well-prepared Burmese food, including its extraordinary signature tea leaf salad, a combo of spicy, salty, crunchy, and sour tastes that is mixed table-side. The modestly decorated, no-reservations restaurant is small and lines can be long during peak times, so leave your number and wait for the call. **Known for:** spicy curries; samusa soup; vegetarian options. [$] *Average main: $15* ✉ *309 Clement St., Richmond* ☎ *415/387–2147* 🌐 *www.burmasuperstar.com.*

Chapeau!

$$$ | **FRENCH** | A husband-and-wife team serves up classic French cooking and wines at this warm neighborhood bistro where you may run into romantic couples on date night or a small but convivial pre-wedding party. Favorites, like bouillabaisse and filet mignon, are beautifully served with loving attention, and the prix fixe three-course menu option is an exceptional value at $60 (for San Francisco prices). **Known for:** garlicky escargot; delicious cassoulet; loyal following. [$] *Average main: $34* ✉ *126 Clement St., Richmond* ☎ *415/7509787* 🌐 *chapeausf.com* 🕓 *No lunch.*

Chili House SF

$$ | **SICHUAN** | Run by Chef Han, this unassuming local establishment serves a fiery hot menu of Sichuan favorites as well as Peking duck and other northern Chinese dishes. Traditional Chinese lanterns, watercolors, and calligraphy decorate the walls, and diners are seated at square tables or larger round tables with revolving trays. **Known for:** fish in flaming chili oil; beef, tripe, and tendon in special chili sauce; cumin lamb. [$] *Average main: $21* ✉ *726 Clement St., Richmond* ☎ *415/387–2658* 🌐 *chilihousesf.com* 🕓 *Closed Tues.*

Mokuku

$$$ | **JAPANESE** | When the fog and wind roll into the Richmond, savvy locals dive straight into this all-you-can-eat Japanese hot pot joint. Guests can pair an inventive soup base, like fire coconut crab or spicy miso, with the restaurant's signature, perfectly marbled Wagyu beef or Kurobuta pork for a satisfying meal. **Known for:** bar-top hot pot service; tatami mat dining room; karaoke night. [$] *Average main: $35* ✉ *332 Clement St., Richmond* ☎ *415/702–6128* 🌐 *www.mokukushabu.com* 🕓 *No lunch.*

Pizzetta 211

$ | **PIZZA** | This shoebox-size spot puts together thin-crust pies topped with the kinds of ingredients that are worth the constant wait (they don't take reservations). Almost half the menu changes on a biweekly basis, while the tomato, basil, and mozzarella pizza; the Sardinian cheese, pine nut, and rosemary pie; and the San Marzano tomato sauce, wild arugula, and mascarpone pizza are dependable favorites. **Known for:** creative topping combinations; good house-made desserts; short, changing menu. [$] *Average main: $16* ✉ *211 23rd Ave., Richmond* ☎ *415/379–9880* 🌐 *www.pizzetta211.com* 🕒 *Closed Tues.*

Tenglong

$ | CHINESE | Plenty of locals come to this tidy space known for remarkably friendly service and the dry chicken wings, fried in garlic and roasted red peppers, as well as for thinly sliced Mongolian beef and *dan dan* noodles. Run by two former Hong Kong restaurant owners, it specializes in mostly southern Chinese fare, like Cantonese cuisine, and has a few Sichuan specialties, too. **Known for:** honey-walnut prawns; spicy seafood noodle soup; local hot spot. [$] *Average main: $14* ✉ *208 Clement St., Richmond* ☎ *415/666–3515* 🌐 *www.tenglongchinese.com* 🕒 *Closed Tues.*

Nightlife

The nightlife in these practical, comfy neighborhoods centers more on reasonably priced restaurants—including Clement Street's good Chinese, Thai, Burmese, and Vietnamese ones—than on bars and nightclubs. What bar scene there is, you'll find low-key and welcoming. Fierce waves and mesmerizing sunsets are just a few of the reasons to make your way to the western reaches of these districts.

BARS

MUSIC CLUBS

The Plough and the Stars

MUSIC CLUBS | A decidedly unglamorous pub where crusty old-timers swap stories over pints of Guinness, this is the city's best bet for traditional Irish music. Bay Area musicians (and, once in a while, big-name bands) perform every night except Monday. Talented locals gather for Tuesday and Sunday *seisiúns,* informal "sessions" where musicians sit around a table and drink and eat while chiming in; anyone skilled at Irish traditional music can play. ✉ *116 Clement St., at 2nd Ave., Richmond* ☎ *415/751–1122* 🌐 *theploughandstars.com.*

Shopping

The Richmond, the vast tract north of Golden Gate Park west from Arguello Boulevard to Ocean Beach, is known for its Asian and other markets. Geary Boulevard is the main drag, but some of the neighborhood's most interesting shops can be found in the dozen blocks of Clement Street west of Arguello, among them the much-loved Green Apple Books.

BOOKS

★ Green Apple Books

BOOKS/STATIONERY | A local favorite with a huge used-book department also carries new books in every field. It's known for its history room and rare-books collection. Two doors down, at 520 Clement Street, is a fiction annex that also sells CDs, DVDs, comic books, and graphic novels. ✉ *506 Clement St., at 6th Ave., Richmond* ☎ *415/387–2272* 🌐 *www.greenapplebooks.com.*

GIFTS AND SOUVENIRS

Park Life

GIFTS/SOUVENIRS | An eclectic assortment of souvenirs, art, books, apparel, stationery, and prints tempt browsers at this design-centric hipster outpost. With a well-curated collection of School of Life philosophy books aiming to tickle your intellect and non-touristy T-shirts to take back home, it's the perfect place to browse for a half hour while waiting for your table at Burma Superstar across the street. ✉ *220 Clement St., Richmond* ☎ *415/386–7275* 🌐 *parklifestore.com.*

The Sunset

Hugging the southern edge of Golden Gate Park and built atop the sand dunes that covered much of western San Francisco into the 19th century, the Sunset is made up of two distinct neighborhoods—the popular Inner Sunset, from Stanyan Street to 19th Avenue, and the foggy Outer Sunset, from 19th to the beach. The Inner Sunset is perhaps the perfect San Francisco "suburb": not too far from the center of things, reachable by public transit, and home to main streets—Irving Street and 9th Avenue just off Golden Gate Park—packed with excellent dining options, with Asian food particularly well represented. Long the domain of surfers and others who love the laid-back beach vibe and the fog, the slow-paced now Outer Sunset finds itself on the radar of locals, with high-quality cafés and restaurants and quirky shops springing up along Judah Street between 42nd and 46th Avenues. The San Francisco Zoo is the district's main tourist attraction.

Sights

San Francisco Zoo

ZOO | FAMILY | Occupying prime ocean-front property, the San Francisco Zoo touts itself as a wildlife-focused recreation center that inspires visitors to become conservationists. Integrated exhibits group different species of animals from the same geographic areas together in enclosures that don't look like cages. More than 2,000 animals and 250 species reside here, including endangered species, such as the snow leopard, Sumatran tiger, and grizzly bear, and a Siberian tiger. The zoo's superstar exhibit is Grizzly Gulch, where orphaned grizzly bear sisters Kachina and Kiona enchant visitors with their frolicking and swimming. The Mexican Gray Wolf grotto houses the smallest gray wolf and the most endangered wolf subspecies in the world. The Lemur Forest has seven varieties of the bug-eyed, long-tailed primates from Madagascar and is the country's largest outdoor lemur habitat. African kikuyugrass carpets the circular outer area of the Jones Family Gorilla Preserve, one of the most natural gorilla habitats of any zoo in the world. Other popular exhibits include Penguin Island, Koala Crossing, and the African Savanna exhibit. The 6-acre Children's Zoo has about 300 mammals, birds, and reptiles, plus a huge playground, a restored 1921 Dentzel carousel, and a mini–steam train. ⊠ Sloat Blvd. and 47th Ave., Sunset ☎ 415/753–7080 ⊕ www.sfzoo. org ⊡ $25, $1 off with Muni transfer (take Muni L–Taraval streetcar from downtown).

16th Avenue Tiled Steps

NEIGHBORHOOD | A community-based project dedicated in 2005, these 163 tiled steps have beautiful designs showing fish, shells, animals, starry skies, and other scenes. The steps are in a residential neighborhood, so it's polite to enjoy the steps and the city views from the top quietly. ⊠ Moraga St., between 15th and 16th Ave., Sunset ⊕ www.16thavenuetiledsteps.com.

🍴 Restaurants

The Sunset neighborhood encompasses the land south of Golden Gate Park, running all the way to the ocean's edge, and has a surf-town or small-town vibe. It's known for its fog, yes, but also bargain eats (U.C. San Francisco is here) that range from pizzas and salads to Eritrean injera (flatbread) and Chinese dumplings, concentrated along Irving Street.

★ Hook Fish Co

$ | SEAFOOD | Unpretentious yet undeniably chic, this neighborhood beach shack is famous for its simple, fresh seafood. The menu changes daily depending on the day's catch, so join hungry surfers and locals as they gobble up tacos, burritos, or fish-and-chips; wash your choice down with beer or wine. **Known for:** serves possibly the best fish and chips in San Francisco; blackboard oysters and specials; lines can be long, so come early. $\boxed{\$}$ *Average main: $16* ✉ *4542 Irving St., Sunset* ☎ *415/569–4984* ⊕ *www. hookfishco.com.*

Outerlands

$$$ | **MODERN AMERICAN** | As infamous for its lines as it is famous for its brunch, this cozy, wood-paneled restaurant serves food that is thoroughly Northern California, from the granola with goat's milk yogurt to the avocado toast drizzled with Meyer lemon vinaigrette. The cast-iron grilled cheese sandwich is legendary, and dinner also offers plenty of charm: just make sure you have some time on your hands and layers to ward off the Sunset chill while you wait. **Known for:** high-quality ingredients; dutch pancakes; house-made bread. $\boxed{\$}$ *Average main: $27* ✉ *4001 Judah St., Sunset* ☎ *415/661–6140* ⊕ *outerlandssf.com.*

San Tung

$ | **CHINESE** | **FAMILY** | The food of China's northeastern province of Shandong is the draw at this bare-bones storefront restaurant where specialties include steamed dumplings—shrimp and leek dumplings are the most popular—and hand-pulled noodles in soup or stir-fried. Especially popular are the platters of excellent dry-fried chicken wings, a cult dish in the city. **Known for:** sauteed string beans; famous chicken wings are a family favorite; long waits. $\boxed{\$}$ *Average main: $15* ✉ *1031 Irving St., Sunset* ☎ *415/242–0828* ⊕ *www.santung.net* ☾ *Closed Wed.*

Terra Cotta Warrior

$ | **NORTHERN CHINESE** | This family-owned restaurant is the best place in the city to sample hard-to-find Muslim Chinese cuisine from northwest China and to carbload. Order classics like wide *biang biang* hand-pulled noodles with cumin lamb or *liangpi* cold noodles, and accompany

them with pita bread soaked in flavorful lamb soup. **Known for:** homey appetizers; food is an excellent value; Chinese hamburger. $\boxed{\$}$ *Average main: $12* ✉ *2555 Judah St., Sunset* ☎ *415/681–3288* ⊕ *tcwus.com* ☾ *Closed Mon. No lunch.*

Nightlife

BARS

The Riptide

BARS/PUBS | A cozy cabin bar that's the perfect finale for beachgoers, the Riptide is a surfer favorite, but you don't have to own a board to feel at home. You'll find classic beers and good food, all at wallet-friendly prices. There's live music most nights, often country, bluegrass, honky-tonk, and open mic. Many tourists fooled by San Francisco's version of summer end up warming their popsicle toes at the bar's fireplace. Sunday features a bacon Bloody Mary, great for hangovers. ✉ *3639 Taraval St, Sunset* ☎ *415/681–8433* ⊕ *www.riptidesf.com.*

Golden Gate Park

Jogging, cycling, skating, picnicking, going to a museum, checking out a concert, dozing in the sunshine … Golden Gate Park is the perfect playground for fast-paced types, laid-back dawdlers, and everyone in between. More than 1,000 acres, stretching from the Haight all the way to the windy Pacific coast, the park is a vast patchwork of woods, trails, lakes, lush gardens, sports facilities, museums—even a herd of bison. You can hit the highlights in a few hours, but it would literally take days to fully explore the entire park. *For more information about the park, see Chapter 10, Golden Gate Park.*

Nightlife

Often shrouded by the city's famous fog and always scented by crisp eucalyptus, Golden Gate Park provides a limited but suitably mellow nightlife experience.

BARS

Beach Chalet

BARS/PUBS | Renovated in 2021, this restaurant-microbrewery, on the second floor of a historic building filled with 1930s Works Project Administration murals (on the first floor), has a stunning view of the Pacific Ocean. It's open for lunch and dinner, but you may want to time your visit and a drink to coincide with the sunset. ■**TIP**➜ **Arrive at least 30 minutes before sunset to beat the dinner crowd.** The house brews are rich and flavorful, and there's a good selection of California wines by the glass. ⊠ *1000 Great Hwy., near John F. Kennedy Dr., Golden Gate Park* ☎ *415/386–8439* ⊕ *www.beachchalet.com.*

Park Chalet

BARS/PUBS | You'll feel like you're in a cabin in the woods as you relax in an Adirondack chair under a heat lamp, enclosed by the greenery of Golden Gate Park. In addition to serving pub food, such as burgers, salads, steaks, and fish-and-chips, the brewery churns out its own beer. On sunny spring and summer weekend days, there's live music on the lawn. The Park Chalet shares a building with the Beach Chalet—but it isn't waterside, so you won't freeze if it's overcast. There's indoor seating too, but the outdoor seating area is the highlight. ⊠ *1000 Great Hwy., near John F. Kennedy Dr., Golden Gate Park* ☎ *415/386–8439* ⊕ *www.parkchalet.com.*

Activities

BOATING AND SAILING

Stow Lake

BOATING | **FAMILY** | If you prefer calm freshwater, you can rent rowboats and pedal boats at Stow Lake in Golden Gate Park. Remember to bring bread for the ducks. ■**TIP**➜ **The lake is open 10–4 on weekends and 11–4 on weekdays for boating; rentals stop one hour before closing.** ⊠ *Stow Lake Boathouse, 50 Stow Lake Dr. E, off John F. Kennedy Dr., Golden Gate Park* ☎ *415/386–2531* ⊕ *stowlakeboathouse. com* ☑ *From $22.50 per hour for boat rentals.*

HIKING

Golden Gate National Recreation Area (*GGNRA*)

HIKING/WALKING | **FAMILY** | This huge, protected area encompasses the San Francisco coastline, the Marin Headlands, and Point Reyes National Seashore, perhaps one of the most beautiful places on the planet. It's veined with hiking trails, including the spectacular Coastal Trail at Lands End in San Francisco (access this from the parking lot near the western end of Point Lobos Avenue), and guided walks are offered in some places. You can find current schedules at visitor centers at Lands End, in the Presidio, and in the Marin Headlands; they're also online. ⊠ *San Francisco* ☎ *415/561–4700* ⊕ *www.nps.gov/goga.*

Chapter 10

GOLDEN GATE PARK

A GREEN RETREAT

Stretching more than 1,000 acres from the ocean to the Haight, Golden Gate Park is a place to slow down and smell the eucalyptus. Stockbrokers and gadget-laden parents stroll the Music Concourse, while speedy tattooed cyclists and wobbly, training-wheeled kids cruise along shaded paths. Seniors and teenagers warm the garden benches, hikers search for waterfalls, and picnickers lounge in the Rhododendron Dell. San Franciscans love their city streets, but the park is where they come to breathe.

PLANNING A PARK VISIT

ORIENTATION

The park breaks down naturally into three chunks. The eastern end attracts the biggest crowds with its cluster of blockbuster sights. It's also the easiest place to dip into the park for a quick trip. Water hobbyists come to the middle section's lake-speckled open space. Sporty types head west to the coastal end for its soccer fields, golf course, and archery range. This windswept western end is the park's least visited and most naturally landscaped part. ⊙ Daily 6 am–10 pm ⊕ www.sfrecpark.org.

WALKING TOURS

San Francisco Botanical Garden (☎ 415/661–1316) has free botanical tours every day (admission not included). Tours start near the main gate daily at 1:30 pm.

San Francisco City Guides (☎ 415/557–4266) offers free year-round tours of the eastern end and the western end of the park and two different tours of the Japanese Tea Garden

BEST TIMES TO VISIT

Time of day: It's best to arrive early at the Conservatory of Flowers, the de Young Museum,

and the Japanese Tea Garden to avoid crowds. At sunset, the only place to be is the park's western end, watching the sun dip into the Pacific.

Time of year: Visit during the week if you can. The long, late summer days of September and October are the warmest times to visit, and many special weekend events are held then.

Blooms: The rhododendrons bloom between February and May. The Queen Wilhelmina Tulip Garden blossoms in February and March. Cherry trees in the Japanese Tea Garden bloom in April, and the Rose Garden is at its best from mid-May to mid-June, in the beginning of July, and during September.

(opposite) Conservatory of Flowers. (top left) The San Francisco Botanical Garden in bloom.

TIPS

■ Carry a map or check online
(See ⊕ www.goldengatepark.
com)—the park's sightlines
usually prevent you from
using city landmarks as reference points. Posted maps
are few and far between,
and they're often out of date.
Paths aren't always clear, so
stick to well-marked trails.

■ In Golden Gate Park, free
public restrooms are fairly
common and mostly clean,
especially around the eastern
end's attractions. Facilities
are available behind the
Conservatory of Flowers or in
the de Young Museum at the
sculpture garden and café
patio. Farther west, behind
Stow Lake's boathouse and
near the Koret Children's
Quarter are facilities.

■ Check out www.goldengate-
park.com for a calendar of
park events. This unofficial
site also has maps and parking info.

BEST WAYS TO SPEND YOUR TIME

The park stretches 3 miles east to west and is a half-
mile wide, so it's possible to cover the whole thing in
a day—by car, public transportation, bike, or even on
foot. But to do so might feel more like a forced march
than a pleasure jaunt. Weigh your time and your interests, choose your top picks, then leave at least an extra
hour to just enjoy being outdoors.

Two hours: Swing by the exquisite Conservatory of Flowers for a 20-minute peek, then head to the de Young Museum. Spend a few minutes assessing its controversial
exterior and perhaps glide through some of the galleries
before heading to the observation tower for a panoramic
view of the city. Cross the Music Concourse to the
spectacular Academy of Sciences.

Half day: Spend a little extra time at the sights described
above, then head to the nearby Japanese Tea Garden to
enjoy its perfectionist landscape. Next, cross the street
to the San Francisco Botanical Garden at Strybing Arboretum and check out the intriguing Primitive Garden. If
you brought supplies, this is a great place for a picnic;
you can also grab lunch at the de Young Café.

Full day: After the half-day tour (above) continue on to
the children's playground if you have kids in tow. Once
your little ones see the playground's tree house–like play
structures and climbing opportunities, you may be here
for the rest of the day. Alternatively, make your way to
the serene National AIDS Memorial Grove. Then head
west, stopping at Stow Lake to climb Strawberry Hill.
Wind up at the Beach Chalet for a sunset drink.

(top) Amateur musicians entertain passersby. (middle) Sundays
are ideal biking days. (bottom) The meandering paths are perfect
for strolling.

GETTING AROUND THE PARK

WALKING

The most convenient entry point is on the eastern edge at Stanyan Street, continuing into the park on JFK Drive, which points you directly toward the Conservatory of Flowers. It's a 10-minute walk there; allow another 10–15 minutes to reach the California Academy of Sciences, de Young Museum, Japanese Tea Garden, and San Francisco Botanical Garden. Stow Lake is another 10 minutes west from these four sights.

BY BIKE

The park is fantastic for cycling, especially on Sunday when cars are barred from John F. Kennedy Drive. Biking the park round-trip is about a 7-mile trip, which usually takes 1–2 hours. The route down John F. Kennedy Drive takes you past the prettiest, well-maintained sections of the park on a mostly flat circuit. The most popular route continues all the way to the beach. Keep in mind that the ride is downhill toward the ocean, uphill heading east.

BY CAR

If you have a car, you'll have no trouble hopping from sight to sight. (But remember, the main road, John F. Kennedy Drive, is closed to cars on Sunday.) Parking within the park is often free and is usually easy to find especially beyond the eastern end. On Sundays or anytime the eastern end is crowded, head for the residential streets north of the park or the underground parking lot; enter on 10th and Fulton (northern edge of the park) or MLK Drive and Concourse (in the park).

BY SHUTTLE

The free Golden Gate Park shuttle runs 9–6 weekends and holidays. It loops through the park every 15–20 minutes, stopping at 14 sights from McLaren Lodge to the Dutch Windmill. If you're driving, leave your car in the free spaces along Ocean Beach (Great Highway between Lincoln and Fulton) and wait at the green shuttle stop sign.

WHERE TO RENT

Parkwide Bike Rentals & Tours (☎ 415/671–8989). The only rental shop in the park is behind the band-shell on the music concourse. For an extra $10 you can return your bike to the Embarcadero/Ferry Building, the Marina, or Union Square. **Golden Gate Park Bike & Skate** (✉ 3038 Fulton St. ☎ 415/668–1117). On the northern edge of the park; good deals on rentals. **San Francisco Bicycle Rentals** (✉ 425 Jefferson St. ☎ 415/922–4537). Customers rave about excellent service and good deals at this Fisherman's Wharf outfit. **Blazing Saddles** (✉ 2715 Hyde St ☎ 415/202–8888). This business operates out of Fisherman's Wharf and North Beach but you can take their bikes to the park, too.

BEST PLACES TO PICNIC ON WEEKENDS

■ Lawn in front of the Conservatory of Flowers.

■ By the pond in the San Francisco Botanical Garden.

■ The benches overlooking the Rustic Bridge at Stow Lake.

■ Rhododendron Dell.

(top) Water lilies adorn the Japanese Tea Garden.

DON'T-MISS SIGHTS

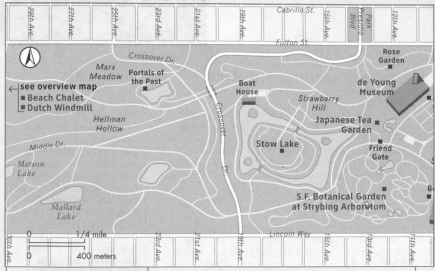

29th Ave. · 27th Ave. · 25th Ave. · 23rd Ave. · 21st Ave. · 19th Ave. · Cabrillo St. · 16th Ave. · Presidio Blvd · Park · 12th Ave.

Fulton St.

Crossover Dr.

Rose Garden

Marx Meadow · Portals of the Past

← see overview map
■ Beach Chalet
■ Dutch Windmill

Boat House

de Young Museum

Strawberry Hill

Hellman Hollow

Japanese Tea Garden

Middle Dr.

Stow Lake

Friend Gate

Metson Lake

Mallard Lake

S.F. Botanical Garden at Strybing Arboretum

Lincoln Way

0   1/4 mile
0   400 meters

30th Ave. · 23rd Ave. · 21st Ave. · 19th Ave. · 16th Ave. · 13th Ave. · 11th Ave.

Conservatory of Flowers
✉ 100 John F. Kennedy Dr. at
   Conservatory Dr.
☎ 415/831–2090
💲 $10 Tues.–Thurs., $12
   Fri.–Sun.
🕐 Tues.–Sun. 10–4:30
🌐 www.conservatoryof
   flowers.org

CONSERVATORY OF FLOWERS

Whatever you do, be sure to at least drive by the Conservatory of Flowers—it's just too darn pretty to miss. The gorgeous, white-framed, 1878 glass structure is topped with a 14-ton glass dome. Stepping inside the giant greenhouse is like taking a quick trip to the rainforest; it's humid, warm, and smells earthy. The undeniable highlight is the Aquatic Plants section, where lily pads float and carnivorous plants dine on bugs to the sounds of rushing water. On the east side of the conservatory (to the right as you face the building), cypress, pine, and redwood trees surround the **Dahlia Garden,** which blooms in summer and fall. To the west is the **Rhododendron Dell,** which contains 850 varieties, more than any other garden of its kind in the country. It's a favorite local Mother's Day picnic spot.

STOW LAKE

Russian seniors feed the pigeons, kids watch turtles sunning themselves, and joggers circle this placid body of water, Golden Gate Park's largest lake. Early park superintendent John McLaren may have snarked that manmade Stow Lake was "a shoestring around a watermelon," but for more than a century visitors have come to walk its paths and bridges, paddle boats, and climb Strawberry Hill (the "watermelon"). Cross one of the bridges—the 19th-century stone bridge on the southwest side is lovely—and ascend the hill; keep your eyes open for the waterfall and an elaborate Chinese Pavilion.

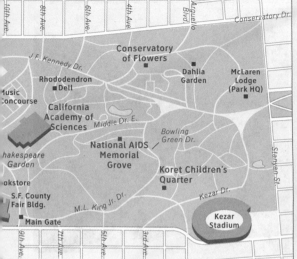

Map labels:
10th Ave. · 8th Ave. · 6th Ave. · 4th Ave. · Arguello Blvd. · Conservatory Dr.
J.F. Kennedy Dr. · Conservatory of Flowers · Dahlia Garden · McLaren Lodge (Park HQ)
Rhododendron Dell · Music Concourse · California Academy of Sciences · Middle Dr. E. · Bowling Green Dr. · Stanyan St.
Shakespeare Garden · National AIDS Memorial Grove · Koret Children's Quarter · Kezar Dr.
Bookstore · S.F. County Fair Bldg. · M.L. King Jr. Dr. · Main Gate · Kezar Stadium
9th Ave. · 7th Ave. · 5th Ave. · 3rd Ave.

SAN FRANCISCO JAPANESE TEA GARDEN

As you amble through the manicured landscape, past Japanese sculptures and perfect miniature pagodas, over ponds of huge carp, you may be transported to a more peaceful plane. Or maybe the shrieks of kids clambering over the almost vertical "humpback" bridges will keep you firmly in the here and now. Either way, this garden is one of those tourist spots that's truly worth a stop (a half-hour will do). And at 5 acres, it's large enough that you'll always be able to find a bit of serenity, even when the tour buses drop by.

■TIP→ The garden is especially lovely in April, when the cherry blossoms are in bloom.

KORET CHILDREN'S QUARTER

Founded in 1888 and impressively renovated, the country's first public children's playground has wave-shaped climbing walls, old-fashioned cement slides, and a 20-plus-foot rope climbing structure that kids love and parents fear. Thankfully, one holdover is the beautiful, handcrafted 1912 Herschell-Spillman Carousel. The lovely stone Sharon Building, next to the playground, offers kids' art classes. Bring a picnic or pick up grub nearby on 9th Avenue and you could spend the entire day here. Be aware that the playground, which has separate areas for toddlers and bigger kids, is unenclosed and sightlines can be obstructed.

Stow Lake
- ✉ Off John F. Kennedy Dr.
- ☎ Boat rental 415/386–2531
- ⏱ Boat rentals 11–4 weekdays, 10–4 weekends
- ⊕ www.stowlakeboathouse.com

San Francisco Japanese Tea Garden
- ✉ 75 Hagiwara Tea Garden Dr.
- ☎ 415/752–1171
- 🎫 $10, free Mon., Wed., and Fri. with entry by 10 am
- ⏱ Mar.–Oct., daily 9–5:45; Nov.–Feb., daily 9–4:45
- ⊕ www.japaneseteagardensf.com

Koret Children's Quarter
- ✉ Bowling Green Dr., off Martin Luther King Jr. Dr
- ☎ 415/861–0778
- 🎫 Playground free, carousel $2
- ⏱ Playground daily dawn–dusk; carousel Memorial Day–Labor Day, weekdays 10:30–5, weekends 10–6, Labor Day–Memorial Day, weekends 10–4.
- ⊕ www.sfrec.org

ᴅE YOUNG MUSEUM

✉ 50 Hagiwara Tea
Garden Dr.

☎ 415/750–3600

⊕ www.deyoung.famsf.org

💲 $15; free 1st Tues.
of month

🕐 Tues.–Sun. 9:30–5:15

TIPS

■ Admission at the de Young
is good for same-day admission to the Legion of Honor
and vice-versa.

■ The de Young is famous
these days first and foremost
for its striking and controversial building and tree-topping
tower. These are accessible
to the public for free, so if it's
not the art you're interested
in seeing, save the cost of
admission and head up the
elevator to 360-degree views
from the glass-walled observation floor.

■ When it's time for a nosh,
head to the de Young Café
and dine in the lovely outdoor
sculpture garden.

Everyone in town has a strong opinion about the
de Young. Some adore the striking copper facade,
while others grimace and hope that the green patina
of age will mellow the effect. The building almost
overshadows the museum's respected collection of
American, African, and Oceanic art.

HIGHLIGHTS
Head through the sprawling concourse level and
begin your visit on the upper level, where you'll
find textiles; art from Africa, Oceana, and New
Guinea; and highlights of the 20th-century American painting collection (such as Wayne Thiebaud,
John Singer Sargent, Winslow Homer, and Richard
Diebenkorn). These are the don't-miss items, so
take your time. Then head back downstairs to see
art from the Americas and contemporary work.

The de Young has had some major international
coups, scoring exhibits such as Tutankhamun and
the Golden Age of the Pharoahs; Van Gogh, Gaugin,
Cezanne, and Beyond: Post-Impressionist Masterpieces from the Musée d'Orsay; and Picasso: Masterpieces from the Musée National Picasso, Paris.
Be sure to check for traveling exhibits while you're
visiting (extra fees apply).

CALIFORNIA ACADEMY OF SCIENCES

✉ 55 Music Concourse Dr.

☎ 415/379-8000

⊕ www.calacademy.org

💳 $30–$40, free one Sun. per quarter, $3 off for visitors who walk, bike, or take public transit.

🕐 Mon.–Sat. 9:30–5, Sun. 11–5

TIPS

■ The academy often hosts gaggles of schoolchildren. Arrive early and allow plenty of time to wait in line.

■ Plan ahead: check Planetarium show times, animal feeding times, etc, before you arrive.

■ Visitors complain about the high cost of food here; consider bringing a picnic.

■ Free days are tempting, but the tradeoff includes extremely long lines and the possibility that you won't get in.

■ With antsy kids, visit Early Explorers Cove and use the academy's in-and-out privileges to run around outside.

■ Take time to examine the structure itself, from denim insulation to weather sensors.

With its native plant–covered living roof, retractable ceiling, three-story rain forest, gigantic planetarium, living coral reef, and frolicking penguins, the Cal Academy is one of the city's most spectacular treasures. Dramatically designed by Renzo Piano, it's an eco-friendly, energy-efficient adventure in biodiversity and green architecture. The roof's large mounds and hills mirror the local topography, and Piano's audacious design completes the dramatic transformation of the park's Music Concourse. Moving away from a restrictive role as a backward-looking museum that catalogued natural history, the new academy is all about sustainability and the future, but you'll still find those beloved dioramas in African Hall.

HIGHLIGHTS

By the time you arrive, hopefully you've decided which shows and programs to attend, looked at the academy's floor plan, and designed a plan to cover it all in the time you have. And if not, here's the quick version: Head left from the entrance to the wooden walkway over otherworldly rays in the Philippine Coral Reef, then continue to the Swamp to see Claude, the famous albino alligator. Swing through African Hall and view the penguins, take the elevator up to the living roof, then return to the main floor and get in line to explore the Rainforests of the World, ducking free-flying butterflies and watching for other live surprises. You'll end up below ground in the Amazonian Flooded Rainforest, where you can explore the academy's other aquarium exhibits. Phew.

ALSO WORTH SEEING

San Francisco Botanical Garden at Strybing Arboretum

SAN FRANCISCO BOTANICAL GARDEN AT STRYBING ARBORETUM

One of the best picnic spots in a very picnic-friendly park, the 55-acre arboretum specializes in plants from areas with climates similar to that of the Bay Area. Walk the Eastern Australian garden to see tough, pokey shrubs and plants with cartoon-like names, such as the hilly-pilly tree. Kids gravitate toward the large shallow fountain and the pond with ducks, turtles, and egrets. Free tours meet at the main gate daily at 1:30. ⊠ *Enter park at 9th Ave. at Lincoln Way* ☎ *415/661–1316* ⊕ *www.sfbg.org* ▧ *$9 weekdays, $12 weekends; Free daily 7:30–9* ☉ *Mar.–Sept., daily 7:30–6; Oct.–early Nov. and Feb.–Mar., daily 7:30–5. Nov.–Jan., daily 7:30–4.*

NATIONAL AIDS MEMORIAL GROVE

This lush, serene 7-acre grove was conceived as a living memorial to the disease's victims. Coast live oaks, Monterey pines, coast redwoods, and other trees flank the grove. There are also two stone circles, one recording the names of the dead and their loved ones, the other engraved with a poem. Free self-guided tours are available to download on any mobile device. ⊠ *Middle Dr. E, west of tennis courts* ☎ *415/765–0498* ⊕ *www.aidsmemorial.org.*

Beach Chalet

BEACH CHALET

Hugging the park's western border, this 1925 Willis Polk–designed structure houses gorgeous Depression-era murals of familiar San Francisco scenes by Lucien Adolphe Labaudt, while verses by local poets adorn niches here and there. Stop by the ground-floor visitors center on your way to indulge in a microbrew upstairs, ideally at sunset. ⊠ *1000 Great Hwy.* ☎ *415/386–8439 restaurant* ⊕ *www.beachchalet.com* ☉ *Restaurant weekdays 11–9, weekends 10–9.*

Dutch Windmill

DUTCH WINDMILL

It may not pump water anymore, but this carefully restored windmill, built in 1903 to irrigate the park, continues to enchant visitors. The Queen Wilhelmina Tulip Garden here is a welcoming respite, particularly lovely during its February and March bloom. The Murphy Windmill is just south of the Dutch Windmill and has a refurbished copper dome; swing by for an interesting comparison. ⊠ *1691 John F. Kennedy Dr., 1/2 block east of Great Hwy., northwest corner of park* ☎ *No phone* ☉ *Dawn–dusk daily.*

THE HAIGHT, THE CASTRO, AND NOE VALLEY

Updated by
Ava Liang Zhao

⦿ Sights	🍴 Restaurants	🛏 Hotels	🛍 Shopping	🍸 Nightlife
★☆☆☆☆	★★★☆☆	★☆☆☆☆	★★★☆☆	★★★☆☆

NEIGHBORHOOD SNAPSHOT

TOP EXPERIENCES

■ **Castro Theatre:** Take in a film at this gorgeous throwback and join the audience shouting out lines, commentary, and songs. Come early and let the Wurlitzer set the mood.

■ **Sunday brunch in the Castro:** Recover from Saturday night (with the entire community) at one of the area's favorite brunch spots.

■ **Vintage shopping in the Haight:** Find the perfect 1930s afternoon dress at Relic Vintage, a pristine faux-leopard coat at Held Over, or the motorcycle jacket of your dreams at Buffalo Exchange.

■ **24th Street stroll:** Take a leisurely ramble down lovable Noe Valley's main drag, lined with unpretentious cafés, comfy eateries, and cute one-of-a-kind shops.

PLANNING YOUR TIME

The Upper Haight is only a few blocks long, and although there are plenty of shops and amusements, an hour or so should be enough unless you're into vintage shopping. Many restaurants cater to the morning-after crowd, so this is a great place for brunch. With the prevalence of panhandling in this area, you may be most comfortable here during the day.

The Castro, with its fun, adult-theme storefronts, invites unhurried exploration; allot at least 60 to 90 minutes. Visit in the evening to check out the lively nightlife, or in the late morning—especially on weekends—when the street scene is hopping.

A loop through Noe Valley takes about an hour. With its popular breakfast spots and cafés, this neighborhood is a good place for a morning stroll. After you've filled up, browse the shops along 24th and Church Streets.

GETTING HERE

■ F-line trolleys serve the Castro. Muni light-rail K–Ingleside, L–Taraval, M–Ocean View, and T–Third trains stop at Castro station; and the J–Church serves the Castro and Noe Valley. The 7–Haight/Noriega bus from Market Street and the 6–Haight/Parnassus from Market serve the Haight. If on foot, know that the hill between the Castro and Noe Valley is steep.

QUICK BITES

■ **Flywheel Coaster Roasters.** Family-owned, this light-filled café with a view of Golden Gate Park roasts its beans in-house for a great cuppa. The cold brew is very good, and the food includes vegan options. ⊠ *672 Stanyan St., Haight* ⊕ *flywheelcoffee.com.*

■ **Lovejoy's Tea Room.** The tearoom is a homey jumble, with its lace-covered tables, couches, and mismatched chairs set among the antiques for sale. High tea and cream tea are served, along with traditional English-tearoom "fayre," such as crustless sandwiches, scones, and crumpets. It's all quite cozy. ⊠ *1351 Church St., at Clipper St., Noe Valley* ⊕ *www.lovejoystearoom.com*

These distinct neighborhoods wear their personalities large and proud, and all are perfect for just strolling around. As if you were watching a slide show of San Francisco's history, you can move from the Haight's residue of 1960s counterculture to the Castro's connection to 1970s and '80s gay life to 1990s gentrification in Noe Valley. Although historic events thrust the Haight and the Castro onto the international stage, both are anything but stagnant—they're still dynamic areas well worth exploring.

The Haight

During the 1960s, the siren song of free love, peace, and mind-altering substances lured thousands of young people to the Haight, a neighborhood just east of Golden Gate Park. By 1966 the area had become a hot spot for rock artists, including the Grateful Dead, Jefferson Airplane, and Janis Joplin. Some of the most infamous flower children, including Charles Manson and People's Temple founder Jim Jones, also called the Haight home.

Today the '60s message of peace, civil rights, and higher consciousness has been distilled into a successful blend of commercialism and progressive causes: the Haight Ashbury Free Clinic, founded in 1967, survives at the corner of Haight and Clayton Streets, while throwbacks like

Bound Together Bookstore (the anarchist book collective), the head shop Pipe Dreams ✉ *(1376 Haight St.)*, and a bevy of tie-dye shops all keep the Summer of Love alive in their own way. The Haight's famous political spirit—it was the first neighborhood in the nation to lead a freeway revolt, and it continues to resist chain stores—survives alongside some of the finest Victorian-lined streets in the city.

The Haight is actually composed of two distinct neighborhoods: the Lower Haight runs from Divisadero to Webster; the Upper Haight, immediately east of Golden Gate Park, is the part people tend to call Haight-Ashbury (and the part that's covered here). San Franciscans come to the Upper Haight for the myriad vintage clothing stores concentrated in its few blocks, bars with character, restaurants where huge breakfast portions take the

Hippie History

The eternal lure for twentysomethings, cheap rent, first helped spawn an indelible part of SF's history and public image. In the early 1960s, young people started streaming into the sprawling, inexpensive Victorian houses in the area around the University of San Francisco, earnestly seeking a new era of communal living, individual empowerment, and expanded consciousness.

Golden Gate Park's Panhandle, a green strip on the Haight's northern edge, was their gathering spot—the site of protests, concerts, food giveaways, and general hanging out. In 1967, George Harrison strolled up the park's Hippie Hill, borrowed a guitar, and played for a while before being recognized. He led the crowd, Pied Piper–style, into the Haight.

A Hippie State of Mind

At first the counterculture was all about sharing and taking care of one another—a good thing, considering most hippies were either broke or had renounced money. The daily free "feeds" in the Panhandle were a staple for many. The Diggers, an anarchist street-theater group, were known for handing out bread shaped like the big coffee cans they baked it in.

At the time, the U.S. government, Harvard professor Timothy Leary, a Stanford student named Ken Kesey, and the kids in the Haight were all experimenting with LSD. Acid was legal, widely available, and usually given away for free. At Kesey's all-night parties, called "acid tests," a buck got you a cup of "electric" Kool-Aid, a preview of psychedelic art, and an earful of the house band, the Grateful Dead. When LSD was made illegal in 1966, the kids responded by staging a Love Pageant Rally, where they dropped acid tabs en masse and rocked out to Janis Joplin and the Dead.

The Peak of the Party

Things crested early in 1967, when between 10,000 and 50,000 people ("depending on whether you were a policeman or a hippie," according to one hippie) gathered at the Polo Field in Golden Gate Park for the "Human Be-In: A Gathering of the Tribes." Poet Allen Ginsberg and Timothy Leary spoke, the Dead and Jefferson Airplane played, and people adorned in beads and feathers waved flags, clanged cymbals, and beat drums. A parachutist dropped onto the field, tossing fistfuls of acid tabs to the crowd. America watched via satellite, gape-mouthed—it was every conservative parent's nightmare.

Burn Out

Later that year, thousands heeded Scott McKenzie's song "San Francisco," which promised, "For those who come to San Francisco, summertime will be a love-in there." The Summer of Love swelled the Haight's population from 7,000 to 75,000; people came to join in and to ogle. But less positive forces soon joined the gentle people, heroin replaced LSD, crime became rampant, and the Haight began a fast slide.

Hippies will tell you the Human Be-In was the pinnacle of their scene, while the Summer of Love was a media creation that turned their movement into a monster. Still, the idea of that fictional summer lingers, and to this day draws pilgrims from all over the world.

edge off a hangover, and Amoeba Music, the best place in town for new and used CDs and vinyl. The Lower Haight is an equally lively stretch with several well-loved pubs and a smattering of niche music shops.

Sights

Buena Vista Park

CITY PARK | The reward for the steep climb to get here is this eucalyptus-filled space with great city views. Dog walkers and homeless folks make good use of the park, and the playground at the top is popular with kids and adults alike. Be sure to scan the stone rain gutters lining many of the walkways for inscribed names and dates; these are the remains of gravestones left unclaimed when the city closed the Laurel Hill cemetery around 1940. A pit stop includes a portable toilet and disposal for used needles and condoms; definitely avoid the park after dark, when these items are left behind. ✉ *Haight St. between Lyon St. and Buena Vista Ave. W, Haight* 🌐 *goldengatepark.com.*

Grateful Dead House

HOUSE | On the outside, this is just one more well-kept Victorian on a street that's full of them, but true fans of the Dead may find some inspiration looking at this legendary structure. The three-story house (closed to the public) is tastefully painted in sedate mauves, tans, and teals—no bright tie-dye colors here. ✉ *710 Ashbury St., just past Waller St., Haight.*

Haight-Ashbury Intersection

NEIGHBORHOOD | On October 6, 1967, hippies took over the intersection of Haight and Ashbury Streets to proclaim the "Death of Hip." If they thought hip was dead then, they'd find absolute confirmation of it today, what with the only tie-dye in sight on the famed corner being a Ben & Jerry's storefront. ✉ *Haight.*

Restaurants

Haight-Ashbury was home base for the country's famed 1960s counterculture, and its café scene still reflects that colorful past.

Over time, the Haight has become two distinct neighborhoods. The Upper Haight is an energetic commercial stretch from Masonic Avenue to Stanyan Street, where head shops and tofu-burger joints still thrive. Meanwhile, the modestly gritty Lower Haight has emerged as a lively bohemian quarter of sorts, with mostly international eateries lining the blocks between Webster and Pierce Streets.

Cha Cha Cha

$$ | CARIBBEAN | A Haight Street institution, boisterous Cha Cha Cha serves island cuisine—a mix of Cajun, Southwestern, and Caribbean influences—tapas style, in a setting with Technicolor tropical plastic decor. The food is hot and spicy: try the fried calamari or chili-spiked cajun shrimp, and wash everything down with a pitcher of Cha Cha Cha's signature sangria. **Known for:** worthy ceviche and paella mixta; ropa vieja (stewed shredded beef and vegetables); lines for dinner can be long;. [$] *Average main: $20* ✉ *1801 Haight St., at Shrader St., Haight* ☎ *415/386–7670* 🌐 *chachachasf.com* 🕒 *Closed Mon.*

Parada 22

$$ | PUERTO RICAN | A small, colorful space sandwiched between larger restaurants on either side, Parada 22 serves up heaping plates of home-style Puerto Rican cuisine—think plantains, seafood, and slow-roasted pork. This still being the Haight, there's also plenty of vegetarian fare on offer. **Known for:** delicious yuca fries; marinated meats and vegetables; lunch specials. [$] *Average main: $17* ✉ *1805 Haight St., near Shrader St., Haight* ☎ *415/750–1111.*

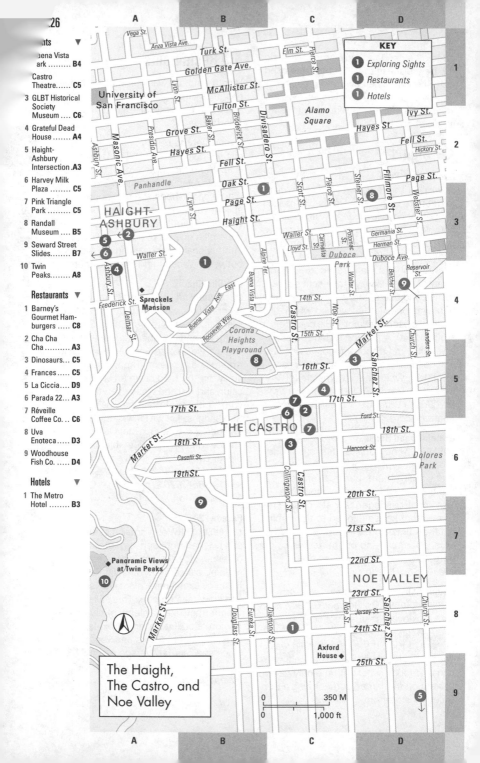

KEY

1 Exploring Sights

1 Restaurants

1 Hotels

The Haight, The Castro, and Noe Valley

Uva Enoteca

$$ | ITALIAN | This casual Italian wine bar hits all the right notes: the mood is convivial, the food is solid, and there's plenty of wine—more than 10 by the glass and a long list of bottles. The menu is straightforward, with assortments of Italian cured meats and cheeses, a selection of salads and vegetable dishes, and a roster of pastas and pizzas. **Known for:** simple but delicious food; good gelato; friendly staff. $ *Average main: $19* ⊠ *568 Haight St., Haight* ☎ *415/829–2024* ⊕ *www.uvaenoteca.com* ☉ *No lunch.*

Hotels

★ The Metro Hotel

$ | HOTEL | These tiny rooms, with simple yet modern decor and equipped with private, if small, bathrooms, are within walking distance to the lively Haight, Hayes Valley, Panhandle, NoPa, and Castro neighborhoods. **Pros:** can't beat the price; out-of-downtown location; friendly staffers. **Cons:** small rooms and bathrooms; street noise; no elevator. $ *Rooms from: $142* ⊠ *319 Divisadero St., Haight* ☎ *415/861–5364* ⊕ *www. metrohotelsf.com* ⇆ *24 rooms* ⦿ *No meals.*

Nightlife

The hippie joints that made the Haight famous may be long gone, but this neighborhood retains a counterculture vibe. Beer connoisseurs should head directly to the Toronado or Magnolia.

BARS

The Alembic

BARS/PUBS | This dark-wood and low-lit space has a certain swagger that is at once charming and classy. It serves full meals but is also a good choice for cocktails and small plates—the polenta fries, Scotch egg, and seasonal salad are all winners. ⊠ *1725 Haight St., at Cole St., Haight* ☎ *415/666–0822* ⊕ *alembicsf. com.*

Magnolia Brewing Company

BREWPUBS/BEER GARDENS | Known for its food as much as its beers, Magnolia is a San Francisco institution, thanks in part to its prime location one block away from the famous Haight-Ashbury intersection. Come for the smoked trout croquettes, falafel salad, and famed burgers, or just grab any one of the over a dozen beers on tap, many made right here in the in-house brewery. There is also a second popular location on 3rd Street in the Dogpatch. ⊠ *1398 Haight St., at Masonic St., Haight* ☎ *415/864–7468* ⊕ *magnolia-brewing.com.*

Noc Noc

BARS/PUBS | A cross between a Tim Burton film and an Oingo Boingo album, this funky, cavelike bar has been making every day Halloween since 1986. Noc Noc's bartenders serve up about 20 or so beers on tap ("No Bud, No Coors, No PBR," proclaims the menu), sake (even unfiltered), and unique twists on traditional drinks, like the Snake Bite, a blend of lager and cider. The house DJ plays acid jazz, industrial, and ambient tunes. When the nearby Toronado gets too busy, head over here. ⊠ *557 Haight St., near Steiner St., Haight* ☎ *415/861–5811* ⊕ *nocnocs.com.*

★ Toronado Pub

BARS/PUBS | You come to one of the city's most popular dive bars for one thing and one thing only: the reasonably priced beers, about four dozen of them on tap. The menu, which runs along the upper wall, will put a kink in your neck as you try to decide. The Toronado opens in the late morning and has a good-size crowd by early afternoon, so show up early to sit at one of the highly coveted tables. Just make sure to bring cash, as they don't accept credit cards. ■TIP➔ **Don't worry about eating beforehand. It's okay to bring in or order in outside food.** ⊠ *547 Haight St., near Fillmore St., Haight* ☎ *415/863–2276* ⊕ *www.toronado.com.*

GAY NIGHTLIFE
Trax Bar
BARS/PUBS | "Laid-back" would be an understatement. Once inside Trax, you won't feel like you're in a gay bar—or in San Francisco. And that's the way the regulars like it. Cheap beer specials draw all types, and though you don't have to don your cruise wear for this place, it's still social. ✉ *1437 Haight St., between Masonic Ave. and Ashbury St., Haight* ☎ *415/864-4213* ⊕ *traxbarsf.com.*

Performing Arts

SPOKEN WORD AND READINGS
Cafe International
READINGS/LECTURES | It's a chill café during the day and a performance venue at night. There's an open-mike session here every Friday night, where spoken-word performances are interspersed with acoustic musical acts. ✉ *508 Haight St., at Fillmore St., Haight* ☎ *415/552-7390* ⊕ *cafeinternationalsf.com.*

Shopping

Largely free of chain stores and big companies, Haight Street is *the* place to find high-quality vintage clothing, funky shoes, folk art from around the world, and used records and CDs.

BOOKS
Booksmith
BOOKS/STATIONERY | This fine bookshop sells current releases, children's titles, and offbeat periodicals. Authors passing through town often make a stop at this neighborhood institution. ✉ *1644 Haight St., between Cole and Clayton Sts., Haight* ☎ *415/863-8688* ⊕ *www.booksmith.com.*

Bound Together Bookstore
BOOKS/STATIONERY | This old-school collective, around since 1976, stocks books on anarchist theory and practice, as well as titles about gender issues, radicalism, and various other left-leaning topics. A portion of the revenue supports anarchist projects and the Prisoners Literature Project. ✉ *1369 Haight St., between Masonic and Central Aves., Haight* ☎ *415/431-8355* ⊕ *boundtogetherbooks.wordpress.com.*

CLOTHING
Buffalo Exchange
CLOTHING | Men and women can find fashionable, high-quality, used clothing at this national chain. Among the items are Levi's, leather jackets, sunglasses, and novelty jewelry. It's also known for its costume offerings and more offbeat merchandise. A sister store is on 23rd Street in the Mission. ✉ *1555 Haight St., between Clayton and Ashbury Sts., Haight* ☎ *415/431-7733* ⊕ *www.buffalo-exchange.com.*

Held Over
CLOTHING | The extensive collection of clothing from the 1920s through the 1980s in this vintage store is organized by decade, saving those looking for flapper dresses from having to wade through lime-green '70s polyester sundresses. Shoes, hats, handbags, and jewelry complete the different looks. There are items for men as well as women. ✉ *1543 Haight St., between Ashbury and Clayton Sts., Haight* ☎ *415/864-0818.*

Relic Vintage
CLOTHING | Offering well-curated clothing, accessories, and jewelry from the roaring '20s to the hippie '60s, this premier vintage shop has a loyal following among retro-conscious gals and pals of San Francisco. Patrons have fun turning back the clock in the well-organized yet funky interior with Hawaiian-theme dressing rooms and a leopard-print chaise lounge. ✉ *1605 Haight St., Haight* ☎ *415/255-7460* ⊕ *www.relicvintagesf.com.*

MUSIC
★ Amoeba Music
MUSIC STORES | With well over a million new and used CDs, DVDs, and records at bargain prices, this warehouselike offshoot of the Berkeley original carries titles you likely can't find on Amazon. No niche is ignored—from electronica and hip-hop to jazz and classical—and the stock changes frequently. ■**TIP➜ Weekly in-store performances attract large crowds.** ⊠ *1855 Haight St., between Stanyan and Shrader Sts., Haight* ☎ *415/831–1200* ⊕ *www.amoeba.com.*

SHOES
John Fluevog
SHOES/LUGGAGE/LEATHER GOODS | The trendy but sturdily made footwear for men and women is among the best in the city. Club girls go gaga over the wacky heels, handing over a pretty penny. They have another small store near Union Square, at 253 Grant Avenue. ⊠ *1697 Haight St., near Cole St., Haight* ☎ *415/436–9784* ⊕ *www.fluevog.com.*

The Castro

The brash and sassy Castro district—the social, political, and cultural center of San Francisco's thriving gay (and, to a much lesser extent, lesbian) community—stands at the western end of Market Street. This neighborhood is one of the city's liveliest and most welcoming, especially on weekends. Streets teem with folks out shopping, pushing political causes, heading to art films, and lingering in bars and cafés. It's also one of the city's most expensive neighborhoods to live in, with an influx of tech money exacerbating an identity crisis that's been simmering for a couple of decades. But you'll still see hard-bodied men in painted-on T-shirts cruising the cutting-edge clothing and novelty stores and pairs of all genders and sexual persuasions holding hands. Brightly painted, intricately restored Victorian houses line the streets here, making the Castro a good place to view striking examples of the architecture San Francisco is famous for.

◉ Sights

★ Castro Theatre
ARTS VENUE | Here's a classic way to join in a beloved Castro tradition: grab some popcorn and catch a flick at this 1,500-seat art-deco theater built in 1922, the grandest of San Francisco's few remaining movie palaces. The neon marquee, which stands at the top of the Castro strip, is the neighborhood's great landmark. The Castro was the fitting host of 2008's red-carpet preview of Gus Van Sant's film *Milk*, starring Sean Penn as openly gay San Francisco supervisor Harvey Milk. The theater's elaborate Spanish baroque interior is fairly well preserved. Before many shows, the theater's pipe organ rises from the orchestra pit and an organist plays pop and movie tunes, usually ending with the Jeanette MacDonald standard "San Francisco" (go ahead, sing along). The crowd can be enthusiastic and vocal, talking back to the screen as loudly as it talks to them. Flicks such as *Who's Afraid of Virginia Woolf?* take on a whole new life, with the assembled beating the actors to the punch and fashioning even snappier comebacks for Elizabeth Taylor. There are often family-friendly sing-alongs to classics like *Mary Poppins*, as well as the occasional niche film festival. ⊠ *429 Castro St., Castro* ☎ *415/621–6120* ⊕ *www.castrotheatre.com* ⊠ *$14.*

GLBT Historical Society Museum
MUSEUM | The small, two-gallery Gay, Lesbian, Bisexual, and Transgender (GLBT) Historical Society Museum, the first of its kind in the United States, presents multimedia exhibits from its vast holdings covering San Francisco's queer history. In the main gallery, you might hear the audiotape Harvey Milk made for the community in the event of his assassination; explore artifacts from "Gayborhoods,"

The Early Days of Gay San Francisco

San Francisco's gay community has been a part of the city since its origins. As a port town and a major hub during the 19th-century gold rush, San Francisco became known for its sexual openness along with all of its other liberalities. But a major catalyst for the rise of the gay community was World War II.

Stationed in San Francisco

During the war, hundreds of thousands of servicemen cycled through "Sodom by the Sea," and for most, San Francisco's permissive atmosphere was an eye-opening experience. The army's "off-limits" lists of forbidden establishments unintentionally (but effectively) pointed the way to the city's gay bars. When soldiers were dishonorably discharged for homosexual activity, many stayed on in the city.

Making the City Home

Scores of these newcomers found homes in what was then called Eureka Valley. When the war ended, the predominantly Irish-Catholic families in that neighborhood began to move out, heading for the burbs. The new arrivals snapped up the Victorians on the main drag, Castro Street.

Beginning of the Movement

The establishment pushed back. In the 1950s, San Francisco's police chief vowed to crack down on "perverts," and the city's gay, lesbian, bisexual, and transgender residents lived in fear of getting caught in police raids. (Arrest meant being outed in the morning paper.) But harassment helped galvanize the community.

The Daughters of Bilitis lesbian organization was founded in the city in 1955; the gay male Mattachine Society, started in Los Angeles in 1950, followed suit with a San Francisco branch.

The Tide Begins to Turn

By the mid-1960s, these clashing interests gave the growing gay population a national profile. The police upped their policy of harassment but overplayed their hand. In 1965 they dramatically raided a New Year's benefit event, and the tide of public opinion began to turn. The police were forced to appoint the first-ever liaison to the gay community. Local gay organizations began to lobby openly. As one gay participant noted, "We didn't go back into the woodwork."

The 1970s and Harvey Milk

The 1970s—thumping disco, raucous street parties, and gay bashing—were a tumultuous time for the gay community. Thousands from across the country flocked to San Francisco's gay milieu. Eureka Valley had more than 60 gay bars, the bathhouse scene in SoMa (where the leather crowd held court) was thriving, and graffiti around town read "Save San Francisco—Kill a Fag." When the Eureka Valley Merchants Association refused to admit gay-owned businesses in 1974, camera-shop owner Harvey Milk founded the Castro Valley Association, and the neighborhood's new moniker was born. Milk was elected to the city's Board of Supervisors in 1977, its first openly gay official (and the inspirational figure for the Oscar-winning film *Milk*).

lost landmarks of the city's gay past; or flip through a memory book with pictures and thoughts on some of the more than 20,000 San Franciscans lost to AIDS. Though perhaps not for everyone (those offended by sex toys and photos of lustily frolicking naked people may, well, be offended), the museum offers an inside look at these communities so integral to the fabric of San Francisco life. ⊠ *4127 18th St., near Castro St., Castro* ☎ *415/621–1107* ⊕ *www.glbthistory.org* ⊠ *$10.*

Harvey Milk Plaza

PLAZA | An 18-foot-long rainbow flag, the symbol of gay pride, flies above this plaza named for the man who electrified the city in 1977 by being elected to its Board of Supervisors as an openly gay candidate. In the early 1970s, Milk's camera store on Castro Street became the center for his campaign to open San Francisco's social and political life to gays and lesbians.

The liberal Milk hadn't served a full year of his term before he and Mayor George Moscone, also a liberal, were shot to death in November 1978 at City Hall. The murderer was a conservative ex-supervisor named Dan White, who had resigned his post and then became enraged when Moscone wouldn't reinstate him. Milk and White had often been at odds on the board. The gay community became infuriated when the "Twinkie defense"—that junk food had led to diminished mental capacity—resulted in only a manslaughter verdict for White. During the so-called White Night Riot of May 21, 1979, gays and their allies stormed City Hall, torching its lobby.

Milk, who had feared assassination, left behind a tape recording in which he urged the community to continue his work. His legacy is the high visibility of gay people throughout city government; a bust of him was unveiled at City Hall in 2008, and the 2008 film *Milk* gives insight into his life. Keep your visiting expectations in check: sandwiched between SoulCycle and a Muni bus stop, this is more of a historical site than an Instagrammable spot. ⊠ *Southwest corner of Castro and Market Sts., Castro.*

Pink Triangle Park

MEMORIAL | On a median near the Castro's huge rainbow flag stands this memorial to the people forced by the Nazis to wear pink triangles. Fifteen triangular granite columns, one for every 1,000 gay, lesbian, bisexual, and transgender people estimated to have been killed during and after the Holocaust, stand in a grassy triangle—a reminder of the gay community's past and ongoing struggle for civil rights. ⊠ *Corner of Market, Castro, and 17th Sts., Castro.*

Randall Museum

MUSEUM | FAMILY | One of the best things about visiting this free nature museum for kids may be its tremendous views of San Francisco. Younger kids who are still excited about petting a rabbit, touching a snakeskin, or seeing a live hawk will enjoy a trip here. The museum sits beneath a hill variously known as Red Rock, Museum Hill, and, correctly, Corona Heights; hike up the steep but short trail for great, unobstructed city views. Just be sure to bring a windbreaker. ⊠ *199 Museum Way, off Roosevelt Way, Castro* ☎ *415/554–9600* ⊕ *randallmuseum.org* ⊠ *Free.*

🍴 Restaurants

The Castro neighborhood, the epicenter of the city's gay community, is chockablock with restaurants and bars. Market Street between Church and Castro Streets is a great stretch for people-watching and café- or bistro-hopping.

Dinosaurs

$ | VIETNAMESE | Most folks think of the Tenderloin or the Richmond for Vietnamese sandwiches, but this small Castro storefront serves up exceptionally fresh *banh mì* and rockin' spring rolls. Service is quick, and a couple of tables take in the scene on Market Street. **Known for:** special banh mi with three kinds of pork; vegetarian options; smoothies and Vietnamese iced coffee. [$] *Average main: $8* ✉ *2275 Market St., near 16th St., Castro* ☎ *415/503–1421* 🌐 *www.eatdinosaurs.com.*

Frances

$$$ | MODERN AMERICAN | Still one of the hottest tickets in town, chef Melissa Perello's simple, sublime restaurant is a consummate date-night destination. Perello's seasonal California-French cooking is its own enduring love affair, with menu standouts including the savory *bavette* steak, grilled Sakura pork chop, and *panisse frites*. For dessert, the lumberjack cake is a perennial favorite. **Known for:** lumberjack cake for dessert; neighborhood gem; tough reservation due to intimate size. [$] *Average main: $34* ✉ *3870 17th St., Castro* ☎ *415/621–3870* 🌐 *www.frances-sf.com* 🕒 *Closed Mon. No lunch.*

Réveille Coffee Co.

$ | CAFÉ | For a perfect, lazy Saturday brunch, head to Réveille Coffee to nosh on a California cuisine–inspired breakfast bowl with coffee in hand and watch colorful Castro characters stroll by. The interior has a fresh, modern look with light birch wood and black-and-white tile at the coffee bar. **Known for:** assorted latte varieties; breakfast sandwiches and toasts; patio seating. [$] *Average main: $12* ✉ *4076 18th St., Castro* ☎ *415/789–6258* 🌐 *www.reveillecoffee.com* 🕒 *No dinner.*

Woodhouse Fish Co.

$$ | SEAFOOD | FAMILY | New Englanders or anyone else hungry for a lobster roll fix need look no further than this super-friendly spot, where the rolls are utterly authentic and accompanied with slaw and fries. Seafood fans will find plenty else to love on the menu, which is stocked with everything from cioppino to crab melts. **Known for:** beer-battered fish-and-chips; popular dollar oysters on Tuesday; nautical-theme decor. [$] *Average main: $19* ✉ *2073 Market St., Castro* ☎ *415/437–2722* 🌐 *www.woodhousefish.com.*

🍸 Nightlife

The gay district is as outrageous as one might expect, if not more so. Leather daddies, costumed club kids, and those who defy "no nudity" laws are among the characters you'll stumble across day or night.

BARS

Blackbird

BARS/PUBS | This neighborhood hangout blends industrial chic and old-world charm with its dark wood paneling and tufted leather seating. The crowd is less casual than others in the Castro, though no one will judge you for wearing Chuck Taylors. Blackbird serves up a good selection of craft beers, along with seasonal cocktails. ✉ *2124 Market St., at Church St., Castro* ☎ *415/872–5310* 🌐 *www.blackbirdbar.com.*

Blush! Wine Bar

BARS/PUBS | A cozy, casual date spot, Blush! serves wines paired with tapas, charcuterie boards, and grilled cheese sandwiches. Sit at the counter for a nice chat with the friendly bartender, and pick a glass or bottle of bubbly or white, rosé, or red wine from its well-curated collection from around the world. This place always buzzes on weekends, so be sure to reserve in advance. ✉ *476 Castro St., Castro* ☎ *415/558–0893* 🌐 *www.blushwinebar.com.*

GAY NIGHTLIFE

The Café

BARS/PUBS | Always comfortable and often packed with a mixed gay, lesbian, and straight crowd, this is a place where you can dance to house or disco music, shoot pool, or meet guys in their twenties at the bar. The outdoor deck—a rarity—makes it a favorite destination for

Gay and Lesbian Nightlife

In the days before the gay liberation movement, bars were more than mere watering holes—they also served as community centers where members of a mostly underground minority could network and socialize. In the 1960s, the bars became hotbeds of political activity; by the 1970s, other social opportunities had become available to gay men and lesbians and the bars' importance as centers of activity decreased.

Old-timers may wax nostalgic about the vibrancy of pre-AIDS, 1970s bar life, but you can still have plenty of fun. A major difference is the one-night-a-week operation of some of the best clubs, which may cater to a different (sometimes straight) clientele on other nights. This type of club tends to come and go, so it's best to pick up one of the two main gay papers to check the latest happenings.

Bay Area Reporter. The weekly *Bay Area Reporter* (⊕ *www.ebar. com*) covers LGBTQ events in its entertainment pages and calendar and has a nightlife section on its website (⊕ *www.ebar.com/events/ nightlife_events*).

San Francisco Bay Times. The biweekly *Bay Times* (⊕ *sfbaytimes. com*) runs features and provides extensive calendar listings of LGBTQ events.

For a place known as a gay mecca, San Francisco has a surprising drought of lesbian bars. The Café is probably the most lesbian-friendly Castro bar, though you'll find queer gals (and many more queer guys) at the Mint, too.

smokers. There's a small weekend cover; expect a line to get in. ⊠ *2369 Market St., near 17th St., Castro* ☎ *415/779–3171* ⊕ *cafesf.com.*

Midnight Sun

BARS/PUBS | One of the Castro's longest-running bars is popular with the polo-shirt-and-khakis crowd and has giant video screens playing the latest music videos, as well as episodes of shows like *Will & Grace* and *Queer Eye.* ⊠ *4067 18th St., at Castro St., Castro* ☎ *415/861–4186* ⊕ *www.midnightsunsf.com.*

Moby Dick

BARS/PUBS | A quintessential neighborhood watering hole outfitted with a pool table and pinball machines has TV screens playing pop videos and music. A giant fish tank sits over the bar, giving shy types a place to rest their gaze while taking a shot of liquid courage. Casually dressed couples and guys with nothing to prove frequent this place, but there's pickup potential, too. Like many smaller dive bars, it's cash only. ⊠ *4049 18th St., at Hartford St., Castro* ☎ *415/294–0731.*

Pilsner Inn

BARS/PUBS | Casual and comfortable—yet still hip and cruise-y—this is the type of neighborhood joint you quickly claim as your own. Kick back with a pint on the fantastic year-round patio (it's covered), and enjoy eye candy of the thirtysomething variety (ranging from conservative yuppie guys to Mission emo boys). The Pilsner is technically a sports bar, which means it has a pool table and TVs tuned to local games. ⊠ *225 Church St., at Market St., Castro* ☎ *415/621–7058* ⊕ *www. pilsnerinn.com.*

● Shopping

The neighborhood that's often called the gay capital of the world is also a major shopping destination for all travelers. It's filled with men's clothing boutiques and home-accessories stores. And if you're looking for something kitschy to shock your Aunt Martha back home, you've come to the right place.

CLOTHING
Rolo
CLOTHING | Selling hard-to-find men's denim, sportswear, shoes, and accessories with a distinct European influence, this store includes clothes designed by Fred Perry, Eton, and Tres Noir. There's another location in SoMa at 1301 Howard Street. ⊠ *2351 Market St., near Castro St., Castro* ☎ *415/431–4545* ⊕ *www.rolo.com.*

COSMETICS AND FRAGRANCES
ZGO Perfumery
PERFUME/COSMETICS | Carrying a unique collection of high-end perfumes, lotions, diffusers, scented candles, and even Mariage Frères teas, this upscale shop is an abiding favorite among discriminating Castro noses. For a respite from the humdrum sex shops dotting Castro Street, duck in here and sample exotic-sounding hand lotions and oils. Shop clerks are knowledgeable and can suggest the perfect gift for yourself or any lucky recipient. ⊠ *600 Castro St., Castro* ☎ *888/789–4753* ⊕ *zgoperfumery.com.*

JEWELRY AND COLLECTIBLES
Brand X Antiques
JEWELRY/ACCESSORIES | The vintage jewelry, mostly from the early part of the 20th century, includes a wide selection of estate pieces and objets d'art. With rings that range in price from $5 to a couple thousand, there's something for everyone. Hours can vary, so it's best to call ahead before visiting. ⊠ *570 Castro St., between 18th and 19th Sts., Castro* ☎ *415/626–8908.*

Noey Valley

There's no better way to stick out like a sore thumb/tourist than to mispronounce Noe Valley as "No" Valley. Look like a local and pronounce it *"Noh-ee"* Valley.

Noe Valley

This upscale but relaxed enclave just south of the Castro is among the city's most desirable places to live, with laid-back cafés, kid-friendly restaurants, and comfortable, old-time shops along Church Street and 24th Street, its main thoroughfares. It was spared the fire that followed the 1906 earthquake and has a large number of prequake homes. You can also see remnants of Noe Valley's agricultural beginnings: Billy Goat Hill (at Castro and 30th Streets), a wild-grass hill often draped in fog and topped by one of the city's best rope-swinging trees, is named for the goats that grazed here right into the 20th century.

● Sights

Seward Street Slides
CITY PARK | FAMILY | A teenager designed these two long, concrete slides back in 1973, saving this mini park from development. Aimed at older kids and adults rather than little ones, the slides offer a fun, steep ride down, so wear sturdy pants. ⊠ *Seward Mini Park, 30 Seward St., Noe Valley* ⊕ *www.sfrecpark.org* ⊙ *Closed Mon.*

★ **Twin Peaks**
VIEWPOINT | Windswept and desolate Twin Peaks—aptly named after a pair of towering peaks overlooking the city—yields sweeping vistas of San Francisco and the neighboring East and North Bay counties. At a hilltop park 922 feet above sea level, you can get a real feel for the city's

A popular photo stop, windswept Twin Peaks has expansive views of the city and nearby counties.

layout, but you'll share it with busloads of other admirers; in summer, arrive before the late-afternoon fog turns the view into pea soup. To drive here, head west from Castro Street up Market Street, which eventually becomes Portola Drive. Turn right (north) on Twin Peaks Boulevard and follow the signs to the top. Muni bus 37–Corbett heads west to Twin Peaks from Market Street. Catch this bus above the Castro Street Muni light-rail station on the island west of Castro at Market Street. ✉ *Noe Valley* ✣ *From Twin Peaks Blvd., follow signs to the top.*

🍴 Restaurants

Barney's Gourmet Hamburgers

$ | **AMERICAN** | **FAMILY** | The Noe Valley location of this family-friendly California burger chain offers a cozy indoor-outdoor dining area, the latter really a patio encased in glass windows for watching foot traffic along 24th Street. The ample menu is loaded with fancier versions of diner classics—think the Gastropub burger, with a fried egg and a pretzel bun, or the Maui Waui, with a teriyaki glaze and grilled pineapple. **Known for:** all kinds of fries; vegetarian options; delicious milkshakes. [$] *Average main: $14* ✉ *4138 24th St., near Castro St., Noe Valley* ☎ *415/282–7770* 🌐 *www.barneyshamburgers.com.*

★ La Ciccia

$$$ | **ITALIAN** | This charming neighborhood trattoria is the only restaurant in the city exclusively serving Sardinian food. The island's classics are all represented—octopus stew in a spicy tomato sauce; spaghetti with *bottariga* (cured roe); and macaroni with sea urchin and cured tuna heart. **Known for:** romantic patio dining; local and restaurant industry favorite, so books up; extensive wine list including Sardinian wines. [$] *Average main: $28* ✉ *291 30th St., at Church St., Noe Valley* ☎ *415/550–8114* 🌐 *www.laciccia.com* ⏲ *Closed Sun. and Mon. No lunch.*

🛍 Shopping

Just south of the Castro on 24th Street, largely residential Noe Valley is an enclave of fancy-food stores, bookshops, women's and children's clothing boutiques, and specialty gift stores.

BOOKS

Omnivore Books on Food

BOOKS/STATIONERY | Love to eat? Love to read? Then this place is paradise. The shelves are bursting with books on growing and cooking food. The store stocks cookbooks on such diverse subjects as the cuisines of colonial Jamaican and Victorian England or 1940s creole cooking. And if you're after a signed first edition by Julia Child or James Beard, you'll find that, too. ⊠ *3885 Cesar Chavez St., at Church St., Noe Valley* ☎ *415/282–4712* ⊕ *omnivorebooks.com.*

CLOTHING

Ambiance

CLOTHING | A well-loved destination for fashion-conscious locals, this is a fun place to find 1920s-inspired dresses, velvet scarves, and dangling silver jewelry. The store has some jaw-dropping sales. There are additional locations on Union and Irving Streets. ⊠ *3979 24th St., between Sanchez and Noe Sts., Noe Valley* ☎ *415/647–5800* ⊕ *ambiancesf.com.*

Small Frys

CLOTHING | **FAMILY** | The colorful cottons carried here are mainly for infants, with some articles for older children. Brands include many Californian and European labels, including Petite Lem, Kanz, and 3 Pommes. There's a sizable section of San Francisco-theme gear and books, and a few shelves of organic and eco-friendly toys as well as whimsical finger puppets round out the selection. ⊠ *3985 24th St., near Noe St., Noe Valley* ☎ *415/648–3954* ⊕ *www.smallfrys.com.*

Two Birds

CLOTHING | A fresh place to find a lacy top or a soft pair of jeans, Two Birds stocks Frēda Salvador, Ulla Johnson, and Smythe. Staying in touch with their city roots, owners Susanna Taylor and Audrey Yang carry sleek jewelry, handbags, and dresses by local designers, too. ⊠ *1309 Castro St., between Jersey and 24th Sts., Noe Valley* ☎ *415/285–1840* ⊕ *www.2birds1store.com.*

FURNITURE, HOUSEWARES, AND GIFTS

Wink SF

GIFTS/SOUVENIRS | Cards, toasters, aprons, books, candles, and a wide selection of SF-theme items line the shelves. You'll also find fridge magnets, wisdom-spouting bags, and bakery-shape pencil erasers. And if you've misplaced your water bottle, the shop stocks a rainbow of colors. ⊠ *4107 24th St., at Castro St., Noe Valley* ☎ *415/401–8881* ⊕ *www.winksf.com.*

HANDICRAFTS AND FOLK ART

Xela Imports

CRAFTS | Africa, Southeast Asia, Europe, and Central America are the sources for the handicrafts sold at Xela (pronounced *shay*-la). They include jewelry, masks, religious icons, and decorative wall hangings. ⊠ *3925 24th St., between Sanchez and Noe Sts., Noe Valley* ☎ *415/695–1323* ⊕ *xelaimports.com.*

Chapter 12

MISSION DISTRICT, DOGPATCH, BERNAL HEIGHTS, AND POTRERO HILL

WITH MISSION BAY

Updated by
Trevor Felch

 Sights
★★☆☆☆

 Restaurants
★★★★★

 Hotels
★☆☆☆☆

 Shopping
★★★☆☆

 Nightlife
★★★★★

NEIGHBORHOOD SNAPSHOT

TOP EXPERIENCES

■ **Vivid murals:** Check out dozens of energetic, colorful public artworks in alleyways and on building exteriors.

■ **Dolores Park:** Join Mission locals and their dogs on this hilly expanse of green that has a glorious view of downtown and, if you're lucky, the Bay Bridge. On sunny days, the whole neighborhood comes out to play.

■ **Phenomenal global food:** Keen appetites and thin wallets will meet their match here. Just try to decide between deliciously fresh burritos, garlicky falafel, thin-crust pizza, savory samosas, and more.

■ **Barhopping:** Embrace your inner (or not-so-inner) hipster. Grab a cocktail at Trick Dog, whose mixologists serve some of the Mission's finest drinks, then peruse the small and mighty menu at the retro-chic Beehive or stop by Elixir, where San Francisco history meets craft cocktails.

■ **One-of-a-kind shopping:** From trendy clothing to pirate supplies (it's true), the Mission is one of the city's prime shopping neighborhoods, especially on perennially hip Valencia Street.

PLANNING YOUR TIME

A walk that includes Mission Dolores and the neighborhood's murals takes about two hours. If you plan to go on a mural tour with the Precita Eyes organization, or if you're a window-shopper, add at least another hour. The Mission is a neighborhood that sleeps in. In the afternoon and evening, the main drags—Mission, Valencia, and 24th Streets—really come to life.

From Sunday through Tuesday, it's relatively quiet here, especially in the evening—a great time to get a café table with no wait. Dogpatch is liveliest during the week, midday to evening, when businesses are hopping. On weekends, this neighborhood relaxes at home.

GETTING HERE

■ The Mission is welcomingly flat, and BART's two Mission District stations drop you in the heart of the action. Get off at 16th Street for Mission Dolores and the shopping, nightlife, and restaurants of the Valencia Corridor or 24th Street to see the neighborhood murals and the increasingly trendy Calle 24 district. Parking is difficult, so take a taxi or rideshare. Dogpatch is well served by the T–Third Muni line, and the 22nd Street Caltrain station is nearby. Bernal Heights and Potrero Hill have slightly easier parking situations (though prepare for steep street-parking angles) and are connected to the Mission by Muni bus lines.

QUICK BITES

■ **La Taqueria.** The most well-known—and quite possibly the best—of the burrito choices around town forgoes rice in the filling (almost all burritos in the Mission include rice) to focus on tender meats. ⊠ *2889 Mission St., Mission*

■ **La Torta Gorda.** Enormous tortas (Mexican sandwiches with meat, avocado, queso fresco, and refried beans on a soft-interior/crunchy-exterior roll) are the specialty of this Mission legend. ⊠ *2833 24th St., Mission* ⊕ *latortagorda. com.*

The Mission has a number of distinct personalities: it's the Latino neighborhood, where working-class folks raise their families and where gangs occasionally clash; it's the hipster hood, where tattooed and pierced twenty- and thirtysomethings hold court in the coolest cafés and bars in town; it's a culinary epicenter, with the strongest concentration of destination restaurants and affordable global cuisines; it's the face of gentrification, where high-tech money prices out longtime commercial and residential renters; and it's the artists' quarter, where murals adorn literally blocks of walls long after their creators have moved to cheaper digs.

It's also the city's equivalent of the Sunshine State—this neighborhood's always the last to succumb to fog. The Mission has ceded the title of neighborhood with the most buzz to Dogpatch, another flat swath on the far side of Potrero Hill, right along the San Francisco Bay coastline. Here artists and industry share space, restaurants draw diners from far-flung neighborhoods, and the city's largest stock of houses that survived the 1906 quake surround a thriving commercial strip with creative flair.

Mission District

Packed with destination restaurants, hole-in-the-wall eateries representing dozens of cuisines, and hip watering holes—plus taquerias, *pupuserías* (places selling thick, filled tortillas), and produce markets—one of the city's hottest hoods strikes an increasingly precarious balance between cutting-edge hot spot and working-class enclave. With longtime businesses being forced out by astronomical rents and city agencies coming together

with community groups to create an action plan to reverse gentrification in the neighborhood, the Mission is in flux once again, a familiar state for almost 100 years.

The eight blocks of Valencia Street between 16th and 24th Streets—what's become known as the Valencia Corridor—typify the Mission District's diversity. Businesses on the block between 16th and 17th Streets, for instance, include a bustling Peruvian restaurant, funky home-decor stores, a New York–style by-the-slice pizzeria, a sushi bar, an upscale matcha-focused café, and bargain and pricey thrift shops. As prices rise, this strip has lost some of its edge as even international publications proclaim its hipness. At the same time, nearby Mission Street is slowly morphing from a row of check-cashing parlors, dollar stores, and residential hotels into overflow for the Valencia Corridor's restaurant explosion. Meanwhile, 24th Street has become the Calle 24 Latino Cultural District in an attempt to protect the mostly Latino-owned businesses that have served this thriving neighborhood for decades.

Italian and Irish in the early 20th century, the Mission became heavily Latino in the late 1960s, when immigrants from Mexico and Central America began arriving. Since the 1970s, groups of muralists have transformed walls and storefronts into canvases, creating art accessible to everyone. Following the example set by the Mexican artist and muralist Diego Rivera, many of the Latino artists address political and social justice issues in their murals. More recently, artists of varied backgrounds, some of whom simply like to paint on a large scale, have expanded the conversation.

The conversations you'll hear on the street these days might unfold in Chinese, Vietnamese, Arabic, and other tongues of the non-Latino immigrants who began settling in the Mission in the 1980s and 1990s along with a young bohemian crowd enticed by cheap rents and the burgeoning arts-and-nightlife scene. These newer arrivals made a diverse and lively neighborhood even more so, setting the stage for the Mission's current hipster cachet. With the neighborhood flourishing, rents have gone through the roof, but the Mission remains scruffy in patches, so as you plan your explorations, take into account your comfort zone.

■ TIP→ **Be prepared for homelessness and drug use around the BART stations, prostitution along Mission Street, and raucous barhoppers along the Valencia Corridor.**

Sights

Balmy Alley murals

PUBLIC ART | Mission District artists have transformed the walls of their neighborhood with paintings, and Balmy Alley is one of the best-executed examples. Many murals adorn the one-block alley, with newer ones continually filling in the blank spaces. In 1971, artists began teaming with local children to create a space to promote peace in Central America, community spirit, and (later) AIDS awareness; since then dozens of muralists have added their vibrant works. The alley's longtime popularity has grown exponentially thanks to its Instagram appeal. ⚠ **Be alert here: the 25th Street end of the alley adjoins a somewhat dangerous area.**

Once you're done at Balmy Alley, head a couple blocks west on 24th Street to another prominent alley of murals on Cypress Street (also between 24th and 25th Streets). ✉ *24th St. between and parallel to Harrison and Treat Sts., alley runs south to 25th St., Mission District* ⊕ *balmyalley.org.*

Mission, Dogpatch, and Portrero Hill

16th St.

280

Jackson Park

18th St.

15

De Haro St.

Kansas St.

Arkansas St.

Missouri St.

Texas St.

Mississippi St.

Indiana St.

20th St.

POTRERO HILL

101

22nd St.

22nd St.

DOGPATCH

10

Potrero Hill Playground

Southern Embarcadero Fwy.

James Lick Fwy.

23rd St.

Dakota St.

25th St.

Cesar Chavez St.

Jerrold Ave.

0   1/2 mile

0   500 meters

KEY

bart BART station

1 Exploring Sights

1 Restaurants

1 Quick Bites

1 Hotels

Lively Dolores Park in the Mission is popular for its playground, special events, and city views.

Clarion Alley murals

PUBLIC ART | Inspired by the work in Balmy Alley, a new generation of muralists began creating a fresh alley-cum-gallery here in 1992, offering a quick but dense glimpse at the Mission's contemporary art scene. The works by the loosely connected artists of the Clarion Alley Mural Project (CAMP) represent a broad range of styles and imagery, such as an exuberant, flowery exhortation to Tax the Rich, a lesbian celebration including donkey heads, and poignant murals honoring the legacies of the late musical artist Prince and George Floyd. ⊠ *Between Valencia and Mission Sts. and 17th and 18th Sts., Mission District* ⊕ *www.clarionalleymuralproject.org.*

★ Dolores Park

CITY PARK | A two-square-block microcosm of life in the district, Mission Dolores Park is one of San Francisco's liveliest green spaces: dog lovers and their pampered pups congregate, kids play at the extravagant playground, and hipsters hold court, drinking beer and rosé cans on sunny days. (Fair warning: if it's over 70°, the place can get packed like traffic at rush hour for picnic-blanket space.) During the summer, Dolores Park hosts movie nights, performances by the San Francisco Mime Troupe, and any number of pop-up events and impromptu parties. Spend a warm day here—maybe sitting at the top of the park with a view of the city and the Bay Bridge —surrounded by locals and that laid-back, still-abundant San Francisco energy, and you may well find yourself plotting your move to the city. The best views are in the southeast corner, near the historic **golden fire hydrant** that saved the neighborhood after the 1906 earthquake. ⊠ *Between 18th and 20th Sts. and Dolores and Church Sts., Mission District* ⊕ *sfrecpark.org.*

Food Chain mural

PUBLIC ART | Brian Barneclo's gigantic *Food Chain* is a retro, 1950s-style celebration of the city's many neighborhoods—and the food chain—complete with an ant birthday party and worms finishing off a human skull (but in a cute way). Fans of the well-known local muralist can see more of his work in the Chase Center, along the Caltrain tracks near the intersection of 7th and Townsend Streets (the largest mural in the city), and in city restaurants, such as St. Francis Fountain and Nopa, as well as at the Facebook headquarters in Menlo Park. ⊠ *Foods Co, 1800 Folsom St., Shotwell St. side of store between 14th and 15th Sts., Mission District* ⊕ *brianbarneclo.com.*

Galería de la Raza

MUSEUM | San Francisco's premier showcase for contemporary Latino art, the gallery exhibits the works of mostly local artists. Events include readings and spoken word by local writers and poets, screenings of Latin American and Spanish films, and theater works by local minority theater troupes. The gallery may close between exhibits, so call ahead. Just across the street, murals and mosaics festoon the 24th Street/York Street Mini Park, a tiny urban playground. A mosaic-covered Quetzalcoatl serpent plunges into the ground and rises, creating hills for little ones to clamber over. ⊠ *1470 Valencia St., Mission District* ☎ *415/826–8009* ⊕ *www.galeriadelaraza. org.*

Golden fire hydrant

LOCAL INTEREST | When all the other fire hydrants went dry during the fire that followed the 1906 earthquake, this one kept pumping. Noe Valley and the Mission District were thus spared the devastation wrought elsewhere in the city, which explains the large number of prequake homes here. Every year on April 18th (the anniversary of the quake), folks gather here to share stories about the disaster, and the famous hydrant gets a fresh coat of gold paint. ⊠ *Church and 20th Sts., southeastern corner of intersection, across from Dolores Park, Mission.*

Vermont Street

With its series of switchbacks, this Potrero Hill roadway is a kind of low-key Lombard Street, but minus the throngs (and the spectacular gardens and views). It's on the east side of the 101 from the Mission. To check it out, head down 24th Street to the end, go left on Vermont, right on 23rd Street past the freeway, left on Rhode Island Street, left on 20th Street, and finally head left down the curvy stretch of Vermont.

Maestrapeace mural

PUBLIC ART | The towering mural that seems to enclose the Women's Building, a community space supporting women and community organizations, celebrates women around the world who work for peace. Created by seven main artists and almost 100 helpers in 1994, this five-story-tall artwork is one of the city's don't-miss murals. ⊠ *Women's Bldg., 3543 18th St. , between Valencia and Guerrero Sts., Mission District* ☎ *415/431–1180* ⊕ *womensbuilding.org.*

Mission Dolores

RELIGIOUS SITE | Two churches stand side by side here, a newer multidomed basilica and the small adobe **Mission San Francisco de Asís,** the latter being the city's oldest standing structure along with the Presidio Officers' Club. Completed in 1791, it's the sixth of the 21 California missions founded by Franciscan friars in the 18th and early 19th centuries. Its ceiling depicts original Ohlone Indian basket designs, executed in vegetable dyes. The tiny chapel includes frescoes and a hand-painted wooden altar.

There's a hidden treasure here, too, a mural forgotten and rediscovered: an original 20-by-22-foot mural with images including a dagger-pierced Sacred Heart

Mission Festivals

Cinco de Mayo is an important event in the Mission: music, dance, and parades commemorate the victory, on May 5, 1862, of Mexicans over French troops who had invaded their country. On Memorial Day weekend the revelers come out in earnest, when Carnaval transforms the neighborhood into a northern Rio de Janeiro for two days. Festivities close down several blocks (usually of Harrison Street), where musicians and dancers perform and crafts and food booths are set up. The Grand Carnaval Parade, along 24th, Mission, and 17th Streets, caps the celebration. Each fall, a festival of the altars for Día de los Muertos (Day of the Dead) is held at the southeastern edge of the Mission at Potrero del Sol Park, followed by a procession around the Mission starting from Bryant and 22nd Streets.

of Jesus, painted with natural dyes by Native Americans in 1791, was found in 2004 behind the altar. Interesting fact: Mission San Francisco de Asís was founded on June 29, 1776, five days before the Declaration of Independence was signed.

The small museum in the mission complex covers its founding and history, and the pretty cemetery—which appears in Alfred Hitchcock's film *Vertigo*—contains the graves of mid-19th-century European immigrants. The remains of an estimated 5,000 Native Americans who died at the mission lie in unmarked graves. ✉ *3321 16th St., at Dolores St., Mission District* ☎ *415/621–8203* 🌐 *www.missiondolores.org* 🎟 *Suggested donation $7.*

Precita Eyes Mural Arts and Visitors Center
LOCAL INTEREST | The muralists of this nonprofit arts organization design and create murals and lead guided walks. Tours start with a 45-minute slide presentation before participants head outside to view murals on Balmy Alley and 24th Street. You can pick up a map of 24th Street's murals at the center and buy art supplies, T-shirts, postcards, and other mural-related items. ✉ *2981 24th St., Mission District* ☎ *415/285–2287* 🌐 *www.precitaeyes.org* 🎟 *Center free, tours $20.*

🍴 Restaurants

You'll never go hungry here, in San Francisco's most jam-packed restaurant neighborhood. From bargain taquerias to hip *izakayas* (a kind of Japanese bar serving small plates and snacks with the drinks), city dwellers know this sector as the go-to area for a great meal. The Valencia Street corridor has been particularly hot, opening new restaurants at a breakneck pace, with many locals declaring it the best food neighborhood in the city.

★ AL's Place
$$ | **MODERN AMERICAN** | AL is chef Aaron London, and his place is a sunny, whitewashed corner spot that serves Michelin-starred, vegetable-forward cooking. London's menu changes frequently, but some dishes, like yellow eye bean stew and grits with goat's milk curd and seasonal produce, stick around, and the wine list is packed with some of the world's finest, largely under-the-radar small producers. **Known for:** fries with a cult following; inventive, vegetable-heavy menu; wonderful sherry and vermouth cocktails. [$] *Average main: $22* ✉ *1499 Valencia St., Mission* ☎ *415/416–6136* 🌐 *www.alsplacesf.com* 🕓 *Closed Mon. and Tues. No lunch.*

San Francisco on Film

With its spectacular cityscape, atmospheric fog, and a camera-ready iconic bridge, it's little wonder that San Francisco has been the setting for hundreds of films. Here are a few of the city's favorite cinematic sites:

■ *Zodiac,* a 2007 drama about an infamous Bay Area serial killer, filmed scenes at the real-life locations where victims were gunned down. (It also recreated the *San Francisco Chronicle* offices, but down south in L.A.)

■ City Hall shows up in the Clint Eastwood cop thrillers *Dirty Harry* and *Magnum Force* and is set aflame in the James Bond flick *A View to a Kill.* Its interior became a nightclub for Robin Williams's *Bicentennial Man* and a courthouse in *Tucker: The Man and His Dream.*

■ Streets in Russian Hill, Potrero Hill, and North Beach were used for the supreme car-chase sequence in *Bullitt.* The namesake detective, played by Steve McQueen, lived in Nob Hill at 1153–57 Taylor Street. And the "King of Cool" did much of his own stunt driving, thank you very much.

■ Brocklebank Apartments, at Mason and Sacramento Streets in Nob Hill, appears in several films, most notably as the posh residence of Kim Novak in Alfred Hitchcock's *Vertigo.* Other key *Vertigo* locations include the cemetery of Mission Dolores and the waterfront at Fort Point.

■ The great Bogie-and-Bacall noir film *Dark Passage* revolves around the art-deco apartment building at 1360 Montgomery Street and the nearby Filbert Steps.

■ Dashiell Hammett's *Thin Man* characters, Nick and Nora Charles, do much of their sleuthing in the city, especially in films like *After the Thin Man,* in which the base of Coit Tower stands in as the entrance to the Charleses' home.

■ North Beach's Tosca Cafe, at 242 Columbus Avenue, is the bar where Michael Douglas unwinds in *Basic Instinct.*

■ The Hilton Hotel at 333 O'Farrell Street became the "Hotel Bristol," the scene of much of the mayhem caused by Barbra Streisand in *What's Up, Doc?*

■ At 2640 Steiner Street in Pacific Heights is the elegant home that Robin Williams infiltrates while disguised as a nanny in *Mrs. Doubtfire.*

■ The Castro of the 1970s comes alive in *Milk,* Gus Van Sant's film starring Sean Penn as slain San Francisco supervisor Harvey Milk.

■ Woody Allen's 2013 drama-comedy *Blue Jasmine* takes place across the city and Marin County and includes a noteworthy scene in SoMa's South Park, a neighborhood favorite near Oracle Park for kids and workers on lunch break.

■ And, of course, there are plenty of movies about the notorious federal prison on Alcatraz Island, including Burt Lancaster's redemption drama *Birdman of Alcatraz,* Clint Eastwood's suspenseful *Escape from Alcatraz,* the goofy *So I Married an Axe Murderer,* and the Sean Connery and Nicolas Cage action flick *The Rock.*

Beretta

$$ | **ITALIAN** | A young crowd flocks to this perennially popular neighborhood favorite with a simple formula: excellent cocktails, affordable Italian food, and that San Francisco rarity, high-quality late-night dining. The long room with a tin ceiling and bare-wood tables is casual and smart but loud, the pizzas respect their Italian heritage (thin crusts, traditional and contemporary toppings), and the antipasti are an appealing mix of vegetables (cauliflower with capers), fish (a light fritto misto), and artisanal *salumi*. **Known for:** carbonara pizza; long waits for a table; frequented by restaurant-industry folks. [$] *Average main: $18* ✉ *1199 Valencia St., Mission District* ☎ *415/695–1199* 🌐 *www.berettasf.com* 🕒 *No lunch weekdays.*

CK Wine Bar

$$ | **MODERN AMERICAN** | California cuisine, via snacks and substantial mains that display all its simple freshness, is on display in this offshoot of flour + water, where you might taste "chicken Caesar" deviled eggs or a half chicken *al mattone* (grilled under a brick) with *romesco* sauce. A planked-and-concrete, tea-light-strung courtyard with a retractable awning shares space with flour + water pasta shop (a daytime deli, café, and larder) and Trick Dog (an energetic cocktail bar). **Known for:** mussels escabeche; excellent wine list; sunny sidewalk seating. [$] *Average main: $20* ✉ *3000 20th St., Mission District* ☎ *415/826–7004* 🌐 *www.centralkitchensf.com* 🕒 *No lunch.*

★ Delfina

$$$ | **ITALIAN** | Crowds are a constant fixture at Craig and Annie Stoll's cultishly adored northern Italian spot, where aluminum-topped tables are squeezed into a casual chic interior with hardwood floors, a room-length mirror, and a tile bar that seems to radiate happiness. Deceptively simple, exquisitely flavored dishes include excellent pastas and consistently great roast chicken; the *panna cotta* is best in class. **Known for:** signature spaghetti with plum tomatoes; hard to get reservations; Monterey Bay calamari with white bean salad. [$] *Average main: $29* ✉ *3621 18th St., Mission District* ☎ *415/552–4055* 🌐 *www.delfinasf.com* 🕒 *No lunch.*

★ flour + water

$$ | **MODERN ITALIAN** | This handsome and boisterous hot spot with slate-gray walls, sturdy wooden tables, and a tiny bar is synonymous with pasta and also serves top-notch, blistery thin-crust Neapolitan pizzas, but the grand experience here is the seven-course pasta-tasting menu (extra charge for wine pairings). Pastas on both menus change constantly with the seasons, but the one standby is a meatless Taleggio *scarpinocc* with aged balsamic drizzled over the bow tie–shaped pasta. **Known for:** difficult-to-get reservations; rarely seen pasta shapes; Italian wines from small producers. [$] *Average main: $25* ✉ *2401 Harrison St., Mission District* ☎ *415/826–7000* 🌐 *www.flourandwater.com* 🕒 *No lunch.*

Foreign Cinema

$$$ | **MODERN AMERICAN** | Classic films are projected on the wall of a large inner courtyard in this hip, loftlike space while you're served stellar seasonal California cooking, and weekend brunch brings throngs fighting for a spot on the patio for some of the city's best egg dishes and Bloody Marys. The main event here is the food (the films are like background decor), and the majestic atmosphere enhances plates of perfectly shucked oysters on the half shell and sesame fried chicken. **Known for:** warm brandade appetizer; excellent cocktails at the restaurant and adjacent Laszlo Bar; pop tarts and croque madame at brunch. [$] *Average main: $34* ✉ *2534 Mission St., Mission District* ☎ *415/648–7600* 🌐 *www.foreigncinema.com* 🕒 *No lunch weekdays.*

★ Lazy Bear

$$$$ | **MODERN AMERICAN** | There's no end to the buzz around chef David Barzelay's 12-plus-course prix-fixe seasonal and imagination-driven dinners, which might

include grilled lamb covered in spring herbs and flowers or delicate San Francisco coast king salmon with English peas and cured roe. An ode to the Western lodge, the high-ceilinged, spacious dining room includes a fireplace, charred wood walls, and wooden rafters. **Known for:** brown bread rolls with butter cultured in-house; sensational friendly yet formal service; dinner-party vibe. $ *Average main: $245 ⊠ 3416 19th St., Mission District ☎ 415/874–9921 ⊕ www.lazybearsf. com ⊘ Closed Mon. and Tues.*

Limón Rotisserie

$$ | PERUVIAN | FAMILY | Cooks in Peru and Ecuador have long argued over which country invented ceviche, but most diners at Limón Rotisserie would probably line up with the Peruvians after eating the myriad delicious versions on offer here. Almost everything is served family-style at this restaurant with four Bay Area locations, including two in the Mission; but as the name suggests, the flavorful marinated roasted chicken (*pollo a la brasa*) gets an especially big nod (a whole chicken is a popular to-go item). **Known for:** tasty empanadas; lomo saltado (a classic Peruvian beef and fries stir-fry); creative, pisco-driven cocktails. $ *Average main: $19 ⊠ 524 Valencia St., Mission District ☎ 415/252–0918 ⊕ www.limonrotisserie.com.*

Lolinda

$$$ | ARGENTINE | Argentine fare, a convivial atmosphere, and talented bartenders help explain the long-running appeal of this contemporary steak house in a sceney two-level former nightclub space with two bars and a rooftop neighbor (El Techo) that offers captivating views—it's no surprise that the crowd sometimes swings young and noisy. Don't miss the chicken empanadas, with flaky pastry and a slight sweetness. **Known for:** wood-fire-grilled meats; lines on Mission Street for El Techo; great new and classic cocktails. $ *Average main: $27 ⊠ 2518 Mission St., Mission District*

☎ *415/550–6970 ⊕ www.lolindasf.com ⊘ Closed Mon. and Tues. No lunch.*

Mission Chinese Food

$$ | CHINESE | While the setting is a bit confusing (the awning still bears the name of its predecessor) and notably informal, the food draws throngs for its bold, cheerfully inauthentic riffs on Chinese cuisine made with quality meats and ingredients, including the fine and super-fiery kung pao pastrami, salt cod fried rice with mackerel confit, and sour chili chicken. Some of the food spikes hot (Chongqing chicken wings), while milder dishes (Westlake rice porridge) are homey and satisfying. **Known for:** thrice-cooked bacon and rice cakes; mapo tofu (tofu in a spicy sauce); party vibe. $ *Average main: $20 ⊠ 2234 Mission St., Mission District ☎ 415/863–2800 ⊕ www.missionchinesefood.com.*

The Morris

$$$ | MODERN AMERICAN | The eastern Mission's seasonal Californian charmer is a delightful stop for a concise menu of "can't ever leave the menu" dishes, plus a few always-changing farmers' market–driven creations. Owner Paul Einbund is one of the city's top sommeliers, so, on cue, the wine list is particularly impressive, and so is the industrial yet cheery, compact dining room, anchored by the small open kitchen, a tidy bar, and a prominent wine storage area. **Known for:** signature smoked duck dish; Chartreuse and Madeira collection; buckwheat doughnuts. $ *Average main: $36 ⊠ 2501 Mariposa St., at Hampshire St., Mission District ☎ 415/612–8480 ⊕ themorris-sf. com ⊘ Closed Mon. No lunch.*

Orenchi Beyond

$ | RAMEN | The namesake ramen bowl at this perennial "best ramen in San Francisco" contender boasts a consistently powerful *tonkotsu* broth base that cooks for 18 hours and chewy noodles that attract the harshest of critics. Its space, at the northern edge of the Mission, is airy and geometric, service is quick and friendly, and the wait is remedied (slightly) by the small front bar that sells sakes and beers. **Known for:** beautifully composed ramen bowls with various broths; excellent vegan ramen; hip vibe. $ *Average main: $15* ⊠ *174 Valencia St., at Duboce Ave., Mission District* ☎ *415/431–3971* ⊕ *www.orenchi-beyond.com.*

Pizzeria Delfina

$$ | **PIZZA** | **FAMILY** | As one of the contenders for the city's best pizza, this offshoot of Delfina is known for perfectly blistered thin crusts and near-constant crowds, as well as super-fresh salads and antipasti. The European-style pizzeria, sandwiched between Tartine Bakery and Delfina, has a few sidewalk tables that can be sublime on a nice day, or you can order takeout and carry the pizza to Dolores Park. **Known for:** seasonally changing pizzas; clam pie; strong wine list that goes way beyond the "pizza wine" norm. $ *Average main: $21* ⊠ *3611 18th St., Mission District* ☎ *415/437–6800* ⊕ *www.pizzeriadelfina.com* ⊘ *No lunch Tues.*

SanJalisco

$ | **MEXICAN** | **FAMILY** | This colorful old-time, sun-filled, family-run restaurant has been a neighborhood favorite since 1988, and not only because it serves breakfast all day—though the hearty *chilaquiles* always hits the spot. On weekends, longtime regulars opt for *birria,* a spicy barbecued goat stew, or *menudo,* a tongue-searing soup made from beef tripe, complemented by beer and sangria. **Known for:** huevos "con amor"; soups change based on day of the week; friendly service. $ *Average main: $13* ⊠ *901 S. Van Ness Ave., Mission District* ☎ *415/648–8383* ⊕ *www. sanjaliscorestaurant.com.*

St. Francis Fountain

$ | **DINER** | **FAMILY** | For an old-fashioned root beer float with a timeless soda fountain atmosphere, stop into the St. Francis Fountain and candy store, a haven for hipsters and kids. Breakfast, burgers, sandwiches, and salads are also on the menu at this San Francisco institution,

open since 1918. **Known for:** nostalgic spot of a kind that's hard to find in San Francisco; worthy milkshakes; aptly named nebulous potato thing. $ *Average main: $11* ⊠ *2801 24th St., at York St., Mission District* ☎ *415/826–4200* ⊕ *www.stfrancisfountainsf.com* ⊘ *No dinner.*

Tartine Manufactory

$$$ | **MODERN AMERICAN** | **FAMILY** | At this sunny, cathedral-like space in the Heath Ceramics building, you'll find Chad Robertson's celebrated breads and Liz Prueitt's pastries but also an all-day dining experience that is a full-service operation after the morning. Excellent cocktails and wine selections make it a draw beyond the carbs and seasonal-produce salads. **Known for:** any tartine (as the name suggests!) or pizza; soft-serve ice cream; coffee roasted in-house. $ *Average main: $28* ⊠ *595 Alabama St., Mission District* ☎ *415/757–0007* ⊕ *tartinebakery.com/ san-francisco/manufactory.*

★ True Laurel

$$ | **MODERN AMERICAN** | Hardly just a plan B for those who didn't score a table at its sibling, Lazy Bear, this excellent cocktail bar and creative small-plates restaurant by the same people offers intriguing combinations and endless conversation starters in a cool modern setting. Menu standouts include the Nashville hot fried chicken sandwich and fried hen-of-the-woods mushrooms. **Known for:** patty melt; inventive cocktails using seasonal produce ; excellent weekend brunch. $ *Average main: $19* ⊠ *753 Alabama St., Mission District* ☎ *415/341–0020* ⊕ *www.truelaurelsf.com* ⊘ *No lunch weekdays.*

Wise Sons Jewish Delicatessen

$ | **DELI** | **FAMILY** | The order of the day (and night) at this simple deli counter and restaurant decorated with old family portraits is Jewish comfort food made with new-wave sensibilities: the pastrami and corned beef are hormone- and antibiotic-free. Breakfast, with bagel sandwiches and challah French toast, is served all day, and no one can stop gushing about

Coffee Breaks in San Francisco

Andytown Coffee Roasters. A neighborhood cornerstone like surfing and frigid sunsets, this charming Outer Sunset roastery and café serves house-baked Irish soda bread, scones, and, of course, coffee drinks. A particular favorite is the Snowy Plover: espresso, simple syrup, sparkling water, and house-made whipped cream. ⊠ *3655 Lawton St.* ☎ *415/753–9775.*

Blue Bottle Coffee. Hidden away on a side street by Patricia's Green in Hayes Valley is this modest kiosk where the organic beans are ground for each cup and the espresso is automatically *ristretto*—a short shot. While Blue Bottle is now a global juggernaut (the blue, boutique equivalent of the green mermaid chain, as locals like to say), Linden Street was the first brick-and-mortar shop, and it's still a San Francisco coffee lover's favorite. ⊠ *315 Linden St., near Gough St.* ☎ *510/653–3394.*

Cafe Réveille. San Francisco has plenty of great food options and coffee destinations, but rarely do the two merge together as well as they do at this Mission Bay roastery and its three other city cafés, which excel equally at sandwiches on fresh focaccia, virtuous lunch bowls, and flat whites. ⊠ *610 Long Bridge St.* ☎ *415/580–7260.*

Farley's. While you're sipping your inky strong cup at friendly Farley's, a neighborhood institution on sunny Potrero Hill, you can play chess, check out the eclectic magazine selection, or catch up on the local gossip. ⊠ *1315 18th St., at Texas St.* ☎ *415/648–1545.*

Four Barrel Coffee. Coffee aficionados should head down Valencia Street to Four Barrel Coffee for excellent house-roasted coffee in a fun and funky space, packed with Mission hipsters, cyclists, and artists (be sure to look at the selection of Mission counterpart Dynamo doughnuts as well). ⊠ *375 Valencia St., between 14th and 15th Sts.* ☎ *415/896–4289.*

Red's Java House. Anyone looking for a real cup of joe (without any sense of pretension) in a bare-bones pine shack should join the savvy dock workers, carpenters, and young suits at decades-old Red's Java House, where the coffee typically follows a cheeseburger and a Bud and the gorgeous view of the East Bay is priceless. ⊠ *Pier 30, between Embarcadero and Bryant St.* ☎ *415/777–5626.*

Ritual Coffee Roasters. In the Mission District, the owners of the popular Ritual Coffee Roasters have plunked their roaster in the back of the café, so you know where your beans—usually single-origin, rather than a blend—were roasted when you order your espresso or drip coffee. ⊠ *1026 Valencia St., between 21st and 22nd Sts.* ☎ *415/641–1011.*

Sightglass Coffee. The stunning interior design of Sightglass's three cafés demands several photographs on each visit, but quickly all eyes settle on the pitch-perfect shots of espresso and cups of robust coffee from beans roasted at their airy SoMa café and roastery. ⊠ *270 7th St.* ☎ *415/861–1313.*

the delicately smoked pastrami heaped between two slabs of house-baked rye. **Known for:** Reuben sandwich; chocolate babka; epic pastrami burger. [$] *Average main: $15* ✉ *3150 24th St., at Shotwell St., Mission District* ☎ *415/590-7955* 🌐 *wisesonsdeli.com.*

Coffee and Quick Bites

La Santaneca de la Mission

$ | **LATIN AMERICAN** | **FAMILY** | The Salvadorans who live in the Mission love to head to this friendly, cash-only, family-run place for *pupusas,* cornmeal rounds stuffed with meat, cheese, and beans. The kitchen also makes the more unusual rice-flour pupusa, as well as other dishes popular in Central America, including seafood soup, tamales, and *chicharrones* (fried pork skins) with yucca. **Known for:** pork and cheese pupusas; atole (hot, frothy corn drink); popular community gathering spot for meals at all times of day. [$] *Average main: $7* ✉ *2815 Mission St., Mission District* ☎ *415/285–2131* 💳 *No credit cards.*

★ Tartine Bakery

$ | **BAKERY** | **FAMILY** | Chad Robertson is America's first modern cult baker, and this tiny Mission District outpost is where you'll find his famed loaves of tangy country bread, beloved pastries like croissants and morning buns, and near-constant lines out the door—good luck finding a seat. They're longest in the morning when locals (and plenty of tourists) need a pastry punch to start the day, and later in the afternoon when the famed loaves emerge freshly baked. **Known for:** anything bread-related; chocolate soufflé cake; indecisive guests who want to order everything. [$] *Average main: $15* ✉ *600 Guerrero St., at 18th St., Mission District* ☎ *415/487–2600* 🌐 *tartinebakery.com* 🕒 *No dinner.*

Hotels

The vibrant Mission has slim choices in the hotel department because it is predominantly residential, but travelers can find vacation rentals as well as under-the-radar B&Bs. The Mission is iffy for wandering around late at night.

The Inn San Francisco

$$ | **B&B/INN** | For decades this Italianate Victorian mansion decked out in ornate poster beds, opulent area rugs, and precious Victorian artifacts has welcomed visitors to the Mission District. **Pros:** charming antiques; garden and sun deck; oozes charm. **Cons:** neighborhood can be sketchy at night; feather beds an issue for those with allergies; a couple rooms lack a private bath. [$] *Rooms from: $285* ✉ *943 S. Van Ness Ave., Mission District* ☎ *415/641–0188, 800/359–0913 for reservations only* 🌐 *www.innsf.com* 🛏 *21 rooms* 🍴 *Breakfast.*

★ The Parker Guest House

$$ | **B&B/INN** | Two yellow 1909 Edwardian houses enchant travelers wanting an authentic San Francisco experience; dark hallways and steep staircases lead to bright, earth-toned rooms with tiled baths (most with tubs), comfortable sitting areas, and cozy linens. **Pros:** handsomely designed, affordable rooms; close to the Castro and Dolores Park; evening wine social hour. **Cons:** long walk or short car ride from the main Mission nightlife; economy rooms have private baths in a hallway; standard rooms are a little tight. [$] *Rooms from: $229* ✉ *520 Church St., Mission District* ☎ *415/621–3222* 🌐 *www.parkerguesthouse.com* 🛏 *21 rooms* 🍴 *Breakfast.*

Nightlife

Once a vibrant mix of Latino street culture and twentysomething dot-com action, the Mission is defined these days by its hipster crowd. This neighborhood rarely sleeps.

BARS

ABV

BARS/PUBS | One of the city's top cocktail bars offers elevated small plates (the burger has a devoted following) late into the night to pair with the excellent cocktail menu, which includes such favorites as a Mumbai Mule featuring saffron vodka. A knowledgeable and friendly staff serves a diverse, energetic crowd that knows their drinks, in a smart modern setting with hard surfaces, bar-stool seating, and a giant mural. The sidewalk tables are popular on sunny days. ■TIP→ **Pay attention to the schedule of the upstairs loft, Over Proof. When open, it's one of the city's best themed cocktail–pairing dinner experiences.** ⊠ 3174 16th St., Mission District ☎ 415/294–1871 ⊕ www.abvsf.com.

The Beehive

BARS/PUBS | The fun-loving, groovy 1960s are the inspiration for the gorgeous setting of this Valencia Street cocktail destination with a busy bar scene up front and a more relaxed, lounge-style atmosphere in the back. However, the cocktails are straight-up modern excellence, always mixing a superb balance of high-quality spirits and homemade ingredients. The glassware and garnishes are gorgeous. ⊠ 842 Valencia St., Mission District ☎ 415/306–8209 ⊕ www. thebeehivesf.com.

★ Elixir

BARS/PUBS | The cocktails are well crafted and affordable at the city's second-oldest saloon location—various watering holes have operated on this site since 1858. It's San Francisco's best example of a retro/vintage neighborhood favorite with all the finest elements of a modern, ingredient-focused cocktail bar. Don't miss the holiday cocktails if a trip happens to be in December. ■TIP→ **Sunday's do-it-yourself Bloody Mary bar is popular with the locals.** ⊠ 3200 16th St., at Guerrero St., Mission District ☎ 415/552–1633 ⊕ www.elixirsf.com.

★ El Rio

BARS/PUBS | A dive bar in the best sense, El Rio has a calendar chock-full of events, from free bands and films to Salsa Sunday (seasonal), all of which keep Mission kids coming back. No matter what day you attend, expect to find a diverse gay and straight crowd enjoying local beers and margaritas. When the weather's warm, the large patio out back is especially popular, and the midday dance parties are the place to be. ⊠ 3158 Mission St., between César Chavez and Valencia Sts., Mission District ☎ 415/282–3325 ⊕ www.elriosf.com.

The Monk's Kettle

BARS/PUBS | Choosing the city's "best beer bar" is an impossible task, but there is no doubt that this intimate, friendly Mission destination is one of them. The tap list captivates the most ardent beer geeks, the bottle list is as deep as many fine-dining restaurants' wine lists, and the gastropub cuisine is particularly impressive. ⊠ 3141 16th St., Mission District ☎ 415/865–9523 ⊕ monkskettle.com.

Nihon Whiskey Lounge

BARS/PUBS | Whiskey lovers need to check this place out, if only to drool over the 150 or so bottles behind the bar. Nihon attracts a super-swank, youngish crowd for decent (if pricey) Japanese tapas; the whiskeys are a strong match with sushi. The dramatic lighting, close quarters, and blood-red tuffets make the bar more suitable for romance than business. ⊠ 1779 Folsom St., near 14th St., Mission District ☎ 415/552–4400 ⊕ dajanigroup.net.

Rite Spot Cafe

BARS/PUBS | A Mission tradition, this classy and casual charmer is like a cabaret club in an aging mobster's garage—it's almost hard to believe you're in 2020s San Francisco. Quirky lounge singers and other musicians entertain most nights. A small menu of affordable sandwiches and Italian food beats your average bar fare. ⊠ 2099

Folsom St., at 17th St., Mission District
☎ 415/552–6066 ⊕ www.ritespotcafe.net.

★ Trick Dog

BARS/PUBS | San Francisco's most talked
about craft cocktail bar for several years
running is still arguably the city's most
innovative one: every drink has at least
one "huh?" ingredient. But no worries,
you're in the hands of some of the most
capable bartenders that you'll ever have
the honor of enjoying a drink from. It gets
very crowded, both for the drinks and for
the outstanding hot dog–shaped burger
and beloved kale salad. ⊠ 3010 20th
St., Mission District ☎ 415/471–2999
⊕ www.trickdogbar.com.

★ Zeitgeist

BARS/PUBS | It's a dive but one of the
city's best beer bars—there are almost
50 on tap—and a great place to relax
with a cold one or an ever-popular Bloody
Mary in the large "garden" (there's not
much greenery) on a sunny day. Burgers
and brats are available, and if you own a
trucker hat, a pair of Vans, and a Pabst
Blue Ribbon T-shirt, you'll fit right in.
This is one of the city's quintessential
experiences, both in terms of bars and
of simply having fun. ⊠ 199 Valencia
St., at Duboce Ave., Mission District
☎ 415/255–7505 ⊕ www.zeitgeistsf.com.

GAY NIGHTLIFE
Martuni's

BARS/PUBS | A mixed crowd enjoys
cocktails in the semi-refined environment
of this piano bar where the Castro, the
Mission, and Hayes Valley intersect;
variations on the martini and different
fruit-flavored lemon drops are a specialty.
This is not the place for innovative mixol-
ogy. In the intimate back room a pianist
plays nightly, and patrons take turns bois-
terously singing show tunes. Martuni's
often gets busy after symphony and
opera performances—Davies Hall and
the Opera House are both within walking
distance. ⊠ 4 Valencia St., at Market St.,
Mission District ☎ 415/241–0205.

THEMED ENTERTAINMENT
Urban Putt

THEMED ENTERTAINMENT | It may be
kid-friendly during the day, but this
14-hole indoor miniature golf course really lights up at night when you can enjoy a
quality cocktail or beer and putt through
the Transamerica Pyramid and those
famous Painted Ladies. It's definitely one
of the city's favorite spots for a first or
second date. ⊠ 1096 S. Van Ness Ave.,
at 22nd St., Mission District ☎ 415/341–
1080 ⊕ www.urbanputt.com.

🎭 Performing Arts

Joe Goode Performance Group

DANCE | Physicality and high-flying style
are the hallmarks of this original group,
a blend of modern dance and theater.
Works include narrative, video projec-
tions, and song and succeed at being
both poignant and funny. ⊠ 401 Alabama
St., Mission ☎ 415/561–6565 ⊕ www.
joegoode.org.

🛍 Shopping

The aesthetic of the hipsters and artist
types who reside in the Mission contributes to the individuality of shopping here.
These night owls keep the city's best
thrift stores, vintage-furniture shops,
alternative bookstores, and increasingly, small clothing boutiques afloat. As
the Mission gentrifies, though, bargain
hunters find themselves trekking farther
afield in search of truly local flavor.

BOOKS
Dog Eared Books

BOOKS/STATIONERY | An eclectic group of
shoppers—gay and straight, fashionable
and practical—wanders the aisles of this
pleasantly ramshackle bookstore. The
diverse stock of literature is mostly used
and unique and includes quirky selections
like local zines, vintage children's books,
and remaindered art books. ⊠ 900 Valencia
St., at 20th St., Mission District ☎ 415/282–
1901 ⊕ www.dogearedbooks.com.

CLOTHING
Lemon Twist
CLOTHING | A fashionable family affair: Danette Scheib is known for her inspired details in women's leisure suits and her signature tulle petticoats that go underneath her A-line skirts. Her husband Eric's T-shirts for men and women in themes like "muscle cars" capture an urban essence. ⊠ *3418 25th St., Mission District* ☎ *415/297–2423* ⊕ *www.lemontwist.net.*

Sunhee Moon
CLOTHING | This San Francisco–based designer uses only American-made fabrics and manufactures all her colorful, compelling, yet low-key women's clothing items locally. Her relaxed contemporary aesthetic is coupled with a good amount of practical mid-century elegance. Appointments take place at her atelier near the border of Bernal Heights and the Mission. ⊠ *3603A 26th St., near Guerrero St., Mission District* ☎ *415/928–1800* ⊕ *www.sunheemoon.com.*

FOOD AND DRINK
Bi-Rite Market
FOOD/CANDY | San Francisco is one of the culinary centers of the world, and this universally adored grocery store by Dolores Park is its beating heart. It's a farmers' market every day inside and well worth browsing around to see the bounty of Northern California, from peak summer tomatoes to local king salmon, plus all kinds of goodies from small producers. If your hotel doesn't have a kitchen, then maybe buy a local peach or blood orange to snack on before strolling across the street for a scoop of salted caramel ice cream from Bi-Rite's equally beloved creamery. ⊠ *3639 18th St., Mission District* ☎ *415/241–9760* ⊕ *biritemarket.com.*

FURNITURE, HOUSEWARES, AND GIFTS
★ Heath Ceramics
CERAMICS/GLASSWARE | Founded in Sausalito in 1948, Heath designs and produces sleek, glossy tiles for the home and newly spun bowls, plates, and cups in rich earth colors to decorate kitchens. You'll also find locally inspired cookbooks and high-quality furniture and silverware from trendy peers throughout Heath's immaculately arranged factory showroom. The company's designs can be found at many of San Francisco's top restaurants and cafés, including the adjacent Tartine Manufactory. ⊠ *2900 18th St., between Alabama and Florida Sts., Mission District* ☎ *415/361–5552* ⊕ *www.heathceramics.com.*

★ Paxton Gate
GIFTS/SOUVENIRS | Elevating gardening to an art, this serene shop offers beautiful earthenware pots, amaryllis and narcissus bulbs, decorative garden items, and coffee-table books, such as a composting book called *Let It Rot!* The collection of taxidermy and preserved bugs provides more unusual gift ideas. A couple storefronts away is too-cute Paxton Gate Curiosities for Kids, jam-packed with retro toys, books, and other stellar finds. ⊠ *824 Valencia St., between 19th and 20th Sts., Mission District* ☎ *415/824–1872* ⊕ *paxtongate.com.*

Therapy
GIFTS/SOUVENIRS | In addition to fun housewares, books, wellness items, and stationery that leans toward retro charm, this local company sells smart San Francisco– and California-theme linens, decor, and accessories that make great souvenirs. ⊠ *545 Valencia St., between 16th and 17th Sts., Mission District* ☎ *415/865–0981* ⊕ *therapystores.com.*

TOYS AND GADGETS
826 Valencia
TOYS | FAMILY | The brainchild of local author Dave Eggers is primarily a center established to help kids with their writing skills via writing programs, tutoring, and storytelling events. But the storefront is also "San Francisco's only independent pirate supply store," a quirky space filled with eye patches, spyglasses, and other pirate-themed paraphernalia. Eggers's quarterly journal, *McSweeney's,* and

other publications are available here. Proceeds benefit the writing center.

On the center's storefront is an intricate mural designed by graphic novelist Chris Ware as a meditation on the evolution of human communication. ⊠ *826 Valencia St., between 18th and 19th Sts., Mission District* ☎ *415/642–5905* ⊕ *826valencia.org.*

Activities

Avital Tours

SPECIAL-INTEREST | The sheer volume of tempting culinary choices in the Mission District can be overwhelming. For food-focused visitors, there's no better tour in the city than joining the insightful guides of this boutique company. Each walk-eat-repeat experience is a delicious, educational morning or afternoon mixing a few dining stops with sights (like the Mission murals and Dolores Park) and history lessons. Tours depart from different locations in the Mission. (A similar North Beach tour is offered as well.) ⊠ *2000 Mission St., Mission District* ☎ *415/355–4044* ⊕ *avitaltours. com* ⊠ *from $99.*

Dogpatch

East of the Mission District and Potrero Hill and a short T–Third Muni light-rail ride from SoMa, the increasingly hip Dogpatch neighborhood has been on the rise since the tech boom of the 2010s started. Red-hot galleries have hit a critical mass, decamping from aging Union Square and even New York to fill the Minnesota Street Project, a giant warehouse of art space; the Museum of Craft and Design is another neighborhood anchor; and the exhibitions at the SF Camerawork gallery continue to include some of the city's most compelling photography. Artisans, designers, and craftspeople eager to protect the area's historical industrial legacy have all moved here in recent years, providing a solid customer base for shops, boutique restaurants, and artisanal food producers (but no bank!). At or near the intersection of 3rd and 22nd Streets, you'll find neighborhood breakfast favorite Just for You Café, pastry standout Neighbor Bakehouse, locally sourced Italian food at sunny yellow Piccino, and small-batch organic ice cream at Mr. and Mrs. Miscellaneous.

⊙ Sights

Museum of Craft and Design

MUSEUM | Right at home in this once-industrial neighborhood now bursting with creative energy, this small, four-room space—definitely a quick view—mounts temporary art and design exhibitions. The focus might be sculpture, metalwork, furniture, or jewelry, though it might also be industrial design, architecture, or very on-trend 2020s subjects like data and computer encoding. The beautifully curated shop is a perfect place for unique souvenirs and imagination-spurring items for the home office. ⊠ *2569 3rd St., near 22nd St., Dogpatch* ☎ *415/773–0303* ⊕ *sfmcd.org* ⊠ *$10* ⊙ *Closed Mon. and Tues.*

Bernal Heights

A neighborhood with a small-town vibe that's home to young families, dog lovers, and a visible lesbian contingent, Bernal Heights draws some locals for its handful of good restaurants and the 360-degree views from the top of Bernal Hill. Less hipster than the neighboring Mission (to the north) and less saturated with the tech money set than Noe Valley (to the west), Bernal Heights feels like a throwback to another time (like at Avedano's, a rarely found classic butcher shop gem), with a beloved community garden, the annual Hillwide Garage Sale, one of the city's most adorable tiny coffee shops (Pinhole Coffee), and hardly a chain store in sight.

Take a stroll down main drag Cortland Avenue, climb the hill at Bernal Heights

Park for one of the city's definitive skyline views (and get a photo sitting in the swing), or explore the stairways in one of San Francisco's lowest-key neighborhoods. The northern part of Bernal Heights, which borders the Mission, is defined by flat, grass-filled Precita Park, a perfect spot for a picnic or game of Frisbee (unlike the very windy, steep Bernal Heights Park). Precita Park is also next to one of the city's most exciting seasonal-modern Californian restaurants, Marlena, at 300 Precita Avenue.

🍴 Restaurants

Cellarmaker House of Pizza

$$ | **PIZZA** | There are several excellent pizzerias and many terrific small breweries in town, but it *almost* seems unfair that quite possibly the best of both genres is one place located where the Mission blurs into Bernal Heights. Cellarmaker is known for its ultra-hoppy beers and unique Coffee & Cigarettes smoked coffee porter; the pizza side focuses on perfect renditions of thick, crispy-edged Detroit-style square slices. **Known for:** constantly changing IPA beers; market-special Detroit-style pizza; constant stream of beer geeks. [$] *Average main: $22* ✉ *3193 Mission St., Bernal Heights* ☎ *415/296–6351* 🌐 *cellarmakerbrewing.com/house-of-pizza/* 🕒 *No lunch Mon.–Sat. No dinner Sun.*

Potrero Hill

Tucked between two freeways east of the Mission and south of SoMa, warm and sunny Potrero Hill is a laid-back, family-friendly neighborhood that can feel like a place apart from the rest of the city. Most of the action happens around 18th and Connecticut Streets. With fantastic views from its slopes; some good shops, restaurants, and bars; and the longtime music club Bottom of the Hill, Potrero Hill is a neighborhood attractive to locals but still off the tourist radar.

🍴 Restaurants

Plow

$$ | **AMERICAN** | **FAMILY** | The brunch lines are as constant as the excellent scrambles, biscuits, and fluffy lemon-ricotta pancakes served at this neighborhood favorite, a former architect's studio. The atmosphere is also winning—bright and pastoral, with rustic wood floors and huge windows—and the Little Plowers menu dishes out smaller-portioned pancakes, French toast, and grilled cheese for younger brunch-loving guests. **Known for:** Plow potatoes; soft scrambled eggs with peak seasonal produce; happiest place in San Francisco at 10 am. [$] *Average main: $19* ✉ *1299 18th St., Potrero Hill* ☎ *415/821–7569* 🌐 *www.eatatplow.com* 🕒 *No dinner.*

🍸 Nightlife

One of the city's less walkable neighborhoods is far from the center of the nightlife scene and sometimes feels downright sleepy. But a strip of 18th Street near Connecticut Street has good food and drinks (try Goat Hill Pizza, Ruby Wine, and Mochica for Peruvian food), and the bottom of the hill is home to the beloved all-things-Boston sports bar Connecticut Yankee, plus the aptly named Bottom of the Hill music club.

BREWPUBS AND BEER GARDENS

Anchor Public Taps/Anchor Brewing

BREWPUBS/BEER GARDENS | Mention "San Francisco" and "beer" and most locals and tourists will immediately think about the one and only Anchor Steam. It's a core part of the city's culture—it's what San Fransiscans drink when the Giants win or after a tough day at work. Anchor started in 1896 and moved to its iconic Potrero Hill home in 1977, where the smell of brewing yeasts, hops, and barley greets the area on most days. The brewery tour and tasting is always a hot ticket (and well worth the time), but it's much easier to grab a flight or pint at their Public Taps bar next door.

✉ *495 De Haro St., Potrero Hill* ☎ *415/863–8350* ⊕ *www.anchorbrewing.com.*

MUSIC CLUBS
Bottom of the Hill
MUSIC CLUBS | This is a great live-music dive—in the best sense of the word—and truly the epicenter of Bay Area indie rock. The club has hosted some great acts over the years, including the Strokes and the Throwing Muses. Rap and hip-hop acts occasionally make it to the stage. ✉ *1233 17th St., at Missouri St., Potrero Hill* ☎ *415/626–4455* ⊕ *www. bottomofthehill.com.*

Shopping

ART GALLERIES
Catharine Clark Gallery
ART GALLERIES | Although nationally known artists—like Masami Teraoka and Andy Diaz Hope—display their modern sculptures, paintings, photographs, and installation artwork here, emerging artists with a Bay Area connection get the spotlight, among them Chester Arnold and Josephine Taylor. The gallery's BOXBLUR space showcases contemporary art both in visual exhibitions and performances. ✉ *248 Utah St., Potrero Hill* ☎ *415/399–1439* ⊕ *cclarkgallery.com.*

Mission Bay

San Francisco is a small city, but it can't really build much more because of zoning rules and because most of its 49 square miles (it's roughly seven miles long by seven miles wide) are already taken up by existing neighborhoods. There is one major exception: Mission Bay. It's confusing because the area isn't attached to the Mission District (it's bordered by Mission Creek), and the neighborhood does have a growing number of residents, but "residents" also often refers to the neighborhood's UCSF medical school students. The newest "locals" in the neighborhood are the NBA's Golden State Warriors, who play at the dazzling Chase Center. In this area between Oracle Park and Dogpatch, it's impossible to miss the construction and hospitals, and the tall, shiny new glass condo buildings (skyscrapers by San Francisco housing standards) feel more like L.A. or Miami. But it's also easy to see the energy of a new neighborhood, which is a rarity in quirky and old San Francisco.

Sights

★ Chase Center
SPORTS VENUE | The National Basketball Association's Golden State Warriors moved across the bay from Oakland to this spectacular arena in 2019. They are the headliners of the city's marquee indoor entertainment complex, which opened with a concert by Metallica with the San Francisco Symphony, followed by global-superstar performances by the likes of Sir Elton John and Janet Jackson. While the action really happens inside, don't miss a walk around the beautiful bayfront grounds; a highlight is Olafur Eliasson's stunning, must-photograph *Seeing Spheres* installation. ✉ *1 Warriors Way, Mission Bay, San Francisco* ☎ *415/479–4667* ⊕ *chasecenter.com.*

PACIFIC HEIGHTS AND JAPANTOWN

WITH THE WESTERN ADDITION

Updated by
Trevor Felch

👁 Sights	🍴 Restaurants	🛏 Hotels	🛍 Shopping	🍸 Nightlife
★★☆☆☆	★★★★☆	★★☆☆☆	★★★☆☆	★★☆☆☆

SAN FRANCISCO'S ARCHITECTURE

California Academy of Sciences

San Francisco's architecture scene underwent a dramatic growth spurt in the first two decades of the 21st century. Boldface international architects spearheaded major projects like the Salesforce Tower (2018), the Chase Center (2019), and SFMOMA's dramatic expansion (2016). And with those additions came heated local debates.

The development flurry is thrown into sharp relief by the previous decades spent carefully preserving the city's historic buildings. Genteel Victorian homes are a San Francisco signature, and this residential legacy is fiercely protected.

Residents aren't shy about voicing opinions on the "starchitect" plans, either. As high-profile designs unfold and new condo neighborhoods break ground, criticism will surely escalate. One thing that gratifies everyone: the impressive advances made in eco-friendly building practices that are a recurring theme in the new, prominent building projects.

SAN FRANCISCO MUSEUM OF MODERN ART (SFMOMA)

Renowned Swiss architect Mario Botta's first shot at designing a museum resulted in the distinctive, sturdy geometrical forms that reflect his signature style. Here a black-and-white cylindrical tower anchors the brick structure. Botta called the huge, slanted skylight the "city's eye, like the Cyclops." A new wing, designed by Snøhetta, opened in 2016, adding more than 100,000 square feet of gallery and public space.

DE YOUNG MUSEUM OF FINE ART

Love it or hate it, the structure is a must-see destination in Golden Gate Park. After the original Egyptian-revival edifice was deemed seismically unsafe, the Pritzker-winning Swiss team Herzog & de Meuron won the commission to rebuild. Their design's copper facade and, in particular, the 144-foot observation tower—a twisted parallelogram grazing the treetops—drew fire from critics, who compared the design to a "rusty aircraft carrier." But the copper hue is mellowing with age, and the panoramic view from the ninth-floor observation deck is a hit.

CALIFORNIA ACADEMY OF SCIENCES

An eco-friendly, energy-efficient adventure in biodiversity, Renzo Piano's audacious design for this natural history museum comes equipped with a rain forest, a planetarium, skylights, and a retractable ceiling over the central courtyard. But it's the "living roof," covered in native plants, that generates the most comment.

MISSION BAY, RINCON HILL, AND TRANSBAY DISTRICT

San Francisco's cityscape is undergoing tremendous change, especially moving south from Market Street

San Francisco Victorian homes

along the waterfront. Glass-sheathed, condo-crammed high-rises are taking over what was a working-class area of warehouses and lofts, led by Oracle Park, the Giants' baseball ballpark. The ultramodern Transbay Terminal, with a rooftop park, opened in 2018, as did the soaring Salesforce Tower, now San Francisco's tallest building. The blocky new Mission Bay Conference Center on the University of California, San Francisco (UCSF) campus, by Mexican architect Ricardo Legorreta, has changed the landscape of nearby Mission Bay, as has the Warriors' new waterfront home, the Chase Center basketball arena and entertainment complex.

PRESIDIO

The development of this parkland continues at a relatively slow pace. Its historic military-base buildings are being put to new uses—everything from a printing press to a spa. Additions include a digital arts center by George Lucas, a Walt Disney Museum, the beautifully renovated mid-century Presidio Theatre, and the hip Inn at the Presidio and Lodge at the Presidio boutique hotels.

de Young Museum of Fine Art

NEIGHBORHOOD SNAPSHOT

TOP EXPERIENCES

■ **Fillmore Street shopping:** Browse the superfine shops along Pacific Heights' main drag.

■ **Picnicking at Lafayette Park:** Gather supplies along Fillmore Street and climb to the top of this park. It's surrounded by spectacular homes and has a sweeping view of the city.

■ **Asian shops in the Japan Center:** Grab an adorable *taiyaki* (a fish-shape cone with soft-serve ice cream) at Uji Time or browse the wonderful Kinokuniya Bookstore and the tea implements at Asakichi.

■ **Spa serenity at Kabuki Springs:** Enter the peaceful lobby and prepare to be transported at the Japanese-style communal baths.

■ **Historical architecture:** Check out the grand vintage houses along the tree-lined streets of Pacific Heights.

GETTING HERE

Steep streets in Pacific Heights make for impressive views and rough walking; consider taking a car or taxi here. For Pacific Heights proper, take the 12–Folsom to its terminus at Van Ness and Pacific Avenues and walk west. For Fillmore Street, catch the 1–California or the 22–Fillmore bus. The 38 and 38R–Geary run right by Japantown, and the 24–Divisadero and 21–Hayes are the routes for the Alamo Square/Western Addition area.

PLANNING YOUR TIME

Give yourself an hour to wander Fillmore Street, more if you're planning to eat here or a picnic in one of the parks. Checking out the stunning homes in Pacific Heights is best done by car, unless you have serious stamina; a half hour is enough. Shops and restaurants are the highlights of Japantown; lunchtime is ideal.

Allow at least an hour to wander around Alamo Square Park and the Divisadero corridor. The street has great restaurants, so plan to eat here.

QUICK BITES

■ **b Patisserie.** Your search for the perfect *kouign-amann* (a traditional glazed, butter-enriched Breton pastry made of croissant dough) ends in this buzzy Pacific Heights café from baking wizard Belinda Leong. ⊠ *2821 California St., at Divisadero St., Pacific Heights* ⊕ *bpatisserie.com.*

■ **Crown and Crumpet Tea Salon.** In the lobby of the New People building, this mini tea shop looks like a little girl's fantasy, with pretty flowered and polka-dotted tablecloths and fancy settings. Stop in for a warm panini or salad, or have high tea with scones, crumpets, and finger sandwiches. ⊠ *1746 Post St., Japantown* ⊕ *www.crown-andcrumpet.com.*

■ **Jane on Fillmore.** After a few blocks of window browsing, stop in this bright, two-story spot for their famous avocado mash, mile-high quiche, homemade baked goods and cookies, and coffee from beans roasted in-house. ⊠ *2123 Fillmore St., Pacific Heights* ⊕ *www.itsjane.com.*

Pacific Heights and Japantown are something of an odd couple: privileged, old-school San Francisco and the workaday commercial center of Japanese American life in the city, stacked virtually on top of each other. The sprawling, extravagant mansions of Pacific Heights gradually give way to the more modest Victorians and unassuming housing tracts of Japantown. The most interesting spots in Japantown huddle in the Japan Center, the neighborhood's two-block centerpiece, and along Post Street. You can find plenty of authentic Japanese treats in the shops and restaurants.

Pacific Heights

Pacific Heights defines San Francisco's most expensive and dramatic real estate. Grand Victorians line the streets, mansions and town houses are priced in the millions, and there are magnificent views from almost any point in the neighborhood. Old money and new, personalities in the limelight and those who prefer absolute media anonymity live here, and few outsiders see anything other than English Tudor imports, baroque bastions, and the pleasing facades of Queen Anne charmers. Nancy Pelosi and Dianne Feinstein, Larry Ellison, and Gordon Getty all own impressive homes here, but not even pockets as deep as those can buy a large garden—space in the city is simply at too much of a premium. Luckily, two of the city's most spectacular parks are located in the area. The boutiques and restaurants along Fillmore Street, which range from glam to funky, are a draw for the whole city as well.

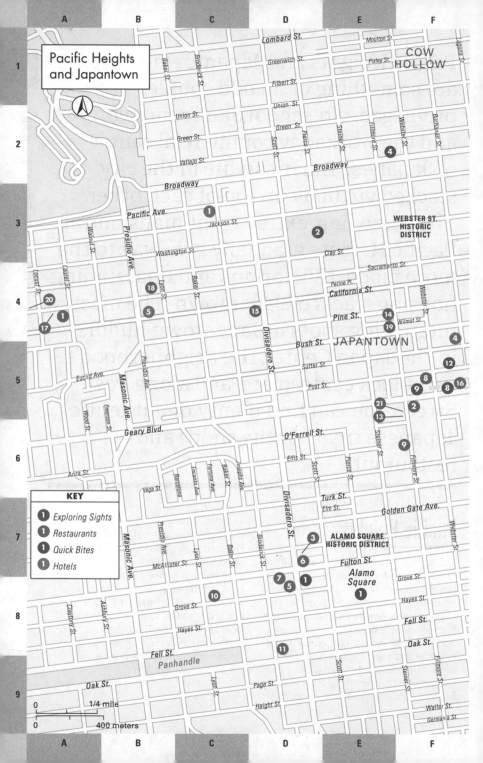

Sights ▼

1 Alamo Square Park...... **E8**
2 Alta Plaza Park.......... **D3**
3 Atherton House......... **G4**
4 Broadway estates....... **E2**
5 Buchanan Mall........... **G6**
6 Cathedral of Saint Mary of the Assumption **H5**
7 Haas-Lilienthal House.. **H3**
8 Japan Center............. **F5**
9 Kabuki Springs & Spa... **F5**
10 Lafayette Park........... **G3**
11 Laguna Street Victorians................ **G4**
12 New People **F5**
13 Two Italianate Victorians................ **H3**
14 Whittier Mansion....... **G3**

Restaurants ▼

1 As Quoted **A4**
2 Avery.................... **F5**
3 Che Fico................. **D7**
4 Daeho **G5**
5 4505 Burgers & BBQ ... **D8**
6 Hina Yakitori............. **D7**
7 Ju-Ni **D8**
8 Marufuku Ramen **F5**
9 Merchant Roots.......... **F6**
10 Nopa **C8**
11 Nopalito.................. **D8**
12 Octavia................... **G4**
13 The Progress............. **F5**
14 Roam Artisan Burgers **E4**
15 Routier **D4**
16 Sasa...................... **F5**
17 Sociale **A4**
18 Sorrel **B4**
19 SPQR..................... **E4**
20 Spruce **A4**
21 State Bird Provisions.... **F5**

Quick Bites ▼

1 The Mill **D8**

Hotels ▼

1 Hotel Drisco **C3**
2 Hotel Kabuki............. **G5**
3 Hotel Majestic **H4**
4 The Kimpton Buchanan Hotel.......... **F4**
5 Laurel Inn................. **B4**
6 Mansion on Sutter....... **H4**
7 Queen Anne Hotel...... **G4**

A Pacific Heights Walk

Start at **Broadway and Webster Streets**, where four notable estates stand within a block of one another. Two are on the north side of Broadway west of the intersection, one is on the same side to the east, and the last is half a block south on Webster. Head south down Webster and hang a right onto Clay to **Alta Plaza Park**, or skip the park and turn left on Jackson to the **Whittier Mansion**, at Jackson and Laguna Streets. Head south down Laguna and cross Washington Street to **Lafayette Park**. Walk on Washington along the edge of the park, past the formal French **Spreckels Mansion** at the corner of Octavia Street, and continue east two more blocks to Franklin Street. Turn left (north); halfway down the block stands the handsome **Haas-Lilienthal House.** Head back south on Franklin Street, stopping to view a handsome Georgian-style residence (1735 Franklin St.) and the Queen Anne–style Coleman House with a gorgeous purple stained-glass window on the home's north side (1701 Franklin St.). At California Street, turn right (west) to see two **Italianate Victorians** and the **Atherton House.** Continue west to Laguna Street and turn left (south); past Pine Street sits a sedate block of **Laguna Street Victorians.**

⊙ Sights

★ Alta Plaza Park

CITY PARK | FAMILY | Golden Gate Park's longtime superintendent, John McLaren, designed the nearly 12-acre park in the early 1900s, modeling its steep south-facing terracing on that of the Grand Casino in Monte Carlo, Monaco. At any time of day, you're guaranteed to find San Francisco's exercise warriors running up the park's south steps like Rocky Balboa in the famous Rocky movies. From the top of those steps, you can see Marin to the north, downtown to the east, Twin Peaks to the south, and Golden Gate Park to the west. ■**TIP→ Kids love the many play structures at the large, enclosed playground at the top; dogs love the off-leash area in the park's southeast corner.** ⊠ Bordered by Clay, Steiner, Jackson, and Scott Sts., Pacific Heights ⊕ www.altaplazapark.com.

Atherton House

HOUSE | The somewhat quirky design of this Victorian-era house incorporates Queen Anne, Stick-Eastlake, and other architectural elements. Many claim the house—now apartments—is haunted by the ghosts of its 19th-century residents, who (supposedly) regularly whisper, glow, and generally cause a mild fuss. It's not open to the public. ⊠ 1990 California St., Pacific Heights.

Broadway estates

HOUSE | Broadway uptown, unlike its garish North Beach stretch, has plenty of prestigious addresses. The three-story palace at 2222 Broadway, which has an intricately filigreed doorway, was built by Comstock silver-mine heir James Clair Flood and later donated to a religious order. The Convent of the Sacred Heart purchased the **Grant House** at 2220 Broadway. These two buildings, along with a Flood property at 2120 Broadway, are used as private school buildings today. A gold-mine heir, William Bowers Bourn II, commissioned Willis Polk to build the nearby brick mansion at 2550 Webster Street. Two blocks away, movie fans will surely recognize the "Mrs. Doubtfire" apartment at Broadway and Steiner (2640 Steiner St.). It's the home where Robin Williams donned his disguise as a lovable British nanny in the beloved 1993 comedy. ⊠ *Pacific Heights.*

Haas-Lilienthal House

HOUSE | A small display of photographs on the bottom floor of this elaborate, gray 1886 Queen Anne house makes clear that despite its lofty stature and striking, round third-story tower, the house was modest compared with some of the giants that fell victim to the 1906 earthquake and fire. San Francisco Heritage, a foundation to preserve San Francisco's architectural history, operates the home, whose carefully kept rooms provide a glimpse into late-19th-century life through period furniture, authentic details (like the antique dishes in the kitchen built-in), and photos of the Haas family, who occupied the house for three generations until 1972. ■TIP➔ **You can admire hundreds of gorgeous San Francisco Victorians from the outside, but this is the only one that's open to the public, and it's worth a visit.** You can download free maps of two nearby walking tours highlighting the neighborhood's historic architecture on the house's website. ⊠ *2007 Franklin St., Pacific Heights* ✛ *between Washington and Jackson Sts.* ☎ *415/441–3000* ⊕ *www.haas-lilienthal-house.org* 🎫 *Tours $10.*

Lafayette Park

CITY PARK | FAMILY | Clusters of trees dot this four-block-square oasis for sunbathers and dog-and-Frisbee teams. On the south side of the park, squat but elegant **2151 Sacramento,** a private condominium, is the site of a home occupied by Sir Arthur Conan Doyle in the late 19th century. Coats of arms blaze in the front stained-glass windows. Across from the park's eastern edge is another eye-catching historic home: the Queen Anne (and distinctly yellow) C. A. Belden House at 2004 Gough Street.

The park's northern border is anchored by the stately Spreckels Mansion, built originally for sugar heir Adolph B. Spreckels and his wife, Alma. It is now the 55-room home of celebrated romance

novelist Danielle Steel. Giant, immaculately trimmed hedges hide most of the mansion from public view—and have been quite the topic of debate among locals for many years. The park itself is a lovely neighborhood space where Pacific Heights residents laze in the sun or exercise their pedigreed canines while gazing at downtown's skyline or the Bay and Marin County hills in the distance to the north. ⊠ *Bordered by Laguna, Gough, Sacramento, and Washington Sts., Pacific Heights* ⊕ *sfrecpark.org.*

Laguna Street Victorians

HOUSE | On the west side of the 1800 block of Laguna Street, these oft-photographed private houses cost between $2,000 and $2,600 when they were built in the 1870s. Nowadays, you'll probably need to add three zeros to those prices; an entire house might sell for upward of $5 million. No bright colors here, though—most of the paint jobs are in soft beiges or pastels. ⊠ *Between Bush and Pine Sts., Pacific Heights.*

Two Italianate Victorians

HOUSE | Two Italianate Victorians stand out on the 1800 block of California. The beauty at 1834, the Wormser-Coleman House, was built in the 1870s. Coleman bought the lot next door, giving this private property an unusually spacious yard for the city, even for this luxurious neighborhood. ⊠ *1818 and 1834 California St., Pacific Heights.*

Whittier Mansion

HOUSE | With a Spanish-tile roof and scrolled bay windows on all four sides, this is one of the most elegant 19th-century houses in the state. Unlike other grand mansions lost in the 1906 quake, the Whittier Mansion was made of solid Arizona sandstone, so only a chimney toppled over during the disaster. Built by William Franklin Whittier, the founder of (what became) the gas and electric utility PG&E, the house served as the German consulate during the Nazi period. Legend has it that the house is haunted. It's not

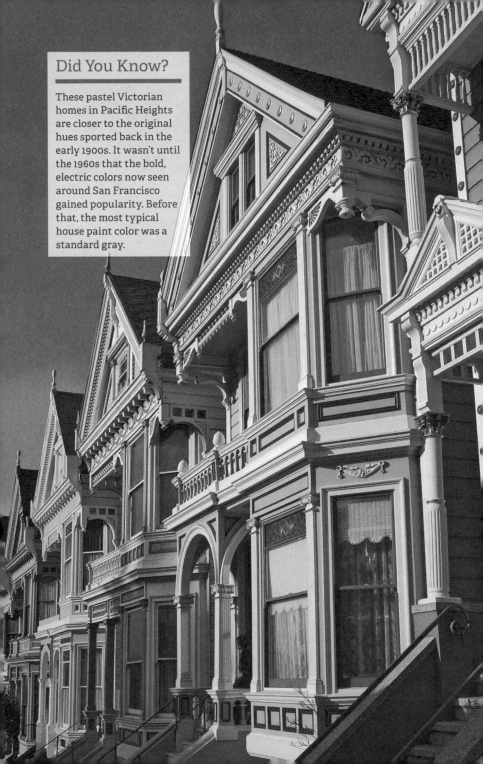

Did You Know?

These pastel Victorian homes in Pacific Heights are closer to the original hues sported back in the early 1900s. It wasn't until the 1960s that the bold, electric colors now seen around San Francisco gained popularity. Before that, the most typical house paint color was a standard gray.

open to the public. ✉ *2090 Jackson St., Pacific Heights.*

🍴 Restaurants

Pacific Heights may well be one of the city's better-known neighborhoods, thanks to Hollywood movies and jaw-dropping mansions. More down-to-earth, and down the hill, is Lower Pac Heights, which attracts professionals and postgrads, who flock to Fillmore Street's bustling eateries. Neighboring Presidio Heights has a handful of upscale dining favorites on Sacramento Street.

As Quoted

$ | **AMERICAN** | **FAMILY** | It's one thing to be a health-focused restaurant, but it's really difficult to be like this sleek Presidio Heights daytime café, where a wellness-centric menu also manages to be so delicious that guests often don't notice how virtuous the dishes are. Bread for the open-faced sandwiches is gluten-free and baked in-house; several items are vegetarian and/or vegan; and even the pappardelle is made of zucchini ribbons instead of wheat. **Known for:** post-yoga healthful meals including salads; excellent gluten-free toasts; freshly made juices and smoothies. [$] *Average main: $16* ✉ *3613 Sacramento St., Presidio Heights* ☎ *415/914–0689* 🌐 *www.eatasquoted.com.*

★ Octavia

$$$ | **MODERN AMERICAN** | Regardless of the time of year, Melissa Perello's second and more upscale restaurant (Frances is the first) is a perennial favorite for diners seeking out what California cuisine really tastes like. The warm, immaculate dining room is a perfect setting for edgier dishes like the popular chilled squid ink noodles starter, along with more comforting produce-driven small plates and entrées. **Known for:** exciting preparations with peak-of-season produce; spicy deviled egg starter; truly professional service. [$] *Average main: $32* ✉ *1701 Octavia St., at Bush St., Lower Pacific Heights* ☎ *415/408–7507* 🌐 *www.octavia-sf.com* 🕒 *No lunch.*

Roam Artisan Burgers

$ | **BURGER** | **FAMILY** | All the burgers at this laid-back spot, part of a popular Bay Area mini-chain, are responsibly sourced, and the beef is 100% grass-fed. Choose a patty (beef, bison, vegetarian, elk, or turkey), then choose a preset "style," or invent your own from the many creative toppings. **Known for:** notable vegetarian burger; popular with families; the "fry-fecta" trio of fry styles for a side. [$] *Average main: $11* ✉ *1923 Fillmore St., Pacific Heights* ☎ *415/800–7801* 🌐 *www.roamburgers.com.*

Sociale

$$$ | **NORTHERN ITALIAN** | The COVID-19 pandemic's outdoor dining requirement led San Francisco diners to discover the city's premier patios—like the one that regulars have known about for years at this Presidio Heights stalwart, hidden from the street down a little alley, almost like a posh, aboveground speakeasy. Whether you're dining on that patio or in the elegant dining room, Italian and seasonal Californian cooking mingle together on the menu. **Known for:** fantastic pastas; chocolate oblivion cake for dessert; Barolo and Barbaresco wine choices. [$] *Average main: $28* ✉ *3665 Sacramento St., Presidio Heights* ☎ *415/921-3200* 🌐 *sfsociale.com* 🕒 *Closed Sun. and Mon.*

★ Sorrel

$$$ | **MODERN AMERICAN** | After a long run as one of San Francisco's most important dining pop-ups, Alex Hong's refined seasonal Californian cooking can be found in one of San Francisco's most dramatic dining settings, with a skylight and floral arrangements that epitomize California "good life" architecture. That vibe is reflected in dishes like a springtime dry-aged duck with green garlic and kumquat, where Hong beautifully blends contemporary techniques and local ingredients. **Known for:** exemplary pastas;

beautifully composed tasting menu; upscale dinner party vibe. $ *Average main: $36* ✉ *3228 Sacramento St., Presidio Heights* ☎ *415/525–3765* 🌐 *www.sorrelrestaurant.com* ⏲ *Closed Mon. and Tues.*

★ SPQR

$$$ | ITALIAN | Open since 2007, Fillmore Street's modern Italian favorite continues to be a special destination for chef Matthew Accarrino's inventive seasonal cooking. You'll find tempting antipasti, superlative pastas like mustard capellini with guinea hen *ragù*, and a few hearty secondi; be sure to save stomach space for the fantastic desserts. **Known for:** chicken liver mousse antipasti; vintages from less-known Italian wine regions; fried chicken on Sundays. $ *Average main: $32* ✉ *1911 Fillmore St., near Bush St., Pacific Heights* ☎ *415/771–7779* 🌐 *www.spqrsf.com* ⏲ *No lunch weekdays.*

Spruce

$$$$ | MODERN AMERICAN | This elegant, grown-up restaurant caters to an older crowd who sink happily into its oversized faux-ostrich leather chairs. The food is equally refined, with ingredients often sourced from the restaurant's farm south of the city and charcuterie made in-house: celeriac velouté with brandied-chestnut mousseline and salmon with horseradish soubise reflect the contemporary Californian menu's elegant French leanings. **Known for:** a beloved burger on an English-muffin bun; giant chocolate chip cookies; well-heeled regulars sipping expensive Napa Valley and French wines. $ *Average main: $40* ✉ *3640 Sacramento St., Pacific Heights* ☎ *415/931–5100* 🌐 *www.sprucesf.com.*

🛏 Hotels

A chic neighborhood—albeit a trek from downtown and many attractions—Pacific Heights pleases celebs, honeymooners, and other travelers with tony B&Bs and boutique properties.

★ Hotel Drisco

$$$$ | HOTEL | You can pretend you're a denizen of one of San Francisco's wealthiest residential neighborhoods while you stay at this understated, elegant Edwardian hotel built in 1903. **Pros:** gorgeous rooms and public spaces; great service and many amenities; quiet residential neighborhood retreat. **Cons:** not a close walk to restaurants or major sights; room prices are as steep as nearby hill; no complimentary chauffeur service in the afternoon or evening. $ *Rooms from: $499* ✉ *2901 Pacific Ave., Pacific Heights* ☎ *415/346–2880, 800/634–7277* 🌐 *hoteldrisco.com* 🛏 *48 rooms* 🍴 *Breakfast.*

Hotel Majestic

$ | HOTEL | Open in 1902, the five-story Majestic is the city's oldest continually operating hotel; its elegant lobby is a graceful haven of antique chandeliers, plush Victorian chairs, antiquarian French books, and Edwardian architecture. **Pros:** nicely upgraded classic hotel; spacious rooms; rates are often a good value. **Cons:** bus ride or over-10-minute walk to activities and restaurants; old style won't appeal to all guests; website works erratically. $ *Rooms from: $130* ✉ *1500 Sutter St., Pacific Heights* ☎ *415/441–1100, 800/869–8966* 🌐 *www.thehotelmajestic.com* 🛏 *58 rooms* 🍴 *No meals.*

Laurel Inn

$ | HOTEL | FAMILY | The blue-and-tan facade of this small hotel, punctuated on two sides by garage entrances, hints at its 1963 motor-inn origins, yet the spacious rooms feel modern. **Pros:** stylish, good-size rooms; family- and pet-friendly rooms; excellent bar. **Cons:** no on-site restaurant; cheapest rooms are very small; additional fee for gym or spa. $ *Rooms from: $179* ✉ *444 Presidio Ave., Pacific Heights* ☎ *415/567–8467, 800/552–8735* 🌐 *www.jdvhotels.com/hotels/california/san-francisco-hotels/laurel-inn* 🛏 *49 rooms* 🍴 *Free Breakfast.*

Mansion on Sutter

$$$ | **B&B/INN** | San Francisco doesn't get much more old-school elegant than this Lower Pac Heights Victorian mansion transformed into a luxurious, intimate lodging with spacious, individually decorated rooms. **Pros:** luxury everywhere in the space; the rare San Francisco Victorian hotel that is pet-friendly; exceptionally comfortable beds. **Cons:** small gym; inconvenient location to downtown and marquee tourist sights; fitness center not on par with rest of hotel. [$] *Rooms from: $300* ✉ *1409 Sutter St., Lower Pacific Heights* ☎ *415/213-2746* 🌐 *www.mansiononsutter.com* 🛏 *12 rooms* 🍴 *Free Breakfast.*

Queen Anne Hotel

$ | **B&B/INN** | Built in the 1890s as a girls' finishing school, this Victorian mansion turned into a hotel is a taste of old San Francisco, with a large parlor and guest rooms that have classic touches, such as painted cherub murals and, in some, wood-burning fireplaces. **Pros:** lots of design character; library/salon will invite you to linger; old-time vibe that is hard to find in SF. **Cons:** substantial walk to downtown or main tourist areas; no restaurant or gym; some guests complain of stuffy, airless rooms. [$] *Rooms from: $179* ✉ *1590 Sutter St., Pacific Heights* ✣ *At Octavia St.* ☎ *415/441–2828* 🌐 *www.queenanne.com* 🛏 *48 rooms* 🍴 *Breakfast.*

Nightlife

The Snug

BARS/PUBS | A welcoming yet refined drinking destination, this Lower Pac Heights bar is exactly what the well-heeled and fun-loving neighborhood needed. It's the rare bar that emphasizes clever cocktails, in-high-demand local craft beer, and smartly selected wine in equal parts. Come hungry, as well, because elevated takes on bar bites like yellowtail poke and sesame naan with shiitake mushroom hummus are created by a chef formerly at some of the country's gastronomic heavyweights (Benu, Alinea). ✉ *2301 Fillmore St., Lower Pacific Heights* 🌐 *www.thesnugsf.com.*

Shopping

With grocery and hardware stores sitting alongside local clothing ateliers and international designer outposts, Pacific Heights' streets manage to mix small-town America with big-city glitz. After you've splurged on a cashmere sweater or a hand-blown glass vase, snag a seat at Blue Bottle or The Grove for coffee or a bite; it's the perfect way to pass an afternoon watching the parade of old money, new money, dogs, and strollers.

BOOKS

Browser Books

BOOKS/STATIONERY | **FAMILY** | Opened in 1976, one of the city's most beloved independent bookstores resides quietly among the chic fashion boutiques lining Fillmore Street. All ages will find ample choices for their next reading material, from contemporary fiction to children's books to a large selection of Buddhist Dharma literature. The store was recently sold to the small, local Green Apple Books group (with two other bookstores in the city), but barely anything has changed at the store with the transition. ✉ *2195 Fillmore St., Lower Pacific Heights* ☎ *415/567–8027* 🌐 *www.greenapplebooks.com.*

CLOTHING

Crossroads Trading Company

CLOTHING | These stores buy, sell, and trade men's and women's new and used clothing, some of it vintage. Previously owned designer items are the specialty at this location. ✉ *1901 Fillmore St., Pacific Heights* ✣ *at Bush St.* ☎ *415/775–8885* 🌐 *crossroadstrading.com.*

Dottie Doolittle

CLOTHING | FAMILY | Pacific Heights mothers shop here for charming silk dresses and other special-occasion outfits for their little ones. Less pricey togs for infants, boys to size 12, and girls to size 16 are also for sale. There are lots of fun toys, from stuffed animals to mini picnic sets, worth glancing at as well. ⊠ *3680 Sacramento St., at Spruce St., Pacific Heights* ☎ *415/563–3244* ⊕ *www.dottiedoolittle.com.*

HeidiSays

CLOTHING | Fanciful windows brimming with bright and festive prints draw passersby into this store. Perky salespeople help women choose between Missoni, Frame, and several other chic designers. ⊠ *2426 Fillmore St., between Washington and Jackson Sts., Pacific Heights* ☎ *415/749–0655* ⊕ *heidisays.com.*

★ Margaret O'Leary

CLOTHING | If you can only buy one piece of clothing in San Francisco, make it a hand-loomed cashmere sweater by this Irish-born local legend. The perfect antidote to the city's wind and fog, the sweaters are so beloved by San Franciscans that some of them never wear anything else. Pick up an airplane wrap for your trip home. ⊠ *2400 Fillmore St., Pacific Heights* ☎ *415/771–9982* ⊕ *www.margaretoleary.com.*

FOOD AND DRINK

D&M Wines and Liquors

WINE/SPIRITS | At first glance, this family-owned business appears to be just another neighborhood liquor store, but it's actually a rare and wonderful specialist. In a city obsessed with wine, these spirits devotees distinguish themselves by focusing on rare, small-production Armagnac and Calvados brandy, and Champagne. Be sure to look up from the bottles and admire the stained-glass lampshades, too. ⊠ *2200 Fillmore St., at Sacramento St., Pacific Heights* ☎ *415/346–1325* ⊕ *dandm.com.*

★ Verve Wine

WINE/SPIRITS | Wine nerds will fall in love with this trendy, upscale destination from one of the country's few master sommeliers, Dustin Wilson. Many wine drinkers will also recognize him from the popular 2012 documentary *Somm* (and its sequels). High-quality, smaller producers from prominent and lesser-known regions share wall space in this exceptionally organized boutique. ⊠ *2358 Fillmore St., between Washington St. and Jackson St., Lower Pacific Heights* ☎ *415/896–4935* ⊕ *vervewine. com.*

FURNITURE, HOUSEWARES, AND GIFTS

Nest

GIFTS/SOUVENIRS | A cross between a Parisian antiques show and a Jamaican flea market, this store could get even the most monochrome New Yorker excited about color. You can turn up the volume on your SF souvenirs with vintage artist journals, rare Oaxacan jewelry, hard-to-find Herb Caen books about his beloved San Francisco, and classic Paris and Barcelona map scarves. ⊠ *2300 Fillmore St., at Clay St., Pacific Heights* ☎ *415/292–6199* ⊕ *www.nestsf.com.*

Sue Fisher King Company

HOUSEHOLD ITEMS/FURNITURE | When Martha Stewart or the buyers at Williams Sonoma need inspiration, they come to see how Sue has set her sprawling table or dressed her stately bed. Her specialty is opulent linens for every room. And when Pacific Heights residents are looking for an impeccable hostess or bridal gift, they come by for a hand-embroidered velvet pillow or a piece of Amanda Moffat pottery. ⊠ *3067 Sacramento St., between Baker and Broderick Sts., Pacific Heights* ☎ *415/922–7276* ⊕ *www.suefisherking.com.*

JEWELRY AND COLLECTIBLES
Goldberry Jewelers

JEWELRY/ACCESSORIES | The former longtime girlfriend of Bob Dylan, Margie Rogerson opened this store to showcase her platinum-only designs. While she carries a large selection of engagement rings, her specialty is colored stones: rubies, sapphires, and emeralds. Their colors really sparkle against the background of this all-white and Lucite space. It's open by appointment only. ✉ *3516 Sacramento St., between Laurel and Locust Sts., Pacific Heights* ☎ *415/225-9336* ⊕ *goldberry.com.*

Japantown

Though still the spiritual center of San Francisco's Japanese American community, Japantown feels somewhat adrift. The Japan Center mall, for instance, comes across as rather sterile, and whereas Chinatown is densely populated and still largely Chinese, Japantown struggles to retain its unique character.

Also called Nihonmachi, Japantown is centered on the southern slope of Pacific Heights, north of Geary Boulevard, between Fillmore and Laguna Streets. The Japanese community in San Francisco started around 1860; after the 1906 earthquake and fire, many of these newcomers settled in the Western Addition. By the 1930s, they had opened shops, markets, meeting halls, and restaurants, and also established Shinto and Buddhist temples. But during World War II the area was virtually gutted when many of its residents, including second- and third-generation Americans, were forced into so-called relocation camps. During the 1960s and 1970s, redevelopment further eroded the neighborhood, and most Japanese Americans now live elsewhere in the city.

Still, when several key properties in the neighborhood were sold in 2007, a group rallied to "save Japantown," and some new blood finally infused the area with energy: Robert Redford's Sundance corporation revived the Kabuki Theatre (now owned by AMC); local, hip hotel group Joie de Vivre (now JdV by Hyatt) took over the Hotel Kabuki; and the J-Pop center, New People, brought Japanese pop culture and a long-missing youthful vibe. ■TIP➡ **Japantown is a relatively safe area, but the Western Addition, south of Geary Boulevard, can be dangerous even during the daytime. Also avoid going too far west of Fillmore Street on either side of Geary.**

Sights

★ Buchanan Mall

STORE/MALL | FAMILY | The shops lining this open-air mall are geared more toward locals—travel agencies, electronics shops—but there are some fun Japanese-goods stores here, too. Start your exploration with fabulous *mochi* (a soft, sweet Japanese rice confection) at **Benkyodo Company** (✉ *1747 Buchanan St.* ☎ *415/922–1244* ⊕ *www.benkyodocompany.com*), a local legend that has been in business since 1906 and still feels like a time warp. It's easy to spend hours among the fabulous origami and craft papers at **Paper Tree** (✉ *1743 Buchanan St.* ☎ *415/921–7100* ⊕ *paper-tree.com*). After shop browsing, have a seat on the steps around local artist Ruth Asawa's twin origami-style fountains, which sit in the middle of the mall. Wrap up a visit with lunch at **Hinodeya Ramen** (✉ *1737 Buchanan St.* ☎ *415/757–0552* ⊕ *hinodeyaramen.com*), serving lighter dashi (clear-broth) ramen, a rarity in the city. ✉ *Buchanan St. between Post and Sutter Sts., Japantown.*

Japan Center

STORE/MALL | **FAMILY** | Cool and curious trinkets, noodle houses and sushi joints, a destination bookstore, and a peek at Japanese culture high and low await at this 5-acre complex designed in 1968 by noted American architect Minoru Yamasaki. The Japan Center includes the shop- and restaurant-filled Kintetsu Mall and Kinokuniya Building; the excellent Kabuki Springs & Spa; the Hotel Kabuki; and the AMC Kabuki reserved-seating cinema/restaurant complex. ✉ *Bordered by Geary Blvd. and Fillmore, Post, and Laguna Sts., Japantown* 🌐 *www.japancentersf.com.*

★ Kabuki Springs & Spa

SPA—SIGHT | The serene spa is one Japantown destination that draws locals from all over town, from hipsters to grandmas, Japanese American or not. Balinese urns decorate the communal bath area of this house of tranquility. The extensive service menu includes facials, salt scrubs, and mud and seaweed wraps, in addition to massage. You can take your massage in a private room with a bath or in a curtained-off area.The communal baths ($30) contain hot and cold tubs, a large Japanese-style bath, a sauna, a steam room, and showers. Bang the gong for quiet if your fellow bathers are speaking too loudly. The clothing-optional baths are open for men only on Monday, Thursday, and Saturday; women bathe on Wednesday, Friday, and Sunday. Bathing suits are required on Tuesday, when the baths are coed. Men and women can reserve a private room daily. ✉ *1750 Geary Blvd., Japantown* ☎ *415/922–6000* 🌐 *kabukisprings.com.*

New People

STORE/MALL | The younger generation's counterpart to the Japan Center, this fresh shopping center combines a cinema, a tea parlor, and shops with a successful synergy. The downstairs New People Cinema shows classic and cutting-edge Asian (largely Japanese) films and is home to the yearly Japan Film Festival. Upstairs you can peruse Japanese pop-culture items and anime-inspired fashion, like handmade, split-toe shoes at SOU • SOU. The latest addition is an immersive, live-puzzle escape room. ✉ *1746 Post St., Japantown* 🌐 *www.newpeopleworld.com.*

🍴 Restaurants

The epicenter of Japantown, which covers about six city blocks, may well be the Japan Center mall, with several restaurants dishing out ramen, sushi, and *donburi* (rice bowl). There's also a glut of karaoke bars, sushi shops, and ramen restaurants along Buchanan Street's pedestrian way, between Post and Sutter.

Daeho

$$ | **KOREAN** | Japantown might be only a few blocks in size, but it's also home to a number of non-Japanese eateries, including this ever-popular specialist in *kalbijjim*, a Korean braised beef short rib soup. Each soup served in the industrial-feeling space, with serene images of mountains on the walls, is large enough to feed a small family and comes with a choice of toppings, like rice cakes or oozing melted cheese (the latter being an Instagram sensation). **Known for:** no reservations, so line can be long; foodie influencers capturing the experience; lively, fun atmosphere. [$] *Average main: $21* ✉ *1620 Post St., Japantown* ☎ *415/563–1388.*

Marufuku Ramen

$$ | **RAMEN** | Hakata-style *tonkotsu* (pork) and extra-intense chicken *paitan* ramen are the specialties of this modern-looking Japan Center restaurant that serves what many San Franciscans consider the city's finest bowl of ramen. As a result, long lines can be daunting, but luckily tables move pretty quickly inside the bustling yet relaxed space decorated wtih wood design elements and dangling Edison bulbs. **Known for:** no reservations, but there's an online wait list; gyoza (pan-fried dumplings) and pork buns to snack on; lively, contemporary vibe. $ *Average main: $18* ✉ *Kinokuniya Bldg., 1581 Webster St., #235, Japantown* ☎ *415/872–9786* ⊕ *www.marufukuramen.com* ☾ *Closed Mon.*

Sasa

$$ | **SUSHI** | Japantown has a host of sushi options at all price points, but this longtime staple on the second floor of the Japan Center stands out from the crowd for its excellent rolls, nigiri, and sashimi. The *omakase* (selections chosen by the chef) menu, with eight pieces of sushi and nigiri, is a fraction of the cost of its downtown peers, but close to equal in quality and diner satisfaction. **Known for:** "mystery box" mini chirashi (rice and raw fish) bowl; uni spoon with quail egg and ikura (cured salmon roe); an oasis in a busy mall. $ *Average main: $26* ✉ *Japan Center East Mall, 22 Peace Plaza, Suite 530, Japantown* ☎ *628/600–6945* ⊕ *sasasf.com.*

 ## Hotels

Though a slight trek from downtown, the bustling Japantown neighborhood pleases travelers who appreciate the neighborhood's cuisine or seek proximity to events at the historic Fillmore music venue.

Hotel Kabuki

$$ | **HOTEL** | Dating back to the 1960s but renovated in 2017, this beautiful Japantown retreat has serenely contemporary rooms, a lobby area with an outdoor garden, a terrific craft-cocktail bar, and a fun record-album wall decoration that is a nod to the neighborhood's music history. **Pros:** spacious rooms; excellent fitness center; terrific restaurant, bar, and virtuous "small farms" breakfast. **Cons:** nightly $30 "destination" fee; confusing in-room thermostat; rooms don't always block outside noise. $ *Rooms from: $249* ✉ *1625 Post St., at Laguna St., Japantown* ☎ *415/922–3200* ⊕ *www.jdvhotels.com* ⮑ *225 rooms* ⦿ *No meals.*

The Kimpton Buchanan Hotel

$$ | **HOTEL** | Local designer Nicole Hollis created a mildly opulent, apartmentlike ambience in the guest rooms and public areas of this boutique hotel. **Pros:** nicely sized, pet-friendly rooms; away from downtown bustle, yet still convenient; complimentary yoga mats in rooms, bicycles at front desk. **Cons:** too far from the action for some travelers; guests must join hotel rewards club to get free Wi-Fi; modern, minimalist room design might not appeal to all tastes. $ *Rooms from: $208* ✉ *1800 Sutter St., Japantown* ☎ *415/921–4000, 855/454–4644* ⊕ *www. thebuchananhotel.com* ⮑ *131 rooms* ⦿ *No meals.*

 # Shopping

Unlike shops in the ethnic enclaves of Chinatown, North Beach, and the Mission, the 5-acre Japan Center (bordered by Laguna, Fillmore, and Post Sts. and Geary Blvd.) is under one roof. The three-block complex includes a reasonably priced public garage and three shop-filled buildings. Especially worthwhile are the West Mall and the Kinokuniya Building, where shops sell things like bonsai trees, tapes and records, jewelry, antique kimonos, *tansu* (Japanese chests), electronics, and colorful glazed dinnerware and teapots.

BOOKS

Kinokuniya Bookstore

BOOKS/STATIONERY | **FAMILY** | The selection of English-language books about Japanese culture—everything from medieval history to origami instructions—is one of the finest in the country. Kinokuniya is also the city's biggest seller of Japanese-language books. Dozens of glossy Asian fashion magazines attract the young and trendy; the manga and anime books and magazines are wildly popular, too. ✉ *Kinokuniya Bldg., 1581 Webster St., at Geary Blvd., Japantown* ☎ *415/567–7625* ⊕ *usa.kinokuniya.com.*

FURNITURE, HOUSEWARES, AND GIFTS

Soko Hardware

HOUSEHOLD ITEMS/FURNITURE | Open since 1925, this shop specializes in beautifully crafted Japanese tools for gardening and woodworking. In addition to the usual hardware-store items, you can find seeds for Japanese plants and books about topics such as making shoji (paper screens). There are also lots of Japanese teapots and cookware vessels to browse. It's a great destination for a unique souvenir and a fun experience to see a truly historic San Francisco business. ⊠ *1698 Post St., at Buchanan St., Japantown* ☎ *415/931–5510* ⊕ *www.sokohardware.com.*

Western Addition

The Western Addition is traditionally one of the city's most diverse neighborhoods. It struggles in some areas with poverty and gang violence, yet the same neighborhood includes the trendy, dining-rich Divisadero corridor and Alamo Square Park with its iconic Painted Ladies. The Lower Fillmore area in its post–World War II heyday was known as the Harlem of the West for its profusion of jazz night spots, where such legends as Billie Holliday, Duke Ellington, and Charlie Parker would play. These days the neighborhood tries to maintain its historic African American cultural core and its link to that heritage with events like the beloved annual Fillmore Jazz Festival in June. More live music rings at The Fillmore, the auditorium made famous in the 1960s by Bill Graham and the iconic bands he booked there, and at the blues-centric Boom Boom Room.

Sights

★ Alamo Square Park

CITY PARK | FAMILY | Whether you've seen them on postcards or on the old TV show *Full House,* the colorful "Painted Ladies" Victorian houses are some of San Francisco's world-renowned icons. The signature view of these beauties with the downtown skyline in the background is from the east side of this hilly park. Tourists love the photo opportunities, but locals also adore the park's tennis courts, dog runs, and ample picnic area—with great views, of course. After taking plenty of photos, swing by the park's northwest corner and admire the William Westerfeld House (*1198 Fulton St.*), a splendid five-story late-19th-century Victorian mansion. ■ **TIP→ If it's a sunny day, grab picnic provisions from Bi-Rite Market** (*550 Divisadero St., at Hayes St.*). **On Fridays and weekends, the Lady Falcon Coffee Club truck is stationed in the park, offering a great caffeine pick-me-up.** ⊠ *Western Addition* ✛ *Bordered by Steiner, Hayes, Scott, and Fulton Sts.* ⊕ *sfrecpark.org.*

Cathedral of Saint Mary of the Assumption

RELIGIOUS SITE | Residing at the prominent intersection of two busy thoroughfares (Geary Boulevard and Gough Street), this striking cathedral stands out with its sweeping contemporary design. Italian architects Pietro Belluschi and Pier Luigi Nervi intended to create a spectacular cathedral that reflects both the Catholic faith and modern technology. It was controversial when it opened in 1971, yet now is applauded for its grand, curving roof that rises to a height of 190 feet, with sections that form a cross highlighted with intricate stained-glass work. The cathedral is open daily for visitors other than during Mass, and it usually has docents on duty in the late morning hours. ⊠ *1111 Gough St., at Geary St., Western Addition* ⊕ *smcsf.org.*

🍴 Restaurants

This area is a patchwork of culturally and economically diverse neighborhoods bordering the Lower Haight, the Fillmore District, and Japantown, and the neighborhood reflects that diversity with Italian, Japanese, and Indian restaurants housed in 1950s-era and Victorian buildings in the span of a couple of city blocks. Some of San Francisco's hottest tables, from morning to late night, can be found along the busy Fillmore and Divisadero commercial corridors.

Automat

$$ | MODERN AMERICAN | FAMILY | The newest marquee pop-up that has turned into a permanent restaurant is this casual establishment on a residential street tucked away from the activity of Divisadero. This all-day restaurant ties together a family-friendly focus with refined technique, featuring excellent sandwiches during the daytime, then the rare prix fixe, counter-service dinner menu. **Known for:** kids' menu for kids of all ages; casual fine-dining menu and vibe; superb house-baked breads. $ *Average main: $20* ✉ *1801 McAllister St., Western Addition* ✛ *at Baker St.* ⊕ *www.automatsf.com.*

Avery

$$$$ | MODERN AMERICAN | With a menu listing caviar bumps, a cheese course in buckwheat tartlet form, and dazzling razor clam *aebleskivers* (Danish beignets), the solo debut of wunderkind chef Rodney Wages is definitely not your average proper fine-dining destination. Then again, with its triple-digit price tags and liberal use of luxe ingredients, it very much fits right into the exclusive San Francisco lavish spectacle dining club. **Known for:** captivating tasting menu with Japanese influences; elegant minimalist decor; strong sake roster. $ *Average main: $189* ✉ *1552 Fillmore St., at Geary St., Western Addition* ☎ *415/817–1187* ⊕ *www.averysf. com* ⊙ *Closed Mon. and Tues.*

Che Fico

$$$ | MODERN ITALIAN | In a city full of Italian restaurants, this consistently popular Divisadero spot on the second floor of a revamped auto body shop sets itself apart with homemade charcuterie, plus antipasti, pastas, and pizza that often take traditional standbys for a creative spin or a California slant from local produce. The clever, beautifully

balanced cocktails and fun twists on homey desserts are both must-orders. **Known for:** pineapple pizza; loud space and hard-to-get reservations; Roman Jewish specialties. $ *Average main: $32* ✉ *838 Divisadero St., Western Addition* ☎ *415/416–6959* ⊕ *www.chefico.com* ⊙ *Closed Sun. and Mon. No lunch.*

4505 Burgers & BBQ

$$ | BARBECUE | FAMILY | The smoker works overtime from noon to night at this hipster-chic barbecue shack, churning out an array of succulent meats that can be had by the plate, the pound, or as a sandwich. Every plate comes with two sides, and you should certainly make the frankaroni one of them: possibly the work of the devil, this is macaroni-and-cheese with pieces of hot dog … deep fried. **Known for:** partially outdoor seating in shipping containers; decadent sides; self-named and possibly correct "Best Damn Cheeseburger". $ *Average main: $20* ✉ *705 Divisadero St., between Grove and Fulton Sts., Western Addition* ☎ *415/231–6993* ⊕ *www.4505burgersandbbq.com.*

Hina Yakitori

$$$$ | JAPANESE | San Franciscans are spoiled with an incredible abundance of cuisines and restaurants specializing in niche dishes—but yakitori (Japanese grilled meat skewers) remained elusive until the Ju-Ni team and chef Tommy Cleary (who previously owned a terrific yakitori restaurant in Oakland) opened this upscale *omakase* (chef's choice) destination near Alamo Square Park, focused on chicken yakitori. The *binchotan* (Japanese charcoal) grill adds the pivotal smoky touch to the skewers that hold all parts of the chicken and make up the heart of the tasting menu. **Known for:** intimate prix-fixe-only dining experience with counter seating; modern arts meet Japanese serene design space; refined, tiny composed dishes to round out the omakase. $ *Average main: $110* ✉ *808 Divisadero St., Western Addition* ☎ *415/817–1944* ⊕ *hinasf.com* ⊙ *Closed Sun. and Mon. No lunch.*

u-Ni

$$$$ | **SUSHI** | With just a dozen counter seats—its name means "12" in Japanese—this NoPa (North of the Panhandle) *omakase* sushi favorite is one of the hardest reservations to get in the entire city and certainly one of the Bay Area's most exquisite sushi experiences. Diners sit in pods of four at the sushi bar, with one sushi chef serving each quartet in the serene-meets-modern room. **Known for:** Wagyu and uni à la carte sushi that can be added to omakase experience; sake selection; high quality with high prices. $ *Average main: $169* ✉ *1335 Fulton St., Western Addition* ☎ *415/655–9924* ⊕ *junisf.com* ⊗ *Closed Mon. and Tues. No lunch.*

Merchant Roots

$$$$ | **CONTEMPORARY** | After starting as part grocer/part lunch café/part tasting menu, this tiny Fillmore spot is now fully devoted to the elaborate tasting menus of chef-owner Ryan Shelton. Themes and dishes change every few months (it could be "flowers" or "Alice in Wonderland"), but the one constant is Shelton's incredible imagination and ability to transform those themes into elaborate, technique-driven composed dishes. **Known for:** SF's best chocolate chip cookies available as a takeout supplement; warm and welcoming ambience; excellent wine program. $ *Average main: $128* ✉ *1365 Fillmore St., Western Addition* ☎ *530/574–7365* ⊕ *www.merchantroots. com* ⊗ *Closed Sun. and Mon. No lunch.*

★ Nopa

$$$ | **AMERICAN** | This is the good-food granddaddy of the hot corridor of the same name (it's hard to tell which came first—Nopa the restaurant or NoPa the North of the Panhandle neighborhood). The Cali-rustic fare here draws dependable crowds regardless of the night, with attractions including a beloved Moroccan vegetable tagine; crisp-skin rotisserie chicken; a juicy hamburger with thick-cut fries; and an outstanding weekend brunch. **Known for:** high-quality comforting food with smart twists; actually good food after 11 pm; a constant and diverse crowd. $ *Average main: $28* ✉ *560 Divisadero St., Western Addition* ☎ *415/864–8643* ⊕ *nopasf.com* ⊗ *No lunch weekdays.*

Nopalito

$$ | **MEXICAN** | **FAMILY** | Those in the mood for a fresh take on both common and seldom-seen Mexican dishes will adore Nopa's nearby little sibling. All the tortillas are made from organic house-ground masa (corn dough), and Mexico's peppers find their way into many of the spice-filled offerings. **Known for:** no reservations, so waits can be long; hearty bowl of pork shoulder–filled pozole rojo; any drink with tequila or mezcal. $ *Average main: $25* ✉ *306 Broderick St., Western Addition* ☎ *415/437–0303* ⊕ *www.nopalitosf.com* ⊗ *Closed Mon.*

The Progress

$$$ | **MODERN AMERICAN** | The second, grander restaurant from the chef-owners of State Bird Provisions is hardly just a little sibling: it features its own type of exciting, seasonally driven cooking, with no shortage of global influences. The lofty, bustling setting within an early-20th-century theater is a stunner of a backdrop, and some regulars love to sit at the small, cheery bar at the front and enjoy their dinner like an audience watching a grand dining-room stage. **Known for:** large BBQ duck platter; superb cocktails; top-notch desserts. $ *Average main: $32* ✉ *1525 Fillmore St., Western Addition* ☎ *415/673–1294* ⊕ *www.theprogress-sf. com* ⊗ *No lunch.*

Routier

$$$ | **BISTRO** | After opening quietly during the COVID-19 pandemic as takeout-only, this *très* charming establishment from an all-star chef trio has quickly become a favorite for classic bistro cooking with plenty of unique elements. A vintage Parisian dining room and marble-topped bar set the stage for fresh takes on

French cuisine with a Californian accent. **Known for:** potato pavé bites; standout cocktails; must-order baguette and desserts. $ *Average main: $28* ✉ *2801 California St., at Divisadero St., Lower Pacific Heights* ☎ *415/766–9997* ⊕ *routiersf.com* ☾ *No lunch.*

★ State Bird Provisions
$$ | **MODERN AMERICAN** | It's more or less impossible to score a reservation for a normal dinner hour at Lower Fillmore's game-changing restaurant, but once you nab a golden ticket, you'll be rewarded with fascinating bites served from roving carts and an à la carte printed menu. The food has an artsy bent to it, and the colorful dining room with pegboard walls adds to a vibe that's part high-school art room, part bohemian dinner party. **Known for:** "State Bird" namesake buttermilk fried quail; long lines at opening time for the no-reservation tables; "World Peace" peanut milk dessert drink. $ *Average main: $26* ✉ *1529 Fillmore St., Western Addition* ☎ *415/795–1272* ⊕ *www.statebirdsf.com* ☾ *No lunch.*

☕ Coffee and Quick Bites

★ The Mill
$ | **BAKERYBAKERY** | "Four-dollar toast" is a phrase used around San Francisco referring to gentrification—and it was inspired by this sun-drenched, Wi-Fi-less café. At this project between one of the city's leading bakers, Josey Baker (yes, that's really his last name and profession!), and the Mission's Four Barrel Coffee, toasts slathered with jam or spreads are the specialty during the day. **Known for:** stellar loaves of bread; precious, post-yoga vibe; one pizza topping served most nights. $ *Average main: $8* ✉ *736 Divisadero St., Western Addition* ☎ *415/345–1953* ⊕ *www.themillsf.com.*

🍸 Nightlife

BARS

Fool's Errand
BARS/PUBS | Excellent wine and top-tier craft beer tend to operate in different spheres when it comes to shops and bars. That isn't the case at this Divisadero bar/shop where some of the world's top boutique wine producers share the space with a rotating who's who of local brewing all-stars. The retail selections are limited but fantastic. If you're lingering with a glass or a pint in the low-ceilinged, cozy space or the Divisadero sidewalk seating, you'll be treated to a choice of hoppy IPAs and beautifully balanced sours on tap or excellent wines from near (maybe an Oakland urban winery) or far (perhaps a biodynamic producer in the Loire Valley). ✉ *639A Divisadero St., Western Addition* ⊕ *foolserrandsf.com.*

Horsefeather
BARS/PUBS | Creative, produce-driven cocktails and a chic, low-key vibe make this Divisadero drinking destination a locals' frequent top choice for a fun night out. The always interesting (but never too bizarre) cocktails range from a breezy California Cooler with celery juice to the rum-and-whiskey-based Breakfast Punch featuring clarified Cinnamon Toast Crunch–infused milk. Weekend brunch is excellent, as is the delightfully messy double cheeseburger. As an added bonus, the kitchen stays open late nightly. ✉ *528 Divisadero St., Western Addition* ☎ *415/817–1939* ⊕ *www.horsefeatherbar.com.*

Madrone Art Bar
BARS/PUBS | Part visual art gallery, part small performing arts space, part neighborhood bar, there's nothing quite like this evening anchor for the NoPa area. Film, music, dance, painting, and other art forms are on rotating display and add up to an always fun, relaxed nightly gathering spot. No two evenings feel the same, and it's a great place to

ember the alternative, free-spirited
aracter that San Francisco is known for
ut which is rapidly vanishing. At the bar,
beers and casual cocktails (specifically
various "mules") are the name of the
game. ⊠ *500 Divisadero St., Western
Addition* ☎ *415/241–0202* ⊕ *madroneart-
bar.com.*

MUSIC CLUBS
Boom Boom Room
MUSIC CLUBS | One of San Francisco's
liveliest music spots is this Fillmore
blues favorite, opened in 1997 by the
"King of the Boogie," John Lee Hooker.
The club has a fun blend of blues, funk,
and hip-hop shows most nights of the
week. ⊠ *1601 Fillmore St., at Geary
Blvd., Western Addition* ☎ *415/673–8000*
⊕ *boomboomroom.com.*

The Fillmore
MUSIC CLUBS | With performances by
everyone from the Counting Crows to
Jimi Hendrix, this legendary auditorium
dating back to 1912 has seen it all. It
remains one of San Francisco's essen-
tial concert destinations for a variety of
music styles. Check out the cool collection of rock posters upstairs before the
show and enjoy complimentary apples
after—a fun tradition for Fillmore concert-
goers. ⊠ *1805 Geary Blvd., at Fillmore
St., Western Addition* ☎ *415/346–6000*
⊕ *www.thefillmore.com.*

The Independent
MUSIC CLUBS | Looking for the next big
indie performer or hip-hop group? This
Divisadero favorite is probably the best
place to find them in the city. The eclectic, 500-person-capacity club/concert
venue opened in 2004 and has become a
key part of San Francisco's concert-going
culture. Headliner names like Zedd and
Foster the People performed their first
SF shows here, while marquee performers like Green Day and John Legend
have appeared on stage in recent years.
⊠ *628 Divisadero St., Western Addition*
☎ *415/771–1421* ⊕ *theindependentsf.
com.*

 Activities

SKATING
The Church of 8 Wheels
IN-LINE SKATING/ROLLER SKATING | Dance
or roll along to disco-era tunes at this
retro-themed skating rink inside an old
church. Friday and Saturday daytime is
open to anyone; after dark is adults only.
⊠ *554 Fillmore St. , at Fell St., Western
Addition* ☎ *415/752–1967* ⊕ *www.chur-
chof8wheels.com* ⊠ *$15, skate rental $5.*

Chapter 14

THE BAY AREA

Updated by
Monique Peterson

⊙ Sights
★★★★☆

🍴 Restaurants
★★★★☆

🛏 Hotels
★★☆☆☆

💼 Shopping
★★☆☆☆

🍸 Nightlife
★★★★☆

WELCOME TO THE BAY AREA

TOP REASONS TO GO

★ **Berkeley's culinary mecca:** Eat your way through this area of North Berkeley, starting with a slice of perfect pizza from Cheese Board Pizza (just look for the line).

★ **Point Reyes National Seashore:** Hike beautifully rugged—and often deserted—beaches at one of the most beautiful places on Earth.

★ **Sitting on a dock by the bay:** Admire the beauty of the Bay Area from the rocky, picturesque shores of Sausalito or Tiburon.

★ **"Beer-hopping" in Oakland's hippest hoods:** Spend time discovering the wealth of unique brewers and award-winning craft-beer makers along the Oakland Ale Trail in a city that takes its beer seriously.

★ **Giant redwoods:** Walking into Muir Woods National Monument, a mere 12 miles north of the Golden Gate Bridge, is like entering a cathedral built by God.

1 Berkeley. Independent bookstores, excellent coffee spots, and thousands of cyclists.

2 Oakland. A diverse, multifaceted city with a lively arts, nightlife, and food scene.

3 The Marin Headlands. Stretching from the Golden Gate Bridge to Muir Beach, these headlands offer spectacular vistas.

4 Sausalito. This Marin County city has stunning views and a bohemian feel.

5 Tiburon. Scenic and quaint, this town has good dining and hiking.

6 Mill Valley. A superb natural setting with a bustling downtown area. Nearby are the towering redwoods of Muir Woods National Monument and breathtaking panoramas of the entire Bay Area from Mt. Tamalpais State Park.

7 Muir Beach. The quiet beach here has a distinctly local feel.

8 Stinson Beach. An expansive stretch of beach and a town with a nonchalant surfer vibe.

9 Point Reyes National Seashore. A dramatic and rocky coastline with miles of sandy beaches.

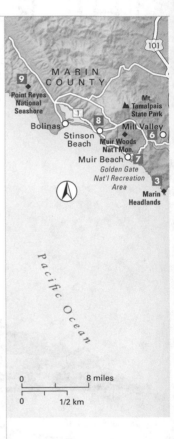

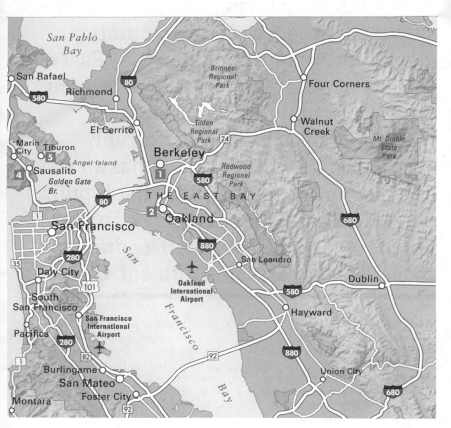

...are for a metropolis to compete ...th its suburbs for visitors, but the view from any of San Francisco's hilltops shows that the Bay Area's temptations extend far beyond the city limits. East of the city are the energetic urban centers of Berkeley and Oakland. Famously radical Berkeley is also comfortably sophisticated, while Oakland has an arts and restaurant scene so hip that it pulls San Franciscans across the bay. To the north is Marin County with its dramatic coastal beauty and chic, affluent villages.

MAJOR REGIONS

The East Bay. The college town of Berkeley has long been known for its liberal ethos, stimulating university community (and perhaps even more stimulating coffee shops), and activist streak. But these days, the lively restaurant and arts scenes are luring even those who wouldn't be caught dead in Birkenstocks. Meanwhile, life in the diverse, harbor-front city of Oakland is strongly defined by a turbulent history. Today, progressive Oakland is an incubator for artisans of all kinds, and the thriving culinary and creative scenes are taking off.

Marin County. Marin is considered the prettiest of the Bay Area counties, primarily because of its wealth of open space. Anchored by water on three sides, the county is mostly parkland, including long stretches of undeveloped coastline along the Marin Headlands, recognizable by the distinguished peak of Mt. Tamalpais. The coastal treasures of Muir Woods National Monument, "Mt. Tam," Stinson and Muir Beaches, and the entire Point Reyes National Seashore are among the country's greatest natural beauties. It's no wonder that the picturesque small towns here—Sausalito, Tiburon, Mill Valley, and Bolinas among them—may sometimes look rustic, but most are home to a dizzyingly high tax bracket.

Planning

When to Go

As with San Francisco, you can visit the rest of the Bay Area any time of year, and it's especially nice in late spring and fall. Unlike San Francisco, though, the surrounding areas are reliably sunny in summer—it gets hotter as you head inland. Even the rainy season has its charms, as otherwise golden hills turn a rich green and wildflowers become plentiful. Precipitation is usually the heaviest between November and March. Berkeley is a university town, so it's easier to navigate the streets and find parking near the university between semesters, but there's also less buzz around town then.

Getting Here and Around

Seamless travel from train to ferry to bus with one fare card is possible—and often preferable to driving on congested freeways and over toll bridges. For trips from one city to the next across the bay, take a tip from locals and save time and money with a Clipper card. They work with BART, Muni, buses, and ferries.
■TIP→ Order a Clipper card before you travel: ⊕ www.clippercard.com.

BART
Using public transportation to reach Berkeley or Oakland is ideal. The under- and aboveground BART (Bay Area Rapid Transit) trains make stops in both cities as well as other East Bay destinations. Trips to either take about a half hour one-way from the center of San Francisco. BART does not serve Marin County.
■TIP→ Check ahead for safety measures and service advisories.

CONTACTS BART. ☎ 510/465–2278 ⊕ www.bart.gov.

BOAT AND FERRY
For sheer romance, nothing beats the ferry; there's service from San Francisco to Sausalito, Tiburon, and Larkspur in Marin County, and to Alameda and Oakland in the East Bay.

The Golden Gate Ferry crosses the bay to Larkspur and Sausalito from San Francisco's Ferry Building (✉ Market St. and the Embarcadero). Blue & Gold Fleet ferries depart daily for Sausalito and Tiburon from Pier 41 at Fisherman's Wharf; weekday commuter ferries leave from the Ferry Building for Tiburon. The trip to either Sausalito or Tiburon takes from 25 minutes to an hour. Purchase tickets from terminal vending machines.

The Angel Island–Tiburon Ferry sails to the island daily from April through October and on weekends the rest of the year. Call ahead to book and to check schedules.

The San Francisco Bay Ferry runs several times daily between San Francisco's Ferry Building or Pier 41 and Oakland's Jack London Square, by way of Alameda. The trip lasts from 25 to 45 minutes and leads to Oakland's waterfront shopping and restaurant district. Purchase tickets on board.

CONTACTS Angel Island–Tiburon Ferry. ☎ 415/435–2131 ⊕ angelislandferry. com. **Blue & Gold Fleet.** ☎ 415/705–8200 ⊕ www.blueandgoldfleet.com. **Golden Gate Ferry.** ☎ 415/921–5858 ⊕ www. goldengate.org. **San Francisco Bay Ferry.** ☎ 707/643–3779, 877/643–3779 ⊕ sanfranciscobayferry.com.

BUS
Golden Gate Transit buses travel north to Sausalito, Tiburon, and elsewhere in Marin County from Perry and 3rd Streets and other points in San Francisco. For Mt. Tamalpais State Park and West Marin (Stinson Beach, Bolinas, and Point Reyes Station), take any route to Marin City and then transfer to the West Marin Stagecoach. San Francisco Muni buses

y serve the city. ■TIP→ Several
.ous options exist for local and region-
.avel throughout the Bay Area, including
.itrak, Greyhound, California Shuttle, and
.iore (www.bayareatransit.net/regional).

Though less speedy than BART, more
than 30 AC Transit bus lines provide service to and from San Francisco throughout the East Bay, even after BART shuts
down. The F and FS lines will get you to
Berkeley, while lines C, P, B, and O take
you to Oakland and Piedmont. Many
lines have been temporarily suspended
due to COVID-19, so check ahead. At this
writing, face masks are required.

CONTACTS AC Transit. ☎ 510/891–4777
⊕ www.actransit.org. Golden Gate Transit.
☎ 511 ⊕ www.goldengate.org. SamTrans.
☎ 800/660–4287 ⊕ www.samtrans.
com. San Francisco Muni. ☎ 311 ⊕ www.
sfmta.com. West Marin Stagecoach. ☎ 511
⊕ marintransit.org/stagecoach.

CAR

To reach the East Bay from San Francisco, take Interstate 80 East across the
San Francisco–Oakland Bay Bridge. For
U.C. Berkeley, merge onto Interstate 580
West and take Exit 11 for University Avenue. For Oakland, merge onto Interstate
580 East. To reach downtown Oakland,
take Interstate 980 West from Interstate
580 East and exit at 14th Street. Travel
time varies depending on traffic but
should take about 30 minutes (or more
than an hour if it's rush hour).

For all points in Marin, head north on U.S.
101 and cross the Golden Gate Bridge.
Sausalito, Tiburon, the Marin Headlands,
and Point Reyes National Seashore are
all accessed off U.S. 101. The scenic
coastal route, Highway 1, also called
Shoreline Highway (and briefly, Panoramic Highway) for certain stretches, can be
accessed off U.S. 101 as well. Follow this
road to Muir Woods, Mt. Tamalpais State
Park, Muir Beach, Stinson Beach, and
Bolinas. From Bolinas, you can continue
north on Highway 1 to Point Reyes.

Hotels

With a few exceptions, hotels in Berkeley
and Oakland tend to be standard-is-
sue, but many Marin hotels package
themselves as cozy retreats. Summer in
Marin is often booked well in advance,
despite weather that can be downright
chilly. Check for special packages during
this season.

*Restaurant prices are the average cost
of a main course at dinner or, if dinner is
not served, at lunch. Hotel prices are the
lowest cost of a standard double room
in high season. Restaurant reviews have
been shortened. For full information, visit
Fodors.com.*

WHAT IT COSTS			
$	$$	$$$	$$$$
RESTAURANTS			
under $17	$17–$26	$27–$36	over $36
HOTELS			
under $200	$200–$300	$301–$400	over $400

Restaurants

The Bay Area is home to many popular
and innovative restaurants, such as
Chez Panisse in Berkeley and Commis in
Oakland—for which reservations must
be made well in advance. There are also
many casual but equally tasty eateries to
test out; expect an emphasis on organic
seasonal produce, locally raised meats,
craft cocktails, and curated wine menus.
Marin's dining scene trends toward the
sleepy side, so be sure to check hours
ahead of time.

Tours

★ **Best Bay Area Tours**
SPECIAL-INTEREST | FAMILY | Morning and afternoon tours of Muir Woods and Sausalito include at least 90 minutes in the redwoods before heading on to Sausalito. On returning to the city, tours make a scenic stop in the Marin Headlands to enjoy fantastic views. Knowledgeable guides lead small tours in comfortable vans, and hotel pickup is included, though park entrance is not. Another tour option includes a visit to Muir Woods plus Wine Country exploration. ☎ *415/543–8687* ⊕ *bestbayareatours. com* ✉ *From $110.*

Berkeley

2 miles northeast of Bay Bridge.

Berkeley is the birthplace of the Free Speech Movement, the radical hub of the 1960s, the home of arguably the nation's top public university, and a frequent site of protests and political movements. The city of 103,000 is also a culturally diverse breeding ground for social trends, a bastion of the counterculture, and an important center for Bay Area writers, artists, and musicians. Berkeley residents, students, and faculty spend hours nursing coffee concoctions while they read, discuss, and debate at the dozens of cafés that surround campus. It's the quintessential university town, with numerous independent bookstores, countless casual eateries, myriad meetups, and thousands of cyclists.

Oakland may have the edge over Berkeley when it comes to ethnic diversity and cutting-edge arts, but unless you're accustomed to sipping hemp-milk lattes while taking in a spontaneous street performance prior to yoga, you'll likely find Berkeley charmingly offbeat.

GETTING HERE AND AROUNᴅ

BART is the easiest way to get to Berkeley from San Francisco. Exit at tʰ Downtown Berkeley Station, and walk a block up Center Street to get to the western edge of campus. AC Transit buses F and FS lines stop near the university and Fourth Street shopping. By car, take Interstate 80 East across the Bay Bridge, merge onto Interstate 580 West, and take the University Avenue exit through downtown Berkeley or take the Ashby Avenue exit and turn left on Telegraph Avenue. Once you arrive, explore on foot. Berkeley is very pedestrian-friendly.

TOURS

Edible Excursions
WALKING TOURS | For an unforgettable foodie experience in Berkeley, book a culinary walking tour, maybe one of North Berkeley. Come hungry for knowledge and noshing. Tours take place Thursday, Saturday, and Sunday. The company also offers tours of San Francisco and Oakland. ☎ *415/806–5970* ⊕ *www.edibleexcursions.net* ✉ *From $114.*

VISITOR INFORMATION

CONTACTS Koret Visitor Center. ✉ *2227 Piedmont Ave., at California Memorial Stadium, Downtown* ☎ *510/642–5215* ⊕ *visit.berkeley.edu.* **Visit Berkeley.** ✉ *2030 Addison St., Suite 102, Downtown* ☎ *510/549–7040, 800/847–4823* ⊕ *www.visitberkeley.com.*

 Sights

★ **BAMPFA (Berkeley Art Museum and Pacific Film Archive)**
MUSEUM | This combined art museum, repertory movie theater, and film archive, known for its extensive collection of some 28,000 works of art and 18,000 films and videos, is now also home to the world's largest collection of African American quilts, thanks to the bequest of art scholar Eli Leon. Artworks span five centuries and include modernist notables Mark Rothko, Jackson Pollock, David

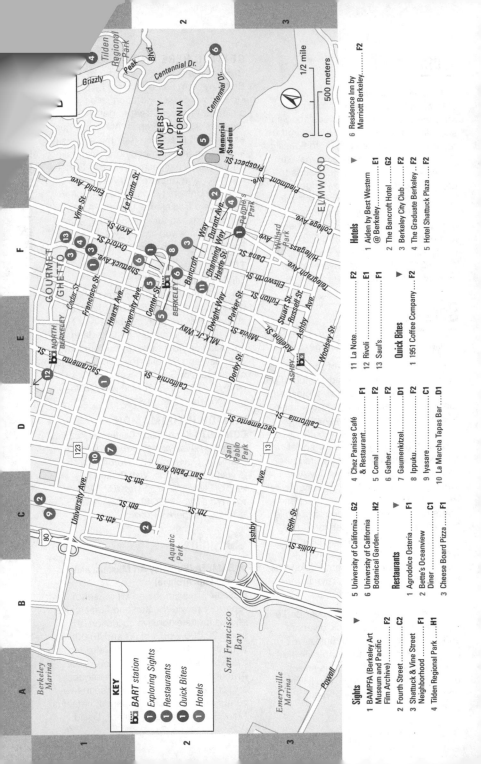

KEY

- BART station
- 1 Exploring Sights
- 1 Restaurants
- 1 Quick Bites
- 1 Hotels

Sights ▶

1 BAMPFA (Berkeley Art Museum and Pacific Film Archive) F2
2 Fourth Street C2
3 Shattuck & Vine Street Neighborhood F1
4 Tilden Regional Park H1
5 University of California ...G2
6 University of California Botanical Garden.......... H2

Restaurants ▶

1 Agrodolce Osteria F1
2 Betta's Oceanview Diner C1
3 Cheese Board Pizza F1
4 Chez Panisse Café & Restaurant.......... F1
5 Comal F2
6 Gather F2
7 Gaumenkitzel.......... D1
8 Ippuku.......... F2
9 Iyasare.......... C1
10 La Marcha Tapas Bar D1
11 La Note.......... F2
12 Rivoli E1
13 Saul's.......... F1

Quick Bites ▶

1 1951 Coffee Company F2

Hotels ▶

1 Aiden by Best Western @ Berkeley.......... E1
2 The Bancroft Hotel G2
3 Berkeley City Club F2
4 The Graduate Berkeley .. F2
5 Hotel Shattuck Plaza F2
6 Residence Inn by Marriott Berkeley.......... F2

Smith, and Hans Hofmann. The Pacific Film Archive includes the largest selection of Japanese films outside Japan and specializes in international films, offering regular screenings, programs, and performances. ✉ 2155 Center St., Downtown ☎ 510/642–0808 ⊕ bampfa.org 💲 $14; free 1st Thurs. of month ⊘ Closed Mon. and Tues.

Fourth Street

NEIGHBORHOOD | Once an industrial area, this walkable stretch of Fourth Street north of University Avenue has transformed into the busiest few blocks of refined shopping and eating in Berkeley. A perfect stop for lovers of design, curated taste experiences, artful living, and fashion, the vibrant district boasts more than 70 shops, specialty stores, cafés, and restaurants. See creation and find inspiration at Castle in the Air, Builders Booksource, and Stained Glass Garden, or sip a "live roast" at Artís, where you can watch small-batch coffee roasting in progress—one pound at a time. ✉ 4th St. between University Ave. and Virginia St., 4th Street ⊕ www.fourthstreet.com.

★ Shattuck & Vine Street Neighborhood

NEIGHBORHOOD | The success of Alice Waters's Chez Panisse defined California cuisine and attracted countless food-related enterprises to a stretch of Shattuck Avenue. Foodies will do well here poking around the shops, grabbing a quick bite, or indulging in a feast.

Tigerlily (✉ 1513 Shattuck) dishes up authentic modern Indian cuisine along with signature cocktails and light fare on the patio. Neighboring **Epicurious Garden** (✉ 1509–1513 Shattuck) food stands sell everything from sushi to gelato. A small terraced garden winds up to the **Imperial Tea Court,** a Zen-like teahouse rife with imports and teaware.

Across Vine Street, the **Vintage Berkeley** (✉ 2113 Vine) wine shop offers regular tastings and reasonably priced bottles within the walls of a historic former

pump house. Coffee lovers can head to the original **Peet's Coffee & Tea** at the corner of Walnut and Vine (2124 Vine).

South of Cedar Street, **The Local Butcher Shop** (✉ No. 1600) sells locally sourced meat and hearty sandwiches of the day. For high-end food at takeout prices, try the salads, sandwiches, and signature potato puffs at **Grégoire,** around the corner on Cedar Street (✉ No. 2109). **Masse's Pastries** (✉ No. 1469 Shattuck) is a museum of edible artwork. We could go on, but you get the idea. ✉ Shattuck Ave. between Delaware and Rose Sts., North Berkeley ⊕ www.northshattuckassociation.org.

★ Tilden Regional Park

NATIONAL/STATE PARK | FAMILY | Stunning bay views, a scaled-down steam train, and a botanic garden with the nation's most complete collection of California plant life are the hallmarks of this 2,077-acre park in the hills just east of the U.C. Berkeley campus. The garden's visitor center offers tours as well as information about Tilden's other attractions, including its picnic spots, Lake Anza swimming site, golf course, and hiking trails (the paved **Nimitz Way,** at Inspiration Point, is a popular hike with wonderful sunset views). ■TIP→ **Children love Tilden's interactive Little Farm and vintage carousel.** ✉ Tilden Regional Park, 2501 Grizzly Peak Blvd., Tilden Park ☎ 510/544–2747 park office ⊕ www.ebparks.org 💲 Free parking and botanic garden.

University of California

COLLEGE | Known simply as "Cal," the founding campus of California's university system is one of the leading intellectual centers in the United States and a major site for scientific research. Chartered in 1868, the university sits on 178 oak-covered acres split by Strawberry Creek; it's bounded by Bancroft Way to the south, Hearst Avenue to the north, Oxford Street to the west, and Gayley Road to the east. Campus highlights include bustling and historic **Sproul Plaza**

The University of California is the epicenter of Berkeley's energy and activism.

(✉ *Bancroft Way and Sather Rd.*), the seven floors and 61-bell carillon of **Sather Tower** (✉ *Campanile Esplanade*), the nearly 3 million artifacts in the **Phoebe A. Hearst Museum of Anthropology** (Kroeber Hall), hands-on **Lawrence Hall of Science** (✉ *1 Centennial Dr.*), the vibrant 34-acre **Botanical Gardens** (✉ *200 Centennial Dr.*), and the historic **Hearst Greek Theatre** (✉ *2001 Gayley Rd.*), the classic outdoor amphitheater designed by John Galen Howard. ✉ *Downtown* ☎ *510/642–6000* 🌐 *www.berkeley.edu.*

University of California Botanical Garden
GARDEN | **FAMILY** | Thanks to Berkeley's temperate climate, more than 10,000 types of plants from all corners of the world flourish in the 34-acre University of California Botanical Garden. Free garden tours are given regularly with paid admission. Benches and shady picnic tables make this a relaxing place for a snack with a breathtaking view. Call or go online before you travel to reserve your visit. ✉ *200 Centennial Dr., Downtown* ☎ *510/643–2755* 🌐 *www.botanicalgarden.berkeley.edu* 🎟 *$15* 🕒 *Closed 1st Tues. every month.*

🍴 Restaurants

Dining in Berkeley may be low-key when it comes to dress, but it's top-of-class in quality, even in less fancy spaces. Late diners beware: Berkeley is an "early to bed" kind of town.

Agrodolce Osteria
$$ | **ITALIAN** | **FAMILY** | Angelo D'Alo's family brings Sicilian flavors and their love for preparing them freshly to the heart of the Shattuck & Vine Street neighborhood, in a setting with black-and-white photos and Italian home decor that add to the old-world atmosphere. The menu features local, sustainable, and organic ingredients in such dishes as house-made orecchiette, seafood risotto, and free-range *pollo allo scarpariello*. **Known for:** oven-roasted heritage pork shoulder; spicy arrabiata; antipasti specialties. [$] *Average main: $22* ✉ *1730 Shattuck Ave., North Berkeley* ☎ *510/848–8748*

🌐 *www.agrodolceberkeley.com* 🕒 *Closed Tues. No lunch.*

Bette's Oceanview Diner

$ | DINER | FAMILY | Checkered floors, vintage burgundy booths, and an old-time jukebox set the scene at this retro-chic diner in the heart of Berkeley's fashionable Fourth Street shopping district. The wait for a seat at breakfast can be quite long; luckily Bette's To Go is always an option. **Known for:** soufflé pancakes; poached egg specialties; meat loaf and gravy. [$] *Average main: $13* ✉ *1807 4th St., near Delaware St., 4th Street* ☎ *510/644–3230* 🌐 *bettesdiner.com* 🕒 *No dinner.*

★ Cheese Board Pizza

$ | PIZZA | A jazz combo often entertains the line that usually snakes down the block outside Cheese Board Pizza; it's that good. The cooperatively owned vegetarian and vegan takeout spot and restaurant draws devoted customers with the smell of just-baked garlic on the pie of the day. **Known for:** cheese varieties; green sauce; live music. [$] *Average main: $12* ✉ *1504–1512 Shattuck Ave., at Vine St., North Berkeley* ☎ *510/549–3183* 🌐 *cheeseboardcollective.coop/pizza* 🕒 *Pizza closed Sun. and Mon., bakery closed Sun.*

★ Chez Panisse Café & Restaurant

$$$$ | MODERN AMERICAN | Alice Waters's legendary eatery, the birthplace of California cuisine, first opened its doors on August 28, 1971. It's still known for a passionate dedication to locally sourced heirloom varieties of fruits and vegetables, heritage breeds, and ethically farmed or foraged ingredients. **Known for:** sustainably sourced meats; attention to detail; simpler fare in upstairs café. [$] *Average main: $150* ✉ *1517 Shattuck Ave., at Vine St., North Berkeley* ☎ *510/548–5525 restaurant, 510/548–5049 café* 🌐 *www.chezpanisse.com* 🕒 *Closed Sun. No lunch in restaurant.*

★ Comal

$ | MODERN MEXICAN | Relaxed ye Comal's cavernous indoor dining s and intimate back patio and firepit a diverse, decidedly casual crowd for cr tive Oaxacan-inspired fare and well-craf ed cocktails. The modern Mexican menu centers on small dishes that lend themselves to sharing and are offered alongside more than 100 tequilas and mezcals. **Known for:** margaritas and mezcal; house-made chicharróns; wood-fired entrées. [$] *Average main: $16* ✉ *2020 Shattuck Ave., near University Ave., Downtown* ☎ *510/926–6300* 🌐 *www.comalberkeley.com* 🕒 *No lunch.*

Gather

$ | MODERN AMERICAN | All things local, organic, seasonal, and sustainable reside harmoniously under one roof at Gather. This haven for vegans, vegetarians, and carnivores alike serves up market and grain salads, shareable grilled local vegetables or cheese plates, roast chicken, and more in a vibrant, well-lit space that boasts funky light fixtures, shiny wood furnishings, and banquettes made of recycled leather belts. **Known for:** heirloom varietals; wood-fired pizzas; house-made liqueurs. [$] *Average main: $16* ✉ *2200 Oxford St., at Allston Way, Downtown* ☎ *510/809–0400* 🌐 *www.gatherberkeley.com.*

Gaumenkitzel

$$ | GERMAN | FAMILY | This award-winning, convivial locale for organic, slow-food German fare is also the spot for the Bay Area's best variety of German beers. With dishes like spätzle and caramelized onions, house-made *brezel* with bratwurst, *jägerschnitzel* with braised red cabbage, and panfried rainbow trout, this kitchen puts a fresh stamp on traditional German favorites. **Known for:** German wine and beer selection; house-made German breads; fresh, sustainable, zero-waste ingredients. [$] *Average main: $20* ✉ *2121 San Pablo Ave., Downtown* ☎ *510/647–5016* 🌐 *www.gaumenkitzel.net* 🕒 *Closed Mon.*

ESE | More Tokyo street n standard sushi house, this a—the Japanese equivalent of r with appetizers—is decked with mboo-screen booths. Servers pour an mpressive array of sakes and *shōchū* and serve up surprising fare. **Known for:** shōchū selection; charcoal-grilled yakitori skewers; selection of small dishes. $ *Average main: $18* ✉ *2130 Center St., Downtown* ☎ *510/665–1969* 🌐 *ippuku-berkeley.com* 🕒 *Closed Mon. No lunch.*

Iyasare

$$ | **JAPANESE** | Reservations are recommended at this Fourth Street hot spot where the outdoor seating is ideal for people-watching and the Japanese country food is uniquely prepared. Locals come back for seasonally changing, eclectic dishes made with a blend of local ingredients, such as burdock root tempura and tamari-kombu cured salmon or sake-steamed Asari clams with squid-ink pasta. **Known for:** Japanese whiskey and specialty sakes; donburi (rice-bowl dishes) and small plates; cured salads. $ *Average main: $20* ✉ *1830 4th St., 4th Street* ☎ *510/845–8100* 🌐 *iyasare-berkeley.com* 🕒 *Closed Sun. and Mon.*

La Marcha Tapas Bar

$$ | **SPANISH** | Delectable samplings of Spanish cuisine and a lively setting with expanded outdoor seating keep this tapas bar brimming with energy amid savory smells of seafood dishes and small plates of peel-and-eat prawns, wild boar meatballs, or goat cheese–stuffed *piquillos rellenos.* The bar's passion for Spanish cuisine and culture is evident in the wines, the Mediterranean flavors, and the cozy setting. **Known for:** paella varieties; happy hour specials; churros con chocolate. $ *Average main: $18* ✉ *2026 San Pablo Ave., Downtown* ☎ *510/647–9525* 🌐 *www.lamarchaberkeley.com.*

★ La Note

$$ | **FRENCH** | A charming taste of Provence in a 19th-century locale with stone floors, country tables, and a seasonal flowering patio, La Note serves rustic French food that is as thoughtfully prepared as the space is lovely. Enjoy breakfast and brunch outdoors with fresh, crusty breads and pastries, eggs Lucas with house-roasted tomatoes, and lemon gingerbread pancakes, or romantic dinners including mussels *mouclade,* ratatouille, and fondue. **Known for:** rustic sandwiches; house-made Merguez sausage; brioche pain perdu. $ *Average main: $20* ✉ *2377 Shattuck Ave., Downtown* ✥ *Between Channing Way and Durant Ave.* ☎ *510/843–1525* 🌐 *www.lanoterestaurant.com* 🕒 *No dinner Sun.–Wed.*

Rivoli

$$$ | **MODERN AMERICAN** | Italian-inspired dishes using fresh California ingredients star on a menu that changes regularly. Inventive offerings are served in a Zen-like modern dining room with captivating views of the lovely back garden. **Known for:** line-caught fish and sustainably sourced meats; curated wine list and specialty cocktails; thoughtfully combined ingredients. $ *Average main: $30* ✉ *1539 Solano Ave., at Neilson St., North Berkeley* ☎ *510/526–2542* 🌐 *www.rivolirestaurant.com* 🕒 *Closed Mon. and Tues. No lunch.*

★ Saul's

$ | **AMERICAN** | **FAMILY** | High ceilings and red-leather booths add to the friendly, retro atmosphere of Saul's deli, a Berkeley institution that is well known for its house-made celery tonic sodas and enormous sandwiches made with Acme bread. Locals swear by the pastrami Reubens, stuffed-cabbage rolls, and challah French toast. **Known for:** hand-rolled organic bagels; chicken schnitzel; corned beef brisket. $ *Average main: $14* ✉ *1475 Shattuck Ave., near Vine St., North Berkeley* ☎ *510/848–3354* 🌐 *www.saulsdeli.com.*

Famed Berkeley restaurant Chez Panisse focuses on seasonal local ingredients.

Coffee and Quick Bites

★ 1951 Coffee Company

$ | **CAFÉ** | Taking its name from the 1951 Refugee Convention at which the United Nations first set guidelines for refugee protections, 1951 Coffee Company is a nonprofit coffee shop inspired and powered by refugees. In addition to crafting high-caliber coffee drinks and dishing out local pastries and savory bites, the colorful café also serves as an inspiring advocacy space and barista training center for refugees. Just three blocks south of campus, this community hub is a favorite meetup spot for locals and students alike. **Known for:** hand-roasted blends; Third Culture Bakery mochi doughnuts and muffins; matcha lattes. [$] *Average main: $8* ✉ *2410 Channing Way, at Dana St., Downtown* ☎ *510/280–6171* 🌐 *www.1951coffee.com* 🕒 *No dinner.*

Hotels

For inexpensive lodging, investigate University Avenue, west of campus. The area can be noisy, congested, and somewhat dilapidated, but it does include a few decent motels and chain properties. All Berkeley lodgings are strictly mid-range.

Aiden by Best Western @ Berkeley

$ | **HOTEL** | One of Berkeley's newest hotels, the Aiden is the first of Best Western's boutique lines to open in California; within a mile of campus and the heart of downtown, it celebrates the culture of Berkeley with posters and wall art that showcase the campus life and spirit the town is known for. **Pros:** private parking; rooftop terrace with firepits and San Francisco Bay views; free bikes. **Cons:** no pets; no capacity for cribs or extra beds; congested area. [$] *Rooms from: $189* ✉ *1499 University Ave., Downtown* ☎ *800/528–1234 toll-free* 🌐 *www.bestwestern.com* 🛏 *39 rooms* 🍴 *No meals.*

…croft Hotel
…TEL | This eco-friendly boutique …—across from the U.C. campus—is …int, charming, and completely green. **…os:** closest hotel in Berkeley to U.C. campus; friendly staff; many rooms have good views. **Cons:** some rooms are quite small; despite renovation, the building shows its age with thin walls; no elevator. [$] *Rooms from: $230* ✉ *2680 Bancroft Way, Downtown* ☎ *510/549–1000, 800/549–1002* 🌐 *bancrofthotel.com* 🛏 *22 rooms* 🍴 *Breakfast.*

★ **Berkeley City Club**
$$ | **HOTEL** | Moorish design and Gothic architecture join with modern amenities at this historic locale steps from the campus, arts venues, and eateries. **Pros:** art gallery and courtyard seating; laundry facilities; on-site salon and skin care. **Cons:** no nonservice pets allowed; limited, fee-only parking; no televisions in rooms. [$] *Rooms from: $245* ✉ *2315 Durant Ave., Downtown* ☎ 🌐 *www.berkeleycityclub.com* 🛏 *38 rooms* 🍴 *Free Breakfast.*

The Graduate Berkeley
$ | **HOTEL** | Fresh, colorful design and Bohemian flair set the tone at this hotel in one of Berkeley's registered historic places, just steps from campus and downtown eating, shopping, and entertainment. **Pros:** convenient location; pet-friendly; complimentary bikes. **Cons:** rooms can be noisy; rooms can be small; fee parking only. [$] *Rooms from: $159* ✉ *2600 Durant Ave., Downtown* ☎ *510/845–8981* 🌐 *www.graduatehotels.com/berkeley* 🛏 *144 rooms* 🍴 *No meals.*

★ **Hotel Shattuck Plaza**
$ | **HOTEL** | This historic boutique hotel sits amid Berkeley's downtown arts district, just steps from the U.C. campus and a short walk from North Berkeley's best bites. **Pros:** central location near public transit; special date night and B&B packages; modern facilities. **Cons:** public and street parking only; limited on-site fitness center; street-facing rooms may be noisy. [$] *Rooms from: $173* ✉ *2086 Allston Way, at Shattuck Ave., Downtown* ☎ *510/845–7300* 🌐 *www.hotelshattuckplaza.com* 🛏 *199 rooms* 🍴 *No meals.*

Residence Inn by Marriott Berkeley
$$$ | **HOTEL** | **FAMILY** | One of Berkeley's newest hotels (planned opening is September 2021), in the heart of the city's arts and cultural district, this Residence Inn reflects the community's dedication to green living, as evident in its Gold LEED certification, use of recycled materials, organic design, and vibrant art that celebrates the city and campus life. **Pros:** views from bar and terrace on 12th floor; steps from campus, arts, fine dining, and sights; state-of-the-art technology. **Cons:** no swimming pool; no free parking; traffic gets very congested in the area. [$] *Rooms from: $301* ✉ *2121 Center St., Downtown* ☎ *510/982–2100* 🌐 *www.marriott.com* 🛏 *331 suites* 🍴 *Free Breakfast.*

🍸 Nightlife

★ **The Freight & Salvage Coffeehouse**
MUSIC CLUBS | Since 1968, the Freight has been a venue for some of the world's finest practitioners of folk, jazz, gospel, blues, world-beat, bluegrass, and storytelling. The nonprofit organization grew from an 87-seat coffee house to a thriving, 500-seat venue in the heart of Berkeley's Arts District. Many tickets cost less than $30. ✉ *2020 Addison St., between Shattuck Ave. and Milvia St., Downtown* ☎ *510/644–2020* 🌐 *thefreight.org.*

★ **Tupper & Reed**
BARS/PUBS | Housed in the former music shop of John C. Tupper and Lawrence Reed, this music-inspired cocktail haven presents a symphony of carefully crafted libations, which are mixed with live music performed by local musicians. The historic 1925 building features a balcony bar, cozy nooks, antique fixtures, a pool table, and romantic fireplaces. ✉ *2271 Shattuck Ave., at Kitteredge St., Downtown* ☎ *510/859–4472* 🌐 *www.tupperandreed.com.*

Performing Arts

More than a hundred arts and cultural organizations championing local artists, performers, and musicians contribute to Berkeley's happening scene, with downtown Berkeley at the epicenter. Many venues have small playhouses and performance spaces, allowing for great sightlines and intimate listening experiences.

Aurora Theatre Company

ARTS CENTERS | Known for critically acclaimed productions like David Mamet's *American Buffalo* and Toni Morrison's *The Bluest Eye*, the Aurora is at the heart of Berkeley storytelling and community engagement. The theater's Alafi Auditorium seats 150 on three sides of the stage for premium viewing, and the smaller Harry's UpStage offers a more intimate experience for 49. New play development and storytelling continue beyond the stage with collaborative audio dramas broadcast weekly. ⊠ *2081 Addison St., Downtown* ☎ *510/843–4822* ⊕ *www.auroratheatre.org.*

Berkeley Repertory Theatre

THEATER | One of the region's most highly respected and innovative repertory theaters, Berkeley Rep performs the work of classic and contemporary playwrights. Well-known pieces mix with world premieres and edgier fare, like steamy Afro-jazz musicals. The theater's complex, which includes the 400-seat Peet's Theatre and the 600-seat Roda Theatre, is in the heart of downtown Berkeley's arts district, near BART's Downtown Berkeley station. ⊠ *2025 Addison St., near Shattuck Ave., Downtown* ☎ *510/647–2949* ⊕ *www.berkeleyrep.org.*

★ California Jazz Conservatory

MUSIC | What started as a music education program in 1977, offering classes with the Bay Area's best jazz players, has become the area's top concert venue for the freshest sounds in jazz from around the world. Two 100-seat performance venues across the street from other, Hardymon Hall (*2087 Add.* and Rendon Hall (*2040 Addison S* intimate viewing of some of the wo most influential musicians. Classes ar workshops continue to serve as the foundation of the conservatory, with regular, affordably priced weekend concerts and weekly performances for the public. ⊠ *2087 Addison St., Downtown* ☎ *510/845–5373* ⊕ *cjc.edu.*

The UC Theatre Taube Family Music Hall

MUSIC | One of Berkeley's oldest theaters opened its doors in 1917 as a first-run movie house with seating for 1,466 filmgoers. For years it served as a famous venue for foreign and domestic classics, closing in 2001. The theater's programming and ongoing renovation are now run by the nonprofit Berkeley Music Group, dedicated to bringing local, national, and international talent to Berkeley's arts district. Limited outdoor drinks and dining are available at the street bar, Out Front at the UC. ⊠ *2036 University Ave., Downtown* ☎ *510/356–4000* ⊕ *theuctheatre. org.*

⬛ Shopping

★ ACCI Gallery

ART GALLERIES | The Arts & Crafts Cooperative, Inc., a collective of Berkeley artists and artisans, has been a stalwart gallery and retail store showcasing ceramics, textiles, paintings, photography, jewelry, and various media since 1959. Explore the amazing range of local talent in a well-lit historic space, and find truly one-of-a-kind gems to take home. ⊠ *1652 Shattuck Ave., North Berkeley ✛ At Lincoln St.* ☎ *510/843–2527* ⊕ *www. accigallery.com.*

★ Amoeba Music

MUSIC STORES | Heaven for audiophiles and movie collectors, this legendary Berkeley favorite is *the* place to head for new and used CDs, vinyl, cassettes, VHS tapes, Blu-ray discs, and DVDs.

e and ever-changing stock
thousands of titles for all music
as well as plenty of Amoeba
. There are branches in San
cisco and Hollywood, but this is the
ginal. ✉ *2455 Telegraph Ave., at Haste
St., Downtown* ☎ *510/549–1125* ⊕ *www.
amoeba.com.*

Hammerling Wines

WINE/SPIRITS | Offering a curated taste of
Central Coast sparkling wines, winemaker Josh Hammerling sources his grapes
from responsibly farmed vineyards with
distinctive fruit. Old-world techniques are
part of the practice for these wines made
entirely by hand. Drop in on weekends
for wines by the glass; it's first come,
first served. ✉ *1350 5th St., 4th Street*
☎ *510/984–0340* ⊕ *www.hammerling-
wines.co.*

★ Moe's Books

BOOKS/STATIONERY | The spirit of Moe—the
creative, cantankerous, cigar-smoking
late proprietor—lives on in this world-famous four-story house full of new and
used books. Since its doors first opened
in 1959, students and professors have
flocked here to browse the large selection, which includes literary and cultural
criticism, art titles, and literature in foreign languages. ✉ *2476 Telegraph Ave.,
near Haste St., Downtown* ☎ *510/849–
2087* ⊕ *www.moesbooks.com.*

Oakland

East of Bay Bridge.

In contrast to San Francisco's buzz and
beauty and Berkeley's storied counter culture, Oakland's allure lies in its amazing
diversity. Here you can find a Nigerian
clothing store, a Gothic revival skyscraper,
a Buddhist meditation center, and a lively
salsa club, all within the same block.

Oakland's multifaceted nature reflects
its colorful and tumultuous history. Once
a cluster of Mediterranean-style homes

and gardens that served as a bedroom
community for San Francisco, the town
had a major rail terminal and port by the
turn of the 20th century. Already a hub of
manufacturing, Oakland became a center
for shipbuilding and industry when the
United States entered World War II. New
jobs in the city's shipyards, railroads, and
factories attracted thousands of laborers
from across the country, including
sharecroppers from the Deep South,
Mexican Americans from the Southwest,
and some of the nation's first female
welders. Neighborhoods were imbued
with a proud but gritty spirit, along with
heightened racial tension. In the wake
of the civil rights movement, racial pride
gave rise to militant groups like the
Black Panther Party, but they were little
match for the economic hardships and
racial tensions that plagued Oakland.
In many neighborhoods the reality was
widespread poverty and gang violence—
subjects that dominated the songs of
such Oakland-bred rappers as the late
Tupac Shakur. The protests of the Occupy
Oakland movement in 2011 and 2012 and
the Black Lives Matter movement more
recently illustrate just how much Oakland
remains a mosaic of its past.

Oakland's affluent reside in the city's
hillside homes and wooded enclaves like
Claremont, Piedmont, and Montclair,
which provide a warmer, more spacious
alternative to San Francisco. A constant
flow of newcomers ensures continued
diversity, vitality, and growing pains.
Neighborhoods to the west and south of
the city center show signs of gentrification as the renovated downtown and
vibrant arts scene continue to inject new
life into the city. Even San Franciscans,
often loath to cross the Bay Bridge,
come to Uptown and Temescal for the
nightlife, arts, and restaurants.

Everyday life here revolves around the
neighborhood. In some areas, such as
Piedmont and Rockridge, you'd swear
you were in Berkeley or San Francisco's

Noe Valley. Along Telegraph Avenue just south of 51st Street, Temescal is littered with hipsters and pulsing with creative culinary and design energy. These are perfect places for browsing, eating, or relaxing between sightseeing trips to Oakland's architectural gems, rejuvenated waterfront, and numerous green spaces.

GETTING HERE AND AROUND

Driving from San Francisco, take Interstate 80 East across the Bay Bridge, then take Interstate 580 East to the Grand Avenue exit for Lake Merritt. To reach downtown and the waterfront, take Interstate 980 West from Interstate 580 East and exit at 12th Street; exit at 18th Street for Uptown. For Temescal, take Interstate 580 East to Highway 24 and exit at 51st Street.

By BART, use the Lake Merritt Station for the Oakland Museum and southern Lake Merritt; the Oakland City Center–12th Street Station for downtown, Chinatown, and Old Oakland; and the 19th Street Station for Uptown, the Paramount Theatre, and the north side of Lake Merritt.

By bus, take the AC Transit's C and P lines to get to Piedmont in Oakland. The O bus stops at the edge of Chinatown near downtown Oakland.

Oakland's Jack London Square is an easy hop on the ferry from San Francisco. Those without cars can take advantage of the free Broadway Shuttle, which runs from Jack London Square to Grand Avenue weekdays, with continued service to 27th Street weeknights from 7 to10 pm. There's no weekend service.

Be aware of how quickly neighborhoods can change. Walking is generally safe downtown and in the Piedmont and Rockridge areas, but be mindful when walking west and southeast of downtown, especially at night.

CONTACTS Broadway Shuttle. ⊕ *www. oaklandca.gov.*

VISITOR INFORMATION

CONTACTS Visit Oakland. ⊠ *481 Wa. St., near Broadway, Jack London Squ* ☎ *510/839–9000* ⊕ *www.visitoakland. com.*

Sights

★ Lake Merritt

NATURE PRESERVE | In the center of Oakland just east of downtown, this tidal lagoon with its unique habitat for more than 100 bird species became the country's first wildlife refuge in 1870. Today, the 3.1-mile path around the lake is also a free refuge for walkers, bikers, joggers, and nature lovers. **Lakeside Park** has **Children's Fairyland** (⊠ *699 Bellevue*) and the **Rotary Nature Center** (⊠ *600 Bellevue*), where monthly bird walks commence every fourth Wednesday. For views from the water, the **Lake Merritt Boating Center** (⊠ *568 Bellevue*) rents kayaks and rowboats (⊕ *www.lakemerritt.org*). Venetian gondolas cruise from the Oakland Boathouse (⊠ *basic tours start at $75 for 45 mins* ⊕ *gondolaservizio. com*), where visitors can also indulge in local artisanal chocolates.

On the lake's south side, the **Camron-Stanford House** (⊠ *1418 Lakeside Dr.*) is the last of the grand Victorians that once dominated the area; it's open Sundays for tours. Nearby, bold **Oakland mural art** offers a more modern feast for the eyes (⊠ *between Madison and Webster Sts. and 7th and 11th Sts.*).

The lake's necklace of lights adds allure for diners heading to the art-deco **Terrace Room** (⊠ *1800 Madison St.*) or **Lake Chalet** (⊠ *1520 Lakeside Dr.*), as well as to a host of tasty options along Grand Avenue, from Ethiopian cuisine at **Enssaro** (⊠ *357a*) and Korean BBQ at **Jong Ga House** (⊠ *372*) to comfort gourmet at **Grand Lake Kitchen** (⊠ *576*). ⊠ *Lake Merritt* ⊠ *Free.*

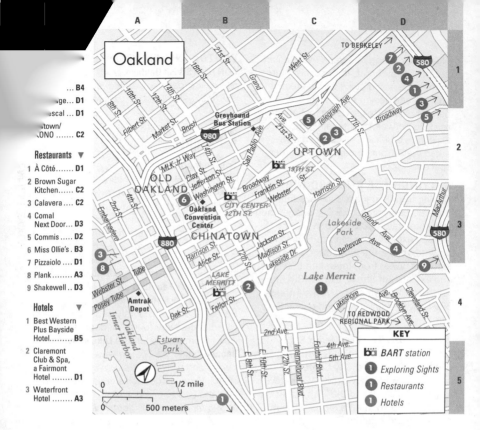

... **B4**

...ge... **D1**

...scal ... **D1**

...town/
...ONO **C2**

Restaurants ▼

1 À Côté....... **D1**

2 Brown Sugar
  Kitchen...... **C2**

3 Calavera **C2**

4 Comal
  Next Door... **D3**

5 Commis **D2**

6 Miss Ollie's . **B3**

7 Pizzaiolo **D1**

8 Plank........ **A3**

9 Shakewell .. **D3**

Hotels ▼

1 Best Western
  Plus Bayside
  Hotel......... **B5**

2 Claremont
  Club & Spa,
  a Fairmont
  Hotel **D1**

3 Waterfront
  Hotel **A3**

★ Oakland Museum of California (*OMCA*)
MUSEUM | FAMILY | Designed by Kevin
Roche, this museum is one of the
country's quintessential examples of
mid-century modern architecture and
home to a capacious collection of nearly
2 million objects in three distinct galleries
celebrating California's history, natural
sciences, and art. Listen to native species and environmental soundscapes in
the Library of Natural Sounds and engage
in stories of the state's past and future,
from Ohlone basket making to emerging
technologies and current events. Not
to be missed are the photographs from
Dorothea Lange's personal archive and
a worthy collection of Bay Area figura-
tive painters, including David Park and
Joan Brown. The museum is also home
to Oakland's freshest culinary destination—star chef Tanya Holland's Town
Fare café. Experience vegetable-centric
California soul food raised to an art form.
■ **TIP→ On Friday evening, the museum bus-
tles with live music, food trucks, and after-
hours gallery access.** ✉ *1000 Oak St., at
10th St., Downtown* ☎ *510/318-8400,
888/625-6873 toll-free* ⊕ *museumca.org*
✎ *$16, free 1st Sun. of month* ☉ *Closed
Mon.–Thurs.*

Rockridge
NEIGHBORHOOD | FAMILY | One of Oak-
land's most desirable places to live is
this fashionable, upscale neighborhood.
Explore the tree-lined streets that
radiate out from **College Avenue,** just
north and south of the Rockridge BART
station for a look at California Crafts-
man bungalows at their finest. By day,
College Avenue between Broadway and
Alcatraz Avenue is crowded with shoppers buying fresh flowers, used books,
and clothing; by night, the same folks

are back for handcrafted meals, artisanal wines, and locally brewed ales. With its specialty food shops and quick bites to go, **Market Hall,** an airy European-style marketplace at Shafter Avenue, is a hub of culinary activity. ✉ *Market Hall, 5655 College Ave., between Alcatraz Ave. and Broadway, Rockridge* 🌐 *www.rockridge-district.com.*

★ Temescal

NEIGHBORHOOD | Centering on Telegraph Avenue between 40th and 51st Streets, Temescal (the Aztec term for "sweat house") is a low-pretension, mon-eyed-hipster hood with young families and middle-aged folks thrown into the mix. Newly redesigned protected bike lanes, bus islands, and a pedestrian plaza add to the vibrancy of this neighborhood. A critical mass of excellent eateries draws diners from around the Bay Area; there are newer favorites like **Co Nam Noodle Bar** (✉ *3936 Telegraph Ave.*) and **Smokin Woods BBQ** (✉ *4307 Telegraph Ave.*), as well as standbys like **Pizzaiolo** (✉ *5008 Telegraph Ave.*) and **Rose's Taproom** (✉ *4930 Telegraph Ave.*). Old-time dive bars and smog-check stations share space with public art installations of murals, sculptures, and mosaic trash cans.

Temescal Alley (✉ *off 49th St.*), a tucked-away lane of tiny storefronts, crackles with the creative energy of local makers. Find botanical wonders at **Crimson Horticultural Rarities** (✉ *No. 470*) or get an old-fashioned straight-edge shave at **Temescal Alley Barbershop** (✉ *No. 470B*). Don't miss grabbing a sweet scoop at **Curbside Creamery** (✉ *No. 482*). ✉ *Temescal* ✣ *Telegraph Ave. between 40th and 51st Sts.* 🌐 *www.temescaldistrict.org.*

Uptown/KONO

NEIGHBORHOOD | Uptown and KONO (Koreatown/Northgate) is where nightlife and cutting-edge art merge. Dozens of galleries cluster around Telegraph Avenue and north of Grand Avenue into KONO, exhibiting everything from photography and installations to glasswork and fiber arts. The first Friday of each month, thousands of people descend for **Art Murmur** (🌐 *www.oaklandartmurmer.org*), a late-night gallery event that has expanded into **First Fridays** (🌐 *www.oaklandfirstfridays.org*), a festival of food trucks, street vendors, and live music along Telegraph Avenue.

Restaurants with a distinctly urban vibe make Uptown/KONO a dining destination every night of the week. Favorites include eclectic Japanese-inspired fare at **Hopscotch** (✉ *1915 San Pablo Ave.*), ramen and *izakaya* offerings at **Shinmai** (✉ *1825-3 San Pablo Ave.*), Oaxacan cuisine at **Agave Uptown** (✉ *2135 Franklin St.*), and soul food with a French-inspired twist at **Brown Sugar Kitchen** (✉ *2295 Broadway*), to name just a few.

Toss in the bevy of bars and there's plenty within walking distance to keep you busy all evening, such as **Drake's Dealership** (✉ *2325 Broadway*), with its spacious, hipster-friendly beer garden, and **Somar** (✉ *1727 Telegraph Ave.*), a bar, music lounge, and art gallery in one. ✉ *Uptown* ✣ *Telegraph Ave. and Broadway from 14th to 27th Sts.*

🍴 Restaurants

À Côté

$$ | **MEDITERRANEAN** | This Mediterranean hot spot is all about seasonal small plates, cozy tables, family-style eating, and excellent wine. Heavy wooden tables, intimate dining nooks, natural light, and a heated patio make this an ideal destination for couples, families, and the after-work crowd. **Known for:** Pernod mussels; Wed. and Thurs. happy hour specials; global and regional wine list. [$] *Average main: $23* ✉ *5478 College Ave., at Taft Ave., Rockridge* ☎ *510/655–6469* 🌐 *www.acoterestaurant.com* ⏲ *No lunch.*

★ Brown Sugar Kitchen

$$ | SOUTHERN | FAMILY | Distinguished chef Tanya Holland dishes up soul food flavored by her African American heritage and French culinary training. This bright, airy, modern Uptown venue is a beloved and bustling community-favorite dining spot, serving local, organic ingredients and sweet and savory dishes—from sweet potato pie to Creole meat loaf—paired with house cocktails and sumptuous wines. **Known for:** fried chicken and cornmeal waffles; bacon-cheddar-scallion biscuits; catfish and oyster po'boys. [$] *Average main: $17* ✉ *2295 Broadway, Uptown* ☎ *510/839–7685* 🌐 *www.brownsugarkitchen.com* 🕒 *Closed Mon. No dinner Tues. and Wed.*

Calavera

$$ | MODERN MEXICAN | FAMILY | This Oaxacan-inspired hot spot offers inventive and elevated plates in an industrial-chic space with lofty ceilings, warm wooden tables, exposed brick walls, and heated outdoor dining. Innovative cocktails like the salt-air margarita come from a beautiful bar with a library of more than 100 agaves. **Known for:** fresh ceviches with shrimp or mushrooms; family-style, wood-fired chicken and whole fish; carnitas tacos in nixtamal heirloom-corn tortillas. [$] *Average main: $22* ✉ *2337 Broadway, at 24th St., Uptown* ☎ *510/338–3273* 🌐 *calaveraoakland.com* 🕒 *Closed Mon.*

Comal Next Door

$ | MEXICAN | A sister restaurant to Berkeley's creative, Oaxacan-inspired Comal, this modern Mexican taqueria centers on mouthwatering, quick-service dishes with freshly grilled ingredients and house-made tortillas, sauces, and salsas. It's easy to see why the lines can be long, thanks to unique bottled mezcal libations and takeaway favorites like *cenas televisiónes*—frozen TV dinners of chicken enchiladas with mole or *rajas* (sliced poblano peppers) and zucchini tamales. **Known for:** burrito bowls and tortas; bottled cocktails and house-made frescas; buttermilk fried chicken and chipotle aioli. [$] *Average main: $11* ✉ *550 Grand Ave., Grand Lake* ☎ *510/422–6625* 🌐 *comalnextdoor.com.*

★ Commis

$$$$ | AMERICAN | A slender, unassuming storefront houses the first East Bay restaurant with a Michelin star (two of them, in fact). The room is minimalist and polished: nothing distracts from the artistry of chef James Syhabout, who creates a multicourse prix-fixe dining experience based on the season and his distinctive vision of modern and classic creations. **Known for:** inventive tasting menu; dizzying variety of wines from around the world; reservations needed well in advance. [$] *Average main: $73* ✉ *3859 Piedmont Ave., at Rio Vista Ave., Piedmont* ☎ *510/653–3902* 🌐 *commisrestaurant.com* 🕒 *Closed Sun. and Mon. No lunch.*

Miss Ollie's

$ | CARIBBEAN | FAMILY | Centrally located in the city's historic district, Miss Ollie's is a colorful, community-minded Afro-Caribbean gem in Swan's Market that packs in mouthwatering flavors. Lunch specialties include the likes of Bajan fried chicken or eggplant sandwiches and Creole salads with persimmon and jicama, while heartier dishes are jerk hen with coconut rice, spicy goat curry, and split-pea and okra fritters. **Known for:** skillet-fried chicken and collard greens; Caribbean meat and vegetable patties; pea and pumpkin soups. [$] *Average main: $16* ✉ *901 Washington St., Old Oakland* ☎ *510/285–6188* 🌐 *www.realmissolliesoakland.com* 🕒 *Closed Tues.*

Pizzaiolo

$$ | ITALIAN | FAMILY | Chez Panisse alum Charlie Hallowell helms the kitchen of this rustic-chic Oakland institution. Diners of all ages perch on wooden chairs with red-leather backs and nosh on farm-to-table Italian fare from a daily-changing menu. **Known for:** seasonal wood-fired pizza; daily house-made breads;

California-Italian entrées. $ *Average main: $21* ✉ *5008 Telegraph Ave., at 51st St., Temescal* ☎ *510/652–4888* ⊕ *www. pizzaiolooakland.com* ◷ *No lunch. Closed Mon. and Tues.*

Plank

$$ | AMERICAN | FAMILY | Food and entertainment come together in an expansive indoor-outdoor space with a waterfront view. Sip from more than 50 handcrafted local beers while playing boccie in the beer garden, lunch on Cuban sandwiches and Cajun mahi tacos during a bowling or billiards match, or try your hand at the arcade before biting into baby back ribs. **Known for:** fun outdoor space with firepits; generous portions; burgers and pizzas with local ingredients. $ *Average main: $17* ✉ *98 Broadway, Jack London Square* ☎ *510/817–0980* ⊕ *www. plankoakland.com.*

★ Shakewell

$$ | MEDITERRANEAN | Two *Top Chef* vets opened this stylish Lakeshore restaurant, which serves creative and memorable Mediterranean small plates in a lively setting that features an open kitchen, wood-fired oven, communal tables, and snug seating. As the name implies, well-crafted cocktails are shaken (or stirred) and poured with panache. **Known for:** wood-oven paella; Spanish and Mediterranean small plates; vegetarian options. $ *Average main: $20* ✉ *3407 Lakeshore Ave., near Mandana Blvd., Grand Lake* ☎ *510/251–0329* ⊕ *www. shakewelloakland.com* ◷ *Closed Mon.*

Hotels

Best Western Plus Bayside Hotel

$ | HOTEL | Sandwiched between the serene Oakland Estuary and an eight-lane freeway, this all-suites property has handsome accommodations with balconies or patios, many overlooking the water. **Pros:** attractive, budget-conscious choice; estuary walkways and views; easy access to and from airport, Jack London Square, and downtown. **Cons:** few shops or restaurants in walking distance; freeway-side rooms can be noisy; some rooms have no views or patios/balconies. $ *Rooms from: $189* ✉ *1717 Embarcadero, off I–880, at 16th St. exit, San Antonio* ☎ *510/356–2450* ⊕ *www. baysidehoteloakland.com* ⇄ *81 rooms* ⦿l *Free Breakfast.*

★ Claremont Club & Spa, a Fairmont Hotel

$$$ | HOTEL | FAMILY | Straddling the Oakland–Berkeley border, this amenities-rich property dating from 1915 beckons like a gleaming white castle in the hills. **Pros:** amazing spa and outdoor fitness pavilion; daily events and special programs for children; solid business amenities. **Cons:** parking is pricey; mandatory facilities charge; remote from shops and restaurants. $ *Rooms from: $339* ✉ *41 Tunnel Rd., at Ashby and Domingo Aves., Claremont* ☎ *510/843–3000, 800/257–7544 reservations* ⊕ *www. fairmont.com/claremont-berkeley* ⇄ *276 rooms* ⦿l *No meals.*

★ Waterfront Hotel

$$ | HOTEL | FAMILY | Thoroughly modern and pleasantly appointed, this JdV by Hyatt hotel sits among the many high-caliber restaurants of Jack London Square and is both a favorite place for locals' family members and a sweet spot for business travelers with its proximity to the square and downtown. **Pros:** outdoor dining in Jack London Square; lovely views, including some water views; free shuttle service to downtown and easy access to SF ferry. **Cons:** passing trains can be noisy on the city side; parking is pricey; limited amenities. $ *Rooms from: $200* ✉ *10 Washington St., Jack London Square* ☎ *510/836–3800 front desk, 888/842–5333 reservations* ⊕ *www.jdvhotels. com* ⇄ *145 rooms* ⦿l *No meals.*

ⓨ Nightlife

Back when rent was still relatively cheap, artists flocked to Oakland, giving rise to a cultural scene—visual arts, indie music, spoken word, film—that's still buzzing, especially in Uptown. Trendy new spaces pop up regularly, and the beer-garden renaissance is well established. Whether you're a self-proclaimed beer snob or just someone who enjoys a cold drink on a sunny day, there's something for everyone. (The Oakland Ale Trail is one way to start exploring craft beer offerings.) Nightlife in Oakland is less crowded and more intimate than what you'll find in San Francisco. Music is just about everywhere, though the most popular venues are downtown.

BARS

★ Heinold's First and Last Chance Saloon

BARS/PUBS | Arguably California's longest continuously active saloon since it opened in 1884, this watering hole, built from the hull of a flat-bottomed stern-wheeler, is the famous place where young Jack London got his start as a writer. Historic photos, artifacts, and turn-of-the-20th-century curios hang from the crooked walls and ceilings, which have been atilt since the 1906 earthquake. Get a peek at the slanted bar, where beers on tap and bottomless stories of Oakland history abound. If the proprietor is in, you'll be in for a treat: a trip through time into the Oakland of old is well worth a visit. ✉ 48 Webster St., Jack London Square ☎ 510/839–6761 ⊕ www.heinoldsfirstandlastchance.com.

Make Westing

BARS/PUBS | Named for a short story by Oakland native Jack London, this sprawling industrial-chic space is always abuzz with hipsters playing bocce, the postwork crowd sipping old-fashioneds, or pretheater couples passing Mason jars of unexpected delectables like Cajun shrimp boil. The patio's your best bet for a conversation on a busy evening. ✉ 1741 Telegraph Ave., at 18th St., Uptown ☎ 510/251–1400 ⊕ makewesting.com.

BREWPUBS AND BEER GARDENS

★ Brotzeit Lokal

BREWPUBS/BEER GARDENS | Wonderfully situated, this tucked-away German biergarten is in Oakland's Brooklyn Basin along the waterfront Bay Trail, with lovely views of the marina, estuary, and Coast Guard Island. Known for its select German beers and a delectable offering of Bavarian dishes, including house-made sausage, schnitzel, sauerkraut, and sandwiches, this family-friendly spot is especially popular on nice days. ✉ 1000 Embarcadero, at 10th Ave., Lake Merritt ☎ 510/ 645–1905 ⊕ brotzeitbiergarten.com.

Buck Wild Brewing

BREWPUBS/BEER GARDENS | Oakland's Jack London District is home to a luxurious taproom that is California's first 100%-gluten-free brewery, specializing in craft beers made without rye, wheat, or barley. The brewery has also partnered with San Francisco's Kitava, which provides a menu with fare (such as fish and chips, loaded fries, Cuban bowls, and small bites) completely free of inflammatory ingredients. ✉ 401 Jackson St., at 4th St., Jack London Square ☎ 510/350–7938 ⊕ www.buckwildbrew.com.

Federation Brewing Company

BREWPUBS/BEER GARDENS | Part of Oakland's Ale Trail, the brewery has a convivial tasting room in the Jack London District with plenty of games for extended sipping of their pilsners, saisons, sours, and hoppy IPAs. Wednesday happy hours and regular rotating comedy and music entertainment usually pack the place, so it's good to check ahead and reserve advance tickets. ✉ 420 3rd St., Jack London Square ☎ 510/496–4228 ⊕ www.federationbrewing.com.

Line 51 Brewing—The Terminal Taproom

BREWPUBS/BEER GARDENS | The bright, airy, 7,500-square-foot brewery and taproom is in many ways a tribute to its early history, when the brewers hauled their kegs on public transit line 51 to their warehouse. Now, Oakland Ale Trail explorers can enjoy freshly tapped beer from a vintage 1971 AC transit bus that serves as a refrigeration unit for their brews. Fermentation tanks are on full display; the owners are passionate about their Red Death ale, IPAs, Short Dog ale, and porters. ⊠ *303 Castro St., at 3rd St., Jack London Square* ☎ *510/985–4181* ⊕ *www. line51beer.com.*

Original Pattern Brewing

BREWPUBS/BEER GARDENS | The love for beer of all varieties is evident in the selection of award-winners at this employee-owned brewery in a brick warehouse space in the Jack London District. The list of IPAs, lagers, sours, fruit-infused beers, Belgian-style ales, and porters is ever changing as the latest brews are tapped. Food pop-ups from Good to Eat Dumplings make outdoor dining possible with dumplings, wontons, and noodles. ⊠ *292 4th St., Jack London Square* ☎ *510/844–4833* ⊕ *www. originalpatternbeer.com.*

★ The Trappist

BREWPUBS/BEER GARDENS | Brick walls, dark wood, soft lighting, and a hum of conversation set a warm and mellow tone inside this Old Oakland Victorian space that has been renovated to resemble a traditional Belgian pub. The setting (which includes two bars and a back patio) is a draw, but the real stars are the artisanal beers—more than 100 Belgian, Dutch, and North American brews. Experience guided tastings and curated offerings by passionate staff well versed in the styles of Trappist and European craft brewing. ⊠ *460 8th St., near Broadway, Old Oakland* ☎ *510/238–8900* ⊕ *www.thetrappist.com.*

CAFÉS

Mua

CAFES—NIGHTLIFE | Cuisine, cocktails, and culture—husband-and-wife-owned Mua puts it all together in an airy converted garage decked out with works by owner/ artist Hi-Suk Dong as well as pieces from his personal collection. The chefs serve up beautifully crafted dishes like blackened catfish and garlic prawns; the bartenders shake up elegant cocktails; and a lively crowd enjoys cultural offerings that include community sketch nights, art shows, and weekend DJ music. This is the perfect stop for any foodie who supports the arts. ⊠ *2442a Webster St., between 24th and 26th Sts., Uptown* ☎ *510/238–1100* ⊕ *muaoakland.com.*

ROCK, POP, HIP-HOP, FOLK, AND BLUES CLUBS

Fox Theater

MUSIC CLUBS | This renovated 1928 theater, Oakland's favorite performance venue, is a remarkable feat of Mediterranean Moorish architecture and has seen the likes of Willie Nelson, the Magnetic Fields, Rebelution, and B.B. King, to name a few. The venue boasts good sight lines, a state-of-the-art sound system, brilliant acoustics, and a restaurant and bar, among other amenities. ⊠ *1807 Telegraph Ave., between 18th and 19th Sts., Uptown* ☎ *510/302–2250* ⊕ *thefox-oakland.com.*

★ Yoshi's

MUSIC CLUBS | Opened in 1972 as a sushi bar, Yoshi's has evolved into one of the area's best jazz and live music venues. The full Yoshi's experience includes traditional Japanese and Asian fusion cuisine in the adjacent restaurant. ⊠ *510 Embarcadero W, between Washington and Clay Sts., Jack London Square* ☎ *510/238–9200* ⊕ *yoshis.com.*

Performing Arts

Paramount Theatre

ARTS CENTERS | A glorious art-deco specimen, the Paramount operates as a venue for concerts and performances of all kinds, from the Oakland Ballet and Oakland Symphony to Jerry Seinfeld and Elvis Costello. The popular classic movie nights start off with a 30-minute Wurlitzer concert. ■TIP➔ **Docent-led tours ($5), offered the first and third Saturday of the month, are fun and informative.** ⊠ *2025 Broadway, at 20th St., Uptown* ☎ *510/465–6400* ⊕ *paramounttheatre.com.*

🛍 Shopping

Pop-up shops and stylish, locally focused stores are scattered throughout the funky alleys of Old Oakland, Uptown, Rockridge, and Temescal, and the streets around Lake Merritt and Grand Lake offer more modest boutiques.

Bay-Made

GIFTS/SOUVENIRS | Owned and operated by women artists, this gift shop showcases the delightful works of more than 120 Oakland artisans and makers. Browse offerings such as handcrafted paper and print art, collage art, chocolate, waxworks, jewelry, ceramics, herbs and oils, and quality art and printing supplies. A rotating gallery wall features the latest works from local artists. ⊠ *3295 Lakeshore Ave., Grand Lake* ☎ *510/520–4600* ⊕ *www.bay-made.com.*

Maison d'Etre

GIFTS/SOUVENIRS | Close to the Rockridge BART station, this store epitomizes the Rockridge neighborhood's funky-chic shopping scene. Look for high-end housewares along with impulse buys like whimsical watches, imported fruit-tea blends, one-of-a-kind gifts, and funky slippers. ⊠ *5640 College Ave., at Keith Ave., Rockridge* ☎ *510/658–2801* ⊕ *www.maisondetre.com.*

★ **Oaklandish**

CLOTHING | The ultimate place for Oakland swag started in 2000 as a public art project of local pride and has become a celebrated brand around the bay, with clothing and accessories for men, women, and kids. A portion of the proceeds from hip Oaklandish-brand T-shirts and accessories supports grassroots nonprofits committed to bettering the local community. It's good-looking stuff for a good cause. ⊠ *1444 Broadway, near 15th St., Uptown* ☎ *510/251–9500* ⊕ *oaklandish.com.*

Activities

Oakland Athletics

BASEBALL/SOFTBALL | FAMILY | Baseball's Oakland Athletics, also called the Oakland A's, has a loyal following among locals in Oakland and enjoys a fierce rivalry with the San Francisco Giants just across the bay. The team hopes to move from its RingCentral Coliseum stadium to a proposed new waterfront ballpark at Jack London Square, perhaps in 2023, but Major League Baseball is also allowing the team to consider relocating to another city; stay tuned. ⊠ *RingCentral Coliseum, 7000 Coliseum Way* ☎ *877/493–2255 box office* ⊕ *mlb.com/athletics.*

The Marin Headlands

Due west of the Golden Gate Bridge's northern end.

The term "Golden Gate" has become synonymous with the world-famous bridge, but it was first given to the narrow waterway that connects the Pacific and San Francisco Bay. To the north of the Golden Gate Strait lie the Marin Headlands, part of the Golden Gate National Recreation Area (GGNRA), with some of the area's most dramatic scenery.

GETTING HERE AND AROUND

Driving from San Francisco, head north on U.S. 101. Just after you cross the Golden Gate Bridge, take Exit 442 for Alexander Avenue. Keep left at the fork and follow signs for San Francisco/U.S. 101 South. Go through the tunnel under the freeway, and turn right up the hill. On weekends and major holidays, Muni bus 76X runs hourly from Sutter and Sansome Streets in the city to the Marin Headlands Visitor Center.

Sights

Marin Headlands

NATIONAL/STATE PARK | FAMILY | The stunning headlands stretch from the Golden Gate Bridge to Muir Beach, drawing photographers who perch on the southern heights for spectacular shots of the city and bridge. Equally remarkable are the views north along the coast and out to the ocean, where the Farallon Islands are visible on clear days. Hawk Hill (accessed from Conzelman Rd.) has a trail with panoramic views and is a great place to watch the fall raptor migration; it's also home to the mission blue butterfly.

The headlands' strategic position at the mouth of San Francisco Bay made them a logical site for military installations from 1890 through the Cold War. Today you can explore the crumbling concrete batteries where naval guns once protected the area. Main attractions are centered on Forts Barry and Cronkhite, which are separated by Rodeo Lagoon and Rodeo Beach, a dark stretch of sand that attracts sandcastle builders and dog owners.

The visitor center is a worthwhile stop for its exhibits on the area's history and ecology, and kids enjoy the educational installations and small play area inside. You can pick up guides to historic sites and wildlife and get information about programming and guided walks. ⊠ *Golden Gate National Recreation Area,*
Visitor Center, Fort Barry Chapel, Fort Barry, Bldg. 948, Field and Bunker Rds., Sausalito ☎ *415/331–1540* ⊕ *www.nps. gov/goga* 🖾 *Free* 🕑 *Closed Tues.* .

Sausalito

2 miles north of Golden Gate Bridge.

Bougainvillea-covered hillsides and an expansive yacht harbor give Sausalito the feel of an Adriatic resort. The town sits on the northwestern edge of San Francisco Bay, where it's sheltered from the ocean by the Marin Headlands; the mostly mild weather here is perfect for strolling and outdoor dining. Nevertheless, morning fog and afternoon winds can roll over the hills without warning, funneling through the central part of Sausalito once known as Hurricane Gulch.

South of Bridgeway, which snakes between the bay and the hills, a waterside esplanade is lined with restaurants on piers that lure diners with good seafood and even better views. Stairs along the west side of Bridgeway and throughout town climb into wooded hillside neighborhoods filled with both rustic and opulent homes. Back on the northern portion of the shoreline, harbors shelter a community of more than 400 houseboats. As you amble along Bridgeway past shops and galleries, you'll notice the absence of basic services. Find them and more on Caledonia Street, which runs parallel to Bridgeway and inland a couple of blocks. While ferry-side shops flaunt kitschy souvenirs, smaller side streets and narrow alleyways offer eccentric jewelry and handmade crafts.

■ TIP➜ **The ferry is the best way to get to Sausalito from San Francisco; you get more romance (and less traffic) and disembark in the heart of downtown.**

First occupied by the Coast Miwok tribe and later visited by Spanish explorers who called the area Saucito (Little

Marin County

0   5 mi

0   5 km

Willow) for the trees growing along its streams, Sausalito was developed as a ranch in 1838 under the ownership of English mariner William Richardson. It served as a port for whaling ships during the 19th century and became a major terminus for transport by rail, ferry, and, eventually, car. By the mid-1800s, wealthy San Franciscans had made Sausalito their getaway across the bay and built lavish Victorian summer homes in the hills. Meanwhile, an influx of hardworking, fun-loving merchants and working-class folk populated the waterfront area, which grew thick with saloons, gambling dens, and bordellos. Bootleggers flourished during Prohibition, and shipyard workers swelled the town's population in the 1940s, at the height of World War II.

Sausalito developed its bohemian flair in the 1950s and '60s, when creative types, including artist Jean Varda, poet Shel Silverstein, and madam Sally Stanford, established an artists' colony and a houseboat community here (this is Otis Redding's "Dock of the Bay"). Both the spirit of the artists and the neighborhood of floating homes persist. For a close-up view of the quirky community, head north on Bridgeway, turn right on Gate Six Road, park where it dead-ends, and enter through the unlocked gates.

GETTING HERE AND AROUND

From San Francisco by car or bike, follow U.S. 101 North across the Golden Gate Bridge and take Exit 442 for Alexander Avenue, just past Vista Point; continue down the winding hill toward the water to where the road becomes Bridgeway. Golden Gate Transit buses will drop you off in downtown Sausalito, and the ferries dock downtown as well. The center of town is flat, with plenty of sidewalks and bay views. It's a pleasure and a must to explore on foot.

VISITOR INFORMATION

CONTACTS Sausalito Chamber of Commerce. ✉ *1913 Bridgeway* ☎ *415/331–7262* 🌐 *www.sausalito.org.*

Sights

The Marine Mammal Center

COLLEGE | FAMILY | This hospital for distressed, sick, and injured marine animals is a leading center for ocean conservancy in the Bay Area and the largest rehabilitation center of its kind in the world. Dedicated to pioneering education, rehabilitation, and research, the center is free and open daily to the public. Tour the facilities and see how elephant seals, sea lions, and pups are cared for and meet the scientists who care for them. Bonus: you'll catch some of the best views of the Marin Headlands and San Francisco Bay along the way. ■ **TIP→ Call ahead or check their website for tour availability.** ✉ *2000 Bunker Rd.* ☎ *415/289–7325* 🌐 *www.marinemammalcenter.org* 🎫 *Free.*

Sally Stanford Drinking Fountain

FOUNTAIN | There's an unusual historic landmark on the Sausalito Ferry Pier—a drinking fountain inscribed "Have a drink on Sally" in remembrance of Sally Stanford, the former San Francisco brothel madam who became Sausalito's mayor in the 1970s. Sassy Sally would have appreciated the fountain's eccentric attachment: a knee-level basin with the inscription "Have a drink on Leland," in memory of her beloved dog. ✉ *Sausalito Ferry Pier, Anchor St. at Humboldt St., off southwest corner of Gabrielson Park* 🌐 *www.oursausalito.com.*

Sausalito Ice House Museum and Visitor Center

INFO CENTER | The local historical society operates this dual educational exhibit and visitor center, where you can get your bearings, learn some history, and find out what's happening around town. The artifacts of indigenous Miwok peoples and photography of turn-of-the-20th-century Sausalito are worth a peek. ✉ *780 Bridgeway, at Bay St.* ☎ *415/332–0505* 🌐 *www.sausalitohistoricalsociety.com* ⏲ *Closed Mon.*

Viña del Mar Plaza and Park

PLAZA | The landmark Plaza Viña del Mar, named for Sausalito's sister city in Chile, marks the center of town. Adjacent to the parking lot and ferry pier, the plaza is flanked by two 14-foot-tall statues of elephants, which were created for the Panama–Pacific International Exposition world's fair held in San Francisco in 1915. A picture-perfect fountain here is great for people-watching. ✉ *Bridgeway and El Portal St.* 🌐 *www.oursausalito.com.*

Restaurants

Arawan Thai

$ | THAI | Tucked along the restaurant row of Caledonia Street for decades, Arawan Thai has been a stalwart destination for some of the tastiest Thai dishes in Marin County. The elegant and cozy interior lends an intimate quality to this hidden gem known for its generous variety of authentic soups, salads, and grilled specialties, along with shareable dishes, such as spicy angel wings (stuffed chicken wings) and prawn and cream cheese puffs. **Known for:** panang, red, and green coconut curries; papaya and mango salads; sizzling wok dishes. [$] *Average main: $14* ✉ *47 Caledonia St.* ☎ *415/729–9395* 🌐 *www.arawansausalito.com.*

Fast Food Français

$ | BISTRO | FAMILY | F3, as it's known, puts a French twist on classic American fast food and dishes up some French nibbles, too, in this casual bistro. The same folks who started Le Garage branch out here with quick bites like French onion burgers with cheddar fondue and double-cream mac-and-cheese, along with Brussels sprouts chips, deviled eggs, and ratatouille. **Known for:** fries and frites; spacious locale; excellent brunch spot. $ *Average main: $16* ✉ *39 Caledonia St.* ☎ *415/887–9047* ⊕ *www.eatf3.com.*

★ Fish

$$ | SEAFOOD | FAMILY | Unsurprisingly, fish—specifically, fresh, sustainably caught fish—is the focus at this gleaming dockside fish house a mile north of downtown. Order at the counter—cash only—and then grab a seat by the floor-to-ceiling windows or at a picnic table on the pier, overlooking the yachts and fishing boats. **Known for:** taco plate; barbecued oysters; fire-grilled entrées. $ *Average main: $23* ✉ *350 Harbor Dr., at Gate 5 Rd., off Bridgeway* ☎ *415/331–3474* ⊕ *www.331fish.com* ⊟ *No credit cards.*

The Joinery

$$ | AMERICAN | Sausalito's popular beer hall and rotisserie offers ample, open, airy indoor seating at long tables and expanded outdoor deck dining with exceptional views of the bay. It's a relaxing spot to enjoy burgers, sandwiches, soups, and salads along with a selection of Belgian beers, IPAs, lagers, and ciders on tap. **Known for:** fried chicken sandwich and grilled cheese; Joinery burger with special sauce; dirty fries and fried Brussels sprouts. $ *Average main: $18* ✉ *300 Tourney St.* ☎ *415/766–8999* ⊕ *www.joineryca.com.*

Le Garage

$$$ | FRENCH | Brittany-born Olivier Souvestre serves traditional French bistro fare in a relaxed, bayside setting that feels more sidewalk café than the converted garage that it is. The restaurant seats only 35 inside and 15 outside, so make reservations or arrive early. **Known for:** PEI mussels and house-cut fries; no-reservation weekend brunch; outstanding bouillabaisse. $ *Average main: $27* ✉ *85 Liberty Ship Way, Suite 109* ☎ *415/332–5625* ⊕ *www.legaragesausalito.com.*

Poggio

$$ | ITALIAN | A hillside dining destination, Poggio serves modern Tuscan-style comfort food in a handsome, old world–inspired space whose charm spills onto the sidewalks. An extensive and ever-changing menu, with ingredients sourced from the restaurant's garden and local farms, features house-made capellini, grilled fish, and wood-fired pizzas. **Known for:** traditional northern Italian dishes; rotisserie chicken with properly-grown organic herbs and vegetables; lobster-roe pasta. $ *Average main: $25* ✉ *777 Bridgeway, at Bay St.* ☎ *415/332–7771* ⊕ *www.poggiotrattoria.com.*

Sausalito Seahorse

$$ | ITALIAN | Live music and dancing complement Tuscan seafood and pasta specialties here and make the Seahorse one of Sausalito's most spirited supper clubs. Sample an abundant antipasti menu and homemade focaccia on outdoor patios or enjoy the band inside with traditional seafood stew or lasagna *classica*. **Known for:** happy hour; schiacciata (a type of Tuscan bread) panini; fun atmosphere. $ *Average main: $23* ✉ *305 Harbor Dr.* ☎ *415/331–2899* ⊕ *www.sausalitoseahorse.com.*

★ Sushi Ran

$$ | JAPANESE | Sushi aficionados swear that this tiny, stylish restaurant—in business since 1986—is the Bay Area's finest option for raw fish, but don't overlook the excellent Pacific Rim fusions, a melding of Japanese ingredients and French cooking techniques. Book in advance or expect a wait, which you can soften by sipping one of the bar's 30 by-the-glass

sakes. **Known for:** fish imported from Tokyo's famous Tsukiji market; local miso-glazed black cod; outstanding sake and wine list. $ *Average main: $25 ⊠ 107 Caledonia St., at Pine St. ☎ 415/332–3620 ⊕ sushiran.com ⊗ No lunch Mon.–Thurs.*

Taste of Rome

$$ | **ITALIAN** | **FAMILY** | From early-morning espresso and frittatas to late-night wine and marsalas, there's something just right at Taste of Rome any time of day. With spacious indoor and outdoor seating and a bountiful menu of fresh and homemade Italian specialties, it's easy to see why this family-owned café is beloved among locals. **Known for:** coffee drinks and desserts; locally sourced organic produce and sustainable seafood; house-made pasta. $ *Average main: $17 ⊠ 1000 Bridgeway ☎ 415/332–7660 ⊕ tasteofrome.co.*

⊖ Coffee and Quick Bites

★ Hamburgers Sausalito

$ | **BURGER** | Patrons queue up daily outside this tiny street-side shop for organic Angus beef patties that are made to order on a wheel-shaped grill. Brave the line (it moves fast) and take your food to the esplanade to enjoy fresh air and bayside views. **Known for:** legendary burgers; bay views; local following. $ *Average main: $9 ⊠ 737 Bridgeway, at Anchor St. ☎ 415/332–9471 ⊗ No dinner.*

Venice Gourmet Deli & Pizza

$ | **ITALIAN** | The traditional Italian deli sandwiches, pizzas made daily, and a shop filled with gourmet delectables, wines, kitchenware, and local flavor have enticed taste buds along picturesque Bridgeway since 1969. Enjoy a meal alfresco at the sidewalk tables, or take a picnic a few steps away to Yee Toch Chee Park for a waterside bite. **Known for:** picnic-perfect sandwiches; service and quality from family owners; plentiful selections. $ *Average main: $12 ⊠ 625 Bridgeway ☎ 415/332–3544 ⊕ www. venicegourmet.com.*

⊨ Hotels

The Inn Above Tide

$$$$ | **B&B/INN** | The balconies at the inn literally hang over the water, and each of its rooms has a "perfect 10" view that takes in wild Angel Island as well as the city lights across the bay. **Pros:** generous continental breakfast; free bikes to tour the area; in-room spa services available. **Cons:** costly daily parking; some rooms are on the small side; ferry-side rooms can be noisy. $ *Rooms from: $425 ⊠ 30 El Portal ☎ 415/332–9535, 800/893–8433 ⊕ www.innabovetide.com ⇄ 33 rooms ⊙I Free Breakfast.*

Tiburon

7 miles north of Sausalito, 11 miles north of Golden Gate Bridge.

On a peninsula that was named Punta de Tiburón (Shark Point) by 18th-century Spanish explorers, this beautiful Marin County community retains the feel of a village—it's more low-key than Sausalito—despite the encroachment of commercial establishments from the downtown area. The harbor faces Angel Island across Raccoon Strait, and San Francisco is directly south across the bay, making the views from the decks of harbor restaurants major attractions. Since 1884, when the San Francisco and North Pacific Railroad relocated their ferry terminal facilities to the harbor town, Tiburon has centered on the waterfront. The ferry is the most relaxing (and fastest) way to get here and allows you to skip traffic and parking problems.

One of the bay's best secrets in plain sight, Angel Island State Park (☎ 415/435–1915 ⊕ www.parks.ca.gov) offers 13 miles of roads and trails from the perimeter up to Mt. Livermore (788 feet), with magnificent panoramic views. The 12-minute ferry ride to Angel Island from Tiburon ($15 round-trip) includes the cost of park admission. ■ **TIP→ To see the sites by bike, rent on the island (www.angelisland.com/bike-rentals) or in Tiburon at Pedego Electric Bikes (10 Main St.).**

GETTING HERE AND AROUND

Blue & Gold Fleet ferries travel between San Francisco and Tiburon daily. By car, head north from San Francisco on U.S. 101 and get off at CA 131/Tiburon Boulevard/East Blithedale Avenue (Exit 447). Turn right onto Tiburon Boulevard and drive just over 4 miles to downtown. Golden Gate Transit serves downtown Tiburon from San Francisco; watch for changes during evening rush hour. Tiburon's Main Street is perfect for wandering, as are the footpaths that frame the water's edge.

VISITOR INFORMATION

CONTACTS destination: Tiburon. ✉ *Town Hall, 1505 Tiburon Blvd.* ☎ *415/435–2298* 🌐 *www.destinationtiburon.org.*

👁 Sights

Ark Row

NEIGHBORHOOD | The historic second block of Main Street is known as Ark Row and has a tree-shaded walk lined with antiques shops, restaurants, and specialty stores. The quaint stretch gets its name from the 19th-century ark houseboats that floated in Belvedere Cove before being beached and transformed into stores. ■ **TIP→ If you're curious about architectural history, the Tiburon Heritage & Arts Commission has a self-guided walking-tour map, available online and at local businesses.** ✉ *Ark Row, Main St., south of Juanita La.* 🌐 *www.townoftiburon.org.*

Old St. Hilary's Landmark and John Thomas Howell Wildflower Preserve

HISTORIC SITE | The architectural centerpiece of this attraction is a stark-white 1888 Carpenter Gothic church that overlooks the town and the bay from its hillside perch. Surrounding the church, which was dedicated as a historical monument in 1959, is a wildflower preserve that's spectacular in May and June, when the rare Tiburon paintbrush and Tiburon black jewel flower bloom. Expect a steep walk uphill to reach the preserve. The Landmarks Society will arrange guided tours by appointment. ■ **TIP→ The hiking trails behind the landmark wind up to a peak that has views of the entire Bay Area.** ✉ *201 Esperanza St., off Mar West St. or Beach Rd.* ☎ *415/435–1853* 🌐 *landmarkssociety.com* 🕒 *Church closed Mon.–Sat. and Nov.–Mar.*

Railroad & Ferry Depot Museum

MUSEUM | A short waterfront walk from the ferry landing, this free museum in Shoreline Park is a well-preserved time capsule of the city's industrial history, complete with working trains. The landmark building has a detailed scale model of Tiburon and its 43-acre rail yard at the turn of the 20th century, when the city served as a major railroad and ferry hub for San Francisco Bay. The Depot House Museum on the second floor showcases a restoration of the stationmaster's living quarters. ✉ *1920 Paradise Dr.* ☎ *415/435–1853* 🌐 *landmarkssociety.com* 🕒 *Closed Mon.–Sat. and Oct.–Apr.*

🍴 Restaurants

Caffè Acri

$ | CAFÉ | This Italian espresso bar and café at the end of the Tiburon Ferry dock is a sweet spot to enjoy a leisurely breakfast or lunch with a cup of locally roasted coffee while waiting for the ferry. In addition to daily-baked pastries and desserts, the menu ranges from omelets and toasted sandwiches to smoothies. **Known for:** farm-fresh salads; espresso drinks; soups and paninis. [$] *Average main: $10* ✉ *1 Main St.* ☎ *415/435–8515* 🌐 *www.caffeacri.com* 🕒 *No dinner.*

★ Luna Blu

$$ | **SICILIAN** | Friendly, informative staff serve Sicilian-inspired seafood in this lively Italian restaurant just a stone's throw from the ferry. Recent renovations have opened up 1,000 square feet of new patio and tripled the capacity of the original dining space. **Known for:** sustainably caught seafood and local, organic ingredients; homemade pastas; rock crab bisque. [$] *Average main: $20* ✉ *35 Main St.* ☎ *415/789–5844* 🌐 *lunablurestaurant.com* 🕒 *Closed Tues. No lunch weekdays.*

Salt & Pepper

$$ | **AMERICAN** | **FAMILY** | Bright and welcoming, this American bistro on Ark Row is known for its seafood starters (oyster poppers, crab stacks, scallops, and steamers) and salads as well as shareable dishes and burgers, chops, and ribs. The airy, rustic space has a pleasant café-like atmosphere that makes it easy to stay and even consider returning for a breakfast of Dungeness crab omelet or ricotta pancakes. **Known for:** clam chowder; kabocha squash and vegetable curry; Mongolian pork chops and rib-eye steaks. [$] *Average main: $24* ✉ *38 Main St.* ☎ *415/435–3594* 🌐 *www.saltandpeppertiburon.com.*

★ Sam's Anchor Cafe

$$ | **AMERICAN** | Open since 1920, this beloved dockside restaurant is the town's most famous eatery, and after 99 years, a bright remodel includes floor-to-ceiling sliding-glass doors and an 80-foot heated bench for deck views on cool days. Remnants of Sam's history are evident in some vintage decor, the hamburger and champagne specials, and the free popcorn. **Known for:** excellent raw bar; pink lemonade and margarita "bowls"; hurricane fries. [$] *Average main: $22* ✉ *27 Main St.* ☎ *415/435–4527* 🌐 *samscafe.com.*

Servino Ristorante

$$ | **SOUTHERN ITALIAN** | **FAMILY** | This family-owned eatery specializes in southern Italian recipes, including lobster agnolotti, seafood stew, pork sausage fondue, house-made pastas, and pizza made with local, sustainable ingredients. With spacious indoor and outdoor seating and waterfront views, the scene is cozy and welcoming even in cooler weather, when there's heated patio dining. **Known for:** alfresco waterfront dining; wines from Italy and California; black truffle raviolacci. [$] *Average main: $23* ✉ *9 Main St.* ☎ *415/435–2676* 🌐 *www.servino.com.*

☕ Coffee and Quick Bites

Waypoint Pizza

$ | **PIZZA** | **FAMILY** | A nautical theme and a tasty "between the sheets" pizza-style sandwich are signatures of this creative pizzeria, which is housed in the 19th-century landmark building that was once home to the Pioneer Boathouse and is now owned by two sailing aficionados. Booths are brightened with blue-checkered tablecloths, and a playful air is added by indoor deck chairs and a picnic table complete with umbrella. **Known for:** pizza-style sandwiches; wild shrimp pesto pizza; soft-serve organic ice cream. [$] *Average main: $15* ✉ *15 Main St.* ☎ *415/435–3440* 🌐 *www.waypointpizza.com.*

🛏 Hotels

Waters Edge Hotel

$$$ | **B&B/INN** | Checking into this stylish downtown hotel feels like tucking away into an inviting retreat by the water—the views are stunning, and the lighting is perfect. **Pros:** complimentary wine and cheese for guests every evening; restaurants and sights are steps away; free bike rentals for guests. **Cons:** downstairs rooms lack privacy and balconies; paid self-parking; 2-night minimum weekends,

3-night minimum holidays. [$] *Rooms from: $309* ✉ *25 Main St., off Tiburon Blvd.* ☎ *415/789–5999, 877/789–5999* 🌐 *www.marinhotels.com* 🛏 *23 rooms* 🍴 *Free Breakfast.*

Shopping

Local Spicery
FOOD/CANDY | This is the place for spices of all varieties from around the world, from adobo to za'atar. Where historic Ark Row curves uphill, the apothecary-like storefront features an aromatic library of assorted loose teas and spices milled in small quantities and prepared in small-batch hand blends to obtain maximum freshness and quality. Not sure where to begin? Ask about pairing flavors with your favorite ingredients and ways of cooking. ✉ *80 Main St.* ☎ *415/435–1100* 🌐 *www.localspicery.com.*

Schoenberg Guitars
MUSIC STORES | Small, narrow, and chockablock with handmade guitars alongside fine vintage classics, this shop is a treat even for those who don't play music. Dozens, if not hundreds, of guitars varying in size, shape, and color hang from the walls and stand against the polished wood floor. There is an organized beauty to the layout of this place and a comforting sense of musical harmony. You may even enjoy an impromptu concert or workshop. ✉ *Ark Row Shopping Center, 106 Main St.* ☎ *415/789–0846* 🌐 *www.om28.com.*

Tiburon Wine
WINE/SPIRITS | Some 200 regional and international wines as well as local Marin Rieslings and pinot noirs line the walls of this cozy shop, which has an indoor tasting room where you can sample more than two dozen. There's also an outdoor seating space for sipping by the glass or bottle. ✉ *84 Main St.* ☎ *415/435–3499* 🌐 *tiburonwine.net.*

Mill Valley

2 miles north of Sausalito, 4 miles north of Golden Gate Bridge.

Chic and woodsy Mill Valley has a dual personality. Here, as elsewhere in the county, the foundation is a superb natural setting. Virtually surrounded by parkland, the town lies at the base of Mt. Tamalpais and contains dense redwood groves traversed by countless creeks. But this is no lumber camp. Smart restaurants and chichi boutiques line streets that have been roamed by more rock stars than one might suspect.

The rustic village flavor isn't a modern conceit, but a holdover from the town's early days as a center for the lumber industry. In 1896, the Mt. Tamalpais Scenic Railroad—dubbed the "Crookedest Railroad in the World" because of its curvy tracks—began transporting visitors from Mill Valley to the top of Mt. Tam and down to Muir Woods, and the town soon became a vacation retreat for city slickers. The trains stopped running in the 1930s as cars became more popular, but the old railway depot still serves as the center of town: the 1929 building has been transformed into the popular Depot Café & Bookstore, at 87 Throckmorton Avenue.

The small downtown area has the constant bustle of a leisure community; even at noon on a Tuesday, people are out shopping for fancy cookware, eco-friendly home furnishings, and boutique clothing.

GETTING HERE AND AROUND

By car from San Francisco, head north on U.S. 101 and get off at CA 131/Tiburon Boulevard/East Blithedale Avenue (Exit 447). Turn left onto East Blithedale Avenue and continue west to Throckmorton Avenue; turn left to reach Depot Plaza, then park. Golden Gate Transit buses serve Mill Valley from San Francisco. Once here, explore the town on foot.

VISITOR INFORMATION

CONTACTS **Mill Valley Chamber of Commerce & Visitor Center.** ⊠ *85 Throckmorton Ave.* ☎ *415/388–9700* ⊕ *www.millvalley. org.*

◉ Sights

Lytton Square

PLAZA | FAMILY | Mill Valley locals congregate on weekends to socialize in the coffeehouses and cafés near the town's central square, but it's buzzing most of the day. The Mill Valley Depot Café & Bookstore at the hub of it all is the place to grab a coffee and sweet treat while reading or playing a game of chess. Shops, restaurants, and cultural venues line the nearby streets. ⊠ *Miller and Throckmorton Aves.*

★ Marin County Civic Center

BUILDING | A wonder of arches, circles, and skylights just 10 miles north of Mill Valley, the Civic Center was Frank Lloyd Wright's largest public project and has been designated a national and state historic landmark, as well as a UNESCO World Heritage Site. It's a performance venue and the locale for the fun and funky Marin County Fair. One-hour docent-led tours leave from the café on the second floor Wednesday and Friday morning at 10:30. ⊠ *3501 Civic Center Dr., off N. San Pedro Rd., San Rafael* ☎ *415/473–6400 Cultural Services department* ⊕ *www.marincounty.org* ⊠ *Free; tour $10* ⊗ *Closed weekends; no tours Mon., Tues., Thurs.*

★ Mill Valley Lumber Yard

HISTORIC SITE | FAMILY | The lumber yard, once a vital center of the region's logging industry, is now a vibrant micro-village of craftsfolk, bread bakers, textile makers, and lifestyle designers, and their boutiques and restaurants. You'll even find a chocolate art studio where custom-designed chocolates and truffles may look almost too good to eat. The preserved brick-red historic structures

are hard to miss along Miller Avenue, and with plenty of parking in the area, plus picnic tables and outdoor space, it's well worth a visit. ⊠ *129 Miller Ave.* ⊕ *www. millvalleylumberyard.com.*

★ Mt. Tamalpais State Park

NATIONAL/STATE PARK | FAMILY | The view of Mt. Tamalpais from all around the bay can be a beauty, but that's nothing compared to the views *from* the mountain, which take in San Francisco, the East Bay, the coast, and beyond. Although the summit of Mt. Tamalpais is only 2,571 feet high, the mountain rises practically from sea level, dominating the topography of Marin County. For years the 6,300-acre park has been a favorite destination for hikers, with more than 200 miles of trails. The park's major thoroughfare, Panoramic Highway, snakes its way up from U.S. 101 to the **Pantoll Ranger Station** and down to Stinson Beach. Parking is free along the roadside, but there's an $8 fee (cash or check only) at the ranger station and additional charges for walk-in campsites and group use.

The **Mountain Theater,** also known as the Cushing Memorial Amphitheatre, is a natural 3,750-seat amphitheater that has showcased summer "Mountain Plays" since 1913.

The **Rock Spring Trail** starts at the Mountain Theater and gently climbs for 1½ miles to the **West Point Inn,** where you can relax at picnic tables before forging ahead via Old Railroad Grade Fire Road and the Miller Trail to Mt. Tam's Middle Peak.

From the Pantoll Ranger Station, the precipitous **Steep Ravine Trail** brings you past stands of coastal redwoods. Hike the connecting **Dipsea Trail** to reach Stinson Beach. ■TIP➜ **If you're too weary to make the 3½-mile trek back up, Marin Transit Bus 61 takes you from Stinson Beach back to the ranger station.** ⊠ *Pantoll Ranger Station, 3801 Panoramic Hwy., at Pantoll Rd.* ✛ *on Mt. Tamalpais* ☎ *415/388–2070* ⊕ *www.parks.ca.gov.*

★ Muir Woods National Monument

NATIONAL/STATE PARK | **FAMILY** | One of the last old-growth stands of redwood (*Sequoia sempervirens*) giants, Muir Woods is nature's cathedral: awe-inspiring and not to be missed. The nearly 560 acres of Muir Woods National Monument contain some of the most majestic redwoods in the world—some more than 250 feet tall.

Part of the Golden Gate National Recreation Area, Muir Woods is a pedestrian's park. The popular 2-mile main trail begins at the park headquarters and provides easy access to streams, ferns, azaleas, and redwood groves. Summer weekends can prove busy, so consider taking a more challenging route, such as the **Dipsea Trail,** which climbs west from the forest floor to soothing views of the ocean and the Golden Gate Bridge. For a complete list of trails, check with rangers.

Picnicking and camping aren't allowed, and neither are pets. Crowds can be large, especially from May through October, so come early in the morning or late in the afternoon. The **Muir Woods Visitor Center** has books and exhibits about redwood trees and the woods' history as well as the latest info on trail conditions; the **Muir Woods Trading Company** serves hot food, organic pastries, and other tasty snacks, and the gift shop offers plenty of souvenirs. **■ TIP→ Muir Woods has no cell service or Wi-Fi, so plan directions and communication ahead of time.**

For parking reservations (required) and shuttle information, visit 🌐 *gomuirwoods.com.* To drive directly from San Francisco, take U.S. 101 North across the Golden Gate Bridge to Exit 445B for Mill Valley/Stinson Beach, then follow signs for Highway 1 North and Muir Woods. ✉ *1 Muir Woods Rd., off Panoramic Hwy.* ☎ *415/561–2850 park reservations,* 🌐 *www.nps.gov/muwo* 🎟 *$15.*

Old Mill Park

CITY PARK | **FAMILY** | To see one of the numerous outdoor oases that make Mill Valley so appealing, follow Throckmorton Avenue a quarter mile west from Lytton Square to Old Mill Park, a shady patch of redwoods that shelters a playground and reconstructed sawmill. The park also hosts September's annual Mill Valley Fall Arts Festival. From the park, Cascade Way winds its way past creek-side homes to the trailheads of several forest paths. ✉ *Throckmorton Ave. and Cascade Dr.* ☎ *415/383–1370 for rental information.* 🌐 *www.millvalleyrecreation.org.*

🍴 Restaurants

Boo Koo

$ | **ASIAN** | Southeast Asian street food with local flair is fired up in this hip and modern street café, where there's outdoor seating and a 10-tap bar. Summer rolls, satays, and skewers complement pho and wok specialties, and the locally sourced, vegan-based menu still has plenty for carnivores, who can customize dishes with grass-fed beef, wild salmon, and free-range chicken. **Known for:** green curry noodles; mint salad; Asian Brussels sprouts. [$] *Average main: $11* ✉ *25 Miller Ave.* ☎ *415/888–8303* 🌐 *eatbookoo.com.*

Buckeye Roadhouse

$$$ | **AMERICAN** | House-smoked meats and fish, grilled steaks, classic salads, and decadent desserts bring locals and visitors back again and again to this 1937 lodge-style roadhouse. Enjoy a Marin martini at the cozy mahogany bar or sip local wine beside the river-rock fireplace. **Known for:** oysters bingo; chili-lime "brick" chicken; ribs and chops. [$] *Average main: $29* ✉ *15 Shoreline Hwy., off U.S. 101* ☎ *415/331–2600* 🌐 *www.buckeyeroadhouse.com.*

Did You Know?

The gorgeous old-growth redwood trees in Muir Woods are often enveloped in fog, which provides the moisture to help them survive the dry summers.

Bungalow 44

$$ | **AMERICAN** | An open, well-lit space with booths and countertop seating from which diners can watch the cooks in action sets the scene at this lively eatery, which serves contemporary California cuisine and inventive cocktails. The menu focuses on locally sourced veggies and seafood. **Known for:** $1 oyster daily happy hour; fresh Marin Farmers' Market ingredients; kickin' fried chicken. $ *Average main: $24* ✉ *44 E. Blithedale Ave., at Sunnyside Ave.* ☎ *415/381–2500* ⊕ *www.bungalow44.com* ⊗ *No lunch.*

La Ginestra

$$ | **ITALIAN** | **FAMILY** | In business since 1964, La Ginestra—named for the flowers that grow on Mt. Vesuvius, in the owners' homeland—is a Mill Valley institution renowned for its no-pretense, family-style Italian meals and impressive wine list. The Sorrento Bar, off the dining room, serves up a delectable array of bar bites, pizzas, and sweets to enjoy while sipping wines and cocktails inspired by the Aversa family's home country. **Known for:** handmade pasta and gnocchi; excellent ravioli; daily fish and small plates. $ *Average main: $20* ✉ *127 Throckmorton Ave., off Miller Ave.* ☎ *415/388–0224* ⊕ *www.laginestramv.com* ⊗ *Closed Mon. and Tues. No lunch.*

Piazza D'Angelo

$$ | **ITALIAN** | **FAMILY** | In the heart of downtown, busy D'Angelo's is known for its authentic and fresh pastas; there are even gluten-free options. Another draw is the scene, especially in the lounge area, which hosts a lively cocktail hour in a traditional trattoria setting. **Known for:** fresh seafood; homemade pasta; top-notch tiramisu. $ *Average main: $22* ✉ *22 Miller Ave., off Throckmorton* ☎ *415/388–2000* ⊕ *www.piazzadangelo.com.*

Playa

$$ | **MODERN MEXICAN** | Modern Mexican farm-to-table creations and inspired cocktails are the focus of this festive indoor-outdoor space that's popular for its firepit, made-to-order masa station, and happy hour. An open kitchen serves up locally sourced, organic, and sustainable dishes like ceviche and flautas, grilled octopus tacos, and braised pork tortas. **Known for:** taco Tuesdays; rare tequilas and mezcals; moles and salsas. $ *Average main: $18* ✉ *41 Throckmorton Ave.* ☎ *415/384–8871* ⊕ *www.playamv.com.*

Vasco

$ | **ITALIAN** | With its wood-fired pizza oven, wine bar, and live music in the evening, this lovely corner restaurant has serious neighborhood charm. Authentic Italian specialties include chicken marsala, seafood stew, and calamari steak. **Known for:** great atmosphere; gluten-free pizza and pasta; memorable tiramisu. $ *Average main: $16* ✉ *106 Throckmorton Ave.* ☎ *415/381–3343* ⊕ *vascorestaurantmillvalley.com* ⊗ *No lunch.*

☕ Coffee and Quick Bites

Avatar's Restaurant

$ | **INDIAN** | The lines can get long at this hole-in-the-wall, no-frills kitchen, where Indian curries are served burrito style while you wait (note: it's cash only). Punjabi burritos or rice plates come with savory lamb, chicken, fish, vegetarian, and vegan ingredients flavored with seasonal fruit chutneys, tamarind sauce, and aromatic blends. **Known for:** curried pumpkin; smoked eggplant; mostly take-out dining. $ *Average main: $8* ✉ *15 Madrona St.* ☎ *415/381–8293* ⊗ *Closed Sun.* ⊟ *No credit cards.*

Equator Coffees

$ | **CAFÉ** | This is the prime spot for a pick-me-up (and people-watching) over a picturesque view of downtown Mill Valley and Mt. Tam. The owners are as serious about coffee as they are about social responsibility, from their fair-chain single-origin beans and organic loose teas down to the locally recycled wood and metal decor. **Known for:** espresso and cappuccino drinks; breakfast sandwiches;

strawberry and chocolate waffles. $ *Average main: $9* ✉ *2 Miller Ave.* ☎ *415/383–1651* ⊕ *www.equatorcoffees. com* ⊙ *No dinner.*

Hotels

Acqua Hotel
$$ | HOTEL | Alongside Richardson Bay, this stylish boutique hotel has modern, elegant rooms decorated in soft Zen-like color schemes. **Pros:** evening wine service; free parking and Wi-Fi; hearty breakfast buffet. **Cons:** next to freeway; traffic audible in rooms facing east; limited amenities within walking distance. $ *Rooms from: $259* ✉ *555 Redwood Hwy., off U.S. 101* ☎ *415/388–9353* ⊕ *www.marinhotels.com* ⊐ *49 rooms* ⦾ *Free Breakfast.*

Mill Valley Inn
$$$ | B&B/INN | The only hotel in downtown Mill Valley is comprised of one of the area's first homes, the Creek House, which has smart-looking Victorian rooms, and two small cottages nestled in a grove beyond a creek. **Pros:** unique rooms in private yet central location; some rooms have balconies, soaking tubs, and fireplaces; free mountain bikes. **Cons:** limited room service; dark in winter because of surrounding trees; some rooms are not accessible via elevator. $ *Rooms from: $329* ✉ *165 Throckmorton Ave., near Miller Ave.* ☎ *415/389–6608, 855/334–7946* ⊕ *millvalleyinn.com* ⊐ *25 rooms* ⦾ *Free Breakfast.*

Mountain Home Inn
$$ | B&B/INN | Abutting 40,000 acres of state and national parks, this airy wooden inn sits on the skirt of Mt. Tamalpais, where you can follow hiking trails all the way to Stinson Beach. **Pros:** amazing terrace and views; peaceful, remote setting; cooked-to-order breakfast. **Cons:** nearest town is a 12-minute drive away; restaurant can get crowded on sunny weekend days; some rooms are tiny and have no TVs. $ *Rooms from: $243* ✉ *810*

Panoramic Hwy., at Edgewood Ave. ☎ *415/381–9000* ⊕ *www.mtnhomeinn. com* ⊐ *10 rooms* ⦾ *Free Breakfast.*

Nightlife

BREWPUBS AND BEER GARDENS
The Junction Beer Garden & Bottle Shop
BREWPUBS/BEER GARDENS | With more than a hundred styles of canned and bottled beers and 30 beers on tap, plus wine and hard kombucha, this enormous indoor and outdoor beer garden is perfectly situated along the Dipsea Trail for a visit before or after a Mt. Tam hike or Tennessee Valley beach visit. The brewers partnered with PizzaHacker, a cult-favorite pizzeria in San Francisco's Bernal Heights, to provide classic pies like their "top-shelf" Margherita, as well as salads and meatballs. The landscaped outdoor space is lined with picnic tables, Adirondack chairs, and firepits. ✉ *226 Shoreline Hwy.* ☎ *415/888–3544* ⊕ *thejunc.com.*

Performing Arts

★ Throckmorton Theatre
ARTS CENTERS | A vibrant cultural hub in the region, the restored cinema and vaudeville house in Mill Valley is known for fostering exceptional arts and education. The darling playhouse seats upward of 260 and features live theater, comedy, and concerts. Two smaller street-side halls, the Tivoli and Crescendo, feature free classical concerts on Wednesday, along with Sunday evening sessions, jazz performances, and new art exhibits every month. ✉ *142 Throckmorton Ave.* ☎ *415/383–9600* ⊕ *www.throckmortont-heatre.org.*

Shopping

Mill Valley Market
FOOD/CANDY | This family-owned market has been the go-to stop for specialty foods, groceries, deli items, and hot food since 1929. Known for the notable beer

and wine selection alongside local and organic produce and healthy grab-and-go foods, this is an ideal place to prepare for a picnic or seek out gourmet gifts, like imported chocolates and 100-year-old balsamic vinegars. ✉ *12 Corte Madera Ave.* ☎ *415/388–3222* 🌐 *millvalleymarket.com.*

Muir Beach

12 miles northwest of Golden Gate Bridge, 6 miles southwest of Mill Valley.

Except on the sunniest of weekends, Muir Beach is relatively quiet, but the drive to this community and beach is a scenic adventure.

GETTING HERE AND AROUND

A car is the best way to reach Muir Beach. From Highway 1, follow Pacific Way southwest ¼ mile.

Beaches

Muir Beach

BEACH—SIGHT | **FAMILY** | Small but scenic, this beach—a rocky patch of shoreline off Highway 1 in the northern Marin Headlands—is a good place to stretch your legs and gaze out at the Pacific Ocean. Locals often walk their dogs here; families and cuddling couples come for picnicking and sunbathing. At the northern end of the beach are waterfront homes (and occasional nude sunbathers), and at the other are the bluffs of the Golden Gate National Recreation Area. A land bridge connects directly from the parking lot to the beach, as well as to a short trail that leads to a scenic overlook and connects to other coastal paths. There are no lifeguards on duty and the currents can be challenging, so swimming is not advised. **Amenities:** parking (free); toilets. **Best for:** solitude; sunset; walking. ✉ *100 Pacific Way, off Shoreline Hwy.* 🌐 *www.nps.gov/gogo.*

Hotels

The Pelican Inn

$$ | **B&B/INN** | From its slate roof to its whitewashed plaster walls, this Tudor-style inn built in the 1970s is English to the core, with its cozy upstairs guest rooms (no elevator) and draped half-tester beds, a sun-filled solarium, and bangers and grilled tomatoes for breakfast. **Pros:** five-minute walk to the beach; great bar and restaurant; peaceful setting. **Cons:** 20-minute drive to nearby attractions; rooms are quite small and rustic; workout and steam room access not on-site. [$] *Rooms from: $224* ✉ *10 Pacific Way, off Hwy. 1* ☎ *415/383–6000* 🌐 *www.pelicaninn.com* 🛏 *7 rooms* 🍴 *Free Breakfast.*

Stinson Beach

20 miles northwest of Golden Gate Bridge.

This laid-back hamlet is all about the beach, and folks come from all over the Bay Area to walk its sandy, often windswept shore. An ideal day trip would include a morning hike at Mt. Tamalpais followed by lunch at one of Stinson's unassuming eateries and a leisurely beach stroll.

GETTING HERE AND AROUND

If you're driving, take U.S. 101 to the Mill Valley/Stinson Beach/Highway 1 exit and follow the road west and then north. By bus, take Golden Gate Transit to Marin City and then transfer to the West Marin Stagecoach (61) for Bolinas.

Beaches

Stinson Beach

BEACH—SIGHT | **FAMILY** | When the fog hasn't rolled in, this expansive stretch of sand is about as close as you can get in Marin to the stereotypical feel of a Southern California beach. There are several clothing-optional areas, among them a section south of Stinson Beach called

Red Rock Beach. ⚠ **Swimming at Stinson Beach can be dangerous; the undertow is strong, and shark sightings, though infrequent, have occurred; lifeguards are on duty May–September.** Pets are not allowed on the national park section of the beach.

On any hot summer weekend, roads to Stinson are packed and the parking lot fills, so factor this into your plans. The town itself—population 600, give or take—has a nonchalant surfer vibe, with a few good eating options and pleasant hippie-craftsy browsing. **Amenities:** food and drink; lifeguards (summer); parking (free); showers; toilets. **Best for:** nudists; sunset; surfing; swimming; walking, windsurfing. ✉ *Hwy. 1, 1 Calle Del Sierra* ☎ *415/868–0942 lifeguard tower* 🌐 *www.nps.gov/goga.*

🍴 Restaurants

Parkside Cafe

$$ | AMERICAN | FAMILY | Though this place is popular for its 1950s beachfront snack bar, the adjoining café, coffee bar, marketplace, and bakery shouldn't be missed either. The full menu serves up fresh ingredients, local seafood, and wood-fired pizzas. **Known for:** espresso and pastry bar; tasty fish-and-chips; rustic house-made breads. [$] *Average main: $26* ✉ *43 Arenal Ave., off Shoreline Hwy.* ☎ *415/868–1272* 🌐 *www.parksidecafe.com.*

Stinson Beach Breakers Cafe

$$ | AMERICAN | Hard to miss along the tiny stretch of Main Street, this café is an easy pre-beach destination for coffee and griddle specialties or post-surf bar bites and cocktails on the heated patio in the afternoon. Beach-cottage hardwood floors and a woodstove add to the warmth of the rustic seaside interior, while a mountain view and firepit enhance the deck. **Known for:** hearty egg breakfast dishes with a Latin twist; fresh oysters; fish tacos. [$] *Average main: $19* ✉ *3465 Hwy. 1* ☎ *415/868–2002* ⏲ *Closed Tues. and Wed. from Nov.–Mar.*

🛏 Hotels

Sandpiper Lodging

$$ | B&B/INN | FAMILY | Recharge, rest, and enjoy the local scenery at this ultrapopular lodging that books up months, even years, in advance. **Pros:** beach chairs, towels, and toys provided; lush garden with grill; minutes from the beach and town. **Cons:** walls are thin; limited amenities; charge for rollaway beds and extra persons. [$] *Rooms from: $262* ✉ *1 Marine Way, off Arenal Ave.* ☎ *415/868–1632* 🌐 *www.sandpiperstinsonbeach.com* 🔑 *11 rooms* 🍽 *No meals.*

Point Reyes National Seashore

Bear Valley Visitor Center is 14 miles north of Stinson Beach.

With sandy beaches stretching for miles, a dramatic rocky coastline, a gem of a lighthouse (Point Reyes Lighthouse: closed at this writing, but check online), and idyllic, century-old dairy farms, Point Reyes National Seashore is one of the most varied and strikingly beautiful corners of the Bay Area.

GETTING HERE AND AROUND

From San Francisco, take U.S. 101 North, head west at Sir Francis Drake Boulevard (Exit 450B) toward San Anselmo, and follow the road just under 20 miles to Bear Valley Road. From Stinson Beach or Bolinas, drive north on Highway 1 and turn left on Bear Valley Road. If you're going by bus, take one of several Golden Gate Transit buses to Marin City; in Marin City, transfer to the West Marin Stagecoach (you'll switch buses in Olema). Once at the visitor center, the best way to get around is on foot.

Did You Know?

The majestic Point Reyes National Seashore offers many attractions for nature lovers: hiking, bird-watching, camping, or whale-watching, depending on the season. But flower picking isn't an approved activity; the wildflowers here are protected.

⊙ Sights

Bear Valley Visitor Center

INFO CENTER | FAMILY | Tucked in the Olema Valley, this welcoming center is a perfect point of orientation for trails and roads throughout the region's unique and diverse ecosystem. It offers a rich glimpse of local cultural and natural heritage with engaging exhibits about the wildlife, history, and ecology of the Point Reyes National Seashore. The rangers at the barnlike facility share their in-depth knowledge about beaches, whale-watching, hiking trails, and camping. Restrooms are available, as well as trailhead parking and a picnic area with barbecue grills. Winter hours may be shorter and summer weekend hours may be longer; call or check the website for details. ⊠ *Bear Valley Visitor Center, 1 Bear Valley Visitor Center Access Rd., west of Hwy. 1, off Bear Valley Rd., Point Reyes Station* ☎ *415/464–5100* ⊕ *www. nps.gov/pore.*

★ Duxbury Reef

NATURE PRESERVE | FAMILY | Excellent tide pooling can be had along the 3-mile shoreline of Duxbury Reef; it's the most extensive tide pool area near Point Reyes National Seashore, as well as one of the largest shale intertidal reefs in North America. Look for sea stars, barnacles, sea anemones, purple urchins, limpets, sea mussels, and the occasional abalone. But check a tide table (⊕ *tidesandcurrents.noaa.gov*) or the local papers if you plan to explore the reef—it's accessible only at low tide. The reef is a 30-minute drive from the Bear Valley Visitor Center. Take Highway 1 South from the center, turn right at Olema Bolinas Road (keep an eye peeled; the road is easy to miss), left on Horseshoe Hill Road, right on Mesa Road, left on Overlook Drive, and then right on Elm Road, which dead-ends at the Agate Beach County Park parking lot.

Excellent tide pooling can be had along the 3-mile shoreline of Duxbury Reef; it's the most extensive tide pool area near Point Reyes National Seashore, as well as one of the largest shale intertidal reefs in North America. Look for sea stars, barnacles, sea anemones, purple urchins, limpets, sea mussels, and the occasional abalone. But check a tide table (⊕ *tidesandcurrents.noaa.gov*) or the local papers if you plan to explore the reef—it's accessible only at low tide. The reef is a 30-minute drive from the Bear Valley Visitor Center. Take Highway 1 South from the center, turn right at Olema Bolinas Road (keep an eye peeled; the road is easy to miss), left on Horseshoe Hill Road, right on Mesa Road, left on Overlook Drive, and then right on Elm Road, which dead-ends at the Agate Beach County Park parking lot. ⊕ *At Duxbury Point, 1 mile west of Bolinas* ⊕ *www.ptreyes.org* 🎫 *Free.*

Palomarin Field Station & Point Reyes Bird Observatory

NATURE PRESERVE | FAMILY | Birders adore Point Blue Conservation Science, which maintains the Palomarin Field Station and the Point Reyes Bird Observatory that are located in the southernmost part of Point Reyes National Seashore. The Field Station has excellent interpretive exhibits, including a comparative display of real birds' talons. The surrounding woods harbor some 200 bird species. As you hike the quiet trails through forest and along ocean cliffs, you're likely to see biologists banding birds to aid in the study of their life cycles. ■TIP→ **Visit Point Blue's website for detailed directions and to find out when banding will occur.** ⊠ *999 Mesa Rd., Bolinas* ☎ *415/868–0655 field station, 707/781–2555 headquarters* ⊕ *www. pointblue.org.*

★ Point Reyes National Seashore

NATIONAL/STATE PARK | FAMILY | One of the Bay Area's most spectacular treasures and the only national seashore on the West Coast, the 71,000-acre Point Reyes National Seashore encompasses hiking trails, secluded beaches, and rugged grasslands, as well as Point Reyes itself, a triangular peninsula that juts into the Pacific. The Point Reyes Lighthouse occupies the peninsula's tip and is a scenic 21-mile drive from Bear Valley Visitor Center; at this writing it is closed for renovations, but check online. The town of **Point Reyes Station** is a one-main-drag affair, with some good places to eat.

The infamous San Andreas Fault runs along the park's eastern edge; take the **Earthquake Trail** from the visitor center to see the impact near the epicenter of the 1906 earthquake that devastated San Francisco. A half-mile path from the visitor center leads to **Kule Loklo,** a reconstructed Miwok village of the region's first known inhabitants.

You can experience the diversity of Point Reyes's ecosystems on the scenic **Coast Trail** through eucalyptus groves and pine forests and along seaside cliffs to beautiful and tiny Bass Lake.

The 4.7-mile-long (one-way) **Tomales Point Trail** follows the spine of the park's northernmost finger of land through the Tule Elk Preserve, providing spectacular ocean views from high bluffs. ⊠ *Bear Valley Visitor Center, 1 Bear Valley Visitor Center Access Rd., Point Reyes Station* ✛ *West of Hwy. 1, off Bear Valley Rd.* ☎ *415/464–5100* ⊕ *www.nps.gov/pore* ⌂ *Free.*

🍴 Restaurants

Cafe Reyes

$ | PIZZA | FAMILY | Sunny patio seating, hand-tossed pizza, and organic local ingredients are the selling points of this laid-back café. The semi-industrial dining room, built around a brick oven, features glazed concrete floors, warm-painted walls, and ceilings high enough to accommodate full-size market umbrellas. **Known for:** wood-fired pizza; Tomales Bay fresh oysters; good salads. $ *Average main: $15* ⊠ *11101 Hwy. 1, Point Reyes Station* ☎ *415/663–9493* ⊕ *cafe-reyes. com* ⌂ *Closed Mon. and Tues.*

Due West

$$ | AMERICAN | A convivial atmosphere and local, sustainable culinary provisions keep this classic Point Reyes tavern a favorite stop among locals. Refurbished and modernized since its days as a horse-and-wagon stop in the 1860s, it now has a farm-to-fork seasonal menu including American classics from burgers and brick-roasted chicken to seafood specialties like shrimp scampi and steamed mussels. **Known for:** artisanal cheese plate; steak frites; regional wine list. $ *Average main: $23* ⊠ *10021 Coastal Hwy. 1, Olema* ☎ *415/663–1264* ⊕ *olemahouse.com/due-west-restaurant/.*

Eleven

$$ | WINE BAR | For a true taste of local culture, this sisters-owned venture welcomes you to sit back, relax, sip some wine, and enjoy the flavors and scene Bolinas is known for, from the town's laid-back lifestyle and quirky decor to the natural beauty and the fresh coastal air. The wine bar and bistro's short but ever-changing creative and thoughtful menus change daily based on what's available and reflect the richness of this region's foodshed—considered one of the nation's most diverse. **Known for:** house-made, locally sourced ingredients; local natural wine selections; pizzas and oysters. $ *Average main: $17* ⊠ *11 Wharf Rd., Bolinas* ☎ *415/868–1133* ⊕ *www.11wharfroad.com* ⌂ *Closed Sun.–Wed.*

★ Hog Island Oyster Co. Marshall Oyster Farm and the Boat Oyster Bar

$$ | SEAFOOD | FAMILY | Take a short trek north on Highway 1 to the gritty mecca of Bay Area oysters—the Hog Island Marshall Oyster Farm. For a real culinary adventure, arrange to shuck and barbecue your own oysters on one of the outdoor grills (all tools supplied, reservations required); or for the less adventurous, the Boat Oyster Bar is an informal outdoor café that serves raw and grilled oysters, local snacks, and tasty beverages. **Known for:** fresh, raw, and grilled oysters; farm tours; Hog Shack shellfish to go. $ *Average main: $24* ⊠ *20215 Shoreline Hwy.* ☎ *415/663–9218* ⊕ *hogislandoysters.com* ◷ *Oyster Bar closed Tues.–Thurs. No dinner.*

Inverness Park Market & Tap Room

$$ | AMERICAN | An organic oasis in the region, this deli, restaurant, and taproom offers a true taste of the Point Reyes foodshed. Classic sandwiches, breakfast bites, burritos, grilled Niman Ranch beef, wild-caught salmon, and vegan burgers are all prepared with fresh local ingredients. **Known for:** Tuesday tacos and Wednesday sushi specials; house-cooked tri-tip and smoked pastrami; grilled oysters. $ *Average main: $18* ⊠ *12301 Sir Francis Drake Blvd., Inverness Park* ☎ *415/663–1491* ⊕ *invernessparkmarket.com.*

Saltwater Oyster Depot

$$ | SEAFOOD | Oysters shucked moments after they're taken out of Tomales Bay and French and California wines sourced from small producers are the keystones of this neighborhood oyster bar. True to the spirit of the region, it is dedicated to sustainable farming, foraging, and fishing. **Known for:** broiled, baked, and chili oysters; clam chowder; natural wines. $ *Average main: $20* ⊠ *12781 Sir Francis Drake Blvd., Inverness* ☎ ⊕ *www.saltwateroysterdepot.com* ◷ *Closed Mon.–Wed.*

★ Side Street Kitchen

$ | AMERICAN | FAMILY | Rotisserie meats and veggies sourced from local farms steal the show at this former mid-20th-century truck stop and diner. It's a go-to for tri-tip and pork belly sandwiches or house-seasoned roasted chicken, best eaten with a host of sides,

sips, and sweets, like crispy Parmesan Brussels sprouts, ginger lemonade, and butterscotch pudding. **Known for:** cold smoked seafood and rotisserie chicken; dog-friendly outdoor patio; apple fritters. $ *Average main: $16* ⊠ *60 4th St., Point Reyes Station* ☎ *415/663–0303* ⊕ *sidestreet-prs.com* ◷ *No dinner after 6pm.*

★ Station House Café

$$ | AMERICAN | Relocated to the space where the restaurant originally opened its doors in 1974, the Station House Café has been a stalwart venue for local music and a staunch supporter of local farms and food artisans. The community-centric eatery serves a blend of modern and classic California dishes comprised of organic seasonal ingredients, sustainable hormone-free meats, and wild-caught seafood. **Known for:** signature popovers and bread pudding; hearty breakfast items; fresh local seafood. $ *Average main: $17* ⊠ *11285 Hwy. 1, at 3rd St., Point Reyes Station* ☎ *415/663–1515* ⊕ *www.stationhousecafe.com* ◷ *Closed Wed. and Thurs.*

Hotels

★ Olema House

$$$$ | B&B/INN | FAMILY | Once a historic 1860s stagecoach stopover, this renovated, luxurious getaway offers just as many reasons to stay on property—with its views of Mt. Wittenberg and garden setting—as to explore the 71,000 acres of national seashore just steps away. **Pros:** steps from trails; convenient parking and horse hitching; friendly and informative staff. **Cons:** steps to some rooms may be steep; street-facing rooms above restaurant may be noisy; Wi-Fi and cell service may be spotty. $ *Rooms from: $480* ⊠ *10021 Coastal Hwy. 1, Olema* ☎ *415/663–9000* ⊕ *olemahouse.com* ⇗ *25 rooms* ❍❙ *Free Breakfast.*

Shopping

★ Cowgirl Creamery

FOOD/CANDY | FAMILY | In this former hay barn, a couple of Berkeley foodies (from Chez Panisse and Bette's Oceanview Diner) started their original creamery for artisanal cheeses. In addition to more than 200 specialty cheeses—local, regional, and international—you'll find Tomales Bay Foods offerings featuring West Marin farm wares. Cowgirl Creamery cheeses harness flavors unique to Point Reyes, such as their award-winning Red Hawk and Mt. Tam made with Straus Family organic milk. Sample seasonal cheeses and see how the cheese is made or order a hot mac-and-cheese at the cantina and stay for a bite at the picnic tables. Abundant deli items, gourmet goodies, and wine selections are perfect for picnicking. ⊠ *80 4th St., Point Reyes Station* ☎ *415/663–9335* ⊕ *cowgirlcreamery.com.*

Gospel Flat Farm Stand

LOCAL SPECIALTIES | This combination art gallery, farm stand, and flower shop captures the true essence of the Bolinas and Olema area, with its dedication to community arts and a bounty of local organic vegetables, fruits, and eggs. The colorful self-serve site is open 24 hours, but what makes it truly special is that the entire stand operates on the honor system. Weigh and log your produce, and slip your payment (cash or check) in the box. The ever-rotating local art on exhibit adds to the allure of this roadside treasure. ⊠ *140 Olema-Bolinas Rd., Bolinas* ☎ *415/868–0921* ⊕ *gospelflatfarm.com.*

★ Toby's Feed Barn

LOCAL SPECIALTIES | The heart of the community since 1942, the barn has a bounty of local gifts and produce, plus an art gallery, yoga studio, and Toby's Coffee Bar for espresso drinks and sell-out pastries. See and hear what's happening locally, catch a live band or literary event, and explore the garden. The internationally renowned all-local, all-organic Point Reyes Farmers' Market is held here on Saturdays during the growing season. ⊠ *11250 Hwy. 1, Point Reyes Station* ☎ *415/663–1223* ⊕ *www.tobysfeedbarn. com.*

Chapter 15

NAPA AND SONOMA

Updated by
Daniel Mangin

⊙ Sights	🍴 Restaurants	🛏 Hotels	👜 Shopping	🍸 Nightlife
★★★★★	★★★★★	★★★★☆	★★★☆☆	★★★☆☆

WELCOME TO NAPA AND SONOMA

TOP REASONS TO GO

★ **Touring wineries:** Let's face it: this is the reason you're here, and the range of excellent sips to sample would make any oeno-phile (or novice drinker, for that matter) giddy.

★ **Biking:** Gentle hills and vineyard-laced farmland make Napa and Sonoma perfect for combining lei-surely back-roads cycling with winery stops.

★ **Spa treatments:** Work-hard, play-hard types and inveterate sybarites flock to Wine Country spas for pampering.

★ **Fine dining:** A meal at a top-tier restaurant can be a revelation about the level of artistry intuitive chefs can achieve and how successfully quality wines pair with food.

★ **Viewing the art:** Several wineries, among them the Hess Collection in Napa, The Donum Estate in Sonoma, and Hall St. Helena, dis-play museum-quality artworks indoors and on their grounds.

The Napa and Sonoma valleys run parallel, southeast to north-west, separated by the Mayacamas Mountains. Northwest of Sonoma Valley are several other important Sonoma County viticultural areas, including the Dry Creek, Alexander, and Russian River valleys. The Carneros, which spans southern Sonoma and Napa counties, is just north of San Pablo Bay.

1 **Napa.**

2 **Yountville.**

3 **Oakville.**

4 **Rutherford.**

5 **St. Helena.**

6 **Calistoga.**

7 **Sonoma.**

8 **Glen Ellen.**

9 **Kenwood.**

10 **Petaluma.**

11 **Healdsburg.**

12 **Geyserville.**

13 **Forestville.**

14 **Guerneville**

15 **Sebastopol.**

16 **Santa Rosa.**

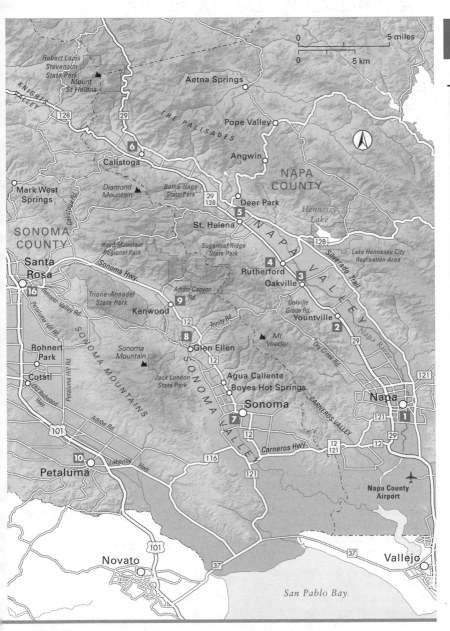

Robert Louis
Stevenson
State Park
Mount
St Helena

Aetna Springs

KNIGHTS VALLEY

128

29

THE PALISADES

Pope Valley

Angwin

6

Calistoga

NAPA COUNTY

Mark West Springs

Diamond Mountain

Bothe-Napa State Park

29
128

Deer Park

Hennessy Lake

SONOMA COUNTY

Calistoga Rd.

St. Helena

5

Santa Rosa

Hood Mountain Regional Park

Sugarloaf Ridge State Park

128

Lake Hennessy City Recreation Area

16

Bennett Valley Rd.

Sonoma Hwy.

Adobe Canyon Rd.

Trione-Annadel State Park

Kenwood

9

Rutherford

4

Oakville

3

Silverado Trail

NAPA VALLEY

Napa River

Petaluma Hill Rd.

12

Trinity Rd.

Oakville Grade Rd.

Yountville

2

29

Rohnert Park

SONOMA MOUNTAINS

8

Glen Ellen

Mt Veeder

12

Dry Creek Rd.

Cotati

Petaluma Hill Rd.

Sonoma Mountain

Jack London State Park

Agua Caliente

121

Old Redwood Hwy.

Boyes Hot Springs

SONOMA VALLEY

CARNEROS VALLEY

Napa

121

Adobe Rd.

Sonoma

7

1

101

10

Laksville Hwy.

12

29

121

Petaluma

116

Carneros Hwy.

12
121

12

121

San Pablo Bay

101

Novato

37

37

Vallejo

Napa County Airport

0   5 miles
0   5 km

In California's premier wine region, the pleasures of eating and drinking are celebrated daily. It's easy to join in at famous wineries and rising newcomers off country roads, or at trendy in-town tasting rooms. Chefs transform local ingredients into feasts, and gourmet groceries sell perfect picnic fare. Yountville, Healdsburg, and St. Helena have small-town charm as well as luxurious inns, hotels, and spas, yet the natural setting is equally sublime, whether experienced from a canoe on the Russian River or the deck of a winery overlooking endless rows of vines.

The Wine Country is also rich in history. In Sonoma you can explore California's Spanish and Mexican pasts at the Sonoma Mission, and the origins of modern California wine making at Buena Vista Winery. Some wineries, among them St. Helena's Beringer and Rutherford's Inglenook, have cellars or tasting rooms dating to the late 1800s. Calistoga is a flurry of late-19th-century Steamboat Gothic architecture, though the town's oldest-looking building, the medieval-style Castello di Amorosa, is a 21st-century creation.

Visits to the Napa Valley's Beringer, Robert Mondavi, and Inglenook—and at Buena Vista in the Sonoma Valley—provide an entertaining overview of Wine Country history. Through the glass walls at Hall St. Helena's tasting room you may glimpse 21st-century wine-making technology in action, and over in Glen Ellen's Benziger Family Winery you can learn how its vineyard managers apply biodynamic farming principles to grape growing. At numerous facilities you can play winemaker at seminars in the fine art of blending wines. If that strikes you as too much effort, you can always pamper yourself at a luxury spa.

To delve further into the fine art of Wine Country living, pick up a copy of *Fodor's Napa and Sonoma*.

MAJOR REGIONS

Napa Valley. Practically speaking, the valley can be divided into its southern and northern parts. The southern Napa Valley encompasses cooler grape-growing areas and the tasting rooms, restaurants, and hotels of **Napa** and **Yountville**, along with slightly warmer **Oakville**. The northern valley begins around **Rutherford,** like Oakville blessed with Cabernet-friendly soils. Beyond it lies hotter **St. Helena,** whose downtown entices with boutiques, galleries, and restaurants. Warmer still is **Calistoga,** known for spas and hot springs.

Sonoma Valley and Petaluma. Modern California wine making began in Sonoma Valley. North of the tasting rooms, restaurants, and lodgings near Sonoma Plaza in downtown **Sonoma** lie the wineries of more pastoral **Glen Ellen** and **Kenwood**. To the valley's west, **Petaluma,** with a burgeoning dining scene, has come into its own as a Wine Country destination.

Northern Sonoma, Russian River, and West County. Its walkable downtown, swank hotels, and restaurant scene make **Healdsburg** the tourist hub of Sonoma County's northern section. North of Healdsburg, mostly rural **Geyserville** has a small, engaging downtown. The Russian River winds through or near **Forestville, Guerneville,** and **Sebastopol,** three West County towns where Chardonnay and Pinot Noir grow well. The county's largest city, **Santa Rosa,** contains non-wine attractions and affordable lodgings.

Planning

When to Go

High season extends from late May through October. In summer, expect the days to be hot and dry. Hotel rates are highest during the height of harvest, in September and October. Then and in summer, book lodgings well ahead. November, except for Thanksgiving week, and December before Christmas are less busy. The weather in Napa and Sonoma is pleasant nearly year-round. Daytime temperatures average from about 55°F during winter to the 80s and 90s (occasionally 100s) in summer. April, May, and October are milder but still warm. The rainiest months are usually from December through March.

Getting Here and Around

AIR TRAVEL

Wine Country regulars often bypass San Francisco and Oakland and fly into Santa Rosa's Charles M. Schulz Sonoma County Airport (STS), which receives direct flights from several western cities. The airport is 15 miles from Healdsburg. ■ TIP→ **Alaska Airlines allows passengers flying out of STS to check up to one case of wine for free.**

BUS TRAVEL

Bus travel is an inconvenient way to explore the Wine Country, though it is possible. Take Golden Gate Transit from San Francisco to connect with Sonoma County Transit buses. VINE connects with BART commuter trains in the East Bay and the San Francisco Bay Ferry in Vallejo. VINE buses serve the Napa Valley.

CAR TRAVEL

A car is the most convenient way to navigate Napa and Sonoma. If you're flying into the area, it's almost always easiest to pick up a car at the airport. You'll also find rental companies in major Wine Country towns. A few rules to note: Smartphone use for any purpose is prohibited, including mapping applications unless the device is mounted to a car's windshield or dashboard and can be activated with a single swipe or finger tap. A right turn after stopping at a red light is legal unless posted otherwise.

Continued on page 334

WINE TASTING *in* NAPA *and* SONOMA

VISITING WINERIES

Tasting rooms range from the grand to the humble, offering everything from a few sips of wine to in-depth tours of facilities and vineyards. Some are open for drop-in visits, usually daily from around 10 or 11 am to 5 pm. Many require guests to make reservations. First-time visitors frequently enjoy the history-oriented focus at Charles Krug, Inglenook, and Buena Vista. The environments at some wineries reflect their owners' or founders' other interests: art at The Donum Estate and Hall St. Helena, movie making at Francis Ford Coppola, and medieval history at the Castello di Amorosa.

Many wineries describe their pourers as "wine educators," and indeed some of them have taken online or other classes and have passed an exam to prove basic knowledge of appellations, grape varietals, vineyards, and wine-making techniques. The one constant, however, is a deep, shared pleasure in the experience of wine tasting.

Fees. Most wineries charge for tasting. In the Napa Valley, expect to pay $35–$65 to sample current releases, $75–$100 or more for reserve, estate, or library wines. Sonoma County tastings generally cost $20–$40 for the former, $40–$75 for the latter. To experience wine making at its highest level, consider splurging for at least one special tasting.

Some wineries waive tasting fees if you join the wine club, purchase a few bottles, or spend a particular dollar amount. At others, the fees are "exclusive of purchase."

Tipping. Many guests tip out of instinct, but it isn't required. Instances when you might consider tipping include when your server has given a few extra pours or a discount on your purchases or has otherwise provided outstanding service. For a basic tasting, $5–$10 per couple will suffice; for a hosted seated tasting, $5–$10 per person, perhaps a little more for extra attention.

Whether you're a serious wine collector making your annual pilgrimage to Northern California's Wine Country or a newbie who doesn't know the difference between a Merlot and Mourvèdre but is eager to learn, you can have a great time touring Napa and Sonoma wineries. Your gateway to the wine world is the tasting room, where staff members are happy to chat with curious guests.

(opposite page) Carneros vineyards in autumn, Napa Valley. (top) Pinot Gris grapes. (bottom) Bottles from Far Niente winery.

WINE TASTING 101

TAKE A GOOD LOOK.

Hold your glass by the stem, raise it to the light, and take a close look at the wine. Check for clarity and color. (This is easiest to do if you can hold the glass in front of a white background.) Any tinge of brown usually means that the wine is over the hill or has gone bad.

BREATHE DEEP.

1. Sniff the wine once or twice to see if you can identify any smells.

2. Swirl the wine gently in the glass. Aerating the wine this way releases more of its aromas. (It's called "volatilizing the esters," if you're trying to impress someone.)

3. Take another long sniff. You might notice that experienced wine tasters spend more time sniffing the wine than drinking it. This is because this step is where the magic happens. The number of scents you might detect is almost endless, from berries, apricots, honey, and wildflowers to leather, cedar, or even tar. Does the wine smell good to you? Do you detect any "off" flavors, like wet dog or sulfur?

AT LAST! TAKE A SIP.

1. Swirl the wine around your mouth so that it makes contact with all your taste buds and releases more of its aromas. Think about the way the wine feels in your mouth. Is it watery or rich? Is it crisp or silky? Does it have a bold flavor, or is it subtle? The weight and intensity of a wine are called its body.

2. Hold the wine in your mouth for a few seconds and see if you can identify any developing flavors. More complex wines will reveal many different flavors as you drink them.

SPIT OR SWALLOW.

The pros typically spit, since they want to preserve their palate (and sobriety) for the wines to come, but you'll find that swallowers far outnumber the spitters in the winery tasting rooms. Whether you spit or swallow, notice the flavor that remains after the wine is gone (the finish).

Swirl

Sniff

Sip

MAKE AN APPOINTMENT

Most Napa and Sonoma wineries accept visitors by appointment only to serve patrons better, though some welcome walk-ins if space is available. To avoid disappointment, make reservations at least a day or two ahead. In summer and early fall, try to visit on weekdays or before 11 am or so when it's less crowded. Also look for wineries off the main drags of Highway 29 in Napa and Highway 12 in Sonoma.

HOW WINE IS MADE

1. CRUSHING
Harvested grapes go into a stemmer-crusher, which separates stems from fruit and crushes the grapes to release "free-run" juice.

2. PRESSING
Remaining juice is gently extracted from grapes. Usually done by pressing grapes against the walls of a tank with an inflatable bladder.

3. FERMENTING
Extracted juice (and also grape skins and pulp, when making red wine) goes into stainless-steel tanks or oak barrels to ferment. During fermentation, sugars convert to alcohol.

4. AGING
Wine is stored in stainless-steel or oak casks or barrels, or sometimes in concrete vessels, to develop flavors.

5. RACKING
Wine is transferred to clean barrels; sediment is removed. Wine may be filtered and fined (clarified) to improve its clarity, color, and sometimes flavor.

6. BOTTLING
Wine is bottled either at the winery or at a special facility, then stored again for bottle-aging.

WHAT'S AN APPELLATION?

American Viticultural Area (AVA) or, more commonly, an appellation. What can be confusing is that some appellations encompass smaller subappellations. The Rutherford, Oakville, and Mt. Veeder AVAs, for instance, are among the Napa Valley AVA's 16 subappellations. Wineries often buy grapes from outside their AVA, so their labels might reference different appellations. A winery in the warmer Napa Valley, for instance, might source Pinot Noir grapes from the cooler Russian River Valley, where they grow better. The appellation listed on a label always refers to where a wine's grapes were grown, not to where the wine was made.

By law, if a label bears the name of an appellation, 85% of the grapes must come from it.

If you base yourself in the Napa Valley towns of Napa, Yountville, or St. Helena, or in Sonoma County's Healdsburg or Sonoma, you can visit numerous tasting rooms and nearby wineries on foot or by bicycle on mostly flat terrain. The free Yountville trolley loops through town, and ride-sharing is viable there and in Napa. Sonoma County sprawls more, but except for far west the public transit and ride-sharing generally work well.

■ TIP→ **When wine tasting, select a designated driver or monitor your intake—the police keep an eye out for tipsy drivers.**

Restaurants

Top Wine Country chefs tend to apply French and Italian techniques to dishes incorporating fresh, local products. Menus are often vegan- and vegetarian-friendly, with gluten-free options. At pricey restaurants you can save money by having lunch instead of dinner. With a few exceptions (noted in individual restaurant listings), dress is informal. *Restaurant reviews have been shortened. For full information, visit Fodors.com.*

Hotels

The fanciest accommodations are concentrated in the Napa Valley towns of Yountville, Rutherford, St. Helena, and Calistoga; Sonoma County's poshest lodgings are in Healdsburg. The cities of Napa, Petaluma, and Santa Rosa are the best bets for budget hotels and inns. On weekends, two- or even three-night minimum stays are commonly required at smaller lodgings. Book well ahead for stays at such places in summer or early fall. Some accommodations aren't suitable for kids, so ask before you book. *Hotel reviews have been shortened. For full information, visit Fodors.com.*

What It Costs

	$	$$	$$$	$$$$
RESTAURANTS				
	under $17	$17–$26	$27–$36	over $36
HOTELS				
	under $200	$200–$300	$301–$400	over $400

Napa

46 miles northeast of San Francisco.

After many years as a blue-collar burg detached from the Wine Country scene, the Napa Valley's largest town (population about 80,000) has evolved into one of its shining stars. Masaharu Morimoto and other chefs of note operate restaurants here, swank hotels and inns can be found downtown and beyond, and the nightlife options include the West Coast edition of the famed Blue Note jazz club. A walkway that follows the Napa River has made downtown more pedestrian-friendly, and the Oxbow Public Market, a complex of high-end food purveyors, is popular with locals and tourists. The market is named for the nearby oxbow bend in the Napa River, a bit north of where Napa was founded in 1848. The first wood-frame building was a saloon, and the downtown area still projects an old-river-town vibe.

GETTING HERE AND AROUND

Downtown Napa lies a mile east of Highway 29—take the 1st Street exit and follow the signs. Ample parking, much of it free for the first three hours and some for the entire day, is available on or near Main Street. Several VINE buses serve downtown and beyond.

Sights

★ Ashes & Diamonds

WINERY/DISTILLERY | Barbara Bestor's sleek white design for this appointment-only winery's glass-and-metal tasting space evokes mid-century modern architecture and with it the era and wines predating the Napa Valley's rise to prominence. Two much-heralded pros lead the wine-making team assembled by record producer Kashy Khaledi: Steve Matthiasson, known for his classic, restrained style and attention to viticultural detail, and Diana Snowden Seysses, who draws on experiences in Burgundy, Provence, and California. Bordeaux varietals are the focus, most notably Cabernet Sauvignon and Cabernet Franc but also the white blend of Sauvignon Blanc and Sémillon and even the rosé (of Cabernet Franc). With a label designer who was also responsible for a Jay-Z album cover and interiors that recall the *Mad Men* in the Palm Springs story arc, the pitch seems unabashedly intended to millennials, but the wines, low in alcohol and with high acidity (good for aging the wines), enchant connoisseurs of all stripes. ⊠ *4130 Howard La., Napa* ✦ *Off Hwy. 29* ☎ *707/666–4777* ⊕ *ashesdiamonds.com* 🍷 *Tastings from $75.*

CIA at Copia

COLLEGE | Full-fledged foodies and the merely curious achieve gastronomical bliss at the Culinary Institute of America's Oxbow District campus, its facade brightened by a wraparound mural inspired by the colorful garden that fronts the facility. When everything's going full tilt, you could easily spend a few hours dining at the indoor and outdoor restaurants; checking out the shop, themed exhibitions, and Vintners Hall of Fame wall; or attending (book ahead) classes and demonstrations. If it's open, head upstairs to the Chuck Williams Culinary Arts Museum. Named for the Williams-Sonoma kitchenwares founder, it holds a fascinating collection of cooking, baking, and other food-related tools, tableware, gizmos, and gadgets, some dating back more than a century. ⊠ *500 1st St., Napa* ✦ *Near McKinstry St.* ☎ *707/967–2500* ⊕ *www.ciaatcopia. com* 🍷 *Facility/museum free, class/demo fees vary.*

★ Domaine Carneros

WINERY/DISTILLERY | A visit to this majestic château is an opulent way to enjoy the Carneros District—especially in fine weather, when the vineyard views are spectacular. The château was modeled after an 18th-century French mansion owned by the Taittinger family. Carved into the hillside beneath the winery, the cellars produce sparkling wines reminiscent of those made by Taittinger, using only Los Carneros AVA grapes. Enjoy flights of sparkling wine or Pinot Noir with cheese and charcuterie plates, caviar, or smoked salmon. Tastings are by appointment only. ⊠ *1240 Duhig Rd., Napa* ✦ *At Hwy. 121* ☎ *707/257–0101, 800/716–2788 Ext. 150* ⊕ *www.domaine-carneros.com* 🍷 *Tastings from $40.*

Etude Wines

WINERY/DISTILLERY | You're apt to see or hear hawks, egrets, Canada geese, and other wildlife on the grounds of Etude, known for sophisticated Pinot Noirs. Although the winery and its light-filled tasting room are in Napa County, the grapes for its flagship Carneros Estate Pinot Noir come from the Sonoma portion of Los Carneros, as do those for the rarer Heirloom Carneros Pinot Noir. Longtime winemaker Jon Priest also excels at single-vineyard Napa Valley Cabernets. In good weather, hosts pour Priest's reds, plus Chardonnay, Pinot Gris, and a few others, on the patio outside the contemporary tasting room. ⊠ *1250 Cuttings Wharf Rd., Napa* ✦ *1 mile south of Hwy. 121* ☎ *707/257–5782* ⊕ *www.etudewines.com* 🍷 *Tastings from $30* ☾ *Closed Tues. and Wed.*

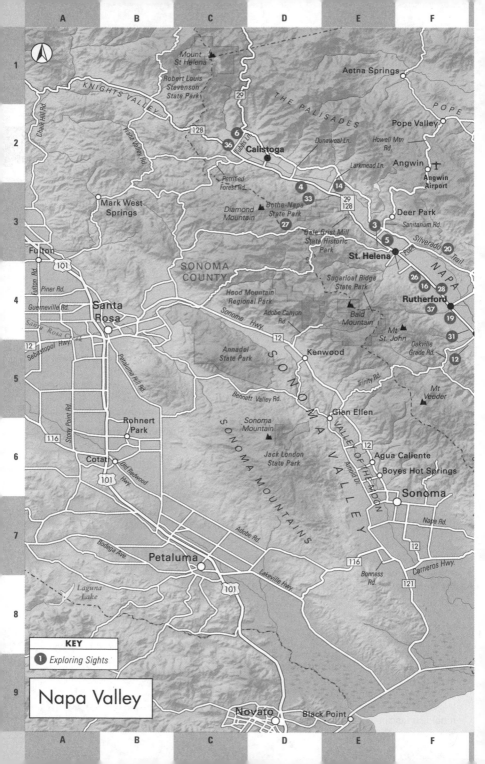

Napa Valley

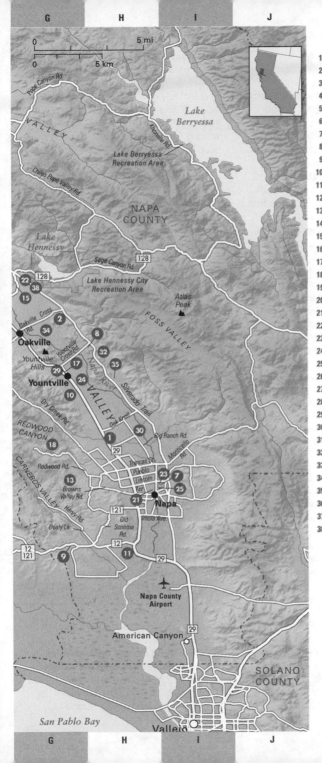

Sights ▼

★ Fontanella Family Winery

WINERY/DISTILLERY | Six miles from the downtown Napa whirl, husband-and-wife Jeff and Karen Fontanella's hillside spread seems a world apart. In addition to his formal studies, Jeff learned about wine making at three prestigious wineries before he and Karen, a lawyer, established their own operation on 81 south-facing Mt. Veeder acres. The couple braved an economic recession, an earthquake, and wildfires in the first decade but emerged tougher, if no less gracious to guests lucky enough to find themselves tasting Chardonnay, Zinfandel, and Cabernet Sauvignon on the patio here. Tastings often end with a Zinfandel-based port-style wine. With the barnlike production facility in the foreground and nearby Cabernet vines ringing a large irrigation pond, the setting represents the very picture of Napa Valley life many visitors imagine. ■TIP➜ **If offered the chance to stroll the estate, take it—the views south to San Francisco and east to Atlas Peak reward the exertion.** ✉ *1721 Partrick Rd., Napa ✛ 1st St. to Browns Valley Rd. west of Hwy. 29* ☎ *707/252–1017* ⊕ *www.fontanellawinery.com* ▨ *Tasting $45.*

Hess Collection

WINERY/DISTILLERY | About 9 miles northwest of Napa, up a winding road ascending Mt. Veeder, this winery is a delightful discovery. The limestone structure, rustic from the outside but modern and airy within, contains Swiss founder Donald Hess's world-class art collection, including large-scale works by contemporary artists such as Andy Goldsworthy, Anselm Kiefer, and Robert Rauschenberg. Cabernet Sauvignon and Chardonnay are strengths, along with small-lot reds (Petite Sirah, Pinot Noir, Syrah, and blends). All visits are by appointment. ■TIP➜ **Guided or self-guided gallery tours are part of most tastings.** ✉ *4411 Redwood Rd., Napa ✛ West off Hwy. 29 at Trancas St./Redwood Rd. exit* ☎ *707/255–1144* ⊕ *www.hesscollection.com* ▨ *Tastings from $45.*

★ Mayacamas Downtown

WINERY/DISTILLERY | Cabernets from Mayacamas Vineyards placed second and fifth respectively on *Wine Spectator* magazine's 2019 and 2020 "Top 100" lists of the world's best wines, two accolades among many for this winery founded atop Mt. Veeder in 1889. One of Napa's leading viticulturists, Annie Favia farms the organic vineyards, elevation 2,000-plus feet, without irrigation; her husband, Andy Favia, is the consulting winemaker. The grapes for the Chardonnay come from 40-year-old vines. Aged in mostly neutral (previously used) French oak barrels to accentuate mountain minerality, the wine is a Napa Valley marvel. The Cabernet Sauvignon ages for three years, spending part of the time in oak barrels more than a century old. Erin Martin, a Napa Valley resident with a hip international reputation, designed the light-filled storefront tasting space. ■TIP➜ **Experiencing these magnificent wines at this downtown tasting room may entice you to visit the estate.** ✉ *First Street Napa, 1256 1st St., Napa ✛ At Randolph St.* ☎ *707/294–1433* ⊕ *www.mayacamas.com* ▨ *Tastings from $35* ⊙ *Closed Mon. and Tues.*

Napa Valley Wine Train

TOUR—SIGHT | Guests on this Napa Valley fixture ride the same 150-year-old rail corridor along which trains once transported passengers as far north as Calistoga's spas. The rolling stock includes restored Pullman cars and a two-story Vista Dome coach with a curved glass roof. The train travels a leisurely, scenic route between Napa and St. Helena. Patrons on some tours enjoy a multicourse meal and tastings at one or more wineries. Some rides involve no winery stops, and themed trips are occasionally scheduled. ■TIP➜ **It's best to make this trip during the day, when you can enjoy the vineyard views.** ✉ *1275 McKinstry St., Napa ✛ Off 1st St.* ☎ *707/253–2111, 800/427–4124* ⊕ *www.winetrain.com* ▨ *From $160.*

★ Oxbow Public Market

MARKET | The 40,000-square-foot market's two dozen stands provide an introduction to Northern California's diverse artisanal food products. Swoon over decadent charcuterie at the Fatted Calf (great sandwiches, too), slurp oysters at Hog Island, enjoy empanadas at El Porteño, or chow down on vegetarian, duck, or salmon tacos at C Casa. Sample wine (and cheese) at the Oxbow Cheese & Wine Merchant, ales at Fieldwork Brewing's taproom, and barrel-aged cocktails at the Napa Valley Distillery. The owner of Kara's Cupcakes operates the adjacent Bar Lucia for (mostly) sparkling wines and rosés. Napa Bookmine is among the few nonfood vendors here. **■ TIP→ Five Dot Ranch and Cookhouse sells quality steaks and other meat to go; if you don't mind eating at the counter, you can order from the small menu and dine on the spot.** ✉ *610 and 644 1st St., Napa* ✣ *At McKinstry St.* 🌐 *www.oxbowpublicmarket.com.*

★ Robert Biale Vineyards

WINERY/DISTILLERY | Here's a surprise: a highly respected Napa Valley winery that doesn't sell a lick of Cabernet. Zinfandel from heritage vineyards, some with vines more than 100 years old, holds the spotlight, with luscious Petite Sirahs in supporting roles. Nearly every pour comes with a fascinating backstory, starting with the flagship Black Chicken Zinfandel. In the 1940s, the Biale family sold eggs, walnuts, and other farm staples, with bootleg Zinfandel a lucrative sideline. Because neighbors could eavesdrop on party-line phone conversations, "black chicken" became code for a jug of Zin. These days the wines are produced on the up-and-up by valley native Tres Goetting, whose vineyard and cellar choices bring out the best in two unsung varietals. The 10-acre property's open-air tasting setting—a stone's throw from Zinfandel vines, with far-off views of two mountain ranges—has a back-porch feel. Visits are by appointment; call ahead for same-day. ✉ *4038 Big Ranch Rd., at Salvador Ave., Napa* ☎ *707/257–7555* 🌐 *biale.com* 🎫 *Tastings from $35.*

Stag's Leap Wine Cellars

WINERY/DISTILLERY | A 1973 Stag's Leap Wine Cellars S.L.V. Cabernet Sauvignon put this winery and the Napa Valley on the enological map by placing first in the famous Judgment of Paris tasting of 1976. The grapes for that wine came from a vineyard visible from the stone-and-glass Fay Outlook & Visitor Center, which has broad views of a second fabled Cabernet vineyard (Fay) and the promontory that gives both the winery and the Stags Leap District AVA their names. The top-of-the-line Cabernets from these vineyards are poured at appointment-only tastings (call ahead for same day visits), some of which include perceptive food pairings by the winery's executive chef. **■ TIP→ When the weather's right, two patios with the same views as the tasting room fill up quickly.** ✉ *5766 Silverado Trail, Napa* ✣ *At Wappo Hill Rd.* ☎ *707/261–6410* 🌐 *www.stagsleapwinecellars.com* 🎫 *Tastings from $50.*

🍴 Restaurants

Angèle

$$$ | **FRENCH** | A vaulted wood-beamed ceiling and paper-topped tables set the scene for romance at this softly lit French bistro inside an 1890s boathouse. Look for clever variations on classic dishes such as croque monsieur (grilled Parisian ham and Gruyère) and Niçoise salad for lunch, with veal sweetbreads and, in season, steamed mussels with white wine–and–saffron broth for dinner. **Known for:** classic bistro cuisine; romantic setting; outdoor seating under bright-yellow umbrellas. [$] *Average main: $33* ✉ *540 Main St., Napa* ✣ *At 5th St.* ☎ *707/252–8115* 🌐 *www.angelerestaurant.com.*

★ Compline

$$$ | **MODERN AMERICAN** | The full name of this enterprise put together by master sommelier Matt Stamp and restaurant wine vet Ryan Stetins is Compline Wine Bar, Restaurant, and Merchant, and indeed you can just sip wine or purchase it here. The place evolved into a hot spot, though, for its youthful vibe and eclectic small and large plates that might include shrimp lumpia (essentially a type of fried spring roll) and citrus-brined chicken but always the Compline burger, best enjoyed with duck-fat fries—and, per Stamp, champagne. **Known for:** upbeat vibe; pastas and vegetarian dishes; by-the-glass wines. [$] *Average main: $29* ✉ *1300 1st St., Suite 312, Napa* ☎ *707/492–8150* 🌐 *complinewine.com* 🕒 *Closed Tues.*

Grace's Table

$$ | **ECLECTIC** | A dependable, varied menu makes this modest corner restaurant occupying a brick-and-glass storefront many Napans' go-to choice for a simple meal. Fish tacos and iron-skillet corn bread with lavender honey and butter show up at all hours, with buttermilk pancakes and chílaquiles scrambled eggs among the brunch staples and cassoulet and roasted young chicken popular for dinner. **Known for:** congenial staffers; good beers on tap; eclectic menu focusing on France, Italy, and the Americas. [$] *Average main: $26* ✉ *1400 2nd St., Napa* ✥ *At Franklin St.* ☎ *707/226–6200* 🌐 *www.gracestable.net.*

★ La Toque

$$$$ | **MODERN AMERICAN** | Chef Ken Frank's La Toque is the complete package: his imaginative French-inspired cuisine, served in a formal dining space, is complemented by a wine lineup that consistently earns the restaurant a coveted *Wine Spectator* Grand Award. Ingredients appearing on the prix-fixe multicourse tasting menu often include caviar, sea scallops, squab, and lamb saddle, in dishes prepared and seasoned to pair with wines jointly chosen by the chefs and master sommelier. **Known for:** chef's tasting menu (á la carte also possible); astute wine pairings; vegetarian tasting menu. [$] *Average main: $150* ✉ *Westin Verasa Napa, 1314 McKinstry St., Napa* ✥ *Off Soscol Ave.* ☎ *707/257–5157* 🌐 *www.latoque.com* 🕒 *Closed Mon. and Tues. No lunch.*

Morimoto Napa

$$$$ | **JAPANESE** | *Iron Chef* star Masaharu Morimoto is the big name behind this downtown Napa restaurant where everything is delightfully over the top, including the desserts. Organic materials such as twisting grapevines above the bar and rough-hewn wooden tables seem simultaneously earthy and modern, creating a fitting setting for the gorgeously plated Japanese fare, from straightforward sashimi to more elaborate seafood, chicken, pork, and beef entrées. **Known for:** theatrical ambience; gorgeous plating; cocktail and sake menu. [$] *Average main: $42* ✉ *610 Main St., Napa* ✥ *At 5th St.* ☎ *707/252–1600* 🌐 *www.morimotonapa.com.*

Oenotri

$$ | **ITALIAN** | Often spotted at local farmers' markets and his restaurant's gardens, Oenotri's ebullient chef-owner and Napa native Tyler Rodde is ever on the lookout for fresh produce to incorporate into his rustic southern-Italian cuisine. His restaurant, a brick-walled contemporary space with tall windows and wooden tables, is a lively spot to sample housemade salumi and pastas, thin-crust pizzas, and entrées that might include seared fresh fish or grilled skirt steak. **Known for:** lively atmosphere; Margherita pizza with San Marzano tomatoes; desserts with flair. [$] *Average main: $26* ✉ *1425 1st St., Napa* ✥ *At Franklin St.* ☎ *707/252–1022* 🌐 *www.oenotri.com.*

★ Torc

$$$ | **MODERN AMERICAN** | *Torc* means "wild boar" in an early Celtic dialect, and owner-chef Sean O'Toole, who formerly helmed kitchens at top Manhattan, San Francisco, and Yountville establishments, occasionally incorporates the restaurant's namesake beast into his eclectic offerings. A recent menu featured baked-stuffed Maine lobster, nettle risotto, three hand-cut pasta dishes, and pork-belly with pole beans, all prepared by O'Toole and his team with style and precision. **Known for:** gracious service; specialty cocktails; Bengali sweet-potato pakora and deviled-egg appetizers. [$] *Average main: $36* ✉ *1140 Main St., Napa* ✣ *At Pearl St.* ☎ *707/252–3292* 🌐 *www.torcnapa.com* 🕒 *Closed Sun. and Mon.*

★ ZuZu

$$$ | SPANISH | At festive ZuZu the focus is on cold and hot tapas, paella, and other Spanish favorites often downed with cava or sangria. Regulars revere the paella, made with Spanish *bomba* rice, and small plates that might include garlic shrimp, jamón Ibérico, lamb chops with Moroccan barbecue glaze, and white anchovies with sliced egg and rémoulade on grilled bread. **Known for:** singular flavors and spicing; Spanish jazz on the stereo; sister restaurant La Taberna three doors south for beer, wine, and bar bites. [$] *Average main: $32* ✉ *829 Main St., Napa* ✣ *Near 3rd St.* ☎ *707/224–8555* 🌐 *www.zuzunapa.com* 🕒 *Closed Mon. and Tues.*

Hotels

Andaz Napa

$$$ | HOTEL | Part of the Hyatt family, this boutique hotel with an urban-hip vibe has spacious guest rooms with white-marble bathrooms stocked with high-quality products. **Pros:** casual-chic feel; proximity to downtown restaurants, theaters, and tasting rooms; cheery, attentive service. **Cons:** unremarkable views from some rooms; expensive on weekends in high season; some room show wear and tear. [$] *Rooms from: $304* ✉ *1450 1st St., Napa* ☎ *707/687–1234* 🌐 *andaznapa.com* 🛏 *141 rooms* 🍴 *No meals.*

★ Archer Hotel Napa

$$$ | HOTEL | Ideal for travelers seeking design pizzazz, a see-and-be-seen atmosphere, and first-class amenities, this five-story downtown Napa property fuses New York City chic and Las Vegas glamour. **Pros:** restaurants and room service by chef Charlie Palmer; Sky & Vine rooftop bar; great views from upper-floor rooms (especially south and west). **Cons:** not particularly rustic; expensive in high season; occasional service, hospitality lapses. [$] *Rooms from: $324* ✉ *1230 1st St., Napa* ☎ *707/690–9800, 855/200–9052* 🌐 *archerhotel.com/napa* 🛏 *183 rooms* 🍴 *No meals.*

★ Carneros Resort and Spa

$$$$ | RESORT | A winning combination of glamour, service, and pastoral seclusion makes this resort with freestanding board-and-batten cottages the perfect getaway for active lovebirds or families and groups seeking to unwind. **Pros:** cottages have lots of privacy; beautiful views from hilltop pool and hot tub; heaters on private patios. **Cons:** long drive to upvalley destinations; least expensive accommodations pick up highway noise; pricey pretty much year-round. [$] *Rooms from: $749* ✉ *4048 Sonoma Hwy./Hwy. 121, Napa* ☎ *707/299–4900, 888/400–9000* 🌐 *www.carnerosresort.com* 🛏 *100 rooms* 🍴 *No meals.*

★ The Inn on First

$$ | B&B/INN | Guests gush over the hospitality at this inn where the painstakingly restored 1905 mansion facing 1st Street contains five rooms, with five additional accommodations, all suites, in a building behind a secluded patio and garden. **Pros:** full gourmet breakfast by hosts-with-the-most owners; gas fireplaces and whirlpool tubs in all rooms; away from downtown but not too far. **Cons:** no TVs; owners "respectfully request no children"; lacks pool, fitness center, and other amenities of larger properties. [$] *Rooms from: $225* ✉ *1938 1st St., Napa* ☎ *707/253–1331* 🌐 *www.theinnonfirst.com* 🛏 *10 rooms* 🍴 *Free breakfast.*

★ Inn on Randolph

$$$ | **B&B/INN** | A few calm blocks from the downtown action on a nearly 1-acre lot with landscaped gardens, the Inn on Randolph—with a Gothic Revival–style main house and its five guest rooms plus five historic cottages out back—is a sophisticated haven celebrated for its gourmet gluten-free breakfasts and snacks. **Pros:** quiet residential neighborhood; spa tubs in cottages and two main-house rooms; romantic setting. **Cons:** a bit of a walk from downtown; expensive in-season; weekend minimum-stay requirement. [$] *Rooms from: $339* ✉ *411 Randolph St., Napa* ☎ *707/257–2886* 🌐 *www.innonrandolph.com* 🛏 *10 rooms* 🍴 *Free breakfast.*

Nightlife

Blue Note Napa

MUSIC CLUBS | The famed New York jazz room's intimate West Coast club hosts national headliners such as Kenny Garrett, KT Tunstall, and Jody Watley. There's a full bar, and you can order a meal or small bites from the kitchen. The larger JaM Cellars Ballroom upstairs books similar artists. ✉ *Napa Valley Opera House, 1030 Main St., Napa* ✣ *At 1st St.* ☎ *707/880–2300* 🌐 *www.bluenotenapa.com.*

Cadet Wine + Beer Bar

WINE BARS—NIGHTLIFE | Cadet plays things urban-style cool with a long bar, high-top tables, and a low-lit, generally loungelike feel. When they opened their bar, the two owners described their outlook as "unabashedly pro-California," but their wine-and-beer lineup circles the globe. The crowd here is youngish, the vibe festive. ✉ *930 Franklin St., Napa* ✣ *At end of pedestrian alley between 1st and 2nd Sts.* ☎ *707/224–4400* 🌐 *www.cadetbeerandwinebar.com* ☞ *Closed Mon. and Tues.*

Shopping

First Street Napa

SHOPPING CENTERS/MALLS | The Archer Hotel Napa anchors this open-air downtown complex of mostly ground-level restaurants, tasting rooms, and national (Anthropologie, Lululemon) and homegrown (Bennington Napa Valley, Habituate Lifestyle + Interiors, Napa Stäk) design, clothing, housewares, and culinary shops. Copperfield's Books and the Visit Napa Valley Welcome Center are also here, along with Milo and Friends for pet necessities and accessories. ✉ *1300 1st St., Napa* ✣ *Between Franklin and Coombs Sts.* ☎ *707/257–6900* 🌐 *www.firststreetnapa.com.*

Activities

Napa Valley Gondola

TOUR—SPORTS | Rides in authentic gondolas that seat up to six depart from downtown Napa's municipal dock. You'll never mistake the Napa River for the Grand Canal, but on a sunny day this is a diverting excursion that often includes a serenade. ✉ *Main Street Boat Dock, 680 Main St., Napa* ✣ *Riverfront Promenade, south of 3rd St. Bridge* ☎ *707/373–2100* 🌐 *napavalleygondola.com* ☞ *From $145 (up to 6 people).*

Yountville

9 miles north of the town of Napa.

Yountville (population 3,000) is something like Disneyland for food lovers. You could stay here several days and not exhaust all the options—a few of them owned by The French Laundry's Thomas Keller—and the tiny town is full of small inns and high-end hotels that cater to those who prefer to walk (not drive) after an extravagant meal. It's also well located for excursions to many big-name Napa wineries, especially those in the Stags Leap District, from which big, bold

Cabernet Sauvignons helped make the Napa Valley's wine-making reputation.

GETTING HERE AND AROUND

Downtown Yountville sits just off Highway 29. Approaching from the south take the Yountville exit—from the north take Madison—and proceed to Washington Street, home to the major shops and restaurants. Yountville Cross Road connects downtown to the Silverado Trail, along which many noted wineries do business. The free Yountville Trolley serves the town daily 10 am–7 pm (on-call service until 11 pm except on Sunday).

 Sights

★ Cliff Lede Vineyards

WINERY/DISTILLERY | Inspired by his passion for classic rock, owner and construction magnate Cliff Lede named the blocks in his Stags Leap District vineyard after hits by the Grateful Dead and other bands. Rock memorabilia and contemporary art like Jim Dine's outdoor sculpture *Twin 6' Hearts,* a magnet for the Instagram set, are two other Lede obsessions. The vibe at his efficient, high-tech winery is anything but laid-back, however. Cutting-edge agricultural and enological science informs the vineyard management and wine making here. Lede produces Sauvignon Blanc, Cabernet Sauvignon, and Bordeaux-style red blends; tastings often include a Chardonnay, Pinot Gris, or Pinot Noir from sister winery FEL. All the wines are well crafted, though the Cabs really rock. ⊠ *1473 Yountville Cross Rd., Yountville* ⊹ *Off Silverado Trail* ☎ *707/944–8642* ⊕ *cliffledevineyards.com* 🍷 *Tastings from $60 (sometimes $40 for weekend garden tastings).*

★ Elyse Winery

WINERY/DISTILLERY | One of his colleagues likens Elyse's winemaker, Russell Bevan, to "a water witch without the walking stick" for his ability to assess a vineyard's weather, soil, and vine positioning and intuit how particular viticultural techniques will affect wines' flavors. Bevan farms judiciously during the growing season, striving later in the cellar to preserve what nature and his efforts have yielded rather than rely on heavy manipulation. Under previous owners for three-plus decades (until 2018), Elyse became known for single-vineyard Zinfandels and Cabernet Sauvignons, with Merlot, Petite Sirah, and red blends other strong suits. A country lane edged by vines leads to this unassuming winery, whose tastings, often outdoors, have a backyard-casual feel. ■TIP→ **Costing much less than the average Napa Valley Cab, Elyse's Holbrook Mitchell Cabernet Sauvignon holds its own against peers priced appreciably higher.** ⊠ *2100 Hoffman La., Napa* ⊹ *1¾ miles south of central Yountville, off Hwy. 29 or Solano Ave.* ☎ *707/944–2900* ⊕ *elysewinery.com* 🍷 *Tastings from $50.*

★ Heron House Yountville

WINERY/DISTILLERY | Nine family-owned wineries specializing in small-batch Cabernet Sauvignon showcase their output at this southern Yountville tasting space that doubles as a boutique for contemporary art, fashion accessories, and household items. Several heavy-duty Napa names are involved, starting with Richard Steltzner, who began growing grapes here in 1965. His daughter, Allison, Heron House's founder, represents his Steltzner Vineyards and her Bench Vineyards, and well-known vintners and winemakers are behind the other operations: Éponymous, Hobel, Lindstrom, Myriad, Perchance, Switchback Ridge, and Zeitgeist. The wineries also make whites, rosés, and other reds. Tasting fees vary depending on the flight, which hosts are happy to adjust to match guests' preferences. Visits are by appointment, but walk-ins are accommodated when possible. ■TIP→ **The King of Kings Cabernet Experience suits collectors and Napa Valley Cab lovers eager to up their game.** ⊠ *6484 Washington St., Suite G, Yountville* ⊹ *At Oak Circle* ☎ *707/947–7039* ⊕ *heronhouseyountville.*

com ✉ *Tastings $65–$125* ⊘ *Closed Tues. and Wed.*

★ Oasis by Hoopes

WINERY/DISTILLERY | Vineyards surround the walk-through organic garden and corral for rescue animals that anchor second-generation vintner Lindsay Hoopes's playfully pastoral, cool-bordering-on-chic wine venue. In conceiving this family- and dog-friendly outdoor-oriented spot— with ample patio and garden seating, an Airstream trailer Instagrammers love, and even a tent—Hoopes aimed to expand the notion of what a Napa Valley wine tasting can entail. To that end, each group or solo visitor pays a table charge the hosts apply to bottles purchased for sipping on-site or later. If you prefer a traditional flight, the fee can go toward that, too. Lindsay's father started Hoopes Vineyard in the 1980s, selling his Oakville AVA Cabernet Sauvignon grapes to A-list producers before starting his boutique label in 1999. The lineup now includes Sauvignon Blanc, Chardonnay, rosé, Merlot, and Syrah. Most are gems, particularly two Oakville Cabs and a Howell Mountain Merlot. ✉ *6204 Washington St., Yountville* ✛ *1 mile south of downtown* ☎ *707/944–1869* ⊕ *hoopesvineyard.com/oasis-by-hoopes* ✉ *Tastings from $75.*

RH Wine Vault

WINERY/DISTILLERY | Gargantuan crystal chandeliers, century-old olive trees, and strategically placed water features provide visual and aural continuity at Restoration Hardware's quadruple-threat food, wine, art, and design compound. An all-day café fronts two steel, glass, and concrete home-furnishings galleries, with a bluestone walkway connecting them to a reboot of the former Ma(i)sonry wine salon here. Centered around a two-story 1904 manor house constructed from Napa River stone, it remains an excellent spot to learn about small-lot Napa and Sonoma wines, served by the glass, flight, or bottle. Collector-revered labels like Corison, Fisher, Lail, Matthiasson, Melka, and Spottswoode are all represented, the wines in good weather poured in "outdoor living rooms" behind the stone structure. Oozing RH fabulousness as it does, the Wine Vault can feel like a scene on a busy day, but the wines are the real deal. All tastings are by appointment. ✉ *6725 Washington St., Yountville* ✛ *At Pedroni St.* ☎ *707/339–4654* ⊕ *www.restorationhardware.com* ✉ *Tastings from $50.*

Robert Sinskey Vineyards

WINERY/DISTILLERY | Although the winery produces a Stags Leap Cabernet Sauvignon (SLD Estate), two Bordeaux-style red blends (Marcien and POV), and white wines, Sinskey is best known for its intense, brambly Carneros District Pinot Noirs. All the grapes are grown in organic, certified biodynamic vineyards. The influence of Robert's wife, Maria Helm Sinskey—a chef and cookbook author and the winery's culinary director—is evident during the tastings, all of which are accompanied by at least a few bites of food. The elevated Terroir Tasting explores the winery's land and farming practices. Chef's Table takes in the winery's culinary gardens and ends with a seated wine-and-food pairing. All visits require an appointment, wisely made a day or two ahead. ✉ *6320 Silverado Trail, Napa* ✛ *At Yountville Cross Rd.* ☎ *707/944–9090* ⊕ *www.robertsinskey.com* ✉ *Tastings $40–$175.*

Restaurants

Ad Hoc

$$$$ | **MODERN AMERICAN** | At this low-key dining room with zinc-top tables and wine served in tumblers, superstar chef Thomas Keller offers a single, fixed-price, nightly menu that might include smoked beef short ribs with creamy herb rice and charred broccolini or sesame chicken with radish kimchi and fried rice. Ad Hoc also serves a small but decadent Sunday brunch, and Keller's Addendum annex, in a separate small building behind the restaurant, sells boxed lunches to go (including moist buttermilk fried chicken) from Thursday to Saturday except in winter. **Known for:** casual cuisine at great prices for a Thomas Keller restaurant; don't-miss buttermilk-fried-chicken night; Burgers & Half Bottles (of wine) pop-up. [$] *Average main: $56* ✉ *6476 Washington St., Yountville* ✣ *At Oak Circle* ☎ *707/944–2487* 🌐 *www.thomaskeller.com/adhoc* ⏲ *Closed Tues. and Wed. No lunch Mon. and Thurs.* ☞ *Check website or call a day ahead for next day's menu.*

★ Bistro Jeanty

$$$ | FRENCH | Escargots, cassoulet, *steak au poivre* (pepper steak), and other French classics are prepared with the utmost precision inside this tan-brick country bistro whose flower-filled window boxes, extra-wide shutters, and red-and-white-striped awning hint at the Old World flair and joie de vivre that infuse the place. Regulars often start with the rich tomato soup in a flaky puff pastry before proceeding to sole meunière or coq au vin, completing the French sojourn with a lemon meringue tart or other authentic dessert. **Known for:** traditional preparations; oh-so-French atmosphere; patio seating. [$] *Average main: $30* ✉ *6510 Washington St., Yountville* ✣ *At Mulberry St.* ☎ *707/944–0103* 🌐 *www.bistrojeanty.com.*

★ Bouchon Bistro

$$$ | FRENCH | The team that created The French Laundry is also behind this place, where everything—the zinc-topped bar, antique sconces, suave waitstaff, and traditional French onion soup—could have come straight from a Parisian bistro. Pan-seared rib eye with béarnaise and mussels steamed with white wine, saffron, and Dijon mustard—both served with crispy, addictive fries—are among the perfectly executed entrées. **Known for:** bistro classics; raw bar; Bouchon Bakery next door. [$] *Average main: $35* ✉ *6534 Washington St., Yountville* ✣ *Near Humboldt St.* ☎ *707/944–8037* 🌐 *thomaskeller.com/bouchonyountville.*

Ciccio

$$ | MODERN ITALIAN | The ranch of Ciccio's owners, Frank and Karen Altamura, supplies some of the vegetables and herbs for the modern Italian cuisine prepared in the open kitchen of this remodeled former grocery store. Seasonal growing cycles dictate the menu, with fried-seafood appetizers (calamari, perhaps, or softshell crabs), a few pasta dishes, herb-crusted fish, and several pizzas among the likely offerings. **Known for:** Negroni bar; pizzas' flavorful cheeses; mostly Napa Valley wines, some from owners' winery. [$] *Average main: $23* ✉ *6770 Washington St., Yountville* ✣ *At Madison St.* ☎ *707/945–1000* 🌐 *www.ciccionapavalley.com* ⏲ *Closed Mon. and Tues. No lunch.*

Coqueta Napa Valley

$$$ | SPANISH | From *pintxos* (small plates) and paellas to Iberian cheeses and fish *a la plancha* (flat-grilled), the chefs at this Wine Country offspring of Michael Chiarello's successful San Francisco restaurant Coqueta reimagine Spanish classics with a 21st-century farm-to-table sensibility. The frenetic pace in the flame-happy open kitchen, inside Yountville's redbrick former railroad depot, keeps the mood lively in the relatively small dining space, with the vibe on the patio out back even more so. **Known for:** sensual flavors; dynamic spicing; seasonal cocktails inspired by Spain and the Napa Valley. [$] *Average main: $32* ✉ *6525 Washington St., Yountville* ✣ *Near Yount St.* ☎ *707/244–4350* 🌐 *www.coquetanv.com/home* ⏲ *Closed Tues. and Wed.*

★ The French Laundry

$$$$ | AMERICAN | An old stone building laced with ivy houses chef Thomas Keller's destination restaurant. Some courses on the two prix-fixe menus, one of which highlights vegetables, rely on luxe ingredients such as *calotte* (cap of the rib eye); others take humble elements like carrots or fava beans and elevate them to art. **Known for:** signature starter "oysters and pearls"; sea urchin, black truffles, and other "supplements"; superior wine list. [$] *Average main: $350* ✉ *6640 Washington St., Yountville* ✣ *At Creek St.* ☎ *707/944–2380* 🌐 *www.frenchlaundry.com* ⏲ *No lunch Mon.–Thurs.* 👔 *Jacket required* ☞ *Reservations essential wks ahead.*

Mustards Grill

$$$ | **AMERICAN** | Cindy Pawlcyn's Mustards Grill fills day and night with fans of her hearty cuisine, equal parts updated renditions of traditional American dishes—what Pawlcyn dubs "deluxe truck stop classics"—and fanciful contemporary fare. Barbecued baby back pork ribs and a lemon-lime tart piled high with brown-sugar meringue fall squarely in the first category, and sweet corn tamales with tomatillo-avocado salsa and wild mushrooms represent the latter. **Known for:** roadhouse setting; convivial mood; hoppin' bar. [$] *Average main: $30* ✉ *7399 St. Helena Hwy./Hwy. 29, Napa* ✣ *1 mile north of Yountville* ☎ *707/944–2424* 🌐 *www.mustardsgrill.com.*

North Block

$$$ | **MODERN AMERICAN** | In his California debut, chef Nick Tamburo, previously of two Manhattan locations of celeb chef David Chang's Momofuku, prepares farm-to-table cuisine with intriguing flavors and ingredients. A recent starter paired oro blanco (a grapefruitlike citrus) and ever-so-thinly sliced kohlrabi (a type of turnip) spiced to marvelous effect with the mildly minty Japanese herb shiso, the chef's artistry repeating itself on the menu's wood-fired pizzas and fish and meat entrées. **Known for:** courtyard patio seating; cocktails and wine list; atmospheric interior. [$] *Average main: $35* ✉ *North Block Hotel, 6757 Washington St., Yountville* ✣ *Near Madison St.* ☎ *707/944–8080* 🌐 *www.northblockhotel.com/dining.*

★ Perry Lang's

$$$$ | **STEAKHOUSE** | An 1870 redbrick former mansion holds this contemporary chophouse whose art-deco accents recall an old-school gentlemen's club—the kind of place to order a stiff cocktail, a wedge salad topped with thick maple-glazed bacon, and a dry-aged rib eye or tomahawk. Chef Adam Perry Lang, a grilling and barbecue artiste, seduces patrons with culinary drama and hand-tooled steak knives so exquisite it's a felony to swipe them, delivering the goods with an experience that satisfies appetite and soul. **Known for:** St. Louis pork ribs with peach barbecue sauce; Cabernet bone-marrow jus and béarnaise and horseradish sauces for steaks; potent craft cocktails. [$] *Average main: $40* ✉ *6539 Washington St., Yountville* ✣ *Just south of Vintage House* ☎ *707/945–4522* 🌐 *perrylangs.com* ⏲ *No lunch.*

Hotels

★ Bardessono

$$$$ | **RESORT** | Tranquility and luxury with a low carbon footprint are among the goals of this ultragreen wood, steel, and glass resortlike property in downtown Yountville, but there's nothing spartan about the accommodations, arranged around four landscaped courtyards. **Pros:** large rooftop lap pool; in-room spa treatments; three luxury villas for extra privacy. **Cons:** expensive year-round; limited view from some rooms; a bit of street traffic on hotel's west side. [$] *Rooms from: $750* ✉ *6526 Yount St., Yountville* ☎ *707/204–6000, 855/232–0450* 🌐 *www.bardessono.com* 🛏 *65 rooms* 🍴 *No meals.*

Maison Fleurie

$$ | **B&B/INN** | A stay at this comfortable, reasonably priced inn, said to be the oldest hotel in the Napa Valley, places you within walking distance of Yountville's fine restaurants. **Pros:** smallest rooms a bargain; outdoor hot tub and pool; free bike rental. **Cons:** lacks amenities of a

full-service hotel; some rooms pick up noise from nearby Bouchon Bakery; hard to book in high season. $ *Rooms from: $229* ✉ *6529 Yount St., Yountville* ☎ *707/944–2056* ⊕ *www.maisonfleurien-apa.com* ⇝ *13 rooms* �‖ *Free breakfast.*

Napa Valley Lodge

$$ | HOTEL | Clean rooms in a convenient motel-style setting draw travelers willing to pay more than at comparable lodgings in the city of Napa to be within walking distance of Yountville's tasting rooms, restaurants, and shops. **Pros:** well-maintained rooms; vineyard-view rooms on north and west sides; large pool area. **Cons:** no elevator; nice enough but lacks panache; pricey on weekends in high season. $ *Rooms from: $285* ✉ *2230 Madison St., Yountville* ☎ *707/944–2468, 888/944–3545* ⊕ *www.napavalleylodge.com* ⇝ *55 rooms* �‖ *Free breakfast.*

★ North Block Hotel

$$$$ | HOTEL | A two-story boutique property near downtown Yountville's northern edge, the North Block attracts sophisticated travelers who appreciate the clever but unpretentious style and offhand luxury. **Pros:** extremely comfortable beds; personalized service; spacious bathrooms. **Cons:** outdoor areas get some traffic noise; weekend minimum-stay requirement; rates soar on high-season weekends. $ *Rooms from: $540* ✉ *6757 Washington St., Yountville* ☎ *707/944–8080* ⊕ *northblockhotel.com* ⇝ *20 rooms* �‖ *No meals.*

Vintage House

$$$$ | RESORT | Part of the 22-acre Estate Yountville complex—other sections include sister lodging Hotel Villagio, the 13,000-square-foot Spa at the Estate, and shops and restaurants—this downtown hotel consists of two-story brick buildings along verdant landscaped paths shaded by mature trees. **Pros:** aesthetically pleasing accommodations; private patios and balconies; secluded feeling yet near shops, tasting rooms, and restaurants. **Cons:** highway noise audible in some

exterior rooms; very expensive on summer and fall weekends; weekend minimum-stay requirement. $ *Rooms from: $429* ✉ *6541 Washington St., Yountville* ☎ *707/944–1112, 877/351–1153* ⊕ *www.vintagehouse.com* ⇝ *80 rooms* �‖ *Free breakfast.*

🛍 Shopping

The Conservatory

CLOTHING | The New York City–based lifestyle company's heavily curated "considered luxury" comes in the form of clothing, accessories, and decor and well-being items created by small, quality-oriented brands for a discerning clientele. Local products include Vintner's Daughter Active Botanical Serum face oil, whose adherents swear nearly stops time. ✉ *6540 Washington St., Yountville* ✛ *Near Humboldt St.* ☎ *707/415–5015* ⊕ *theconservatorynyc.com/pages/napa-store.*

🏃 Activities

BALLOONING

Napa Valley Aloft

BALLOONING | Passengers soar over the Napa Valley in balloons that launch from downtown Yountville. Flights are from 40 minutes to an hour-plus, depending on the wind speed, with the entire experience taking from three to four hours. ✉ *The Estate Yountville, 6525 Washington St., Yountville* ✛ *Near Mulberry St.* ☎ *707/944–4400, 855/944–4408* ⊕ *www.nvaloft.com* 🎫 *$250 per person.*

BICYCLING

Napa Valley Bike Tours

BICYCLING | With dozens of wineries within 5 miles, this shop makes a fine starting point for guided and self-guided vineyard and wine-tasting excursions. Rental bikes are also available. ✉ *6500 Washington St., Yountville* ✛ *At Mulberry St.* ☎ *707/251–8687* ⊕ *www.napavalleybiketours.com* 🎫 *From $124 (½-day guided tour).*

SPAS

The Spa at The Estate

FITNESS/HEALTH CLUBS | The joint 13,000-square-foot facility of Vintage House and the Hotel Villagio is a five-minute walk from the former's lobby, even less from the latter's. Private spa suites are popular with couples, who enjoy the separate relaxation areas, indoor and outdoor fireplaces, steam showers, saunas, and extra-large tubs. Many treatments involve Omorovicza products based on Hungarian thermal waters and minerals. For a quick uplift, book 20 minutes in the spa's oxygen chair, designed to optimize breathing and promote relaxation. Facials, lip plumping, and massages are among the other à la carte services. The ground-floor retail area, open to the public, is well stocked with beauty products. ⊠ *The Estate Yountville, 6481 Washington St., Yountville* ⬧ *At Oak Circle* ☎ *707/948–5050* ⊕ *www.villagio. com/spa* ⬛ *Treatments from $85.*

Oakville

2 miles northwest of Yountville.

A large butte that runs east–west just north of Yountville blocks the cooling fogs from the south, facilitating the myriad microclimates of the Oakville AVA, home to several high-profile wineries.

GETTING HERE AND AROUND

Driving along Highway 29, you'll know you've reached Oakville when you see the Oakville Grocery on the east side of the road. You can reach Oakville from the Sonoma County town of Glen Ellen by heading east on Trinity Road from Highway 12. The twisting route, along the mountain range that divides Napa and Sonoma, eventually becomes the Oakville Grade. The views on this drive are breathtaking, though the continual curves make it unsuitable for those who suffer from motion sickness.

 Sights

B Cellars

WINERY/DISTILLERY | The chefs take center stage in the open-hearth kitchen of this boutique winery's hospitality house, and with good reason: creating food-friendly wines is B Cellars's raison d'être. Visits to the Oakville facility—all steel beams, corrugated metal, and plate glass yet remarkably cozy—often begin with a tour of the winery's culinary garden and vineyard, with a pause for sips of wine still aging in barrel. A seated tasting of finished wines paired with small bites follows the tour. Kirk Venge, whose fruit-forward style suits the winery's food-oriented approach, crafts red and white blends and single-vineyard Cabernets from estate fruit and grapes from Beckstoffer and other noteworthy vineyards. All visits are strictly by appointment. ⊠ *703 Oakville Cross Rd., Oakville* ⬧ *West of Silverado Trail* ☎ *707/709–8787* ⊕ *www. bcellars.com* ⬛ *Tastings from $80* ⊗ *Closed Tues. and Wed.*

Far Niente

WINERY/DISTILLERY | Hamden McIntyre, a prominent winery architect of his era also responsible for Inglenook and what's now the Culinary Institute of America at Greystone, designed the centerpiece 1885 stone winery here. Abandoned in the wake of Prohibition and only revived beginning in 1979, Far Niente now ranks as one of the Napa Valley's most beautiful properties. Guests participating in the Estate Tasting learn some of this history while sipping the flagship wines, a Chardonnay and a Cabernet Sauvignon blend, along with Russian River Valley Pinot Noir from the affiliated EnRoute label and Dolce, a late-harvest Sémillon and Sauvignon Blanc wine. The Extended Estate Tasting takes in the winery and its aging caves, while the Library Wine Tasting compares older vintages. ⊠ *1350 Acacia Dr., Oakville* ⬧ *Off Oakville Grade Rd.* ☎ *707/944–2861* ⊕ *www.farniente. com* ⬛ *Tastings from $80.*

Robert Mondavi Winery

WINERY/DISTILLERY | Arguably the most influential participant in the Napa Valley's rise to international prominence, the late Robert Mondavi established his namesake winery in the 1960s after losing a battle with his brother over the direction of their family's Charles Krug Winery. In an era when tasting rooms were mostly downscale affairs, Mondavi commissioned architect Cliff May to create a grand Mission-style space to receive visitors. May's design still resonates, the graceful central arch framing the lawn and the vineyard behind, inviting a stroll under the arcades. The Estate Tour & Tasting and Vintner's Tasting provide an introduction to the winery, its portfolio, and Mondavi's life. Another offering focuses on whites and caviar, with a third involving Cabernet Sauvignon from the Mondavi section of the famed To Kalon Vineyard. All visits require a reservation, with last-minute requests often granted. ⊠ *7801 St. Helena Hwy./Hwy. 29, Oakville* ☎ *888/766–6328* ⊕ *www. robertmondaviwinery.com* ⊠ *Tastings and tours from $40.*

★ Silver Oak

WINERY/DISTILLERY | The first review of this winery's Napa Valley Cabernet Sauvignon declared the debut 1972 vintage not all that good and, at $6 a bottle, overpriced. Oops. The celebrated Bordeaux-style Cabernet blend, still the only Napa Valley wine bearing its winery's label each year, evolved into a cult favorite, and founders Ray Duncan and Justin Meyer received worldwide recognition for their signature use of exclusively American oak to age the wines. At the Oakville tasting room, constructed out of reclaimed stone and other materials from a 19th-century Kansas flour mill, the Silver Oak Tasting includes sips of the current Napa Valley vintage, its counterpart from Silver Oak's Alexander Valley operation in Sonoma County, and a library wine. Hosts of vertical tastings pour six Cabernet vintages. All visits require an appointment. ⊠ *915 Oakville Cross Rd., Oakville* ✛ *Off Hwy. 29* ☎ *707/942–7022* ⊕ *www.silveroak. com* ⊠ *Tastings $30–$85.*

Rutherford

2 miles northwest of Oakville.

With its singular microclimate and soil, Rutherford is an important viticultural center, with more big-name wineries than you can shake a corkscrew at. Cabernet Sauvignon is king here. The well-drained, loamy soil is ideal for those vines, and since this part of the valley gets plenty of sun, the grapes develop exceptionally intense flavors.

GETTING HERE AND AROUND

Wineries around Rutherford are dotted along Highway 29 and the parallel Silverado Trail north and south of Rutherford Road/Conn Creek Road, on which wineries can also be found.

Sights

★ Frog's Leap

WINERY/DISTILLERY | If you're a novice, the tour at eco-friendly Frog's Leap is a fun way to begin your education. Conducted by hosts with a sense of humor, the tour stops by a barn built in 1884, 5 acres of organic gardens, and a frog pond topped with lily pads. The winery produced its first vintage, small batches of Sauvignon Blanc and Zinfandel, in 1981, adding Chardonnay and Cabernet Sauvignon the next year. These days Chenin Blanc is another white, with Merlot, Petite Sirah, and the Heritage Blend of classic Napa Valley varietals among the other reds. All visits require a reservation. ■**TIP→ The tour is recommended, but you can forgo it and taste on a garden-view porch.** ⊠ *8815 Conn Creek Rd., Rutherford* ☎ *707/963–4704* ⊕ *www.frogsleap.com* ⊠ *Tastings $45–$95, tour and tasting $75.*

★ Inglenook
WINERY/DISTILLERY | *Wine Enthusiast* magazine bestowed a lifetime-achievement award on vintner-filmmaker Francis Ford Coppola, whose wine-world contributions include resurrecting the historic Inglenook estate. Over the decades he reunited the original property acquired by Inglenook founder Gustave Niebaum, remodeled Niebaum's ivy-covered 1880s château, and purchased the rights to the Inglenook name. The winery's place in Napa Valley history is among the topics discussed at tastings, some of which involve cheese, charcuterie, or other wine-food pairings. Most sessions see a pour of the signature Rubicon wine, a Cabernet Sauvignon–based blend. All visits require an appointment; call the winery or check at the visitor center for same-day. **■ TIP→ In lieu of a tasting, you can book a table at The Bistro, a wine bar with a picturesque courtyard, to sip wine by the glass or bottle.** ✉ *1991 St. Helena Hwy./Hwy. 29, Rutherford* ✥ *At Hwy. 128* ☎ *707/968–1100* 🌐 *www.inglenook.com* 🎫 *Tastings from $60* ⏲ *Closed Mon.–Wed.*

Mumm Napa
WINERY/DISTILLERY | When Champagne Mumm of France set about establishing a California sparkling-wine outpost, its winemaker chose the Napa Valley, where today the winery sources grapes from more than 50 local producers. Made in the *méthode traditionelle* style from Chardonnay, Pinot Noir, Pinot Meunier, and occasionally Pinot Gris, the wines are all fermented in the bottle. Most guests enjoy them alfresco, by the glass or flight, on a patio above the surrounding vineyards or one at eye level. Book an Oak Terrace Tasting to sample top-of-the-line cuvées under the sprawling branches of a blue oak nearly two centuries old. Tasting is by appointment only. ✉ *8445 Silverado Trail, Rutherford* ✥ *1 mile south of Rutherford Cross Rd.* ☎ *707/967–7700* 🌐 *www.mummnapa.com* 🎫 *Tastings $40–$75.*

ZD Wines
WINERY/DISTILLERY | Founded in 1969 and still run by the same family, this winery specializing in Chardonnay, Pinot Noir, and Cabernet Sauvignon is respected for its organic practices, local philanthropy, and Abacus blend. Made "solera-style," Abacus contains wine from every ZD Reserve Cabernet Sauvignon vintage since 1992. The Chardonnay and Pinot Noir come from a Carneros property, the Cabernet from the winery's Rutherford estate, where the wines are made and presented to the public. Appointment-only tastings (same-day often possible) take place in a second-floor space with broad valley views west to the Mayacamas Mountains. For an introduction to ZD and its wine-making philosophy, book a current-release flight. Barrel tastings, small bites, and small-batch reserve wines are all part of the Abacus Experience, which concludes with a current and older Abacus blend. ✉ *8383 Silverado Trail, Rutherford* ☎ *800/487–7757* 🌐 *www.zdwines.com* 🎫 *Tastings from $40.*

🍴 Restaurants

★ Restaurant at Auberge du Soleil
$$$$ | MODERN AMERICAN | Possibly the most romantic roost for brunch or dinner in all the Wine Country is a terrace seat at the Auberge du Soleil resort's illustrious restaurant, and the Mediterranean-inflected cuisine more than matches the dramatic vineyard views. The prix-fixe dinner menu (three or four courses), which relies mainly on local produce, might include caviar or diver scallop starters, delicately prepared fish or vegetable middle-course options, and mains like prime beef pavé with béarnaise, spiced lamb loin, or Japanese Wagyu. **Known for:** polished service; comprehensive wine list; special-occasion feel. [$] *Average main: $135* ✉ *Auberge du Soleil, 180 Rutherford Hill Rd., Rutherford* ✥ *Off Silverado Trail* ☎ *707/963–1211, 800/348–5406* 🌐 *www.aubergedusoleil.com.*

Frog's Leap's picturesque country charm extends all the way to the white picket fence.

Rutherford Grill

$$$ | **AMERICAN** | Dark-wood walls, subdued lighting, and red-leather banquettes make for a perpetually clubby mood at this Rutherford hangout where the patio, popular for its bar, fireplace, and rocking chairs, opens for full meal service or drinks and appetizers when the weather's right. Many entrées—steaks, burgers, fish, rotisserie chicken, and barbecued pork ribs—emerge from an oak-fired grill operated by master technicians. **Known for:** iron-skillet corn bread direct from the oven; signature French dip sandwich and grilled jumbo artichokes; reasonably priced wine list with rarities. [$] *Average main: $29* ✉ *1180 Rutherford Rd., Rutherford* ✣ *At Hwy. 29* ☎ *707/963–1792* 🌐 *www.rutherfordgrill.com.*

Hotels

★ Auberge du Soleil

$$$$ | **RESORT** | Taking a cue from the olive-tree-studded landscape, this hotel with a renowned restaurant and spa cultivates a luxurious look that blends French and California style. **Pros:** stunning valley views; spectacular pool and spa areas; Deluxe-category suites fit for a superstar. **Cons:** stratospheric prices; least expensive rooms get some noise from the bar and restaurant; weekend minimum-stay requirement. [$] *Rooms from: $925* ✉ *180 Rutherford Hill Rd., Rutherford* ☎ *707/963–1211, 800/348–5406* 🌐 *www.aubergedusoleil.com* 🛏 *52 rooms* 🍴 *Free breakfast.*

★ Rancho Caymus Inn

$$$ | **HOTEL** | A romantic hacienda-away-from-home that off-season may well be the Napa Valley's best value in its price range, this upscale-contemporary boutique hotel near Inglenook and the Rutherford Grill contains rooms whose decor and artworks evoke the area's Mexican heritage. **Pros:** courtyard pool area; smallest rooms are 400 square feet, with several 600 or more; well-trained staff. **Cons:** all rooms have only showers (albeit nice ones); king beds in all rooms (no sofa beds, though a few

rollaways available); no spa or fitness center. $ *Rooms from: $396* ✉ *1140 Rutherford Rd., Rutherford* ☎ *707/200–9300* 🌐 *www.ranchocaymusinn.com* 🛏 *26 rooms* 🍴 *Free breakfast.*

St. Helena

2 miles northwest of Oakville.

Downtown St. Helena is the very picture of good living in the Wine Country: sycamore trees arch over Main Street (Highway 29), where visitors flit between boutiques, cafés, and storefront tasting rooms housed in sun-faded redbrick buildings. The genteel district pulls in rafts of tourists during the day, though like most Wine Country towns St. Helena more or less rolls up the sidewalks after dark.

The Napa Valley floor narrows between the Mayacamas and Vaca mountains around St. Helena. The slopes reflect heat onto the vineyards below, and since there's less fog and wind, things get pretty toasty. This is one of the valley's hottest AVAs, with midsummer temperatures often reaching the mid-90s. Bordeaux varietals are the most popular grapes grown here—especially Cabernet Sauvignon but also Merlot, Cabernet Franc, and Sauvignon Blanc.

GETTING HERE AND AROUND

Downtown stretches along Highway 29, called Main Street here. Many wineries lie north and south of downtown along Highway 29. More can be found off Silverado Trail, and some of the most scenic spots are on Spring Mountain, which rises southwest of town.

👁 Sights

Beringer Vineyards

WINERY/DISTILLERY | Brothers Frederick and Jacob Beringer opened the winery that still bears their name in 1876. One of California's earliest bonded wineries, it's the oldest one in the Napa Valley never to have missed a vintage—no mean feat, given Prohibition. Reserve tastings of a limited release Chardonnay, a few big Cabernets, and a Sauterne-style dessert wine take place on the veranda (also inside when possible) at Frederick's grand Rhine House Mansion, built in 1884 and surrounded by mature landscaped gardens. Beringer is known for several widely distributed wines, but many poured here are winery exclusives. Visits require a reservation; same-day guests are accommodated if possible. ✉ *2000 Main St./Hwy. 29, St. Helena* ✣ *Near Pratt Ave.* ☎ *707/963–8989* 🌐 *www.beringer.com* 🎟 *Tastings from $35.*

Charles Krug Winery

WINERY/DISTILLERY | A historically sensitive renovation of its 1874 Redwood Cellar Building transformed the former production facility of the Napa Valley's oldest winery into an epic hospitality center. Charles Krug, a Prussian immigrant, established the winery in 1861 and ran it until his death in 1892. Italian immigrants Cesare Mondavi and his wife, Rosa, purchased Charles Krug in 1943, operating it with their sons Peter and Robert (who later opened his own winery). Still run by Peter's family, Charles Krug specializes in small-lot Yountville and Howell Mountain Cabernet Sauvignons plus Sauvignon Blanc, Chardonnay, Merlot, and Pinot Noir. All visits are by appointment. ✉ *2800 Main St./Hwy. 29, St. Helena* ✣ *Across from Culinary Institute of America* ☎ *707/967–2229* 🌐 *www.charleskrug.com* 🎟 *Tasting $45, tour $75 (includes tasting).*

Hall St. Helena

WINERY/DISTILLERY | The Cabernet Sauvignons produced here are works of art born of the latest in organic-farming science and wine-making technology. A glass-walled tasting room allows guests to see some of the high-tech equipment winemaker Megan Gunderson employs to craft wines that also include Merlot, Cabernet Franc, and Sauvignon Blanc. Looking westward from the second-floor tasting area, rows of neatly spaced Cabernet vines capture the eye, beyond them the tree-studded Mayacamas Mountains. Hard to miss as you arrive along Highway 29, Lawrence Argent's 35-foot-tall *Bunny Foo Foo,* a stainless-steel sculpture of a rabbit leaping out of the vineyard, is one of many museum-quality artworks on display at appointment-only Hall (call for same-day). ■TIP→ **Sister winery Hall Rutherford hosts an exclusive wine-and-food pairing atop a Rutherford hillside.** ✉ *401 St. Helena Hwy./Hwy. 29, St. Helena ✛ Near White La.* ☎ *707/967-2626* ⊕ *www.hallwines. com* ☐ *Tastings from $40.*

★ **Joseph Phelps Vineyards**
WINERY/DISTILLERY | An appointment is required for tastings at the winery started by the late Joseph Phelps, but it's worth the effort—all the more so after an inspired renovation of the main redwood structure, a classic of 1970s Northern California architecture. Phelps produces very fine whites, along with Pinot Noir from its Sonoma Coast vineyards, but the blockbusters are the Bordeaux reds, particularly the Cabernet Sauvignons and Insignia, a luscious-yet-subtle Cab-dominant blend. Insignia, which often receives high-90s scores from respected wine publications, is always among the current releases poured at the one-hour seated Terrace Tasting overlooking grapevines and oaks. Several other experiences involve food pairings; participants in the blending seminar mix the varietals that go into Insignia. ✉ *200 Taplin Rd., St. Helena ✛ Off Silverado Trail* ☎ *707/963–2745, 800/707–5789* ⊕ *www.josephphelps.com* ☐ *Tastings from $90.*

Prager Winery & Port Works
WINERY/DISTILLERY | "If door is locked, ring bell," reads a sign outside the weathered-redwood tasting shack at this family-run winery known for red, white,

and tawny ports. The sign, the bell, and the thousands of dollar bills tacked to the walls and ceilings inside are your first indications that you're drifting back in time with the old-school Pragers, who have been making regular and fortified wines in St. Helena since the late 1970s. Five members of the second generation, along with two spouses, run this homespun operation founded by Jim and Imogene Prager. In addition to ports the winery makes Petite Sirah and Sweet Claire, a late-harvest Riesling dessert wine. Some tastings take place in a garden outside the tasting room or on the crush pad. ✉ *1281 Lewelling La., St. Helena ✛ Off Hwy. 29* ☎ *707/963–7678* ⊕ *www.pragerport.com* ☐ *Tastings $40 (includes glass).*

★ **Pride Mountain Vineyards**
WINERY/DISTILLERY | This winery 2,200 feet up Spring Mountain straddles Napa and Sonoma counties, confusing enough for visitors but even more complicated for the wine-making staff: government regulations require separate wineries and paperwork for each side of the property. It's one of several Pride Mountain quirks, but winemaker Sally Johnson's "big red wines," including a Cabernet Sauvignon · that earned 100-point scores from a major wine critic two years in a row, are serious business. On a visit, by appointment only, you can learn about the farming and cellar strategies behind Pride's acclaimed Cabs (the winery also produces Syrah, a Cab-like Merlot, Viognier, and Chardonnay among others). ■TIP→ **The views here are knock-your-socks-off gorgeous.** ✉ *4026 Spring Mountain Rd., St. Helena ✛ Off St. Helena Rd. (extension of Spring Mountain Rd. in Sonoma County)* ☎ *707/963–4949* ⊕ *www.pridewines. com* ☐ *Tastings $30–$90* ◷ *Closed Tues.*

The Prisoner Wine Company
WINERY/DISTILLERY | The iconoclastic brand opened an industrial-chic space with interiors by the wildly original Napa-based designer Richard Von Saal

to showcase its flagship The Prisoner red blend. "Getting the varietals to play together" is winemaker Chrissy Wittmann's mission with that wine (Zinfandel, Cabernet Sauvignon, Petite Sirah, Syrah, Charbono) and siblings like the Blindfold white (Chardonnay plus Rhône and other varietals). The Line-up Tasting of current releases unfolds either in the Tasting Lounge (more hip hotel bar than traditional tasting room) or outside in the casual open-air The Yard. When offered, The Makery Experience (indoors) involves boldly flavored plates that pair well with Wittman's fruit-forward wines. The Prisoner's tasting space is quite the party, for which a reservation is required. ⊠ 1178 Galleron Rd., St. Helena ⊹ At Hwy. 29 ☎ 707/967–3823, 877/283–5934 ⊕ www.theprisonerwinecompany.com ▤ Tastings from $45.

★ Tres Sabores Winery

WINERY/DISTILLERY | A long, narrow lane with two sharp bends leads to splendidly workaday Tres Sabores, where the sight of sheep, golden retrievers, guinea hens, pomegranate and other trees and plants, a slew of birds and bees, and a heaping compost pile reinforce a simple point: despite the Napa Valley's penchant for glamour this is, first and foremost, farm country. Owner-winemaker Julie Johnson specializes in single-vineyard wines that include Cabernet Sauvignon and Zinfandel from estate-grown certified-organic Rutherford bench vines. She also excels with Petite Sirah from dry-farmed Calistoga fruit, Sauvignon Blanc, and the zippy ¿Por Qué No? (Why not?) red blend. Tres sabores is Spanish for "three flavors," which to Johnson represents the land, her vines, and, as she puts it, "the spirit of the company around the table." Tastings by appointment only are informal and usually held outside. ⊠ 1620 S. Whitehall La., St. Helena ⊹ West of Hwy. 29 ☎ 707/967–8027 ⊕ www.tressabores. com ▤ Tasting $50.

🍴 Restaurants

Brasswood Bar + Bakery + Kitchen

$$$ | ITALIAN | After Napa Valley fixture Tra Vigne lost its lease, many staffers regrouped a few miles north at the restaurant (the titular Kitchen) of the Brasswood complex, which also includes a bakery, shops, and a wine-tasting room. Along with dishes developed for the new location, chef David Nuno incorporates Tra Vigne favorites such as mozzarella-stuffed arancini (rice balls) into his Mediterranean-leaning menu. **Known for:** mostly Napa-Sonoma wine list; no corkage on first bottle; Tra Vigne favorites. $ Average main: $31 ⊠ 3111 St. Helena Hwy. N, St. Helena ⊹ Near Ehlers La. ☎ 707/968–5434 ⊕ www.brasswood. com.

The Charter Oak

$$$ | MODERN AMERICAN | Christopher Kostow's reputation rests on his swoon-worthy haute cuisine for The Restaurant at Meadowood, but he and his Charter Oak team adopt a more straightforward approach—fewer ingredients chosen for maximum effect—at this high-ceilinged, brown-brick downtown restaurant. On the ever-evolving menu this strategy might translate into dishes like celery-leaf chicken with preserved lemon, herbs, and pan drippings, and red kuri squash with caramelized koji and goat cheese (or just go for the droolworthy cheeseburger and thick fries). **Known for:** exceedingly fresh produce from nearby Meadowood farm; patio dining in brick courtyard; top chef's affordable cuisine. $ Average main: $29 ⊠ 1050 Charter Oak Ave., at Hwy. 29, St. Helena ☎ 707/302–6996 ⊕ www.thecharteroak.com ☽ No lunch Mon. and Tues.

★ Cook St. Helena

$$ | ITALIAN | A curved marble bar spotlit by contemporary art-glass pendants adds a touch of style to this downtown restaurant whose northern Italian cuisine pleases with understated sophistication.

Mussels with house-made sausage in a spicy tomato broth, chopped salad with pancetta and pecorino, and the daily changing risotto are among the dishes regulars revere. **Known for:** top-quality ingredients; reasonably priced local and international wines; intimate dining. [$] *Average main: $26* ✉ *1310 Main St., St. Helena* ✣ *Near Hunt Ave.* ☎ *707/963–7088* 🌐 *www.cooksthelena.com* 🕒 *Closed weekends (check website for updates).*

★ Farmstead at Long Meadow Ranch

$$$ | MODERN AMERICAN | In a high-ceilinged former barn with plenty of outside seating, Farmstead revolves around an open kitchen whose chefs prepare meals with grass-fed beef and lamb, fruits and vegetables, and eggs, olive oil, wine, honey, and other ingredients from nearby Long Meadow Ranch. Entrées might include wood-grilled trout with fennel, mushroom, onion, and bacon-mustard vinaigrette; caramelized beets with goat cheese; or a wood-grilled heritage pork chop with jalapeño grits. **Known for:** Tuesday fried-chicken night; house-made charcuterie; on-site general store, café, and Long Meadow Wines tasting space. [$] *Average main: $27* ✉ *738 Main St., St. Helena* ✣ *At Charter Oak Ave.* ☎ *707/963–4555* 🌐 *www.longmeadowranch.com/eat-drink/restaurant.*

Goose & Gander

$$$ | MODERN AMERICAN | A Craftsman bungalow whose 1920s owner reportedly used the cellar for bootlegging during Prohibition houses this restaurant where the pairing of food and drink is as likely to involve a craft cocktail as a sommelier-selected wine. Main courses such as brick-cooked chicken, a heritage-pork burger, and dry-aged New York steak with black-lime and pink-peppercorn butter follow starters that might include blistered Brussels sprouts and roasted octopus. **Known for:** intimate main dining room with fireplace; alfresco patio dining; basement bar among Napa's best watering holes. [$] *Average main: $31* ✉ *1245 Spring St., St. Helena* ✣ *At Oak St.* ☎ *707/967–8779* 🌐 *www.goosegander.com* 🕒 *No lunch.*

Gott's Roadside

$ | AMERICAN | A 1950s-style outdoor hamburger stand goes upscale at this spot whose customers brave long lines to order breakfast sandwiches, juicy burgers, root-beer floats, and garlic fries. Choices not available a half century ago include ahi tuna and Impossible burgers and kale and Vietnamese chicken salads. **Known for:** tasty 21st-century diner cuisine; shaded picnic tables (arrive early or late for lunch to get one); second branch at Napa's Oxbow Public Market. [$] *Average main: $14* ✉ *933 Main St./Hwy. 29, St. Helena* ✣ *Near Charter Oak Ave.* ☎ *707/963–3486* 🌐 *www.gotts.com* ☞ *Reservations not accepted.*

★ Press

$$$$ | MODERN AMERICAN | For years this cavernous restaurant with a contempo-barn interior and wraparound patio steps from neighboring vineyards was northern Napans' preferred stop for a top-shelf cocktail, grass-fed dry-aged steak, and high-90s-scoring local Cabernet. It still is, but since arriving in 2019, chef Philip Tessier, formerly of Yountville's The French Laundry and Bouchon Bistro and New York City's Le Bernardin, has expanded the menu to include more refined preparations, much of whose produce is grown nearby. **Known for:** extensive wine cellar; impressive cocktails; casual-chic ambience. [$] *Average main: $45* ✉ *587 St. Helena Hwy./Hwy. 29, St. Helena* ✣ *At White La.* ☎ *707/967–0550* 🌐 *www.pressnapavalley.com* 🕒 *No lunch Mon.–Thurs.*

🛏 Hotels

Alila Napa Valley

$$$$ | HOTEL | An upscale-casual ultra-contemporary adults-only resort formerly known as Las Alcobas Napa Valley but as of 2021 in the Hyatt Alila brand's fold, this hillside beauty sits adjacent to Beringer Vineyards six blocks north of Main Street shopping and dining. **Pros:** vineyard views from most rooms; Acacia House restaurant; pool, spa, and fitness center. **Cons:** expensive much of the year; per website no children under age 18 permitted; no self-parking. [$] *Rooms from: $700* ✉ *1915 Main St., St. Helena* ☎ *707/963–7000* 🌐 *www.alilanapavalley.com* 🛏 *68 rooms* 🍴 *No meals.*

El Bonita Motel

$ | **HOTEL** | A classic 1950s-style neon sign marks the driveway to this well-run roadside motel that—when it isn't sold out—offers great value to budget-minded travelers. **Pros:** cheerful rooms; family-friendly; microwaves and mini-refrigerators. **Cons:** noise issues in roadside and ground-floor rooms; expensive on high-season weekends; lacks amenities of fancier properties. [$] *Rooms from: $160* ✉ *195 Main St./Hwy. 29, St. Helena* ☎ *707/963–3216* 🌐 *www.elbonita.com* 🛏 *52 rooms* 🍴 *Free breakfast.*

Harvest Inn

$$$ | **HOTEL** | Although this inn sits just off Highway 29, its patrons remain mostly above the fray, strolling 8 acres of gardens, enjoying views of the vineyards adjoining the property, partaking in spa services, and drifting to sleep in beds adorned with fancy linens and down pillows. **Pros:** garden setting; spacious rooms; near choice wineries, restaurants, and shops. **Cons:** some lower-price rooms lack elegance; high weekend rates; occasional service lapses. [$] *Rooms from: $359* ✉ *1 Main St., St. Helena* ☎ *707/963–9463* 🌐 *www.harvestinn.com* 🛏 *81 rooms* 🍴 *No meals.*

Inn St. Helena

$$$ | **B&B/INN** | A large room at this spiffed-up downtown St. Helena inn is named for author Ambrose Bierce *(The Devil's Dictionary)*, who lived in the main Victorian structure in the early 1900s, but sensitive hospitality and modern amenities are what make a stay worth writing home about. **Pros:** aim-to-please staff and owner; outdoor porch and swing; convenient to shops, tasting rooms, restaurants. **Cons:** no pool, gym, room service, or other typical amenities; two-night minimum on weekends (three with Monday holiday); per website "children 16 and older are welcome." [$] *Rooms from: $309* ✉ *1515 Main St., St. Helena* ☎ *707/963–3003* 🌐 *www.innsthelena.com* 🛏 *8 rooms* 🍴 *Free breakfast.*

Meadowood Napa Valley

$$$$ | **RESORT** | This elite 250-acre resort's celebrated restaurant and more than half its accommodations were destroyed in the 2020 Glass Fire, but the spa, pools, tennis courts, fitness center, and a fair number of cottages in one part survived and are set to reopen in late summer 2021, with reconstruction in other areas not expected to affect the guest experience. **Pros:** scrupulously maintained rooms; all-organic spa; gracious service. **Cons:** still recovering from fire; far from downtown St. Helena; weekend minimum-stay requirement. [$] *Rooms from: $825* ✉ *900 Meadowood La., St. Helena* ☎ *707/963–3646, 866/987–8212* 🌐 *www.meadowood.com* 🛏 *31 rooms* 🍴 *No meals.*

Wine Country Inn

$$$ | **B&B/INN** | Vineyards flank the three buildings, containing 24 rooms, and five cottages of this pastoral retreat, where blue oaks, maytens, and olive trees provide shade, and gardens feature lantana (small butterflies love it) and lavender. **Pros:** staff excels at anticipating guests' needs; good-size swimming pool; vineyard views from most rooms. **Cons:** some rooms let in noise from neighbors; expensive in high season; weekend minimum-stay requirement. [$] *Rooms from: $329* ✉ *1152 Lodi La., St. Helena* ✣ *East of Hwy. 29* ☎ *707/963–7077, 888/465–4608* 🌐 *www.winecountryinn.com* 🛏 *29 rooms* 🍴 *Free breakfast.*

★ Wydown Hotel

$$$ | HOTEL | This smart boutique hotel near downtown shopping and dining delivers comfort with a heavy dose of style: the storefront lobby's high ceiling and earth tones, punctuated by rich-hued splashes of color, hint at the relaxed grandeur owner-hotelier Mark Hoffmeister and his design team achieved in the rooms upstairs. **Pros:** well run; eclectic decor; downtown location. **Cons:** lacks the amenities of larger properties; large corner rooms pick up some street noise; two-night minimum on weekends. [$] *Rooms from: $339* ✉ *1424 Main St., St. Helena* ☎ *707/963–5100* 🌐 *www.wydownhotel.com* 🛏 *12 rooms* 🍴 *No meals.*

Nightlife

The Saint

WINE BARS—NIGHTLIFE | This high-ceilinged downtown wine bar benefits from the grandeur and gravitas of its setting inside a stone-walled late-19th-century former bank. Lit by chandeliers and decked out in contemporary style with plush sofas and chairs and Lucite stools at the bar, it's a classy, loungelike space to expand your enological horizons. ✉ *1351 Main St., St. Helena* ✣ *Near Adams St.* ☎ *707/302–5130* 🌐 *www.thesaintnapavalley.com* ☞ *Closed Mon.–Wed. (but check).*

Calistoga

3 miles northwest of St. Helena.

With false-fronted, Old West–style shops and 19th-century inns and hotels lining its main drag, Lincoln Avenue in Calistoga comes across as more down-to-earth than its more polished neighbors. Don't be fooled, though. On its outskirts lie some of the Wine Country's swankest (and priciest) resorts and its most fanciful piece of architecture, the medieval-style Castello di Amorosa winery.

Calistoga was developed as a spa-oriented getaway from the start. Sam Brannan, a gold rush–era entrepreneur, planned to use the area's natural hot springs as the centerpiece of a resort complex. His venture failed, but old-time hotels and bathhouses—along with some glorious new spas—still operate. You can come for an old-school mud bath, or go completely 21st century and experience lavish treatments based on the latest innovations in skin and body care.

GETTING HERE AND AROUND

Highway 29 heads east (turn right) at Calistoga, where in town it is signed as Lincoln Avenue. If arriving via the Silverado Trail, head west at Highway 29/Lincoln Avenue.

Sights

Castello di Amorosa

WINERY/DISTILLERY | An astounding medieval structure complete with drawbridge and moat, chapel, stables, and secret passageways, the Castello commands Diamond Mountain's lower eastern slope. Some of the 107 rooms contain artist Fabio Sanzogni's replicas of 13th-century frescoes (cheekily signed with his website address), and the dungeon has an iron maiden from Nuremberg, Germany. You must pay for a tour, when offered, to see most of Dario Sattui's extensive eight-level property, though with general admission you'll have access to part of the complex. Bottlings of note include several Italian-style wines, including La Castellana, a robust "super Tuscan" blend of Cabernet Sauvignon, Sangiovese, and Merlot; and Il Barone, a deliberately big Cab primarily of Rutherford grapes. All visits are by appointment. ✉ *4045 N. St. Helena Hwy./Hwy. 29, Calistoga* ✣ *Near Maple La.* ☎ *707/967–6272* 🌐 *www.castellodiamorosa.com* 🎟 *Check with winery for tasting and tour prices.*

Chateau Montelena

WINERY/DISTILLERY | Set amid a bucolic northern Calistoga landscape, this winery helped establish the Napa Valley's reputation for high-quality wine making. At the pivotal Paris tasting of 1976, the Chateau Montelena 1973 Chardonnay took first place, beating out four white Burgundies from France and five other California Chardonnays, an event immortalized in the 2008 movie *Bottle Shock*. A 21st-century Napa Valley Chardonnay is always part of A Taste of Montelena—the winery also makes Sauvignon Blanc, Riesling, a fine estate Zinfandel, and Cabernet Sauvignon—or you can opt for the Montelena Estate Collection tasting of Cabernets from several vintages. When tours are offered, there's one that takes in the grounds and covers the history of this stately property whose stone winery building was erected in 1888. All visits require a reservation. ⊠ *1429 Tubbs La., Calistoga* ⊹ *Off Hwy. 29* ☎ *707/942–5105* ⊕ *www.montelena.com* 🍷 *Tastings from $40.*

Frank Family Vineyards

WINERY/DISTILLERY | As a former Disney film and television executive, Rich Frank knows a thing or two about entertainment, and it shows in the chipper atmosphere that prevails in the winery's bright-yellow Craftsman-style tasting room. The site's wine-making history dates from the 19th century, and portions of an original 1884 structure, reclad in stone in 1906, remain standing today. From 1952 until 1990, Hanns Kornell made sparkling wines on this site. Frank Family makes sparklers itself, but the high-profile wines are the Carneros Chardonnay and several Cabernet Sauvignons, particularly the Rutherford Reserve and the Winston Hill red blend. Tastings are sit-down affairs, indoors, on the back veranda, or under 100-year-old elms. Reservations are required. ⊠ *1091 Larkmead La., Calistoga* ⊹ *Off Hwy. 29* ☎ *707/942–0859* ⊕ *www.frankfamilyvineyards.com* 🍷 *Tastings from $50.*

★ Schramsberg

WINERY/DISTILLERY | On a Diamond Mountain site the German-born Jacob Schram planted to grapes in the early 1860s, Schramsberg pours its esteemed *méthode traditionnelle* (aka *méthode champenoise*) sparkling wines. Author Robert Louis Stevenson was among Schram's early visitors. After the vintner's death in 1905 the winery closed and fell into disrepair, but in 1965 Jack and Jamie Davies purchased the 200-acre Schramsberg property and began restoring its buildings and caves. Chinese laborers dug some of the latter in the 1870s. In the 1990s, the family set about replanting the vineyard to Cabernet Sauvignon and other Bordeaux varietals for the Davies Vineyards label's still red wines. Tastings at Schramsberg can include pours of only sparkling wines, only still wines, or a combination of the two. All visits are by appointment. ⊠ *1400 Schramsberg Rd., Calistoga* ⊹ *Off Hwy. 29* ☎ *707/942–4558, 800/877–3623* ⊕ *www.schramsberg.com* 🍷 *Tastings from $50.*

Tamber Bey Vineyards

WINERY/DISTILLERY | Endurance riders Barry and Jennifer Waitte share their passion for horses and wine at their glam-rustic winery north of Calistoga. Their 22-acre Sundance Ranch remains a working equestrian facility, but the site has been revamped to include a state-of-the-art winery with separate fermenting tanks for grapes from Tamber Bey's vineyards in Yountville, Oakville, and elsewhere. The winemakers produce Chardonnay, Sauvignon Blanc, and Pinot Noir, but the showstoppers are several subtly powerful reds, including the flagship Oakville Cabernet Sauvignon and a Yountville Merlot. The top-selling wine, Rabicano, is a Cabernet Sauvignon-heavy Bordeaux-style blend. Visits here require an appointment. ⊠ *1251 Tubbs La., Calistoga* ⊹ *At Myrtledale Rd.* ☎ *707/942–2100* ⊕ *www.tamberbey.com* 🍷 *Tastings from $45.*

The astounding Castello di Amorosa has 107 rooms.

🍴 Restaurants

★ Lovina

$$$ | **MODERN AMERICAN** | A vintage-style neon sign outside this bungalow restaurant announces "Great Food," and the chefs deliver with imaginative, well-plated dishes served on two floors or a streetside patio that in good weather is especially festive during weekend brunch. Entrée staples on the seasonally changing menu include cioppino and slow-roasted half-chicken, with heirloom-tomato gazpacho a summer starter and chicken-dumpling soup its warming winter counterpart. **Known for:** imaginative cuisine; weekend brunch scene; Wine Wednesdays no corkage, discounts on wine list. [$] *Average main: $34* ✉ *1107 Cedar St., Calistoga* ✣ *At Lincoln Ave.* ☎ *707/942–6500* 🌐 *www.lovinacalistoga.com* 🕒 *No lunch weekdays.*

Sam's Social Club

$$$ | **MODERN AMERICAN** | Tourists, locals, and spa guests—some of the latter in bathrobes after treatments—assemble inside this resort restaurant or on its extensive patio for breakfast, lunch, bar snacks, or dinner. Lunch options include thin-crust pizzas, sandwiches, an aged-cheddar burger, and entrées such as chicken paillard, with the burger reappearing for dinner along with pan-seared fish, rib-eye steak frites, and similar fare. **Known for:** casual atmosphere; cocktail-friendly starters; hearty salads. [$] *Average main: $31* ✉ *Indian Springs Resort and Spa, 1712 Lincoln Ave., Calistoga* ✣ *At Wappo Ave.* ☎ *707/942–4969* 🌐 *www.samssocialclub.com.*

★ Solbar

$$$$ | **MODERN AMERICAN** | The restaurant at Solage attracts the resort's clientele, upvalley locals, and guests of nearby lodgings for sophisticated farm-to-table cuisine served in the high-ceilinged dining area or alfresco on a sprawling patio warmed by shapely heaters and a mesmerizing fire pit. Dishes on the lighter side might include house-made pasta or well-executed sole, with duck breast, crispy pork, or prime New York steak

among the heartier options. **Known for:** artisanal cocktails; festive patio; Sunday brunch. $ *Average main: $40* ✉ *Solage, 755 Silverado Trail, Calistoga* ✛ *At Rosedale Rd.* ☎ *866/942–7442* ⊕ *solage. aubergeresorts.com/dine.*

Hotels

★ Embrace Calistoga

$$$ | B&B/INN | Extravagant hospitality defines the Napa Valley's luxury properties, but Embrace Calistoga takes the prize in the "small lodging" category. **Pros:** attentive owners; marvelous breakfasts; restaurants, tasting rooms, and shopping within walking distance. **Cons:** light hum of street traffic; no pool or spa; two-night minimum some weekends. $ *Rooms from: $309* ✉ *1139 Lincoln Ave., Calistoga* ☎ *707/942–9797* ⊕ *embracecalistoga.com* ⇨ *5 rooms* ⦿ *Free breakfast.*

Four Seasons Resort and Residences Napa Valley

$$$$ | RESORT | Opened in 2021, this suave luxury resort entices high rollers with farmhouse-eclectic interiors and amenities that include a spa, a destination restaurant, two pools, 7-plus acres of vines, and a working winery. **Pros:** estate villa and one-bedroom suites offer maximum luxury and privacy; destination restaurant Truss; on-site vineyard and winery. **Cons:** expensive year-round; casual-chic yet may feel too formal for some guests; minimum two-night weekend requirement. $ *Rooms from: $1400* ✉ *400 Silverado Trail N, Calistoga* ☎ *707/709–2100, 800/819–5053 for reservations* ⊕ *www.fourseasons.com/napavalley* ⇨ *83 rooms* ⦿ *No meals.*

Indian Springs Calistoga

$$$ | RESORT | Palm-studded Indian Springs—operating as a spa since 1862—ably splits the difference between laid-back and chic in accommodations that include lodge rooms, suites, cottages, stand-alone bungalows, and two houses. **Pros:** palm-studded grounds with outdoor seating areas; on-site Sam's Social Club restaurant; enormous mineral pool. **Cons:** lodge rooms are small; many rooms have showers but no tubs; two-night minimum on weekends (three with Monday holiday). $ *Rooms from: $309* ✉ *1712 Lincoln Ave., Calistoga* ☎ *707/709–8139* ⊕ *www.indiansprings-calistoga.com* ⇨ *113 rooms* ⦿ *No meals.*

★ Solage

$$$$ | RESORT | The aesthetic at this 22-acre property, where health and wellness are priorities, is Napa Valley barn meets San Francisco loft: guest rooms have high ceilings, sleek contemporary furniture, all-natural fabrics in soothingly muted colors, and an outdoor patio. **Pros:** great service; complimentary bikes; separate pools for kids and adults. **Cons:** vibe might not suit everyone; longish walk from some lodgings to spa and fitness center; expensive in-season. $ *Rooms from: $749* ✉ *755 Silverado Trail, Calistoga* ☎ *866/942–7442, 707/226–0800* ⊕ *www.solagecalistoga.com* ⇨ *89 rooms* ⦿ *No meals.*

Shopping

Mad Mod Shop

CLOTHING | Find the new polka-dotted, patent-leathered you at this quirky stop for vintage-inspired dresses, skirts, tops, and accessories in all sizes. ✉ *1410 Lincoln Ave., Calistoga* ✛ *At Washington St.* ☎ *707/942–1059* ⊕ *madmodshop.com.*

Activities

BICYCLING
Calistoga Bikeshop

BICYCLING | Options here include regular and fancy bikes that rent for $28 and up for two hours, and there's a self-guided Cool Wine Tour ($110) with stops for tastings at three or four small wineries. ✉ *1318 Lincoln Ave., Calistoga* ✛ *Near Washington St.* ☎ *707/942–9687* ⊕ *www.calistogabikeshop.net.*

SPAS

Indian Springs Spa

FITNESS/HEALTH CLUBS | Even before Sam Brannan constructed a spa·on this site in the 1860s, the Wappo Indians built sweat lodges over its thermal geysers. Treatments include a Calistoga-classic, pure volcanic-ash mud bath followed by a mineral bath, after which clients are wrapped in a flannel blanket for a 15-minute cool-down session or until called for a massage if they've booked one. Oxygen-infusion facials are another specialty. Before or following a treatment, guests unwind at the serene Buddha Pool, fed by one of the property's four geysers. ✉ *1712 Lincoln Ave., Calistoga* ✛ *At Wappo Ave.* ☎ *707/942–4913* ⊕ *indianspringscalistoga.com/spa-overview* ✎ *Treatments from $95.*

★ Spa Solage

FITNESS/HEALTH CLUBS | This 20,000-square-foot eco-conscious spa reinvented the traditional Calistoga mud-and-mineral-water regimen with the hour-long "Mudslide." The three-part treatment includes a mud body mask applied in a heated lounge, a soak in a thermal bath, and a power nap in a sound-vibration chair. The mud here, less gloppy than at other resorts, is a mix of clay, volcanic ash, and essential oils. Traditional spa services—combination Shiatsu-Swedish and other massages, foot reflexology, facials, and waxes—are available, as are yoga and wellness sessions. ✉ *755 Silverado Trail, Calistoga* ✛ *At Rosedale Rd.* ☎ *707/226–0825* ⊕ *solage.aubergeresorts.com/spa* ✎ *Treatments from $110.*

Sonoma

14 miles west of Napa, 45 miles northeast of San Francisco.

One of the few towns in the valley with multiple attractions unrelated to food and wine, Sonoma has plenty to keep you busy for a couple of hours before you head out to tour the wineries. And you needn't leave town to taste wine. About three dozen tasting rooms are within steps of tree-filled Sonoma Plaza. The valley's cultural center, Sonoma was founded in 1835 when California was still part of Mexico.

GETTING HERE AND AROUND

Highway 12 (signed as Broadway near Sonoma Plaza) heads north into Sonoma from Highway 121 and south from Santa Rosa into downtown Sonoma. Parking is relatively easy to find on or near the plaza, and you can walk to many restaurants, shops, and tasting rooms. Signs point the way to several wineries a mile or more east of the plaza. Sonoma County Transit buses serve the town.

 Sights

★ Bedrock Wine Co.

WINERY/DISTILLERY | Zinfandel and other varietals grown in heritage vineyards throughout California are the focus of Bedrock, a young winery whose backstory involves several historical figures. Tastings take place in a home east of Sonoma Plaza owned in the 1850s by General Joseph Hooker. By coincidence, Hooker planted grapes at what's now the estate Bedrock Vineyard a few miles away. General William Tecumseh Sherman was his partner in the vineyard (a spat over it affected their Civil War interactions), which newspaper magnate William Randolph Hearst's father, George, replanted in the late 1880s. Some Hearst vines still produce grapes, whose current owner-winemaker, Morgan Twain-Peterson, learned about Zinfandel from his dad, Ravenswood founder Joel Peterson. Twain-Peterson's bottlings, many of them field blends containing multiple varietals grown and fermented together, are as richly textured as his winery's prehistory. ✉ *General Joseph Hooker House, 414 1st St. E, Sonoma* ✛ *Near E. Spain St.* ☎ *707/343–1478* ⊕ *www.bedrockwineco.com* ✎ *Tastings from $30* ✆ *Closed Mon. and Tues.*

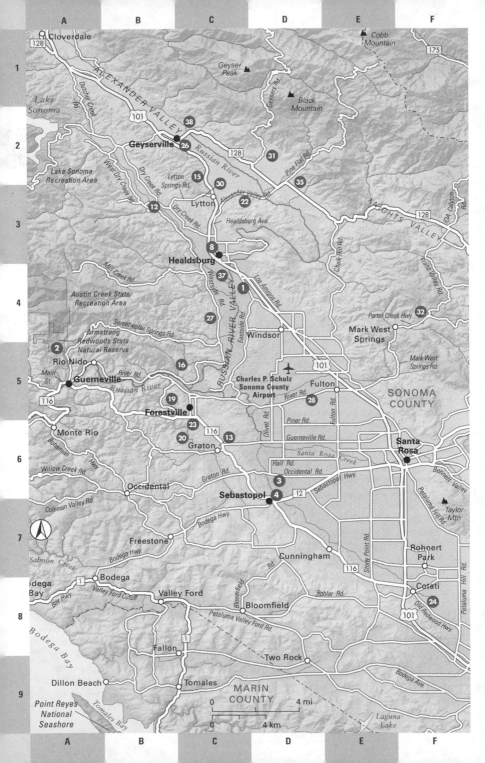

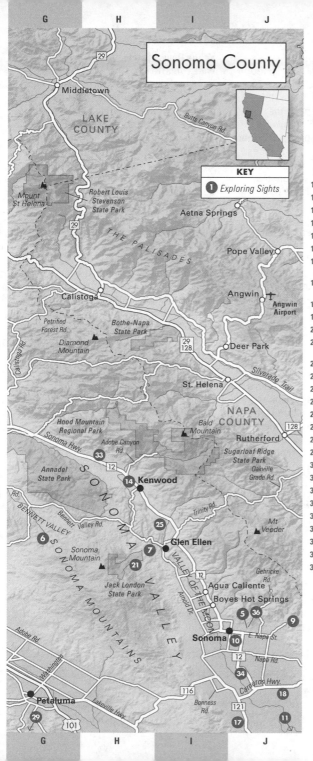

Sonoma County

KEY

1 Exploring Sights

Buena Vista Winery

WINERY/DISTILLERY | A local actor in top hat and 19th-century garb often greets guests as Count Agoston Haraszthy at this entertaining homage to the birthplace of modern California wine making. Haraszthy's rehabilitated former press house (used for pressing grapes into wine), completed in 1864, is the architectural focal point, with photos, banners, plaques, and artifacts providing historical context. Chardonnay, Pinot Noir, and several red blends are the strong suits among the two-dozen-plus wines produced. During appointment-only visits (walk-ins sometimes possible), you can taste some of them solo or preorder a box lunch from the affiliated Oakville Grocery. ⊠ 18000 Old Winery Rd., Sonoma ⊹ Off E. Napa St. ☎ 800/926–1266 ⊕ www.buenavistawinery.com ⧖ Tastings from $20.

Corner 103

WINERY/DISTILLERY | After leading an effort to revive a troubled local winery, Lloyd Davis, an African American financier and oenophile, turned his attention to a new passion: making the experience of learning about wine and food-wine pairings less daunting. To that end he opened a light-filled space, diagonally across from Sonoma Plaza, for tastings of Sonoma County wines usually paired with cheeses or other pertinent bites. The lineup includes a Brut Rosé sparkler, Chardonnay and Marsanne-Roussanne whites, a rosé of Pinot Noir, and several reds. Corner 103's welcoming atmosphere, which earned it the top slot on USA Today's Best Tasting Room list for 2020, makes it an excellent choice for wine novices seeking to expand their knowledge. Visits are by appointment only, though hosts usually accommodate drop-ins seeking wine-only tastings. ⊠ 103 W. Napa St., Sonoma ⊹ At 1st St. W ☎ 707/931–6141 ⊕ www.corner103.com ⧖ Tastings from $20.

★ The Donum Estate

WINERY/DISTILLERY | The wine-making team of this prominent Chardonnay and Pinot Noir producer prizes viticulture—selecting vineyards with superior soils and microclimates, planting compatible clones, then farming with rigor—over wine-making wizardry. The Donum Estate, whose white board-and-batten tasting room affords guests hilltop views of Los Carneros, San Pablo Bay, and beyond, farms two vineyards surrounding the structure, one in the Russian River Valley, and another in Mendocino County's Anderson Valley. All the wines exhibit the "power yet elegance" that sealed the winery's fame in the 2000s. Tastings are by appointment only. Forty large-scale museum-quality contemporary sculptures placed amid the vines, including works by Ai Weiwei, Lynda Benglis, Louise Bourgeois, Keith Haring, and Anselm Kiefer, add a touch of high culture to a visit here. ■ TIP→ The winery offers an invigorating 1½-hour guided stroll past the artworks without the tasting. ⊠ 24500 Ramal Rd., Sonoma ⊹ Off Hwy. 121/12 ☎ 707/732–2200 ⊕ www.thedonumestate.com ⧖ Tastings from $95, art tour $50.

Gloria Ferrer Caves and Vineyards

WINERY/DISTILLERY | On a clear day this Spanish hacienda–style winery's Vista Terrace lives up to its name as guests at seated tastings sip delicate sparkling wines while taking in views of gently rolling Carneros hills and beyond them San Pablo Bay. The Chardonnay and Pinot Noir grapes from the vineyards in the foreground are the product of old-world wine-making knowledge—generations of the founding Ferrer family made cava in Spain—but also contemporary soil management techniques and clonal research. Hosts well-acquainted with the winery's sustainability practices and history as the Carneros District's first sparkling-wine house serve the wines accompanied by food that varies from cheese and charcuterie to caviar or a full lunch. All visits are by appointment. ■ **TIP→ For the cheese-and-charcuterie option you can upgrade from the standard flight, which includes still wines, to an all-bubbles one.** ✉ *23555 Carneros Hwy./Hwy. 121, Sonoma* ☎ *707/933–1917* 🌐 *www.gloriaferrer.com* 🎟 *Tastings from $55.*

Hanson of Sonoma Distillery
WINERY/DISTILLERY | The Hanson family makes grape-based organic vodkas, one traditional, the rest infused with cucumbers, ginger, mandarin oranges, Meyer lemons, or habanero and other chili peppers. A surprise to many visitors, the Hansons make a blended white wine before distilling it into vodka. The family pours its vodkas, along with single-malt whiskey, in an industrial-looking tasting room heavy on the steel, with wood reclaimed from Deep South smokehouses adding a rustic note. In good weather some sessions take place on the landscaped shore of a small pond. Per state law, there's a limit to the amount poured, but it's sufficient to get to know the product. ✉ *22985 Burndale Rd., Sonoma* ✥ *At Carneros Hwy. (Hwy. 121)* ☎ *707/343–1805* 🌐 *hansonofsonoma.com* 🎟 *Tastings from $25, tours from $50 (includes tasting).*

★ Sangiacomo Family Wines
WINERY/DISTILLERY | Several dozen wineries produce vineyard-designate Chardonnays and Pinot Noirs from grapes grown by the Sangiacomo family, whose Italian ancestors first started farming in Sonoma in 1927. The family didn't establish its own label until 2016, but its cool-climate wines and a Napa Valley Cabernet are already earning critical plaudits. Chardonnay vines and the Carneros District's western hills form the backdrop for tastings, usually outdoors, at the 110-acre Home Ranch, the first of a dozen-plus vineyards the Sangiacomos acquired or lease. At appointment-only visits you're apt to encounter one or more third-generation members, all of whom enjoy meeting guests and sharing their family's legacy. ■ **TIP→ On Fridays, the winery hosts Sunset on the Terrace, with wines served by the glass or bottle from 3:30 pm until sundown.** ✉ *21545 Broadway, Sonoma* ✥ *2½ miles south of Sonoma Plaza* ☎ *707/934–8445* 🌐 *www.sangiacomowines.com* 🎟 *Tastings from $30.*

Sonoma Mission
RELIGIOUS SITE | The northernmost of the 21 missions established by Franciscan friars in California, Sonoma Mission was founded in 1823 as Mission San Francisco Solano. These days it serves as the centerpiece of **Sonoma State Historic Park,** which includes several other sites in Sonoma and nearby Petaluma. Some early mission structures fell into ruin, but all or part of several remaining buildings date to the era of Mexican rule over California. The **Sonoma Barracks,** a half block west of the mission at 20 East Spain Street, housed troops under the command of General Mariano Guadalupe Vallejo, who controlled vast tracts of land in the region. **General Vallejo's Home,** a Victorian-era structure, is a few blocks west. ✉ *114 E. Spain St., Sonoma* ✥ *At 1st St. E* ☎ *707/938–9560* 🌐 *www.parks.ca.gov* 🎟 *$3, includes same-day admission to other historic sites.*

🍴 Restaurants

★ Cafe La Haye
$$$ | **AMERICAN** | In a postage-stamp-size open kitchen (the dining room, its white walls adorned with contemporary art, is nearly as compact), chef Jeffrey Lloyd turns out understated, sophisticated fare emphasizing seasonably available local ingredients. Meats, pastas, and seafood get deluxe treatment without fuss or fanfare—and the daily risotto special is always worth trying. **Known for:** Napa-Sonoma wine list with French complements; signature butterscotch pudding; owner Saul Gropman on hand to greet diners. [$] *Average main: $27* ✉ *140 E. Napa St., Sonoma* ✥ *East of Sonoma Plaza* ☎ *707/935–5994* 🌐 *www.cafelahaye.com* 🕒 *Closed Sun. and Mon. No lunch.*

El Dorado Kitchen

$$$ | **MODERN AMERICAN** | This restaurant owes its visual appeal to its clean lines and handsome decor, but the eye inevitably drifts westward to the open kitchen, where longtime chef Armando Navarro and his team craft dishes full of subtle surprises. The menu might include cod ceviche or fried calamari with spicy marinara sauce as starters and pan-roasted salmon or paella awash with seafood and dry-cured Spanish chorizo sausage among the entrées. **Known for:** subtle tastes and textures; truffle-oil fries with Parmesan; bar menu's pizzas and burger. [$] *Average main: $29* ✉ *El Dorado Hotel, 405 1st St. W, Sonoma* ✥ *At W. Spain St.* ☎ *707/996–3030* 🌐 *eldoradokitchen.com.*

★ **Girl & the Fig**

$$ | **FRENCH** | At this hot spot for inventive French cooking inside the historic Sonoma Hotel bar, you can always find a dish with the signature figs on the menu, whether it's a fig-and-arugula salad or an aperitif blending sparkling wine with fig liqueur. Also look for duck confit, a burger with matchstick fries, and wild flounder meunière. **Known for:** Rhône-wines emphasis; artisanal cheese platters; Sunday brunch. [$] *Average main: $26* ✉ *Sonoma Hotel, 110 W. Spain St., Sonoma* ✥ *At 1st St. W* ☎ *707/938–3634* 🌐 *www.thegirlandthefig.com.*

★ **LaSalette Restaurant**

$$$ | **PORTUGUESE** | Born in the Azores and raised in Sonoma, chef-owner Manuel Azevedo serves cuisine inspired by his native Portugal in this warmly decorated spot. The wood-oven-roasted fish is always worth trying, and there are usually boldly flavored pork dishes, along with stews, salted cod, and other hearty fare. **Known for:** authentic Portuguese cuisine; sophisticated spicing; local and Portuguese wine flights. [$] *Average main: $29* ✉ *452 1st St. E, Sonoma* ✥ *Near E. Spain St.* ☎ *707/938–1927* 🌐 *www.lasaletterestaurant.com* ⏲ *Closed Wed.*

Taub Family Outpost

$$ | **AMERICAN** | Its varied initiatives and location across from Sonoma Plaza's southwest corner ensure steady traffic to this combination all-day restaurant, gourmet marketplace, wine shop, café, bar, and wine-tasting space whose updated-country-store decor suits its 1912 building's Mexican period/Old West flourishes. Items that might appear on the menu range from the healthful (ancient-grain burgers; smoked-beet salad) to the sinfully delicious (grilled cheese with bacon; fried chicken) and in-between (prosciutto with honeydew melon). **Known for:** coffee and cocktails; wines from many lands; patio dining. [$] *Average main: $22* ✉ *497 1st St. W, Sonoma* ✥ *At W. Napa St.* ☎ *707/721–1107* 🌐 *taubfamilyoutpost.com* ⏲ *Closed Mon.*

★ **Wit & Wisdom Tavern**

$$$ | **MODERN AMERICAN** | A San Francisco culinary star with establishments worldwide, Michael Mina debuted his first Wine Country restaurant in 2020, its interior of charcoal grays, browns, and soft whites dandy indeed, if by evening vying with outdoor spaces aglow with fire pits and lighted water features. Seasonal regional ingredients—Pacific Coast fish, pasture-raised meats, freshly plucked produce—go into haute-homey dishes, prepared open-fire, that include pizzas, handmade pastas, and the signature lobster potpie with brandied lobster cream and black truffle. **Known for:** shellfish and duck-wing apps; extensive local wines; large outdoor patio. [$] *Average main: $35* ✉ *The Lodge at Sonoma, 1325 Broadway, Sonoma* ✥ *At Leveroni Rd.* ☎ *707/931–3405* 🌐 *www.witandwisdomsonoma.com.*

Hotels

Inn at Sonoma

$$ | **B&B/INN** | Little luxuries delight at this well-run inn ¼-mile south of Sonoma Plaza whose guest rooms, softly lit and done in pastels, have comfortable beds topped with feather comforters and plenty of pillows. **Pros:** last-minute specials are a great deal; afternoon wine, cheese, and freshly baked cookies; good soundproofing blocks out Broadway street noise. **Cons:** on a busy street rather than right on the plaza; pet-friendly rooms book up quickly; some rooms on the small side. [$] *Rooms from: $259* ✉ *630 Broadway, Sonoma* ☎ *707/939–1340* 🌐 *www.innatsonoma.com* 🛏 *27 rooms* 🍴 *Free breakfast.*

★ **Ledson Hotel**

$$$ | **B&B/INN** | With just six rooms the Ledson feels intimate, and the furnishings and amenities—down beds, mood lighting, gas fireplaces, whirlpool tubs, and balconies for enjoying breakfast or a glass of wine—stack up well against Wine Country rooms costing more, especially in high season. **Pros:** convenient Sonoma Plaza location; spacious, individually decorated rooms; whirlpool tub in all rooms. **Cons:** two people maximum occupancy in all rooms; children must be at least 12 years old; front rooms have plaza views but pick up some street noise. [$] *Rooms from: $350* ✉ *480 1st St. E, Sonoma* ☎ *707/996–9779* 🌐 *www.ledsonhotel.com* 🛏 *6 rooms* 🍴 *No meals.*

★ **MacArthur Place Hotel & Spa**

$$$$ | **HOTEL** | Guests at this 7-acre boutique property five blocks south of Sonoma Plaza bask in ritzy seclusion in plush accommodations set amid landscaped gardens. **Pros:** verdant garden setting; restaurant among Sonoma's best; great for a romantic getaway. **Cons:** a bit of a walk from the plaza; some traffic noise audible in street-side rooms; pricey in high season. [$] *Rooms from: $459* ✉ *29 E. MacArthur St., Sonoma* ☎ *707/938–2929, 800/722–1866* 🌐 *www.macarthurplace.com* 🛏 *64 rooms* 🍴 *Free breakfast.*

Nightlife

Sigh!

WINE BARS—NIGHTLIFE | From the oval bar and walls the color of a fine Blanc de Blancs to retro chandeliers that mimic champagne bubbles, everything about this sparkling-wine bar's frothy space screams "have a good time." That owner Jayme Powers and her posse are trained in the fine art of *sabrage* (opening a bottle of sparkling with a saber) only adds to the festivity. ■ **TIP→ Sigh! opens at noon, so it's a good daytime stop, too.** ✉ *120 W. Napa St., Sonoma* ✥ *At 1st St. W* ☎ *707/996–2444* 🌐 *www.sighsonoma.com.*

Shopping

Chateau Sonoma

HOUSEHOLD ITEMS/FURNITURE | The fancy furniture, lighting fixtures, and objets d'art at this upscale shop make it a dangerous place to enter: within minutes you may find yourself reconsidering your entire home's aesthetic. The owner's keen eye for French style makes a visit here a pleasure. ✉ *453 1st St. W, Sonoma* ✥ *Between W. Napa and W. Spain Sts.* ☎ *707/309–1993* 🌐 *www.chateausonoma.com.*

Activities

SPAS

Willow Stream Spa at Fairmont Sonoma Mission Inn & Spa

FITNESS/HEALTH CLUBS | By far the Wine Country's largest spa, the Fairmont resort's 40,000-square-foot facility provides every amenity you could want, including pools and hot tubs fed by local thermal springs. Each of the three signature treatments achieves a specific objective. Starting with a lavender bubble bath, followed by a botanical body wrap and a massage, the Couples Lavender Kur focuses on pampering, whereas the Neroli Blossom Kur—a body polish, a full-body massage, a moisture mask, and a facial and scalp massage—is all about restoring balance. For clients in need of a detox, the Wine Country Kur begins with exfoliation, a soak, and a wrap, concluding with a grape-seed oil massage. ⊠ *100 Boyes Blvd./Hwy. 12, Sonoma ⊕ 2½ miles north of Sonoma Plaza ☎ 707/938–9000 ⊕ www.fairmont.com/sonoma/willow-stream ☒ Treatments from $79.*

Glen Ellen

7 miles north of Sonoma.

Craggy Glen Ellen epitomizes the difference between the Napa and Sonoma valleys. Whereas small Napa towns like St. Helena get their charm from upscale boutiques and restaurants lined up along well-groomed sidewalks, Glen Ellen's crooked streets are shaded with stands of old oak trees and occasionally bisected by the Sonoma and Calabazas creeks. Tucked among the trees of a narrow canyon where Sonoma Mountain and the Mayacamas pinch in the valley floor, Glen Ellen looks more like a town of the Sierra foothills gold country than a Wine Country village.

GETTING HERE AND AROUND

Glen Ellen sits just off Highway 12. From the north or south , take Arnold Drive west and follow it south less than a mile. The walkable downtown straddles a half-mile stretch of Arnold Drive. Sonoma County Transit buses serve Glen Ellen.

Sights

Benziger Family Winery

WINERY/DISTILLERY | One of the best-known Sonoma County wineries sits on a sprawling estate in a bowl with 360-degree sun exposure. Hosts conducting popular tram tours explain the benefits of the vineyard's natural setting and how biodynamic farming yields healthier, more flavorful fruit. The eco-friendly agricultural practices include extensive plantings to attract beneficial insects and the deployment of sheep to trim vegetation between the vines while simultaneously tilling the soil with their hooves and fertilizing to boot. Known for Chardonnay, Cabernet Sauvignon, Merlot, Pinot Noir, and Sauvignon Blanc, the winery is a beautiful spot for an alfresco tasting, whether you take the tour or not. All visits are by appointment; in summer and early fall, reserve a tram tour at least a day or two ahead. ⊠ *1883 London Ranch Rd., Glen Ellen ⊕ Off Arnold Dr. ☎ 888/490–2739 ⊕ www.benziger.com ☒ Tasting $30, tram tour and tasting $60 ⊗ Closed Tues. and Wed.*

★ Jack London State Historic Park

NATIONAL/STATE PARK | The pleasures are pastoral and intellectual at author Jack London's beloved Beauty Ranch, where you could easily spend the afternoon hiking some of the 30-plus miles of trails that loop through meadows and stands of oaks, redwoods, and other trees. Manuscripts and personal artifacts depicting London's travels are on view at the House of Happy Walls Museum, which provides an overview of the writer's life, literary passions, humanitarian and conservation efforts, and promotion of organic farming. A short hike away lie the ruins of Wolf House, which burned down just before London was to move in. Also open to visitors are a few outbuildings and the restored wood-framed cottage where London penned many of his later works. He's buried on the property. ■TIP➔ **The park's Broadway Under the Stars series, a hot summer ticket, is expected to resume in 2021.** ⊠ *2400 London Ranch Rd., Glen Ellen ⊕ Off Arnold Dr. ☎ 707/938–5216 ⊕ www.jacklondonpark.com ☒ Parking $10 ($5 walk-in or bike), includes admission to museum; cottage $4.*

Benziger tram tours take to the fields to show biodynamic farming techniques in action.

★ Lasseter Family Winery

WINERY/DISTILLERY | Immaculately groomed grapevines dazzle the eye at John and Nancy Lasseter's secluded winery, and it's no accident: Phil Coturri, Sonoma Valley's premier organic vineyard manager, tends them. Even the landscaping, which includes an insectary to attract beneficial bugs, is meticulously maintained. Come harvesttime, the wine-making team oversees gentle processes that transform the fruit into wines of purity and grace, among them a Sémillon–Sauvignon Blanc blend, two rosés, and Bordeaux and Rhône reds. Evocative labels illustrate the tale behind each wine. In good weather, guests enjoy these well-told stories at tastings on the winery's outdoor patio, whose views include the vineyard and the Mayacamas Mountains. All visits are by appointment. ✉ *1 Vintage La., Glen Ellen* ✥ *Off Dunbar Rd.* ☎ *707/933–2814* 🌐 *www.lasseterfamilywinery.com* 🎟 *Tastings from $25.*

🍴 Restaurants

★ Glen Ellen Star

$$$ | **ECLECTIC** | Chef Ari Weiswasser honed his craft at The French Laundry, Daniel, and other bastions of culinary finesse, but at his Wine Country outpost he prepares haute-rustic cuisine, much of it emerging from a wood-fired oven that burns a steady 600°F. Crisp-crusted, richly sauced Margherita and other pizzas thrive in the torrid heat, as do tender whole fish entrées and vegetables roasted in small iron skillets. **Known for:** outdoor dining area; prix-fixe Wednesday "neighborhood night" menu with free corkage; Weiswasser's sauces, emulsions, and spices. [$] *Average main: $30* ✉ *13648 Arnold Dr., Glen Ellen* ✥ *At Warm Springs Rd.* ☎ *707/343–1384* 🌐 *glenellenstar.com* 🕒 *No lunch.*

★ Les Pascals

$ | **FRENCH** | A bright-yellow slice of France in downtown Glen Ellen, this combination pâtisserie, boulangerie, and café takes its name from its husband-and-wife owners,

Pascal and Pascale Merle. Pascal whips up croissants, breads, turnovers, and sweet treats like Napoleons, galettes, and eclairs, along with quiches, potpies, and other savory fare; Pascale creates an upbeat environment for customers to enjoy them. **Known for:** memorable French onion soup; shaded back patio; high-test French and Italian coffee drinks. ⓢ *Average main: $10* ⊠ *13758 Arnold Dr., Glen Ellen* ✛ *Near London Ranch Rd.* ☎ *707/934–8378* ⊕ *www.lespascalspatisserie.com* ⊙ *Closed Wed. No dinner.*

Hotels

★ Gaige House + Ryokan

$$$ | B&B/INN | There's no other place in Sonoma or Napa quite like the Gaige House + Ryokan, which blends the best elements of a traditional country inn, a boutique hotel, and a longtime expat's classy Asian hideaway. **Pros:** short walk to Glen Ellen restaurants, shops, and tasting rooms; freshly baked cookies; full breakfasts, afternoon wine and appetizers. **Cons:** sound carries in the main house; the least expensive rooms are on the small side; oriented more toward couples than families with children. ⓢ *Rooms from: $302* ⊠ *13540 Arnold Dr., Glen Ellen* ☎ *707/935–0237, 800/935–0237* ⊕ *www.thegaigehouse.com* ⋧ *23 rooms* ⦿ *Free breakfast.*

★ Olea Hotel

$$$ | B&B/INN | Husband-and-wife team Ashish and Sia Patel operate this down-home country casual yet sophisticated boutique lodging. **Pros:** beautiful style; complimentary wine; filling two-course breakfasts. **Cons:** minor road noise in some rooms; fills up quickly on weekends; weekend minimum-stay requirement. ⓢ *Rooms from: $309* ⊠ *5131 Warm Springs Rd., Glen Ellen* ✛ *West off Arnold Dr.* ☎ *707/996–5131* ⊕ *www.oleahotel.com* ⋧ *15 rooms* ⦿ *Free breakfast.*

Kenwood

4 miles north of Glen Ellen.

Tiny Kenwood consists of little more than a few restaurants, shops, tasting rooms, and a historic train depot, now used for private events. But hidden in this pretty landscape of meadows and woods at the north end of Sonoma Valley are several good wineries, most just off the Sonoma Highway. Varietals grown here at the foot of the Sugarloaf Mountains include Sauvignon Blanc, Chardonnay, Zinfandel, and Cabernet Sauvignon.

GETTING HERE AND AROUND

To get to Kenwood from Glen Ellen, head northeast on Arnold Drive and north on Highway 12. Sonoma Transit buses serve Kenwood from Glen Ellen and Sonoma.

Sights

★ En Garde Winery

WINERY/DISTILLERY | Sommeliers, critics, and collectors extol the Pinot Noirs and Cabernet Sauvignons of Csaba Szakál, En Garde's Hungarian-born winemaker and owner. Striving to create what he describes as "aromatic, complex, lush, and juicy" wines, Szakál selects top Sonoma County vineyards for the Pinots and the Napa Valley's Diamond Mountain, Mt. Veeder, and other high-elevation sites for the Cabernets. Not afraid to heavy up the oak on the Cabernets, he nevertheless achieves elegance as well. The winemaker is equally precise about hiring staffers for his modest highway's-edge tasting room along Kenwood's brief commercial strip. Well-acquainted with his goals and methods, they provide a wealth of knowledge about wine making and California viticulture. If you're lucky, Szakál himself will be around to discuss his wines (he loves to), which also include Chardonnay, Viognier, and rosé of Pinot Noir. Visits are by reservation, with same-day appointments sometimes possible. ⊠ *9077 Sonoma Hwy., Kenwood* ✛ *At Shaw Ave.*

☎ *707/282–9216* 🌐 *www.engardewinery.com* 🎫 *Tastings $25–$40.*

St. Francis Winery

WINERY/DISTILLERY | Nestled at the foot of Mt. Hood, St. Francis has earned national acclaim for its pairings of wines and small bites. With its red-tile roof and bell tower and views of the Mayacamas Mountains to the east, the winery's California Mission–style visitor center occupies one of Sonoma County's most scenic locations. The charm of the surroundings is matched by the mostly red wines, among them rich, earthy Zinfandels from the Dry Creek, Russian River, and Sonoma valleys. The five-course pairings might include Chardonnay with lobster bisque or Cabernet Sauvignon with wine-braised beef ribs. ✉ *100 Pythian Rd., Kenwood* ✣ *Off Hwy. 12* ☎ *707/538–9463, 888/675–9463* 🌐 *www.stfranciswinery.com* 🎫 *Tastings from $20* 🕒 *Closed Tues. and Wed.*

🍴 Restaurants

Salt & Stone

$$$ | **MODERN AMERICAN** | The menu at this upscale roadhouse with a sloping wood-beamed ceiling focuses on seafood and meat—beef, lamb, chicken, duck, and other options—with many dishes in both categories grilled. Start with the classics, perhaps a martini and oysters Rockefeller, before moving on to well-plated contemporary entrées that might include crispy-skin salmon or duck breast, a fish stew, or grilled rib-eye. **Known for:** mountain-view outdoor seating area; weekend brunch; weekday happy hour 2:30–5:30 except holidays. [$] *Average main: $29* ✉ *9900 Sonoma Hwy., Kenwood* ✣ *At Kunde Winery Rd.* ☎ *707/833–6326* 🌐 *www.saltstonekenwood.com* 🕒 *No lunch Tues. and Wed.*

🛏 Hotels

★ Kenwood Inn and Spa

$$$ | **B&B/INN** | Fluffy feather beds, custom Italian furnishings, and French doors in most cases opening onto terraces or balconies lend this inn's uncommonly spacious guest rooms a romantic air—more than a few guests are celebrating honeymoons or anniversaries. **Pros:** large rooms; lavish furnishings; romantic setting. **Cons:** far from nightlife; expensive in high season; geared more to couples than families with children. [$] *Rooms from: $381* ✉ *10400 Sonoma Hwy./Hwy. 12, Kenwood* ☎ *707/833–1293, 800/353–6966* 🌐 *www.kenwoodinn.com* 🛏 *29 rooms* 🍴 *Free breakfast.*

Petaluma

24 miles southwest of Kenwood, 39 miles north of San Francisco.

The first thing you should know about Petaluma is that this is a farm town—with more than 62,500 residents, a large one—and the residents are proud of it. Recent years have seen an uptick in the quality of Petaluma cuisine, fueled in part by the proliferation of local organic and artisanal farms and boutique wine production. With the 2018 approval of the Petaluma Gap AVA, the city even has its name on a wine appellation.

GETTING HERE AND AROUND

Petaluma lies west of Sonoma and southwest of Glen Ellen and Kenwood. From Highway 12 or Arnold Drive, take Watmaugh Road west to Highway 116 west. Sonoma Transit buses serve Petaluma. From San Francisco take U.S. 101 (or Golden Gate Transit Bus 101) north.

◉ Sights

Lagunitas Brewing Company

WINERY/DISTILLERY | These days owned by Heineken International, Lagunitas began as a craft brewery in Marin County in 1993 before moving to Petaluma in 1994. In addition to its large facility, the company operates a taproom, the Schwag Shop for gifts, and an outdoor beer garden that in good weather bustles even midday. Guides leading the brewery tour, which when offered includes a beer flight, provide an irreverent version of the company's rise to international acclaim. An engaging tale involves the state alcohol board's sting operation commemorated by Undercover Investigation Shut-down Ale, one of several small-batch brews made here. ■ **TIP→ The taproom closes on Monday and Tuesday, but the gift shop stays open and tours may take place.** ⊠ 1280 N. McDowell Blvd., Petaluma ✛ ½ mile north of Corona Rd. ☎ 707/769–4495 ⊕ lagunitas.com/taproom/petaluma ☞ Tour free ⊙ Taproom closed Mon. and Tues.

★ McEvoy Ranch

WINERY/DISTILLERY | The late Nan McEvoy's retirement project after departing as board chair of the San Francisco Chronicle, the ranch produces organic extra virgin olive oil as well as Pinot Noir and other wines, the estate ones from the Petaluma Gap AVA. Relaxing tastings of oils or wines unfold on a pond's-edge flagstone patio with views of alternating rows of Syrah grapes and mature olive trees. Two wine tastings include a simple lunch; the Taste of the Season spread involves wine served with artisanal cheeses, charcuterie, and other items. Walkabout Ranch Tours of four guests or more take in vineyards, gardens, and a Chinese pavilion. All visits require an appointment. ⊠ 5935 Red Hill Rd., Petaluma ✛ 6½ miles south of downtown ☎ 866/617–6779 ⊕ www.mcevoyranch. com ☞ Tastings from $25 (olive oil), $35 (wine); tours from $55.

🍴 Restaurants

★ Central Market

$$ | MODERN AMERICAN | A participant in the Slow Food movement, Central Market serves creative, upscale Cal-Mediterranean dishes—many of whose ingredients come from the restaurant's organic farm—in a century-old building with an exposed brick wall and an open kitchen. The menu, which changes daily depending on chef Tony Najiola's inspiration and what's ripe and ready, might include smoked duck wings as a starter, a slow-roasted-beets salad, pizzas, stews, two or three pasta dishes, and wood-grilled fish and meat. **Known for:** chef's tasting menus; superior wine list; historic setting. $ Average main: $26 ⊠ 42 Petaluma Blvd. N, Petaluma ✛ Near Western Ave. ☎ 707/778–9900 ⊕ www. centralmarketpetaluma.com ⊙ Closed Mon. and Tues. No lunch.

★ Pearl Petaluma

$$ | MEDITERRANEAN | Regulars of this southern Petaluma "daytime café" with indoor and outdoor seating rave about its eastern Mediterranean–inflected cuisine—then immediately downplay their enthusiasm lest this unassuming gem become more popular. The menu changes often, but mainstays include shakshuka (a tomato-based stew with baked eggs) and a lamb burger dripping with tzatziki. **Known for:** weekend brunch; fun beverage lineup, both alcoholic and non; menu prices include gratuity. $ Average main: $20 ⊠ 500 1st St., Petaluma ✛ At G St. ☎ 707/559–5187 ⊕ pearlpetaluma. com ⊙ Closed Tues. No dinner.

Healdsburg

17 miles north of Santa Rosa, 32 miles northwest of Petaluma.

Sonoma County's ritziest town and the star of many a magazine spread or online feature, Healdsburg is located at the intersection of the Dry Creek Valley, Russian River Valley, and Alexander Valley AVAs. Several dozen wineries bear a Healdsburg address, and around downtown's plaza you'll find fashionable boutiques, spas, hip tasting rooms, and art galleries, and some of the Wine Country's best restaurants.

Especially on weekends, you'll have plenty of company as you tour the downtown area. You could spend a day just exploring the tasting rooms and shops surrounding Healdsburg Plaza, but be sure to allow time to venture into the surrounding countryside. With orderly rows of vines alternating with beautifully overgrown hills, this is the setting you dream about when planning a Wine Country vacation.

GETTING HERE AND AROUND

Healdsburg sits just off U.S. 101. Heading north, take the Central Healdsburg exit to reach Healdsburg Plaza; heading south, take the Westside Road exit and pass east under the freeway. Sonoma County Transit buses serve Healdsburg from Santa Rosa.

Sights

★ Aperture Cellars

WINERY/DISTILLERY | As a youth, Jesse Katz tagged along with his photographer father, Andy Katz, to wineries worldwide, stimulating curiosity about wine that led to stints at august operations like the Napa Valley's Screaming Eagle and Bordeaux's Petrús. In 2009, still in his 20s, Katz started Aperture, a success from the get-go for his single-vineyard Cabernets and Bordeaux blends. Among the whites are Sauvignon Blanc and an old-vine Chenin Blanc that's one of California's best. Katz's wines, which benefit from rigorous farming and cellar techniques, are presented by appointment only in an ultracontemporary hospitality center that opened in 2020 about 2½ miles south of Healdsburg Plaza. One tasting explores Aperture's

various wine-growing sites, the other the single-vineyard wines. The center's shutterlike windows and other architectural elements evoke Andy Katz's photography career; his images of the Russian River Valley and beyond hang on the walls. ⊠ 12291 Old Redwood Hwy. ✛ ¼ mile south of Limerick La. ☎ 707/200–7891 ⊕ www.aperture-cellars.com ⊠ Tastings from $50.

Breathless Wines

WINERY/DISTILLERY | The mood's downright bubbly (pardon that pun) at the oasis-like garden patio of this sparkling-wine producer tucked away in an industrial park northwest of Healdsburg Plaza. Established by three sisters in memory of their mother, Breathless sources grapes from appellations in Sonoma, Napa, and Mendocino counties that find their way into sparklers and a few still wines. The small indoor tasting area, decorated flapper-era-style, was ingeniously fashioned out of shipping containers, though nearly everyone sips in the umbrella-shaded garden in fine weather. You can sample wine by the glass, flight, or bottle; all visits require an appointment, with same-day reservations sometimes possible. ■TIP→ **Splurge on the Sabrage Experience to learn how to open a bottle with a saber, a tradition supposedly initiated by Napoléon's soldiers.** ⊠ 499 Moore La. ✛ Off North St. ☎ 707/395–7300 ⊕ www.breathlesswines.com ⊠ Tastings from $13 per glass, $20 per flight ⊘ Closed Tues. and Wed. (sometimes changes).

Dry Creek Vineyard

WINERY/DISTILLERY | Loire-style Sauvignon Blanc marketed as Fumé Blanc brought instant success to the Dry Creek Valley's first new winery since Prohibition, but this stalwart established in 1972 also does well with Zinfandel and Cabernet Sauvignon and other Bordeaux-style reds. Founder David Stare's other contributions include leading the drive to develop the Dry Creek Valley appellation and coining the term "old-vine Zinfandel." The winery's history and wine-making evolution are among the topics addressed at tastings—outdoors under the shade of a magnolia and several redwood trees or in the nautical-themed tasting room. ✉ *3770 Lambert Bridge Rd.* ⊹ *Off Dry Creek Rd.* ☎ *707/433–1000, 800/864–9463* ⊕ *www.drycreekvineyard.com* 🍷 *Tastings from $25.*

Gary Farrell Vineyards & Winery

WINERY/DISTILLERY | Pass through an impressive metal gate and wind your way up a steep hill to reach this winery with knockout Russian River Valley views from the elegant two-tiered tasting room and terrace outside. In 2017 *Wine Enthusiast Magazine* named a Gary Farrell Chardonnay wine of the year, one among many accolades for this winery known for sophisticated single-vineyard Chardonnays and Pinot Noirs. Farrell departed in the early 2000s, but current winemaker Theresa Heredia acknowledges that her philosophy has much in common with his. For the Pinots, this means picking on the early side to preserve acidity and focusing on "expressing the site." The Elevation Tasting of single-vineyard wines provides a good introduction. All visits are by appointment; same-day reservations are possible during the week, but call ahead. ✉ *10701 Westside Rd.* ☎ *707/473–2909* ⊕ *www.garyfarrellwinery.com* 🍷 *Tastings from $35.*

★ Jordan Vineyard and Winery

WINERY/DISTILLERY | Founders Tom and Sally Jordan erected the French-style château here in part to emphasize their goal of producing Sonoma County Chardonnays and Cabernet Sauvignons—one of each annually—to rival those from the Napa Valley and France itself. Their son John, now at the helm, has instituted numerous improvements, among them the replanting of many vines and a shift to all-French barrels for aging. Most tastings revolve around executive chef Todd Knoll's small bites, whose ingredients come mainly from Jordan's organic garden. The Library Tasting of current releases concludes with an older Cabernet for comparison. An enchanting themed lunch and wine pairing, Paris on the Terrace, unfolds on the château's terrace from spring to early fall, when the winery often hosts a three-hour Estate Tour & Tasting. The latter's pièce de résistance is the stop at a 360-degree vista point overlooking the 1,200-acre property's vines, olive trees, and countryside. Visits are strictly by appointment. ✉ *1474 Alexander Valley Rd.* ⊹ *1½ miles east of Healdsburg Ave.* ☎ *800/654–1213, 707/431–5250* ⊕ *www.jordanwinery.com* 🍷 *Tastings from $45* ⊗ *Closed Tues. and Wed. Dec.–Mar.*

MacRostie Estate House

WINERY/DISTILLERY | A driveway off Westside Road curls through undulating vineyard hills to the steel, wood, and heavy-on-the-glass tasting space of this longtime Chardonnay and Pinot Noir producer. Moments after you've arrived and a host has offered a glass of wine, you'll already feel transported to a genteel, rustic world. Hospitality is clearly a priority, but so, too, is seeking out top-tier grape sources—30 for the Chardonnays, 15 for the Pinots—among them Dutton Ranch, Sangiacomo, and owner Steve MacRostie's Wildcat. With fruit this renowned, current winemaker Heidi Bridenhagen downplays the oak and other tricks of her trade, letting the vineyard settings, grape clones, and vintage do the talking. Tastings, inside or on balcony terraces with views across the Russian River Valley, are all seated and by appointment. ✉ *4605 Westside Rd.* ⊹ *Near Frost Rd.* ☎ *707/473–9303* ⊕ *macrostiewinery.com* 🍷 *Tastings from $35.*

★ Ridge Vineyards

WINERY/DISTILLERY | Ridge stands tall among local wineries, and not merely because its 1971 Monte Bello Cabernet Sauvignon rated second-highest among California reds competing with French ones at the famous Judgment of Paris blind tasting of 1976. The winery built its reputation on Cabernets, Zinfandels, and Chardonnays of unusual depth and complexity, but you'll also find blends of Rhône varietals. Ridge makes wines using grapes from several California locales—including the Dry Creek Valley, Sonoma Valley, Napa Valley, and Paso Robles—but the focus is on single-vineyard estate wines such as the Lytton Springs Zinfandel from fruit grown near the tasting room. In good weather you can sit outside, taking in views of rolling vineyard hills while you sip. ✉ *650 Lytton Springs Rd.* ✣ *Off U.S. 101* ☎ *408/867–3233* 🌐 *www.ridgewine.com/visit/lytton-springs* 🎫 *Tastings from $20.*

★ Silver Oak

WINERY/DISTILLERY | The views and architecture are as impressive as the wines at the Sonoma County outpost of the same-named Napa Valley winery. In 2018, six years after purchasing a 113-acre parcel with 73 acres planted to grapes, Silver Oak debuted its ultramodern, environmentally sensitive winery and glass-walled tasting pavilion. As in Napa, the Healdsburg facility produces just one wine each year: a well-balanced Alexander Valley Cabernet Sauvignon aged in American rather than French oak barrels. One tasting includes the current Alexander Valley and Napa Valley Cabernets plus an older vintage. Two or more wines of sister operation Twomey Cellars, which produces Sauvignon Blanc, Pinot Noir, and Merlot, begin a second offering that concludes with the current Cabernets. Hosts at a third pour current and older Cabernets from either Napa or Sonoma. Make a reservation for all visits. ✉ *7300 Hwy. 128* ✣ *Near Chaffee Rd.* ☎ *707/942–7082* 🌐 *www.silveroak.com* 🎫 *Tastings from $40.*

★ Tongue Dancer Wines

WINERY/DISTILLERY | Down a country lane less than 2 miles south of Healdsburg Plaza, James MacPhail's modest production facility seems well away from the upscale fray. MacPhail makes wines for The Calling, Sangiacomo, and other labels, but Tongue Dancer's Chardonnays and Pinot Noirs are his handcrafted labors of love. Made from small lots of grapes from choice vineyard sites, the wines impress, sometimes stun, with their grace, complexity, and balance. The flagship Sonoma Coast Pinot Noir, a blend from two or more vineyards, is poured at most tastings, in a mezzanine space above oak-aging barrels or on an outdoor patio. Either the winemaker or his co-owner and wife, Kerry Forbes-MacPhail—she's credited on bottles as the "Knowledgeable One" (and she is)—will host you. As James describes it, they aim to "create an approachable experience for guests we hope will leave as friends." Appointment-only visits are best made a day or more ahead. ✉ *851 Magnolia Dr.* ✣ *Off Westside Rd.* ☎ *707/433–4780* 🌐 *tonguedancerwines.com* 🎫 *Tastings from $25* ⏲ *Closed Sun.*

🍴 Restaurants

★ Barndiva

$$$$ | **AMERICAN** | Music plays quietly in the background while servers carry inventive seasonal cocktails at this restaurant that abandons the homey vibe of many Wine Country spots in favor of a more urban feel. Make a light meal out of yellowtail tuna crudo or homemade linguine, or settle in for the evening with pan-seared day scallops or a grass-fed strip loin. **Known for:** good cocktails; stylish cuisine; open-air patio. [$] *Average main: $38* ✉ *231 Center St.* ✣ *Near Matheson St.* ☎ *707/431–0100* 🌐 *www.barndiva.com* ⏲ *Closed Mon. and Tues. No lunch weekdays.*

Bravas Bar de Tapas

$$$ | **SPANISH** | Spanish-style tapas and an outdoor patio in perpetual party mode make this restaurant, headquartered in a restored 1920s bungalow, a popular downtown perch. Contemporary Spanish mosaics set a perky tone inside, but unless something's amiss with the weather, nearly everyone heads out back for flavorful croquettes, paella, jamón, *pan tomate* (tomato toast), grilled octopus, skirt steak, and crispy fried chicken. **Known for:** casual small plates; specialty cocktails, sangrias, and beer; sherries from dry to sweet. $ *Average main: $28* ✉ *420 Center St.* ✣ *Near North St.* ☎ *707/433–7700* 🌐 *www.barbravas.com* 🕒 *Closed Mon. and Tues.*

Campo Fina

$$ | **ITALIAN** | Chef Ari Rosen serves up contemporary-rustic Italian cuisine at this converted storefront that once housed a bar notorious for boozin' and brawlin'. Sandblasted red brick, satin-smooth walnut tables, and old-school lighting fixtures (and a large back patio) strike a retro note for a menu built around pizzas and gems such as Rosen's variation on his grandmother's tomato-braised chicken with creamy-soft polenta. **Known for:** outdoor patio's boccie court out of an Italian movie set; lunch sandwiches; wines from California and Italy. $ *Average main: $23* ✉ *330 Healdsburg Ave.* ✣ *Near North St.* ☎ *707/395–4640* 🌐 *www.campofina.com.*

Costeaux French Bakery

$ | **FRENCH** | Breakfast, served all day at this bright-yellow French-style bakery and café, includes the signature omelet (sun-dried tomatoes, bacon, spinach, and Brie) and French toast made from thick slabs of cinnamon-walnut bread. French onion soup and cranberry-turkey, French dip, and (on the cinnamon-walnut bread) Monte Cristo sandwiches are among the lunch favorites. **Known for:** breads, croissants, and fancy pastries; quiche and omelets; front patio. $ *Average main: $15* ✉ *417 Healdsburg Ave.* ✣ *At North St.* ☎ *707/433–1913* 🌐 *www.costeaux.com* 🕒 *Closed Mon. and Tues. (check to be sure). No dinner.*

★ SingleThread Farms Restaurant

$$$$ | **ECLECTIC** | The seasonally oriented, multicourse Japanese dinners known as *kaiseki* inspired the prix-fixe vegetarian, meat, and seafood menu at the spare, elegant restaurant—redwood walls, walnut tables, mesquite-tile floors, muted-gray yarn-thread panels—of internationally renowned culinary artists Katina and Kyle Connaughton (she farms, he cooks). As Katina describes the endeavor, the microseasons of their nearby farm (ask about visiting it) plus SingleThread's rooftop garden of fruit trees and greens dictate Kyle's rarefied fare, prepared in a theatrically lit open kitchen. **Known for:** culinary precision; instinctive service; impeccable wine pairings. $ *Average main: $295* ✉ *131 North St.* ✣ *At Center St.* ☎ *707/723–4646* 🌐 *www.singlethreadfarms.com* 🕒 *No lunch weekdays.*

★ Valette

$$$ | **MODERN AMERICAN** | Northern Sonoma native Dustin Valette opened this homage to the area's artisanal agricultural bounty with his brother, who runs the high-ceilinged dining room, where the playful contemporary lighting tempers the austerity of the exposed concrete walls and butcher-block-thick wooden tables. Charcuterie is an emphasis, but also consider the signature day-boat scallops *en croûte* (in a pastry crust) or dishes that might include Szechuan-crusted duck breast or a variation on Niçoise salad with albacore poached in olive oil. **Known for:** "Trust me" (the chef) tasting menu; mostly Northern California and French wines; chef's nearby The Matheson for wine tasting, pairings, and rooftop dining. $ *Average main: $36* ✉ *344 Center St.* ✣ *At North St.* ☎ *707/473–0946* 🌐 *www.valettehealdsburg.com* 🕒 *No lunch.*

🛏 Hotels

★ Harmon Guest House

$$$ | **HOTEL** | A boutique sibling of the h2hotel two doors away, this downtown delight debuted in late 2018 having already earned LEED Gold status for its eco-friendly construction and operating practices. **Pros:** rooftop bar's cocktails, food menu, and views; connecting rooms and suites; similarly designed sister property h2hotel two doors south. **Cons:** minor room-to-room noise bleed-through; room gadgetry may flummox some guests; minimum-stay requirements some weekends. $ *Rooms from: $389* ✉ *227 Healdsburg Ave.* ☎ *707/922–5262* ⊕ *harmonguesthouse.com* ↩ *39 rooms* ¶⊙¶ *Free breakfast.*

Hotel Trio Healdsburg
$$ | HOTEL | Named for the three major wine appellations—the Russian River, Dry Creek, and Alexander valleys—whose confluence it's near, this Residence Inn by Marriott 1¼ miles north of Healdsburg Plaza caters to families and extended-stay business travelers with spacious rooms equipped with full kitchens. **Pros:** cute robot room service; full kitchens; rooms sleep up to four or six. **Cons:** 30-minute walk to downtown; slightly corporate feel; pricey in high season. $ *Rooms from: $242* ✉ *110 Dry Creek Rd.* ☎ *707/433–4000* ⊕ *www. hoteltrio.com* ↩ *122 rooms* ¶⊙¶ *Free breakfast.*

★ Montage Healdsburg
$$$$ | RESORT | Its bungalowlike guest rooms deftly layered into oak- and Cabernet-studded hills a few miles north of Healdsburg Plaza, this architectural sensation that opened fully in 2021 significantly upped Sonoma County's ultraluxury game. **Pros:** vineyard views from spa, restaurant, and swimming pool; outdoor living spaces with daybeds and fire pits; recreational options on-property or nearby. **Cons:** expensive year-round; hefty resort fee; car trip required for off-property visits. $ *Rooms from: $845* ✉ *100 Montage Way* ☎ *707/979–9000* ⊕ *www. montagehotels.com/healdsburg* ↩ *130 bungalows* ¶⊙¶ *No meals.*

★ River Belle Inn
$$ | B&B/INN | An 1875 Victorian with a storied past and a glorious colonnaded wraparound porch anchors this boutique property along the Russian River. **Pros:**

riverfront location near a dozen-plus tasting rooms; cooked-to-order full breakfasts; attention to detail. **Cons:** about a mile from Healdsburg Plaza; minimum-stay requirement on weekends; lacks on-site pool, fitness center, and other amenities. $ *Rooms from: $280* ✉ *68 Front St.* ☎ *707/955–5724* ⊕ *www.riverbelleinn. com* ↩ *12 rooms* ¶⊙¶ *Free breakfast.*

🛍 Shopping

ART GALLERIES
★ Gallery Lulo
ART GALLERIES | A collaboration between a local artist and jewelry maker and a Danish-born curator, this gallery presents changing exhibits of jewelry, sculpture, and objets d'art. ✉ *303 Center St.* ✛ *At Plaza St.* ☎ *707/433–7533* ⊕ *www. gallerylulo.com.*

FOOD AND WINE
Dry Creek General Store
FOOD/CANDY | For breakfasts, sandwiches, bread, cheeses, and picnic supplies, stop by the general store, established in 1881 and still a popular spot for locals to hang out on the porch or in the bar. Beer and wine are also for sale, along with artisanal sodas, ciders, and juices. ✉ *3495 Dry Creek Rd.* ✛ *At Lambert Bridge Rd.* ☎ *707/433–4171* ⊕ *www.drycreekgeneralstore1881.com.*

🏃 Activities

BICYCLING
Getaway Adventures / Wine Country Bikes
TOUR—SPORTS | This shop several blocks southeast of Healdsburg Plaza is perfectly located for setting up single or multiday treks into the Dry Creek and Russian River valleys by bike, kayak, or both. Private and group tours might include wineries, organic farms, and other stops. If you prefer to explore on your own, you can rent equipment. ✉ *61 Front St.* ✛ *At Hudson St.* ☎ *800/499–2453* ⊕ *getawayadventures.com* 🚲 *Daily rentals from $39 per day, full-day tours from $139.*

SPAS

★ A Simple Touch Spa

FITNESS/HEALTH CLUBS | Skilled in Swedish, deep-tissue, sports, and other massage modalities, this soothing but unpretentious day spa's therapists routinely receive post-session raves. The most popular treatment involves heated basalt stones applied to the client's body, followed by a massage of choice. Foot reflexology, reiki, and facials are among the other specialties. ■ **TIP➜ Couples can enjoy any of the massages performed side-by-side by two therapists.** ✉ *239 Center St., Suite C ✛ Near Matheson St.* ☎ *707/433–6856* ⊕ *asimpletouchspa.com* ✆ *Treatments $55–$300.*

Geyserville

8 miles north of Healdsburg.

Several high-profile Alexander Valley AVA wineries, including the splashy Francis Ford Coppola Winery, can be found in the town of Geyserville, a small part of which stretches west of U.S. 101 into northern Dry Creek. Not long ago this was a dusty farm town, and downtown Geyserville retains its rural character, but the restaurants, shops, and tasting rooms along the short main drag hint at Geyserville's growing sophistication.

GETTING HERE AND AROUND

From Healdsburg, the quickest route to downtown Geyserville is north on U.S. 101 to the Highway 128/Geyserville exit. Turn right at the stop sign onto Geyserville Avenue and follow the road north to the small downtown. For a more scenic drive, head north from Healdsburg Plaza along Healdsburg Avenue. About 3 miles north, jog west (left) for a few hundred feet onto Lytton Springs Road, then turn north (right) onto Geyserville Avenue. In town the avenue merges with Highway 128. Sonoma County Transit buses serve Geyserville from downtown Healdsburg.

◉ Sights

Francis Ford Coppola Winery

WINERY/DISTILLERY | The fun at what the film director has called his "wine wonderland" is all in the excess. You may find it hard to resist having your photo snapped standing next to Don Corleone's desk from *The Godfather* or beside other memorabilia from Coppola films (including some directed by his daughter, Sofia). A bandstand reminiscent of one in *The Godfather Part II* is the centerpiece of a large pool area where you can rent a changing room, complete with shower, and spend the afternoon lounging poolside, perhaps ordering food from the adjacent café. A more elaborate restaurant, Rustic, overlooks the vineyards. As for the wines, the excess continues in the cellar, where Coppola's team produces several dozen varietal bottlings and blends. ✉ *300 Via Archimedes ✛ Off U.S. 101* ☎ *707/857–1400* ⊕ *www.franciscoppolawinery.com* ✆ *Tastings from $35.*

★ Locals Tasting Room

WINERY/DISTILLERY | If you're serious about wine, Carolyn Lewis's tasting room is worth the trek 8 miles north of Healdsburg Plaza to downtown Geyserville. Connoisseurs who appreciate Lewis's ability to spot up-and-comers head here regularly to sample the output of a dozen or so small wineries, most without tasting rooms of their own. There's no fee for tasting—extraordinary for wines of this quality—and the extremely knowledgeable staff are happy to pour you a flight of several wines so you can compare, say, different Cabernet Sauvignons. ✉ *21023A Geyserville Ave. ✛ At Hwy. 128* ☎ *707/857–4900* ⊕ *www.localstastingroom.com* ✆ *Tasting free.*

★ Robert Young Estate Winery

WINERY/DISTILLERY | Panoramic Alexander Valley views unfold at Scion House, the stylish yet informal knoll-top tasting space of this longtime Geyserville grower. The first Youngs began farming this land in the mid-1800s, raising cattle and growing wheat, prunes, and other crops. In the 1960s the late Robert Young, of the third generation, began cultivating grapes, eventually planting two Chardonnay clones now named for him. Grapes from them go into the Area 27 Chardonnay, among the best whites. The reds—small-lot Cabernet Sauvignons plus individual bottlings of Cabernet Franc, Malbec, Merlot, and Petit Verdot—shine even brighter. Tastings at Scion House, named for the fourth generation, whose members built on Robert Young's legacy and established the winery, are by appointment. Call ahead for same-day reservations. **■TIP→ Cab fanatics should consider the Ultimate Cabernet Lovers Experience of top-tier estate wines.** *✉ 5120 Red Winery Rd. ✥ Off Hwy. 128 ☎ 707/431–4811 🌐 www.ryew.com 🎫 Tastings from $30 🕒 Closed Tues.*

★ Zialena

WINERY/DISTILLERY | Sister-and-brother team Lisa and Mark Mazzoni (she runs the business, he makes the wines) debuted their small winery's first vintage in 2014, but their Italian American family's wine-making heritage stretches back more than a century. Named for the siblings' great aunt Lena, known for her hospitality, Zialena specializes in estate-grown Zinfandel and Cabernet Sauvignon, some of whose lush mouthfeel derives from techniques Mark absorbed while working for the international consultant Philippe Melka. The Zin and Cab grapes, along with those for the Chardonnay and seductive rosé of Sangiovese, come from the 120-acre Mazzoni Vineyard, from which larger labels like Jordan also source fruit. Tastings are by appointment only, with same-day visits often possible. *✉ 21112 River Rd. ✥ Off Hwy. 128 ☎ 707/955–5992 🌐 www.zialena.com 🎫 Tastings from $15.*

🍴 Restaurants

Diavola Pizzeria & Salumeria

$$ | ITALIAN | A dining area with hardwood floors, a pressed-tin ceiling, and exposed-brick walls provides a fitting setting for the rustic cuisine at this Geyserville mainstay. Chef Dino Bugica studied with artisanal cooks in Italy before opening this restaurant specializing in wood-fired pizzas and house-cured meats, with a few salads and meaty main courses rounding out the menu. **Known for:** talented chef; smoked pork belly, pancetta, and spicy Calabrese sausage; casual setting. *[$] Average main: $23 ✉ 21021 Geyserville Ave. ✥ At Hwy. 128 ☎ 707/814–0111 🌐 www.diavolapizzeria.com.*

🛏 Hotels

Geyserville Inn

$$ | HOTEL | Clever travelers give the Healdsburg hubbub and prices the heave-ho but still have easy access to outstanding Dry Creek and Alexander Valley wineries from this modest, motel-like inn with a boutique-hotel sensibility. **Pros:** outdoor pool; vineyard-view decks from second-floor rooms in back; picnic area. **Cons:** rooms facing pool or highway can be noisy; weekend two-night minimum requirement; not for party types. *[$] Rooms from: $209 ✉ 21714 Geyserville Ave. ☎ 707/857–4343, 877/857–4343 🌐 www.geyservilleinn.com 🔑 41 rooms 🍽 No meals.*

Forestville

13 miles southwest of Healdsburg.

To experience the Russian River Valley AVA's climate and rusticity, follow the river's westward course to the town of Forestville, home to a highly regarded restaurant and inn and a few wineries producing Pinot Noir from the Russian River Valley and well beyond.

GETTING HERE AND AROUND

To reach Forestville from U.S. 101, drive west from the River Road exit north of Santa Rosa. From Healdsburg, follow Westside Road west to River Road and then continue west. Sonoma County Transit buses serve Forestville.

Sights

★ Hartford Family Winery

WINERY/DISTILLERY | Pinot Noir lovers appreciate the subtle differences in the wines Hartford's team crafts from grapes grown in several Sonoma County AVAs, along with fruit from nearby Marin and Mendocino counties and Oregon. The winery also produces highly rated Chardonnays and old-vine Zinfandels. If the weather's good, enjoy a flight on the patio outside the opulent main winery building. At private library tastings, guests sip current and older vintages. All visits are by appointment; call ahead on the same day. ✉ *8075 Martinelli Rd.* ✣ *Off Hwy. 116 or River Rd.* ☎ *707/887–8030* 🌐 *www.hartfordwines.com* 🎫 *Tastings from $25* ⏲ *Closed Tues. and Wed.*

Joseph Jewell Wines

WINERY/DISTILLERY | Pinot Noirs from the Russian River Valley and Humboldt County to the north are the strong suit of this winery sourcing from prestigious vineyards like Bucher and Hallberg Ranch. Owner-winemaker Adrian Manspeaker, a Humboldt native, spearheaded the foray into Pinot Noir grown in the coastal redwood country. His playfully rustic storefront tasting room in downtown Forestville (visits by appointment) provides the opportunity to experience what's unique about the varietal's next Northern California frontier. There are plenty of whites here, too—Sauvignon Blanc, two Chardonnays, Pinot Gris, and Vermentino—plus rosé of Pinot, and Zinfandel from 1970s vines. ■ **TIP→ In 2021 the winery expects to begin offering outdoor tastings and vineyard tours at Raymond Burr Vineyards in Healdsburg.** ✉ *6542 Front St.* ✣ *Near 1st St.* ☎ *707/820–1621* 🌐 *www.josephjewell.com* 🎫 *Tastings from $25* ⏲ *Closed Mon.–Wed.*

Restaurants

Backyard

$$$ | MODERN AMERICAN | The couple behind this casually rustic modern American restaurant, who met while working at Thomas Keller restaurants in Yountville, regard Sonoma County's farms and gardens as their "backyard." Dinner entrées, which change seasonally, usually include buttermilk fried chicken with buttermilk biscuits, coleslaw, and honey butter. **Known for:** husband-and-wife chef-owners; ingredients from high-quality local purveyors; poplar-shaded outdoor front patio. [$] *Average main: $28* ✉ *6566 Front St./Hwy. 116* ✣ *At 1st St.* ☎ *707/820–8445* 🌐 *backyardforestville.com* ⏲ *Closed Tues.–Thurs.*

Hotels

★ The Farmhouse Inn

$$$$ | B&B/INN | With a farmhouse-meets-modern-loft aesthetic, this low-key but upscale getaway with a pale-yellow exterior contains spacious rooms filled with king-size four-poster beds, whirlpool tubs, and hillside-view terraces. **Pros:** fantastic restaurant; luxury bath products; full-service spa. **Cons:** mild road noise audible in rooms closest to the street; two-night minimum on weekends; pricey, especially during high season. [$] *Rooms from: $518* ✉ *7871 River Rd.* ☎ *707/887–3300, 800/464–6642* 🌐 *www.farmhouseinn.com* 🔑 *25 rooms* 🍴 *Free breakfast.*

Activities

Burke's Canoe Trips

CANOEING/ROWING/SKULLING | You'll get a real feel for the Russian River's flora and fauna on a leisurely 10-mile paddle downstream from Burke's to Guerneville. A shuttle bus returns you to your car at the end of the journey, which is best taken from late May through mid-October and, in summer, on a weekday—summer weekends can be crowded and raucous. ✉ *8600 River Rd.* ✣ *At Mirabel Rd.* ☎ *707/887–1222* 🌐 *www.burkescanoetrips.com* 🎟 *$75 per canoe.*

Guerneville

7 miles northwest of Forestville, 15 miles southwest of Healdsburg.

Guerneville's tourist demographic has evolved over the years—Bay Area families in the 1950s, lesbians and gays starting in the 1970s, and these days a mix of both groups, plus techies and outdoorsy types—with coast redwoods and the Russian River always central to the town's appeal. The area's most famous winery is Korbel Champagne Cellars, established nearly a century and a half ago. Even older are the stands of trees that except on the coldest winter days make Armstrong Redwoods State Natural Reserve such a perfect respite from wine tasting.

GETTING HERE AND AROUND

To get to Guerneville from Healdsburg, follow Westside Road south to River Road and turn west. From Forestville, head west on Highway 116; alternatively, you can head north on Mirabel Road to River Road and then head west. Sonoma County Transit buses serve Guerneville.

Sights

★ Armstrong Redwoods State Natural Reserve

NATIONAL/STATE PARK | **FAMILY** | Here's your best opportunity in the western Wine Country to wander amid *Sequoia sempervirens,* also known as coast redwood trees. The oldest example in this 805-acre state park, the Colonel Armstrong Tree, is thought to be more than 1,400 years old. A half mile from the parking lot, the tree is easily accessible, and you can hike a long way into the forest before things get too hilly. **■ TIP→ During hot summer days, Armstrong Redwoods's tall trees help the park keep its cool.** ✉ *17000 Armstrong Woods Rd.* ✣ *Off River Rd.* ☎ *707/869–2958 for visitor center, 707/869–2015 for park headquarters* 🌐 *www.parks.ca.gov* 🎟 *$8 per vehicle, free to pedestrians and bicyclists.*

Restaurants

★ boon eat+drink

$$ | **MODERN AMERICAN** | A casual storefront restaurant on Guerneville's main drag, boon eat+drink has a menu built around salads, smallish shareable plates, and entrées that might include a vegan bowl, chili-braised pork shoulder, and local cod with beluga lentils. Like many of chef-owner Crista Luedtke's dishes, the signature polenta lasagna—creamy ricotta salata cheese and polenta served on greens sautéed in garlic, all of it floating upon a spicy marinara sauce—deviates significantly from the lasagna norm but succeeds on its own merits. **Known for:** adventurous culinary sensibility; Sonoma County wine selection; local organic ingredients. [$] *Average main: $23* ✉ *16248 Main St.* ✣ *At Church St.* ☎ *707/869–0780* 🌐 *eatatboon.com* ⏲ *Closed Mon. and Tues.*

Hotels

boon hotel+spa

$$ | **HOTEL** | Redwoods, Douglas firs, and palms supply shade and seclusion at this lushly landscaped resort ¾ mile north of downtown Guerneville. **Pros:** filling breakfasts; pool area and on-site spa; complimentary bikes. **Cons:** lacks amenities of larger properties; pool rooms too close to the action for some guests; can be pricey in high season. [$] *Rooms from: $213* ✉ *14711 Armstrong Woods Rd.* ☎ *707/869–2721* 🌐 *boonhotels.com* 🛏 *15 rooms* 🍴 *Free breakfast.*

Sebastopol

14 miles southeast of Guerneville.

A stroll through downtown Sebastopol—a town formerly known more for Gravenstein apples than for grapes but these days a burgeoning wine hub—reveals glimpses of the distant and recent past and perhaps the future, too. Many hippies settled here in the 1960s and 70s and, as the old Crosby, Stills, Nash & Young song goes, they taught their children well: the town remains steadfastly, if not entirely, countercultural.

GETTING HERE AND AROUND

Sebastopol can be reached from Guerneville by taking Highway 116 south. From Santa Rosa, head west on Highway 12. Sonoma County Transit buses serve Sebastopol.

Sights

The Barlow

MARKET | A multibuilding complex on a former apple-cannery site, The Barlow celebrates Sonoma County's "maker" culture with tenants who produce or sell wine, beer, spirits, crafts, clothing, art, and artisanal food and herbs. The anchor wine tenant, Kosta Browne, receives only club members and allocation-list guests, but other tasting rooms are open to the public, and Region wine bar promotes small Sonoma County producers. Crooked Goat Brewing makes and sells ales, Golden State Cider pours apple-driven beverages, and you can have a nip of vodka, gin, sloe gin, or wheat and rye whiskey at Spirit Works Distillery. Over at Fern Bar, the zero-proof (as in nonalcoholic) cocktails entice as much as the traditional ones. The bar serves food, as do Sushi Koshō, Blue Ridge Kitchen (Southern-influenced comfort fare), and a few other spots. ⊠ *6770 McKinley St.* ✢ *At Morris St., off Hwy. 12* 📱 *707/824–5600* ⊕ *www.thebarlow.net* 🖃 *Complex free; fees for tasting.*

★ Dutton-Goldfield Winery

WINERY/DISTILLERY | An avid cyclist whose previous credits include developing the wine-making program at Hartford Court, Dan Goldfield teamed up with fifth-generation farmer Steve Dutton to establish this small operation devoted to cool-climate wines. Goldfield modestly strives to take Dutton's meticulously farmed fruit and "make the winemaker unnoticeable," but what impresses the most about these wines, which include Chardonnay, Gewürztraminer, Riesling, Pinot Noir, and Zinfandel, is their sheer artistry. Among the ones to seek out are the Angel Camp Pinot Noir, from Anderson Valley (Mendocino County) grapes, and the Morelli Lane Zinfandel, from fruit grown on the remaining 1.8 acres of an 1880s vineyard Goldfield helped revive. One tasting focuses on current releases, another on single-vineyard Pinot Noirs. ⊠ *3100 Gravenstein Hwy. N/Hwy. 116* ✢ *At Graton Rd.* 📱 *707/827–3600* ⊕ *www.duttongoldfield.com* 🖃 *Tastings from $30.*

★ Iron Horse Vineyards

WINERY/DISTILLERY | A meandering one-lane road leads to this winery known for its sparkling wines and estate Chardonnays and Pinot Noirs. The sparklers have made history: Ronald Reagan served them at his summit meetings with Mikhail Gorbachev; George H. W. Bush took some along to Moscow for treaty talks; and Barack Obama included them at official state dinners. Despite Iron Horse's brushes with fame, a casual rusticity prevails at its outdoor tasting area (large heaters keep things comfortable on chilly days), which gazes out on acres of rolling, vine-covered hills. Tastings are by appointment only. ⊠ *9786 Ross Station Rd.* ✢ *Off Hwy. 116* 📱 *707/887–1507* ⊕ *www.ironhorsevineyards.com* 🖃 *Tasting $30.*

Iron Horse produces sparklers that make history.

🍴 Restaurants

★ Handline Coastal California

$ | MODERN AMERICAN | FAMILY | Sebastopol's former Foster's Freeze location, now a 21st-century fast-food palace, won design awards for its rusted steel frame and translucent panel-like windows. The menu, a paean to coastal California cuisine, includes oysters raw and grilled, fish tacos, ceviche, tostadas, three burgers (beef, vegetarian, and fish), and, honoring the location's previous incarnation, chocolate and vanilla soft-serve ice cream. **Known for:** upscale comfort food; outdoor patio; sustainable seafood and other ingredients. [$] *Average main: $14* ✉ *935 Gravenstein Hwy. S* ✥ *Near Hutchins Ave.* ☎ *707/827–3744* 🌐 *www.handline.com.*

Ramen Gaijin

$$ | JAPANESE | Inside a tall-ceilinged, brick-walled, vaguely industrial-looking space with reclaimed wood from a coastal building backing the bar, the chefs at Ramen Gaijin turn out richly flavored ramen bowls brimming with crispy pork belly, woodear mushrooms, seaweed, and other well-proportioned ingredients. *Izakaya* (Japanese pub grub) dishes like *donburi* (meat and vegetables over rice) are another specialty, like the ramen made from mostly local proteins and produce. **Known for:** artisanal cocktails, beer, wine, and cider; gluten-free, vegetarian dishes; karage (fried chicken) and other small plates. [$] *Average main: $18* ✉ *6948 Sebastopol Ave.* ✥ *Near Main St.* ☎ *707/827–3609* 🌐 *www.ramengaijin.com* 🕓 *Closed Sun. and Mon. No lunch.*

Santa Rosa

6 miles east of Sebastopol, 55 miles north of San Francisco.

Urban Santa Rosa isn't as popular with tourists as many Wine Country destinations—which isn't surprising, seeing as there are more office parks than wineries within its limits. Nevertheless, this hardworking town is home to a couple of interesting cultural offerings and a few noteworthy restaurants and vineyards. The city's chain motels and hotels can be handy if you're finding that everything else is booked up, especially since Santa Rosa is roughly equidistant from Sonoma, Healdsburg, and the western Russian River Valley, three of Sonoma County's most popular wine-tasting destinations.

GETTING HERE AND AROUND

To get to Santa Rosa from Sebastopol, drive east on Highway 12. From San Francisco, cross the Golden Gate Bridge and continue north on U.S. 101. Santa Rosa's hotels, restaurants, and wineries are spread over a wide area; factor in extra time when driving around the city, especially during morning and evening rush hour. From San Francisco or Marin County, take Golden Gate Transit Bus 101. Sonoma County Transit buses serve Santa Rosa and the surrounding area.

 Sights

Balletto Vineyards

WINERY/DISTILLERY | A few decades ago Balletto was known more for quality produce than grapes, but the new millennium saw vineyards emerge as the core business. About 90% of the fruit from the family's 650-plus acres goes to other wineries, with the remainder destined for Balletto's estate wines. The house style is light on the oak, high in acidity, and low in alcohol content, a combination that yields exceptionally food-friendly wines. Sipping a Pinot Gris, rosé of Pinot Noir, or brut rosé sparkler on the outdoor patio can feel transcendent on a warm day, though the Chardonnays and Pinot Noirs, starting with the very reasonably priced Teresa's Unoaked Chard and flagship Estate Pinot, steal the show. ⊠ *5700 Occidental Rd.* ✛ *2½ miles west of Hwy. 12* ☎ *707/568–2455* ⊕ *www.ballettovineyards.com* ⊠ *Tastings from $15.*

★ Belden Barns

WINERY/DISTILLERY | Experiencing the enthusiasm this winery's owners radiate supplies half the pleasure of a visit to Lauren and Nate Belden's Sonoma Mountain vineyard, where at elevation 1,000 feet they grow fruit for their all-estate lineup. Grüner Veltliner, a European white grape, isn't widely planted in California, but the crisp yet softly rounded wine they produce from it makes a case for an increase. Critics also hail the Grenache, Pinot Noir, Syrah, and a nectarlike late-harvest Viognier, but you're apt to like anything poured. Tastings take place in a high-ceilinged former milking barn whose broad doorway frames a view of grapevines undulating toward a hilltop. The Beldens tailor visits to guests' interests but will nearly always whisk you into the vineyard, past a 2-acre organic garden, and over to a wishing tree whose results Lauren swears by. ■**TIP**➔ **The tasting fee here is a two-bottle purchase per adult.** ⊠ *5561 Sonoma Mountain Rd.* ✛ *10 miles south of downtown off Bennett Valley Rd.; 5½ miles west of Glen Ellen off Warm Springs Rd.* ☎ *415/577–8552* ⊕ *www.beldenbarns.com* ⊠ *Tastings from $50 (for two bottles).*

★ Martinelli Winery

WINERY/DISTILLERY | In a century-old hop barn with the telltale triple towers, Martinelli has the feel of a traditional country store, but sophisticated wines are made here. The winery's reputation rests on its complex Pinot Noirs, Syrahs, and Zinfandels, including the Jackass Hill Vineyard Zin, made with grapes from vines planted mostly in the 1880s. Noted winemaker Helen Turley set the Martinelli style—fruit-forward, easy on the oak, reined-in tannins—in the 1990s, and the current team continues this approach. Tastings held (weather permitting) on a vineyard's-edge terrace survey the current releases. All visits are by appointment, best made online. ■**TIP**➔ **Call the winery directly about library or collector flights.** ⊠ *3360 River Rd., Windsor*

✥ East of Olivet Rd. ☎ *707/525–0570, 800/346–1627* 🌐 *www.martinelliwinery.com* 🎫 *Tastings from $25* ⏲ *Closed days may vary; check with winery.*

Safari West
NATURE PRESERVE | FAMILY | An unexpected bit of wilderness in the Wine Country, this preserve with African wildlife covers 400 acres. Begin your visit with a stroll around enclosures housing lemurs, cheetahs, giraffes, and rare birds like the brightly colored scarlet ibis. Next, climb with your guide onto open-air vehicles that spend about two hours combing the expansive property, where more than 80 species—including gazelles, cape buffalo, antelope, wildebeests, and zebras—inhabit the hillsides. **■ TIP→ If you'd like to extend your stay, lodging in swank Botswana-made tent cabins is available.** ✉ *3115 Porter Creek Rd.* ✥ *Off Mark West Springs Rd.* ☎ *707/579–2551, 800/616–2695* 🌐 *www.safariwest.com* 🎫 *$93–$103 Sept.–May, $108–$128 June–Aug.*

🍴 Restaurants

Grossman's Noshery and Bar
$$ | DELI | The menu at this homage to Jewish delicatessens plays the greatest hits—blintzes, latkes, lox, chopped liver, and knishes, plus pastrami, corned beef, and Reuben sandwiches—but mashes things up with chicken shawarma kebabs, fish-and-chips, and other atypical deli dishes. It's all executed with panache, and the retro-eclectic decor (black-and-white ceramic tile floors, colorful tropical-bird-print wallpaper, chunky stone fireplace) feels nostalgic yet of the moment. **Known for:** baked goods; happy-hour (daily 3–5) frozen vodka shots; picnic-table seating beside the building. [$] *Average main: $18* ✉ *Hotel La Rose, 308½ Wilson St.* ✥ *Near 4th St.* ☎ *707/595–7707* 🌐 *grossmanssr.com.*

★ Walter Hansel Wine & Bistro
$$$ | FRENCH | Tabletop linens and lights softly twinkling from this ruby-red roadhouse restaurant's low wooden ceiling raise expectations the Parisian-style bistro cuisine consistently exceeds. A starter of cheeses or lobster bisque in a puff pastry awakens the palate for entrées like chicken cordon bleu, steak au poivre, or what this place does best: seafood dishes that might include scallops in white-truffle cream sauce or subtly sauced wild Alaskan halibut. **Known for:** romantic setting for classic cuisine; prix-fixe option; vegan and vegetarian dishes. [$] *Average main: $35* ✉ *3535 Guerneville Rd.* ✥ *At Willowside Rd., 6 miles northwest of downtown* ☎ *707/546–6462* 🌐 *walterhanselbistro.com* ⏲ *Closed Mon. and Tues. No lunch.*

🛏 Hotels

★ Vintners Resort
$$$$ | HOTEL | With a countryside location, a reserved sense of style, and spacious rooms with comfortable beds, the Vintners Resort further seduces with a slew of amenities and a scenic vineyard landscape. **Pros:** John Ash & Co. restaurant; vineyard jogging path; personalized service. **Cons:** occasional noise from adjacent events center; trips to downtown Santa Rosa or Healdsburg require a car; pricey on summer and fall weekends. [$] *Rooms from: $415* ✉ *4350 Barnes Rd.* ☎ *707/575–7350, 800/421–2584* 🌐 *www.vintnersresort.com* 🛏 *78 rooms* 🍴 *No meals.*

Index

Photo Credits

Front Cover: Matteo Colombo [Description: Aerial of downtown district Bay bridge and Oakland in the background at dusk, San Francisco, California, USA.]. **Back cover, from left to right:** Jaspe/Dreamstime, Serrnovik/Dreamstime, Lunamarina/Dreamstime. **Spine:** Tholbox / Shutterstock. **Interior, from left to right:** IM_photo/Shutterstock (1). travelview/Shutterstock (2). Robert Holmes (5). **Chapter 1: Experience San Francisco:** f11photo/Shutterstock (6-7). Scott Wilson / Alamy Stock Photo (8). Ekaterina Pokrovsky/shutterstock (9). Jill Krueger (9). Steve Wood/shutterstock (10). Pung/shutterstock (10). Tetra Images, LLC / Alamy Stock Photo (10). canyalcin/shutterstock (10). Dan Henson/shutterstock (11). Matt Boyle/shutterstock (11). Gene X Hwang/Orange Photography (12). Della Huff / Alamy Stock Photo (12). Maciej Bledowski/shutterstock (12). Alex Zyuzikov/shutterstock (12). Zachary Frank / Alamy Stock Photo (13). TJ Muzeni (14). eye35 stock / Alamy Stock Photo (14). TJ Muzeni (14). Courtesy of Tonga Room (14). dibrova/shutterstock (15). Engel Ching/shutterstock (15). Sundry Photography/shutterstock (16). Courtesy of Musée Mécanique (16). Paul Juser/shutterstock.com (16). Courtesy of Tartine Bakery (16). Matthew Kiernan / Alamy Stock Photo (17). Courtesy of Bluxome Street Winery (22). Marc Fiorito - Gamma Nine Photography (22). Courtesy of Boudin Bakery (22). Courtesy of Blue Bottle Coffee (23). SFCVB (23). Jill Krueger (24). TJ Muzeni (24). Jemny/Shutterstock (24). ESB Professional/ Shutterstock (24). Morenovel/Shutterstock (25). MNStudio/Shutterstock (25). Eug Png/Shutterstock (25). kropic1/Shutterstock (25). Book Club of California (26). Courtesy of Kabuki Springs & Spa (26). Courtesy of TreasureFest (26). Alison Taggart-Barone/Parks Conservancy (26). JHVEPhoto/Shutterstock (27). canadastock/Shutterstock (33). Pius Lee/Shutterstock (35). San Francisco Municipal Railway Historical Archives (36). **Chapter 3: Union Square and Chinatown:** Victoria R/Shutterstock (63). Santirf | Dreamstime.com (69). Kongomonkey | Dreamstime. com (81). CURAphotography/Shutterstock (83). Library of Congress Prints and Photographs Division (84). Arnold Genthe (Public Domain) (84). Sandor Balatoni/SFCVB (85). Library of Congress Prints and Photographs Division (85). Library of Congress (86). f11photo/Shutterstock (88). **Chapter 4: SoMa and Civic Center with the Tenderloin and Hayes Valley:** V_E/Shutterstock (91). **Chapter 5: Nob Hill and Russian Hill with Polk Gulch:** F11photo | Dreamstime.com (119). **Chapter 6: North Beach:** randy andy/Shutterstock (135). Tinamou | Dreamstime.com (139). yhelfman/iStockphoto (146). **Chapter 7: On the Waterfront Fisherman's Wharf, Embarcadero, and the Financial District:** rramirez125/iStockphoto (149). IM_photo/Shutterstock (161). f11photo/Shutterstock (169). Daniel DeSlover/Shutterstock (170). Public Domain (171). POPPERFOTO / Alamy (171). Wikipedia (171). Eliza Snow/iStockphoto (173). Steve Rosset/Shutterstock (174). **Chapter 8: The Marina and the Presidio with Cow Hollow:** Andrew Zarivny/Shutterstock (179). ESB Professional/Shutterstock (180). Phitha Tanpairoj/Shutterstock (181). Steve Holderfield/Shutterstock (181). **Chapter 9: The Western Shoreline:** Robert Holmes (199). bteimages/Shutterstock (205). **Chapter 10: Golden Gate Park:** California Travel and Tourism Co. (211). Robert Holmes (212-214). Natalia Bratslavsky/iStockphoto (215). Robert Holmes (216-218). Janet Fullwood (219, All). Donna & Andrew/Flickr (220). Andrew Zarivny/Shutterstock (220). Robert Holmes (220). **Chapter 11: The Haight, the Castro, and Noe Valley:** Luciano Mortula - LGM/Shutterstock (221). Sepavo | Dreamstime.com (235). **Chapter 12: Mission District, Dogpatch, Bernal Heights, and Potrero Hill With Mission Bay:** Kārlis Dambrāns/Flickr, [CC BY 2.0] (237). Held Jurgen / age fotostock (240). jejim/Shutterstock (244). **Chapter 13: Pacific Heights and Japantown with the Western Addition:** Della Huff / Alamy (259). Andreistanescu | Dreamstime.com (260). Lunamarina | Dreamstime. com (261). Checubus | Dreamstime.com (261). Rafael Ramirez Lee/iStockphoto (268). **Chapter 14: The Bay Area:** Jon Chica/Shutterstock (281). Sundry Photography/iStockkphoto (290). Nancy Hoyt Belcher / Alamy (293). topseller/Shutterstock (315). S. Greg Panosian/iStockphoto (320). **Chapter 15: Napa and Sonoma:** cheng cheng/Shutterstock (325). Robert Holmes (330). Far Niente+Dolce+Nickel & Nickel (331). kevin miller/iStockphoto (331) Agence Images / Alamy (332). Cephas Picture Library / Alamy (332). PHILIPPE ROY / Alamy (332). Warren H. White (333, All). Terry Joanis/Frog's Leap (351). Smcfeeters | Dreamstime.com (359). Benziger Family Winery (369). Laurence G. Sterling/Iron Horse Vineyards (383). **About Our Writers:** All photos are courtesy of the writers.

*Every effort has been made to trace the copyright holders, and we apologize in advance for any accidental errors. We would be happy to apply the corrections in the following edition of this publication.

Notes

Notes

Notes

Fodor's SAN FRANCISCO

Publisher: Stephen Horowitz, *General Manager*

Editorial: Douglas Stallings, *Editorial Director*; Jill Fergus, Amanda Sadlowski, Caroline Trefler, *Senior Editors*; Kayla Becker, Alexis Kelly, *Editors*

Design: Tina Malaney, *Director of Design and Production*; Jessica Gonzalez, *Graphic Designer*; Mariana Tabares, *Design and Production Intern*

Production: Jennifer DePrima, *Editorial Production Manager*; Elyse Rozelle, *Senior Production Editor*; Monica White, *Production Editor*

Maps: Rebecca Baer, *Senior Map Editor*; Mark Stroud (Moon Street Cartography), *Cartographer*

Photography: Viviane Teles, *Senior Photo Editor*; Namrata Aggarwal, Ashok Kumar, *Photo Editors*; Rebecca Rimmer, *Photo Intern*

Business and Operations: Chuck Hoover, *Chief Marketing Officer*; Robert Ames, *Group General Manager*; Devin Duckworth, *Director of Print Publishing*; Amber Zhou, *Business Analyst*

Public Relations and Marketing: Joe Ewaskiw, *Senior Director of Communications and Public Relations*

Fodors.com: Jeremy Tarr, *Editorial Director*; Rachael Levitt, *Managing Editor*

Technology: Jon Atkinson, *Director of Technology*; Rudresh Teotia, *Lead Developer*; Jacob Ashpis, *Content Operations Manager*

Writer: Trevor Felch, Daniel Mangin, Monique Peterson, Coral Sisk, Ava Liang Zhao

Editor: Linda Cabasin, Jacinta O'Halloran

Production Editor: Jennifer DePrima

31st Edition

ISBN 978-1-64097-398-5

ISSN 1525–1829

All details in this book are based on information supplied to us at press time. Always confirm information when it matters, especially if you're making a detour to visit a specific place. Fodor's expressly disclaims any liability, loss, or risk, personal or otherwise, that is incurred as a consequence of the use of any of the contents of this book.

SPECIAL SALES

This book is available at special discounts for bulk purchases for sales promotions or premiums. For more information, e-mail SpecialMarkets@fodors.com.

PRINTED IN CANADA

10 9 8 7 6 5 4 3 2 1

About Our Writers

 Trevor Felch is a lifelong Bay Area resident who has spent countless days catching his breath after climbing San Francisco's hills. He spends most of his time eating and drinking around San Francisco, then writing about those experiences for several local and national publications. When he isn't staring at a laptop or a bakery case full of sourdough loaves and croissants, he's usually swimming or preparing for the next half marathon (remember all those sourdough loaves and croissants?), exploring around town with his girlfriend's dog, or some other activity for soaking up the California sun. He is the author of *San Francisco Cocktails*, a recipe collection and in-depth guide to the Bay Area's cocktail history and leading bars.

 Daniel Mangin has been a Fodor's Travel writer and editor for over a quarter of a century. The writer of all editions of *Fodor's Napa and Sonoma*, he also contributed to its predecessor *Fodor's InFocus Napa & Sonoma*. As the editorial director of the Compass American Guides, Daniel was the series editor of *California Wine Country*. He has also written about wine and wineries for *The California Directory of Fine Wineries*, *Napa Valley Life Magazine*, *Marin Magazine*, and other print and online outlets.

 A Northern California native, writer and editor, **Monique Peterson** navigates Bay Area cities and landscapes with ease to share her insights on favorite places and new experiences, from Lake Merritt and San Pablo Avenue to Sausalito and Point Reyes Station. A former Napa Valley broadast journalist, Monique produced live coverage of the wine industry and local and regional news. She later pursued New York City publishing ventures, writing and editing books about art, science, history, and nature for The Walt Disney Company, Discovery Channel School, and Random House. She presently lives in the California foothills, where she writes fiction and screenplays when she's not hiking, biking, or pursuing new adventures.

 Coral Sisk is an American-born food writer with an Italian-Iranian background. She holds a sommelier certification and a bachelor's degree in Italian Studies and Geography from the University of Washington, Seattle. After graduating college, she moved to Florence and started a local blog, Curious Appetite, parlaying it into a business of gourmet gifts and culinary wine tours in Florence and Bologna and around Tuscany. Coral splits her time between Italy and San Francisco. In Florence, she conducts tours and contributes dining guides and profiles on the country's makers to international publications and travel guides, including *Condé Nast Traveler*, Eater, and *The Guardian*. In San Francisco she covers food and drink in North Beach, the city's Italian district.

 Ava Liang Zhao is a China-born, Hawaii-raised adventurer who has called San Francisco home since 2009. A recovering lawyer, she has recently traded in her legal briefs for a career as a full-time creative. When she is not hiking her favorite trails on Mt. Tam or exploring the best hidden eats of vista points in San Francisco, she can be found indoors doodling with watercolors, practicing yoga, or cooking her grandma's recipes in the kitchen. As of late, she is learning to be an urban farmer, ceramacist, and UX designer.

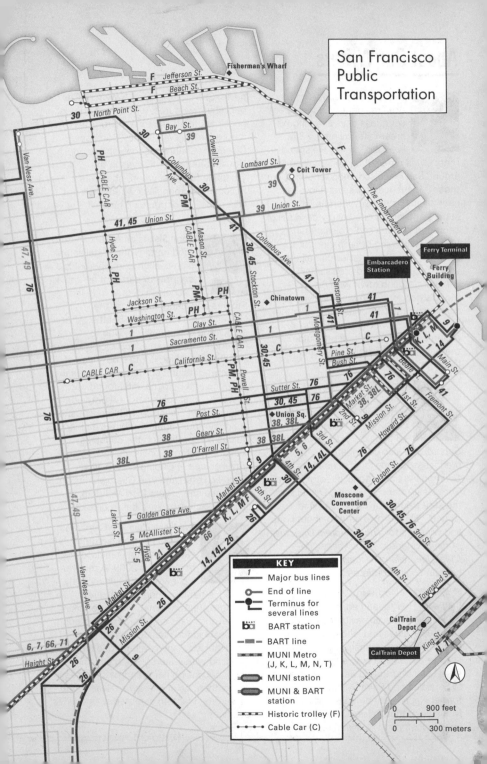

San Francisco Public Transportation

KEY

——1——	Major bus lines
⊸	End of line
●—○	Terminus for several lines
🚇	BART station
▬ ▬ ▬	BART line
▭▭▭	MUNI Metro (J, K, L, M, N, T)
▬▬▬	MUNI station
▬▬▬	MUNI & BART station
●▬●▬●	Historic trolley (F)
•—•—•	Cable Car (C)

Fisherman's Wharf

Jefferson St.
Beach St.
North Point St.
Bay St.
Lombard St.
Coit Tower
Union St.
Columbus Ave.
Union St.
Jackson St.
Washington St.
Clay St.
Sacramento St.
California St.
Sutter St.
Post St.
Geary St.
O'Farrell St.
Golden Gate Ave.
McAllister St.
Market St.
Mission St.
Haight St.

Van Ness Ave.
Hyde St.
Mason St.
Stockton St.
Powell St.
Montgomery St.
Powell St.
Larkin St.
Hyde St.

CABLE CAR
Chinatown
Union Sq.
Moscone Convention Center

The Embarcadero
Ferry Terminal
Ferry Building
Embarcadero Station

Sansome St.
Pine St.
Bush St.
Battery St.
Main St.
1st St.
2nd St.
3rd St.
4th St.
5th St.
Fremont St.
Howard St.
Folsom St.
Townsend St.
King St.

CalTrain Depot
CalTrain Depot

PH
PM
CABLE CAR

30
39
41
45
38
38L
76
1
5
6
9
14
14L
21
26
47
49
66
6, 7, 66, 71
K, L, M
K, L, M, F
J, K, L, M, N, T
5, 6
30, 45, 76

0   900 feet
0   300 meters

N, T